C0-APY-060

CHRIS AND MARK,
BEST WISHES

RVers BEST
PUBLIC
CAMPGROUNDS

Second Edition

State and County Campgrounds, Corps of Engineers, National Forest, National Park, National Monument, and Bureau of Land Management Parks, for fees typically $23 or less.

By Lee Zaborowski

DAD & JEANNE

RVers BEST PUBLIC CAMPGROUNDS, Second Edition, copyright © 2014 by Lee Zaborowski. All rights reserved. No part of this publication may be reproduced, stored in a retrieval system or transmitted in any form or by any means, electronic, mechanical, recording or otherwise without the prior written permission of the author.

While every effort has been made to insure the accuracy of this publication, the author and publisher shall have neither liability nor responsibility to any person or entity with respect to any loss or damage caused, or alleged to be caused, directly or indirectly by the information contained in this publication.

ISBN-10: 1939784026
ISBN-13: 978-1-939784-02-5

Contents

Quick Start Guide

About the Book. As they RVed the country, Lee and Jeanne Zaborowski became enamored with the wonderful network of public campgrounds across the country - there are over 12,000 in all! They enjoyed the sylvan environment of public camps, the relative quiet, lower fees, and sense of duty and responsibility shown by the vast majority of state, federal & county hosts and rangers.

The individual campgrounds will accommodate most RVs and were selected for amenities, conveniences and reviews. Occasionally you will encounter a challenging route or road getting to one of the campgrounds. We tried to keep those situations to a minimum.

Feedback in reviews on the First Edition reported the desire for campgrounds away from Interstate highways. As a result, the author has added almost 200 campgrounds on scenic and coastal highways, as well as to National Parks.

In this Second Edition, Lee has also expanded the campground information and amenities with a table of around 40 specifications per campground.

Given the many thousands of turn and mileage directions, there is probably the inevitable error or two in the book. Lee especially apologies in advance if you experience one. Email errors/changes to the address in this section if you have something to report.

State Chapter Introductions. Each state presents a unique blend of public park and campground providers, services, fees, and reservation options. You should become familiar with a state's introduction content before looking at individual campgrounds.

Camp Map Numbers. The numbering of campgrounds in a state is lowest to highest Interstate number, and lowest to highest Exit number on each Interstate. Non-Interstate roads are south to north.

Finding a Park/Campground. Use whatever combination you prefer - Highway information; nearby town and Directions; or GPS coordinates. Any mix of these will lead you to the Park/Campground location.

Abbreviations. There are some abbreviations, most should be familiar:

BLM - Bureau of Land Management
Bus - Interstate Business Route
Blvd - Boulevard
COE - Corps of Engineers
Cty - County
FM - Farm to Market (road designation)
FS - Forest Service
Fwy - Freeway
Hwy - Highway
NA - Not Applicable
NF - National Forest
NM - National Monument
NP - National Park
NPS - National Park Service
NRA - National Recreation Area
Rd - Road
St - Street
TVA - Tennessee Valley Authority

Fees. The one true statement about fees is that they constantly change. Fees in this book were compiled during 2014. The fee range given with each camp is from basic to best set-up for that camp. If there is a notable discount, that is also noted. State park systems are noted for add-on additional fees beyond the site fee. Possible additional fees include some combination of - vehicles being towed or towing, park entrance fees, and assorted use surcharges.

Phone Numbers. Numbers given are, with few exceptions, for the destination park or camp, not a remote location.

Websites. Listed websites are typically for the destination park or camp. Nevertheless, some States have chosen to send people directly to a reservation system for basic information and site reservations.

Directions. Distance segments should be correct within a few tenths of a mile. At turns, compass information is often given (east, etc.) unless curvy roads confuse orientation. It is always wise to confirm directions against onboard maps, GPS, etc. A good habit is to call the park about recent changes or possible road construction issues.

America the Beautiful Senior Pass. This is a lifetime Pass available to U.S. Citizens and permanent residents who are 62 years and older, which provides access to recreation areas managed by five Federal agencies. It also provides the pass owner a discount on some Expanded Amenity Fees such as camping.

The cost of the Senior Pass is $10, and it is valid for the lifetime of the pass owner. Golden Age Passports continue to be valid for a lifetime and are equivalent to the new Senior Pass. For current information or changes go to -

http://store.usgs.gov/pass/senior.html

Types of Camp Sites. Sites are categorized and named differently, as defined by the state. Most common labels are basic or primitive (dry), electric, electric/water (standard), full hook up (water/electric/sewer), premium (waterfront).

Camp Accommodations. The number of sites given is usually the number of RV sites. It is not uncommon to see a lower than official number as group and tent sites are not counted. The length number (i.e. 40 feet) is the maximum length RV the campground normally will accommodate. The majority of states will not allow you to bring firewood into a park. The best advice is not to carry firewood. Many camps will sell you wood, which is a good pest control option, and sales help park budgets.

Security. A majority of the campgrounds listed have one or more forms of the following types of on-site security - ranger, host, patrol, gate. That information is not consistently known, so if this is a concern for you, call the camp to inquire.

Online Registration. The majority of states use their own online registration system; or like the Federal Government use *Reserve America* (RA) or *Recreation.gov* as their registration system service provider. Everyone charges an online registration service fee, as well as assorted fees to cancel or change a reservation. Most states also have a statewide telephone reservation system, while some states do it on a park-by-park basis. Generally, calling the Park directly in advance of your arrival to gauge demand and the actual necessity of getting a reservation is a good idea. For some selected parks, a year ahead is not too soon.

Pets. As a rule public campgrounds will allow pets (3 or more dogs can be a problem) out in the camp if on a leash. Leash length varies by state between 6-10 feet. The exceptions most often found are no pets on beaches, in buildings, or certain parks (this is rare).

Points of Interest. Every park and campground stop is a unique experience. The space in Chapters for each campground region could never do any community or area justice. Two or three highlights are noted

to get you thinking about possible visitor destinations.

Corrections and Cautions. The Author is not responsible for any mishaps you may experience. Readers should plan ahead and proceed cautiously, especially with respect to routing information. If you should find an error, enhancement or update please let us know. We're also open to suggestions to improve this book. Send your information or comments to -

leezabo@gmail.com

About the Author. Lee Zaborowski is a retired educator, both as a teacher and administrator in Adult and Continuing Education programs. Lee has authored before, this is the second edition of his fourth book. He has three children and six grandchildren.

Lee fell in love with the outdoors, as a youth during the 40s and 50s, during the then annual summer trip to a resort in northern Wisconsin. Since those days he's lugged canvas tents around Idaho to fly fish, and progressed to long bicycle touring/camping trips all over the United States, carrying clothes, camping gear, tools, etc. in panniers on the bike.

Today, Lee and his wife, Jeanne, and the two family cats tour the States in their RV. Both Lee and Jeanne enjoy photography.

"May the road rise up to meet you.
May the wind be always at your back.
May the warm rays of sun fall upon your home.
And may the hand of a friend always be near."

Irish prayer/blessing

About Alabama's Public Campgrounds

Alabama has roughly the same number of state campground parks as you will find federal campgrounds. There are relatively few local government campgrounds.

Based on location and access for RVs, a majority of the campgrounds selected are state parks. The RV traveler should find variety and much to enjoy in each of these parks. The parks listed here vary in site size from 13 to 496 with 105 being the average number of sites for the locations selected. You can learn more about the State Parks at -

http://www.alapark.com/

The Alabama State Parks offer diverse options in addition to the usual campground amenities including restaurants, expansive fishing facilities with equipped harbors, as well as lodges. Many park campgrounds offer senior discounts, allow pets, have onsite picnic tables and grills and ample parking for visitors.

Advance reservations are recommended. There is no statewide, centralized campground information and registration system for the Alabama State Parks. Each park has a detailed website and registration process (online or call in). Campsites fees were typically in the $20-$35 range. The websites and telephone numbers for each park are listed in the book

[1] Meaher State Park	[10] Gunter Hill Campground
[2] Blakeley State Park	[11] Oak Mountain State Park
[3] Gulf State Park	[12] Rickwood Caverns State Park
[4] Florala State Park	[13] Monte Sano State Park
[5] Jennings Ferry Camp	[14] Joe Wheeler State Park
[6] Lake Lurleen State Park	[15] Chewacla State Park
[7] Cheaha State Park	[16] Lakepoint Resort State Park
[8] DeSoto State Park	[17] Six Mile Creek
[9] Chickasabogue Park	[18] Foscue Creek

NOTES:

Alabama

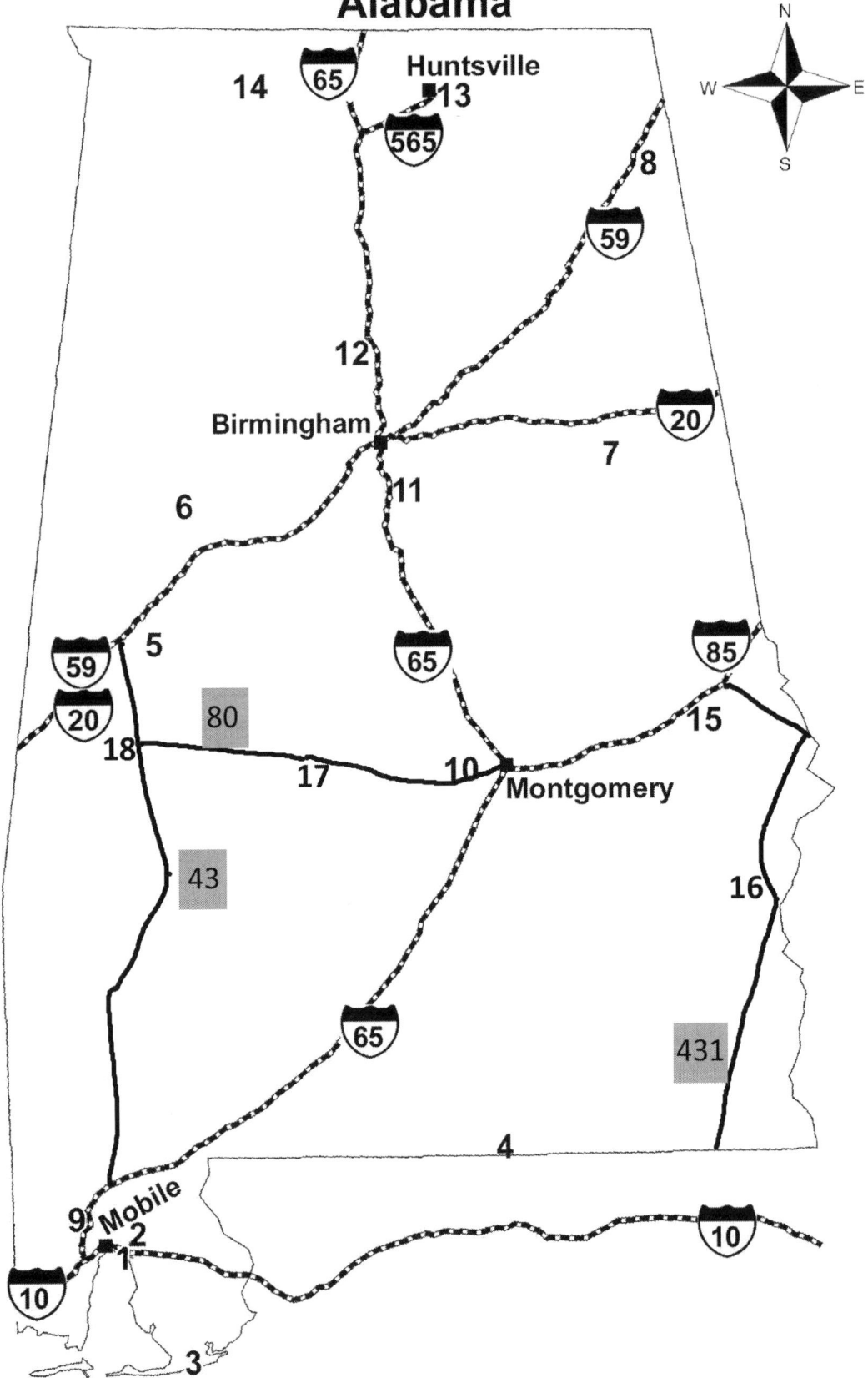

14

65

Huntsville
■13

565

8

59

12

Birmingham ■

20

7

6

11

59

5

65

85

20

80

15

18

17

10

Montgomery

43

16

431

65

4

9 Mobile
2
1

10

10

3

N
W E
S

9

[1] Meaher State Park
I-10, Exit 35
Near Mobile
N30 40.224 W87 55.857
State Rate: $34, 15% Senior Discount
(251) 626-5529
http://www.alapark.com/Meaher/

Directions

2 miles. From Exit 35 take Battleship Pkwy (Hwy 90/98) north and west to the park entrance.

Points of Interest

There is a new bathhouse with laundry facilities for overnight campers. Experience the rich history of Mobile at the Museum of Mobile, the Conde-Charlott Museum House, the Bellington Gardens or the Carnival Museum. Be sure to visit the Southern Market. Coastal activities include Delta Excursions & lots of fresh seafood.

RV Sites		Water		Laundry	Y
Number	56	None		Wi-Fi	
Shaded	Y	At Site	Y	Fishing	Y
By Water	Y	Spigots		Hiking	Y
Paved	Y	Sewer		Biking	
Pull Thru	Y	None		Swimming	
ADA	Y	At Site	Y	Watch Wildlife	Y
Max RV Size	45 ft	Dump Station		Pets	Y
Electric		Amenities		Security	
None		Restrooms	Y	Host(s)	Y
20 Amp	Y	Showers	Y	Rangers(s)	Y
30 Amp	Y	Reserve Sites		Gate	
50 Amp	Y	Store		Patrolled	
		Grill/Table	Y		

[2] Blakeley State Park
I-10, Exit 35
Near Mobile
N30 42.824 W87 54.099
State Rate: $30
(251) 626-5581
www.BlakeleyPark.com

Directions

7 miles. From Exit 35 go north on US Highway 98 to US Highway 31 and take a right. Turn left on Highway 225 and go 4 1/2 miles. Park is on left.

Points of Interest

Blakeley State Park hosts year around events including Bluegrass Festival events, boat tours of the Mobile-Tensaw Delta (one of Alabama's Ten Natural Wonders), and significant area Civil War locations. Be sure to visit Blakeley, one of the oldest towns in the State of Alabama.

RV Sites		Water		Laundry	
Number	28	None		Wi-Fi	
Shaded	Y	At Site	Y	Fishing	
By Water	Y	Spigots		Hiking	Y
Paved		Sewer		Biking	
Pull Thru	Y	None		Swimming	
ADA		At Site	Y	Watch Wildlife	Y
Max RV Size	40 ft	Dump Station		Pets	Y
Electric		Amenities		Security	
None		Restrooms	Y	Host(s)	Y
20 Amp	Y	Showers		Rangers(s)	Y
30 Amp	Y	Reserve Sites		Gate	
50 Amp	Y	Store		Patrolled	
		Grill/Table			

[3] Gulf State Park
I-10, Exit 44
Near the Gulf of Mexico
N30 16.068 W87 39.021
State Rate: $31-44, 15% Senior Discount
(251) 948-7275
http://www.alapark.com/GulfState/

Directions

30 miles. From Exit 44 go due south on US 59 to the City of Gulf Shores. At Hwy 180 turn left (east) to State Park Road.

Points of Interest

Located on the coast of Alabama in the City of Gulf Shores, you will find two miles of white sand beaches. Enjoy nature programs & events, hiking trails, & geocaching. Visit the Ft. Morgan National Historic Landmark. There is tennis, golf & a large lake for fishing & swimming.

RV Sites		Water		Laundry	Y
Number	496	None		Wi-Fi	Y
Shaded	Y	At Site	Y	Fishing	Y
By Water	Y	Spigots		Hiking	Y
Paved	Y	Sewer		Biking	Y
Pull Thru	Y	None		Swimming	Y
ADA	Y	At Site	Y	Watch Wildlife	
Max RV Size	45 ft	Dump Station		Pets	Y
Electric		Amenities		Security	
None		Restrooms	Y	Host(s)	Y
20 Amp	Y	Showers	Y	Rangers(s)	Y
30 Amp	Y	Reserve Sites	Y	Gate	
50 Amp	Y	Store	Y	Patrolled	Y
		Grill/Table	Y		

[4] Florala State Park
I-10, Exit 56 or 85 (both in Florida)
In Florala on the AL state line
N30 59.888 W86 19.066
State Rate: $23-$29, 15% Senior Discount
(334) 858-6425
http://www.alapark.com/Florala/

Directions

27 miles. From the west take Florida Exit 56, go north on US 85, turn right on US 54 to the Park. From the east take Florida Exit 85 on Hwy 331 north, turn left at US 54 to the Park.

Points of Interest

The Park stretches along the shores of Lake Jackson. Within walking, the City of Florala has many antique shops, Victorian mansions, & art galleries. The oldest Masonic Celebration is also there. The Worlds Domino Tournament and the Rattle Snake Rodeo are big attractions.

RV Sites		Water		Laundry	Y
Number	28	None		Wi-Fi	Y
Shaded	Y	At Site	Y	Fishing	Y
By Water	Y	Spigots		Hiking	
Paved		Sewer		Biking	Y
Pull Thru	Y	None		Swimming	Y
ADA		At Site	Y	Watch Wildlife	
Max RV Size	45 ft	Dump Station		Pets	Y
Electric		Amenities		Security	
None		Restrooms	Y	Host(s)	Y
20 Amp	Y	Showers	Y	Rangers(s)	Y
30 Amp	Y	Reserve Sites	Y	Gate	
50 Amp	Y	Store		Patrolled	
		Grill/Table	Y		

[5] Jennings Ferry Camp
I-20/59, Exit 40
Southwest of Tuscaloosa
N32 48.617 W87 48.406
COE Rate: $18
America/Beautiful Rate: $9
(205) 372-1217
http://www.recreation.gov/

Directions

10 miles. From Exit 40 take Hwy 14 towards and through Eutaw. Look for signs to turn right off Hwy 14 at Jennings Ferry Rd.

Points of Interest

The camp is on the Black Warrior River. Who can forget that Tuscaloosa is the Home of Forrest Gump. Be sure to visit the University of Alabama campus, for football fans the Paul W. Bryant Museum is not to be missed. Historic homes are located on the Black Warrior River.

RV Sites		Water		Laundry	Y
Number	52	None		Wi-Fi	
Shaded	Y	At Site	Y	Fishing	Y
By Water	Y	Spigots		Hiking	Y
Paved	Y	Sewer		Biking	
Pull Thru	Y	None		Swimming	
ADA	Y	At Site	Y	Watch Wildlife	Y
Max RV Size	40+	Dump Station	Y	Pets	Y
Electric		Amenities		Security	
None		Restrooms	Y	Host(s)	Y
20 Amp	Y	Showers	Y	Rangers(s)	Y
30 Amp	Y	Reserve Sites	Y	Gate	
50 Amp	Y	Store		Patrolled	
		Grill/Table	Y		

[6] Lake Lurleen State Park
I-20/59, Exit 68
North of Tuscaloosa
State Rate: $22-28, 15% Senior Discount
N33 17.752 W87 40.612
(205) 339-1558
http://www.alapark.com/lakelurleen/

Directions

12 miles. From Exit 68 take Black Warrior Pkwy north for 7 miles. Turn left on   McFarland (Hwy 6/82) then immediate right on Mt. Olive (Cty 23), 5 miles to Park.

Points of Interest

Who can forget that Tuscaloosa is the Home of Forrest Gump. Be sure to visit the University of Alabama campus, and if you're a football fan the Paul W. Bryant Museum is not to be missed. Many historic homes are located on the Black Warrior River.

RV Sites		Water		Laundry	
Number	91	None		Wi-Fi	
Shaded	Y	At Site	Y	Fishing	Y
By Water	Y	Spigots		Hiking	Y
Paved	Y	Sewer		Biking	Y
Pull Thru	Y	None		Swimming	Y
ADA	Y	At Site	some	Watch Wildlife	Y
Max RV Size	45	Dump Station	Y	Pets	Y
Electric		Amenities		Security	
None		Restrooms	Y	Host(s)	Y
20 Amp	Y	Showers	Y	Rangers(s)	Y
30 Amp	Y	Reserve Sites	Y	Gate	Y
50 Amp		Store	Y	Patrolled	
		Grill/Table	Y		

[7] Cheaha State Park
I-20, Exit 191
East of Birmingham
State Rate: $22-27, 15% Senior Discount
N33 28.629 W85 48.492
(256) 488-5111
www.alapark.com/CheahaResort/

Directions

12 miles. From Exit 191 take Hwy 1/431 south 4 miles to the Skyway Mountainway (Hwy 281). Turn right, go 8 miles to the camp.

Points of Interest

In Birmingham, for vehicle & aviation buffs, the Barber Vintage Motorsports Museum (the largest collection of motorcycles in the world) and the Southern Museum of Flight hold unique collections of artifacts. Other possibilities include the Ruffiner Mountain Nature Center and the Botanical Gardens.

RV Sites		Water		Laundry	
Number	73	None		Wi-Fi	Y
Shaded	Y	At Site	Y	Fishing	Y
By Water		Spigots		Hiking	Y
Paved	Y	**Sewer**		Biking	Y
Pull Thru	Y	None		Swimming	Y
ADA	Y	At Site	Y	Watch Wildlife	Y
Max RV Size	45	Dump Station		Pets	Y
Electric		**Amenities**		**Security**	
None		Restrooms	Y	Host(s)	Y
20 Amp	Y	Showers	Y	Rangers(s)	Y
30 Amp	Y	Reserve Sites	Y	Gate	
50 Amp	Y	Store	Y	Patrolled	
		Grill/Table	Y		

[8] DeSoto State Park
I-59, Exit 231
Near GA State Line
State Rate: $29, 15% Senior Discount
N34 30.059 W85 37.088
(256) 845-5075
www.alapark.com/DeSotoResort/

Directions

14 miles. From Exit 231 follow Hwy 117 for 7 miles to County Roads 630 and then 106 (Wester Rd) for 7 miles to the Park

Points of Interest

Visit Fort Payne, home of the country music group "Alabama." Fort Payne is within 30 miles of substantial water recreational areas notably Guntersville Lake and Lake Weiss and Mentone, a popular mountain resort. Fort Payne Depot Museum is a good place to discover local history.

RV Sites		Water		Laundry	Y
Number	94	None		Wi-Fi	Y
Shaded	Y	At Site	Y	Fishing	Y
By Water		Spigots		Hiking	Y
Paved		**Sewer**		Biking	Y
Pull Thru	Y	None		Swimming	Y
ADA	Y	At Site	Y	Watch Wildlife	Y
Max RV Size	45	Dump Station		Pets	Y
Electric		**Amenities**		**Security**	
None		Restrooms	Y	Host(s)	Y
20 Amp	Y	Showers	Y	Rangers(s)	Y
30 Amp	Y	Reserve Sites	Y	Gate	
50 Amp	Y	Store	Y	Patrolled	
		Grill/Table	Y		

[9] Chickasabogue Park
I-65, Exit 13
Near Chickasaw
County Rate: $18
N30 46.710 W88 06.469
(251) 574-2267
www.mobilecountyal.gov/

Directions

4 miles. From Exit 13, on west side of exit take Hwy 213 (N. Shelton Beach Rd.), go south 2.2 mi to Whistler then east (left) 0.7 mi to Aldock Rd and north (left) 1 mi. follow signs.

Points of Interest

Near the Park office is the oldest Methodist/Episcopal church in Alabama. It is now a museum with exhibits from various periods of foreign, Indian, and local occupation. Also visit Bellingrath Gardens and the USS Alabama Battleship.

RV Sites		Water		Laundry	Y
Number	50	None		Wi-Fi	
Shaded	Y	At Site	Y	Fishing	Y
By Water		Spigots		Hiking	Y
Paved	Y	**Sewer**		Biking	Y
Pull Thru	Y	None		Swimming	
ADA	Y	At Site	Y	Watch Wildlife	
Max RV Size	40+	Dump Station		Pets	Y
Electric		**Amenities**		**Security**	
None		Restrooms	Y	Host(s)	Y
20 Amp	Y	Showers	Y	Rangers(s)	
30 Amp	Y	Reserve Sites		Gate	
50 Amp	Y	Store		Patrolled	Y
		Grill/Table	Y		

[10] Gunter Hill Campground
I-65, Exit 167
West of Montgomery
COE Rate: $18
America/Beautiful Rate: $9
N32 21.602 W86 28.908
(334) 872-9554
http://www.reserveamerica.com/

Directions

15 miles. From Exit 167 go west on US 80 for 9 miles. Turn right on County Road 7 for 5 miles to Old Selma Road. Turn left for 1 mile, follow signs.

Points of Interest

Close to Montgomery & Selma where both cities have a wide variety of Civil Rights & Civil War locations worth visiting. The Montgomery Motor Speedway is nearby for race buffs but some weekends may be a bit noisy.

RV Sites		Water		Laundry	Y
Number	142	None		Wi-Fi	
Shaded	Y	At Site	Y	Fishing	Y
By Water	Y	Spigots		Hiking	Y
Paved	Y	Sewer		Biking	Y
Pull Thru		None		Swimming	
ADA		At Site	Y	Watch Wildlife	Y
Max RV Size	45	Dump Station	Y	Pets	Y
Electric		Amenities		Security	
None		Restrooms	Y	Host(s)	Y
20 Amp	Y	Showers	Y	Rangers(s)	Y
30 Amp	Y	Reserve Sites	Y	Gate	
50 Amp	Y	Store	Y	Patrolled	
		Grill/Table	Y		

[11] Oak Mountain State Park
I-65, Exit 246
South of Birmingham
State Rate: $24-30, 15% Senior Discount
N33 21.164 W86 43.083
(205) 620-2527
http://www.alapark.com/OakMountain/

Directions

3 miles. From Exit 246, on west side of exit take Oak Mountain Park Rd. south to John Findley Dr. (State Park Rd), follow the signs.

Points of Interest

In Birmingham, vehicle & aviation buffs will enjoy the Barber Vintage Motorsports Museum or the Southern Museum of Flight. Other possibilities include the Ruffiner Mountain Nature Center and the Botanical Gardens. Also see and tour the Russell Cave National Monument near Bridgeport.

RV Sites		Water		Laundry	Y
Number	85	None		Wi-Fi	Y
Shaded	Y	At Site	Y	Fishing	Y
By Water	Y	Spigots		Hiking	Y
Paved	road	Sewer		Biking	Y
Pull Thru	Y	None		Swimming	Y
ADA	Y	At Site	Y	Watch Wildlife	Y
Max RV Size	40+	Dump Station		Pets	Y
Electric		Amenities		Security	
None		Restrooms	Y	Host(s)	Y
20 Amp	Y	Showers	Y	Rangers(s)	Y
30 Amp	Y	Reserve Sites	Y	Gate	
50 Amp		Store	Y	Patrolled	
		Grill/Table	Y		

[12] Rickwood Caverns State Park
I-65, Exit 289
North of Birmingham
State Rate: $20-23, 15% Senior Discount
N33 52.580 W86 51.900
(205) 647-9692
http://www.alapark.com/RickwoodCaverns/

Directions

3 miles. From Exit 289, on west side of exit take Rickwood Caverns Rd. west and turn south to Rickwood Park Rd.

Points of Interest

Offering more than a mile of underground wonder in Rickwood Cave, this park offers unique opportunities to examine an underground pool and 260 million-year-old formations. Cave tours are $10 (adults). For your safety & convenience, access to the cave is available only with a tour guide.

RV Sites		Water		Laundry	
Number	13	None		Wi-Fi	Y
Shaded	Y	At Site	Y	Fishing	
By Water		Spigots		Hiking	Y
Paved		Sewer		Biking	
Pull Thru		None		Swimming	pool
ADA	Y	At Site		Watch Wildlife	
Max RV Size	40	Dump Station	Y	Pets	Y
Electric		Amenities		Security	
None		Restrooms	Y	Host(s)	Y
20 Amp	Y	Showers	Y	Rangers(s)	Y
30 Amp	Y	Reserve Sites		Gate	
50 Amp		Store	Y	Patrolled	
		Grill/Table	y		

[13] Monte Sano State Park
I-65, Exit 340
East of Huntsville
State Rate: $19-$25, 15% Senior Discount
N34 44.633 W86 30.731
(256) 534-6589
www.alapark.com/MonteSano/Camping/

Directions

28 miles. From Exit 340 go 17 miles east on I-565 to Exit 17. Follow Governors Drive east (becomes US 431) for 7 miles. Turn left on Monte Sano Blvd. Go 2.5 miles and turn right on Nolen Ave for 1 mile to the park.

Points of Interest

The vistas of Monte Sano (Spanish for "Mountain of Health") are 1,600 feet above sea level. There are ample hiking trails and wildlife. The planetarium is open on weekends. Huntsville, home of the 'Space & Rocket Center' is close by.

RV Sites		Water		Laundry	
Number	89	None		Wi-Fi	
Shaded	Y	At Site	Y	Fishing	
By Water		Spigots		Hiking	Y
Paved		**Sewer**		Biking	Y
Pull Thru	Y	None		Swimming	Y
ADA	Y	At Site	Y	Watch Wildlife	Y
Max RV Size	45	Dump Station		Pets	Y
Electric		**Amenities**		**Security**	
None		Restrooms	Y	Host(s)	Y
20 Amp	Y	Showers	Y	Rangers(s)	Y
30 Amp	Y	Reserve Sites	Y	Gate	
50 Amp	Y	Store	Y	Patrolled	
		Grill/Table	Y		

[14] Joe Wheeler State Park
i-65, Exit 351
West of Athens
State Rate: $22-25, 15% Senior Discount
N34 47.581 W87 22.796
(256) 247-1184
http://www.alapark.com/JoeWheeler/

Directions

30 miles. From Exit 351 go west for 26 miles on Hwy 2/72 to Hwy 101 (Wheeler Dam Hwy). Go south 4 miles to Park.

Points of Interest

Decatur, known as "the River City" or "Chicago of the South" combines with Huntsville for a unique feel of the south. The area hosts air balloon festivals, horse racing and a variety of festivals throughout the year for visitors. Decatur is the home of Mellow Mix Cat Food.

RV Sites		Water		Laundry	Y
Number	116	None		Wi-Fi	Y
Shaded	Y	At Site	Y	Fishing	Y
By Water	Y	Spigots		Hiking	Y
Paved	Y	**Sewer**		Biking	Y
Pull Thru	Y	None		Swimming	Y
ADA	Y	At Site	Y	Watch Wildlife	Y
Max RV Size	45	Dump Station		Pets	Y
Electric		**Amenities**		**Security**	
None		Restrooms	Y	Host(s)	Y
20 Amp	Y	Showers	Y	Rangers(s)	Y
30 Amp	Y	Reserve Sites	Y	Gate	Y
50 Amp	Y	Store	Y	Patrolled	
		Grill/Table	Y		

[15] Chewacla State Park
I-85, Exit 51
South of Auburn
State Rate: $19-29, 15% Senior Discount
N32 33.240 W85 28.829
(334) 887-5621
http://www.alapark.com/Chewacla/

Directions

One mile. From I-85, Exit 51, go south on Hwy 15/29 but turn immediately left on Shell Toomer Pkwy for a mile to the Park entrance.

Points of Interest

Area attractions include historic downtown Opelika, the Tuskegee Airman National Historic Site, the Julie Collins Smith Museum of Fine Art, Auburn University, and plenty of retail and restaurant options.

RV Sites		Water		Laundry	
Number	36	None		Wi-Fi	Y
Shaded	Y	At Site	Y	Fishing	Y
By Water	Y	Spigots		Hiking	Y
Paved	road	**Sewer**		Biking	Y
Pull Thru	Y	None		Swimming	Y
ADA	Y	At Site	Y	Watch Wildlife	Y
Max RV Size	45	Dump Station		Pets	Y
Electric		**Amenities**		**Security**	
None		Restrooms	Y	Host(s)	Y
20 Amp	Y	Showers	Y	Rangers(s)	Y
30 Amp	Y	Reserve Sites	Y	Gate	
50 Amp	Y	Store		Patrolled	
		Grill/Table	Y		

[16] Lakepoint Resort State Park
Hwy 431
North of Eufaula
N31 59.256 W85 06.866
State Rate: $19-28, 15% Senior Discount
334-687-6026
http://www.alapark.com/LakePointResort

Directions

7 miles. From the intersection of Hwys 82 and 431 in Eufaula go north on Hwy 431 for 7 miles to the campground

Points of Interest

Picturesque Lakepoint is located on Lake Eufaula, known as "The Bass Capital of the World." The Park is near several interesting attractions - the Shorter Mansion, Fendall Hall and the Eufaula National Wildlife Refuge. Start an historic walk at the Shorter Mansion, located near other historic homes and buildings.

RV Sites		Water		Laundry	Y
Number	190	None		Wi-Fi	Y
Shaded	Y	At Site	Y	Fishing	Y
By Water	Y	Spigots		Hiking	Y
Paved	Y	Sewer		Biking	Y
Pull Thru	Y	None		Swimming	Y
ADA	Y	At Site	Y	Watch Wildlife	Y
Max RV Size	45	Dump Station	Y	Pets	Y
Electric		Amenities		Security	
None		Restrooms	Y	Host(s)	Y
20 Amp	Y	Showers	Y	Rangers(s)	Y
30 Amp	Y	Reserve Sites	Y	Gate	Y
50 Amp	Y	Store	Y	Patrolled	
		Grill/Table	Y		

[17] Six Mile Creek
County Road 139
South of Selma
32 19.27 W87 0.57
COE Rate: $18
America/Beautiful Rate: $9
(334)872-9554
http://www.recreation.gov

Directions

10 miles. From Hwy 80/22 in south Selma follow US 80 south for 3 miles. Turn right on Hwy 41 for 4.5 miles to County Road 139, go north 1.5 miles to County Rd 77 and 1 mile to the camp.

Points of Interest

The city is best known for the Battle of Selma and for the Selma to Montgomery Marches. Selma is home to the largest contiguous historic district in the State of Alabama.

RV Sites		Water		Laundry	Y
Number	31	None		Wi-Fi	
Shaded	Y	At Site	Y	Fishing	Y
By Water	Y	Spigots		Hiking	Y
Paved	Y	Sewer		Biking	
Pull Thru		None		Swimming	
ADA	Y	At Site	Y	Watch Wildlife	Y
Max RV Size	45	Dump Station	Y	Pets	Y
Electric		Amenities		Security	
None		Restrooms	Y	Host(s)	
20 Amp	Y	Showers	Y	Rangers(s)	Y
30 Amp	Y	Reserve Sites	Y	Gate	
50 Amp	Y	Store		Patrolled	
		Grill/Table	Y		

[18] Foscue Creek
Lock and Dam Road
West Side of Demopolis
N32 30.56, W87 52.10
COE Rate: $24
America/Beautiful Rate: $12
(334) 289-5535
http://www.recreation.gov/

Directions

4.0 miles. From Hwys 43/80 drive 1.5 miles west on Hwy 80, turn right at Maria St. Go 1.5 miles north to Lock & Dam Rd. Turn left & follow signs a mile to the campground.

Points of Interest

Demopolis is blessed with a number of well preserved historical sites, nationally recognized festivals and events. Close by, the Tombigee and Black Warrior Rivers provide the opportunity for world class fishing & water sports.

RV Sites		Water		Laundry	Y
Number	54	None		Wi-Fi	
Shaded	Y	At Site	Y	Fishing	Y
By Water	Y	Spigots		Hiking	Y
Paved	Y	Sewer		Biking	Y
Pull Thru	Y	None		Swimming	
ADA	Y	At Site	Y	Watch Wildlife	Y
Max RV Size	45	Dump Station	Y	Pets	Y
Electric		Amenities		Security	
None		Restrooms	Y	Host(s)	Y
20 Amp	Y	Showers	Y	Rangers(s)	Y
30 Amp	Y	Reserve Sites	Y	Gate	
50 Amp	Y	Store		Patrolled	
		Grill/Table	Y		

About Arizona's Public Campgrounds

There are close to 250 public campgrounds in Arizona (many are remote and/ or not RV accessible). Almost 75% are located on Federal Lands, the balance managed by State or Local Government agencies. The parks listed here vary in site size from 11 to over 400 with 85 being the average number of sites for the locations selected. A majority of the parks listed are part of the Arizona State Park System. They have an excellent webpage at:

http://azstateparks.com/

You will find a wealth of useful information, such as park closings, five day schedules, and special events. There is a limited statewide registration system for the Arizona State Parks. Fifteen Parks offer 24/7 Online Campground Reservations (There is a $5 non-refundable reservation fee per site). Call the Reservation Call Center at (520) 586-2283. You can call 7 days a week, from 8 am to 5 pm MST. Campsites fees were typically in the $15-$30 range, $50 for double sites. The websites and telephone numbers for each park listed in the book are noted in the campground entry.

[1] Dome Rock Mountain (Quartzite)	**[12] Kaibab Lake Campground**
[2] Lost Dutchman State Park	**[13] Dogtown Lake Camp**
[3] Picacho Peak State Park	**[14] Bonito Campground**
[4] Catalina State Park	**[15] Homolovi Ruins State Park**
[5] Kartchner Caverns State Park	**[16] Gila County RV Park**
[6] Roper Lake State Park	**[17] Fool Hollow Lake Recreation Area**
[7] Virgin River Canyon	**[18] Willow Beach Campground - Lake Mead NRA**
[8] Lake Pleasant County Park	
[9] Cave Creek Regional Park	**[19] Wahweap Campground - Glen Canyon NRA**
[10] Dead Horse Ranch State Park	
[11] Patagonia Lake State Park	

NOTES:

Arizona

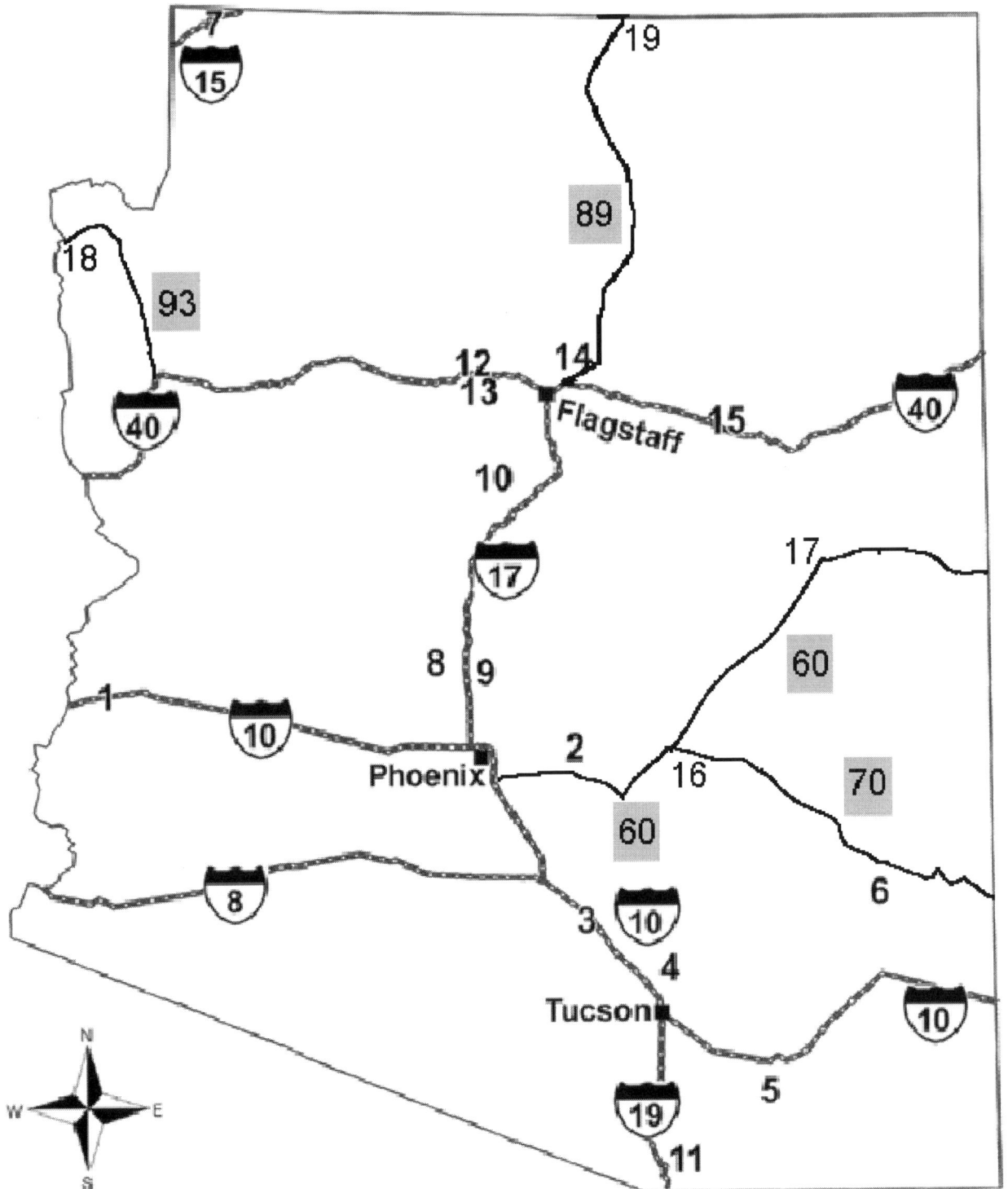

[1] Dome Rock Mountain (Quartzite)
I-10, Exit 19
Near Town of Quartzsite
N 33 38.869 W 114 16.982
BLM Rate: NA
(928) 317-3200
http://www.blm.gov/az/st/en/prog/recreation/camping/dev_camps/dome-rock.html

Directions

2 miles. From Exit 19 in the town of Quartzsite go west on the Frontage Road (Kuehn Street). The camping area is south and north of the Frontage Road.

Points of Interest

RVers go to Quartzsite during the winter months. Folks form groups based on RV brand or extended relationships. The flea markets are memorable! If you know how to manage your electricity/water for a week this place is worth experiencing.

RV Sites		Water		Laundry	
Number	NA	None	Y	Wi-Fi	
Shaded		At Site		Fishing	
By Water		Spigots		Hiking	Y
Paved		**Sewer**		Biking	Y
Pull Thru	Y	None	Y	Swimming	
ADA		At Site		Watch Wildlife	Y
Max RV Size	ANY	Dump Station		Pets	Y
Electric		**Amenities**		**Security**	
None	Y	Restrooms		Host(s)	Call 911
20 Amp		Showers		Rangers(s)	
30 Amp		Reserve Sites		Gate	
50 Amp		Store		Patrolled	
		Grill/Table			

[2] Lost Dutchman State Park
I-10, Exit 154
Near Phoenix
N 33 27.852 W 111 28.918
State Rate: $15-$30
(480) 982-4485
http://azstateparks.com/parks/lodu/index.html

Directions

33 miles. From Exit 154 take US 60 (divided highway) east 25 miles to Exit 196. Go left on S. Idaho Rd for 2.5 miles & bear right on N. Apache Trail (Hwy 88) for 5 miles to park.

Points of Interest

Lost Dutchman State Park offers a variety of hiking trails and nature trails, such as the Superstition Mountains (a source of mystery and legend since early times). Park trails offer good opportunities for bird watching & wildlife viewing.

RV Sites		Water		Laundry	
Number	70	None		Wi-Fi	
Shaded	Semi	At Site	Y	Fishing	
By Water		Spigots	Y	Hiking	Y
Paved	Y	**Sewer**		Biking	Y
Pull Thru	Y	None		Swimming	
ADA		At Site		Watch Wildlife	Y
Max RV Size	ANY	Dump Station	Y	Pets	Y
Electric		**Amenities**		**Security**	
None		Restrooms	Y	Host(s)	Y
20 Amp	Y	Showers	Y	Rangers(s)	Y
30 Amp	Y	Reserve Sites	Y	Gate	
50 Amp	Y	Store	Y	Patrolled	
		Grill/Table	Y		

[3] Picacho Peak State Park
I-10, Exit 219
South of Casa Grande
N 32 38.757 W 111 24.069
State Rate: $15-$25
(520) 466-3183
http://azstateparks.com/Parks/PIPE/index.html

Directions

The park is within sight of Exit 219 of I-10.

Points of Interest

As you approach the park you will see 1,500 foot Picacho Peak, located in the Park. You can enjoy the view along the peak as you hike the trails that wind up to the top. The park and surrounding area encompass unique geological characteristics, which includes varied desert growth.

RV Sites		Water		Laundry	
Number	100	None		Wi-Fi	
Shaded		At Site		Fishing	
By Water		Spigots	Y	Hiking	Y
Paved	Y	**Sewer**		Biking	Y
Pull Thru	Y	None		Swimming	
ADA	Y	At Site		Watch Wildlife	Y
Max RV Size	ANY	Dump Station	Y	Pets	Y
Electric		**Amenities**		**Security**	
None		Restrooms	Y	Host(s)	Y
20 Amp	Y	Showers	Y	Rangers(s)	Y
30 Amp	Y	Reserve Sites	Y	Gate	
50 Amp	Y	Store	Y	Patrolled	
		Grill/Table	Y		

[4] Catalina State Park, I-10
Exit 240
North Side of Tucson
N 32 25.007 W 110 56.255
State Rate: $15-$25
(520) 628-5798
http://azstateparks.com/parks/CATA/index.html

Directions

15 miles. From Exit 240 go east on Tangerine Road for 14 miles, then right on N. Oracle for a mile to the park entrance.

Points of Interest

Visit the Sonora Desert Museum and the Old Tucson Studio (a movie studio & theme park), which holds various festivals, fairs, & with museums will provide visitors many opportunities to experience the uniqueness of the area. Tucson is the home of the University of Arizona.

RV Sites		Water		Laundry	N
Number	120	None		Wi-Fi	N
Shaded	Yes	At Site	Y	Fishing	N
By Water	N	Spigots		Hiking	Y
Paved	Y	Sewer		Biking	Y
Pull Thru	Y	None		Swimming	N
ADA		At Site		Watch Wildlife	Y
Max RV Size	Any	Dump Station	Y	Pets	Y
Electric		Amenities		Security	
None		Restrooms	Y	Host(s)	Y
20 Amp	Y	Showers	Y	Rangers(s)	Y
30 Amp	Y	Reserve Sites	Y	Gate	
50 Amp	Y	Store	Y	Patrolled	
		Grill/Table	Y		

[5] Kartchner Caverns State Park, I-10
Exit 302
South of Bensen
N 31 50.134 W 110 20.621
State Rate: $25
(520) 586-2283
http://azstateparks.com/Parks/KACA/index.html

Directions

9 miles. From Exit 302 go south on Hwy 90. Park is on the right.

Points of Interest

Enjoy the Visitor Center, deli and exhibits. The main attraction is Kartchner Caverns. The Caverns is home to one of the world's longest soda straw stalactites (over 21 feet) & other unusual formations such as shields, totems, helictites, & rimstone dams.

RV Sites		Water		Laundry	
Number	62	None		Wi-Fi	
Shaded	N	At Site	Y	Fishing	
By Water	N	Spigots		Hiking	Y
Paved	Y	Sewer		Biking	Y
Pull Thru	Y	None		Swimming	
ADA	Y	At Site	Y	Watch Wildlife	Y
Max RV Size	Any	Dump Station	Y	Pets	Y
Electric		Amenities		Security	
None		Restrooms	Y	Host(s)	Y
20 Amp	Y	Showers	Y	Rangers(s)	Y
30 Amp	Y	Reserve Sites	Y	Gate	
50 Amp	Y	Store	Y	Patrolled	
		Grill/Table	Y		

[6] Roper Lake State Park, I-10
Exits 352/355 or
Hwy 191, go south at Hwy 70/191
South of Safford
N 32 45.517 W 109 42.447
State Rate: $15-$23
(928) 428-6760
http://azstateparks.com/Parks/ROLA/index.html

Directions

In Stafford, take 1st Ave. (Hwy 191) south for 5.5 miles to W. Roper Lake Rd. & the Park on the left: or *29 miles from I-10*. From either Exit 352 or 355 go north on Hwy 191 to W. Roper Lake Rd. Park is on the right.

Points of Interest

The stone hot springs are inviting. The Dos Arroyos Trail leads to a re-created Indian village containing replicas of dwellings, grinding stones, roasting pits, & other tools and artifacts. There is a Visitor Center.

RV Sites		Water		Laundry	
Number	60	None		Wi-Fi	
Shaded	Y	At Site	Y	Fishing	Y
By Water	Y	Spigots		Hiking	Y
Paved	Y	Sewer		Biking	Y
Pull Thru	Y	None		Swimming	Y
ADA		At Site		Watch Wildlife	Y
Max RV Size	Any	Dump Station	Y	Pets	Y
Electric		Amenities		Security	
None		Restrooms	Y	Host(s)	Y
20 Amp	Y	Showers	Y	Rangers(s)	Y
30 Amp	Y	Reserve Sites	Y	Gate	
50 Amp	Y	Store	Y	Patrolled	
		Grill/Table	Y		

[7] Virgin River Canyon, I-15 & I-17
Exit 18 of I-15
Between Mesquite & St. George
N36 57.058 W113 47.613
BLM Rate: $8
America/Beautiful Rate: $4
(435) 688-3200
http://www.blm.gov/az/st/en/prog/recreation/camping/dev_camps/vrg.html

Directions

The park is within sight of Exit 18, on the south side of I-15.

Points of Interest

Located in the Virgin River Gorge, the campground is surrounded by colorful cliffs and rocky canyons. Enjoy river access, wildlife viewing, hiking, and scenic views. Notable area destinations and sights include Zion National Park, Snow Canyon, and Quail Creek.

RV Sites		Water		Laundry	
Number	75	None		Wi-Fi	
Shaded	Y	At Site	Y	Fishing	
By Water		Spigots		Hiking	Y
Paved	Y	**Sewer**		Biking	Y
Pull Thru	Y	None		Swimming	
ADA	Y	At Site		Watch Wildlife	Y
Max RV Size	Any	Dump Station	Y	Pets	Y
Electric		**Amenities**		**Security**	
None	Y	Restrooms	Y	Host(s)	Y
20 Amp		Showers		Rangers(s)	Y
30 Amp		Reserve Sites		Gate	
50 Amp		Store		Patrolled	
		Grill/Table	Y		

[8] Lake Pleasant County Park, I-17
Exit 223
North of Phoenix
N33 51.839 W112 19.121
Maricopa County Rate: $17-$35
(928) 501-1710
http://www.maricopa.gov/parks/lake_pleasant/Camping.aspx

Directions

17 miles. From Exit 223 take Hwy 74 (Carefree Hwy) west. Go 15 miles to Castle Hot Spring Road. Turn right (north) 2 miles to park entrance.

Points of Interest

Lake Pleasant provides ample campsite views of the water & a variety of water sports - half the sites are close to water's edge, the other are on a bluff overlooking the water. Shopping opportunities abound on I-17. Phoenix is close by with many sights & Baseball Spring Training.

RV Sites		Water		Laundry	
Number	148	None		Wi-Fi	
Shaded	Y	At Site	Y	Fishing	Y
By Water	Y	Spigots		Hiking	Y
Paved	Y	**Sewer**		Biking	Y
Pull Thru	Y	None		Swimming	Y
ADA		At Site		Watch Wildlife	Y
Max RV Size	Any	Dump Station	Y	Pets	Y
Electric		**Amenities**		**Security**	
None		Restrooms	Y	Host(s)	Y
20 Amp	Y	Showers	Y	Rangers(s)	Y
30 Amp	Y	Reserve Sites	Y	Gate	
50 Amp	Y	Store		Patrolled	
		Grill/Table	Y		

[9] Cave Creek Regional Park, I-17
Exit 223
North of Phoenix
N33 49.424 W112 00.916
Maricopa County Rate: $15-$20
(623) 465-0431
http://www.maricopa.gov/parks/cave_creek/Camping.aspx

Directions

8 miles. From Exit 223 take Hwy 74 (Carefree Hwy) east 7 miles to 32nd St. Turn left (north) one mile to the Park entrance.

Points of Interest

Hohokam Indians resided here around 800-1400 A.D. Stone huts, pit houses, terraced field & irrigation ditches remain, as well as petroglyphs. The County sponsors a star gazing program. Shopping opportunities are on I-17. Phoenix is close with sights & Baseball Spring Training.

RV Sites		Water		Laundry	
Number	38	None		Wi-Fi	
Shaded	N	At Site	Y	Fishing	
By Water	N	Spigots		Hiking	Y
Paved	Y	**Sewer**		Biking	Y
Pull Thru	Y	None		Swimming	
ADA		At Site		Watch Wildlife	Y
Max RV Size	Any	Dump Station	Y	Pets	Y
Electric		**Amenities**		**Security**	
None		Restrooms	Y	Host(s)	Y
20 Amp	Y	Showers	Y	Rangers(s)	Y
30 Amp	Y	Reserve Sites	Y	Gate	
50 Amp	Y	Store		Patrolled	
		Grill/Table	Y		

[10] Dead Horse Ranch State Park, I-17
Exit 287 of I-17
(or from Sedona via Hwy 89)
Southwest of Sedona
N 34 45.185 W 112 01.327
State Rate: $15-$30
(928) 634-5283
http://azstateparks.com/Parks/DEHO/index.html

Directions

13 miles. From Exit 287 go west on Hwy 260 11 miles to Main St. Cottonwood (Hwy 89A), turn left. Go 2 miles to N 10th Street. You'll see a brown Park sign before the 10th Street turn.

Points of Interest

Dead Horse Ranch State Park adjoins Verde River Greenway State Natural Area. Use the Park as base camp to enjoy the natural surroundings of the Greenway. Be sure to visit Sedona & Jerome.

RV Sites		Water		Laundry	
Number	133	None		Wi-Fi	
Shaded	Y	At Site	Y	Fishing	Y
By Water	N	Spigots		Hiking	Y
Paved	Y	Sewer		Biking	Y
Pull Thru	Y	None		Swimming	Y
ADA	Y	At Site		Watch Wildlife	Y
Max RV Size	Any	Dump Station	Y	Pets	Y
Electric		Amenities		Security	
None		Restrooms	Y	Host(s)	Y
20 Amp	Y	Showers	Y	Rangers(s)	Y
30 Amp	Y	Reserve Sites	Y	Gate	
50 Amp	Y	Store	Y	Patrolled	
		Grill/Table	Y		

[11] Patagonia Lake State Park, I-19
Exit 1
North of Mexico Border
N 31 29.293 W 110 51.223
State Rate: $17-$28
(520) 287-6965
http://azstateparks.com/Parks/PALA/index.html

Directions

15 miles. From Exit 1 go 2 miles north on I-19 BUS. Turn left at AZ-82 E/W Patagonia Hwy. Go 11 miles then turn left. Go 2 miles on Patagonia Lake Rd. to the Park.

Points of Interest

Railroad buffs note that the tracks of the New Mexico/Arizona railroad lie beneath the lake! Fishermen catch bass, crappie, blue gill, catfish, & rainbow trout. Birdwatchers see the canyon towhee, Inca dove, vermilion flycatcher, black vulture, & hummingbird species.

RV Sites		Water		Laundry	
Number	105	None		Wi-Fi	
Shaded	Y	At Site	Y	Fishing	Y
By Water	Y	Spigots		Hiking	Y
Paved	Y	Sewer		Biking	Y
Pull Thru	Y	None		Swimming	Y
ADA	Y	At Site		Watch Wildlife	Y
Max RV Size	Any	Dump Station	Y	Pets	Y
Electric		Amenities		Security	
None		Restrooms	Y	Host(s)	Y
20 Amp	Y	Showers	Y	Rangers(s)	Y
30 Amp	Y	Reserve Sites	Y	Gate	
50 Amp	Y	Store	Y	Patrolled	
		Grill/Table	Y		

[12] Kaibab Lake Campground, I-40
Exit 165
West of Flagstaff
N35 16.871 W112 09.424
Kaibab NF Rate: $18 - $30
America/Beautiful Rate: $9 - $15
(928) 699-1239
http://www.fs.usda.gov/recarea/kaibab/recarea/?recid=11659

Directions

2 miles. From Exit 165 turn north on Hwy 64 for 1 mile to campground sign. Turn left 1 mile to campground.

Points of Interest

Sites are spacious and some overlook the lake. The campground is convenient to Williams. Take the Grand Canyon Railway train to the south rim of the Grand Canyon National Park. Spend a day in Old Town Flagstaff.

RV Sites		Water		Laundry	Y
Number	73	None		Wi-Fi	
Shaded	Y	At Site		Fishing	Y
By Water	Y	Spigots	Y	Hiking	Y
Paved	Y	Sewer		Biking	Y
Pull Thru	Y	None	N	Swimming	
ADA	Y	At Site		Watch Wildlife	Y
Max RV Size	40	Dump Station		Pets	Y
Electric		Amenities		Security	
None	N	Restrooms	Y	Host(s)	Y
20 Amp		Showers		Rangers(s)	Y
30 Amp		Reserve Sites	Y	Gate	
50 Amp		Store	Y	Patrolled	
		Grill/Table	Y		

[13] Dogtown Lake Camp, I-40
Exit 167
West of Flagstaff
N35 12.779 W112 07.565
Kaibab NF Rate: $18 - $30
America/Beautiful Rate: $9 - $15
(928) 699-1239
http://www.fs.usda.gov/recarea/
kaibab/recreation/wateractivities/
recarea/?recid=11656&actid=78

Directions

6 miles. From Exit 167 go south on Garland Prairie Road for about six miles.

Points of Interest

The area was a 'prairie dog town' before the lake was formed. Go to Williams & take the Grand Canyon Railway train to the south rim of the Grand Canyon National Park. Spend a day in Old Town Flagstaff with quaint shops & restaurants.

RV Sites		Water		Laundry	Y
Number	50	None		Wi-Fi	
Shaded	Yes	At Site		Fishing	Y
By Water	Y	Spigots	Y	Hiking	Y
Paved		Sewer		Biking	Y
Pull Thru	Y	None	N	Swimming	
ADA	Y	At Site		Watch Wildlife	Y
Max RV Size	40	Dump Station		Pets	Y
Electric		Amenities		Security	
None	N	Restrooms	Y	Host(s)	Y
20 Amp		Showers		Rangers(s)	Y
30 Amp		Reserve Sites	Y	Gate	
50 Amp		Store	Y	Patrolled	
		Grill/Table	Y		

[14] Bonito Campground, I-40
Exit 201
North of Flagstaff
N35 22.332 W111 33.372
Coconino NF Rate: $18
America/Beautiful Rate: $9
(928) 527-3600
http://www.fs.usda.gov/recarea/co-conino/recreation/camping-cabins/
recarea/?recid=55072&actid=29

Directions

14 miles. From Exit 201 take Rt. 89 north 12.5 miles to Sunset Crater/Wupaiki signs. Turn right at sign & go 1.9 miles to campground sign, turn left into camp.

Points of Interest

In Sunset Crater Volcano National Monument see volcano cinder cones, expanses of lava, still black in color. Wupatki National Monument contains pueblos with a deep red color. Spend a day in Old Town Flagstaff.

RV Sites		Water		Laundry	
Number	44	None		Wi-Fi	
Shaded	Y	At Site		Fishing	
By Water	N	Spigots	Y	Hiking	Y
Paved	Y	Sewer		Biking	Y
Pull Thru	Y	None	N	Swimming	
ADA	Y	At Site		Watch Wildlife	Y
Max RV Size	42	Dump Station		Pets	Y
Electric		Amenities		Security	
None	N	Restrooms	Y	Host(s)	Y
20 Amp		Showers		Rangers(s)	Y
30 Amp		Reserve Sites		Gate	
50 Amp		Store	Y	Patrolled	
		Grill/Table	Y		

[15] Homolovi Ruins State Park, I-40
Exit 257
Borders Winslow
N 35 01.524 W 110 37.733
State Rate: $15-$25
(928) 289-4106
http://azstateparks.com/Parks/HORU/index.html

Directions

1 mile. From Exit 257 go 1 mile north

Points of Interest

Hopi consider Homolovi part of their homeland & still make pilgrimages here. To protect this site, the Hopi supported the idea of Homolovi Ruins State Park. Visit the La Posada Hotel, the "last great railroad hotel" and 'Stand on a Corner' with The Eagles. Meteor Crater is close by.

RV Sites		Water		Laundry	
Number	52	None		Wi-Fi	
Shaded	Y	At Site	Y	Fishing	
By Water	N	Spigots	Y	Hiking	Y
Paved	Y	Sewer		Biking	Y
Pull Thru	Y	None		Swimming	
ADA	Y	At Site		Watch Wildlife	Y
Max RV Size	Any	Dump Station	Y	Pets	Y
Electric		Amenities		Security	
None		Restrooms	Y	Host(s)	Y
20 Amp	Y	Showers	Y	Rangers(s)	Y
30 Amp	Y	Reserve Sites	Y	Gate	
50 Amp	Y	Store	Y	Patrolled	
		Grill/Table	Y		

[16] Gila County RV Park, Hwy 60
In Globe
N 33 23.624 W 110 47.212
Gila County Rate: $20 - $28
(800) 436-8083
http://www.gilamini.com/index.html

Directions

0.3 miles. Turn east on W. Oak St. Go 2 blocks to S. Broad St., then right for 2 blocks to W. Cottonwood St. Go right again, one block to the campground.

Points of Interest

Antique shops, restaurants, a haunted jail, and Globe's beautifully restored train depot are within walking distance in the Historic Downtown District. Visit the Besh Ba Gowah Archeological Park. You'll see the Salado Ruins and Ethno-botanical & Botanical Gardens, said to be the largest collection of Salado pottery artifacts in the world.

RV Sites		Water		Laundry	
Number	20	None		Wi-Fi	Y
Shaded	Y	At Site	Y	Fishing	
By Water	Y	Spigots		Hiking	
Paved		Sewer		Biking	Y
Pull Thru		None		Swimming	
ADA		At Site	Y	Watch Wildlife	
Max RV Size	40	Dump Station		Pets	Y
Electric		Amenities		Security	
None		Restrooms	Y	Host(s)	Y
20 Amp	Y	Showers		Rangers(s)	
30 Amp	Y	Reserve Sites	Y	Gate	
50 Amp	Y	Store	Y	Patrolled	
		Grill/Table	Y		

[17] Fool Hollow Lake Recreation Area, Hwy 260
NW of Hwy 60
NW of Show Low
N 34 15.80 W 110 04.578
State Rate: $17 - $30
(928) 537-3680
http://azstateparks.com/Parks/FOHO/index.html

Directions

3.0 miles. Go NW for 2.0 miles on Hwy 260 from the intersection of Hwy 260 & Hwy 60 to W Old Linden Rd. Go right on W Old Linden Rd. for 0.6 miles to Fool Hollow Lake Rd. Turn left, go 0.5 miles to the park entrance.

Points of Interest

Show Low is the tourism hub of the White Mountains. Find championship golf courses for both leisure players and serious golfers. The White Mountains Trail system provides areas where you can go for a gentle walking or do some strenuous, heart pumping hiking, or try you hand at white water rafting.

RV Sites		Water		Laundry	
Number	123	None		Wi-Fi	
Shaded	Y	At Site	Y	Fishing	Y
By Water	Y	Spigots		Hiking	Y
Paved	Y	Sewer		Biking	Y
Pull Thru		None		Swimming	Y
ADA	Y	At Site	Y	Watch Wildlife	Y
Max RV Size	40	Dump Station	Y	Pets	Y
Electric		Amenities		Security	
None		Restrooms	Y	Host(s)	Y
20 Amp	Y	Showers	Y	Rangers(s)	Y
30 Amp	Y	Reserve Sites	Y	Gate	Y
50 Amp	Y	Store		Patrolled	
		Grill/Table	Y		

[18] Willow Beach Campground - Lake Mead NRA, Hwy 93
Southeast of Boulder City
N 35 52.168 W 114 39.614
Lake Mead NRA Rate: $35
(928) 767-4747
http://foreverresorts.com/foreverinfo.cfm?PropertyKey=129&ContentKey=429248

Directions

4.2 miles. On the Colorado River. From the junction of Hwy 93 & Willow Beach Rd (between mile markers 14 & 15), go NW for 4.2 miles on Willow Beach Rd to the campground/marina.

Points of Interest

The park offers scenic views of the Colorado river, the Black Canyon, solitude of the desert with mountains in the distance. The park is also just minutes from Hoover Dam. The location is perfect for those that want to be in the great outdoors, yet close to Las Vegas.

RV Sites		Water		Laundry	Y
Number	29	None		Wi-Fi	Y
Shaded		At Site	Y	Fishing	Y
By Water	Y	Spigots		Hiking	Y
Paved	Y	Sewer		Biking	Y
Pull Thru	Y	None		Swimming	Y
ADA	Y	At Site	Y	Watch Wildlife	
Max RV Size	45	Dump Station		Pets	Y
Electric		Amenities		Security	
None		Restrooms	Y	Host(s)	Y
20 Amp	Y	Showers	Y	Rangers(s)	Y
30 Amp	Y	Reserve Sites	Y	Gate	
50 Amp	Y	Store	Y	Patrolled	
		Grill/Table	Y		

[19] Wahweap Campground- Glen Canyon NRA, Hwy 89
On the Arizona/Utah State Line
N 36 59.947 W 111 29.891
Glen Canyon NRA Rate: $26-$48
(800) 528-6154

http://www.nps.gov/glca/planyourvisit/campgrounds.htm

Directions

3.5 miles south of the Arizona/Utah state line on Hwy 89, go east on Lakeshore Drive. Go 2.4 miles to the Lake Powell shore, then bear left on Lakeshore Drive for 0.4 miles to the campground entrance on your left.

Points of Interest

Check out the NPS Amphitheater programs. There are also a lot of other wonders of nature within a short drive - Antelope Canyons, Horseshoe Bend, Coyote Buttes and the Wave, White Pocket, Toadstools, Painted Desert, Glen & Marble Canyons.

RV Sites		Water		Laundry	Y
Number	202	None		Wi-Fi	Y
Shaded		At Site	Y	Fishing	Y
By Water	Y	Spigots	Y	Hiking	Y
Paved	Y	Sewer		Biking	Y
Pull Thru	Y	None		Swimming	Y
ADA	Y	At Site	Y	Watch Wildlife	
Max RV Size	45	Dump Station	Y	Pets	Y
Electric		Amenities		Security	
None		Restrooms	Y	Host(s)	Y
20 Amp	Y	Showers	Y	Rangers(s)	Y
30 Amp	Y	Reserve Sites	Y	Gate	
50 Amp	Y	Store	Y	Patrolled	
		Grill/Table	Y		

NOTES:

About Arkansas's Public Campgrounds

Campgrounds managed by the Corps of Engineers and the State of Arkansas tended to be the most accessible and best suited for RVers. Sixty percent of the camps listed here are in State Parks, the rest are on COE lands. The typical campground cited in the book has close to 70 sites & the fee will be around $24.

The State Parks of Arkansas have a comprehensive website, where you can book a campsite online, by phone, or at the park. Go to the following website and scroll to the bottom of the page for the Registration window-

http://www.arkansasstateparks.com/park-finder/

Arkansas State Parks generally are located on or near water. Most of the park campsites have water and electric hookups, dump stations, picnic tables, grills and lantern hangers. You need to call the individual campground to get information related to paved sites. All parks are pet friendly.

RV camping rates for all the state parks are:

Class AAA (Water/50 Amp/Sewer)-$30

Class AA (Electricity/Water/Sewer)-$27

Class A (Water/50 Amp)-$24

Class B (Water/30 Amp)-$19

Class C (Electricity or Water)-$15

Class D (no hookups)-$12

Discounts for all the state parks are:

Arkansas citizens over age 62 is 50%/Su-Th; 25%/Fr-Sa & holidays.

Out-of-State citizens over age 62 is 25%/Su-Th.

100% Disabled U.S. citizen is 50% anytime with written proof.

(See State website for details)

[1] Millwood State Park	**[12] Lake Poinsett State Park**
[2] Crater of Diamonds State Park	**[13] Tar Camp**
[3] White Oak State Park	**[14] Rising Star**
[4] DeGray Lake State Park	**[15] Lake Fort Smith State Park**
[5] Lake Catherine State Park	**[16] Devils Den State Park**
[6] Brady Mountain Camp	**[17] Horseshoe Bend Camp**
[7] Aux Arc Campground	**[18] Lake Chicot State Park**
[8] Lake Dardanelle State Park	**[19] Cane Creek State Park**
[9] Toad Suck Ferry Camp	**[20] Lake Frierson State Park**
[10] Willow Beach Camp	**[21] Crowley's Ridge State Park**
[11] Village Creek State Park	

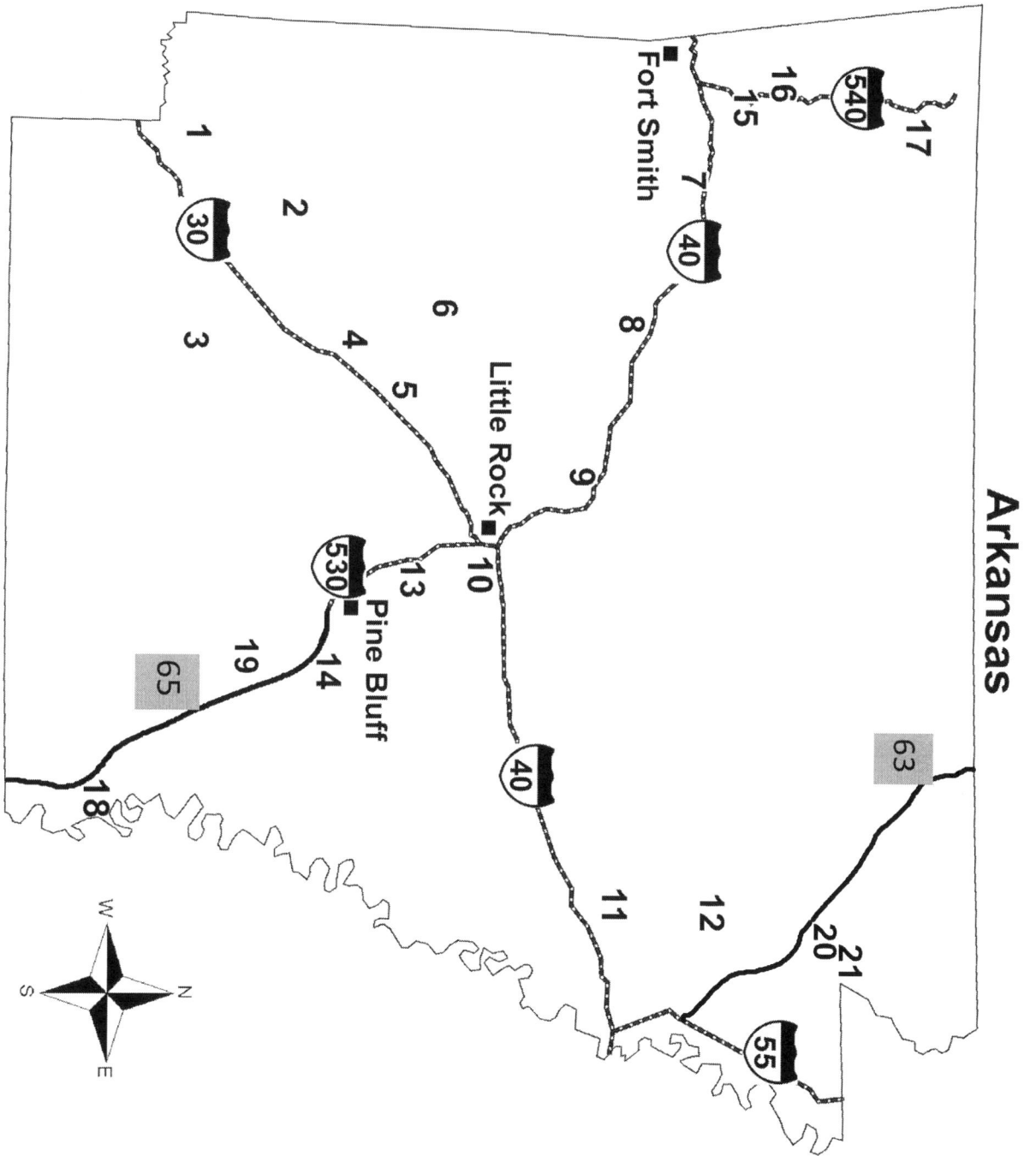

Arkansas

Fort Smith

16
15
540
17

1

30

2

3

7

40

6

4

5

8

Little Rock

9

530

13

10

Pine Bluff

19

65

14

40

18

11

12

63

20
21

55

N
E
S
W

[1] Millwood State Park
I-30, Exit 223 in Texas
(In TX on the AR/TX state line)
North of Texarkana
N33 40.870 W94 00.001
State Rates - See AR Introduction Page
(870) 898-2800
http://www.arkansasstateparks.com/Millwood/

Directions

25 miles. From Exit 223 drive 16 miles north on Hwy 71 to Ashdown, then 9 miles east on Hwy 32 to the park entrance.

Points of Interest

In Texarkana visit the Ace of Clubs house built in the shape of a playing card. Tour Historic Washington State Park. Music buff's will seek the mural of favorite son Scott Joplin. Check out the Perot Theater (an Italian Renaissance Theater built in 1924), & find Photographer's Island.

RV Sites		Water		Laundry	
Number	117	None		Wi-Fi	
Shaded	Y	At Site	Y	Fishing	Y
By Water	Y	Spigots		Hiking	Y
Paved		**Sewer**		Biking	Y
Pull Thru		None		Swimming	Y
ADA	Y	At Site	y	Watch Wildlife	Y
Max RV Size	45	Dump Station	Y	Pets	Y
Electric		**Amenities**		**Security**	
None		Restrooms	Y	Host(s)	Y
20 Amp	Y	Showers	Y	Rangers(s)	Y
30 Amp	Y	Reserve Sites	Y	Gate	
50 Amp	Y	Store	Y	Patrolled	
		Grill/Table	Y		

[2] Crater of Diamonds State Park
I-30, Exit 30
Northeast of Nashville, AR
N34 02.489 W93 40.573
State Rates - See AR Introduction Page
(870) 285-3113
http://www.craterofdiamondsstatepark.com/

Directions

43 miles. From Exit 30 go north on Hwy 278 for 27 miles to Nashville. Take Hwy 27 north and go 13 miles to Murfreesboro, then Hwy 301 southeast 3 miles to the park.

Points of Interest

This camp is farther off the Interstate for parks selected for the book but the unique appeal of the Crater of Diamonds made it a must addition. This is the only site in the world where the public can search for diamonds and "finder's keepers!" About 800 gems are found each year!

RV Sites		Water		Laundry	
Number	52	None		Wi-Fi	Y
Shaded	Y	At Site	Y	Fishing	
By Water	Y	Spigots		Hiking	Y
Paved	Y	**Sewer**		Biking	Y
Pull Thru		None		Swimming	Y
ADA	Y	At Site	Y	Watch Wildlife	Y
Max RV Size	45	Dump Station	Y	Pets	Y
Electric		**Amenities**		**Security**	
None		Restrooms	Y	Host(s)	Y
20 Amp	Y	Showers	Y	Rangers(s)	Y
30 Amp	Y	Reserve Sites	Y	Gate	
50 Amp	Y	Store	Y	Patrolled	
		Grill/Table	Y		

[3] White Oak Lake State Park
I-30, Exit 44
South of Arkadelphia
N33 41.323 W93 07.042
State Rates - See AR Introduction Page
(870) 685-2748
http://www.arkansasstateparks.com/whiteoaklake/

Directions

22 miles. From Exit 44 drive 20 miles east on Hwy 24. At Bluff City go 100 yards south on Hwy 299, then 2 miles southeast on Hwy 387 to Park entrance.

Points of Interest

In Prescott, with it's historic downtown, visit the Depot Museum. For the history buff, Civil War history abounds in the area. Visit President Clinton's Home Museum in Hope, just 15 miles away.

RV Sites		Water		Laundry	
Number	45	None		Wi-Fi	
Shaded	Y	At Site	Y	Fishing	Y
By Water	Y	Spigots		Hiking	Y
Paved	Y	**Sewer**		Biking	Y
Pull Thru	Y	None		Swimming	
ADA	Y	At Site		Watch Wildlife	Y
Max RV Size	45	Dump Station	Y	Pets	Y
Electric		**Amenities**		**Security**	
None		Restrooms	Y	Host(s)	Y
20 Amp	Y	Showers	Y	Rangers(s)	Y
30 Amp	Y	Reserve Sites	Y	Gate	
50 Amp	Y	Store	Y	Patrolled	
		Grill/Table	Y		

[4] DeGray Lake State Park
I-30, Exit 78
North of Arkadelphia
N34 15.355 W93 07.729
State Rates - See AR Introduction Page
(501) 865-5810
http://www.degray.com/

Directions

6 miles. From Exit 78 drive 6 miles north on Scenic 7 Byway to the park.

Points of Interest

DeGray, Arkansas's only resort state park, is set in the foothills of the Ouachita Mountains. Enjoy park guided lake cruises, kayak tours, Elderhostel, arts/crafts workshops, safaris, snorkeling, owl prowls, & square dances. Visit Garvan Woodland Gardens (University of Arkansas' Botanical Garden) or Hot Springs, AR, 'America's First Resort' & have a thermal springs spa.

RV Sites		Water		Laundry	
Number	113	None		Wi-Fi	
Shaded	Y	At Site	Y	Fishing	Y
By Water	Y	Spigots		Hiking	Y
Paved	Y	Sewer		Biking	Y
Pull Thru	Y	None		Swimming	Y
ADA	Y	At Site		Watch Wildlife	Y
Max RV Size	45	Dump Station	Y	Pets	Y
Electric		Amenities		Security	
None		Restrooms	Y	Host(s)	Y
20 Amp	Y	Showers	Y	Rangers(s)	Y
30 Amp	Y	Reserve Sites	Y	Gate	
50 Amp	Y	Store	Y	Patrolled	
		Grill/Table	Y		

[5] Lake Catherine State Park
I-30, Exit 97
Near Hot Springs
N34 26.223 W92 55.141
State Rates - See AR Introduction Page
(501) 844-4176
http://www.arkansasstateparks.com/lakecatherine/

Directions

12 miles. From Exit 97 near Malvern go 12 miles northwest on Hwy 171 to the park.

Points of Interest

The Park features rustic style facilities using native stone & wood, constructed by the CCC in the 1930s. Campsites offer lake and woodland views. Two of the park's campgrounds underwent recent total renovations. Near by, Diamondhead, a private resort community offers golf, snack bar, restaurant & Olympic-size swimming pool that park visitors are welcome to enjoy.

RV Sites		Water		Laundry	
Number	68	None		Wi-Fi	
Shaded	Y	At Site	Y	Fishing	Y
By Water	Y	Spigots		Hiking	Y
Paved	Y	Sewer		Biking	Y
Pull Thru		None		Swimming	Y
ADA	Y	At Site	Y	Watch Wildlife	Y
Max RV Size	45	Dump Station	Y	Pets	Y
Electric		Amenities		Security	
None		Restrooms	Y	Host(s)	Y
20 Amp	Y	Showers	Y	Rangers(s)	Y
30 Amp	Y	Reserve Sites	Y	Gate	
50 Amp	Y	Store	Y	Patrolled	
		Grill/Table	Y		

[6] Brady Mountain Camp
I-30, Exit 98
Northwest of Hot Springs
N34 34.814 W93 15.779
COE Rate: $14-$16
America/Beautiful Rate: $7-$8
(501) 760-1146
http://www.recreation.gov

Directions

33 miles. From Exit 98 drive 17 miles northwest on Hwy 270 to Hot Springs, then west 10 miles to Brady Mountain Access Road. Turn right and follow access road 6 miles north to the park.

Points of Interest

Visit Hot Springs. Enjoy a thermal springs spa. Wander downtown, with its classic hotels, Victorian architecture, art studios & renowned Bathhouse Row. Enjoy antique, crystal & rock shops, boutiques, specialty malls & a variety of restaurants.

RV Sites		Water		Laundry	
Number	74	None		Wi-Fi	
Shaded	Y	At Site	Y	Fishing	Y
By Water	Y	Spigots		Hiking	Y
Paved	Y	Sewer		Biking	Y
Pull Thru		None		Swimming	Y
ADA	Y	At Site		Watch Wildlife	Y
Max RV Size	45	Dump Station	Y	Pets	Y
Electric		Amenities		Security	
None		Restrooms	Y	Host(s)	
20 Amp	Y	Showers	Y	Rangers(s)	Y
30 Amp	Y	Reserve Sites	Y	Gate	
50 Amp	Y	Store		Patrolled	
		Grill/Table	Y		

[7] Aux Arc Campground
I-40, Exit 35
South of Ozark
N35 28.059 W93 49.329
COE Rate: $10-18
America/Beautiful Rate: $5-9
(479) 667-1100
http://www.recreation.gov

Directions

4 miles. From Exit 35 drive 2 miles on Hwy 23 to Ozark, continue 2 mi. to Hwy 309. Turn left and follow signs to the park.

Points of Interest

The City of Ozark has that wonderful small town feel. The square is filled with antique and gift shops. Venture into nearby Arkansas Wine Country, among the largest and oldest wine producing areas in the South, notably Altus, which is the Wine Capitol of Arkansas.

RV Sites		Water		Laundry	
Number	60	None		Wi-Fi	
Shaded	Y	At Site	Y	Fishing	Y
By Water	Y	Spigots		Hiking	Y
Paved	Y	Sewer		Biking	Y
Pull Thru		None		Swimming	
ADA	Y	At Site		Watch Wildlife	Y
Max RV Size	45	Dump Station	Y	Pets	Y
Electric		Amenities		Security	
None		Restrooms	Y	Host(s)	Y
20 Amp	Y	Showers	Y	Rangers(s)	Y
30 Amp	Y	Reserve Sites	Y	Gate	
50 Amp	Y	Store		Patrolled	
		Grill/Table	Y		

[8] Lake Dardanelle State Park
I-40, Exit 81
South of Russellville
N35 14.939 W93 12.784
State Rates - See AR Introduction Page
(479) 967-5516
http://www.arkansasstateparks.com/lakedardanelle/

Directions

11 miles. From Exit 81 at Russellville, take Hwy 7 south for 7 miles to the town of Dardanelle, turn right on Hwy 22 and travel 4 miles to the main park.

Points of Interest

The Park features a large Visitor Center over-looking the Lake. As a major bass fishing tournament site, the fishing tournament weigh-in pavilion is the first of its kind in the nation. Visit the main streets of Dardanelle & Russellville.

RV Sites		Water		Laundry	
Number	74	None		Wi-Fi	
Shaded	Y	At Site	Y	Fishing	Y
By Water	Y	Spigots		Hiking	Y
Paved	Y	Sewer		Biking	Y
Pull Thru		None		Swimming	Y
ADA	Y	At Site		Watch Wildlife	Y
Max RV Size	45	Dump Station	Y	Pets	Y
Electric		Amenities		Security	
None		Restrooms	Y	Host(s)	Y
20 Amp	Y	Showers	Y	Rangers(s)	Y
30 Amp	Y	Reserve Sites	Y	Gate	
50 Amp	Y	Store	Y	Patrolled	
		Grill/Table	Y		

[9] Toad Suck Ferry Camp
I-40, Exit 129
West of Conway
N35 04.663 W92 32.652
COE Rate: $18-$20
America/Beautiful Rate: $9-$10
(501)759-2005
http://www.recreation.gov

Directions

7 miles. From Exit 129 drive west for 7 miles on Hwy 60, follow signs into the campground.

Points of Interest

The river provides the perfect atmosphere to relax & watch riverboats & barges. Visit Conway, the second fastest growing city in Arkansas and home to 3 colleges, earning it the nickname "The City of Colleges." Enjoy the Conway Symphony, Community Arts, & Arkansas Shakespeare Theatre.

RV Sites		Water		Laundry	
Number	48	None		Wi-Fi	
Shaded	Y	At Site	Y	Fishing	Y
By Water	Y	Spigots		Hiking	
Paved	Y	Sewer		Biking	Y
Pull Thru		None		Swimming	Y
ADA	Y	At Site		Watch Wildlife	Y
Max RV Size	45	Dump Station	Y	Pets	Y
Electric		Amenities		Security	
None		Restrooms	Y	Host(s)	
20 Amp	Y	Showers	Y	Rangers(s)	Y
30 Amp	Y	Reserve Sites	Y	Gate	
50 Amp	Y	Store		Patrolled	
		Grill/Table	Y		

[10] Willow Beach Camp
I-40, Exit 159
East of Little Rock
N34 42.052 W92 08.289
COE Rate: $19
America/Beautiful Rate: $10
(501) 534-0451
http://www.recreation.gov/

Directions

10 miles. From Exit 159 drive 3 miles south on I-440 to Hwy 165, then east for 3 miles. Go south 3 miles on Colonel Maynard Road & west 1 mile on Blue Heron to the campground.

Points of Interest

Discover Little Rock by 'Little Rocks Tour' bus. Little Rock is the place to be with the bustling River Market District featuring restaurants, shops, bars, & museums. The Clinton Presidential Center is a significant addition to Little Rock.

RV Sites		Water		Laundry	
Number	23	None		Wi-Fi	
Shaded	Y	At Site	Y	Fishing	Y
By Water	Y	Spigots		Hiking	Y
Paved		Sewer		Biking	Y
Pull Thru		None		Swimming	
ADA	Y	At Site		Watch Wildlife	Y
Max RV Size	45	Dump Station	Y	Pets	Y
Electric		Amenities		Security	
None		Restrooms	Y	Host(s)	
20 Amp	Y	Showers	Y	Rangers(s)	Y
30 Amp	Y	Reserve Sites	Y	Gate	
50 Amp	Y	Store		Patrolled	
		Grill/Table	Y		

[11] Village Creek State Park
I-40, Exit 242
North of Forrest City
N35 10.284 W90 43.647
State Rates - See AR Introduction Page
(870) 238-9406
http://www.arkansasstateparks.com/villagecreek

Directions

13 miles From Exit 242 at Forrest City drive 13 miles north on Hwy 284 to the park entrance.

Points of Interest

Find the trail path crossing the 'Trail of Tears,' the relocation of Native Americans from their homelands to Indian Territory (present day Oklahoma). Forrest City, on Crowley's Ridge, the rugged & beautiful outcropping that runs from Missouri through Arkansas is a popular destination.

RV Sites		Water		Laundry	
Number	96	None		Wi-Fi	
Shaded	Y	At Site	Y	Fishing	Y
By Water	Y	Spigots		Hiking	Y
Paved	Y	Sewer		Biking	Y
Pull Thru	Y	None		Swimming	Y
ADA	Y	At Site	Y	Watch Wildlife	Y
Max RV Size	45	Dump Station	Y	Pets	Y
Electric		Amenities		Security	
None		Restrooms	Y	Host(s)	Y
20 Amp	Y	Showers	Y	Rangers(s)	Y
30 Amp	Y	Reserve Sites	Y	Gate	
50 Amp	Y	Store	Y	Patrolled	
		Grill/Table	Y		

[12] Lake Poinsett State Park
I-55, Exit 23
South of Jonesboro
N35 32.022 W90 41.272
State Rates - See AR Introduction Page
(870) 578-2064
http://www.arkansasstateparks.com/lakepoinsett/

Directions

25 miles. From Exit 23 drive 13 miles northwest on Hwy 63 to Hwy 14 then 10 miles west to Hwy 163 then 2 miles south to the park entrance.

Points of Interest

Downtown Jonesboro is filled with gift shops, restaurants, and art galleries. Arkansas State University offers one of the mid-South's finest museums & a fine arts center. Check out the Forum Civic Center and Theatre, known for its special productions as well as its art galleries.

RV Sites		Water		Laundry	
Number	29	None		Wi-Fi	
Shaded	Y	At Site	Y	Fishing	Y
By Water	Y	Spigots		Hiking	Y
Paved	some	Sewer		Biking	Y
Pull Thru		None		Swimming	
ADA		At Site		Watch Wildlife	Y
Max RV Size	45	Dump Station	Y	Pets	Y
Electric		Amenities		Security	
None		Restrooms	Y	Host(s)	Y
20 Amp	Y	Showers	Y	Rangers(s)	Y
30 Amp	Y	Reserve Sites	Y	Gate	
50 Amp	Y	Store	Y	Patrolled	
		Grill/Table	Y		

[13] Tar Camp
I-530, Exit 20
South of Little Rock
N34 27.741 W92 06.820
COE Rate: $19
America/Beautiful Rate: $10
(501) 397-5101
http://www.recreation.gov

Directions

5 miles. From Exit 20 go east on Hwy 46 through town for 0.9 miles to N. Brodie St. Go left for 2 blocks then turn right. Follow River Rd for 4 miles east to Tar Camp Park.

Points of Interest

The nearby town of Pine Bluff is the home for the Arkansas Railroad Museum, Pine Bluff Regional Park, the Martha Mitchell Home and other points of interest, as well as shopping and groceries.

RV Sites		Water		Laundry	
Number	53	None		Wi-Fi	
Shaded	Y	At Site	Y	Fishing	Y
By Water	Y	Spigots		Hiking	Y
Paved		Sewer		Biking	
Pull Thru		None		Swimming	
ADA		At Site		Watch Wildlife	Y
Max RV Size	45	Dump Station	Y	Pets	Y
Electric		Amenities		Security	
None		Restrooms	Y	Host(s)	
20 Amp	Y	Showers	Y	Rangers(s)	Y
30 Amp	Y	Reserve Sites	Y	Gate	
50 Amp	Y	Store		Patrolled	
		Grill/Table	Y		

[14] Rising Star
I-530, Exit 46
East of Pine Bluff
N34 09.925 W91 44.210
COE Rate: $19
America/Beautiful Rate: $10
(870) 534-0451
http://www.recreation.gov/

Directions

12 miles. From Exit 46 take Hwy 65 south for 8 miles then left for 4 miles on Blankenship Road to Rising Star Campground.

Points of Interest

Visit Pine Bluff, the 'City of Murals.' Enjoy The Arts and Science Center, which features theatrical performances and workshops. Pine Bluff has the only museum dedicated to the history of band music and instruments. Visit the Arkansas Railroad Museum and the Martha Mitchell Home.

RV Sites		Water		Laundry	
Number	25	None		Wi-Fi	
Shaded	Y	At Site	Y	Fishing	Y
By Water	Y	Spigots		Hiking	Y
Paved		Sewer		Biking	Y
Pull Thru		None		Swimming	
ADA	Y	At Site		Watch Wildlife	Y
Max RV Size	45	Dump Station	Y	Pets	Y
Electric		Amenities		Security	
None		Restrooms	Y	Host(s)	Y
20 Amp	Y	Showers	Y	Rangers(s)	Y
30 Amp	Y	Reserve Sites	Y	Gate	
50 Amp	Y	Store		Patrolled	
		Grill/Table	Y		

[15] Lake Fort Smith State Park
I-540, Exit 29
North of Fort Smith
N35 41.721 W94 07.141
State Rates - See AR Introduction Page
(479) 369-2469
http://www.arkansasstateparks.com/lakefortsmith/

Directions

9 miles. Take Exit #29 off I-540. Go east on Ark. 282 for 1.8 miles to U.S. 71, then north for 7.5 miles to Shepherd Springs Road, turn east and go 2 miles to the park.

Points of Interest

Sightsee the Fort Smith riverfront and Belle Grove Historic District. Walk the downtown riverfront areas & you'll find boutiques, cafes and clothing stores from consignment to elegant antique shops including an old west cowboy store.

RV Sites		Water		Laundry	
Number	30	None		Wi-Fi	
Shaded	Y	At Site	Y	Fishing	Y
By Water	Y	Spigots		Hiking	Y
Paved	Y	Sewer		Biking	Y
Pull Thru	Y	None		Swimming	Y
ADA	Y	At Site		Watch Wildlife	Y
Max RV Size	45	Dump Station	Y	Pets	Y
Electric		Amenities		Security	
None		Restrooms	Y	Host(s)	Y
20 Amp	Y	Showers	Y	Rangers(s)	Y
30 Amp	Y	Reserve Sites	Y	Gate	
50 Amp	Y	Store	Y	Patrolled	
		Grill/Table	Y		

[16] Devils Den State Park
I-50, Exit 53
South of Fayetteville
N35 46.941 W94 14.974
State Rates - See AR Introduction Page
(479) 761-3325
http://www.arkansasstateparks.com/devilsden

Directions

17 miles. From Exit 53 go 17 miles southwest on Hwy 170 to the park (RVs over 26 feet are advised not to use Exit 45 and Hwy 74 - a mountainous road).

Points of Interest

RVers can explore one or more of the Park's many caves and crevices. Nearby, Fayetteville is a unique mix of college town, outdoor-lovers delight, cultural/arts center, & home to the University of Arkansas; and recognized by Forbes magazine as a top five smaller town.

RV Sites		Water		Laundry	
Number	93	None		Wi-Fi	
Shaded	Y	At Site	Y	Fishing	
By Water	Y	Spigots		Hiking	Y
Paved	Y	**Sewer**		Biking	Y
Pull Thru		None		Swimming	Y
ADA		At Site	Y	Watch Wildlife	Y
Max RV Size	45	Dump Station	Y	Pets	Y
Electric		**Amenities**		**Security**	
None		Restrooms	Y	Host(s)	Y
20 Amp	Y	Showers	Y	Rangers(s)	
30 Amp	Y	Reserve Sites	Y	Gate	
50 Amp	Y	Store	Y	Patrolled	
		Grill/Table	Y		

[17] Horseshoe Bend Camp
I-540, Exit 83
East of Bentonville/Rogers
N36 17.193 W94 01.448
COE Rate: $18
America/Beautiful Rate: $9
(479) 925-2561
http://www.recreation.gov

Directions

11 miles From Exit 83 take Hwy 94 east (W New Hope Rd.) for 5.3 miles to Monte NE Rd. Bear right, go 1.6 miles to Hwy 94 Rd. Turn left, go 0.8 miles to Panorama Rd. Turn right, go 3.2 miles to the Camp.

Points of Interest

Visit Bentonville, enjoy Opera in the Ozarks, the Northwest Arkansas Symphony, Walton Arts Center & Arends Arts Center. Discover Roger's many historically significant buildings with an historic aura.

RV Sites		Water		Laundry	
Number	136	None		Wi-Fi	
Shaded	Y	At Site	Y	Fishing	Y
By Water	Y	Spigots		Hiking	Y
Paved		**Sewer**		Biking	Y
Pull Thru	Y	None		Swimming	
ADA	Y	At Site	Y	Watch Wildlife	Y
Max RV Size	45	Dump Station	Y	Pets	Y
Electric		**Amenities**		**Security**	
None		Restrooms	Y	Host(s)	
20 Amp	Y	Showers	Y	Rangers(s)	Y
30 Amp	Y	Reserve Sites	Y	Gate	Y
50 Amp	Y	Store		Patrolled	
		Grill/Table	Y		

[18] Lake Chicot State Park
Hwy 144
Northeast of Lake Village.
N33 22.683 W91 11.542
State Rates - See AR Introduction Page
(870) 265-5480
http://www.arkansasstateparks.com/lakechicot/

Directions

8 miles. At St. Mary's St. in Lake Village turn east for 0.6 miles to Lake Shore Drive (Hwy 144). Turn left, go 7.2 miles to Hwy 257 & the campground.

Points of Interest

The Mississippi Delta's captivating beauty & recreational opportunities come together at Arkansas's largest natural lake, Lake Chicot. Cut off centuries ago when the Mississippi River changed course, this peaceful setting offers some of the best birding opportunities in Arkansas.

RV Sites		Water		Laundry	Y
Number	122	None		Wi-Fi	Y
Shaded	Y	At Site	Y	Fishing	Y
By Water	Y	Spigots		Hiking	Y
Paved		**Sewer**		Biking	Y
Pull Thru	Y	None		Swimming	Y
ADA	Y	At Site	Y	Watch Wildlife	Y
Max RV Size	45	Dump Station	Y	Pets	Y
Electric		**Amenities**		**Security**	
None		Restrooms	Y	Host(s)	Y
20 Amp	Y	Showers	Y	Rangers(s)	Y
30 Amp	Y	Reserve Sites	Y	Gate	
50 Amp	Y	Store	Y	Patrolled	
		Grill/Table	Y		

[19] Cane Creek State Park
Hwy 425
South Side of Star City
N33 54.780 W91 45.882
State Rates - See AR Introduction Page
(870) 628-4714
http://www.arkansasstateparks.com/canecreek/

Directions

6 miles From Hwy 425 take Hwy 293 on the south side of Star City. Go 5.5 miles east to the park.

Points of Interest

With great fishing and a 15.5 mile multipurpose hiking trail (the only one of its kind in south Arkansas and parts of Mississippi) provides a challenging adventure for hikers, and bicyclist alike. Just across Cane Creek Lake timber-filled lake, anglers and paddlers can also explore Bayou Bartholomew, the world's longest bayou.

RV Sites		Water		Laundry	
Number	29	None		Wi-Fi	
Shaded	Y	At Site	Y	Fishing	Y
By Water	Y	Spigots		Hiking	Y
Paved	Y	Sewer		Biking	Y
Pull Thru		None		Swimming	
ADA	Y	At Site		Watch Wildlife	Y
Max RV Size	45	Dump Station	Y	Pets	Y
Electric		Amenities		Security	
None		Restrooms	Y	Host(s)	Y
20 Amp	Y	Showers	Y	Rangers(s)	Y
30 Amp	Y	Reserve Sites	Y	Gate	
50 Amp	Y	Store	Y	Patrolled	
		Grill/Table	Y		

[20] Lake Frierson State Park
Hwy 141
North of Jonesboro
State Rates - See AR Introduction Page
N35 58.349 W90 42.940
(870) 932-2615
http://www.arkansasstateparks.com/lakefrierson/

Directions

12 miles. In southwest Joneboro, where Hwy 49 meets Hwy 63, go northeast on Southwest Dr., which becomes Main St., then Hwy 141. Follow Hwy 141 for 12 miles north to the campground

Points of Interest

The park is a peaceful place to relax and enjoy the year-round fishing. *A bathhouse and sanitary dump station are at nearby Crowley's Ridge State Park. Jonesboro has the venues to satisfy the music lover and patron of the visual and performing arts.

RV Sites		Water		Laundry	
Number	4	None		Wi-Fi	
Shaded	Y	At Site	Y	Fishing	Y
By Water	Y	Spigots		Hiking	Y
Paved	Y	Sewer		Biking	Y
Pull Thru		None		Swimming	
ADA	Y	At Site		Watch Wildlife	Y
Max RV Size	40	Dump Station	*	Pets	Y
Electric		Amenities		Security	
None		Restrooms	Y	Host(s)	
20 Amp	Y	Showers	Y	Rangers(s)	Y
30 Amp	Y	Reserve Sites	Y	Gate	
50 Amp		Store	Y	Patrolled	
		Grill/Table	Y		

[21] Crowley's Ridge State Park
Hwy 141
North of Jonesboro
State Rates - See AR Introduction Page
N36 2.691" W90 40.007
(870) 573-6751
http://www.arkansasstateparks.com/crowleysridge/

Directions

18 miles. In southwest Joneboro, where Hwy 49 meets Hwy 63, go northeast on Southwest Dr., which becomes Main St., then Hwy 141. Follow Hwy 141 for 18 miles to Walcott, then 0.2 miles to the campground

Points of Interest

Native log and stone structures, constructed by the Civilian Conservation Corps in the 1930s, set the mood for this park's rustic warmth. The park offers fishing boat, kayak, & pedal boat rentals & Interpretive programs.

RV Sites		Water		Laundry	
Number	18	None		Wi-Fi	
Shaded	Y	At Site	Y	Fishing	Y
By Water	Y	Spigots		Hiking	Y
Paved		Sewer		Biking	Y
Pull Thru	Y	None		Swimming	Y
ADA	Y	At Site		Watch Wildlife	Y
Max RV Size	45	Dump Station	Y	Pets	Y
Electric		Amenities		Security	
None		Restrooms	Y	Host(s)	
20 Amp	Y	Showers	Y	Rangers(s)	Y
30 Amp	Y	Reserve Sites	Y	Gate	
50 Amp		Store	Y	Patrolled	
		Grill/Table	Y		

About California's Public Campgrounds

The State Parks System has a very helpful and comprehensive website -

http://www.parks.ca.gov/

Campground reservations for over 560 public campgrounds in California can be made though Reserve America (**http://www.reserveamerica.com**) including most State Parks. Many campgrounds fill-up months ahead so plan in advance. Of the almost 120 State Parks less than 15 currently can accommodate an RV of 36 feet or more.

Be advised that the basic California length law for vehicles is 40 feet unless specifically exempted. The California Vehicle Code (CVC) does allow motorhomes over 40 feet in length, up to 45 feet, on certain routes. Over-length motorhomes are allowed on interstates and on those State routes that can accommodate them. Over-length motorhomes may travel on virtually every State route EXCEPT those signed with a 30-foot kingpin-to-rear-axle (KPRA) advisory sign.

In light of the State's RV length law many State Parks are restrictive on RV lengths over 35-40 feet so there are a limited number of State Parks listed in this chapter. On the other hand the California Counties have an exceptional collection of RV friendly parks, a number of which are cataloged here. The strong presence of National Forests (NF) shows in the list of some of the campgrounds noted here.

As you might expect the State Park Camps are higher priced ($35-$62), while county parks fall in the $16-$27 range. As is typical for other states, the Federal campgrounds represent the fee bargain at $5-$18 with an America the Beautiful card.

[1] Guajome County Park	[12] Dos Picos County Park
[2] San Onofre State Beach	[13] Lake Elsinore County Park
[3] Bolsa Chica State Beach	[14] Table Mountain
[4] Los Alamos Camp	[15] Calico Ghost Town
[5] Kern River County Park	[16] Loggers Campground
[6] Dos Reis County Park	[17] El Capitan State Beach
[7] Sycamore Grove	[18] Pismo State Beach - North Beach
[8] Antlers	[19] Standish-Hickey SRA
[9] Burnt Rancheria	[20] Richardson Grove State Park
[10] Cottonwood Camp	[21] Humboldt Redwoods State Park
[11] Mayflower County Park	[22] Redwood National and State Parks

California

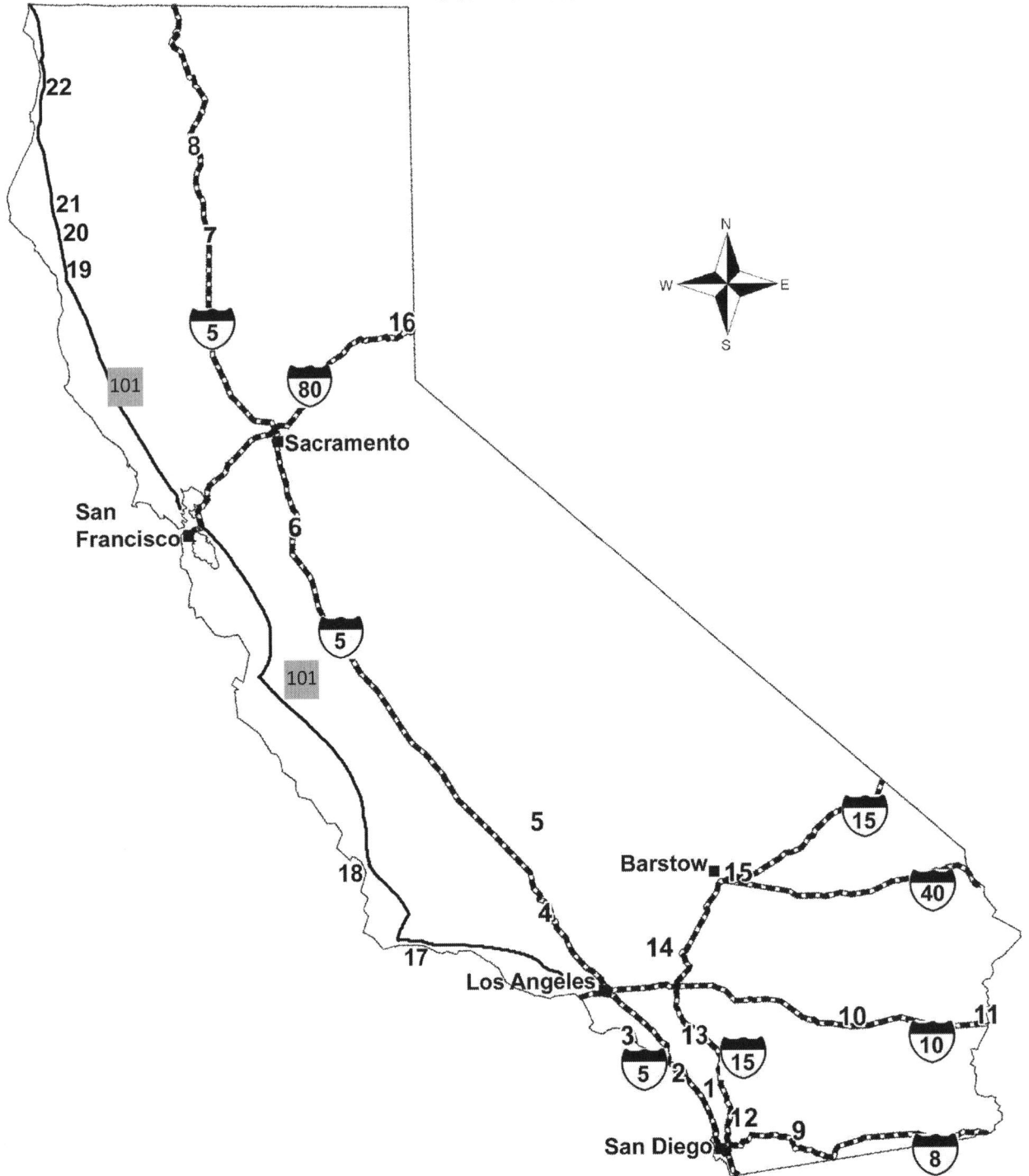

[1] Guajome County Park
I-5, Exit 54
In City of Oceanside
N33 14.829 W117 16.348
County Rate: $29
(760) 724 4489
http://www.co.san-diego.ca.us/parks/Camping/
guajome.html

Directions

7 miles. From Exit 54 drive east on Hwy 76 for 8 miles to Guajome Lake Rd. Turn right on Guajome Lake Rd. and proceed to the park main entrance on your right.

Points of Interest

The Park is located in the coastal community of Oceanside & has good access to San Diego County activities. The Park ponds attract migratory birds. Five miles of park trails wander through woodland, chaparral, wetland, & mixed grassland habitats.

RV Sites		Water		Laundry	
Number	33	None		Wi-Fi	
Shaded	Y	At Site	Y	Fishing	Y
By Water		Spigots		Hiking	
Paved	Y	**Sewer**		Biking	Y
Pull Thru		None		Swimming	
ADA	Y	At Site		Watch Wildlife	
Max RV Size	45	Dump Station	Y	Pets	Y
Electric		**Amenities**		**Security**	
None		Restrooms	Y	Host(s)	Y
20 Amp	Y	Showers	Y	Rangers(s)	Y
30 Amp	Y	Reserve Sites	Y	Gate	
50 Amp		Store		Patrolled	
		Grill/Table	Y		

[2] San Onofre State Beach
I-5, Exit 71
San Mateo Campground
Near San Clemente
N33 22.444 W117 33.735
State Rate: $45 - $60
(949) 492-4872
http://www.parks.ca.gov/?page_id=647

Directions

1.5 mile. From Exit 71 (Exit Basilone) turn toward the ocean and follow Old Pacific Hwy for 1.5 mile. Turn right on to Beach Club Rd. to the Park.

Points of Interest

The campground is just inland from the sandy beaches of San Onofre State Beach. A 1.5-mile nature trail connects the campground to the well known surf of Trestles Beach. View wetland habitats, which host some rare, endangered species.

RV Sites		Water		Laundry	
Number	70	None		Wi-Fi	
Shaded	Y	At Site	Y	Fishing	Y
By Water	Y	Spigots		Hiking	Y
Paved	Y	**Sewer**		Biking	
Pull Thru		None		Swimming	Y
ADA	Y	At Site		Watch Wildlife	
Max RV Size	36	Dump Station	Y	Pets	Y
Electric		**Amenities**		**Security**	
None		Restrooms	Y	Host(s)	Y
20 Amp	Y	Showers	Y	Rangers(s)	Y
30 Amp	Y	Reserve Sites	Y	Gate	
50 Amp		Store		Patrolled	
		Grill/Table	Y		

[3] Bolsa Chica State Beach
I-5, Exit 107
In Huntington Beach
N33 41.558 W118 02.657
State Rate: $50-$65
(714) 846-3460
http://www.parks.ca.gov/?page_id=642

Directions:

The beach extends from Pacific Coast Highway at Golden West to Pacific Coast Highway at Warner Ave.

Points of Interest

The camp is a popular place for surf fishing and bare-handed fishing for California grunion. The beach extends 3 miles from Seal Beach to Huntington Beach City Pier. There is a bikeway. Watchable wildlife options are also available. Bolsa Chica Ecological Reserve is close by.

RV Sites		Water		Laundry	
Number	55	None		Wi-Fi	
Shaded		At Site	Y	Fishing	Y
By Water	Y	Spigots		Hiking	Y
Paved	Y	**Sewer**		Biking	Y
Pull Thru		None		Swimming	Y
ADA	Y	At Site		Watch Wildlife	Y
Max RV Size	40	Dump Station	Y	Pets	Y
Electric		**Amenities**		**Security**	
None		Restrooms	Y	Host(s)	Y
20 Amp	Y	Showers	Y	Rangers(s)	Y
30 Amp	Y	Reserve Sites	Y	Gate	
50 Amp	Y	Store		Patrolled	
		Grill/Table	Y		

[4] Los Alamos Camp
I-5, Exit 195
North of Santa Clarita
N34 42.198 W118 48.337
Angeles NF Rate: $20 - $25
America/Beautiful Rate: $10 - $12
(805) 434-1996
http://www.forestcamping.com/dow/pacficsw/
angcmp.htm#los%20alamos

Directions

4 miles. From Exit 195 turn southwest on Smokey Bear Rd. to Pyramid Lake Rd. Go 1.5 miles south on Pyramid Lake Rd. Turn right at sign and go 2 miles north on Hard Luck Rd. to campground.

Points of Interest

Just south, in Santa Clarita enjoy the golf courses, dining, & a rich western heritage. Also visit Mentryville, the William S. Hart Museum.

RV Sites		Water		Laundry	
Number	93	None		Wi-Fi	
Shaded	some	At Site		Fishing	Y
By Water	Y	Spigots	Y	Hiking	Y
Paved	Y	**Sewer**		Biking	Y
Pull Thru	Y	None		Swimming	Y
ADA	Y	At Site		Watch Wildlife	Y
Max RV Size	45	Dump Station	Y	Pets	Y
Electric		**Amenities**		**Security**	
None	Y	Restrooms	Y	Host(s)	Y
20 Amp		Showers		Rangers(s)	Y
30 Amp		Reserve Sites	Y	Gate	
50 Amp		Store	Y	Patrolled	
		Grill/Table	Y		

[5] Kern River County Park
I-5, Exit 257
East of Bakersfield
N35 26.730 W118 55.193
County Rate: $22-$27
(661) 872-5149
http://www.co.kern.ca.us/parks/kern-river-camp.asp

Directions

33 miles. From Exit 257 follow Hwy 58 east. Go 20.6 miles on Hwy 58. At Hwy 99 continue straight, now on Hwy 178, for 7 miles to Fairfax Rd. Turn left for 2.2 miles to Alfred Harrell Hwy. Turn right, go 3.2 miles to the camp.

Points of Interest

Enjoy Bakersfield, its proximity to Sequoia National Forest and largest collection of Basque restaurants in the US. Visit the California Living Museum (CALM) California's Premier Native Zoo/Garden.

RV Sites		Water		Laundry	
Number	50	None		Wi-Fi	
Shaded	Y	At Site	Y	Fishing	
By Water	Y	Spigots		Hiking	
Paved		**Sewer**		Biking	
Pull Thru	Y	None		Swimming	
ADA		At Site		Watch Wildlife	
Max RV Size	45	Dump Station	Y	Pets	fee
Electric		**Amenities**		**Security**	
None	Y	Restrooms	Y	Host(s)	Y
20 Amp		Showers	Y	Rangers(s)	
30 Amp		Reserve Sites		Gate	
50 Amp		Store		Patrolled	
		Grill/Table	Y		

[6] Dos Reis County Park
I-5, Exit 463
South of Stockton
N37 49.805 W121 18.646
County Rate: $25 - $30
(209) 953-8800
http://www.sjparks.com/parks/dos-reis-regional-park.aspx

Directions

2 miles. From Exit 463 go west to the frontage road, Matheny Rd., then 0.5 miles north to Dos Reis Rd. Turn west for 1 mile to the park.

Points of Interest

Stockton is close by with many sightseeing venues plus opportunities to enjoy music, theater, dance, literary events, and other cultural and entertainment programs. The City has its own symphony and opera company and hosts the popular Asparagus Festival.

RV Sites		Water		Laundry	
Number	26	None		Wi-Fi	
Shaded	Y	At Site	Y	Fishing	
By Water	Y	Spigots		Hiking	Y
Paved	Y	**Sewer**		Biking	Y
Pull Thru	Y	None		Swimming	
ADA	Y	At Site	Y	Watch Wildlife	
Max RV Size	45	Dump Station		Pets	fee
Electric		**Amenities**		**Security**	
None		Restrooms	Y	Host(s)	Y
20 Amp	Y	Showers	Y	Rangers(s)	
30 Amp	Y	Reserve Sites	Y	Gate	
50 Amp		Store		Patrolled	
		Grill/Table	Y		

[7] Sycamore Grove
I-5, Exit 649
Southeast of Red Bluff
N40 09.364 W122 12.251
Mendocino NF Rate: $16-$30
America/Beautiful Rate: $8-$15
(530) 527-1196
http://www.reserveamerica.com/

Directions

3 miles. From Exit 649 go east on Hwy 36 (Antelope Blvd) 0.3 miles, turn south on Sale Lane for 2.2 miles to the park.

Points of Interest

In Red Bluff visit Gaumer's Mineral Museum & find gems, minerals, fossils, Native American carvings, and a mining exhibit. The Kelly-Griggs House Museum is a trip into the past, through this classic Victorian home decorated with pioneer, early Chinese & Native American artifacts.

RV Sites		Water		Laundry	
Number	30	None		Wi-Fi	
Shaded	Y	At Site	Y	Fishing	Y
By Water	Y	Spigots		Hiking	Y
Paved	Y	**Sewer**		Biking	Y
Pull Thru	Y	None	Y	Swimming	Y
ADA	Y	At Site		Watch Wildlife	Y
Max RV Size	45	Dump Station		Pets	Y
Electric		**Amenities**		**Security**	
None		Restrooms	Y	Host(s)	Y
20 Amp	Y	Showers	Y	Rangers(s)	
30 Amp	Y	Reserve Sites	Y	Gate	Y
50 Amp	Y	Store	Y	Patrolled	
		Grill/Table	Y		

[8] Antlers
I-5, Exit 702
North of Redding
N40 53.155 W122 22.847
Shasta NF Rate: $20-$35
America/Beautiful Rate: $10-$17
(530) 275-1589
http://www.recreation.gov/

Directions

1 mile. From Exit 702 go east to the Antlers Rd. frontage road, then right for 1 mile to the park.

Points of Interest

In Redding walk the Sundial Bridge at Turtle Bay. Explore nature's underground works, thousands of years in the making, at Lake Shasta Caverns. Visit Lassen Volcanic National Park. In 1914 the volcano erupted, beginning a 7-year cycle of sporadic volcanic outbursts.

RV Sites		Water		Laundry	
Number	45	None		Wi-Fi	
Shaded	Y	At Site	Y	Fishing	Y
By Water	Y	Spigots		Hiking	
Paved	Y	**Sewer**		Biking	
Pull Thru		None	Y	Swimming	Y
ADA	Y	At Site		Watch Wildlife	Y
Max RV Size	45	Dump Station		Pets	Y
Electric		**Amenities**		**Security**	
None	Y	Restrooms	Y	Host(s)	Y
20 Amp		Showers		Rangers(s)	Y
30 Amp		Reserve Sites	Y	Gate	
50 Amp		Store	Y	Patrolled	
		Grill/Table	Y		

[9] Burnt Rancheria
I-8, Exit 47
Northeast of Pine Valley
N32 51.655 W116 25.252
Cleveland NF Rate: $20
America/Beautiful Rate: $10
(619) 473-0120
http://www.recreation.gov/

Directions

10 miles. From Exit 47 take Sunrise Hwy S1 northeast for 10 miles to Milepost 23. Stop at entrance for campground information and site location.

Points of Interest

The San Diego State University Observatory sponsors 'Star Parties' for campers. Enjoy a hike along the Desert View Nature Trail and interpretive programs. Visit the old country Our Lady of the Pines Catholic Church.

RV Sites		Water		Laundry	
Number	49	None	Y	Wi-Fi	
Shaded	Y	At Site		Fishing	
By Water		Spigots		Hiking	Y
Paved		**Sewer**		Biking	Y
Pull Thru		None		Swimming	
ADA	Y	At Site	Y	Watch Wildlife	Y
Max RV Size	45	Dump Station		Pets	Y
Electric		**Amenities**		**Security**	
None	Y	Restrooms	Y	Host(s)	Y
20 Amp		Showers	Y	Rangers(s)	Y
30 Amp		Reserve Sites	Y	Gate	
50 Amp		Store		Patrolled	
		Grill/Table	Y		

[10] Cottonwood Camp
I-10, Exit 168
East of Indio
N33 44.889 W115 49.482
Joshua Tree NP Rate: $15
America/Beautiful Rate: $8
(877) 444-6777
http://www.nps.gov/jotr/planyourvisit/camping.htm

Directions

4 miles. From Exit 168 take Cottonwood Spring Rd. north for 4 miles to the park entrance for campground information and site location.

Points of Interest

A highlight is the night sky. The desert environment allows for great views of the moon over the mountains. With its mild winter & rock formations, plants & wildlife, Joshua Tree is excellent for hiking.

RV Sites		Water		Laundry	
Number	62	None		Wi-Fi	
Shaded		At Site		Fishing	
By Water		Spigots	Y	Hiking	Y
Paved	Y	**Sewer**		Biking	
Pull Thru	Y	None		Swimming	
ADA	Y	At Site		Watch Wildlife	Y
Max RV Size	40	Dump Station	Y	Pets	Y
Electric		**Amenities**		**Security**	
None	Y	Restrooms	Y	Host(s)	Y
20 Amp		Showers		Rangers(s)	Y
30 Amp		Reserve Sites	Y	Gate	
50 Amp		Store		Patrolled	
		Grill/Table	Y		

[11] Mayflower County Park
I-10, Exit 241
West of Quartzsite
N33 40.250 W114 32.038
County Rate: $20-$35
(760) 922-4665
http://www.rivcoparks.org/parks/mayflower/mayflower-park-home/

Directions

7 miles. From Exit 241 go north on Hwy 95 (Intake Blvd.) for 4 miles, then east on 6th Ave. for 3 miles to Colorado River Rd., then left into the park.

Points of Interest

The Blythe Intaglios, a group of gigantic figures are found 15 miles north of Blythe, the largest is 171 feet. The figures are between 450 & 2,000 years old. On hikes, watch for the Chuckwalla, a stocky wide-bodied lizard up to 16 inches long!

RV Sites		Water		Laundry	
Number	152	None		Wi-Fi	Y
Shaded	Y	At Site	Y	Fishing	Y
By Water	Y	Spigots		Hiking	
Paved		**Sewer**		Biking	Y
Pull Thru	Y	None		Swimming	
ADA	Y	At Site		Watch Wildlife	
Max RV Size	45	Dump Station	Y	Pets	Y
Electric		**Amenities**		**Security**	
None		Restrooms	Y	Host(s)	Y
20 Amp	Y	Showers	Y	Rangers(s)	Y
30 Amp	Y	Reserve Sites	Y	Gate	
50 Amp	Y	Store		Patrolled	
		Grill/Table	Y		

[12] Dos Picos County Park
I-15, Exit 17
Northeast of San Diego
N32 59.944 W116 56.473
County Rate: $24-$29
(760) 789-2220
http://www.sdcounty.ca.gov/parks/Camping/dos_picos.html

Directions

18 miles. From Exit 17 go east on Scripps Poway Pkwy. for 8.6 miles to Hwy 67. Turn north for 7.5 miles to Mussey Grade Rd. Turn right for 2 mile to Dos Picos Park Rd. and follow this 1 mile to the park.

Points of Interest

With 30 museums & 9 theatres, Balboa Park is the cultural heart. Visit the Timken Museum of Art, Opera or the Air & Space Museum or try a show at The Old Globe.

RV Sites		Water		Laundry	
Number	57	None		Wi-Fi	
Shaded	Y	At Site	Y	Fishing	Y
By Water	Y	Spigots		Hiking	Y
Paved		**Sewer**		Biking	Y
Pull Thru	Y	None		Swimming	
ADA	Y	At Site		Watch Wildlife	
Max RV Size	40	Dump Station	Y	Pets	fee
Electric		**Amenities**		**Security**	
None		Restrooms	Y	Host(s)	Y
20 Amp	Y	Showers	Y	Rangers(s)	Y
30 Amp	Y	Reserve Sites	Y	Gate	
50 Amp		Store		Patrolled	
		Grill/Table	Y		

[13] Lake Elsinore County Park
I-15, *Exit Lake Elsinore/Central Ave.*
South of Carona
N33 40.594 W117 22.423
County Rate: $25-$35
(800) 416-6992
http://www.rockymountainrec.com/lake-elsinore/

Directions

3 miles. Take the Lake Elsinore/Central Ave Exit southwest toward the lake. Turn right onto Collier (Hwy 74). Go 0.5 miles. Turn left on Riverside Dr. for 2.2 miles to the park entrance on the left.

Points of Interest

Lake Elsinore is the largest natural freshwater lake in Southern California and is set against the Ortega Mountains. You are surrounded by outdoor activities, historic sites, Hollywood, Los Angeles, Disneyland.

RV Sites		Water		Laundry	Y
Number	120	None		Wi-Fi	
Shaded	Y	At Site	Y	Fishing	Y
By Water	Y	Spigots	Y	Hiking	Y
Paved		Sewer		Biking	Y
Pull Thru		None		Swimming	Y
ADA	Y	At Site		Watch Wildlife	
Max RV Size	40	Dump Station	Y	Pets	Y
Electric		Amenities		Security	
None		Restrooms	Y	Host(s)	Y
20 Amp	Y	Showers	Y	Rangers(s)	
30 Amp	Y	Reserve Sites	Y	Gate	Y
50 Amp		Store	Y	Patrolled	
		Grill/Table	some		

[14] Table Mountain
I-15, Exit *Hwy 138/Wrightwood*
West of Wrightwood
N34 22.882 W117 41.408
Angeles NF Rate: $20-$40
America/Beautiful Rate: $10-$20
(760) 249-3526
http://www.recreation.gov/

Directions

18 miles. From Hwy 138/Wrightwood Exit go west 8.4 miles on Hwy 138 to Hwy 2, then left 8.8 miles, to Big Pines. Turn right on Table Mountain Rd for 0.7 mile to the campground.

Points of Interest

Visit Hesperia in the Mojave Desert, with many unique restaurants. See the Radio Control Model Aircraft Park. Enjoy watching or flying radio controlled aircraft. Dozens of movies were filmed in Victorville at The New Reflections concert venue Downtown.

RV Sites		Water		Laundry	
Number	39	None		Wi-Fi	
Shaded		At Site		Fishing	
By Water		Spigots	Y	Hiking	Y
Paved	Y	Sewer		Biking	Y
Pull Thru	Y	None	Y	Swimming	
ADA	Y	At Site		Watch Wildlife	Y
Max RV Size	45	Dump Station		Pets	Y
Electric		Amenities		Security	
None	Y	Restrooms	Y	Host(s)	Y
20 Amp		Showers		Rangers(s)	Y
30 Amp		Reserve Sites	Y	Gate	
50 Amp		Store		Patrolled	
		Grill/Table	Y		

[15] Calico Ghost Town
I-15, Exit *Ghost Town Road*
Northeast of Barstow
N34 56.485 W116 52.011
County Park Rate: $30-$35, Fee includes
Ghost town Admission, Senior Discounts
(877) 387-2757
http://cms.sbcounty.gov/parks/Parks/CalicoGhostTown.aspx

Directions

3 miles. Take the Ghost Town Road Exit. Drive north for 3.4 miles on Ghost Town Rd. to the camp on your left.

Points of Interest

An authentic silver mining town where hundreds of mines, 22 saloons, mercantile stores, & The U.S. Borax Co. left their mark. Events & living history are hallmarks of Calico (first preserved by Walter Knott, Knott's Berry Farm Founder).

RV Sites		Water		Laundry	
Number	265	None		Wi-Fi	
Shaded		At Site	Y	Fishing	
By Water		Spigots		Hiking	Y
Paved		Sewer		Biking	Y
Pull Thru	Y	None		Swimming	
ADA		At Site	Y	Watch Wildlife	
Max RV Size	45	Dump Station	Y	Pets	Y
Electric		Amenities		Security	
None		Restrooms	Y	Host(s)	Y
20 Amp	Y	Showers	Y	Rangers(s)	
30 Amp	Y	Reserve Sites	Y	Gate	
50 Amp	Y	Store	Y	Patrolled	
		Grill/Table	Y		

[16] Loggers Campground
I-80, Exit 194
North of Truckee
N39 27.841 W120 07.833
Tahoe NF Rate: $22
America/Beautiful Rate: $11
(530) 587-9281
http://www.recreation.gov/

Directions

9 miles. From Exit 194 take Hirshdale Rd. 0.5 miles northeast to Boca. Bare right on Cty Rd 894Aa1 (Stampede Meadows Rd). Go 6.6 miles to Cty Rd. 261 (Dog Valley Rd.). Turn left, go 2 miles to campground.

Points of Interest

Truckee is an historic mountain town. The Donner Party ordeal is Truckee's most famous historical event. See a lot of the old west. Visit the National Automobile Museum.

RV Sites		Water		Laundry	
Number	200	None		Wi-Fi	
Shaded	Y	At Site		Fishing	Y
By Water	Y	Spigots	Y	Hiking	Y
Paved	Y	Sewer		Biking	Y
Pull Thru	Y	None		Swimming	Y
ADA		At Site		Watch Wildlife	Y
Max RV Size	40	Dump Station	Y	Pets	Y
Electric		Amenities		Security	
None	Y	Restrooms	Y	Host(s)	Y
20 Amp		Showers		Rangers(s)	Y
30 Amp		Reserve Sites	Y	Gate	
50 Amp		Store	Y	Patrolled	
		Grill/Table	Y		

[17] El Capitan State Beach
Hwy 101, Exit 117
West of Santa Barbara
N34 27.762 W120 01.293
State Rate: $35 - $45
(805) 968-1033
http://www.parks.ca.gov/?page_id=601

Directions

1 mile. Exit 117 to El Capitan State Beach Road. Turn toward the ocean and the campground.

Points of Interest

Santa Barbara, 15 minutes away, combines big city culture with backwoods outdoor adventures. Explore galleries and year-round arts events. Try these itineraries - Secret Gardens, Santa Barbara on Stage, Gallery Hop 'Til You Drop. Sign up for the Arts & Culture enewsletter to plan your visit.

RV Sites		Water		Laundry	
Number	133	None	Y	Wi-Fi	
Shaded	Y	At Site		Fishing	Y
By Water	Y	Spigots		Hiking	Y
Paved	Y	Sewer		Biking	Y
Pull Thru	Y	None	Y	Swimming	Y
ADA		At Site		Watch Wildlife	
Max RV Size	42	Dump Station		Pets	Y
Electric		Amenities		Security	
None	Y	Restrooms	Y	Host(s)	Y
20 Amp		Showers	Y	Rangers(s)	Y
30 Amp		Reserve Sites	Y	Gate	
50 Amp		Store	Y	Patrolled	
		Grill/Table	Y		

[18] Pismo State Beach - North Beach
Hwy 101, Exit 190 or 190A
In Oceano
N35 07.943 W120 38.035
State Rate: $25 - $35
(805) 473-7220
http://www.parks.ca.gov/?page_id=595

Directions

1-2 miles. *101N* Exit 190 to Ocean View Ave. Turn left on Hwy 1 for 0.5 mile to the camp. *101S* Exit 190B to Hinds. Turn right, then left on Price St. for 2 blocks to Ocean View Ave. Turn left on Hwy 1 for 0.5 mile to the camp.

Points of Interest

Dig for the famous Pismo clam. There are tree-lined dunes & bird watching. The park has the largest wintering colony of monarch butterflies in the U.S. A trolly service provides access to the surrounding community.

RV Sites		Water		Laundry	
Number	103	None	Y	Wi-Fi	
Shaded	Y	At Site		Fishing	Y
By Water	Y	Spigots		Hiking	Y
Paved	Y	Sewer		Biking	
Pull Thru	Y	None		Swimming	Y
ADA	Y	At Site		Watch Wildlife	
Max RV Size	36	Dump Station	Y	Pets	Y
Electric		Amenities		Security	
None	Y	Restrooms	Y	Host(s)	Y
20 Amp		Showers	Y	Rangers(s)	
30 Amp		Reserve Sites	Y	Gate	
50 Amp		Store		Patrolled	
		Grill/Table	Y		

[19] Standish-Hickey SRA
Hwy 101
North of Leggett
N39 52.683 W123 43.599
State Rate: $35 - $45
(707) 925-6482
http://www.parks.ca.gov/?page_id=423

Directions

1.7 miles. From Leggett go 1.7 miles north on Hwy 101 to the campground entrance.

Points of Interest

Standish-Hickey is at the gateway to the tall trees country. Ten miles of trails weave through steep canyon bluffs, second-growth forests and pockets of old-growth redwood and Douglas-fir. The tallest redwood, the Miles Standish Tree (225 feet tall, 13 feet in diameter) is easy to spot from a distance.

RV Sites		Water		Laundry	
Number	73	None		Wi-Fi	
Shaded	Y	At Site		Fishing	Y
By Water	Y	Spigots	Y	Hiking	Y
Paved		Sewer		Biking	Y
Pull Thru	Y	None	Y	Swimming	Y
ADA	Y	At Site		Watch Wildlife	Y
Max RV Size	27	Dump Station		Pets	Y
Electric		Amenities		Security	
None	Y	Restrooms	Y	Host(s)	Y
20 Amp		Showers	Y	Rangers(s)	Y
30 Amp		Reserve Sites	Y	Gate	
50 Amp		Store		Patrolled	
		Grill/Table	Y		

[20] Richardson Grove State Park
Hwy 101
South of Garberville
N40 00.954 W123 47.477
State Rate: $35 - $45
(707) 247-3318
http://www.parks.ca.gov/?page_id=422

Directions

Between Leggett and Garberville. 15.5 miles north of Leggett. 8 miles south of Garberville.

Points of Interest

The most notable natural feature of Richardson Grove is the old-growth redwood forest, which thrives in the area's mild climate. The South Fork of the Eel River, named for the Pacific lamprey, runs through the park. The first known inhabitants of this region where the Athabascan-speaking Sinkyone people.

RV Sites		Water		Laundry	
Number	100	None		Wi-Fi	
Shaded	Y	At Site		Fishing	Y
By Water	Y	Spigots	Y	Hiking	Y
Paved	Y	Sewer		Biking	Y
Pull Thru		None	Y	Swimming	Y
ADA	Y	At Site		Watch Wildlife	Y
Max RV Size	35	Dump Station		Pets	Y
Electric		Amenities		Security	
None	Y	Restrooms	Y	Host(s)	Y
20 Amp		Showers	Y	Rangers(s)	Y
30 Amp		Reserve Sites	Y	Gate	
50 Amp		Store	Y	Patrolled	
		Grill/Table	Y		

[21] Humboldt Redwoods State Park
Hwy 101, along State Route 254
Between Myers Flat and Weott
State Rate: $35
N40 18.574 W123 54.643
(707) 946-2409
http://www.parks.ca.gov/?page_id=425

Directions

20 miles. Park headquarters and the Visitor Center are located on the Avenue of the Giants, State Route 254, between the towns of Weott and Myers Flat.

Points of Interest

This Park (a diverse ecosystem) includes the Rockefeller Forest, the largest old growth redwood forest in the world. The Park protects an environment unique on earth. Favorite locations are Founders Grove Nature Trail, Avenue of the Giants, and Humboldt Redwoods Visitor Center.

RV Sites		Water		Laundry	
Number	252	None		Wi-Fi	
Shaded	Y	At Site		Fishing	Y
By Water	Y	Spigots	Y	Hiking	Y
Paved		Sewer		Biking	Y
Pull Thru		None	Y	Swimming	Y
ADA	Y	At Site		Watch Wildlife	Y
Max RV Size	33	Dump Station		Pets	Y
Electric		Amenities		Security	
None		Restrooms	Y	Host(s)	Y
20 Amp		Showers	Y	Rangers(s)	Y
30 Amp		Reserve Sites	Y	Gate	
50 Amp		Store	Y	Patrolled	
		Grill/Table	Y		

[22] Redwood National and State Parks
Hwy 101
Between Crescent City & Orick
N41 17.089 W124 05.329 (Info Ctr)
Site Fees: $35 - $43
America The Beautiful & State Passes: $17.50
(707) 465-7335
http://www.reserveamerica.com/

Directions

Redwood National & State Parks is generally oriented along the Hwy 101 corridor between Crescent City & Orick. Five information centers are located along this north-south corridor.

Points of Interest

Four campgrounds - Jedediah Smith, Mill Creek, Elk Prairie and Gold Bluffs Beach - provide unparalleled camping opportunities for families with vehicles. Plan ahead on where you want to stay and what activities you'll do. Be sure to check on reservations.

RV Sites		Water		Laundry	
Number	332	None		Wi-Fi	
Shaded	Y	At Site		Fishing	Y
By Water	Y	Spigots	Y	Hiking	Y
Paved		Sewer		Biking	Y
Pull Thru	Y	None		Swimming	Y
ADA	Y	At Site		Watch Wildlife	Y
Max RV Size	36	Dump Station	Y	Pets	Y
Electric		Amenities		Security	
None	Y	Restrooms	Y	Host(s)	Y
20 Amp		Showers	Y	Rangers(s)	Y
30 Amp		Reserve Sites	Y	Gate	
50 Amp		Store	Y	Patrolled	
		Grill/Table	Y		

NOTES:

About Colorado's Public Campgrounds

With many Colorado State Parks close to Interstate roads it is not surprising that most entries for this state come from the Colorado State Parks System.

Attracting over 11 million visitors per year, Colorado's 42 State Parks are a vital cornerstone in Colorado's economy and quality of life, offering some of the highest quality outdoor recreation destinations in the state. You can find those parks at their website -

www.parks.state.co.us/

State Park advanced reservations are available at:

http://coloradostateparks.reserveamerica.com/

A few notes you should be aware of -

- Reservations can be made a maximum of six months in advance of arrival date, depending on the parks open date.
- Do not bring firewood from out of state.
- All state camps require a $6-$8 per day per vehicle pass.

We generally found most National lands to be too remote and inaccessible for most sizable RVs. The parks listed here vary in site size from 16 to over 363 with the 105 being the average number for the locations selected. State Park campground fees are -

- Full campground hookup $24 per night.
- Electrical campground $20 per night.
- Basic campground $16 per night.
- Camping fees do not include vehicle entrance fees. The CO annual pass ($70/ nonresident) reduces camp fees on weekdays & covers the daily access fee.

[1] Trinidad Lake State Park	[13] Bear Creek Lake Park
[2] Lathrop State Park	[14] Jackson Lake State Park
[3] Lake Pueblo State Park	[15] North Sterling State Park
[4] Cheyenne Mountain State Park	[16] Crawford State Park
[5] Cherry Creek State Park	[17] Black Canyon Of The Gunnison
[6] St. Vrain State Park	[18] Curecanti NRA
[7] Boyd Lake State Park	[19] Eleven Mile State Park
[8] Highline Lake State Park	[20] Mueller State Park
[9] Saddlehorn Camp	[21] Yampa River State Park
[10] Rifle Gap State Park	[22] Stagecoach State Park
[11] Gore Creek	[23] Rocky Mountain National Park
[12] Heaton Bay	

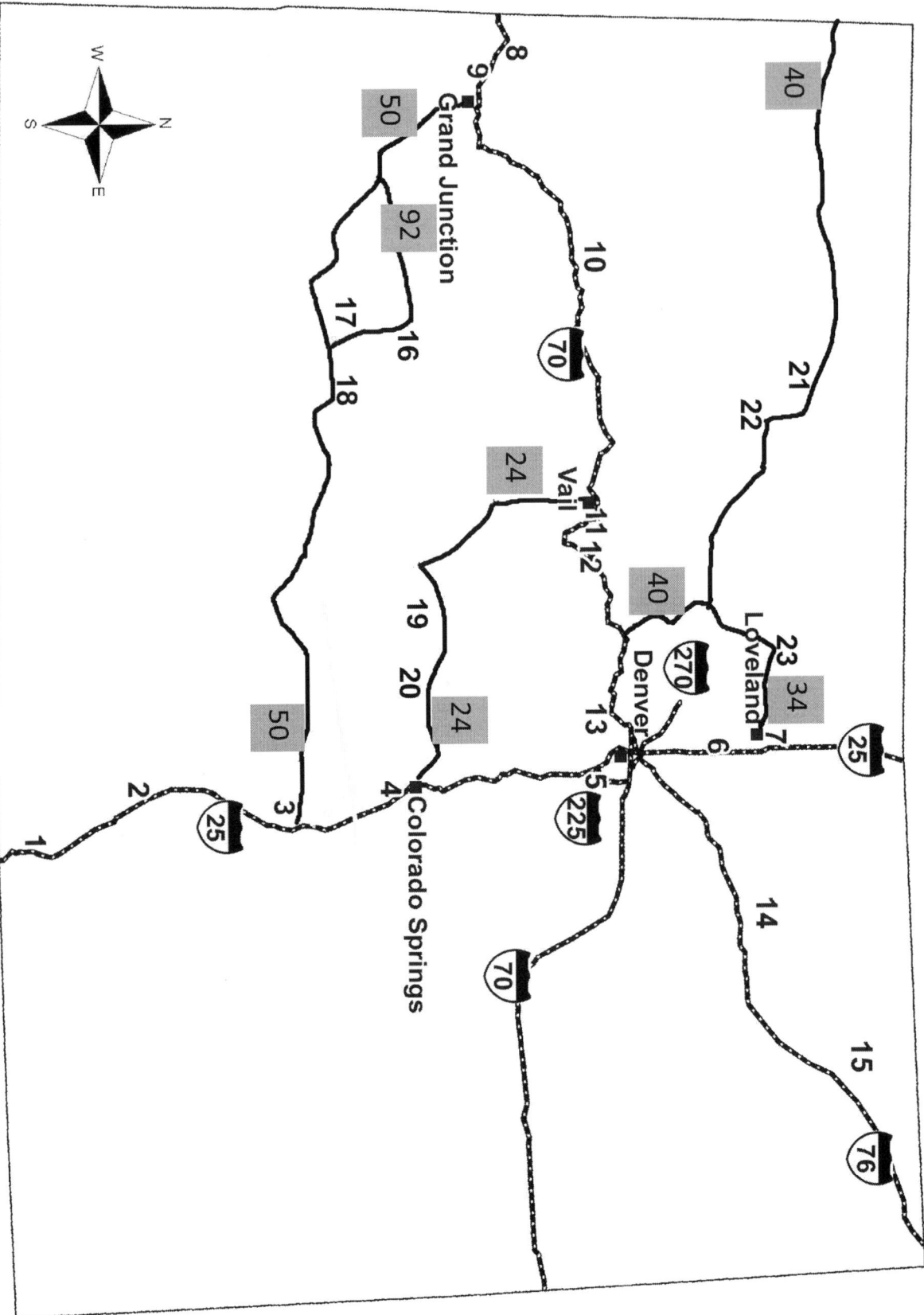

Colorado

[1] Trinidad Lake State Park
I-25, Exit 13
West of Trinidad
N37 09.003 W104 34.247
State Rate: $16-$24
(719) 846-6951
www.parks.state.co.us/parks/trinidadlake/

Directions

5 miles. From Exit 13 go east on West Main St. to the first four-way stop, turn left onto Nevada. At the next four-way stop turn left on to Hwy 12 for 4 miles to the Park.

Points of Interest

The camp is a beautiful mountain setting in southern Colorado, on a mesa approximately 200 feet above the lake. Ride the free Trinidad trolley and discover winding brick streets, historic architecture, art history, archaeology and museums. Musical and gallery events occur year around.

RV Sites		Water		Laundry	Y
Number	73	None		Wi-Fi	
Shaded	Y	At Site	Y	Fishing	Y
By Water	Y	Spigots		Hiking	Y
Paved		**Sewer**		Biking	Y
Pull Thru	Y	None		Swimming	
ADA	Y	At Site	Y	Watch Wildlife	Y
Max RV Size	45	Dump Station	Y	Pets	Y
Electric		**Amenities**		**Security**	
None		Restrooms	Y	Host(s)	Y
20 Amp	Y	Showers	Y	Rangers(s)	Y
30 Amp	Y	Reserve Sites	Y	Gate	
50 Amp	Y	Store	Y	Patrolled	
		Grill/Table	Y		

[2] Lathrop State Park
I-25, Exit Walsenburg Hwy 160
West of Walsenburg
N37 36.071 W104 49.998
State Rate: $16-$24
(719) 738-2376
http://parks.state.co.us/parks/lathrop

Directions

3 miles. From Exit Walsenburg Hwy 160, go west on Hwy 160 for 3 miles to the Park.

Points of Interest

The Spanish Peaks tower over Colorado's first State Park, which is close by Martin and Horseshoe Lakes. Drive the scenic 'Highway of Legends,' which begins near the campground and wends its way through some of Colorado's most interesting historic locales and beautiful scenery.

RV Sites		Water		Laundry	
Number	95	None		Wi-Fi	
Shaded	Y	At Site		Fishing	Y
By Water	Y	Spigots	Y	Hiking	Y
Paved	Y	**Sewer**		Biking	Y
Pull Thru	Y	None		Swimming	Y
ADA	Y	At Site	Y	Watch Wildlife	Y
Max RV Size	45	Dump Station	Y	Pets	Y
Electric		**Amenities**		**Security**	
None		Restrooms	Y	Host(s)	Y
20 Amp	Y	Showers	Y	Rangers(s)	Y
30 Amp	Y	Reserve Sites	Y	Gate	
50 Amp	Y	Store	Y	Patrolled	
		Grill/Table	Y		

[3] Lake Pueblo State Park
I-25, Exits 94 or 101
West of Pueblo
N38 14.852 W104 43.375
State Rate: $16-$20
(719) 561-9320
http://parks.state.co.us/Parks/lakepueblo

Directions

10 miles. From Exit 94 go west/north on Hwy 45 for 5 miles to Hwy 96, then 4 miles west to park. From Exit 101 go 3 miles west on Hwy 50, then Hwy 45 south 4 miles to Hwy 96 & 4 miles west to the park.

Points of Interest

So large there is never a crowded feeling. Pueblo, 'America's Home of Heroes' hosts National Medal of Honor Day. Pueblo is also home to the State Fair & the National Hot Rod Association's Rocky Mountain Street Rod Nationals.

RV Sites		Water		Laundry	Y
Number	363	None		Wi-Fi	
Shaded		At Site		Fishing	Y
By Water	Y	Spigots	Y	Hiking	Y
Paved	Y	**Sewer**		Biking	Y
Pull Thru	Y	None		Swimming	
ADA	Y	At Site	Y	Watch Wildlife	Y
Max RV Size	45	Dump Station	Y	Pets	Y
Electric		**Amenities**		**Security**	
None		Restrooms	Y	Host(s)	Y
20 Amp	Y	Showers	Y	Rangers(s)	Y
30 Amp	Y	Reserve Sites	Y	Gate	
50 Amp		Store		Patrolled	
		Grill/Table	Y		

[4] Cheyenne Mountain State Park
I-25, Exit 135
South of Colorado Springs
N38 44.283 W104 48.529
State Rate: $16-$26
(719) 576-2016
http://parks.state.co.us/Parks/cheyennemountain

Directions

4 miles. From Exit 135 go west 2 miles on Hwy 83 to Hwy 115, then south 2 miles to Nelson Blvd (Fort Carson, Gate 1 is on the left). Turn right onto JL Ranch Heights and into the park.

Points of Interest

Tour the Air Force Academy. Drive up Pikes Peak or to the Garden of the Gods Park, Seven Falls, or Cave Of The Winds. There are a number of military installations and the U. S. Olympic Training Center.

RV Sites		Water		Laundry	Y
Number	51	None		Wi-Fi	
Shaded		At Site	Y	Fishing	Y
By Water		Spigots		Hiking	Y
Paved		**Sewer**		Biking	Y
Pull Thru	Y	None		Swimming	
ADA	Y	At Site	Y	Watch Wildlife	Y
Max RV Size	45	Dump Station		Pets	Y
Electric		**Amenities**		**Security**	
None		Restrooms	Y	Host(s)	Y
20 Amp	Y	Showers	Y	Rangers(s)	Y
30 Amp	Y	Reserve Sites	Y	Gate	
50 Amp	Y	Store	Y	Patrolled	
		Grill/Table	Y		

[5] Cherry Creek State Park
I-25, Exits 199/200
In Southeast Denver
N39 38.838 W104 49.738
State Rate: $16-$26
(303) 690-1166
http://parks.state.co.us/parks/cherrycreek/

Directions

5 miles. From Exit 199 or 200 go east on I-225 for 4 miles to Hwy 83 (S. Parker Rd.). Exit south and go 1 mile to the Park.

Points of Interest

This modern park has a mature, grassy and tree landscape, lake and so many amenities you could stay busy with all the park has to offer. However, Denver beckons and is close by. The park can be a great base camp for exploring a city with so much to see and do.

RV Sites		Water		Laundry	Y
Number	122	None		Wi-Fi	Y
Shaded	Y	At Site	Y	Fishing	Y
By Water	Y	Spigots		Hiking	Y
Paved	Y	**Sewer**		Biking	Y
Pull Thru	Y	None		Swimming	Y
ADA	Y	At Site	Y	Watch Wildlife	Y
Max RV Size	45	Dump Station	Y	Pets	Y
Electric		**Amenities**		**Security**	
None		Restrooms	Y	Host(s)	Y
20 Amp	Y	Showers	Y	Rangers(s)	Y
30 Amp	Y	Reserve Sites	Y	Gate	
50 Amp	Y	Store	Y	Patrolled	
		Grill/Table	Y		

[6] St. Vrain State Park (Barbour Ponds)
I-25, Exit 240
East of Longmont
N40 09.649 W104 59.912
State Rate: $16-$24
(303) 678-9402
http://parks.state.co.us/Parks/StVrain

Directions

2 miles. From Exit 240 take Hwy 119 west for 1 mile then turn north and go 1 mile on County Rd. 7 and Weld County Rd. 24 1/2 to the Park.

Points of Interest

You are a short drive from Boulder, Longmont, Loveland and Greeley. Boulder - Pearl St.; Longmont - The Community Theater; Loveland - bronze sculpture artists using three foundries, many art galleries and annual sculpture show; Greeley - James Michener Library.

RV Sites		Water		Laundry	
Number	87	None		Wi-Fi	
Shaded	Y	At Site	Y	Fishing	Y
By Water	Y	Spigots	Y	Hiking	Y
Paved	Y	**Sewer**		Biking	Y
Pull Thru	Y	None		Swimming	
ADA	Y	At Site	Y	Watch Wildlife	Y
Max RV Size	42	Dump Station	Y	Pets	Y
Electric		**Amenities**		**Security**	
None		Restrooms	Y	Host(s)	Y
20 Amp	Y	Showers	Y	Rangers(s)	Y
30 Amp	Y	Reserve Sites	Y	Gate	
50 Amp	Y	Store		Patrolled	
		Grill/Table	Y		

[7] Boyd Lake State Park
I-25, Exit 257
East of Loveland
N40 25.797 W105 03.509
State Rate: $20
(970) 669-1739
http://parks.state.co.us/Parks/BoydLake/

Directions

6 miles. From Exit 257 go west on Hwy 34 for 4 miles to Madison Ave., then north for 2 miles to Cty Rd 24E. Turn east and follow signs to the park.

Points of Interest

Loveland is a magnet for bronze sculpture artists. You'll find many art galleries and an annual sculpture show. The park is a good base for visiting Rocky Mountain National Park. In Estes Park, lunch at the magnificent Stanley Hotel, which inspired Steven King's 'The Shining.'

RV Sites		Water		Laundry	Y
Number	130	None		Wi-Fi	
Shaded	Y	At Site		Fishing	Y
By Water	Y	Spigots	Y	Hiking	Y
Paved	Y	Sewer		Biking	Y
Pull Thru	Y	None		Swimming	Y
ADA	Y	At Site	few	Watch Wildlife	
Max RV Size	45	Dump Station	Y	Pets	Y
Electric		Amenities		Security	
None		Restrooms	Y	Host(s)	Y
20 Amp	Y	Showers	Y	Rangers(s)	Y
30 Amp	Y	Reserve Sites	Y	Gate	
50 Amp	Y	Store	Y	Patrolled	
		Grill/Table	Y		

[8] Highline Lake State Park
I-70, Exit 15
Northwest of Grand Junction
N39 16.192 W108 50.171
State Rate: $16-$18
(970) 858-7208
http://parks.state.co.us/Parks/highlinelake

Directions

8 miles. From Exit 15 go north on Hwy 139 for 6 miles to Q Rd. Turn west for just over a mile to 11 8/10 Rd., then north for a mile to the Park.

Points of Interest

An ideal base for discovering the Grand Junction area. Bird watchers should note that The Audubon Society has designated the park an important bird area. Enjoy a dramatic red rock landscape & the wine country environment of Grand Junction with great shops, restaurants, & galleries.

RV Sites		Water		Laundry	Y
Number	31	None		Wi-Fi	
Shaded	Y	At Site		Fishing	Y
By Water	Y	Spigots	Y	Hiking	Y
Paved		Sewer		Biking	Y
Pull Thru	Y	None		Swimming	
ADA	Y	At Site		Watch Wildlife	Y
Max RV Size	40	Dump Station	Y	Pets	Y
Electric		Amenities		Security	
None	Y	Restrooms	Y	Host(s)	Y
20 Amp		Showers	Y	Rangers(s)	Y
30 Amp		Reserve Sites	Y	Gate	
50 Amp		Store		Patrolled	
		Grill/Table	Y		

[9] Saddlehorn Camp
I-70, Exit 19
Colorado National Monument
West of Grand Junction
N39 07.277 W108 43.917
NM Rate: $20; America Beautiful Pass: $10
(970) 858-3617
http://www.nps.gov/colm/planyourvisit/saddle-horn-campground.htm

Directions

7 miles. From Exit 19 go south on Hwy 340 for 3 miles to the Park entrance at Rimrock Dr. Turn right and follow the road 4 miles to the campground.

Points of Interest

Colorado National Monument is one of the grand landscapes of the American West. Towering monoliths exist within a vast plateau-and-canyon panorama. Climb Independence Monument.

RV Sites		Water		Laundry	
Number	80	None		Wi-Fi	
Shaded	Y	At Site		Fishing	
By Water		Spigots	Y	Hiking	Y
Paved	Y	Sewer		Biking	Y
Pull Thru	Y	None	Y	Swimming	
ADA	Y	At Site		Watch Wildlife	Y
Max RV Size	40	Dump Station		Pets	Y
Electric		Amenities		Security	
None	Y	Restrooms	Y	Host(s)	Y
20 Amp		Showers		Rangers(s)	Y
30 Amp		Reserve Sites	Y	Gate	
50 Amp		Store	Y	Patrolled	
		Grill/Table	Y		

[10] Rifle Gap State Park
I-70, Exit 90
West of Glenwood Springs
N39 38.096 W107 44.045
State Rate: $16-$24
(970) 625-1607
http://parks.state.co.us/Parks/RifleGap/

Directions

9 miles. From Exit 90 take Hwy 13 for 3 miles north through Rifle and to Hwy 325. Turn right on Hwy 325 and go 6 miles to Rifle Gap Rd. on left, into the Park.

Points of Interest

Rifle is one of the top outdoor sports towns in the country. Enjoy the world's largest hot springs swimming pool in Glenwood Springs. You'll find both the Roaring Fork & Colorado Rivers so river rafting is popular; or enjoy lunch on the veranda of the historic Hotel Colorado.

RV Sites		Water		Laundry	
Number	89	None		Wi-Fi	Y
Shaded	some	At Site	Y	Fishing	Y
By Water	Y	Spigots		Hiking	Y
Paved	Y	Sewer		Biking	Y
Pull Thru	Y	None		Swimming	
ADA	Y	At Site	Y	Watch Wildlife	Y
Max RV Size	45	Dump Station	Y	Pets	Y
Electric		Amenities		Security	
None		Restrooms	Y	Host(s)	Y
20 Amp	Y	Showers	Y	Rangers(s)	Y
30 Amp	Y	Reserve Sites	Y	Gate	
50 Amp	Y	Store	Y	Patrolled	
		Grill/Table	Y		

[11] Gore Creek
I-70, Exit 180
East of Vail
N39 37.631 W106 16.486
White River NF Rate: $18
America/Beautiful Rate: $9
(970) 319-2670
http://www.fs.usda.gov/recarea/whiteriver/recarea/?recid=41347

Directions

3 miles. From Exit 180 (E. Vail Entrance) turn south & follow Bighorn Rd. southeast, go 3 miles to campground sign. Turn left into campground at Gore Creek Campground.

Points of Interest

The closest camp to Vail & Beaver Creek. Vail streets are closed to autos. You walk or ride the free shuttle in an alpine village with world class views, shops, restaurants, & entertainment.

RV Sites		Water		Laundry	
Number	18	None		Wi-Fi	
Shaded	Y	At Site		Fishing	
By Water		Spigots	Y	Hiking	Y
Paved		Sewer		Biking	Y
Pull Thru	Y	None	Y	Swimming	
ADA		At Site		Watch Wildlife	Y
Max RV Size	40	Dump Station		Pets	Y
Electric		Amenities		Security	
None	Y	Restrooms	Y	Host(s)	
20 Amp		Showers		Rangers(s)	Y
30 Amp		Reserve Sites		Gate	
50 Amp		Store		Patrolled	
		Grill/Table	Y		

[12] Heaton Bay Campground
I-70, Exit 203
Between Frisco and Dillon
N39 36.245 W106 04.689
White River NF Rate: $19
America/Beautiful Rate: $10
(970) 319-2670
http://www.recreation.gov/

Directions

1 mile. From Exit 203 on the south side of I-70, take County Rd. 7 (Dillon Dam Rd.) northeast 1 mile to the campground on the east (right) side of the road.

Points of Interest

The towns of Frisco, Dillon, and Breckenridge are close, as are the ski areas of Copper Mountain, Keystone. There is much to see & do with unlimited sightseeing, shopping, large outlet malls, restaurants and après-ski destinations.

RV Sites		Water		Laundry	
Number	59	None		Wi-Fi	
Shaded	some	At Site		Fishing	Y
By Water		Spigots	Y	Hiking	Y
Paved	Y	Sewer		Biking	Y
Pull Thru	Y	None	Y	Swimming	
ADA	Y	At Site		Watch Wildlife	Y
Max RV Size	45	Dump Station		Pets	Y
Electric		Amenities		Security	
None		Restrooms	Y	Host(s)	Y
20 Amp	Y	Showers		Rangers(s)	Y
30 Amp	Y	Reserve Sites	Y	Gate	
50 Amp	Y	Store		Patrolled	
		Grill/Table	Y		

[13] Bear Creek Lake Park
I-70, Exit 251
Southwest Denver
N39 39.219 W105 10.611
City of Lakewood Park Rate: $20
(303) 697-6159
http://www.lakewood.org/bclp/

Directions

6 miles. From Exit 251 go south on Hwy 470 for 5 miles to Hwy 8 (Morrison Rd.). Exit east to the Bear Creek Lake Regional Park, immediately on the right.

Points of Interest

Convenient to Bandimere Speedway & Red Rocks Amphitheatre. Visit William Frederick Hayden Park on Green Mountain. Denver also beckons. The park can be a great base camp for exploring a city with so much to see and do.

RV Sites		Water		Laundry	
Number	47	None		Wi-Fi	
Shaded		At Site		Fishing	Y
By Water		Spigots	Y	Hiking	Y
Paved		**Sewer**		Biking	Y
Pull Thru	Y	None		Swimming	Y
ADA		At Site		Watch Wildlife	
Max RV Size	45	Dump Station	Y	Pets	Y
Electric		**Amenities**		**Security**	
None		Restrooms	Y	Host(s)	Y
20 Amp	Y	Showers	Y	Rangers(s)	
30 Amp	Y	Reserve Sites	Y	Gate	Y
50 Amp	Y	Store	Y	Patrolled	
		Grill/Table	Y		

[14] Jackson Lake State Park
I-76, Exit 66
North of Wiggins
N40 22.725 W104 05.370
State Rate: $16-$20
(970) 645-2551
http://parks.state.co.us/parks/jacksonlake

Directions

11 miles. From Exit 66 go north on Hwy 39 (becomes Cty Rd 5) for 7.6 miles, then west on Cty Rd. Y5/10 for 1.5 miles to Cty Rd 3, then north for 1.5 miles into the Park.

Points of Interest

In Ft. Morgan take the Pioneer Trail Scenic & Historic Byway north to Pawnee Buttes, a key setting in James Michener's novel, Centennial. Hike the trails of Pawnee National Grassland. See the Rainbow Arch Bridge just north of town, a rare example of this style of bridge architecture.

RV Sites		Water		Laundry	
Number	259	None		Wi-Fi	
Shaded	Y	At Site		Fishing	Y
By Water	Y	Spigots	Y	Hiking	Y
Paved		**Sewer**		Biking	Y
Pull Thru	Y	None		Swimming	Y
ADA	Y	At Site		Watch Wildlife	Y
Max RV Size	45	Dump Station	Y	Pets	Y
Electric		**Amenities**		**Security**	
None		Restrooms	Y	Host(s)	Y
20 Amp	Y	Showers	Y	Rangers(s)	Y
30 Amp	Y	Reserve Sites	Y	Gate	
50 Amp	Y	Store	Y	Patrolled	
		Grill/Table	Y		

[15] North Sterling State Park
I-76, Exit 125
North of Sterling
N40 45.830 W103 16.037
State Rate: $16-$20
(970) 522-3657
http://parks.state.co.us/Parks/northsterling

Directions

21 miles. From Exit 125 go west on Chestnut 1.6 mile Turn right at 3rd (Hwy 138), go north, merging with Broadway. Go 9 mile to Hwy 113. Turn left for 1.7 mile to Cty Rd. 46. Go west for 8 mile to the 'T.' Turn right 0.2 mile to the Park on the left.

Points of Interest

Enjoy majestic bluffs & views of the high plains. Sterling, the 'Queen City of the Plains,' is close by the Overland Trail and is home to The Overland Tail Museum.

RV Sites		Water		Laundry	
Number	135	None		Wi-Fi	
Shaded		At Site		Fishing	Y
By Water	Y	Spigots	Y	Hiking	Y
Paved		**Sewer**		Biking	Y
Pull Thru	Y	None		Swimming	
ADA	Y	At Site		Watch Wildlife	Y
Max RV Size	45	Dump Station	Y	Pets	Y
Electric		**Amenities**		**Security**	
None		Restrooms	Y	Host(s)	Y
20 Amp	Y	Showers	Y	Rangers(s)	Y
30 Amp	Y	Reserve Sites	Y	Gate	
50 Amp	Y	Store	Y	Patrolled	
		Grill/Table	Y		

[16] Crawford State Park
Hwy 92
South of Crawford
N38 40.701 W107 35.802
State Rate: $16-$20
(970) 921-5721
www.parks.state.co.us/Parks/Crawford/

Directions

1 mile From Crawford Center go on Hwy 92 for 2.5 miles south of town to the Park.

Points of Interest

A nice retreat for outdoor recreation. The Black Canyon of the Gunnison is close by, visit there to enjoy some inspiring scenery. A few minutes drive from Crawford, a narrow opening canyon with sheer walls as much as 1,200 feet deep displays the Gunnison River Gorge like no where else. National Forest areas offer mountain biking, hiking and horseback riding.

RV Sites		Water		Laundry	
Number	60	None		Wi-Fi	
Shaded		At Site	Y	Fishing	Y
By Water	Y	Spigots		Hiking	Y
Paved		Sewer		Biking	Y
Pull Thru	Y	None		Swimming	
ADA	Y	At Site		Watch Wildlife	Y
Max RV Size	45	Dump Station	Y	Pets	Y
Electric		Amenities		Security	
None		Restrooms	Y	Host(s)	Y
20 Amp	Y	Showers	Y	Rangers(s)	Y
30 Amp	Y	Reserve Sites	Y	Gate	
50 Amp		Store		Patrolled	
		Grill/Table	Y		

[17] Black Canyon Of The Gunnison - South Rim Campground
Hwy 347 off Hwy 50
East of Montrose
N38 32.459 W107 41.387
NPS Rate: $12-$18
America/Beautiful Rate: $6-$9
(970) 641-2337
http://www.nps.gov/blca/index.htm

Directions

14 miles. From Montrose go 7.5 miles east on Hwy 50 to Hwy 347. Turn north for 6 miles to the camp.

Points of Interest

Black Canyon of Gunnison National Park is a beautiful getaway for sightseeing, rock climbing & hiking. The park protects the most dramatic section of the Gunnison River Canyon; no other canyon in North America combines the narrow opening, sheer walls, and startling depths of Black Canyon.

RV Sites		Water		Laundry	
Number	88	None		Wi-Fi	
Shaded	Y	At Site		Fishing	
By Water		Spigots	Y	Hiking	Y
Paved		Sewer		Biking	Y
Pull Thru	Y	None	Y	Swimming	
ADA	Y	At Site		Watch Wildlife	Y
Max RV Size	40	Dump Station		Pets	Y
Electric		Amenities		Security	
None		Restrooms	Y	Host(s)	Y
20 Amp	Y	Showers		Rangers(s)	Y
30 Amp	Y	Reserve Sites	Y	Gate	
50 Amp	Y	Store	Y	Patrolled	
		Grill/Table	Y		

[18] Curecanti NRA
Hwy 50
West of Gunnison
N38 28.176 W107 09.800
NRA Rate: $12-$18
America/Beautiful Rate: $6-$9
(970) 641-2337
http://www.nps.gov/cure/planyourvisit/camping.htm

Directions (Elk Creek Campground)

16 miles west of Gunnison Center on Hwy 50.

Points of Interest

Curecanti NRA is a series of three reservoirs along the Gunnison River. There are 10 campgrounds with a variety of services for RVs. At Elk Creek, catch large salmon & rainbow trout, or try windsurfing and water skiing. Swimming is permitted and birders can find bald eagles in winter. At 7,540 feet, Elk Creek is surrounded by sagebrush.

RV Sites		Water		Laundry	
Number	75	None		Wi-Fi	
Shaded	Y	At Site		Fishing	Y
By Water	Y	Spigots	Y	Hiking	Y
Paved	Y	Sewer		Biking	Y
Pull Thru	Y	None		Swimming	Y
ADA	Y	At Site		Watch Wildlife	Y
Max RV Size	45	Dump Station	Y	Pets	Y
Electric		Amenities		Security	
None		Restrooms	Y	Host(s)	Y
20 Amp	Y	Showers	Y	Rangers(s)	Y
30 Amp	Y	Reserve Sites	Y	Gate	
50 Amp	Y	Store	Y	Patrolled	
		Grill/Table	Y		

[19] Eleven Mile State Park
County Rd 92
East of Hartsel
N38 56.079 W105 30.077
State Rate: $16-$20
(719) 748-3401
www.parks.state.co.us/Parks/ElevenMile/Pages/

Directions (Rocky Ridge Campground)

From Hartsel Center go east on Hwy 24 for 11 miles to County Road 23 (at Glentiver). Turn south and drive 2.8 miles to County Road 59. Turn east and drive 2.5 miles to the intersection of County Road 59 and 92. Continue east on County Road 92 for 5 miles to the camp.

Points of Interest

Enjoy outstanding fishing as well as miles of scenic hiking and biking trails. Canoe around the shores of the backcountry. Many species of birds reside in or migrate through the park.

RV Sites		Water		Laundry	Y
Number	144	None		Wi-Fi	
Shaded	Y	At Site		Fishing	Y
By Water	Y	Spigots	Y	Hiking	Y
Paved		Sewer		Biking	Y
Pull Thru	Y	None		Swimming	Y
ADA	Y	At Site		Watch Wildlife	Y
Max RV Size	45	Dump Station	Y	Pets	Y
Electric		Amenities		Security	
None		Restrooms	Y	Host(s)	Y
20 Amp	Y	Showers	Y	Rangers(s)	Y
30 Amp	Y	Reserve Sites	Y	Gate	
50 Amp		Store	Y	Patrolled	
		Grill/Table	Y		

[20] Mueller State Park
Hwy 24
South of Divide
N38 53.383 W105 09.550
State Rate: $20-$22
(719) 687-2366
http://www.parks.state.co.us/Parks/Mueller/

Directions

Just west of Divide turn left onto Hwy 67 for 3.6 miles to the campground.

Points of Interest

A popular Watchable Wildlife Area, Mueller is home to abundant wildlife. You are less than a hour from Colorado Springs. Destination there could be - Royal Gorge Bridge and Park, Florissant Fossil Beds National Monument, Molly Kathleen Gold Mine, Pikes Peak Highway, Pikes Peak Cog Railway, or take the Gold Belt Scenic Byway Tour.

RV Sites		Water		Laundry	Y
Number	135	None		Wi-Fi	
Shaded	Y	At Site		Fishing	Y
By Water		Spigots	Y	Hiking	Y
Paved	Y	Sewer		Biking	Y
Pull Thru	Y	None		Swimming	
ADA	Y	At Site		Watch Wildlife	Y
Max RV Size	45	Dump Station	Y	Pets	Y
Electric		Amenities		Security	
None		Restrooms	Y	Host(s)	Y
20 Amp	Y	Showers	Y	Rangers(s)	Y
30 Amp	Y	Reserve Sites	Y	Gate	
50 Amp	Y	Store	Y	Patrolled	
		Grill/Table	Y		

[21] Yampa River State Park
Hwy 40
West of Hayden
N40 29.518 W107 18.373
State Rate: $16-$20
(970) 276-2061
http://www.parks.state.co.us/Parks/YampaRiver/

Directions

2.6 miles west of Hayden just off Hwy 40.

Points of Interest

A 134 mile stretch of the Yampa River, the heart of Yampa River State Park, has 13 access points stretching from Hayden to the Dinosaur National Monument. The Elkhead Reservoir is another component of the Yampa River State Park system. Visitors can enjoy swimming, boating, fishing, camping and picnicking at the lake. Steamboat Springs is only 30 minutes away!

RV Sites		Water		Laundry	Y
Number	50	None		Wi-Fi	
Shaded		At Site		Fishing	Y
By Water	Y	Spigots	Y	Hiking	Y
Paved		Sewer		Biking	Y
Pull Thru	Y	None		Swimming	Y
ADA	Y	At Site		Watch Wildlife	Y
Max RV Size	45	Dump Station	Y	Pets	Y
Electric		Amenities		Security	
None		Restrooms	Y	Host(s)	Y
20 Amp	Y	Showers	Y	Rangers(s)	Y
30 Amp	Y	Reserve Sites	Y	Gate	
50 Amp	Y	Store	Y	Patrolled	
		Grill/Table	Y		

[22] Stagecoach State Park
Hwy 131
South of Steamboat Springs
N40 16.895 W106 52.116
State Rate: $16-$20
(970) 736-2436
http://www.parks.state.co.us/Parks/Stagecoach/

Directions

Travel 4.5 miles southeast on U.S. 40, then south on Colorado 131 for 6.5 miles to Cty Rd 14. Drive 6 miles south on County Road 14 to the park entrance.

Points of Interest

Many visitors make Stagecoach their base-camp when exploring nearby outdoor recreation opportunities including the Flattops Wilderness, Sarvice Creek Wilderness and Blacktail Mountain. Steamboat Springs is less than 30 minutes away!

RV Sites		Water		Laundry	
Number	100	None		Wi-Fi	
Shaded		At Site		Fishing	Y
By Water	Y	Spigots	Y	Hiking	Y
Paved		Sewer		Biking	Y
Pull Thru	Y	None		Swimming	Y
ADA	Y	At Site		Watch Wildlife	Y
Max RV Size	45	Dump Station	Y	Pets	Y
Electric		Amenities		Security	
None		Restrooms	Y	Host(s)	Y
20 Amp	Y	Showers	Y	Rangers(s)	Y
30 Amp	Y	Reserve Sites	Y	Gate	
50 Amp		Store		Patrolled	
		Grill/Table	Y		

[23] Rocky Mountain National Park - Moraine Park Campground
Hwy 36
West of Estes Park
N40 21.517 W105 35.144
NPS Rate: $20
America/Beautiful Rate: $10
(970) 586-1206
http://www.nps.gov/romo/planyourvisit/camping.htm

Directions

From Estes Park take Hwy 36 west into the Park, go 2 miles to Bear Lake Rd. Turn left for 1.3 miles to the campground.

Points of Interest

Scenic driving, hiking, backpacking, fishing, horseback riding and wildlife viewing are popular activities. Access the free summer shuttle buses to Bear Lake & Estes Park from the campground.

RV Sites		Water		Laundry	
Number	244	None		Wi-Fi	
Shaded	Y	At Site		Fishing	Y
By Water		Spigots	Y	Hiking	Y
Paved	some	Sewer		Biking	Y
Pull Thru		None		Swimming	
ADA	Y	At Site		Watch Wildlife	Y
Max RV Size	40	Dump Station	Y	Pets	Y
Electric		Amenities		Security	
None	Y	Restrooms	Y	Host(s)	Y
20 Amp		Showers		Rangers(s)	Y
30 Amp		Reserve Sites	Y	Gate	
50 Amp		Store	Y	Patrolled	Y
		Grill/Table	Y		

About Connecticut and Rhode Island's Public Campgrounds

CONNECTICUT

There are 17 public campgrounds in total in Connecticut with camping sites, 14 of which are State Parks or Forests. The State lands are overseen by the Connecticut Department of Energy & Environmental Protection (DEEP). Their website is -

http://www.ct.gov/deep/cwp/view.asp?a=2716&q=325086

State regulations state "TRAILERS AND RV's EXCEEDING 35' IN LENGTH ARE NOT PERMITTED IN STATE PARKS. PETS ARE PROHIBITED IN A MAJORITY OF STATE PARK CAMPING AREAS."

The Department of Energy & Environmental Protection (DEEP) has a toll free telephone and on-line system to reserve campsites at state park and forest campgrounds. Reservations for all state campgrounds are available online at Reserve America or by calling toll free (877) 668-2267.

The State Park camping season is mid-April - September 30. However, some campgrounds are open on a restricted basis prior to Memorial Day Weekend or after Labor Day. Fires are permitted in designated fireplaces. Ground fires are strictly prohibited at all State campgrounds. Except as specifically authorized, no firearms, archery equipment or other weapons may be possessed in any campground or recreation area.

RHODE ISLAND

There are less than 10 public campgrounds in total in Rhode Island, 5 of which are State Parks, Ponds or Recreation Areas. The Rhode Island Department of Environmental Management (RI DEM) provides oversight. The website is -

http://www.riparks.com/index.html

The RI DEM uses ReserveAmerica to provide its online reservation system. There is a fee for this. Reservations are also available through the call center or walk-in camping. Most of the parks are pet friendly.

[1] Kettletown State Park (CT)	**[5] West Thompson Lake (CT)**
[2] Hammonasset Beach State Park (CT)	**[6] Burlingame State Park (RI)**
[3] Rocky Neck State Park (CT)	**[7] Fishermen's State Park (RI)**
[4] Salt Rock State Park (CT)	**[8] George Washington Campground (RI)**

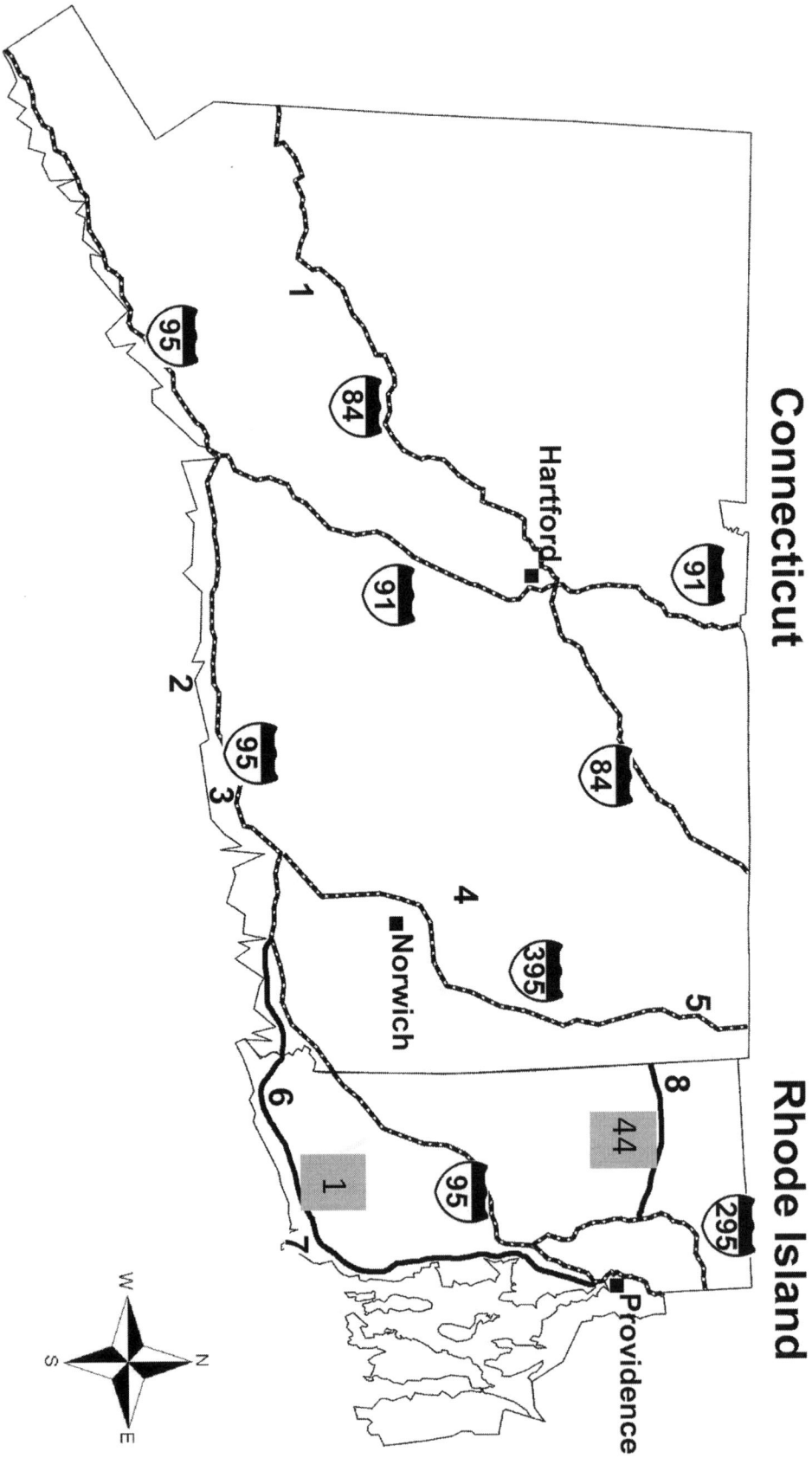

[1] Kettletown State Park (CT)
I-84, Exit 15
East of Danbury
N41 25.751 W73 12.045
State Rate: $17-$27
(203) 264-5678
http://www.ct.gov/deep/cwp/view.
asp?a=2716&q=325230#map

Directions

4.5 miles. From Exit 15 take Kettletown Rd. south for 3.5 miles to Georges Hill Rd. Turn right for 0.7 miles to the park entrance.

Points of Interest

The park was originally inhabited by the Pootatuck Indians, members of the Algonquin group. The Pootatucks developed a drum communications system which could carry a message over 200 miles in just two hours.

RV Sites		Water		Laundry	
Number	63	None		Wi-Fi	
Shaded	Y	At Site		Fishing	Y
By Water	Y	Spigots	Y	Hiking	Y
Paved		Sewer		Biking	Y
Pull Thru	Y	None		Swimming	Y
ADA	Y	At Site		Watch Wildlife	Y
Max RV Size	28	Dump Station	Y	Pets	
Electric		Amenities		Security	
None	Y	Restrooms		Host(s)	Y
20 Amp		Showers	Y	Rangers(s)	Y
30 Amp		Reserve Sites	Y	Gate	
50 Amp		Store		Patrolled	Y
		Grill/Table	Y		

[2] Hammonasset Beach State Park (CT)
I-95, Exit 62
East of New Haven
N41 16.420 W72 33.740
State Rate: $20-$45
(203) 245-2785
http://www.ct.gov/deep/cwp/view.
asp?a=2716&q=325210&deepNav_GID=1650

Directions

1.2 miles. Go approximately 1 mile south. Go straight through the traffic light crossing Rt. 1 (Boston Post Road) into the park.

Points of Interest

"Hammonasset" means "where we dig holes in the ground." Swim in the salt water, collect shells, build a sandcastle, sunbathe, relax, and walk along the 3/4 mile boardwalk. Bring your own fire ring for a fire.

RV Sites		Water		Laundry	
Number	558	None		Wi-Fi	
Shaded	Y	At Site		Fishing	Y
By Water	Y	Spigots	Y	Hiking	Y
Paved		Sewer		Biking	Y
Pull Thru		None		Swimming	Y
ADA	Y	At Site		Watch Wildlife	Y
Max RV Size	35	Dump Station	Y	Pets	
Electric		Amenities		Security	
None		Restrooms	Y	Host(s)	Y
20 Amp	Y	Showers	Y	Rangers(s)	Y
30 Amp	Y	Reserve Sites	Y	Gate	
50 Amp	Y	Store	Y	Patrolled	Y
		Grill/Table			

[3] Rocky Neck State Park (CT)
I-95, Exit 72
In East Lyme
N41 19.015 W72 14.562
State Rate: $20-$30
(860) 424-3200
http://www.ct.gov/deep/cwp/view.
asp?A=2716&Q=325256

Directions

1.0 mile. Exit south on Rocky Neck for 0.6 miles to Hwy 156. Turn left and go east 0.3 mile to the park.

Points of Interest

Rocky Neck was known to Indians & colonists as a place of abundant fish & wildlife. A large marine estuary bisects the park providing saltwater fishing opportunities. Spring tides allow alewives to swim to spawning grounds. Osprey, cranes, & herons wade among cattails & rose mallow.

RV Sites		Water		Laundry	
Number	160	None		Wi-Fi	
Shaded	Y	At Site		Fishing	Y
By Water	Y	Spigots	Y	Hiking	Y
Paved	Y	Sewer		Biking	Y
Pull Thru		None		Swimming	Y
ADA	Y	At Site		Watch Wildlife	Y
Max RV Size	35	Dump Station	Y	Pets	
Electric		Amenities		Security	
None		Restrooms	Y	Host(s)	Y
20 Amp		Showers	Y	Rangers(s)	Y
30 Amp		Reserve Sites	Y	Gate	
50 Amp		Store	Y	Patrolled	Y
		Grill/Table	Y		

[4] Salt Rock State Park (CT)
I-395, Exit 83
Southeast of Willamantic
N41 38.564 W72 05.311
State Rate: $33-$40
(860) 822-0884
www.reserveamerica.com

Directions

5.0 miles. Go left, follow Rt. 97 north through Baltic for 5.2 miles. Park will be on the left just north of Salt Rock Road.

Points of Interest

Salt Rock is the only State Campground with many amenities of a modern campground. A dominant theme that appears in Willimantic is frogs. The amphibians decorating The Frog Bridge are 11 feet tall, and they sit atop spools of thread. Both rooted in the town's history

RV Sites		Water		Laundry	
Number	71	None		Wi-Fi	
Shaded	Y	At Site	Y	Fishing	Y
By Water	Y	Spigots		Hiking	Y
Paved	Y	Sewer		Biking	Y
Pull Thru	Y	None		Swimming	Y
ADA	Y	At Site	Y	Watch Wildlife	
Max RV Size	35	Dump Station	Y	Pets	Y
Electric		Amenities		Security	
None		Restrooms	Y	Host(s)	Y
20 Amp	Y	Showers	Y	Rangers(s)	Y
30 Amp	Y	Reserve Sites	Y	Gate	
50 Amp	Y	Store	Y	Patrolled	Y
		Grill/Table	Y		

[5] West Thompson Lake (CT)
I-395, Exit 99
West of Thompson
N41 57.255 W71 53.651
COE Rate: $15-$30
America/Beautiful Rate: $8-$15
(860) 923-3121
www.reserveamerica.com

Directions

4 miles. From Exit 99 go east on Hwy 200 one mile, then south on Hwy 193 for 2 miles. Go north on Reardon Rd. 1/2 mile to the Park on the left.

Points of Interest

Visit Thompson International Speedway, with the highest banked race track in New England. The speedway holds one of the biggest race programs in New England - "The World Series of Auto Racing", 14 divisions and 600 cars.

RV Sites		Water		Laundry	
Number	25	None		Wi-Fi	
Shaded	Y	At Site		Fishing	Y
By Water	Y	Spigots	Y	Hiking	Y
Paved		Sewer		Biking	Y
Pull Thru		None		Swimming	
ADA	Y	At Site		Watch Wildlife	
Max RV Size	45	Dump Station	Y	Pets	Y
Electric		Amenities		Security	
None		Restrooms	Y	Host(s)	Y
20 Amp	Y	Showers	Y	Rangers(s)	Y
30 Amp	Y	Reserve Sites	Y	Gate	
50 Amp		Store		Patrolled	
		Grill/Table	Y		

[6] Burlingame State Park (RI)
Hwy 1, Old Post Rd Exit
West of Charleston
N41 21.981 W71 42.687
State Rate: $14-$20
(401) 322-7337
http://www.riparks.com/

Directions

1 mile. Take the Old Post Rd exit to Klondike Rd.4. Proceed 0.3 miles to the park.

Points of Interest

The Audubon Society operates the nearby Kimball Wildlife Sanctuary. The Sanctuary abuts Burlingame State Park and trails lead from the campground to the sanctuary. The campground is minutes from the Connecticut casinos and historic Mystic. Charlestown's Ninigret Park is the site of not-to-be-missed events - the Seafood Festival and/or the Rhythm and Roots Festival.

RV Sites		Water		Laundry	
Number	700	None		Wi-Fi	
Shaded	Y	At Site		Fishing	Y
By Water	Y	Spigots	Y	Hiking	Y
Paved		Sewer		Biking	Y
Pull Thru	Y	None		Swimming	Y
ADA	Y	At Site	Y	Watch Wildlife	Y
Max RV Size	45	Dump Station	Y	Pets	Y
Electric		Amenities		Security	
None	Y	Restrooms	Y	Host(s)	Y
20 Amp		Showers	Y	Rangers(s)	Y
30 Amp		Reserve Sites	Y	Gate	
50 Amp		Store	Y	Patrolled	Y
		Grill/Table	Y		

[7] Fishermen's State Park (RI)
Hwy 1, Hwy 108 Exit
South of Warwick
N41 22.836 W71 29.280
State Rates: $18-$35
(401) 789-8374
http://www.riparks.com/

Directions

24 miles. From Hwy 1 take the Hwy 108, then south 4 miles along Hwy 108 to the Park.

Points of Interest

Visitors will find neatly trimmed grass & tree lined paths. You will be close to popular state beach areas like Roger Wheeler, Salty Brine, and Scarborough. You are a short drive from tourist mecca's such as Newport & Wickford. The camp is 1 mile from the Block Island Ferry Dock.

RV Sites		Water		Laundry	
Number	147	None		Wi-Fi	
Shaded	Y	At Site	Y	Fishing	Y
By Water	Y	Spigots		Hiking	Y
Paved	Y	**Sewer**		Biking	Y
Pull Thru	Y	None		Swimming	Y
ADA	Y	At Site		Watch Wildlife	
Max RV Size	45	Dump Station	Y	Pets	Y
Electric		**Amenities**		**Security**	
None		Restrooms	Y	Host(s)	Y
20 Amp	Y	Showers	Y	Rangers(s)	Y
30 Amp	Y	Reserve Sites	Y	Gate	
50 Amp		Store		Patrolled	Y
		Grill/Table	Y		

[8] George Washington State Park (RI)
I-295, Exit 7
Northwest of Providence
N41 55.185 W71 45.298
State Rates: $14-$20
(401) 568-6700
http://www.riparks.com/

Directions

14 miles from I-295. From Exit 7 follow Hwy 44 (Putnam Pike) west approximately 14 miles to the camp entrance on your right.

Points of Interest

Providence is a top travel destination. Visit Roger Williams Park, comprised of waterways, walks, a Botanical Center, a Carousel Village, and Museum of Natural History and Planetarium. History buffs will be attracted to rich and varied architecture, which ranges from Colonial to Modern.

RV Sites		Water		Laundry	
Number	45	None		Wi-Fi	
Shaded	Y	At Site		Fishing	Y
By Water	Y	Spigots	Y	Hiking	Y
Paved		**Sewer**		Biking	Y
Pull Thru	few	None	Y	Swimming	Y
ADA	Y	At Site		Watch Wildlife	Y
Max RV Size	45	Dump Station		Pets	Y
Electric		**Amenities**		**Security**	
None	Y	Restrooms	Y	Host(s)	Y
20 Amp		Showers		Rangers(s)	Y
30 Amp		Reserve Sites	Y	Gate	
50 Amp		Store		Patrolled	Y
		Grill/Table	Y		

About Delaware and Maryland's
Public Campgrounds

DELAWARE

Camping is available at five Delaware state parks. The campgrounds are open from March 1 through November 30. You can learn more at the State Parks at their website -

www.destateparks.com

You may make a reservation up to 7 months or as little as 1 day in advance of your visit. Reservations at -

http://delawarestateparks.reserveamerica.com/

All of the campgrounds provide drinking water outlets, modern shower and sanitary facilities, and sewage dumping stations. Campsites are equipped with a picnic table and may include a fire ring (campfire regulations). Many have electric and water hookups.

MARYLAND

The National Geographic Magazine calls Maryland's extraordinary public lands "America in Miniature." Maryland has the Appalachian Mountains, Chesapeake Bay, marshland on the Eastern Shore, and the Atlantic Ocean. You can learn more at -

http://www.dnr.state.md.us/publiclands/campinginfo.asp

On-line reservations may be made at -

reservations.dnr.state.md.us

There are 25 State Parks that have campgrounds, of which 11 have sites which will accommodate RVs of 35 feet or more and 16 of which have hook ups. Most of Maryland's State Forests and National Parks supply equipment rentals for boating, canoeing, and kayaking, Camping season is generally mid-April through mid-October. The America the Beautiful Pass allows free entry to all State Parks that charge service fees. The pass is also valid for half price camping Sunday through Thursday.

[1] Trap Pond State Park (DE)	[9] Greenbelt Park (DC)
[2] Cape Henlopen State Park (DE)	[10] Elk Neck State Park (MD)
[3] Killens Pond State Park (DE)	[11] Little Bennett County Campground (MD)
[4] Lums Pond State Park (DE)	[12] Janes Island State Park (MD)
[5] New Germany State Park (MD)	[13] Pocomoke River State Park, Shad Hill (MD)
[6] Rocky Gap State Park (MD)	
[7] Cunningham Falls State Park (MD)	[14] Assateague State Park (MD)
[8] Patapsco Valley State Park (MD)	[15] Tuckahoe State Park (MD)

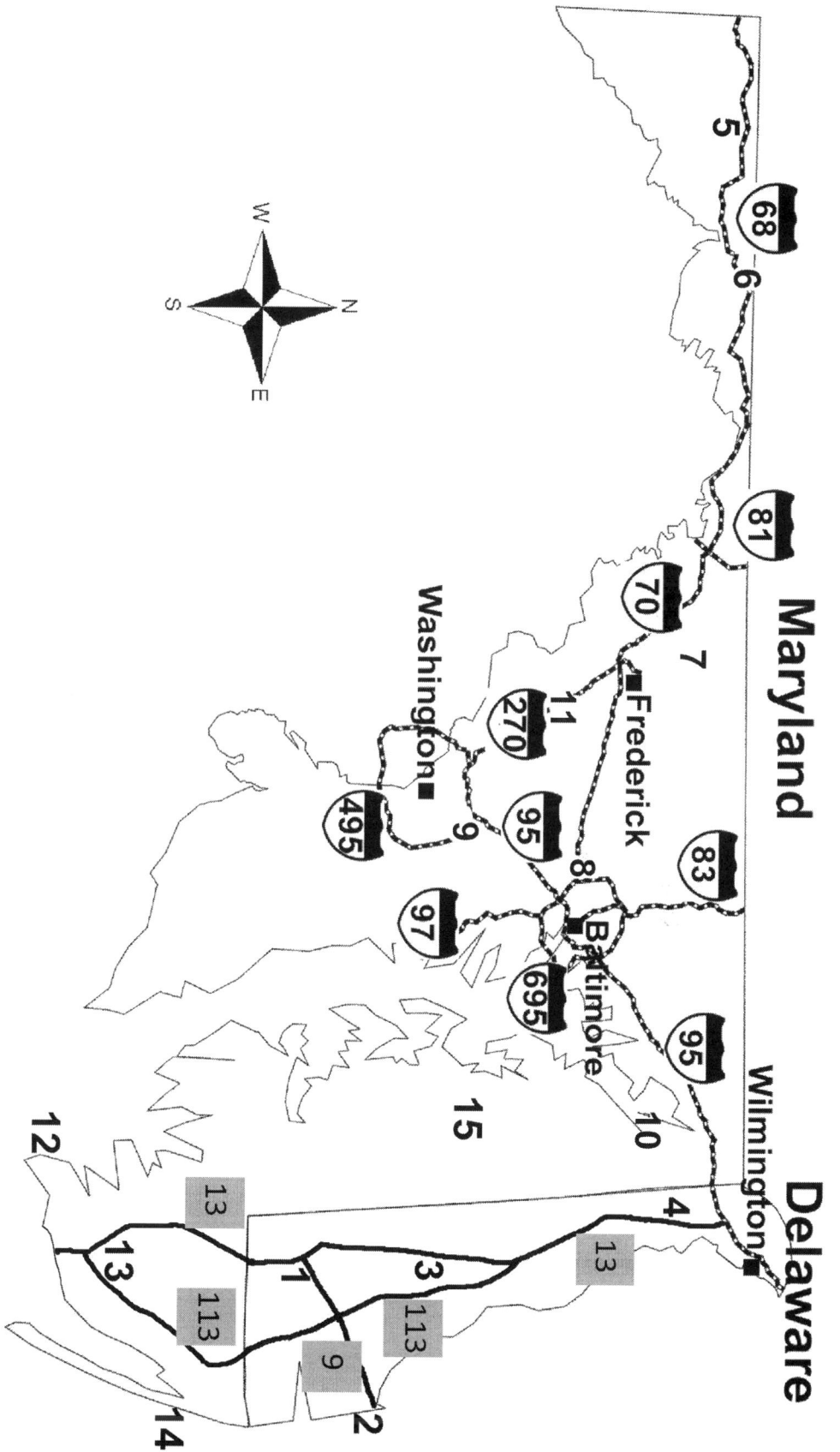

[1] Trap Pond State Park (DE)
Hwy 13, East on Hwy 24
East of Laurel
N38 31.863 W75 28.602
State Rate: $30, Senior Discount
(302) 875-2392
www.destateparks.com/camping/trap-pond/

Directions

6 miles. From Hwy 13 go 4.6 miles east on Hwy 24 (Laurel Rd) to Trap Pond Rd. Turn right for 1 mile to Goose Nest Rd. Turn left for 0.2 mile the park entrance.

Points of Interest

Trap Pond is the northernmost natural stand of bald cypress on the Eastern seaboard. Many birds flock to stands of bald cypress, including Great Blue Herons, owls, warblers, and Pileated Woodpeckers. Birdwatchers can also see hummingbirds & Bald Eagles in season

RV Sites		Water		Laundry	
Number	130	None		Wi-Fi	
Shaded	Y	At Site	Y	Fishing	Y
By Water	Y	Spigots		Hiking	Y
Paved		**Sewer**		Biking	Y
Pull Thru	Y	None		Swimming	
ADA	Y	At Site		Watch Wildlife	Y
Max RV Size	40	Dump Station	Y	Pets	Y
Electric		**Amenities**		**Security**	
None		Restrooms	Y	Host(s)	Y
20 Amp	Y	Showers	Y	Rangers(s)	Y
30 Amp	Y	Reserve Sites	Y	Gate	
50 Amp	Y	Store	Y	Patrolled	Y
		Grill/Table	Y		

[2] Cape Henlopen State Park (DE)
Hwy 113, East from Georgetown on Hwy 9
East of Lewes
N38 46.809 W75 07.203
State Rate: $33-$35, Senior Discount
(302) 645-8983
www.destateparks.com/camping/cape-henlopen/

Directions

17 miles. From Georgetown Center go east on Hwy 9 for 12.3 miles to Hwy 1. Turn right for 1 mile to Dartmouth Dr. then left for 0.2 mile then left on Kings Hwy for 2.8 mile, & right 0.3 miles to the campground.

Points of Interest

Visitors will witness the historical impact and the natural beauty that first moved William Penn to protect this area of pine-covered dunes for the public. This is the largest of the Delaware State Parks.

RV Sites		Water		Laundry	Y
Number	151	None		Wi-Fi	
Shaded	Y	At Site	Y	Fishing	Y
By Water	Y	Spigots		Hiking	Y
Paved		**Sewer**		Biking	Y
Pull Thru		None		Swimming	Y
ADA	0	At Site		Watch Wildlife	Y
Max RV Size	35	Dump Station	Y	Pets	Y
Electric		**Amenities**		**Security**	
None	Y	Restrooms	Y	Host(s)	Y
20 Amp		Showers	Y	Rangers(s)	Y
30 Amp		Reserve Sites	Y	Gate	
50 Amp		Store	Y	Patrolled	Y
		Grill/Table	Y		

[3] Killens Pond State Park (DE)
Hwy 13, Southeast of Reeves Crossing
South of Felton
N38 58.467 W75 32.085
State Rate: $31, Senior Discount
www.destateparks.com/camping/killens-pond/
(302) 284-3412

Directions

1.5 miles. From Hwy 13, just south of Reeves Pond go east on Paradise Alley Rd for 1.5 miles, past the Primitive Campground, to the RV campground.

Points of Interest

Pine woods and a picturesque millpond provide a great setting. The Park is conveniently located 15 miles south of Dover, 45 miles from the Delaware Beaches and within 2 hours of Philadelphia, Baltimore, Annapolis, Northern Virginia and Washington, DC.

RV Sites		Water		Laundry	
Number	59	None		Wi-Fi	
Shaded	Y	At Site	Y	Fishing	Y
By Water	Y	Spigots		Hiking	Y
Paved		**Sewer**		Biking	Y
Pull Thru		None		Swimming	
ADA		At Site		Watch Wildlife	Y
Max RV Size	40	Dump Station	Y	Pets	Y
Electric		**Amenities**		**Security**	
None		Restrooms	Y	Host(s)	Y
20 Amp	Y	Showers	Y	Rangers(s)	Y
30 Amp	Y	Reserve Sites	Y	Gate	
50 Amp		Store	Y	Patrolled	Y
		Grill/Table	Y		

[4] Lums Pond State Park (DE)
I-95, Exit 1
South of Glasgow
N39 32.898 W75 43.090
State Rate: $25-$30, Senior Discount
(302) 368-6989
www.destateparks.com/camping/lums-pond/

Directions

8 miles. From Exit 1 take 896/301 south for 6.2 miles. Turn east (left) on Hwy 71 (Red Lion Rd.) for 1.4 miles to the Park entrance

Points of Interest

The campground is within the Brandywine Valley, where the Du Pont mansions and gardens at Longwood, Winterthur, Hagley and Nemours attract millions of visitors from around the world. The camp is also a good stopover for those going down the eastern shore.

RV Sites		Water		Laundry	
Number	68	None		Wi-Fi	
Shaded	Y	At Site		Fishing	Y
By Water	Y	Spigots		Hiking	Y
Paved		Sewer		Biking	Y
Pull Thru	Y	None		Swimming	
ADA		At Site		Watch Wildlife	Y
Max RV Size	45	Dump Station	Y	Pets	Y
Electric		Amenities		Security	
None	few	Restrooms	Y	Host(s)	Y
20 Amp	few	Showers	Y	Rangers(s)	Y
30 Amp		Reserve Sites	Y	Gate	
50 Amp		Store		Patrolled	Y
		Grill/Table	Y		

[5] New Germany State Park (MD)
I-68, Exit 22
West of Frostburg
N39 37.839 W79 07.721
State Rate: $19, Senior Discounts
(301) 895-5453
http://www.dnr.state.md.us/publiclands/western/newgermany.asp

Directions

5 miles. From Exit 22 go south on Chestnut Ridge Rd. for 3 miles to New Germany Rd. Continue south (left) for 2 miles to the Park.

Points of Interest

Located in the forested peaks and valleys of the Blue Ridge and Allegheny Mountains. Visit Frostburg, a historic main street community. Ride the Western Maryland Scenic Railroad or tour the Thrasher Carriage Museum, where costumed docents transport you back in time.

RV Sites		Water		Laundry	
Number	35	None		Wi-Fi	
Shaded	Y	At Site		Fishing	Y
By Water	Y	Spigots	Y	Hiking	Y
Paved		Sewer		Biking	Y
Pull Thru		None		Swimming	Y
ADA		At Site		Watch Wildlife	Y
Max RV Size	40	Dump Station	Y	Pets	Y
Electric		Amenities		Security	
None	Y	Restrooms	Y	Host(s)	Y
20 Amp		Showers	Y	Rangers(s)	Y
30 Amp		Reserve Sites	Y	Gate	
50 Amp		Store	Y	Patrolled	Y
		Grill/Table	Y		

[6] Rocky Gap State Park (MD)
I-68, Exit 50
Northeast of Cumberland
N39 41.755 W78 39.047
State Rate: $22-$28, Senior Discounts
(301) 722-1480
http://www.dnr.state.md.us/publiclands/western/rockygap.asp

Directions

Adjoins I-68. From Exit 50 go north directly into the Park entrance.

Points of Interest

The Chesapeake and Ohio Canal's towpath is a favorite of hikers, joggers, and bicyclists. Go on the 'All Aboard For Cumberland' National Register of Historic Places Travel Itinerary, which explores Cumberland's past through 27 historic places listed in the National Register.

RV Sites		Water		Laundry	
Number	227	None		Wi-Fi	
Shaded	Y	At Site		Fishing	Y
By Water	Y	Spigots	Y	Hiking	Y
Paved		Sewer		Biking	Y
Pull Thru	Y	None		Swimming	Y
ADA	Y	At Site		Watch Wildlife	Y
Max RV Size	45	Dump Station	Y	Pets	Y
Electric		Amenities		Security	
None		Restrooms	Y	Host(s)	Y
20 Amp	Y	Showers	Y	Rangers(s)	Y
30 Amp	Y	Reserve Sites	Y	Gate	
50 Amp		Store	Y	Patrolled	Y
		Grill/Table	Y		

[7] Cunningham Falls State Park (MD)
I-70, Exit 52
North of Frederick
N39 34.925 W77 26.167
State Rate: $22-$28, Senior Discounts
(800) 825-7275
www.dnr.state.md.us/publiclands/western/
cunningham.asp

Directions

13 or 19 miles. From Exit 52 go north on Hwy 15 for 13 miles to the **Manor Camp** crossover left turn. **Or** continue 3 more miles to Thurmont, turn west on Hwy 77 for 4 miles, then left on Catoctin Hollow Rd. to **Houck Camp**.

Points of Interest

In the Catoctin Mountains the camp area is known for its history and scenic beauty. Scenic byways lead to wineries & orchards. You are an hour from Washington, Baltimore, Gettysburg & Antietam.

RV Sites		Water		Laundry	
Number	158	None		Wi-Fi	
Shaded	Y	At Site		Fishing	Y
By Water	Y	Spigots	Y	Hiking	Y
Paved		Sewer		Biking	Y
Pull Thru		None		Swimming	Y
ADA	Y	At Site		Watch Wildlife	Y
Max RV Size	35	Dump Station	Y	Pets	Y
Electric		Amenities		Security	
None		Restrooms	Y	Host(s)	Y
20 Amp	some	Showers	Y	Rangers(s)	Y
30 Amp	some	Reserve Sites	Y	Gate	
50 Amp		Store	Y	Patrolled	Y
		Grill/Table	Y		

[8] Patapsco Valley State Park (MD)
I-70, Exit 87
West Side of Baltimore
N39 17.692 W76 47.243
State Rate: $19-$25, Senior Discounts
(410) 461-5005
www.dnr.state.md.us/publiclands/central/patap-sco.asp

Directions

4 miles. If your RV is over 11' 1" high, you must enter the park by the Hwy 40 east-bound entrance. From Exit 87 go south for 2 miles on Hwy 29. Turn east on Hwy 40 for 2 miles to the park.

Points of Interest

See the Elkridge Furnace & forge in the park. In Baltimore see baseball at Camden Yards or tour the inner harbor of Washington. Go to Ellicott City and visit the B&O Railroad Museum.

RV Sites		Water		Laundry	
Number	26	None		Wi-Fi	
Shaded	Y	At Site		Fishing	Y
By Water		Spigots	Y	Hiking	Y
Paved	Y	Sewer		Biking	Y
Pull Thru		None		Swimming	Y
ADA	Y	At Site		Watch Wildlife	Y
Max RV Size	35	Dump Station	Y	Pets	Y
Electric		Amenities		Security	
None		Restrooms	Y	Host(s)	Y
20 Amp	Y	Showers	Y	Rangers(s)	Y
30 Amp	Y	Reserve Sites	Y	Gate	Y
50 Amp		Store	Y	Patrolled	Y
		Grill/Table	Y		

[9] Greenbelt Park (District of Columbia)
I-95, Exit 23
Northwest Side of Washington, D. C.
N38 59.748 W76 53.708
NP Rate: $16
America/Beautiful Rate: $8
(301) 344-3948
www.recreation.gov/CCC

Directions

1 mile from I-95. From Exit 23 take Hwy 201 (Kenilworth Avenue) south 0.5 mile. Turn left on Hwy 193 (Greenbelt Rd.) 0.3 mile to the park entrance on the right.

Points of Interest

The camp is known for its safe, peaceful surroundings in an urban setting, plus great NPS hospitality. The campground is located in suburban Maryland just ten miles from Washington, D.C. The camp is 1.5 mi. from the D.C. Metro.

RV Sites		Water		Laundry	
Number	100	None		Wi-Fi	
Shaded	Y	At Site		Fishing	
By Water		Spigots	Y	Hiking	Y
Paved	Y	Sewer		Biking	Y
Pull Thru		None		Swimming	
ADA	Y	At Site		Watch Wildlife	
Max RV Size	35	Dump Station	Y	Pets	Y
Electric		Amenities		Security	
None	Y	Restrooms	Y	Host(s)	Y
20 Amp		Showers	Y	Rangers(s)	Y
30 Amp		Reserve Sites	Y	Gate	
50 Amp		Store		Patrolled	
		Grill/Table	Y		

[10] Elk Neck State Park (MD)
I-95, Exit 100
South of North East Town
N39 28.829 W75 59.103
State Rate: $22-$37, Senior Discounts
(410) 287-5333
http://www.dnr.state.md.us/publiclands/central/elkneck.asp

Directions

12 miles. From Exit 100 take Hwy 272 south, through the Town of North East, for 12 miles to the Park.

Points of Interest

Located on a peninsula with beaches, marshlands & bluffs. Walk to the scenic Turkey Point Lighthouse with a view of the Elk River and Chesapeake Bay. Downtown North East offers antique shops, stores, & restaurants. St. Mary Anne's Episcopal Church dates to the 1700's.

RV Sites		Water		Laundry	
Number	229	None		Wi-Fi	Y
Shaded	Y	At Site	Y	Fishing	Y
By Water	Y	Spigots	Y	Hiking	Y
Paved		**Sewer**		Biking	Y
Pull Thru	Y	None		Swimming	Y
ADA	Y	At Site	Y	Watch Wildlife	Y
Max RV Size	45	Dump Station	Y	Pets	Y
Electric		**Amenities**		**Security**	
None		Restrooms		Host(s)	Y
20 Amp	Y	Showers	Y	Rangers(s)	Y
30 Amp	Y	Reserve Sites	Y	Gate	
50 Amp	Y	Store	Y	Patrolled	Y
		Grill/Table	Y		

[11] Little Bennett County Campground (MD)
I-270, Exit 18
South of Frederick
N39 14.793 W77 17.453
CP Rate: $31-$31-$49
(301) 528-3430
www.montgomeryparks.org/enterprise/park_facilities/little_bennett/little_bennett_campground.shtm

Directions

2 miles. From Exit 18 go northeast on Hwy 121 (Clarksburg Rd.) 1/2 mile to Hwy 355 (Frederick Rd.). Turn left, go 1 mile to the park entrance on the right.

Points of Interest

Civil War sites & historic monuments are nearby. If you are planning a visit to the Nation's Capital, be sure to ask staff for information on public transportation, including Metrorail service. In Frederick discover a great American main street.

RV Sites		Water		Laundry	Y
Number	91	None		Wi-Fi	
Shaded	Y	At Site		Fishing	
By Water		Spigots	Y	Hiking	Y
Paved		**Sewer**		Biking	Y
Pull Thru	Y	None		Swimming	
ADA	Y	At Site		Watch Wildlife	
Max RV Size	45	Dump Station	Y	Pets	Y
Electric		**Amenities**		**Security**	
None		Restrooms	Y	Host(s)	Y
20 Amp	Y	Showers	Y	Rangers(s)	
30 Amp	Y	Reserve Sites	Y	Gate	
50 Amp	Y	Store		Patrolled	
		Grill/Table	Y		

[12] Janes Island State Park (MD)
Hwy 13, Crisfield Hwy (413) Exit
Northwest of Crisfield
N38 00.491 W75 50.616
State Rate: $22-$37, Senior Discounts
(410) 968-1565
http://www.dnr.state.md.us/publiclands/eastern/janesisland.asp

Directions

13.5 miles. From the Crisfield Hwy (413) Exit off Hwy 13, go southwest for 12 miles to Plantation Rd. Go right for 0.6 miles to Airport Rd, then left 0.8 miles to Lawson Rd. Go right to the campground.

Points of Interest

The waterfront sites are some of the best. Janes Island is crabbing - where you learn why 'Maryland is for Crabs!' Crisfield, the blue shell capital of the world, is close by with local catches to eat.

RV Sites		Water		Laundry	
Number	102	None		Wi-Fi	Y
Shaded	Y	At Site		Fishing	Y
By Water	Y	Spigots	Y	Hiking	Y
Paved		**Sewer**		Biking	Y
Pull Thru	Y	None		Swimming	Y
ADA	Y	At Site	Y	Watch Wildlife	Y
Max RV Size	45	Dump Station	Y	Pets	Y
Electric		**Amenities**		**Security**	
None		Restrooms	Y	Host(s)	Y
20 Amp	Y	Showers	Y	Rangers(s)	Y
30 Amp	Y	Reserve Sites	Y	Gate	
50 Amp		Store	Y	Patrolled	Y
		Grill/Table	Y		

[13] Pocomoke River State Park, Shad Hill (MD)
Hwy 113
South of Snow Hill
N38 07.735 W75 26.409
State Rate: $22-$28, Senior Discounts
(410) 632-2566
http://www.dnr.state.md.us/publiclands/eastern/pocomokeriver.asp

Directions

4 miles. From Hwys 113 and 12 go south on Hwy 113 for 4 miles to the Campground.

Points of Interest

The Park is well known for its stand of loblolly pine and cypress swamps which border the wild and scenic Pocomoke River. Snow Hill boasts fine examples of Federal, Queen Anne, Gothic Revival, and Victorian style architecture in its houses.

RV Sites		Water			Laundry	
Number	188	None			Wi-Fi	Y
Shaded	Y	At Site			Fishing	Y
By Water	Y	Spigots	Y		Hiking	Y
Paved		Sewer			Biking	Y
Pull Thru		None			Swimming	Y
ADA	Y	At Site			Watch Wildlife	Y
Max RV Size	45	Dump Station	Y		Pets	Y
Electric		Amenities			Security	
None		Restrooms	Y		Host(s)	Y
20 Amp	Y	Showers	Y		Rangers(s)	Y
30 Amp	Y	Reserve Sites	Y		Gate	
50 Amp		Store	Y		Patrolled	Y
		Grill/Table	Y			

[14] Assateague State Park (MD)
Hwy 113, Ocean Gateway (Hwy 50) Exit
Southeast of Berlin
N38 14.308 W75 08.331
State Rate: $22-$28, Senior Discounts
(410) 641-2918
http://www.dnr.state.md.us/publiclands/eastern/assateague.asp

Directions

14 miles. Go 5.5 miles east on Hwy 50 to Stephen Decatur Highway (Rt 611). Turn south and follow Stephen Decatur Highway for 8.2 miles to the campground.

Points of Interest

The historic town of Berlin is eight miles away. Quaint shops, an historic hotel, and small restaurants give visitors the chance to step back in time. Berlin was the filming location for two major motion pictures.

RV Sites		Water			Laundry	
Number	312	None			Wi-Fi	
Shaded	Y	At Site			Fishing	Y
By Water	Y	Spigots	Y		Hiking	Y
Paved	Y	Sewer			Biking	Y
Pull Thru		None			Swimming	Y
ADA	Y	At Site			Watch Wildlife	Y
Max RV Size	45	Dump Station	Y		Pets	Y
Electric		Amenities			Security	
None		Restrooms	Y		Host(s)	Y
20 Amp	Y	Showers	Y		Rangers(s)	Y
30 Amp	Y	Reserve Sites	Y		Gate	
50 Amp		Store	Y		Patrolled	Y
		Grill/Table	Y			

[15] Tuckahoe State Park (MD)
Hwy 50/301
East of Annapolis
N38 57.997 W75 55.869
State Rate: $22-$28, Senior Discounts
(410) 820-1668
http://www.dnr.state.md.us/publiclands/eastern/tuckahoe.asp

Directions

30 miles. Go 20 miles east on Hwys 50/301 across the Bay Bridge, bearing right with Hwy 50. Make a left at the intersection of Hwy 50 and 404, go 7 miles to Hwy 480. Make a left then immediate left on Eveland Rd, go 3.3 miles to the campground.

Points of Interest

There is much to see and do by bike or walking in the park. Denton and St. Michaels are good sightseeing and eating destinations.

RV Sites	54	Water			Laundry	
Number		None			Wi-Fi	
Shaded	some	At Site			Fishing	Y
By Water	Y	Spigots	Y		Hiking	Y
Paved		Sewer			Biking	Y
Pull Thru		None			Swimming	
ADA	Y	At Site			Watch Wildlife	Y
Max RV Size	45	Dump Station	Y		Pets	Y
Electric		Amenities			Security	
None		Restrooms	Y		Host(s)	Y
20 Amp	Y	Showers	Y		Rangers(s)	Y
30 Amp	Y	Reserve Sites	Y		Gate	
50 Amp		Store			Patrolled	Y
		Grill/Table	Y			

About Florida's Public Campgrounds

There are 160 State Parks, many of which will accommodate RVs. The State Park System represents over 50% of public campgrounds in the state, the balance being primarily county parks. State Park RV campsites range in length from 20 to 76 feet. Most campsites maintain a soft gravel pad and each is equipped with water and electricity. Most parks have a centrally located dump station. Some parks offer pull through and waterfront locations. Camping fees range from $16.00 to $42.00 per night. You can find information on the State Parks at -

http://www.floridastateparks.org/

Florida state parks are open from 8 a.m. until sundown 365 days a year. Domestic pets are permitted in designated day-use areas at ALL Florida State Parks. Service animals are welcome in all areas.

Visitors to Florida State Parks can reserve campsites as much as 11 months in advance, by dialing 1-800 326-3521. If you prefer, you can make your reservation online at:

http://floridastateparks.reserveamerica.com

Reservations in advance are always a good idea in Florida!

[1] Lake Louisa State Park	[14] Markham Park
[2] Wekiwa Springs State Park	[15] Collier-Seminole State Park
[3] Blue Springs State Park	[16] Koreshan State Historic Site Park
[4] Big Lagoon State Park	[17] Lake Manatee State Park
[5] Blackwater River State Park	[18] Alafia River State Park
[6] Fred Gannon Rocky Bayou State Park	[19] Hillsborough River State Park
[7] Falling Waters State Park	[20] Lake Griffin Park
[8] Florida Caverns State Park	[21] Paynes Prairie Preserve State Park
[9] Three Rivers State Park	[22] O'Leno State Park
[10] Suwannee River State Park	[23] Stephen Foster Folk Culture Center State Park
[11] Ocean Pond	[24] St. Lucie South
[12] John Pennekamp Coral Reef State Park	[25] Jetty Park Campground
[13] Lone Pine Key	[26] Anastasia State Park
	[27] Fort Clinch State Park

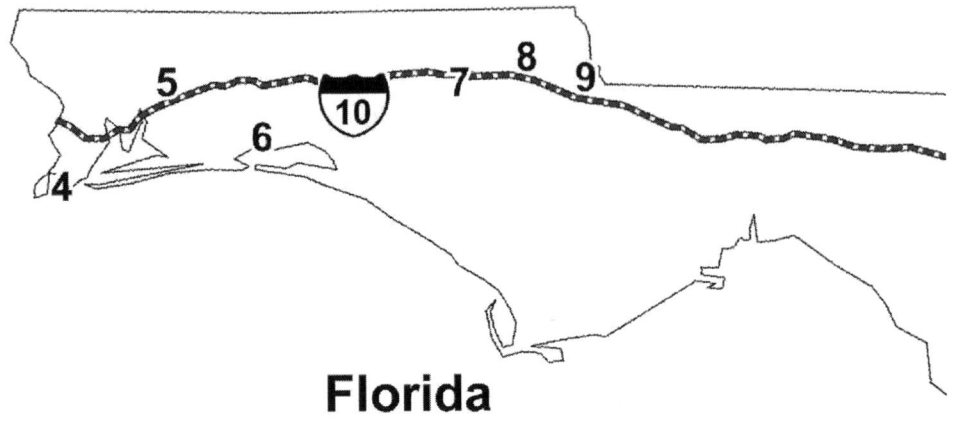

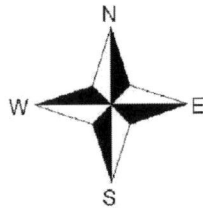

Florida

Florida

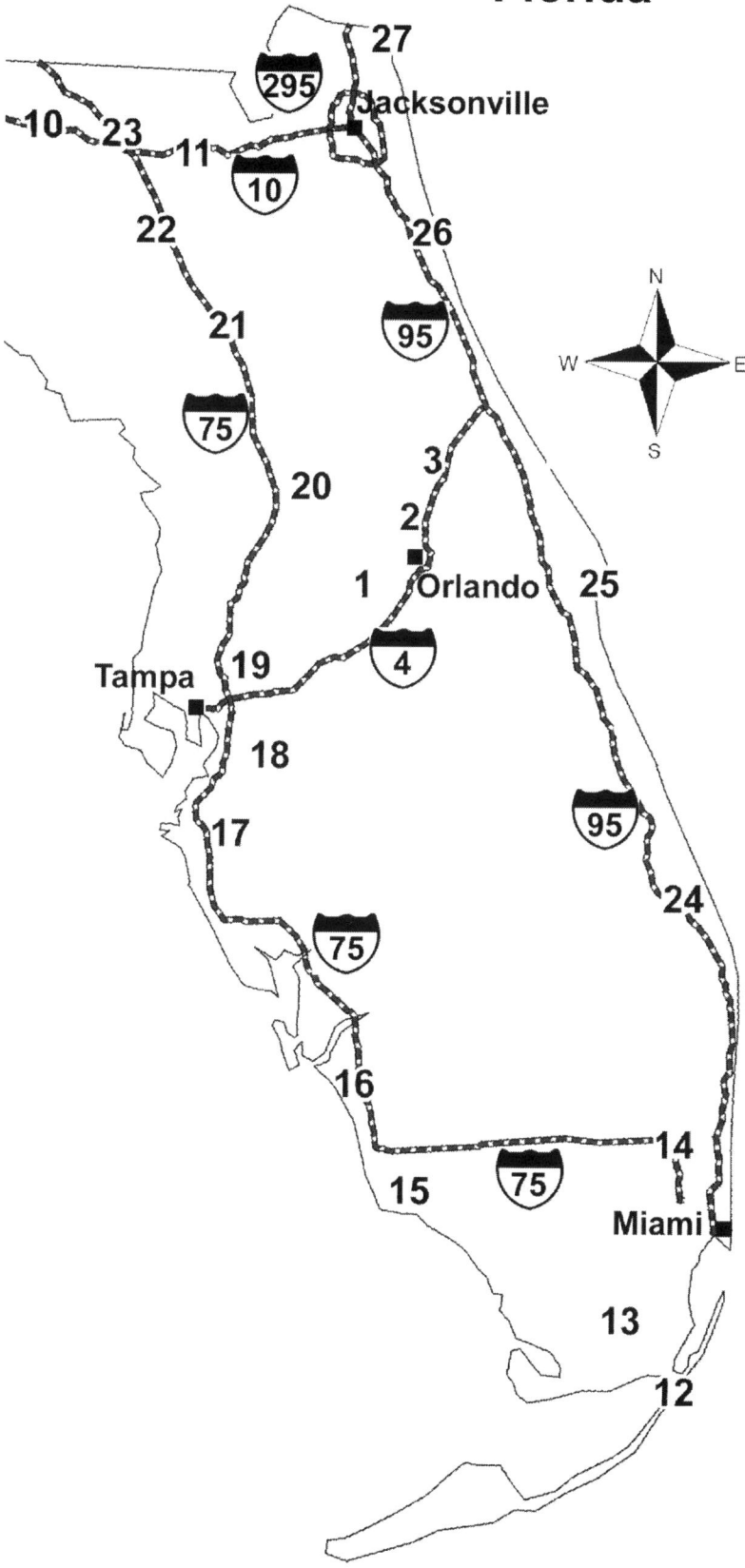

27

295

Jacksonville

-10 23 11

10

22

21

26

95

75

20

3

2

1 Orlando 25

N

W   E

S

Tampa 19

4

18

17

75

95

24

16

14

15 75

Miami

13

12

[1] Lake Louisa State Park
I-4, Exit 55
West of Orlando
N28 27.386 W81 43.263
State Rate: $24
(352) 394-3969
http://www.floridastateparks.org/lakelouisa/
default.cfm

Directions

16 miles. From Exit 55 go north on Hwy 27/25 for 16 miles to the entrance on the left.

Points of Interest

The Park is noted for its beautiful lakes, rolling hills, and scenic landscapes. Lake Louisa is in a chain of 13 lakes connected by the Palatlakaha River. If you park at the highest park point at night you may see the fireworks shows from Walt Disney World Theme Park near by.

RV Sites		Water		Laundry	
Number	60	None		Wi-Fi	
Shaded		At Site	Y	Fishing	Y
By Water	Y	Spigots		Hiking	Y
Paved		Sewer		Biking	Y
Pull Thru	Y	None		Swimming	Y
ADA	Y	At Site	Y	Watch Wildlife	Y
Max RV Size	45	Dump Station	Y	Pets	Y
Electric		Amenities		Security	
None		Restrooms	Y	Host(s)	Y
20 Amp	Y	Showers	Y	Rangers(s)	Y
30 Amp	Y	Reserve Sites	Y	Gate	Y
50 Amp	Y	Store		Patrolled	Y
		Grill/Table	Y		

[2] Wekiwa Springs State Park
I-4, Exit 94
North of Orlando
N28 42.568 W81 27.768
State Rate: $24
(407) 884-2008
http://www.floridastateparks.org/wekiwasprings/default.cfm

Directions

5 miles. From Exit 94 go west on Hwy 434 for 1/2 mile. Turn right on Wekiva Springs Rd. and go 4 miles to the entrance on the right.

Points of Interest

At the Wekiwa River headwaters, vistas offer a glimpse of what Central Florida looked like when Timucuan Indians inhabited the area. You should see wildlife in the park. You are located less than an hour from most Central Florida attractions, many in Orlando.

RV Sites		Water		Laundry	
Number	60	None		Wi-Fi	
Shaded	Y	At Site	Y	Fishing	Y
By Water	Y	Spigots		Hiking	Y
Paved		Sewer		Biking	Y
Pull Thru		None		Swimming	Y
ADA	Y	At Site	Y	Watch Wildlife	Y
Max RV Size	45	Dump Station	Y	Pets	Y
Electric		Amenities		Security	
None		Restrooms	Y	Host(s)	Y
20 Amp	Y	Showers	Y	Rangers(s)	Y
30 Amp	Y	Reserve Sites	Y	Gate	
50 Amp		Store	Y	Patrolled	Y
		Grill/Table	Y		

[3] Blue Springs State Park
I-4, Exit 114
West of Orange City
N28 57.142 W81 20.010
State Rate: $24
(386) 775-3663
http://www.floridastateparks.org/bluespring/
default.cfm

Directions

7 miles. From Exit 114 go northwest on Hwy 472 for 3 miles. Turn south on Hwy 17/92 for 2 miles to West French Avenue (in Orange City). Turn right about 2 miles to the Park.

Points of Interest

Manatee viewing is possible in winter. Visit the 1872 Thursby House, siting atop an ancient Timucuan shell midden (centuries of Timucuan oyster shell accumulation). It was an early site for orange crop shipping, now a museum.

RV Sites		Water		Laundry	
Number	51	None		Wi-Fi	
Shaded	Y	At Site	Y	Fishing	Y
By Water	Y	Spigots	Y	Hiking	Y
Paved		Sewer		Biking	Y
Pull Thru		None		Swimming	Y
ADA	Y	At Site		Watch Wildlife	Y
Max RV Size	40	Dump Station	Y	Pets	Y
Electric		Amenities		Security	
None		Restrooms	Y	Host(s)	Y
20 Amp	Y	Showers	Y	Rangers(s)	Y
30 Amp	Y	Reserve Sites	Y	Gate	
50 Amp		Store	Y	Patrolled	Y
		Grill/Table	Y		

[4] Big Lagoon State Park
I-10, Exit 7
South of Pensacola
N30 19.313 W87 24.222
State Rate: $20
(850) 492-1595
http://www.floridastateparks.org/biglagoon/default.cfm

Directions

20 miles. Go south on Hwy 297 for 3.2 miles to Hwy 90. Turn right, go 1.1 miles to Hwy 173. Turn left, proceed for 10 miles to Hwy 292. Turn right, go 5 miles to the Gulf Beach Hwy. Turn left, go 1.2 miles to the Park.

Points of Interest

Visit Pensacola, America's first settlement. The flags of five nations have flown over the city in past centuries. As the Cradle of Naval Aviation, Pensacola also boasts a proud military history.

RV Sites		Water		Laundry	
Number	75	None		Wi-Fi	
Shaded	Y	At Site	Y	Fishing	Y
By Water	Y	Spigots	Y	Hiking	Y
Paved		Sewer		Biking	Y
Pull Thru		None		Swimming	Y
ADA	Y	At Site		Watch Wildlife	Y
Max RV Size	40	Dump Station	Y	Pets	Y
Electric		Amenities		Security	
None		Restrooms	Y	Host(s)	Y
20 Amp	Y	Showers	Y	Rangers(s)	Y
30 Amp	Y	Reserve Sites	Y	Gate	
50 Amp	Y	Store		Patrolled	Y
		Grill/Table	Y		

[5] Blackwater River State Park
I-10, Exits 31 or 45
Northeast of Pensacola
N30 42.483 W86 52.956
State Rate: $20
(850) 983-5363
http://www.floridastateparks.org/blackwater-river/

Directions

11 or 13 miles. **East bound**, Exit 31. Go 1 mi. north on Hwy 87 then east on Hwy 90 for 7 mi. to Harold. Go north on Deaton Bridge Rd 3 mi. to Park. **West bound**, Exit 45. Go 1/2 mi. north to Hwy 90, then west 9 mi. to Harold. Turn north as noted above.

Points of Interest

The park is certified as a Registered State Natural Feature - possessing exceptional value in illustrating the natural history of Florida.

RV Sites		Water		Laundry	
Number	30	None		Wi-Fi	
Shaded	Y	At Site	Y	Fishing	Y
By Water	Y	Spigots		Hiking	Y
Paved	some	Sewer		Biking	Y
Pull Thru		None		Swimming	Y
ADA	Y	At Site	Y	Watch Wildlife	Y
Max RV Size	45	Dump Station	Y	Pets	Y
Electric		Amenities		Security	
None		Restrooms	Y	Host(s)	Y
20 Amp	Y	Showers	Y	Rangers(s)	Y
30 Amp	Y	Reserve Sites	Y	Gate	
50 Amp	Y	Store		Patrolled	Y
		Grill/Table	Y		

[6] Fred Gannon Rocky Bayou State Park
I-10, Exits 56 or 70
East of Niceville
N30 29.762 W86 25.967
State Rate: $16
(850) 833-9144
www.floridastateparks.org/rockybayou/default.cfm

Directions

21 miles. **East bound,** Exit 56, take Hwy 85 south 15.7 mi. Go east on Hwy 20 for 4.3 miles to Park. **West bound**, Exit 70, take Hwy 285 south for 17.4 mi. Go east on Hwy 20 for 3.4 mi. to the Park.

Points of Interest

See Destin, on a peninsula separating the Gulf of Mexico from Choctawhatchee Bay & experience Florida's Emerald Coast. The city claims the biggest Florida fishing fleet & is known for white beaches & emerald-colored waters.

RV Sites		Water		Laundry	Y
Number	42	None		Wi-Fi	
Shaded	Y	At Site	Y	Fishing	Y
By Water	Y	Spigots		Hiking	Y
Paved	some	Sewer		Biking	Y
Pull Thru		None		Swimming	
ADA	Y	At Site		Watch Wildlife	Y
Max RV Size	45	Dump Station	Y	Pets	Y
Electric		Amenities		Security	
None		Restrooms	Y	Host(s)	Y
20 Amp	Y	Showers	Y	Rangers(s)	Y
30 Amp	Y	Reserve Sites	Y	Gate	
50 Amp	Y	Store		Patrolled	Y
		Grill/Table	Y		

[7] Falling Waters State Park
Exit 120
South of Chipley
N30 43.783 W85 31.683
State Rate: $18
(850) 638-6130
http://www.floridastateparks.org/fallingwaters/default.cfm

Directions

2.5 miles. From Exit 120 go south on Hwy 77 for 0.7 mile. Turn east on State Park Rd for 1.8 mile to the Park.

Points of Interest

The park has a beautiful waterfall (highest in Florida) & lots of trails to explore. Impressive trees & fern-covered sinkholes line Sink Hole Trail, the boardwalk that leads campers to the waterfall. Also enjoy beautiful native and migrating butterflies in the butterfly garden.

RV Sites		Water		Laundry	
Number	24	None		Wi-Fi	
Shaded	Y	At Site	Y	Fishing	Y
By Water		Spigots		Hiking	Y
Paved		**Sewer**		Biking	Y
Pull Thru	Y	None		Swimming	Y
ADA	Y	At Site		Watch Wildlife	Y
Max RV Size	45	Dump Station	Y	Pets	Y
Electric		**Amenities**		**Security**	
None		Restrooms	Y	Host(s)	Y
20 Amp	Y	Showers	Y	Rangers(s)	Y
30 Amp	Y	Reserve Sites	Y	Gate	
50 Amp	Y	Store		Patrolled	Y
		Grill/Table	Y		

[8] Florida Caverns State Park
I-10, Exit 142
North of Marianna
N30 48.507 W85 12.742
State Rate: $20
(850) 82-9598
www.floridastateparks.org/floridacaverns/default.cfm

Directions

8 miles. From Exit 142, turn north on Hwy 71 for 2 miles to Hwy 90. Go west 3 miles to Hwy 166 (Jefferson St, then Caverns Rd). Go north for 3 miles to Park.

Points of Interest

The only Florida park offering cave tours; with impressive formations of stalactites, stalagmites, soda straws, flowstones, & draperies. There is a Panhandle Pioneer Settlement about 30 minutes south. Visit Marianna & historic Russ House.

RV Sites		Water		Laundry	
Number	32	None		Wi-Fi	
Shaded	Y	At Site	Y	Fishing	Y
By Water		Spigots		Hiking	Y
Paved		**Sewer**		Biking	Y
Pull Thru		None		Swimming	Y
ADA	Y	At Site	Y	Watch Wildlife	Y
Max RV Size	40	Dump Station	Y	Pets	Y
Electric		**Amenities**		**Security**	
None		Restrooms	Y	Host(s)	Y
20 Amp	Y	Showers	Y	Rangers(s)	Y
30 Amp	Y	Reserve Sites	Y	Gate	
50 Amp	Y	Store	Y	Patrolled	Y
		Grill/Table	Y		

[9] Three Rivers State Park
I-10, Exit 158
West of Tallahassee
N30 44.362 W84 56.211
State Rate: $16
(850) 482-9006
http://www.floridastateparks.org/threerivers/default.cfm

Directions

8 miles. From Exit 158 go 5 miles north on Hwy 286 into Sneads to Hwy 90. Go west 0.5 miles to River Road. Turn north for 2.2 miles to the park.

Points of Interest

Looking for trees dripping with Spanish moss, and a great view of the water, wildlife and birds? This camp is for you. Situated on Lake Seminole, this is a great camp to relax, walk, fish, read, or take that nap.

RV Sites		Water		Laundry	
Number	30	None		Wi-Fi	
Shaded	Y	At Site	Y	Fishing	Y
By Water	Y	Spigots		Hiking	Y
Paved		**Sewer**		Biking	Y
Pull Thru	Y	None		Swimming	Y
ADA	Y	At Site		Watch Wildlife	Y
Max RV Size	45	Dump Station	Y	Pets	Y
Electric		**Amenities**		**Security**	
None		Restrooms	Y	Host(s)	Y
20 Amp	Y	Showers	Y	Rangers(s)	Y
30 Amp	Y	Reserve Sites	Y	Gate	
50 Amp	Y	Store		Patrolled	Y
		Grill/Table	Y		

[10] Suwannee River State Park
I-10, Exit 275
West of Live Oak
N30 22.650 W83 09.952
State Rate: $22
(386) 362-2746
http://www.floridastateparks.org/suwan-neeriver/default.cfm

Directions

5 miles. From Exit 275 go northwest on Hwy 10/90 for 6 miles to the park.

Points of Interest

Historic landmarks show the importance of the Suwannee River to Florida history. Along the Suwannee, long mounds of earthworks built during the Civil War guard incursions by Union Navy gunboats. Remnants include one of the State's oldest cemeteries, and a paddle-wheel shaft.

RV Sites		Water		Laundry	
Number	30	None		Wi-Fi	
Shaded	Y	At Site	Y	Fishing	Y
By Water	Y	Spigots		Hiking	Y
Paved		Sewer		Biking	Y
Pull Thru		None		Swimming	
ADA	Y	At Site	Y	Watch Wildlife	Y
Max RV Size	45	Dump Station		Pets	Y
Electric		Amenities		Security	
None		Restrooms	Y	Host(s)	Y
20 Amp	Y	Showers	Y	Rangers(s)	Y
30 Amp	Y	Reserve Sites	Y	Gate	
50 Amp	Y	Store		Patrolled	Y
		Grill/Table	Y		

[11] Ocean Pond
I-10, Exit 324
North of Olustee
N30 14.364 W82 25.120
Osceola NF Rate: $8-$16
America/Beautiful Rate: $4-$8
(386) 752-2577
http://www.stateparks.com/osceola.html

Directions

9 miles. From Exit 324 go 6.5 miles east on Hwy 10/90 to Cty Rd. 250/266 (Forest Rd.), just before Olustee. Turn north for 2.5 miles to the camp.

Points of Interest

Visit the Olustee Battlefield Historic State Park, which commemorates Florida's largest Civil War battle in 1864 where over 10,000 troops fought a five-hour battle. The Battlefield Park & Interpretive Center are open daily.

RV Sites		Water		Laundry	Y
Number	67	None		Wi-Fi	
Shaded	Y	At Site	Y	Fishing	Y
By Water	Y	Spigots		Hiking	Y
Paved	Y	Sewer		Biking	
Pull Thru		None		Swimming	Y
ADA	Y	At Site		Watch Wildlife	Y
Max RV Size	45	Dump Station	Y	Pets	Y
Electric		Amenities		Security	
None		Restrooms	Y	Host(s)	
20 Amp	Y	Showers	Y	Rangers(s)	Y
30 Amp	Y	Reserve Sites		Gate	
50 Amp		Store		Patrolled	
		Grill/Table	Y		

[12] John Pennekamp Coral Reef State Park
I-75, Exit 5
North of Key Largo
N25 07.646 W80 24.575
State Rate: $36
(305) 451-1202
www.floridastateparks.org/pennekamp/

Directions

25 mi. from Florida's Turnpike. From Exit 5 of I-75 go south on the Florida's Turnpike for 39.5 miles to its terminus at Hwy 1. Continue south 25 miles on Hwy 1 to the Park at Mile Marker 102.5, just north of Key Largo.

Points of Interest

This park is said to be one of the main attractions near Key Largo. Be sure to take a boat, or glass-bottom boat tour, out to the coral reef as it is the coral reefs and marine life that bring most visitors to the park.

RV Sites		Water		Laundry	Y
Number	47	None		Wi-Fi	Y
Shaded	Y	At Site	Y	Fishing	Y
By Water	Y	Spigots		Hiking	Y
Paved		Sewer		Biking	Y
Pull Thru		None		Swimming	Y
ADA	Y	At Site	Y	Watch Wildlife	Y
Max RV Size	45	Dump Station	Y	Pets	Y
Electric		Amenities		Security	
None		Restrooms	Y	Host(s)	Y
20 Amp	Y	Showers	Y	Rangers(s)	Y
30 Amp	Y	Reserve Sites	Y	Gate	
50 Amp	Y	Store	Y	Patrolled	Y
		Grill/Table	Y		

[13] Lone Pine Key
I-75, Exit 5 (see [12] for 1st leg of directions)
West of Homestead
N25 25.033 W80 38.814
Everglades NP Rate: $14
America/Beautiful Rate: $7
(800) 365-2267
http://www.everglades.national-park.com/camping.htm

Directions

15 miles from Florida's Turnpike terminus. At Hwy 1 go west on Palm Dr., 1.6 mile to 192nd Ave., then south 2 mile to Hwy 9336 (Ingram Hwy) & west on 9336, 10 mile to the camp road. Turn left, go 1.3 mile to camp.

Points of Interest

Learn about the unique Everglades ecosystem. Look for Mahogany Hammock (largest Mahogany tree in the US). Check the 'Artist in Residence Program.'

RV Sites		Water		Laundry	
Number	108	None		Wi-Fi	
Shaded	Y	At Site		Fishing	Y
By Water	Y	Spigots	Y	Hiking	Y
Paved		Sewer		Biking	Y
Pull Thru	Y	None		Swimming	
ADA		At Site		Watch Wildlife	Y
Max RV Size	45	Dump Station	Y	Pets	Y
Electric		Amenities		Security	
None	Y	Restrooms	Y	Host(s)	Y
20 Amp		Showers		Rangers(s)	Y
30 Amp		Reserve Sites		Gate	
50 Amp		Store		Patrolled	
		Grill/Table	Y		

[14] Markham Park
I-75, Exit 15
West of Ft. Lauderdale
N26 07.601 W80 21.590
County Rate: $40
(954) 357-8868
http://www.broward.org/Parks/Camping/Pages/Default.aspx

Directions

3 miles. From Exit 15 go west onto Royal Palm Blvd, immediately turn at the first right on Weston Rd. Go north on Hwy 84 for 3 miles to the Park.

Points of Interest

In Ft. Lauderdale, find the Riverwalk Arts and Entertainment District. The brick-lined promenade features the Broward Center for the Performing Arts, Museum of Discovery & Science, Florida Grand Opera, Ft. Lauderdale Historical Center, Stranahan House and Museum of Art.

RV Sites		Water		Laundry	
Number	60	None		Wi-Fi	Y
Shaded	Y	At Site	Y	Fishing	
By Water	Y	Spigots		Hiking	
Paved	Y	Sewer		Biking	Y
Pull Thru	Y	None		Swimming	Y
ADA	Y	At Site	Y	Watch Wildlife	
Max RV Size	45	Dump Station	Y	Pets	Y
Electric		Amenities		Security	
None		Restrooms	Y	Host(s)	Y
20 Amp	Y	Showers	Y	Rangers(s)	
30 Amp	Y	Reserve Sites	Y	Gate	
50 Amp	Y	Store	Y	Patrolled	Y
		Grill/Table	Y		

[15] Collier-Seminole State Park
I-75, Exit 101
Southeast of Naples
N25 59.534 W81 35.390
State Rate: $22
(239) 394-3397
http://www.floridastateparks.org/collierseminole/default.cfm

Directions

16 miles. From Exit 101 go south on Cty Rd 951 (Collier Rd.), 7 miles to Hwy 41. Turn east, go 9 miles. The Park will be on the right.

Points of Interest

The park has a wealth of vegetation & wildlife typical of the Everglades & a forest of tropical trees. Although rare elsewhere, the Florida royal palm is common here. The restaurants of Marco Island will delight with fresh seafood & island creations. Explore Ten Thousand Islands.

RV Sites		Water		Laundry	
Number	120	None		Wi-Fi	
Shaded	Y	At Site	Y	Fishing	Y
By Water	Y	Spigots		Hiking	Y
Paved		Sewer		Biking	Y
Pull Thru		None		Swimming	
ADA	Y	At Site		Watch Wildlife	Y
Max RV Size	40	Dump Station	Y	Pets	Y
Electric		Amenities		Security	
None		Restrooms	Y	Host(s)	Y
20 Amp	Y	Showers	Y	Rangers(s)	Y
30 Amp	Y	Reserve Sites	Y	Gate	
50 Amp	Y	Store	Y	Patrolled	Y
		Grill/Table	Y		

[16] Koreshan State Historic Site Park
I-75, Exit 123
South of San Carlos Park
N26 25.868 W81 48.885
State Rate: $26
(239) 992-0311
www.floridastateparks.org/koreshan/default.cfm

Directions

2 miles. From Exit 123 go west 2.2 miles on Corkscrew Rd. After crossing Hwy 41/45 look for entrance to park on right.

Points of Interest

Cyrus Teed brought followers to Estero in 1894 to build New Jerusalem for his new faith, Koreshanity. The colony faded and deeded the land to the State. Tour Founders House, Planetary Court, and Bamboo Landing. Contact the Park Curator for more information.

RV Sites		Water		Laundry	Y
Number	60	None		Wi-Fi	
Shaded	Y	At Site	Y	Fishing	Y
By Water	Y	Spigots		Hiking	Y
Paved		Sewer		Biking	Y
Pull Thru		None		Swimming	Y
ADA	Y	At Site		Watch Wildlife	Y
Max RV Size	40	Dump Station	Y	Pets	Y
Electric		Amenities		Security	
None		Restrooms	Y	Host(s)	Y
20 Amp	Y	Showers	Y	Rangers(s)	Y
30 Amp	Y	Reserve Sites	Y	Gate	
50 Amp		Store	Y	Patrolled	Y
		Grill/Table	Y		

[17] Lake Manatee State Park
I-75, Exit 220
East of Bradenton
N27 28.514 W82 20.920
State Rate: $22
(941) 741-3028
www.floridastateparks.org/lakemanatee/default.cfm

Directions

9 miles. From Exit 220 go 9 miles east on Hwy 64, just past Dam Rd, to the park on your left.

Points of Interest

Try the award winning Bradenton Riverfront Theatre. Visit South Florida Museum, Bishop Planetarium & Parker Manatee Aquarium. Shop the Village of Arts -studios, galleries & small restaurants, mostly catering to the arts. One of the Top 10 cities in the country for working artists.

RV Sites		Water		Laundry	
Number	60	None		Wi-Fi	
Shaded	Y	At Site	Y	Fishing	Y
By Water	Y	Spigots		Hiking	Y
Paved		Sewer		Biking	Y
Pull Thru		None		Swimming	Y
ADA	Y	At Site		Watch Wildlife	Y
Max RV Size	40	Dump Station	Y	Pets	Y
Electric		Amenities		Security	
None		Restrooms	Y	Host(s)	Y
20 Amp	Y	Showers	Y	Rangers(s)	Y
30 Amp	Y	Reserve Sites	Y	Gate	
50 Amp		Store		Patrolled	Y
		Grill/Table	Y		

[18] Alafia River State Park
I-75, Exit 240
Southeast of Tampa
N27 46.867 W82 08.734
State Rate: $22
(813) 72-5320
www.floridastateparks.org/alafiariver/default.cfm

Directions

20 miles. From Exit 240 go east on Hwy 674 for 15 miles. Turn north on Cty Rd. 39 for 5 miles to the park entrance on the right.

Points of Interest

Tampa/St. Petersburg are close. Try Heritage Park, St. Petersburg Museum of History, Salvador Dali Museum, Old Hyde Park Village, Sunken Gardens, Florida Holocaust Museum, and much more. See *http://www.tampaguide.com/Todo/TodoCat22.asp*

RV Sites		Water		Laundry	
Number	18	None		Wi-Fi	
Shaded	Y	At Site	Y	Fishing	Y
By Water	Y	Spigots		Hiking	Y
Paved	Y	Sewer		Biking	Y
Pull Thru	Y	None		Swimming	
ADA	Y	At Site		Watch Wildlife	Y
Max RV Size	45	Dump Station	Y	Pets	Y
Electric		Amenities		Security	
None		Restrooms	Y	Host(s)	Y
20 Amp	Y	Showers	Y	Rangers(s)	Y
30 Amp	Y	Reserve Sites	Y	Gate	
50 Amp	Y	Store		Patrolled	Y
		Grill/Table	Y		

[19] Hillsborough River State Park
I-75, Exit 265
Northeast of Tampa
N28 08.674 W82 13.463
State Rate: $24
(813) 987-6771
www.floridastateparks.org/hillsboroughriver/
default.cfm

Directions

11 miles. From Exit 265 take Fowler Ave 1.5 miles east to Hwy 301. Go northeast on Hwy 301 for 9.5 miles to the park entrance on the left.

Points of Interest

Fort Foster, a replica of an 1837 fort from the Second Seminole War, is located on the park grounds. Tampa-St. Petersburg are close by. For a list of activities go to entry [18] and/or see - *http://www. tampaguide.com/Todo/TodoCat22.asp*

RV Sites		Water		Laundry	
Number	112	None		Wi-Fi	Y
Shaded	Y	At Site	Y	Fishing	Y
By Water	Y	Spigots		Hiking	Y
Paved	Y	**Sewer**		Biking	Y
Pull Thru	Y	None		Swimming	Y
ADA	Y	At Site		Watch Wildlife	Y
Max RV Size	40	Dump Station	Y	Pets	Y
Electric		**Amenities**		**Security**	
None		Restrooms	Y	Host(s)	Y
20 Amp	Y	Showers	Y	Rangers(s)	Y
30 Amp	Y	Reserve Sites	Y	Gate	
50 Amp	Y	Store	Y	Patrolled	Y
		Grill/Table	Y		

[20] Lake Griffin State Park
I-75, Exit 329
North of Leesburg
N28 51.450 W81 54.182
State Rate: $18
(352) 360-6760
www.floridastateparks.org/lakegriffin/default.
cfm

Directions

17 miles. From Exit 329 go east 13.5 miles on Hwy 44 to Leesburg. Turn north on Hwy 27/25 for 3.5 miles to park on the right.

Points of Interest

The Park is located within an hour of central Florida attractions & theme parks. Visit Leesburg, the 'Lakefront City.' Lake Griffin, in the world-renowned Harris Chain of Lakes, is one of central Florida's largest freshwater lakes and is host to the Bassmasters Tournament.

RV Sites		Water		Laundry	Y
Number	40	None		Wi-Fi	
Shaded	Y	At Site	Y	Fishing	Y
By Water		Spigots		Hiking	Y
Paved		**Sewer**		Biking	Y
Pull Thru	Y	None		Swimming	
ADA	Y	At Site	some	Watch Wildlife	Y
Max RV Size	40	Dump Station	Y	Pets	Y
Electric		**Amenities**		**Security**	
None		Restrooms	Y	Host(s)	Y
20 Amp	Y	Showers	Y	Rangers(s)	Y
30 Amp	Y	Reserve Sites	Y	Gate	
50 Amp	Y	Store		Patrolled	Y
		Grill/Table	Y		

[21] Paynes Prairie Preserve State Park
I-75, Exit 374
South of Gainesville
N29 31.146 W82 17.892
State Rate: $18
(352) 466-3397
www.floridastateparks.org/paynesprairie/de-
fault.cfm

Directions

2 miles. From Exit 374 go east on Cty Rd. 234 for 1.4. Turn left on Hwy 441 and go 0.6 miles to Savannah Blvd. and the Park on the right.

Points of Interest

In a 22,000-acre preserve, the Park is in one of the most significant natural & historic areas in Florida. In 1774, noted artist and naturalist William Bartram called it the "great Alachua Savannah." Gainesville has much to offer in museums, historic sites, live theater, & shopping.

RV Sites		Water		Laundry	
Number	31	None		Wi-Fi	
Shaded	Y	At Site	Y	Fishing	Y
By Water		Spigots		Hiking	Y
Paved		**Sewer**		Biking	Y
Pull Thru		None		Swimming	
ADA	Y	At Site		Watch Wildlife	Y
Max RV Size	40	Dump Station	Y	Pets	Y
Electric		**Amenities**		**Security**	
None		Restrooms	Y	Host(s)	Y
20 Amp	Y	Showers	Y	Rangers(s)	Y
30 Amp	Y	Reserve Sites	Y	Gate	Y
50 Amp	Y	Store	Y	Patrolled	Y
		Grill/Table	Y		

[22] O'Leno State Park
I-75, Exit 414
O'Leno State Park
North of Gainesville
N29 55.181 W82 36.514
State Rate: $18
(386) 454-1853
www.floridastateparks.org/oleno/default.cfm

Directions

6 miles. From Exit 414 go 6 miles south on Hwy 41 to Sprite Loop and the park entrance on the left.

Points of Interest

Enjoy a rustic 1930's Civilian Conservation Corps era atmosphere on the banks of the scenic Santa Fe River. Discover nearby Cross Creek, the home of author Marjorie Kinnan Rawlings, who wrote The Yearling and Cross Creek, both made into movies.

RV Sites		Water		Laundry	
Number	61	None		Wi-Fi	
Shaded	Y	At Site	Y	Fishing	Y
By Water	Y	Spigots		Hiking	Y
Paved		Sewer		Biking	Y
Pull Thru	Y	None		Swimming	Y
ADA	Y	At Site		Watch Wildlife	Y
Max RV Size	40	Dump Station	Y	Pets	Y
Electric		Amenities		Security	
None		Restrooms	Y	Host(s)	Y
20 Amp	Y	Showers	Y	Rangers(s)	Y
30 Amp	Y	Reserve Sites	Y	Gate	
50 Amp	Y	Store		Patrolled	Y
		Grill/Table	Y		

[23] Stephen Foster Folk Culture Center State Park
Exit 439 of I-75
North of I-10
N30 19.794 W82 45.616
State Rate: $20
(386) 397-2733
www.floridastateparks.org/stephenfoster/

Directions

4 miles. From Exit 439 travel east on Hwy 136 for 3 miles. Turn left on Hwy 25/41. Park entrance is on the left.

Points of Interest

On the legendary Suwannee River, the Park honors the memory of American composer Stephen Foster. A wide variety of artisans populate Craft Square monthly. Tour the Museum and Carillon Tower. Participate in workshops & retreat events or get involved as a crafter or demonstrator.

RV Sites		Water		Laundry	
Number	45	None		Wi-Fi	
Shaded	Y	At Site	Y	Fishing	Y
By Water	Y	Spigots		Hiking	Y
Paved		Sewer		Biking	Y
Pull Thru	Y	None		Swimming	
ADA	Y	At Site		Watch Wildlife	Y
Max RV Size	45	Dump Station	Y	Pets	Y
Electric		Amenities		Security	
None		Restrooms	Y	Host(s)	Y
20 Amp	Y	Showers	Y	Rangers(s)	Y
30 Amp	Y	Reserve Sites	Y	Gate	
50 Amp	Y	Store	Y	Patrolled	Y
		Grill/Table	Y		

[24] St. Lucie South
I-95, Exit 101
South of Stuart
N27 06.680 W80 17.041
COE Rate: $20-$24
America/Beautiful Rate: $10-$12
(772) 287-1382
www.reserveamerica.com/

Directions

2 miles. From Exit 101 go 0.5 mile south on Hwy 76 to Locks Rd. Turn right, drive 1.3 miles to the camp.

Points of Interest

Enjoy the view of boats & manatees passing through the lock & dam as they travel the Okeechobee Waterway. Visit the City of Stuart, known as the 'Sailfish Capital of the World,' because of the many sailfish found in the ocean off Martin County. Charter a boat, catch your own!

RV Sites		Water		Laundry	
Number	9	None		Wi-Fi	
Shaded		At Site	Y	Fishing	Y
By Water	Y	Spigots		Hiking	Y
Paved	Y	Sewer		Biking	Y
Pull Thru		None		Swimming	
ADA	Y	At Site		Watch Wildlife	Y
Max RV Size	42	Dump Station	Y	Pets	Y
Electric		Amenities		Security	
None		Restrooms	Y	Host(s)	Y
20 Amp	Y	Showers	Y	Rangers(s)	Y
30 Amp	Y	Reserve Sites	Y	Gate	
50 Amp	Y	Store		Patrolled	
		Grill/Table	Y		

[25] Jetty Park Campground
I-95, Exit 205
Cape Canaveral
N28 24.330 W80 35.693
Port Authority Rate: $32-$47
(321) 783-7111
http://www.jettyparkbeachandcampground.
com/camp_index

Directions

14 miles. From Exit 205 go 12 miles east on Hwy 528 (Beachline Expressway), merge into Hwy A1A, to George J. King Blvd. Exit and go east 1.7 miles to the park entrance.

Points of Interest

Watch giant cruise ships or submarines come in with the dolphins. One of this park's best features is the 1,200 foot Malcolm E. McLouth Fishing Pier (accessible to physically challenged). Cocoa Beach is just a few minutes drive.

RV Sites		Water		Laundry		Y
Number	126	None		Wi-Fi		Y
Shaded	Y	At Site	Y	Fishing		Y
By Water	Y	Spigots		Hiking		Y
Paved	Y	Sewer		Biking		Y
Pull Thru	Y	None		Swimming		
ADA	Y	At Site	Y	Watch Wildlife		Y
Max RV Size	45	Dump Station	Y	Pets		Y
Electric		Amenities		Security		
None		Restrooms	Y	Host(s)		Y
20 Amp	Y	Showers	Y	Rangers(s)		
30 Amp	Y	Reserve Sites	Y	Gate		Y
50 Amp	Y	Store	Y	Patrolled		Y
		Grill/Table	Y			

[26] Anastasia State Park
I-95, Exit 311
South of St. Augustine
N29 52.835 W81 17.170
State Rate: $28
(904) 461-2033
www.floridastateparks.org/anastasia/default.cfm

Directions

9 miles. From Exit 311 travel northeast 3.6 miles on Hwy 207 to Hwy 312. Turn east on Hwy 312, go 3.6 miles to Hwy A1A. Travel 1.5 miles north to the park entrance on the right.

Points of Interest

At the park, shop the Farmer's Market on Saturday. St. Augustine is the oldest European established city in the U.S. There is much to see - St. Augustine Lighthouse, Avero House, Castillo de San Marcos National Monument, Old St. Johns County Jail, & Zorayda Castle to name a few.

RV Sites		Water		Laundry	
Number	139	None		Wi-Fi	
Shaded	Y	At Site	Y	Fishing	Y
By Water	Y	Spigots		Hiking	Y
Paved		Sewer		Biking	Y
Pull Thru		None		Swimming	Y
ADA	Y	At Site	Y	Watch Wildlife	Y
Max RV Size	40	Dump Station	Y	Pets	Y
Electric		Amenities		Security	
None		Restrooms	Y	Host(s)	Y
20 Amp	Y	Showers	Y	Rangers(s)	Y
30 Amp	Y	Reserve Sites	Y	Gate	
50 Amp		Store	Y	Patrolled	Y
		Grill/Table	Y		

[27] Fort Clinch State Park
I-95, Exit 373
At Fernandina Beach
N30 40.077 W81 26.056
State Rate: $26
(904) 277-7274
www.floridastateparks.org/fortclinch/default.cfm

Directions

16 miles. From Exit 373 travel east & north, 15 miles, on Hwy 200/A1A. In Fernandina the street name is 8th St. At Atlantic (A1A) turn east (right) for 1 mile to the Park.

Points of Interest

Enjoy hiking in the maritime hammock, explore Atlantic beaches, experience the Living History Program at 19th century Historic Fort Clinch. Special events occur monthly. Fernandina Beach has a historic district with Victorian homes & shops.

RV Sites		Water		Laundry		Y
Number	61	None		Wi-Fi		
Shaded	Y	At Site	Y	Fishing		Y
By Water	Y	Spigots		Hiking		Y
Paved		Sewer		Biking		Y
Pull Thru		None		Swimming		
ADA	Y	At Site	Y	Watch Wildlife		Y
Max RV Size	45	Dump Station	Y	Pets		Y
Electric		Amenities		Security		
None		Restrooms	Y	Host(s)		Y
20 Amp	Y	Showers	Y	Rangers(s)		Y
30 Amp	Y	Reserve Sites	Y	Gate		
50 Amp	Y	Store	Y	Patrolled		Y
		Grill/Table	Y			

About Georgia's Public Campgrounds

Forty-three Georgia State Parks offer over 2,400 campsites. Rates average around $23-$28 per night.

Sites offer electrical and water hookups, grills or fire rings, and picnic tables. Some are specially designed just for tents, while others have pull-through access for large RVs. Modern bath houses with hot showers, flush toilets and electrical outlets are conveniently located. All camp grounds have dump stations, and several offer cable TV hookups. A few campgrounds have sewage hookups. Most state parks have laundry facilities and sell camping supplies, offer accessible campsites, fishing piers, nature trails and picnic areas. Pets are welcome in campgrounds if kept on a six-foot leash and attended at all times. Every Tuesday the State Park website will show which campsites are available for the upcoming weekend. You can get details at -

www.georgiastateparks.org/

Reservations are accepted up to 13 months in advance (to the day) of your arrival date. Go to -

www.georgiastateparks.org/reservations/

Annual ParkPass discounts of 50% are available for seniors who present a copy of their drivers license. Seniors, 62 and older, receive $20 off individual or family membership in Friends of Georgia State Parks & Historic Sites. Seniors also receive 20% off campsite rates (year-round). The discount applies only when vehicle is registered to a senior. The daily (entrance) fee is $5 and RVers pay only one fee for the duration of the stay.

[1] Little Ocmulgee State Park	[12] McKinney Campround
[2] George L. Smith State Park	[13] R. Shaefer Heard Campground
[3] John Tanner State Park	[14] Fort Yargo State Park
[4] Hard Labor Creek State Park	[15] Tugaloo State Park
[5] A.H. Stephens Historic Park	[16] Crooked River State Park
[6] Big Hart Campground	[17] Fort McAllister Historic Park
[7] Petersburg Campground	[18] F.D. Roosevelt State Park
[8] Cloudland Canyon State Park	[19] Magnolia Springs State Park
[9] Reed Bingham Historic Park	[20] Elijah Clark State Park
[10] Georgia Veterans State Park	[21] Hart State Outdoor Recreation Area
[11] Indian Springs State Park	

Georgia

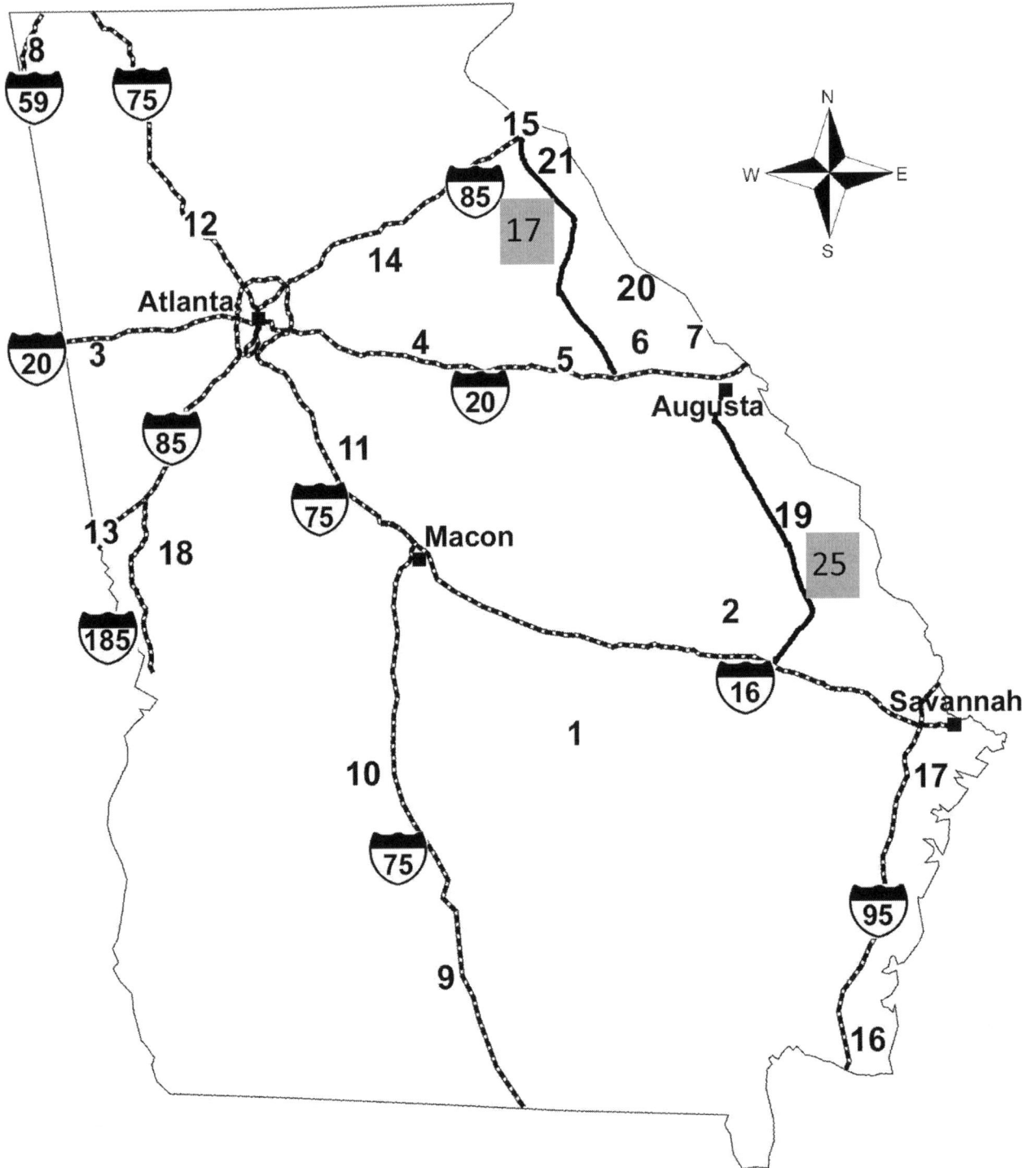

8
59
75

15
21
85
17

12
14

Atlanta

20
3

4
5
6
7
20
Augusta

85

11

75

13
18

Macon

185

19
25

2
16

1

Savannah

10

17

75

9

95

16

[1] Little Ocmulgee State Park
I-16, Exit 51
South of Dublin
N32 05.513 W82 53.078
State Rate: $23-$25, Senior Discount
(229) 868-7474
http://gastateparks.org/info/liocmulgee/

Directions

28 miles. From Exit 51 go south on Hwy 319/441 for 28 miles to the entrance on the right, just before entering McRae.

Points of Interest

The lodge restaurant is said to offer a good meal. Visit Dublin, known for its St Patrick's festival, also tour the Laurens Museum originally built by Andrew Carnegie as a library. Check out the Statue of Liberty replica, one-twelfth actual size, in downtown McRae's Liberty Square.

RV Sites		Water		Laundry	
Number	55	None		Wi-Fi	Y
Shaded	Y	At Site	Y	Fishing	Y
By Water	Y	Spigots		Hiking	Y
Paved		**Sewer**		Biking	Y
Pull Thru	Y	None		Swimming	Y
ADA	Y	At Site	Y	Watch Wildlife	
Max RV Size	45	Dump Station	Y	Pets	Y
Electric		**Amenities**		**Security**	
None		Restrooms	Y	Host(s)	Y
20 Amp	Y	Showers	Y	Rangers(s)	Y
30 Amp	Y	Reserve Sites	Y	Gate	
50 Amp	Y	Store	Y	Patrolled	Y
		Grill/Table	Y		

[2] George L. Smith State Park
I-16, Exit 104
North of Metter
N32 32.686 W82 07.512
State Rate: $25-$28, Senior Discount
(478) 763-2759
http://gastateparks.org/info/georgels/

Directions

15 miles. From Exit 104 go 1.6 miles north on Hwy 23/121 to Hwy 46 in Metter. Turn left for 3 blocks to Hwy 23 (College St). Turn north on Hwy 23 for 11.3 miles to George L. Smith Rd, then right 2 miles to the Park.

Points of Interest

The Park is known for the Parrish Mill. Hikers have 7 miles of trails, & look for the lumbering Gopher Tortoise, Georgia's state reptile. In Statesboro visit the Georgia Southern University Museum & Georgia Southern Botanical Garden.

RV Sites		Water		Laundry	Y
Number	25	None		Wi-Fi	
Shaded	Y	At Site	Y	Fishing	Y
By Water	Y	Spigots		Hiking	
Paved		**Sewer**		Biking	Y
Pull Thru	Y	None		Swimming	
ADA	Y	At Site	Y	Watch Wildlife	Y
Max RV Size	40	Dump Station	Y	Pets	Y
Electric		**Amenities**		**Security**	
None		Restrooms	Y	Host(s)	Y
20 Amp	Y	Showers	Y	Rangers(s)	Y
30 Amp	Y	Reserve Sites	Y	Gate	
50 Amp	Y	Store	Y	Patrolled	Y
		Grill/Table	Y		

[3] John Tanner County Park
I-20, Exit 11
Northwest of Carrollton
N33 36.111 W85 10.005
County Rate: $30
(770) 830-2222
http://gastateparks.org/info/jtanner/

Directions

7 miles. From Exit 11 go south on Hwy 27 for 1.3 miles to Bowdon Junction Rd. Turn right, go 3 miles to Hwy 16. Go left, drive 1.6 miles, then right on Tanner Beach Rd 0.7 mile to the Park.

Points of Interest

Explore shops, restaurants & galleries of historic Carrollton. Visit Pickett's Mill, one of the best preserved Civil War battlefields in the nation. Travel roads used by Federal & Confederate troops, see earthworks constructed by these men, & walk the same ravine where hundreds died.

RV Sites		Water		Laundry	
Number	31	None		Wi-Fi	
Shaded	Y	At Site	Y	Fishing	Y
By Water	Y	Spigots		Hiking	Y
Paved		**Sewer**		Biking	Y
Pull Thru	Y	None		Swimming	Y
ADA	Y	At Site	Y	Watch Wildlife	Y
Max RV Size	40	Dump Station	Y	Pets	Y
Electric		**Amenities**		**Security**	
None		Restrooms	Y	Host(s)	Y
20 Amp	Y	Showers	Y	Rangers(s)	
30 Amp	Y	Reserve Sites	Y	Gate	
50 Amp	Y	Store		Patrolled	Y
		Grill/Table	Y		

[4] Hard Labor Creek State Park
I-20, Exit 105
Northwest of Madison
N33 39.582 W83 36.121
State Rate: $25-$29, Senior Discount
(706) 557-3001
http://gastateparks.org/info/hardlabor/

Directions

5 miles. From Exit 105 go north on Newborn for 2.5 miles (bare left at Hawkins Ave). Turn left on E. Dixie Hwy, go one block, turn right on Fairplay St. Go 2.6 miles into the Park.

Points of Interest

The Park is best known for The Creek Golf Course, used by the pros for practice before Augusta. It is one of Georgia's best golf values, with special rates for seniors. Visit historic Madison, with the largest designated historic district in Georgia. It is the City Sherman refused to burn!

RV Sites		Water		Laundry	Y
Number	46	None		Wi-Fi	Y
Shaded	Y	At Site	Y	Fishing	Y
By Water	Y	Spigots		Hiking	Y
Paved		Sewer		Biking	Y
Pull Thru	Y	None		Swimming	Y
ADA	Y	At Site		Watch Wildlife	Y
Max RV Size	45	Dump Station	Y	Pets	Y
Electric		Amenities		Security	
None		Restrooms	Y	Host(s)	Y
20 Amp	Y	Showers	Y	Rangers(s)	Y
30 Amp	Y	Reserve Sites	Y	Gate	
50 Amp	Y	Store		Patrolled	Y
		Grill/Table	Y		

[5] A.H. Stephens Historic Park
I-20, Exit 148
North of Crawfordville
N33 33.477 W82 53.815
State Rate: $24-$26, Senior Discount
(706) 456-2602
http://gastateparks.org/info/ahsteph/

Directions

4 miles. **Due to low bridge, especially if your RV is taller than 12' 10"**, from Exit 148 go 2.2 miles on Hwy 22, cross Hwy 278. Turn right onto MLK Jr. Dr. Go 1 mile (keeping left), then turn left on Alexander St. to park.

Points of Interest

Tour Liberty Hall, home of Confederate Vice President Alexander Stephens & governor of Georgia. The Park features a Confederate museum with one of the finest collections of Civil War artifacts in Georgia.

RV Sites		Water		Laundry	
Number	22	None		Wi-Fi	
Shaded	Y	At Site	Y	Fishing	Y
By Water	Y	Spigots		Hiking	Y
Paved		Sewer		Biking	Y
Pull Thru	Y	None		Swimming	
ADA	Y	At Site		Watch Wildlife	Y
Max RV Size	45	Dump Station	Y	Pets	Y
Electric		Amenities		Security	
None		Restrooms	Y	Host(s)	Y
20 Amp	Y	Showers	Y	Rangers(s)	Y
30 Amp	Y	Reserve Sites	Y	Gate	
50 Amp	Y	Store		Patrolled	Y
		Grill/Table	Y		

[6] Big Hart Campground
I-20, Exit 172
Northwest of Augusta
N33 36.881 W82 30.772
COE Rate: $24-$26
America/Beautiful Rate: $12-$13
(706) 595-8613
www.recreation.gov/

Directions

8.5 miles. From Exit 172 go north 6 miles on Hwy 78 to Russell Landing Rd. Turn right and travel east 2.5 miles to campground.

Points of Interest

Nearby Augusta is Georgia's second oldest city. Known as the South's "Garden City," it is full of history, atmosphere & Southern charm. Discover Augusta's tree-lined streets & majestic antebellum mansions. Enjoy dozens of shops, restaurants, cultural attractions & entertainment.

RV Sites		Water		Laundry	
Number	32	None		Wi-Fi	
Shaded	Y	At Site	Y	Fishing	Y
By Water	Y	Spigots		Hiking	Y
Paved		Sewer		Biking	Y
Pull Thru		None		Swimming	Y
ADA	Y	At Site		Watch Wildlife	Y
Max RV Size	45	Dump Station	Y	Pets	Y
Electric		Amenities		Security	
None		Restrooms	Y	Host(s)	Y
20 Amp	Y	Showers	Y	Rangers(s)	Y
30 Amp	Y	Reserve Sites	Y	Gate	Y
50 Amp	Y	Store		Patrolled	Y
		Grill/Table	Y		

[7] Petersburg Campground
I-20, Exit 183
Northwest of Augusta
N33 39.593 W82 15.634
COE Rate: $18-$26
America/Beautiful Rate: $9-$13
(706) 541-9464
http://www.reserveamerica.com/

Directions

13 miles. From Exit 183 go north on Hwy 221 for 11.5 miles to Petersburg Rd. Turn left, go 1 miles to the campground.

Points of Interest

Nearby Augusta is Georgia's second oldest city. Known as the South's "Garden City," it is full of history, atmosphere & Southern charm. Discover Augusta's tree-lined streets & majestic antebellum mansions. Enjoy dozens of shops, restaurants, cultural attractions & entertainment.

RV Sites		Water		Laundry	Y
Number	93	None		Wi-Fi	
Shaded	Y	At Site	Y	Fishing	Y
By Water	Y	Spigots		Hiking	Y
Paved		**Sewer**		Biking	Y
Pull Thru	Y	None		Swimming	
ADA	Y	At Site		Watch Wildlife	Y
Max RV Size	45	Dump Station	Y	Pets	Y
Electric		**Amenities**		**Security**	
None		Restrooms	Y	Host(s)	Y
20 Amp	Y	Showers	Y	Rangers(s)	Y
30 Amp	Y	Reserve Sites	Y	Gate	Y
50 Amp	Y	Store		Patrolled	Y
		Grill/Table	Y		

[8] Cloudland Canyon State Park
I-59, Exit 11
Southwest of Chattanooga, TN
N34 48.930 W85 29.376
State Rate: $25-$30, Senior Discount
(706) 657-4050
http://gastateparks.org/info/cloudland/

Directions

7 miles. From Exit 11 go southeast 2 blocks to Main St. Turn right, go 2 blocks to Hwy 136 (Lafayette St.) Turn left on Hwy 136, go 6.2 miles to Cloudland Canyon Park Rd. Turn left in to the Park.

Points of Interest

Don't miss Lookout Mountain. Visit Dalton's Prater's Mill (on the National Register of Historic Places). Its heritage runs back to the days of the Cherokee Indians. At the Tunnel Hill Heritage Center, one of the South's oldest railroad tunnels still stands.

RV Sites		Water		Laundry	
Number	72	None		Wi-Fi	
Shaded	Y	At Site	Y	Fishing	Y
By Water		Spigots		Hiking	Y
Paved		**Sewer**		Biking	Y
Pull Thru	Y	None		Swimming	
ADA	Y	At Site		Watch Wildlife	Y
Max RV Size	40	Dump Station	Y	Pets	Y
Electric		**Amenities**		**Security**	
None		Restrooms	Y	Host(s)	Y
20 Amp	Y	Showers	Y	Rangers(s)	Y
30 Amp	Y	Reserve Sites	Y	Gate	Y
50 Amp	Y	Store	Y	Patrolled	Y
		Grill/Table	Y		

[9] Reed Bingham Historic Park
I-75, Exit 39
West of Adel/Sparks
N31 09.683 W83 32.380
State Rate: $25-$35, Senior Discount
(229) 896-3551
http://gastateparks.org/info/reedbing/

Directions

6 miles. From Exit 39 go 5.4 miles west on Hwy 37 to Reed Bingham Rd. Turn right, go 0.9 miles in to the Park.

Points of Interest

RVers can see abundant wildlife, rare and endangered species. Volunteers can assist with Gopher Tortoise Management projects and may witness hatching of tortoises. In winter, thousands of "buzzards," large black vultures and turkey vultures, roost in the trees and soar overhead.

RV Sites		Water		Laundry	Y
Number	46	None		Wi-Fi	
Shaded	Y	At Site	Y	Fishing	Y
By Water	Y	Spigots		Hiking	Y
Paved		**Sewer**		Biking	Y
Pull Thru	Y	None		Swimming	Y
ADA	Y	At Site	Y	Watch Wildlife	Y
Max RV Size	45	Dump Station	Y	Pets	Y
Electric		**Amenities**		**Security**	
None		Restrooms	Y	Host(s)	Y
20 Amp	Y	Showers	Y	Rangers(s)	Y
30 Amp	Y	Reserve Sites	Y	Gate	
50 Amp	Y	Store		Patrolled	Y
		Grill/Table	Y		

[10] Georgia Veterans State Park
I-75, Exit 101
West of Cordele
N31 58.082 W83 54.737
State Rate: $25-$28, Senior Discount
(229) 276-2371
http://gastateparks.org/info/georgiavet/

Directions

10 miles. From Exit 101 go 10 miles west on Hwy 30/280 through Cordele to Cannon Rd. Turn left into the Park.

Points of Interest

The park museum has Revolutionary through Gulf War items. The golf course and lake make this one of Georgia's most popular parks. The SAM Shortline Excursion Train covers Cordele-Plains via the park. Riders see a telephone museum and President Jimmy Carter's boyhood farm.

RV Sites		Water		Laundry	
Number	77	None		Wi-Fi	
Shaded	Y	At Site	Y	Fishing	Y
By Water	Y	Spigots		Hiking	Y
Paved		Sewer		Biking	Y
Pull Thru	Y	None		Swimming	Y
ADA	Y	At Site	Y	Watch Wildlife	Y
Max RV Size	45	Dump Station	Y	Pets	Y
Electric		Amenities		Security	
None		Restrooms	Y	Host(s)	Y
20 Amp	Y	Showers	Y	Rangers(s)	Y
30 Amp	Y	Reserve Sites	Y	Gate	
50 Amp	Y	Store	Y	Patrolled	Y
		Grill/Table	Y		

[11] Indian Springs State Park
I-75, Exits 188 or 205
North of Forsyth
N33 14.719 W83 55.229
State Rate: $25-$29, Senior Discount
(770) 504-2277
http://gastateparks.org/info/indspr/

Directions

15 miles. **Northbound**, take Exit 188, proceed north on Hwy 42, 15 mi. to Spring Rd & the Park. **Southbound**, take Exit 205, go east 8.6 mi. on Hwy 16 to Jackson; then south 5.2 miles on Hwy 23/42 to Spring Rd & the Park.

Points of Interest

In Macon, see the Georgia Music Hall of Fame - country, big band & southern rock; or Hay House - William Butler Johnston was Confederate treasurer, but the mansion he built is the real treasure; or Tubman African American Museum.

RV Sites		Water		Laundry	
Number	60	None		Wi-Fi	
Shaded	Y	At Site	Y	Fishing	Y
By Water	Y	Spigots		Hiking	Y
Paved		Sewer		Biking	Y
Pull Thru	few	None		Swimming	Y
ADA	Y	At Site	Y	Watch Wildlife	Y
Max RV Size	45	Dump Station	Y	Pets	Y
Electric		Amenities		Security	
None		Restrooms	Y	Host(s)	Y
20 Amp	Y	Showers	Y	Rangers(s)	Y
30 Amp	Y	Reserve Sites	Y	Gate	
50 Amp	Y	Store		Patrolled	Y
		Grill/Table	Y		

[12] McKinney Campground
I-75, Exit 278
North of Atlanta
N34 06.895 W84 41.552
COE Rate: $26-$30
America/Beautiful Rate: $13-$15
(678) 721-6700
http://www.recreation.gov

Directions

4 miles. From Exit 278 go north 2.7 miles on Glade Rd. to Kings Camp Rd. Turn left and go west 0.7 mile to McKinney Campground Rd. Turn south (left) 0.5 mile to the campground.

Points of Interest

In Cartersville experience the Cowboy way at the Booth Western Art Museum. Very new is the Smithsonian Affiliate Tellus: Northwest Georgia Science Museum. Or just shop, enjoy and have lunch in historic downtown Cartersville.

RV Sites		Water		Laundry	Y
Number	150	None		Wi-Fi	
Shaded	Y	At Site	Y	Fishing	Y
By Water	Y	Spigots		Hiking	Y
Paved		Sewer		Biking	Y
Pull Thru	Y	None		Swimming	Y
ADA	Y	At Site		Watch Wildlife	Y
Max RV Size	45	Dump Station	Y	Pets	Y
Electric		Amenities		Security	
None		Restrooms	Y	Host(s)	Y
20 Amp	Y	Showers	Y	Rangers(s)	Y
30 Amp	Y	Reserve Sites	Y	Gate	Y
50 Amp	Y	Store		Patrolled	Y
		Grill/Table	Y		

[13] R. Shaefer Heard Campground
I-85, Exit 2
Southwest of LaGrange
N32 55.304 W85 09.376
COE Rate: $22
America/Beautiful Rate: $11
(706) 645-2404
www.recreation.gov/

Directions

5 miles. From Exit 2 go west 1.3 miles on Hwy 18 (10th Av.) to Ave. E (Westpoint Rd). Turn right & travel 3.3 miles on Hwy 29 to the campground road (just past Reed Rd) on the left.

Points of Interest

Visit LaGrange, a classic Georgia town (the 'City Of Elms and Roses'). Classic antebellum homes proudly attest to the rich history of LaGrange. In Pine Mountain experience the thrill of a steeplechase. The city is also the gateway to Callaway Gardens.

RV Sites		Water		Laundry	Y
Number	117	None		Wi-Fi	
Shaded	Y	At Site	Y	Fishing	Y
By Water	Y	Spigots		Hiking	Y
Paved		Sewer		Biking	Y
Pull Thru	Y	None		Swimming	Y
ADA	Y	At Site		Watch Wildlife	Y
Max RV Size	45	Dump Station	Y	Pets	Y
Electric		Amenities		Security	
None		Restrooms	Y	Host(s)	Y
20 Amp	Y	Showers	Y	Rangers(s)	Y
30 Amp	Y	Reserve Sites	Y	Gate	Y
50 Amp	Y	Store		Patrolled	Y
		Grill/Table	Y		

[14] Fort Yargo State Park
I-85, Exit 126
East of Lawrenceville
N33 59.098 W83 44.015
State Rate: $28-$30, Senior Discount
(770) 867-3489
http://gastateparks.org/info/ftyargo/

Directions

10.5 miles. From Exit 126 go 9.6 miles southeast on Hwy 211 to Winder. At Hwy 81 (Broad St.) turn right for 1 mile to the park on the left.

Points of Interest

You are close to Athens, Atlanta, and Stone Mountain. Stone Mountain is well-known for the enormous bas-relief on its north face, the largest in the world. Three figures of the Confederate States of America are carved there: Stonewall Jackson, Robert E. Lee, and Jefferson Davis.

RV Sites		Water		Laundry	Y
Number	52	None		Wi-Fi	
Shaded	Y	At Site	Y	Fishing	Y
By Water	Y	Spigots		Hiking	Y
Paved		Sewer		Biking	Y
Pull Thru	Y	None		Swimming	Y
ADA	Y	At Site		Watch Wildlife	Y
Max RV Size	45	Dump Station	Y	Pets	
Electric		Amenities		Security	
None		Restrooms	Y	Host(s)	Y
20 Amp	Y	Showers	Y	Rangers(s)	Y
30 Amp	Y	Reserve Sites	Y	Gate	
50 Amp	Y	Store	Y	Patrolled	Y
		Grill/Table	Y		

[15] Tugaloo State Park
I-85, Exit 173
At South Carolina State Line
N34 30.115 W83 04.938
State Rate: $25-$32, Senior Discount
(706) 356-4362
http://gastateparks.org/info/tugaloo/
Directions

7.5 miles. From Exit 173 turn south on Hwy 17 toward Lavonia, go 1.1 miles to Hwy 59. Turn left, follow Hwy 59 1.1 miles to Hwy 328. Bare left on Hwy 328, go 4 miles to Tugaloo Park Rd. Turn right, drive 1.3 miles in to the Park.

Points of Interest

Spectacular views of Lake Hartwell in every direction. Visit the Ty Cobb Museum in Royston that honors the Baseball Hall of Fame player. The museum contains art, memorabilia, film, video, books and historical archives of Cobb.

RV Sites		Water		Laundry	Y
Number	113	None		Wi-Fi	
Shaded	Y	At Site	Y	Fishing	Y
By Water	Y	Spigots		Hiking	Y
Paved		Sewer		Biking	Y
Pull Thru	Y	None		Swimming	Y
ADA	Y	At Site		Watch Wildlife	Y
Max RV Size	35	Dump Station	Y	Pets	Y
Electric		Amenities		Security	
None		Restrooms	Y	Host(s)	Y
20 Amp	Y	Showers	Y	Rangers(s)	Y
30 Amp	Y	Reserve Sites	Y	Gate	
50 Amp		Store	Y	Patrolled	Y
		Grill/Table	Y		

[16] Crooked River State Park
I-95, Exit 3
East of Kingsland
N30 50.438 W81 33.711
State Rate: $25-$28, Senior Discount
(912) 882-5256
http://www.gastateparks.org/info/crookriv/

Directions

12 miles. From Exit 3 go east 5.6 miles on Hwy 40 to Spur 40 (Charlie Smith Sr. Hwy). Turn north and go 6.3 miles to the park.

Points of Interest

Birding enthusiasts will enjoy the large bird blind that provides close views. Visitors may venture to the nearby ruins of the tabby (a mixture of limestone, sand, and sea shells) "McIntosh Sugar Works" mill. Close by is the ferry and visitor center for Cumberland Island National Seashore.

RV Sites		Water		Laundry	Y
Number	62	None		Wi-Fi	Y
Shaded	Y	At Site	Y	Fishing	Y
By Water	Y	Spigots		Hiking	Y
Paved		**Sewer**		Biking	Y
Pull Thru	Y	None		Swimming	
ADA	Y	At Site		Watch Wildlife	Y
Max RV Size	45	Dump Station	Y	Pets	Y
Electric		**Amenities**		**Security**	
None		Restrooms	Y	Host(s)	Y
20 Amp	Y	Showers	Y	Rangers(s)	Y
30 Amp	Y	Reserve Sites	Y	Gate	
50 Amp		Store	Y	Patrolled	Y
		Grill/Table	Y		

[17] Fort McAllister Historic Park
I-95, Exit 90
South of Savannah
N31 53.143 W81 12.695
State Rate: $27-$30, Senior Discount
(912) 727-2339
http://gastateparks.org/info/ftmcallister/

Directions

10 miles. From Exit 90 go 6.4 miles southeast on Hwy 144 to Spur 144 (Fort McAllister Rd). Turn left, go 3.2 miles to the Park.

Points of Interest

The park is the home of the best preserved earthwork fortification of the Confederacy. The park's Civil War museum contains exhibits and artifacts. Enjoy Savannah, one of the most beautiful cities in the world. The Historic District of Savannah is a must visit location.

RV Sites		Water		Laundry	Y
Number	65	None		Wi-Fi	
Shaded	Y	At Site	Y	Fishing	Y
By Water	Y	Spigots		Hiking	Y
Paved		**Sewer**		Biking	Y
Pull Thru	Y	None		Swimming	
ADA	Y	At Site		Watch Wildlife	Y
Max RV Size	45	Dump Station	Y	Pets	Y
Electric		**Amenities**		**Security**	
None		Restrooms	Y	Host(s)	Y
20 Amp	Y	Showers	Y	Rangers(s)	Y
30 Amp	Y	Reserve Sites	Y	Gate	
50 Amp		Store	Y	Patrolled	Y
		Grill/Table	Y		

[18] F.D. Roosevelt State Park
I-185, Exit 34
East of Pine Mountain
N32 50.334 W84 48.893
State Rate: $25-$28, Senior Discount
(706) 663-4858
http://gastateparks.org/info/fdr/

Directions

11 miles. From Exit 34 go east 6.5 miles on Hwy 18. Southwest of Pine Mountain go straight on Hwy 354 for 3.8 miles to Hwy 190. Turn right 0.3 miles to the Park entrance.

Points of Interest

The Park is close to Callaway Gardens & the town of Pine Mountain. In addition, visit the FDR Little White House or take in one of the local festivals. Spend a day in downtown Pine Mountain's & Chipley Village's shops, with boutiques & antiques, from fine art to handcrafted birdhouses.

RV Sites		Water		Laundry	Y
Number	140	None		Wi-Fi	
Shaded	Y	At Site	Y	Fishing	Y
By Water	Y	Spigots		Hiking	Y
Paved		**Sewer**		Biking	Y
Pull Thru	Y	None		Swimming	Y
ADA	Y	At Site		Watch Wildlife	Y
Max RV Size	40	Dump Station	Y	Pets	Y
Electric		**Amenities**		**Security**	
None		Restrooms	Y	Host(s)	Y
20 Amp	Y	Showers	Y	Rangers(s)	Y
30 Amp	Y	Reserve Sites	Y	Gate	
50 Amp		Store	Y	Patrolled	Y
		Grill/Table	Y		

[19] Magnolia Springs State Park
Hwy 25
North of Millen
N32 52.412 W81 57.677
State Rate: $25-$28, Senior Discount
(478) 982-1660
http://gastateparks.org/MagnoliaSprings

Directions

5 miles. From Millen Center (Hwys 25 & 17) go 5 miles north on Hwy 25 to the Park.

Points of Interest

Magnolia Springs State Park, known for its crystal clear springs, has a boardwalk that spans the cool spring water, allowing visitors to look for alligators, turtles and other wildlife near the springs. Historic Savannah & Augusta are short drives. During the Civil War, this site was called Camp Lawton and served as "the world's largest prison."

RV Sites		Water		Laundry	Y
Number	26	None		Wi-Fi	
Shaded	Y	At Site	Y	Fishing	Y
By Water	Y	Spigots		Hiking	Y
Paved		**Sewer**		Biking	
Pull Thru	Y	None		Swimming	Y
ADA	Y	At Site		Watch Wildlife	Y
Max RV Size	40	Dump Station	Y	Pets	Y
Electric		**Amenities**		**Security**	
None		Restrooms	Y	Host(s)	Y
20 Amp	Y	Showers	Y	Rangers(s)	Y
30 Amp	Y	Reserve Sites	Y	Gate	
50 Amp	Y	Store		Patrolled	Y
		Grill/Table	Y		

[20] Elijah Clark State Park
Hwy 378
Northeast of Lincolnton
N33 50.988 W82 23.861
State Rate: $25-$28, Senior Discount
(706) 359-3458
http://gastateparks.org/ElijahClark

Directions

23 miles. From the junction of 17/78/378 on the east side of Washington go 22.5 miles east, through Lincolnton, on Hwy 378 to the Park.

Points of Interest

The park is located on the shore of Clarks Hill Lake, one of the largest lakes in the Southeast. With its boat ramps & accessible fishing pier it is popular with anglers & boaters. A sandy swimming beach welcomes visitors to cool off. The Park is named for frontiersman and Georgia war hero Elijah Clark.

RV Sites		Water		Laundry	
Number	165	None		Wi-Fi	
Shaded	Y	At Site	Y	Fishing	Y
By Water	Y	Spigots		Hiking	Y
Paved		**Sewer**		Biking	Y
Pull Thru	Y	None		Swimming	Y
ADA	Y	At Site		Watch Wildlife	Y
Max RV Size	40	Dump Station	Y	Pets	Y
Electric		**Amenities**		**Security**	
None		Restrooms	Y	Host(s)	Y
20 Amp	Y	Showers	Y	Rangers(s)	Y
30 Amp	Y	Reserve Sites	Y	Gate	
50 Amp	Y	Store	Y	Patrolled	Y
		Grill/Table	Y		

[21] Hart State Outdoor Recreation Area
Hwy 29
North of Hartwell
N34 22.421 W82 54.399
State Rate: $19-$26, Senior Discount
(706) 376-8756
http://gastateparks.org/Hart

Directions

15 miles. From the junction of Hwy 17/29 in Royston go east, through Hartwell on Hwy 29, for 13 miles. Turn left on Ridge Road and proceed 2 miles to the park.

Points of Interest

This self-registration campground is open on a first-come, first-served basis from March 15 until September 15. Swimming, boating, water skiing and fishing on Lake Hartwell are prime reasons to visit Hart. Most sites are located on the scenic lake shore.

RV Sites		Water		Laundry	Y
Number	62	None		Wi-Fi	Y
Shaded	Y	At Site	Y	Fishing	Y
By Water	Y	Spigots		Hiking	Y
Paved		**Sewer**		Biking	Y
Pull Thru	Y	None		Swimming	Y
ADA	Y	At Site		Watch Wildlife	
Max RV Size	40	Dump Station	Y	Pets	Y
Electric		**Amenities**		**Security**	
None		Restrooms	Y	Host(s)	Y
20 Amp	Y	Showers	Y	Rangers(s)	Y
30 Amp	Y	Reserve Sites		Gate	
50 Amp		Store	Y	Patrolled	Y
		Grill/Table	Y		

About Idaho's Public Campgrounds

There are 30 Idaho State Parks. Detailed information is available at -

http://www.idaho.gov/recreation/parks_camping.html

You can register online up to 9 months in advance at -

http://idahostateparks.reserveamerica.com/

Discounts may be available on reservations and/or use fees for currently registered Idaho RV sticker holders, disabled Idaho veterans, low income Idahoans, and senior citizens. Discounts are only available on reservations made through the call center (1-888-922-6743) or may be claimed when registering at the park. Those 62 or older will receive 50% off camping fees within select Idaho State Parks. The discount is valid mid-week on stays Monday – Thursday (excluding holidays).

Standard Campsite: $12 - $18. Any campsite, tent or RV.

Serviced Campsite/ W or E: $18 - $20. Any campsite, tent or RV with water or electricity.

Serviced Campsite /W, E: $22 - $24. Any campsite, tent pad or RV with water and electricity.

Serviced Campsite /W, E, SWR: $24 - $26. Any campsite, tent pad or RV, with water, electricity, and sewer.

Pets are welcome in most parks, but you must keep them on a leash no longer than six feet, or confined to your RV.

[1] Scout Mountain Campground	**[7] Craters of the Moon National Monument**
[2] Stoddard Creek Campground	**[8] Joe T. Fallini Recreation Site**
[3] Three Island Crossing State Park	**[9] Hells Gate State Park**
[4] Lake Walcott State Park	**[10] Heyburn State Park**
[5] Massacre Rocks State Park	**[11] Farragut State Park**
[6] Beauty Creek Campground	**[12] Priest Lake State Park**

NOTES:

Idaho

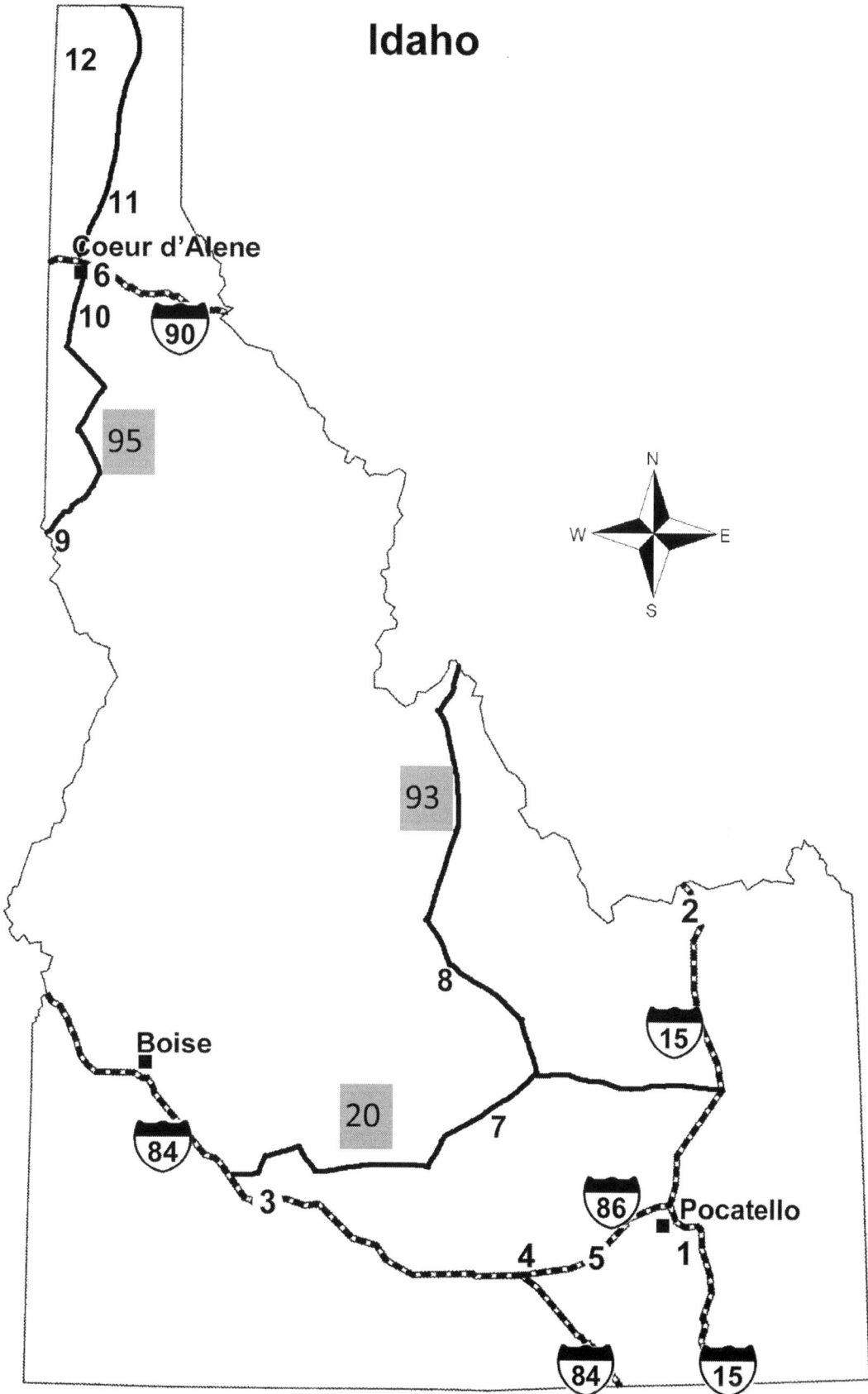

[1] Scout Mountain Campground
I-15, Exit 63
South of Pocatello
N42 41.503 W112 21.541
Caribou NF Rate: $10-$20
America/Beautiful Rate: $5-$10
(208) 236-7500
http://www.recreation.gov/

Directions

14 miles. From Exit 63 go south 0.3 mi. to Portneuf Rd. Go east 2 miles to Bannock Hwy then south 5 miles to E. Fork of Mink Creek Rd. Turn left, go 6 miles up to campground.

Points of Interest

The road in is paved and there are switch-backs but RVs should be OK. In Pocatello, you can find rodeos, a casino, attend an Indian Pow Wow, seek out historic sites or see living history with a Fur Traders Encampment.

RV Sites		Water			Laundry	
Number	13	None			Wi-Fi	
Shaded	Y	At Site			Fishing	
By Water		Spigots	Y		Hiking	Y
Paved	some	**Sewer**			Biking	Y
Pull Thru	Y	None	Y		Swimming	
ADA	Y	At Site			Watch Wildlife	Y
Max RV Size	45	Dump Station			Pets	Y
Electric		**Amenities**			**Security**	
None	Y	Restrooms	Y		Host(s)	
20 Amp		Showers			Rangers(s)	Y
30 Amp		Reserve Sites	Y		Gate	
50 Amp		Store			Patrolled	
		Grill/Table	Y			

[2] Stoddard Creek Campground
I-15, Exit 184
North of Dubois
N44 25.064 W112 12.809
Targhee NF Rate: $10
America/Beautiful Rate: $5
(208) 374-5422
http://www.recreation.gov/

Directions

1 mile. From Exit 184 go west on Stoddard Creek Rd (FR 002) 1 mile to the Stoddard Creek Camp Ground Rd. (FR 003).

Points of Interest

Drive to Craters of the Moon National Monument & St. Anthony Sand Dunes. This 10,600 acre area of clear, shifting, white quartz sand is known for its unique beauty, recreation opportunities, and is home to one of the largest herds of wintering elk in the United States.

RV Sites		Water			Laundry	
Number	21	None			Wi-Fi	
Shaded	Y	At Site			Fishing	Y
By Water		Spigots	Y		Hiking	Y
Paved		**Sewer**			Biking	Y
Pull Thru	Y	None	Y		Swimming	
ADA	Y	At Site			Watch Wildlife	Y
Max RV Size	45	Dump Station			Pets	Y
Electric		**Amenities**			**Security**	
None	Y	Restrooms	Y		Host(s)	Y
20 Amp		Showers			Rangers(s)	Y
30 Amp		Reserve Sites			Gate	
50 Amp		Store			Patrolled	
		Grill/Table	Y			

[3] Three Island Crossing State Park
I-84, Exit 121
South of Glenns Ferry
N42 56.718 W115 19.077
State Rate: $22-$38, Senior Discount
(208) 366-2394
http://parksandrecreation.idaho.gov/parks/three-island-crossing

Directions

2 miles. From Exit 121, turn south, follow 1st Ave for 0.7 miles. Go left on Commercial Ave for 0.5 miles then right on Madison Ave. Drive 1 mile to the park.

Points of Interest

The Park is home to The Oregon Trail History & Education Center. Close by is the Carmela Winery & Golf Course. South of town is Hagerman Fossil Beds National Monument, with the largest concentration of Hagerman Horse fossils in North America.

RV Sites		Water			Laundry	
Number	82	None			Wi-Fi	Y
Shaded	Y	At Site	Y		Fishing	Y
By Water	Y	Spigots			Hiking	Y
Paved	Y	**Sewer**			Biking	Y
Pull Thru	Y	None			Swimming	
ADA	Y	At Site			Watch Wildlife	Y
Max RV Size	45	Dump Station	Y		Pets	Y
Electric		**Amenities**			**Security**	
None		Restrooms	Y		Host(s)	Y
20 Amp	Y	Showers	Y		Rangers(s)	Y
30 Amp	Y	Reserve Sites	Y		Gate	
50 Amp		Store	Y		Patrolled	Y
		Grill/Table	Y			

[4] Lake Walcott State Park
I-84, Exit 211
Northeast of Rupert
N42 40.515 W113 29.011
State Rate: $12-$22, Senior Discount
(208) 436-1258
http://parksandrecreation.idaho.gov/parks/
lake-walcott

Directions

16 miles. From Exit 211 go northeast on Hwy 24 through Rupert, 10.4 miles in all to 400 North Rd (Minidoka Dam Rd.), just past Acequia. Turn right for 5.3 miles to the campground.

Points of Interest

Drive to Craters of the Moon National Monument. Try the Shoshone Ice Caves. Guides explain the geologic, volcanic, & historical background in these large lava ice caves. A museum contains Indian artifacts, gems, & minerals of interest.

RV Sites		Water		Laundry	
Number	22	None		Wi-Fi	Y
Shaded	Y	At Site	Y	Fishing	Y
By Water	Y	Spigots		Hiking	Y
Paved		Sewer		Biking	Y
Pull Thru	Y	None		Swimming	Y
ADA	Y	At Site		Watch Wildlife	Y
Max RV Size	45	Dump Station	Y	Pets	Y
Electric		Amenities		Security	
None		Restrooms	Y	Host(s)	Y
20 Amp	Y	Showers	Y	Rangers(s)	Y
30 Amp	Y	Reserve Sites	Y	Gate	
50 Amp		Store		Patrolled	Y
		Grill/Table	Y		

[5] Massacre Rocks State Park
I-86, Exit 28
Southwest of American Falls
N42 40.692 W112 59.135
State Rate: $14-$38, Senior Discount
(208) 548-2672
http://parksandrecreation.idaho.gov/parks/
massacre-rocks

Directions

1 mile from I-86. From Exit 28, turn to the northwest side of the Interstate. Take the frontage road right for 1 mile to campground.

Points of Interest

The Park, along The Oregon Trail, has excellent vistas. Visit Register Rock, two miles from the park, that holds the signatures of Oregon Trail emigrants who stopped for an evening of rest before continuing on their journeys. Discover the "Gate of Death" & "Devil's Gate."

RV Sites		Water		Laundry	
Number	42	None		Wi-Fi	Y
Shaded	Y	At Site	Y	Fishing	Y
By Water	Y	Spigots		Hiking	Y
Paved		Sewer		Biking	Y
Pull Thru	Y	None		Swimming	
ADA	Y	At Site		Watch Wildlife	Y
Max RV Size	45	Dump Station	Y	Pets	Y
Electric		Amenities		Security	
None		Restrooms	Y	Host(s)	Y
20 Amp	Y	Showers	Y	Rangers(s)	Y
30 Amp	Y	Reserve Sites	Y	Gate	
50 Amp		Store		Patrolled	Y
		Grill/Table	Y		

[6] Beauty Creek Campground
I-90, Exit 22
East of Coeur d'Alene
N47 36.408 W116 40.092
Coeur d'Alene NF Rate: $18
America/Beautiful Rate: $9
(208) 765-7287
http://www.recreation.gov/

Directions

3 miles. From Exit 22 go south on Hwy 97 for 2.4 mile to Beauty Creek Rd. Turn left, go 0.7 miles to the campground.

Points of Interest

The campground is 0.5 mile from Lake Coeur d'Alene. The lake is very large with much to do - rent paddle boats, take a ferry or sea plane ride, go parasailing, or just swim and relax. Go horseback riding or try a cattle drive outing; or kayaking, perhaps even white water rafting!

RV Sites		Water		Laundry	
Number	20	None		Wi-Fi	
Shaded	Y	At Site		Fishing	Y
By Water	Y	Spigots	Y	Hiking	Y
Paved	Y	Sewer		Biking	Y
Pull Thru		None	Y	Swimming	Y
ADA	Y	At Site		Watch Wildlife	Y
Max RV Size	40	Dump Station		Pets	Y
Electric		Amenities		Security	
None	Y	Restrooms	Y	Host(s)	Y
20 Amp		Showers		Rangers(s)	Y
30 Amp		Reserve Sites	Y	Gate	
50 Amp		Store		Patrolled	Y
		Grill/Table	Y		

[7] Craters of the Moon National Monument
Hwy 20
Northeast of Carey
N43 27.717 W113 33.796
National Monument Rate: $10
America/Beautiful Rate: $5
(208) 527-1335
http://www.recreation.gov/

Directions

25 miles northeast on Hwy 20. Go 0.25 miles from the Visitor Center on Craters Loop Drive.

Points of Interest

Craters of the Moon is a vast ocean of lava flows with scattered islands of cinder cones & sagebrush. Your only chance to camp on the moon. A unique environment, camping in the lava flows. Rangers do interesting nightly programs in the campground amphitheater. You are welcome to fill jugs but please fill RV tanks elsewhere.

RV Sites		Water		Laundry	
Number	51	None		Wi-Fi	
Shaded		At Site		Fishing	Y
By Water		Spigots	Y	Hiking	Y
Paved		**Sewer**		Biking	Y
Pull Thru	Y	None	Y	Swimming	Y
ADA	Y	At Site		Watch Wildlife	
Max RV Size	45	Dump Station		Pets	Y
Electric		**Amenities**		**Security**	
None	Y	Restrooms	Y	Host(s)	Y
20 Amp		Showers		Rangers(s)	Y
30 Amp		Reserve Sites		Gate	
50 Amp		Store	Y	Patrolled	Y
		Grill/Table	Y		

[8] Joe T. Fallini Recreation Site
Hwy 93
North of Mackay
N43 57.399 W113 40.154
BLM Rate: $14
America/Beautiful Rate: $7
(208) 879-6200
http://www.blm.gov/id/st/en/visit_and_play/places_to_see/challis_field_office/Joe_T_Fallini_Recreation_Site.html

Directions

4 miles. Go northwest out of Mackay on Hwy 93 to the campground on the southern tip of Mackay Reservoir.

Points of Interest

The Joe T. Fallini scenic area has a gorgeous view of the Lost River Range and offers reservoir recreational opportunities.

RV Sites		Water		Laundry	
Number	18	None		Wi-Fi	
Shaded		At Site	Y	Fishing	Y
By Water	Y	Spigots	Y	Hiking	Y
Paved	Y	**Sewer**		Biking	Y
Pull Thru		None		Swimming	
ADA	Y	At Site		Watch Wildlife	
Max RV Size	45	Dump Station	Y	Pets	Y
Electric		**Amenities**		**Security**	
None		Restrooms	Y	Host(s)	Y
20 Amp	Y	Showers		Rangers(s)	Y
30 Amp	Y	Reserve Sites		Gate	
50 Amp	Y	Store		Patrolled	Y
		Grill/Table	Y		

[9] Hells Gate State Park
Hwys 12/95
South of Lewiston
N46 22.441 W117 02.913
State Rate: $14-$22, Senior Discount
(208) 799-5015
http://parksandrecreation.idaho.gov/parks/hells-gate

Directions

6 miles. From the junction of Hwys 12 & 95 take Hwy 12 west 2.8 miles to Snake River Ave. Go south 3.3 miles to Hells Gate Park Rd.

Points of Interest

Drive 8 miles up Old Spiral Highway for a panoramic view from the top of the Lewiston Hill. Go ghost hunting on a walking tour where "ghosts" have been encountered in historic downtown Lewiston. Relax by the fountain in Brackenbury Square while shopping. Take a jet boat trip into Hells Canyon.

RV Sites		Water		Laundry	
Number	80	None		Wi-Fi	
Shaded	Y	At Site	Y	Fishing	Y
By Water	Y	Spigots		Hiking	Y
Paved		**Sewer**		Biking	Y
Pull Thru	Y	None		Swimming	Y
ADA	Y	At Site	Y	Watch Wildlife	Y
Max RV Size	45	Dump Station	Y	Pets	Y
Electric		**Amenities**		**Security**	
None		Restrooms	Y	Host(s)	Y
20 Amp	Y	Showers	Y	Rangers(s)	Y
30 Amp	Y	Reserve Sites	Y	Gate	
50 Amp	Y	Store	Y	Patrolled	Y
		Grill/Table	Y		

[10] Heyburn State Park
Hwy 95
East of Plummer
N47 21.12 W116 46.19
State Rate: $12-$24, Senior Discount
(208) 686-1308
http://parksandrecreation.idaho.gov/parks/
heyburn

Directions

6 miles. From Plummer go 6 miles east on Hwy 5. Take a left onto Chatcolet Rd. The Visitor's Center is visible as soon as you turn onto Chatcolet Road.

Points of Interest

Heyburn is the oldest park in the Pacific Northwest. Towering ponderosa pines give way to flower-filled meadows & placid waters. There are 2 RV campgrounds. Hawleys Landing has reservations. Benewah is first-come, first-served.

RV Sites		Water		Laundry	
Number	57	None		Wi-Fi	Y
Shaded	Y	At Site	Y	Fishing	Y
By Water	Y	Spigots		Hiking	Y
Paved	Y	Sewer		Biking	Y
Pull Thru	Y	None		Swimming	Y
ADA	Y	At Site	Y	Watch Wildlife	Y
Max RV Size	45	Dump Station	Y	Pets	Y
Electric		Amenities		Security	
None		Restrooms	Y	Host(s)	Y
20 Amp	Y	Showers	Y	Rangers(s)	Y
30 Amp	Y	Reserve Sites	Y	Gate	
50 Amp	Y	Store	Y	Patrolled	Y
		Grill/Table	Y		

[11] Farragut State Park
Hwy 95
East of Athol
N47 57.167 W116 36.132
State Rate: $12-$26, Senior Discount
(208) 683-2425
http://www.visitidaho.org/attraction/parks/
farragut-state-park/

Directions

4.5 miles. From Hwy 95, just east of Athol, go 4.5 miles on Hwy 54 to the Park.

Points of Interest

Athol, on the shores of Lake Pend Oreille, was once Idaho's largest city & the world's second largest naval training station. The U. S, Navy conducts research with large-scale submarine models in the deepwater lake. Today, the 4,000-acre park provides a variety of recreation opportunities. Silverwood Theme Park is 8 miles away.

RV Sites		Water		Laundry	
Number	222	None		Wi-Fi	
Shaded	Y	At Site	Y	Fishing	Y
By Water	Y	Spigots		Hiking	Y
Paved	Y	Sewer		Biking	Y
Pull Thru	Y	None		Swimming	Y
ADA	Y	At Site	Y	Watch Wildlife	Y
Max RV Size	40	Dump Station	Y	Pets	Y
Electric		Amenities		Security	
None		Restrooms	Y	Host(s)	Y
20 Amp	Y	Showers	Y	Rangers(s)	Y
30 Amp	Y	Reserve Sites	Y	Gate	
50 Amp	Y	Store	Y	Patrolled	Y
		Grill/Table	Y		

[12] Priest Lake State Park
Hwy 2/95
North of Priest River
N48 36.340 W116 49.727 (Indian Creek)
State Rate: $12-$26, Senior Discount
(208) 443-2200
http://www.visitidaho.org/attraction/parks/
priest-lake-state-park/

Directions

61 miles. From Sandpoint go 22 miles on Hwy 2 to Priest River. From Priest River travel north on Hwy 57 approximately 22 miles, go east on Dickensheet Rd to Dickensheet Unit. Continue north on Cavanaugh Bay Rd approximately 17 miles to Indian Creek Unit. Continue approximately 9 miles north to Lionhead Unit.

Points of Interest

The Park is surrounded by the natural beauty of Northern Idaho and mile high mountains.

RV Sites		Water		Laundry	
Number	151	None		Wi-Fi	
Shaded	Y	At Site	Y	Fishing	Y
By Water	Y	Spigots		Hiking	Y
Paved		Sewer		Biking	Y
Pull Thru	Y	None		Swimming	Y
ADA	Y	At Site	Y	Watch Wildlife	Y
Max RV Size	45	Dump Station	Y	Pets	Y
Electric		Amenities		Security	
None		Restrooms	Y	Host(s)	Y
20 Amp	Y	Showers	Y	Rangers(s)	Y
30 Amp	Y	Reserve Sites	Y	Gate	
50 Amp	Y	Store	Y	Patrolled	Y
		Grill/Table	Y		

About Illinois's Public Campgrounds

State and COE Parks dominate the Illinois countryside. There are 81 State Parks with RV camp sites. The Army Corps of Engineers also has a number of campgrounds that RVers will find appealing.

The Illinois Department of Natural Resources (IDNR) does not charge an entrance fee to any of their campgrounds. The fee schedule listed below is for all sites with RV category camping. Generally, throughout the state, camping is available year round weather permitting. Camp roads are usually paved, sites typically are gravel. You can get more DNR camping information at -

http://dnr.state.il.us/lands/landmgt/programs/camping/

IDNR camping and shelter reservations are no longer taken through the mail or over the phone. Campground reservations are made through Reserve America -

http://www.reserveamerica.com/

The fee schedule is:

Class AA: $25-$35 (Showers, electricity, sewer, and vehicular access).

Class A: $20-$30 (Showers, electricity, and vehicular access).

Class B/E: $18-$20 (Electricity and vehicular access).

Class B/S: $10-$12 (Showers and vehicular access).

Class C: $8 (Vehicular access without showers access).

For Memorial Day, July 4th, and Labor Day there is a $10/day premium. All Discounts apply only to Illinois residents. The reservation fee surcharge is $5.

Note - with the large number of Interstate Roads in close proximity in Illinois, a number of the parks can easily be reached from more than one Interstate highway.

[1] Ferne Clyffe State Park	[11] Ramsey Lake State Park
[2] Starved Rock State Park	[12] Fox Ridge State Park
[3] Shabbona Lake State Park	[13] Siloam Springs State Park
[4] Rock Cut State Park	[14] Clinton Lake State Recreation Area
[5] Sangchris Lake State Park	[15] Moraine View State Park
[6] Giant City State Park	[16] Kickapoo State Recreation Area
[7] Gun Creek Campground	[17] Fisherman's Corner
[8] Dam West Recreation Area	[18] Johnson-Sauk Trail State Recreation Area
[9] Lithia Springs Camp	
[10] Kankakee River State Park	[19] Morrison-Rockwood State Park

Illinois

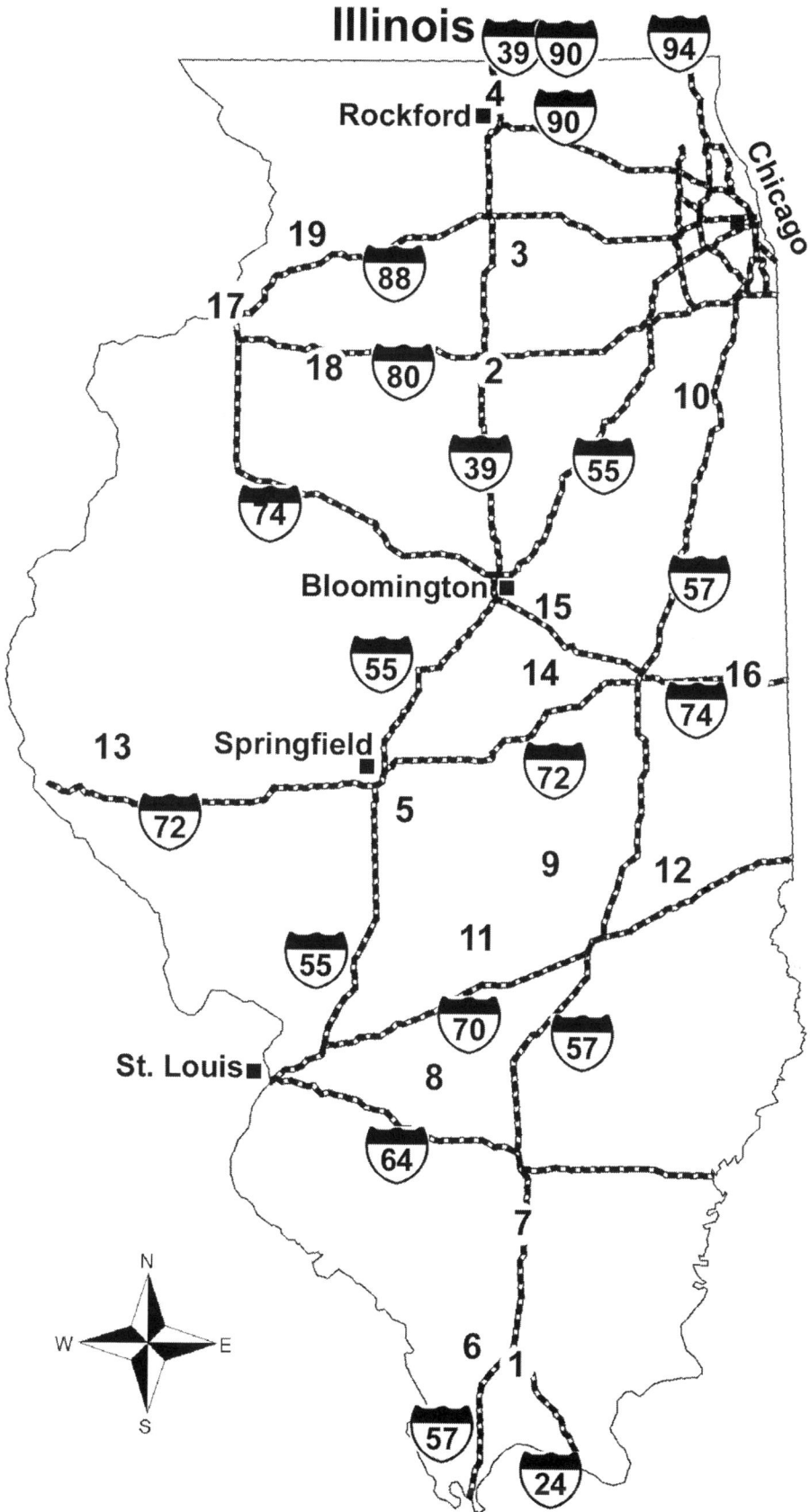

[1] Ferne Clyffe State Park
I-24, Exit 7
South of Goreville
N37 31.954 W88 57.986
State Rate: $8-$35
(618) 995-2411
http://dnr.state.il.us/lands/landmgt/PARKS/
R5/FERNE.HTM#Camping

Directions

3 miles. From Exit 7 turn west for 2.4 miles on Cty Hwy 12 to Hwy 37 (S Broadway). Turn left (south) and go 0.6 miles to park entrance.

Points of Interest

The Park is known as an outstanding natural scenic spot, walkers will enjoy the experience. The Park is a great base for exploring the southern Illinois region, from the Tunnel Hill State Bike Trail in Vienna, to Golconda on the Ohio River, and The Garden of the Gods south of Harrisburg.

RV Sites		Water		Laundry	
Number	59	None		Wi-Fi	
Shaded	Y	At Site		Fishing	Y
By Water	Y	Spigots	Y	Hiking	Y
Paved		**Sewer**		Biking	Y
Pull Thru	Y	None		Swimming	
ADA	Y	At Site		Watch Wildlife	Y
Max RV Size	42	Dump Station	Y	Pets	Y
Electric		**Amenities**		**Security**	
None		Restrooms	Y	Host(s)	Y
20 Amp	Y	Showers	Y	Rangers(s)	Y
30 Amp	Y	Reserve Sites	Y	Gate	
50 Amp	few	Store		Patrolled	Y
		Grill/Table	Y		

[2] Starved Rock State Park
I-39, Exits 54 or 59
South of LaSalle
N41 19.278 W89 00.648
State Rate: $8-$35
(815) 667-4726
http://dnr.state.il.us/lands/Landmgt/PARKS/
i&m/east/starve/park.htm

Directions

5.5 miles. **Northbound,** from Exit 54 go east 2.1 mi. on Walnut to Ed Hand (Hwy 23). Turn north for 1 mi. to Hwy 71. Turn right for 1.3 mi. to Hwy 178. Turn north for 0.8 mi. to the Park. **Southbound,** from Exit 59 go 2.2 mi. east on I-80 to Exit 81. Turn south on Hwy 178 for 3.2 mi. to Park.

Points of Interest

What makes this park unique are the 18 canyons formed by glacial meltwater & erosion. The park is best known for its fascinating rock formations.

RV Sites		Water		Laundry	
Number	122	None		Wi-Fi	
Shaded	Y	At Site		Fishing	Y
By Water		Spigots	Y	Hiking	Y
Paved		**Sewer**		Biking	Y
Pull Thru		None		Swimming	
ADA	Y	At Site		Watch Wildlife	Y
Max RV Size	42	Dump Station	Y	Pets	Y
Electric		**Amenities**		**Security**	
None		Restrooms	Y	Host(s)	Y
20 Amp	Y	Showers	Y	Rangers(s)	Y
30 Amp	Y	Reserve Sites	Y	Gate	
50 Amp	Y	Store	Y	Patrolled	Y
		Grill/Table	Y		

[3] Shabbona Lake State Park
I-39, Exit 87
South of DeKalb
N41 45.666 W88 52.184
State Rate: $8-$35
(815) 824-2106
http://dnr.state.il.us/lands/Landmgt/PARKS/
R1/SHABBONA.HTM

Directions

7 miles. From Exit 87 take Hwy 30 east 5.5 miles toward Shabbona. Before town turn right on Preserve Road. Go 1.6 mile to the Park.

Points of Interest

The 1,550 acres of Park land is rolling prairie and features a 319 acre man-made fishing lake. In Shabbona, you'll find some great restaurants, shopping at stores that take you back to another time, and history to keep you busy learning for hours.

RV Sites		Water		Laundry	
Number	88	None		Wi-Fi	
Shaded	Y	At Site		Fishing	Y
By Water	Y	Spigots	Y	Hiking	Y
Paved		**Sewer**		Biking	Y
Pull Thru		None		Swimming	
ADA	Y	At Site		Watch Wildlife	Y
Max RV Size	40	Dump Station	Y	Pets	Y
Electric		**Amenities**		**Security**	
None		Restrooms	Y	Host(s)	Y
20 Amp	Y	Showers	Y	Rangers(s)	Y
30 Amp	Y	Reserve Sites	Y	Gate	
50 Amp	Y	Store	Y	Patrolled	Y
		Grill/Table	Y		

[4] Rock Cut State Park
I-39/90, Hwy 173 Exit (mile marker 70)
North Side of Rockford
N42 22.193 W88 58.699
State Rate: $8-$35
(815) 885-3311
http://dnr.state.il.us/lands/Landmgt/PARKS/
R1/ROCKCUT.HTM

Directions

0.5 miles. From Hwy 173 Exit (at mile marker 70) go 0.6 miles west to the Park.

Points of Interest

Rockford is home to many quality antique stores, intriguing curiosities, boutiques and plain old junk shops. Some examples - Fire Station Antique Mall, Angela's Attic on Gardner, and Roscoe Antiques. Or visit homes located within the eight historic neighborhoods of Rockford's urban core.

RV Sites		Water		Laundry	
Number	199	None		Wi-Fi	
Shaded	Y	At Site		Fishing	Y
By Water	Y	Spigots	Y	Hiking	Y
Paved		Sewer		Biking	Y
Pull Thru		None		Swimming	Y
ADA	Y	At Site		Watch Wildlife	Y
Max RV Size	45	Dump Station	Y	Pets	Y
Electric		Amenities		Security	
None		Restrooms	Y	Host(s)	Y
20 Amp	Y	Showers	Y	Rangers(s)	Y
30 Amp	Y	Reserve Sites	Y	Gate	
50 Amp	Y	Store	Y	Patrolled	Y
		Grill/Table	Y		

[5] Sangchris Lake State Park
I-55, Exits 82 or 96A
Southeast of Springfield
N39 39.317 W89 29.279
State Rate: $8-$35
(217) 498-9208
http://dnr.state.il.us/Lands/Landmgt/PARKS/
R4/SANGCH.HTM

Directions

13-15 mi. **Northbound**, from Exit 82 go east on Hwy 104 for 6 mi. to Cty 37. Turn north 5.5 mi. to New City Rd (Cty 9). Turn right 3.4 mi. to the Park. **Southbound**, from Exit 96A, take Hwy 29 south 4.1 mi. to Rochester. Go right at Walnut (Hwy 37). Go south 5.7 mi. to New City Rd then left 3.4 mi. to the Park.

Points of Interest

Springfield has many historic sites - Abraham Lincoln Library & Museum for example.

RV Sites		Water		Laundry	
Number	120	None		Wi-Fi	
Shaded	Y	At Site		Fishing	Y
By Water	Y	Spigots	Y	Hiking	Y
Paved		Sewer		Biking	Y
Pull Thru		None		Swimming	
ADA	Y	At Site		Watch Wildlife	Y
Max RV Size	40	Dump Station	Y	Pets	Y
Electric		Amenities		Security	
None		Restrooms	Y	Host(s)	Y
20 Amp	Y	Showers	Y	Rangers(s)	Y
30 Amp	Y	Reserve Sites	Y	Gate	
50 Amp	Y	Store	Y	Patrolled	Y
		Grill/Table	Y		

[1] Ferne Clyffe State Park
I-57, Exit 40
South of Goreville
N37 31.954 W88 57.986
State Rate: $8-$35
(618) 995-2411
http://dnr.state.il.us/lands/landmgt/PARKS/
R5/FERNE.HTM#Camping

Directions

5 miles. From Exit 40 go east for 3.2 miles on Hwy 13 (Goreville Rd.) to Goreville. Turn south on Hwy 37. Go 1.7 miles to the park entrance.

Points of Interest

The Park is known as an outstanding natural scenic spot, walkers will enjoy the experience. The Park is a great base for exploring the southern Illinois region, from the Tunnel Hill State Bike Trail in Vienna, to Golconda on the Ohio River, and The Garden of the Gods south of Harrisburg.

RV Sites		Water		Laundry	
Number	59	None		Wi-Fi	
Shaded	Y	At Site		Fishing	Y
By Water	Y	Spigots	Y	Hiking	Y
Paved		Sewer		Biking	Y
Pull Thru	Y	None		Swimming	
ADA	Y	At Site		Watch Wildlife	Y
Max RV Size	42	Dump Station	Y	Pets	Y
Electric		Amenities		Security	
None		Restrooms	Y	Host(s)	Y
20 Amp	Y	Showers	Y	Rangers(s)	Y
30 Amp	Y	Reserve Sites	Y	Gate	
50 Amp	few	Store		Patrolled	Y
		Grill/Table	Y		

[6] Giant City State Park
I-57, Exit 45
South of Carbondale
N37 36.266 W89 11.653
State Rate: $8-$35
(618) 457-4836
http://dnr.state.il.us/Lands/Landmgt/PARKS/
R5/GC.HTM

Directions

16 miles. From Exit 45 go northwest on Hwy 148 for 2.4 mi. Turn left on Grassy Rd. Follow Grassy Rd for 4.3 mi. Turn left at the 'Y', staying on Grassy for 4.4 more mi. to Giant City Rd. Turn south on Giant City Rd 4.5 mi. to the Park.

Points of Interest

Hike the Giant City Nature Trail, home of the "Giant City Streets" formed 12,000 years ago by huge bluffs of sandstone. Enjoy the rustic beauty of the Lodge. Drive the Southern Illinois Wine Trail.

RV Sites		Water		Laundry	
Number	85	None		Wi-Fi	
Shaded	Y	At Site		Fishing	Y
By Water		Spigots	Y	Hiking	Y
Paved		Sewer		Biking	Y
Pull Thru	Y	None		Swimming	
ADA	Y	At Site		Watch Wildlife	Y
Max RV Size	40	Dump Station	Y	Pets	Y
Electric		Amenities		Security	
None		Restrooms	Y	Host(s)	Y
20 Amp	Y	Showers	Y	Rangers(s)	Y
30 Amp	Y	Reserve Sites	Y	Gate	
50 Amp	few	Store	Y	Patrolled	Y
		Grill/Table	Y		

[7] Gun Creek Campground
I-57, Exit 77
North of Benton
N38 04.686 W88 55.833
COE Rate: $16-$24
America/Beautiful Rate: $8-$12
(618) 724-2493
http://www.reserveamerica.com/

Directions

1 mile. From Exit 77 go 0.3 miles west on Hwy 154. Go south for 0.3 miles to Gun Creek Trail. Turn right on Golf Course Drive, go 0.5 miles to the campground.

Points of Interest

Enjoy the Rend Lake Visitor Center, Ranger-led programs, educational programs, environmental education, and Rend Lake Wildlife Refuge. Auto touring and "Watchable Wildlife" viewing opportunities abound at the lake.

RV Sites		Water		Laundry	
Number	101	None		Wi-Fi	
Shaded	Y	At Site		Fishing	Y
By Water	Y	Spigots	Y	Hiking	Y
Paved	Y	Sewer		Biking	Y
Pull Thru	few	None		Swimming	
ADA	Y	At Site		Watch Wildlife	Y
Max RV Size	45	Dump Station	Y	Pets	Y
Electric		Amenities		Security	
None		Restrooms	Y	Host(s)	Y
20 Amp	Y	Showers	Y	Rangers(s)	Y
30 Amp	Y	Reserve Sites	Y	Gate	
50 Amp	Y	Store		Patrolled	Y
		Grill/Table	Y		

[8] Dam West Recreation Area
I-57, Exit 116
North of Carlyle
N38 37.923 W89 21.647
COE Rate: $18-$52
America/Beautiful Rate: $9-$26
(618) 594-4410
http://www.reserveamerica.com/

Directions

24 miles. From Exit 116 go 22 miles west on Hwy 50 to Carlyle. Go north on Hwy 127 for 1.3 mile to William Rd. Turn east, go 0.6 mile to Lake Road (Cty Rd 1430 N), turn north 0.3 miles to the campground.

Points of Interest

Carlyle Lake is the largest in-land lake in Illinois, with much to offer. Some area museums of note include the Bock Sculpture Museum, American Farm Heritage Museum, & Pioneer Log Cabin Village.

RV Sites		Water		Laundry	
Number	109	None		Wi-Fi	
Shaded	Y	At Site	Y	Fishing	Y
By Water	Y	Spigots		Hiking	Y
Paved	Y	Sewer		Biking	Y
Pull Thru		None		Swimming	Y
ADA	Y	At Site	Y	Watch Wildlife	Y
Max RV Size	45	Dump Station	Y	Pets	Y
Electric		Amenities		Security	
None		Restrooms	Y	Host(s)	Y
20 Amp	Y	Showers	Y	Rangers(s)	Y
30 Amp	Y	Reserve Sites	Y	Gate	
50 Amp	Y	Store	Y	Patrolled	Y
		Grill/Table	Y		

[9] Lithia Springs Camp
I-57, Exit 190
West of Mattoon
N39 26.062 W88 45.626
COE Rate: $18-$36
America/Beautiful Rate: $9-$18
(217) 774-3951
www.reserveamerica.com/

Directions

27 miles. From Exit 190 go 24 miles west on Hwy 16. East of Shelbyville turn north on Cty Rd. 2200E for 1.5 miles to Cty Rd. 1500N, then west 1.5 miles to the campground.

Points of Interest

A favorite trip is the Amish destination of Rockome Gardens, north of Mattoon, with Elvan's Soda Fountain, Enchanted Cave, Horse Powered Sawmill, & Blacksmith Shop. Master craftsmen & artisans demonstrate century-old skills.

RV Sites		Water		Laundry	Y
Number	115	None		Wi-Fi	
Shaded	Y	At Site	Y	Fishing	Y
By Water	Y	Spigots		Hiking	Y
Paved		Sewer		Biking	Y
Pull Thru	Y	None		Swimming	Y
ADA	Y	At Site	Y	Watch Wildlife	Y
Max RV Size	45	Dump Station	Y	Pets	Y
Electric		Amenities		Security	
None		Restrooms	Y	Host(s)	Y
20 Amp	Y	Showers	Y	Rangers(s)	Y
30 Amp	Y	Reserve Sites	Y	Gate	
50 Amp	Y	Store		Patrolled	Y
		Grill/Table	Y		

[10] Kankakee River State Park
I-57, Exit 315
Northwest of Kankakee
N41 12.248 W87 58.750
State Rate: $8-$35
(815) 933-1383
http://dnr.state.il.us/Lands/Landmgt/PARKS/R2/KANKAKEE.HTM

Directions

9 miles. From Exit 315 go south 0.5 mile to Armour Rd. Turn right, go 2 miles to Hwy 102. Turn right, go 7 miles to the Park entrance.

Points of Interest

The park puts you within an hour of the southern suburbs of Chicago as well as the Indiana state line. Frank Lloyd Wright designed two houses in the Riverview section of Kankakee - The B. Harley Bradley House & Stable and the Warren Hickox House, both still stand today.

RV Sites		Water		Laundry	
Number	260	None		Wi-Fi	
Shaded	Y	At Site		Fishing	Y
By Water	Y	Spigots	Y	Hiking	Y
Paved		Sewer		Biking	Y
Pull Thru		None		Swimming	
ADA	Y	At Site		Watch Wildlife	Y
Max RV Size	42	Dump Station	Y	Pets	Y
Electric		Amenities		Security	
None		Restrooms	Y	Host(s)	Y
20 Amp	Y	Showers	Y	Rangers(s)	Y
30 Amp	Y	Reserve Sites	Y	Gate	Y
50 Amp	Y	Store		Patrolled	Y
		Grill/Table	Y		

[8] Dam West Recreation Area
I-64, Exit 50
North of Carlyle
N38 37.923 W89 21.647
COE Rate: $18-$52
America/Beautiful Rate: $9-$26
(618) 594-4410
http://www.reserveamerica.com/

Directions

18 miles. From Exit 50 go 16.8 miles north on Hwy 127 to the north side of Carlyle. Turn east (right) on William Rd, go 0.6 mile to Lake Rd (Cty Rd 1430 N), turn north 0.3 miles on Lake Rd to the Camp.

Points of Interest

Carlyle Lake is the largest in-land lake in Illinois, with much to offer. Some area museums of note include the Bock Sculpture Museum, American Farm Heritage Museum, & Pioneer Log Cabin Village.

RV Sites		Water		Laundry	
Number	109	None		Wi-Fi	
Shaded	Y	At Site	Y	Fishing	Y
By Water	Y	Spigots		Hiking	Y
Paved	Y	Sewer		Biking	Y
Pull Thru		None		Swimming	Y
ADA	Y	At Site	Y	Watch Wildlife	Y
Max RV Size	45	Dump Station	Y	Pets	Y
Electric		Amenities		Security	
None		Restrooms	Y	Host(s)	Y
20 Amp	Y	Showers	Y	Rangers(s)	Y
30 Amp	Y	Reserve Sites	Y	Gate	
50 Amp	Y	Store	Y	Patrolled	Y
		Grill/Table	Y		

[11] Ramsey Lake State Park
I-70, Exit 63
North of Vandalia
N39 09.566 W89 07.500
State Rate: $8-$35
(618) 423-2215
http://dnr.state.il.us/Lands/Landmgt/PARKS/
R5/RAMSEY.HTM

Directions

14 miles. From Exit 63 go 12.8 miles north on Hwy 51. Just north of Ramsey turn west on Cty Rd. 2900 (Ramsey Lake Rd.) for 1.4 mile to the Park.

Points of Interest

Vandalia is the oldest existing Capitol & served the State from 1819-1839. You can tour The Vandalia State House, which is also notable for its association with Abraham Lincoln, who served in the House of Representatives.

RV Sites		Water		Laundry	
Number	155	None		Wi-Fi	
Shaded	Y	At Site		Fishing	Y
By Water	Y	Spigots	Y	Hiking	Y
Paved		Sewer		Biking	Y
Pull Thru	Y	None		Swimming	
ADA	Y	At Site		Watch Wildlife	Y
Max RV Size	45	Dump Station	Y	Pets	Y
Electric		Amenities		Security	
None		Restrooms	Y	Host(s)	Y
20 Amp	Y	Showers	Y	Rangers(s)	Y
30 Amp	Y	Reserve Sites	Y	Gate	
50 Amp	Y	Store	Y	Patrolled	Y
		Grill/Table	Y		

[12] Fox Ridge State Park
I-70, Exit 119
South of Charleston
N39 24.166 W88 08.091
State Rate: $8-$35
(217) 345-6416
http://dnr.state.il.us/Lands/Landmgt/PARKS/
R3/FOX/FOX.HTM

Directions

11 miles I-70. From Exit 119 go 11 miles north on Hwy 130 to the Park entrance at State Park Rd.

Points of Interest

Tour the Lincoln Log Cabin Historic Site. The site preserves the 1840s farm of Thomas and Sarah Bush Lincoln, father and stepmother of our 16th president. Close by is the Moore Home Historic Site, where Lincoln bid his stepmother farewell before assuming the Presidency.

RV Sites		Water		Laundry	
Number	43	None		Wi-Fi	
Shaded	Y	At Site		Fishing	Y
By Water		Spigots	Y	Hiking	Y
Paved		Sewer		Biking	Y
Pull Thru	few	None		Swimming	
ADA	Y	At Site		Watch Wildlife	Y
Max RV Size	40	Dump Station	Y	Pets	Y
Electric		Amenities		Security	
None		Restrooms	Y	Host(s)	Y
20 Amp	Y	Showers	Y	Rangers(s)	Y
30 Amp	Y	Reserve Sites	Y	Gate	
50 Amp	Y	Store		Patrolled	Y
		Grill/Table	Y		

[13] Siloam Springs State Park
I-72, Exit 20
East of Quincy
N39 53.749 W90 57.305
State Rate: $8-$35
(217) 894-6205
http://dnr.state.il.us/Lands/Landmgt/PARKS/
R4/SILOAMSP.HTM

Directions

19 miles. From Exit 20 go 7.7 mi. north on Cty Rd 4/24. Turn right on Cty 22 (400 N) for 1 mi., then left on Cty Rd 2500 for 0.5 mi. to Hwy 104. Go right 3.5 mi. to Road 2873 (Siloam Rd.). Turn left, go 5.8 mi. to the park.

Points of Interest

Visit The Old Carthage Jail, where Mormon leader, Joseph Smith Jr., & his brother Hyrum, were killed by an angry mob in 1844. Relax at Baxter's Winery, the oldest Winery in Illinois, in Nauvoo.

RV Sites		Water		Laundry	
Number	182	None		Wi-Fi	
Shaded	Y	At Site		Fishing	Y
By Water	Y	Spigots	Y	Hiking	Y
Paved		Sewer		Biking	Y
Pull Thru	Y	None		Swimming	Y
ADA	Y	At Site		Watch Wildlife	Y
Max RV Size	45	Dump Station	Y	Pets	Y
Electric		Amenities		Security	
None		Restrooms	Y	Host(s)	Y
20 Amp	Y	Showers	Y	Rangers(s)	Y
30 Amp	Y	Reserve Sites	Y	Gate	
50 Amp	few	Store	Y	Patrolled	Y
		Grill/Table	Y		

[14] Clinton Lake State Recreation Area
I-72, Exit 156
West of Champaign
N40 09.794 W88 47.266
State Rate: $8-$35
(217) 935-8722
http://dnr.state.il.us/Lands/Landmgt/PARKS/
R3/CLINTON.HTM

Directions

12 miles. From Exit 156 go 7.5 miles north on Hwy 48 to Hwy 10. Turn west, go 2 miles to Hwy 14 (Friends Creek Rd.). Go north on Cty 14 for 2.5 miles to the park entrance.

Points of Interest

There is easy access to the lake for fishing or boating & nature trails nearby for walking. Nevertheless, you are within 30 minutes drive of Champaign-Urbana, Decatur or Bloomington-Normal if you want to sightsee or shop.

RV Sites		Water		Laundry	
Number	308	None		Wi-Fi	
Shaded	Y	At Site		Fishing	Y
By Water	Y	Spigots	Y	Hiking	Y
Paved		**Sewer**		Biking	Y
Pull Thru		None		Swimming	Y
ADA	Y	At Site	few	Watch Wildlife	Y
Max RV Size	40	Dump Station	Y	Pets	Y
Electric		**Amenities**		**Security**	
None		Restrooms	Y	Host(s)	Y
20 Amp	Y	Showers	Y	Rangers(s)	Y
30 Amp	Y	Reserve Sites	Y	Gate	
50 Amp	Y	Store	Y	Patrolled	Y
		Grill/Table	Y		

[15] Moraine View State Recreation Area
I-74 Exit 149
East of Bloomington
N40 24.808 W88 43.654
State Rate: $8-$35
(309) 724-8032
http://dnr.state.il.us/Lands/Landmgt/PARKS/
R3/MORAINE.HTM

Directions

7 miles. From Exit 149 take Chestnut (Cty 21) north 0.5 miles to Hwy 150. Turn left, follow Hwy 150 north for 0.6 miles through LeRoy to N West St. Turn north, still on Cty 21 (2600 East Rd), going 5.2 miles in all to E 900 Rd N. Turn right, go 2.1 miles to the park.

Points of Interest

The road around the lake is a great walking/biking loop. There are several of Illinois' finest wineries located just a short drive from Bloomington-Normal.

RV Sites		Water		Laundry	
Number	137	None		Wi-Fi	
Shaded	Y	At Site		Fishing	Y
By Water	Y	Spigots	Y	Hiking	Y
Paved	few	**Sewer**		Biking	Y
Pull Thru		None		Swimming	Y
ADA	Y	At Site		Watch Wildlife	Y
Max RV Size	35	Dump Station	Y	Pets	Y
Electric		**Amenities**		**Security**	
None		Restrooms	Y	Host(s)	Y
20 Amp	Y	Showers	Y	Rangers(s)	Y
30 Amp	Y	Reserve Sites	Y	Gate	
50 Amp		Store	Y	Patrolled	Y
		Grill/Table	Y		

[16] Kickapoo State Recreation Area
I-74, Exit 210
West of Danville
N40 08.323 W87 45.185
State Rate: $8-$35
(217) 442-4915
http://dnr.state.il.us/Lands/Landmgt/PARKS/
R3/KICKAPOO.HTM

Directions

4.2 miles. From Exit 210 go 2.2 miles southwest on Hwy 150 to 1000 East Rd. Turn north, go 2 miles to Kickapoo Park Rd. Turn right in to the Park.

Points of Interest

Hikers, wildflower enthusiasts, and wildlife lovers will enjoy this park. The Danville Vermilion downtown area has many antique, collectible and specialty shops. In Rossville the Depot Museum features railroad memorabilia.

RV Sites		Water		Laundry	
Number	92	None		Wi-Fi	
Shaded	Y	At Site		Fishing	Y
By Water	Y	Spigots	Y	Hiking	Y
Paved		**Sewer**		Biking	Y
Pull Thru	Y	None		Swimming	
ADA	Y	At Site		Watch Wildlife	Y
Max RV Size	45	Dump Station	Y	Pets	Y
Electric		**Amenities**		**Security**	
None		Restrooms	Y	Host(s)	Y
20 Amp	Y	Showers	Y	Rangers(s)	Y
30 Amp	Y	Reserve Sites	Y	Gate	
50 Amp	Y	Store	Y	Patrolled	Y
		Grill/Table	Y		

[17] Fisherman's Corner
I-80, Exit 1
Northeast of Moline
N41 34.006 W90 23.767
COE Rate: $16-$18
America/Beautiful Rate: $9
(815) 259-3628
http://www.recreation.gov/

Directions

2 miles. From Exit 1 go 2 mile southwest on Hwy 84 to the camp entrance.

Points of Interest

Moline is part of the Quad Cities area. Of note there is The John Deere Pavilion, which contains exhibits celebrating the history of the agricultural implements industry in the Midwest and showcases a variety of past and present John Deere plows, tractors, combines, and other machinery.

RV Sites		Water		Laundry	
Number	29	None		Wi-Fi	
Shaded	Y	At Site		Fishing	Y
By Water	Y	Spigots	Y	Hiking	Y
Paved	Y	**Sewer**		Biking	Y
Pull Thru		None		Swimming	
ADA	Y	At Site		Watch Wildlife	
Max RV Size	45	Dump Station	Y	Pets	Y
Electric		**Amenities**		**Security**	
None		Restrooms	Y	Host(s)	Y
20 Amp	Y	Showers	Y	Rangers(s)	Y
30 Amp	Y	Reserve Sites	Y	Gate	
50 Amp	Y	Store		Patrolled	Y
		Grill/Table	Y		

[18] Johnson-Sauk Trail State Recreation Area
I-80, Exit 33
North of Kewanee
N41 19.777 W89 53.455
State Rate: $8-$35
(309) 853-5589
http://dnr.state.il.us/Lands/Landmgt/PARKS/ R1/JOHNSON.HTM

Directions

7 miles. From Exit 33 go 5.6 miles south on Hwy 78 to N 1200th Ave. Turn left, go 1.2 miles to the park entrance.

Points of Interest

Tour the Park's feature - a 1910 round barn. One of the largest round barns in the country, this architectural marvel is 80 feet high & 85 feet in diameter, with a 16-foot wide silo inside! Round barns originally were built by religious groups as they "left no corners for the devil to hide."

RV Sites		Water		Laundry	
Number	70	None		Wi-Fi	
Shaded	Y	At Site		Fishing	Y
By Water		Spigots	Y	Hiking	Y
Paved		**Sewer**		Biking	Y
Pull Thru		None		Swimming	
ADA	Y	At Site		Watch Wildlife	Y
Max RV Size	40	Dump Station	Y	Pets	Y
Electric		**Amenities**		**Security**	
None		Restrooms	Y	Host(s)	Y
20 Amp	Y	Showers	Y	Rangers(s)	Y
30 Amp	Y	Reserve Sites	Y	Gate	
50 Amp	Y	Store	Y	Patrolled	Y
		Grill/Table	Y		

[19] Morrison-Rockwood State Park
I-88, Exit 26
North of Morrison
N41 50.474 W89 58.004
State Rate: $8-$35
(815) 772-4708
http://dnr.state.il.us/lands/landmgt/PARKS/ R1/MORRISON.HTM

Directions

11 miles. From Exit 26 take Hwy 78 north 6 miles into Morrison. Turn left at Hwy 30 for 1.5 miles. Turn north on Hwy 78, go 1 mile to Damen Rd. Turn right for 1.1 mile to Crosby Rd. Turn left, go 1 mile to the Park.

Points of Interest

Visit Ronald Reagan's birthplace in Tampico and tour the Ronald Reagan Birthplace and Museum. Then drive to Dixon and visit President Regan's boyhood home.

RV Sites		Water		Laundry	
Number	92	None		Wi-Fi	
Shaded	Y	At Site		Fishing	Y
By Water		Spigots	Y	Hiking	Y
Paved		**Sewer**		Biking	Y
Pull Thru	Y	None		Swimming	
ADA	Y	At Site		Watch Wildlife	Y
Max RV Size	40	Dump Station	Y	Pets	Y
Electric		**Amenities**		**Security**	
None		Restrooms	Y	Host(s)	Y
20 Amp	Y	Showers	Y	Rangers(s)	Y
30 Amp	Y	Reserve Sites	Y	Gate	
50 Amp	Y	Store	Y	Patrolled	Y
		Grill/Table	Y		

About Indiana's Public Campgrounds

The Indiana Department of Natural Resources website has helpful information relevant to RV camping. Go to -

www.in.gov/dnr/parklake/

Online reservations for campgrounds can be found at

www.camp.IN.gov

Many campgrounds are seasonal and may not be available for the dates you select. Dogs and cats must be attended at all times and kept on a leash no longer than six feet. Fires may be built only in the fire rings provided. Collecting firewood in state parks is prohibited. Firewood is for sale at the park concession or campground store. Bring firewood from home only with bark removed, or purchase firewood with a state or federal compliance stamp. It is also possible to bring scrap kiln dried lumber.

Camping fees are -

	Sun - Wed	Thu - Sat	Holiday Weekends
Full Hookup	$26.00	$36.00	$40.00
Electric	$19.00	$26.00	$29.00
Non-Electric	$12.00	$15.00	$18.00

A gate fee may be applicable.

[1] Harmonie State Park

[2] Lynnville Park Campground

[3] Indian-Celina Lake Recreation Area

[4] Charlestown State Park

[5] Muscatatuck County Park

[6] Brown County State Park

[7] Ouabache State Park

[8] Johnny Appleseed Campground

[9] Chain O' Lakes State Park

[10] McCormick's Creek State Park

[11] Whitewater Memorial State Park

[12] Turkey Run State Park

[13] Indiana Dunes State Park

[14] Lincoln State Park

[15] Shakamak State Park

[16] Prophetstown State Park

[17] Tippecanoe River State Park

[18] Potato Creek State Park

NOTES:

Indiana

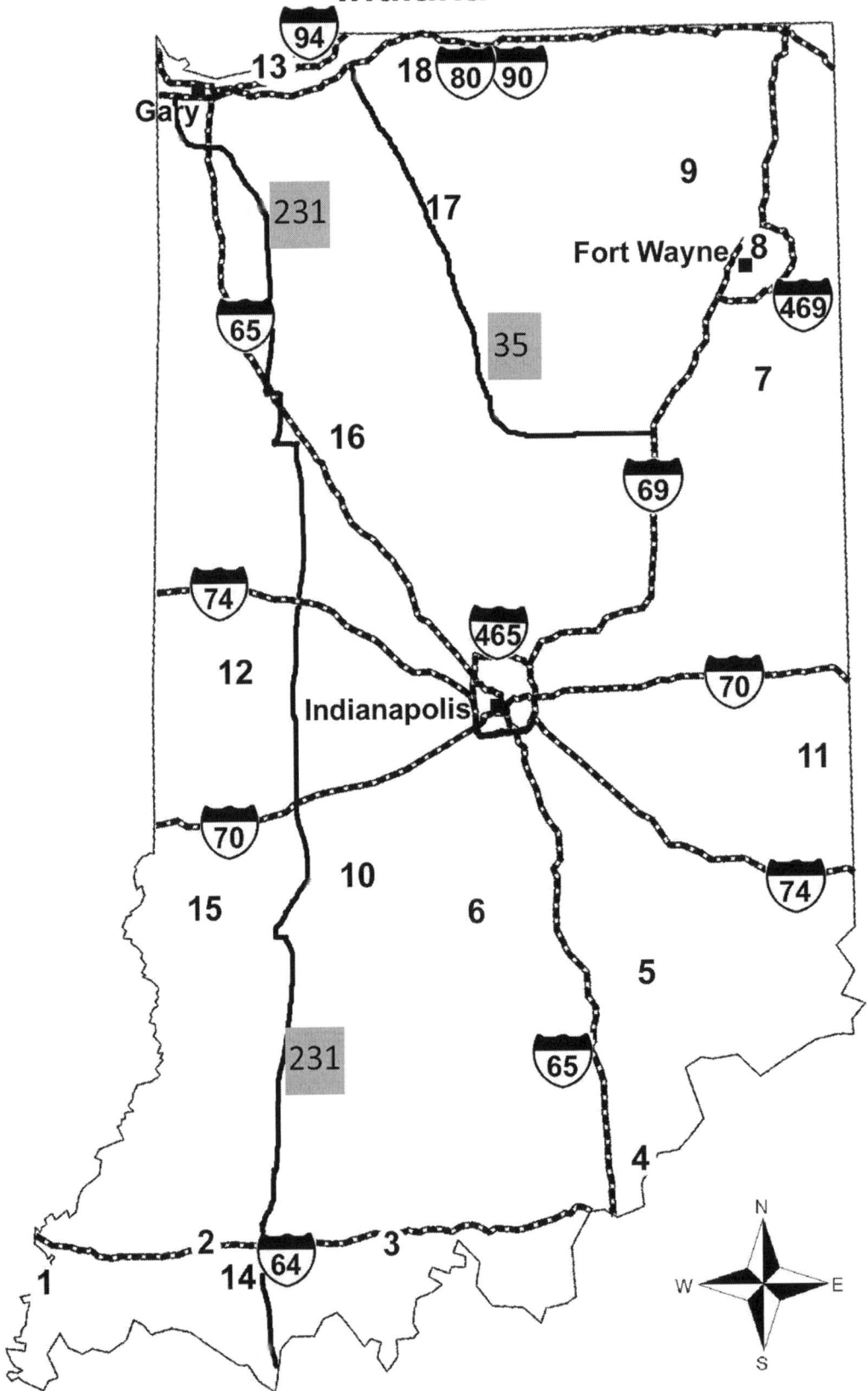

94

13

18 80 90

Gary

9

231

17

Fort Wayne 8

35

469

7

65

16

69

74

12

465

Indianapolis

70

11

70

10

6

15

5

74

231

65

4

2   3

1   14 64

N
W   E
S

[1] Harmonie State Park
I-64, Exit 4
Northwest of Evansville
N38 05.415 W87 56.656
State Rate: $12-$29
(812) 682-4821
http://www.in.gov/dnr/parklake/2981.htm

Directions

11 miles. From Exit 4 turn south for 10 miles on Hwy 69 to Hwy 269 (Cty Rd 325N). Turn right for 1 miles to the park entrance.

Points of Interest

Two communal living experiments give the RVer a chance to visit Historic New Harmony which retains some of the colorful history for public interest. Here, utopian experiments - The Harmonists of the Rappite Community and the Owen Community - originated in New Harmony in the 1800's.

RV Sites		Water		Laundry	
Number	200	None		Wi-Fi	
Shaded	Y	At Site		Fishing	Y
By Water	Y	Spigots	Y	Hiking	Y
Paved		**Sewer**		Biking	Y
Pull Thru	Y	None		Swimming	Y
ADA	Y	At Site		Watch Wildlife	Y
Max RV Size	45	Dump Station	Y	Pets	Y
Electric		**Amenities**		**Security**	
None		Restrooms	Y	Host(s)	Y
20 Amp	Y	Showers	Y	Rangers(s)	Y
30 Amp	Y	Reserve Sites	Y	Gate	
50 Amp	Y	Store	Y	Patrolled	Y
		Grill/Table	Y		

[2] Lynnville Park Campground
I-64, Exit 39
West of Lynnville
N38 11.591 W87 19.733
County Rate: $20
(812) 922-5144
http://www.rvparklist.com/rvpark/8373/

Directions

2 miles. From Exit 39 turn north for 0.2 mile on Hwy 61 to Hwy 68. Turn west and go just under 2 miles to the park entrance on the right.

Points of Interest

Visit the Park's Wahnsiedler Observatory & home of the Evansville Astronomical Society. Spend some quality night time gazing at the stars. Check out the observatory's two telescopes: a 14 inch Celestron Schmitt-Cassegrain reflector & a 12.5 inch Cave Newtonian reflector.

RV Sites		Water		Laundry	
Number	54	None		Wi-Fi	
Shaded	Y	At Site	Y	Fishing	Y
By Water	Y	Spigots		Hiking	Y
Paved		**Sewer**		Biking	Y
Pull Thru	Y	None		Swimming	
ADA		At Site	Y	Watch Wildlife	
Max RV Size	40	Dump Station		Pets	Y
Electric		**Amenities**		**Security**	
None		Restrooms	Y	Host(s)	Y
20 Amp	Y	Showers	Y	Rangers(s)	
30 Amp	Y	Reserve Sites		Gate	
50 Amp	Y	Store		Patrolled	Y
		Grill/Table	Y		

[3] Indian-Celina Lake Recreation Area
I-64, Exit 79
South of St. Croix
N38 11.927 W86 36.223
Hoosier NF Rate: $17-$31
America/Beautiful Rate: $9-$16
(812) 843-4891
http://www.reserveamerica.com/

Directions

3 miles. From Exit 79 go 2 miles south on Hwy 37 to Cty Rd 501. Turn right, go 0.3 miles to Cty Rd 502. Turn left into the campgrounds.

Points of Interest

Swimming is excellent at Tipsaw Lake Beach, with its excellent swimming beach, modern bath-house/showers, dressing facilities, & restrooms. Drive to Holiday World, an hour away. It's a great place to walk, enjoy the sights, food & take in some of the shows and other entertainment.

RV Sites		Water		Laundry	
Number	23	None		Wi-Fi	
Shaded	Y	At Site		Fishing	Y
By Water	Y	Spigots	Y	Hiking	Y
Paved		**Sewer**		Biking	Y
Pull Thru		None		Swimming	Y
ADA	Y	At Site		Watch Wildlife	Y
Max RV Size	35	Dump Station	Y	Pets	Y
Electric		**Amenities**		**Security**	
None		Restrooms	Y	Host(s)	Y
20 Amp	Y	Showers	Y	Rangers(s)	Y
30 Amp	Y	Reserve Sites	Y	Gate	
50 Amp		Store		Patrolled	Y
		Grill/Table	Y		

[4] Charlestown State Park
I-65, Exit 9
North of Louisville, KY
N38 26.964 W85 38.777
State Rate: $12-$40
(812) 256-5600
http://www.in.gov/dnr/parklake/2986.htm

Directions

9 miles. From Exit 9 go northeast on Hwy 331 for 1 mile to Hwy 403. Turn right, go 5.6 miles to Hwy 3. Turn right, go 1.2 mile to Hwy 62. Turn left and proceed 1 mile to the Park on the right.

Points of Interest

The park has 200 foot overlooks above the Ohio River. This area is known for its diversity of topography, which will interest walkers, as well as excellent watchable wildlife - birders can seek out the 70+ species of birds. Of course Louisville is a 25 minute drive for sightseers and shoppers.

RV Sites		Water		Laundry	
Number	192	None		Wi-Fi	
Shaded	Y	At Site	Y	Fishing	Y
By Water	Y	Spigots	Y	Hiking	Y
Paved	Y	Sewer		Biking	Y
Pull Thru		None		Swimming	
ADA	Y	At Site	Y	Watch Wildlife	Y
Max RV Size	42	Dump Station	Y	Pets	Y
Electric		Amenities		Security	
None		Restrooms	Y	Host(s)	Y
20 Amp	Y	Showers	Y	Rangers(s)	Y
30 Amp	Y	Reserve Sites	Y	Gate	
50 Amp	Y	Store		Patrolled	Y
		Grill/Table	Y		

[5] Muscatatuck County Park
I-65, Exit 50
East of Seymour
N38 59.377 W85 36.969
County Rate: $16-$25
(812) 346-2953
http://www.muscatatuckpark.com/camping.htm

Directions

13 miles. From Exit 50 turn east for 12.4 miles on Hwy 50 to Hwy 3/7. Turn south and go 1.2 mile to the park entrance on the right.

Points of Interest

Two Wildlife Refuges, 2 State Fish & Wildlife Areas, a State Forest & a State Nature Preserve surround the Park. The local towns are rich in history. Vernon is a Historic District. Enjoy "Indiana's best mid-19th century towns," with antique shops, festivals, herb farms & quaint dining.

RV Sites		Water		Laundry	
Number	26	None		Wi-Fi	
Shaded	Y	At Site	Y	Fishing	Y
By Water		Spigots	Y	Hiking	Y
Paved		Sewer		Biking	Y
Pull Thru	Y	None		Swimming	
ADA	Y	At Site	Y	Watch Wildlife	Y
Max RV Size	45	Dump Station	Y	Pets	Y
Electric		Amenities		Security	
None		Restrooms	Y	Host(s)	Y
20 Amp	Y	Showers	Y	Rangers(s)	
30 Amp	Y	Reserve Sites	Y	Gate	
50 Amp		Store		Patrolled	Y
		Grill/Table	Y		

[6] Brown County State Park
I-65, Exit 68
West of Bloomington
N39 10.606 W86 16.232
State Rate: $12-$29
(812) 988-6406
http://www.in.gov/dnr/parklake/2988.htm

Directions

18 miles. You must use the West Entrance. From Exit 68 go 16 miles west on Hwy 46, through Gnaw Bone, to Nashville. Turn south on Hwy 46 for 2.3 miles to the West Entrance.

Points of Interest

This is the largest Indiana State park, with 15,776-acres. The Ogle Hollow Nature Preserve contains a self-guided nature trail. Naturalist services are available year-round. Visit the Abe Martin Lodge and Restaurant. Nashville features specialty shops, art galleries, and historic homes.

RV Sites		Water		Laundry	
Number	424	None		Wi-Fi	
Shaded	Y	At Site		Fishing	Y
By Water		Spigots	Y	Hiking	Y
Paved		Sewer		Biking	Y
Pull Thru	Y	None		Swimming	Y
ADA	Y	At Site		Watch Wildlife	Y
Max RV Size	45	Dump Station	Y	Pets	Y
Electric		Amenities		Security	
None		Restrooms	Y	Host(s)	Y
20 Amp	Y	Showers	Y	Rangers(s)	Y
30 Amp	Y	Reserve Sites	Y	Gate	
50 Amp		Store	Y	Patrolled	Y
		Grill/Table	Y		

[7] Ouabache ('Wabash') State Park
I-69, Exit 86
South of Ft. Wayne
N40 43.515 W85 07.365
State Rate: $12-$29
(260) 824-0926
http://www.in.gov/dnr/parklake/2975.htm

Directions

16.5 miles. From Exit 86 go east onto Hwy 224, then immediately turn right on Hwy 116. Drive 13 miles to Bluffton. Turn left on Hwy 124 for 1.8 miles to Hwy 201. Turn right for 1.6 mile on 201 to the Park.

Points of Interest

The park area was occupied by the Miami Indians. In Fort Wayne see world-class art venues & museums. Check out the renowned Vera Bradley bags & DeBrand Fine Chocolates. Use the largest public genealogical collection in America.

RV Sites		Water			Laundry	
Number	124	None			Wi-Fi	
Shaded	Y	At Site			Fishing	Y
By Water	Y	Spigots	Y		Hiking	Y
Paved	Y	**Sewer**			Biking	Y
Pull Thru		None			Swimming	Y
ADA	Y	At Site			Watch Wildlife	Y
Max RV Size	45	Dump Station	Y		Pets	Y
Electric		**Amenities**			**Security**	
None		Restrooms	Y		Host(s)	Y
20 Amp	Y	Showers	Y		Rangers(s)	Y
30 Amp	Y	Reserve Sites	Y		Gate	
50 Amp	Y	Store	Y		Patrolled	Y
		Grill/Table	Y			

[8] Johnny Appleseed Campground
I-69, Exit 109
North side of Fort Wayne
N41 06.730 W85 07.136
County Rate: $18
(260) 427-6720
www.fortwayneparks.org/

Directions

4 miles. From Exit 109 turn southeast a block to Hwy 33/930, Coliseum Blvd. Turn left, go 3.8 miles to N Harry Baals Dr and the park entrance, on the right.

Points of Interest

See Fort Wayne's world-class art venues & museums. Check out the renowned Vera Bradley bags & DeBrand Fine Chocolates, made here. Use the largest public genealogical collection in America. Enjoy world-class arts & theatre. Enjoy a touring Broadway show or concert.

RV Sites		Water			Laundry	Y
Number	41	None			Wi-Fi	Y
Shaded	Y	At Site	Y		Fishing	Y
By Water	Y	Spigots	Y		Hiking	Y
Paved		**Sewer**			Biking	Y
Pull Thru	Y	None			Swimming	
ADA	Y	At Site			Watch Wildlife	
Max RV Size	42	Dump Station	Y		Pets	Y
Electric		**Amenities**			**Security**	
None		Restrooms	Y		Host(s)	Y
20 Amp	Y	Showers	Y		Rangers(s)	
30 Amp	Y	Reserve Sites			Gate	
50 Amp	Y	Store			Patrolled	Y
		Grill/Table	Y			

[9] Chain O' Lakes State Park
I-69, Exit 129
Northwest of Ft. Wayne
N41 20.482 W85 24.138
State Rate: $10-$29
(260) 636-2654
http://www.in.gov/dnr/parklake/2987.htm

Directions

20.5 miles. From Exit 129 go west on Hwy 8 for 7.1 miles to Hwy 3. Turn south 1 mile to E Baseline Rd. Turn west again for 10.6 miles to Hwy 9. Turn south for 0.7 miles to the E 75 S Rd. Turn left, go 1.1 miles to the Park.

Points of Interest

Paddle the chain of lakes, hike trails, or attend a nature program in the park's 'old schoolhouse' nature center. Visit the Auburn Cord Duesenburg Museum. Area sights include the Mid America Windmill Museum & Old Jail Museum.

RV Sites		Water			Laundry	
Number	380	None			Wi-Fi	
Shaded	Y	At Site			Fishing	Y
By Water	Y	Spigots	Y		Hiking	Y
Paved		**Sewer**			Biking	Y
Pull Thru		None			Swimming	Y
ADA	Y	At Site			Watch Wildlife	Y
Max RV Size	45	Dump Station	Y		Pets	Y
Electric		**Amenities**			**Security**	
None		Restrooms	Y		Host(s)	Y
20 Amp	Y	Showers	Y		Rangers(s)	Y
30 Amp	Y	Reserve Sites	Y		Gate	
50 Amp	Y	Store	Y		Patrolled	Y
		Grill/Table	Y			

[10] McCormick's Creek State Park
I-70, Exit 41
South of Cloverdale
N39 16.992 W86 43.572
State Rate: $12-$29
(812) 829-2235
http://www.in.gov/dnr/parklake/2978.htm

Directions

20 miles. From Exit 41 go 18.3 miles south on Hwy 231 to Spencer. Turn east on Hwy 46 for 1.7 miles to the Park entrance on your left.

Points of Interest

Indiana's first State Park is noted for mani-cured grounds, unique limestone formations, & scenic waterfalls. At the Saddle Barn go on trail/hayrides. Play racquetball, handball, basketball, volleyball or use the shuffleboard courts in the Recreation Center, then enjoy a meal at the Canyon Inn.

RV Sites		Water			Laundry	
Number	189	None			Wi-Fi	Y
Shaded	Y	At Site			Fishing	Y
By Water		Spigots	Y		Hiking	Y
Paved		Sewer			Biking	Y
Pull Thru	Y	None			Swimming	Y
ADA	Y	At Site			Watch Wildlife	Y
Max RV Size	40	Dump Station	Y		Pets	Y
Electric		Amenities			Security	
None		Restrooms	Y		Host(s)	Y
20 Amp	Y	Showers	Y		Rangers(s)	Y
30 Amp	Y	Reserve Sites	Y		Gate	Y
50 Amp		Store	Y		Patrolled	Y
		Grill/Table	Y			

[11] Whitewater Memorial State Park
I-70, Exit 151
South of Richmond
N39 36.724 W84 56.538
State Rate: $10-$29
(765) 458-5565
http://www.in.gov/dnr/parklake/2962.htm

Directions

19 miles. From Exit 151 turn south on Hwy 27 for 17 miles to Liberty. In Liberty, continue 1.8 miles south on Hwy 101 to the Park entrance.

Points of Interest

Ride the Whitewater Valley Railroad. Visit his-toric Metamora, observe a horse-drawn canal boat at the Whitewater Canal State Historic Site. Take a short cruise on the Ben Franklin, which passes through the Duck Creek Aque-duct, believed to be the only structure of its kind still in existence.

RV Sites		Water			Laundry	
Number	236	None			Wi-Fi	
Shaded	Y	At Site			Fishing	Y
By Water	Y	Spigots	Y		Hiking	Y
Paved		Sewer			Biking	Y
Pull Thru	Y	None			Swimming	Y
ADA	Y	At Site			Watch Wildlife	Y
Max RV Size	45	Dump Station	Y		Pets	Y
Electric		Amenities			Security	
None		Restrooms	Y		Host(s)	Y
20 Amp	Y	Showers	Y		Rangers(s)	Y
30 Amp	Y	Reserve Sites	Y		Gate	
50 Amp		Store	Y		Patrolled	Y
		Grill/Table	Y			

[12] Turkey Run State Park
I-74, Exit 15
Southwest of Crawfordsville
N39 52.925 W87 12.115
State Rate: $12-$29
(765) 597-2635
http://www.in.gov/dnr/parklake/2964.htm

Directions

19 miles. From Exit 15 turn south on Hwy 41 for 17.3. Turn east on Hwy 47 for 1.7 miles to the Park entrance on the left.

Points of Interest

Enjoy the Park's geologic wonders and wood-lands. Explore sandstone ravines, stands of aged forests, and scenic views along Sugar Creek. Dine at Turkey Run Inn's Narrows Res-taurant, one of the finest in the area. Relax by the fireplace after a hike. Don't miss Billie Creek Village.

RV Sites		Water			Laundry	
Number	213	None			Wi-Fi	
Shaded	Y	At Site			Fishing	Y
By Water	Y	Spigots	Y		Hiking	Y
Paved		Sewer			Biking	Y
Pull Thru	Y	None			Swimming	Y
ADA	Y	At Site			Watch Wildlife	Y
Max RV Size	45	Dump Station	Y		Pets	Y
Electric		Amenities			Security	
None		Restrooms	Y		Host(s)	Y
20 Amp	Y	Showers	Y		Rangers(s)	Y
30 Amp	Y	Reserve Sites	Y		Gate	
50 Amp	Y	Store	Y		Patrolled	Y
		Grill/Table	Y			

[13] Indiana Dunes State Park
I-80/90, Exit 31; I-94, Exit 26
North of Chesterton
N41 39.391 W87 03.757
State Rate: $19-$29
(219) 926-1952
http://www.in.gov/dnr/parklake/2980.htm

Directions

6 miles. From Exit 31 go north 6 miles on Hwy 49 (Cty Rd 25) to the Park.

2.5 miles. From Exit 26 go north 2.5 miles on Hwy 49 (Cty Rd 25) to the Park.

Points of Interest

This campground is an adventure in itself. The grounds & trails are great for bikes or walking. There are different trails over the dunes, one with an interesting wooden stairs, great for photographs. Walk up, along, down the dunes. Walk the Lake Michigan beach, Chicago on the horizon.

RV Sites		Water		Laundry	
Number	140	None		Wi-Fi	
Shaded	Y	At Site		Fishing	Y
By Water	Y	Spigots	Y	Hiking	Y
Paved	Y	Sewer		Biking	Y
Pull Thru		None		Swimming	Y
ADA	Y	At Site		Watch Wildlife	Y
Max RV Size	45	Dump Station	Y	Pets	Y
Electric		Amenities		Security	
None		Restrooms	Y	Host(s)	Y
20 Amp	Y	Showers	Y	Rangers(s)	Y
30 Amp	Y	Reserve Sites	Y	Gate	
50 Amp	Y	Store	Y	Patrolled	Y
		Grill/Table	Y		

[14] Lincoln State Park
I-64, Exit 57A
South of Lincoln City
N38 06.802 W87 01.388
State Rate: $12-$40
(812) 937-4710
http://www.in.gov/dnr/parklake/2979.htm

Directions

7 miles. From Exit 57A go south through Dale on Hwy 231 for 6.4 miles to Hwy 162. Turn east for 0.4 miles to the Park.

Points of Interest

Discover the boyhood home of the 16th president of the United States, Abraham Lincoln. Tour the Colonel Jones Home, the historic home of the merchant and Civil War officer who employed young Lincoln. The Little Pigeon Creek Baptist Church and Cemetery, located on the property, is where Lincoln's sister Sarah is buried.

RV Sites		Water		Laundry	
Number	233	None		Wi-Fi	
Shaded	Y	At Site		Fishing	Y
By Water	Y	Spigots	Y	Hiking	Y
Paved		Sewer		Biking	Y
Pull Thru	Y	None		Swimming	Y
ADA	Y	At Site		Watch Wildlife	Y
Max RV Size	40	Dump Station	Y	Pets	Y
Electric		Amenities		Security	
None		Restrooms	Y	Host(s)	Y
20 Amp	Y	Showers	Y	Rangers(s)	Y
30 Amp	Y	Reserve Sites	Y	Gate	
50 Amp		Store	Y	Patrolled	Y
		Grill/Table	Y		

[15] Shakamak State Park
Hwy 41, East of Shelburn
South of Terre Haute
N39 10.637 W87 13.936
State Rate: $12-$29
(812) 665-2158
http://www.in.gov/dnr/parklake/2969.htm

Directions

9.5 miles. Take I-70, Exit 7 south on Hwy 41. From Hwy 41 take Hwy 48 east for 9.5 miles to the park.

Points of Interest

Man-made lakes offer acres of water for fishing and boating. A family aquatic center provides swimming fun. About two-thirds of the campsites are in a wooded area, offering cool shade in the summer and beautiful fall colors in autumn. Nearby is a play field area for family fun. Terre Haute is a short drive north.

RV Sites		Water		Laundry	
Number	172	None		Wi-Fi	
Shaded	Y	At Site		Fishing	Y
By Water	Y	Spigots	Y	Hiking	Y
Paved		Sewer		Biking	Y
Pull Thru	Y	None		Swimming	Y
ADA	Y	At Site		Watch Wildlife	Y
Max RV Size	45	Dump Station	Y	Pets	Y
Electric		Amenities		Security	
None		Restrooms	Y	Host(s)	Y
20 Amp	Y	Showers	Y	Rangers(s)	Y
30 Amp	Y	Reserve Sites	Y	Gate	
50 Amp		Store		Patrolled	Y
		Grill/Table	Y		

[16] Prophetstown State Park
I-65, Exit 178
North of West Lafayette
N40 29.814 W86 50.594
State Rate: $12-$40
(765) 567-4919
http://www.in.gov/dnr/parklake/2971.htm

Directions

3 miles. From I-65, take exit 178. Go 0.3 miles south on Hwy 43 to Burnett Rd. Turn left, go 0.4 miles to 9th St. Go right 0.5 mile to Swisher Rd, then left on Swisher 1.6 miles to the Park

Points of Interest

Indiana's newest park is named for a Native American village established by Tecumseh, & his brother Tenskwatawa (The Prophet) in 1808. The park is unique because of expanses of tall prairie grasses, native wildflowers, and wetlands. Tippecanoe Battlefield Museum is close by.

RV Sites		Water		Laundry	
Number	110	None		Wi-Fi	
Shaded	Y	At Site	Y	Fishing	Y
By Water	Y	Spigots	Y	Hiking	Y
Paved		Sewer		Biking	Y
Pull Thru	Y	None		Swimming	
ADA	Y	At Site	Y	Watch Wildlife	Y
Max RV Size	45	Dump Station	Y	Pets	Y
Electric		Amenities		Security	
None		Restrooms		Host(s)	Y
20 Amp	Y	Showers	Y	Rangers(s)	Y
30 Amp	Y	Reserve Sites	Y	Gate	Y
50 Amp	Y	Store		Patrolled	Y
		Grill/Table	Y		

[17] Tippecanoe River State Park
Hwy 35
North of Winamac
N41 07.039 W86 36.164
State Rate: $12-$29
(574) 946-3213
http://www.in.gov/dnr/parklake/2965.htm

Directions

5 miles. Go 5 miles north of Winamac on Hwy 35 to the Park entrance.

Points of Interest

The Park borders seven miles of the Tippecanoe River. This is a must for canoe lovers, bring your own canoe or make arrangements with the local canoe livery. Visit Rochester and the Round Barn Museum, located in Fulton Country, with the most round barns in Indiana. For circus lovers, Rochester was the home of Clyde Beatty and the Cole Bros. Circus.

RV Sites		Water		Laundry	
Number	112	None		Wi-Fi	
Shaded	Y	At Site		Fishing	Y
By Water	Y	Spigots	Y	Hiking	Y
Paved		Sewer		Biking	Y
Pull Thru	Y	None		Swimming	
ADA	Y	At Site		Watch Wildlife	Y
Max RV Size	40	Dump Station	Y	Pets	Y
Electric		Amenities		Security	
None		Restrooms		Host(s)	Y
20 Amp	Y	Showers	Y	Rangers(s)	Y
30 Amp	Y	Reserve Sites	Y	Gate	Y
50 Amp	Y	Store		Patrolled	Y
		Grill/Table	Y		

[18] Potato Creek State Park
Hwy 31, South from South Bend
Southwest of South Bend
N41 32.096 W86 21.618
State Rate: $12-$29
(574) 656-8186
http://www.in.gov/dnr/parklake/2972.htm

Directions

11 miles. From the south side of South Bend at Hwys 20 & 41, go 6 miles south on Hwy 41 to Hwy 4, then 4.6 miles west to the Park.

Points of Interest

There is much to do in South Bend. Experience the legendary traditions of Notre Dame University. HealthWorks! Kids' Museum merges children's museums & health education. The Chocolate Museum houses a collection among the worlds largest. Experience transportation history at the Studebaker Museum.

RV Sites		Water		Laundry	
Number	287	None		Wi-Fi	
Shaded	Y	At Site		Fishing	Y
By Water	Y	Spigots	Y	Hiking	Y
Paved		Sewer		Biking	Y
Pull Thru	Y	None		Swimming	Y
ADA	Y	At Site		Watch Wildlife	Y
Max RV Size	45	Dump Station	Y	Pets	Y
Electric		Amenities		Security	
None		Restrooms	Y	Host(s)	Y
20 Amp	Y	Showers	Y	Rangers(s)	Y
30 Amp	Y	Reserve Sites	Y	Gate	
50 Amp		Store	Y	Patrolled	Y
		Grill/Table	Y		

About Iowa's Public Campgrounds

Learn about Iowa's State Parks at -

www.iowadnr.gov/Destinations/StateParksRecAreas/IowasStateParks.aspx

Reservations can be made 3 months ahead, 24 hours a day, 7 days a week & are accepted for 50% - 75% of the campsites online at -

http://iowastateparks.reserveamerica.com/

The Reservation Call Center, (877) 427-2757, will operate from 7:00 am - 7:00 pm (CDT), Monday - Friday; & 8:00 am - 4:00 pm Saturday - Sunday (CDT).

RV camp fees, during the peak season (May 1 to September 30) per night are:

Modern electric -	$16	**Entrance Fees -**	None
Modern, non-electric -	$11	**Off-Season Site Fee -**	Subtract $ 3
Non-modern, electric -	$14	**Water/sewer, all year -**	Add $ 3
Non-modern, non-electric -	$ 9		

(**Modern** - camping area which has showers and flush toilets. **Non-modern** - camping area in which no showers are provided, containing only pit-type latrines or flush toilets. Water may or may not be available to campers.)

It is in direct violation of the USDA APHIS quarantine for you to bring firewood from quarantined states into Iowa. You may bring your dog to the park as long as it is on a leash no more than 6 feet in length.

There is also an excellent Country Park System in Iowa, with over 40 parks with substantial campgrounds. Go to - **http://www.mycountyparks.com**

[1] Waubonsie State Park	[12] Sugar Bottom
[2] Wilson Island State Recreation Area	[13] West Lake County Park
[3] Lewis & Clark State Park	[14] Squaw Creek County Park
[4] Nine Eagles State Park	[15] Black Hawk County Park
[5] Lake Ahquabi State Park	[16] Viking Lake State Park
[6] Cherry Glen Campground	[17] Green Valley State Park
[7] Briggs Woods County Park	[18] Geode State Park
[8] Clear Lake State Park	[19] Black Hawk State Park
[9] Prairie Rose State Park	[20] Brushy Creek State Recreation Area
[10] Lake Anita State Park	[21] Backbone State Park
[11] Rock Creek State Park	

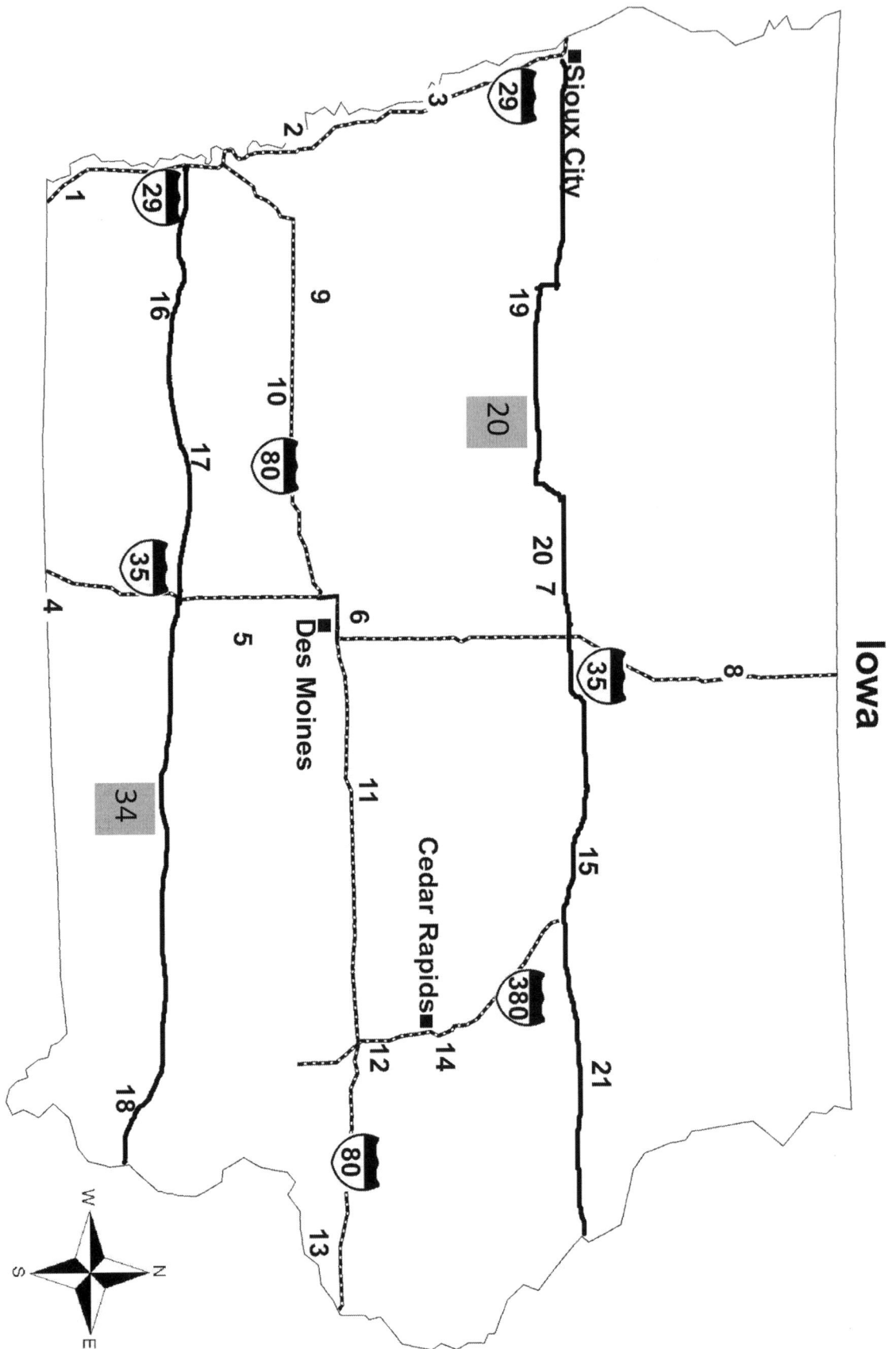

Iowa

Sioux City

Des Moines

Cedar Rapids

[1] Waubonsie State Park
I-29, Exit 10
Southeast of Percival
N40 40.845 W95 40.912
State Rate: $6-$16
(712) 382-2786
www.iowadnr.gov/Destinations/StatePark-sRecAreas/IowasStateParks.aspx

Directions

5.5 miles. From Exit 10 go 5.3 miles east on Hwy 2 to Hwy 239, turn right into the Park.

Points of Interest

The Park is in the "Loess Hills," a landform found only along the Missouri River & in China. Interpretive Trails provide visitors a chance to learn of the important plants & trees, as well as enjoy the views. Waubonsie State Park is a site on the national Lewis & Clark Historical Trail.

RV Sites		Water		Laundry	
Number	40	None		Wi-Fi	
Shaded	Y	At Site		Fishing	Y
By Water		Spigots	Y	Hiking	Y
Paved		**Sewer**		Biking	Y
Pull Thru	Y	None		Swimming	
ADA	Y	At Site		Watch Wildlife	Y
Max RV Size	45	Dump Station	Y	Pets	Y
Electric		**Amenities**		**Security**	
None		Restrooms	Y	Host(s)	Y
20 Amp	Y	Showers	Y	Rangers(s)	Y
30 Amp	Y	Reserve Sites	Y	Gate	
50 Amp	Y	Store		Patrolled	Y
		Grill/Table	Y		

[2] Wilson Island State Recreation Area
I-29, Exit 72
North of Council Bluffs
N41 29.503 W96 00.574
State Rate: $6-$16
(712) 642-2069
www.iowadnr.gov/Destinations/StatePark-sRecAreas/IowasStateParks.aspx

Directions

6 miles. From Exit 72 turn west and follow DeSoto Ave. for 6 miles to the Park.

Points of Interest

Quiet, shady and spacious campsites are some of the Park's assets. Just north is the Bertrand Museum (sunken paddleboat sternwheeler) and The DeSoto National Wildlife Refuge. Both are terrific places to visit. The sights of Council Bluffs and Omaha are close by.

RV Sites		Water		Laundry	
Number	135	None		Wi-Fi	
Shaded	Y	At Site		Fishing	Y
By Water	Y	Spigots	Y	Hiking	Y
Paved		**Sewer**		Biking	Y
Pull Thru	Y	None		Swimming	Y
ADA	Y	At Site		Watch Wildlife	Y
Max RV Size	45	Dump Station	Y	Pets	Y
Electric		**Amenities**		**Security**	
None		Restrooms	Y	Host(s)	Y
20 Amp	Y	Showers	Y	Rangers(s)	Y
30 Amp	Y	Reserve Sites	Y	Gate	
50 Amp		Store		Patrolled	Y
		Grill/Table	Y		

[3] Lewis & Clark State Park
I-29, Exit 112
North of Onawa
N42 01.597 W96 09.715
State Rate: $6-$16
(712) 423-2829
www.iowadnr.gov/Destinations/StateParksRecAreas/IowasStateParks.aspx

Directions

1.5 miles. From Exit 112 go 1.5 miles west on Hwy 175 to Hwy 324. Turn north in to the Park.

Points of Interest

Lewis and Clark State Park is perfect for a hike. You can view the full-sized reproduction of Lewis and Clark's keelboat/barge, "Best Friend." Blue Lake is great for a variety of water sports, the beach is a fine place for sunbathing, swimming or reading your book.

RV Sites		Water		Laundry	
Number	112	None		Wi-Fi	
Shaded	Y	At Site	Y	Fishing	Y
By Water	Y	Spigots	Y	Hiking	Y
Paved		**Sewer**		Biking	Y
Pull Thru	Y	None		Swimming	Y
ADA	Y	At Site	Y	Watch Wildlife	Y
Max RV Size	45	Dump Station	Y	Pets	Y
Electric		**Amenities**		**Security**	
None		Restrooms	Y	Host(s)	Y
20 Amp	Y	Showers	Y	Rangers(s)	Y
30 Amp	Y	Reserve Sites	Y	Gate	
50 Amp	Y	Store		Patrolled	
		Grill/Table	Y		

[4] Nine Eagles State Park
I-35, Exit 4
Southeast of Davis City
N40 35.298 W93 45.254
State Rate: $6-$16
(641) 442-2855
www.iowadnr.gov/Destinations/StatePark-
sRecAreas/IowasStateParks.aspx

Directions

10 miles. From Exit 4 go 3.9 miles east on
Hwy 69. Turn south on Cty Rd J66 for 5.6
miles to the Park entrance on the left.

Points of Interest

Wooded hills & valleys make this one of southern
Iowa's most scenic parks. Enjoy 9 miles of trails
meandering through wooded hills & valleys. The
beach offers swimming & is a great place for
swimmers and sunbathers. For local flavor La-
moni, Davis City, Pleasanton & Leon are close.

RV Sites		Water		Laundry	
Number	68	None		Wi-Fi	
Shaded	Y	At Site		Fishing	Y
By Water	Y	Spigots	Y	Hiking	Y
Paved		**Sewer**		Biking	Y
Pull Thru	Y	None		Swimming	Y
ADA	Y	At Site		Watch Wildlife	Y
Max RV Size	45	Dump Station	Y	Pets	Y
Electric		**Amenities**		**Security**	
None		Restrooms	Y	Host(s)	Y
20 Amp	Y	Showers	Y	Rangers(s)	Y
30 Amp	Y	Reserve Sites	Y	Gate	
50 Amp	Y	Store		Patrolled	Y
		Grill/Table	Y		

[5] Lake Ahquabi State Park
I-35, Exit 56
South of Des Moines
N41 17.743 W93 34.952
State Rate: $6-$16
(515) 961-7101
www.iowadnr.gov/Destinations/StatePark-
sRecAreas/IowasStateParks.aspx

Directions

20 miles. From Exit 56 go 13.3 mi. east on Hwy
92 to Indianola. Turn south on Hwy 65/69 for
5.1 mi. to the intersection where Hwy 65 turns
east. Turn west (right) for 1 mi. on Cty Rd. 58
to 118th Ave. Go north 0.6 mi. to the Park.

Points of Interest

In Indianola visit The National Balloon Museum.
The town square provides an array of unique
shops & restaurants. Dine in or patio, enjoy the
ambiance of the present day & not so distant past.

RV Sites		Water		Laundry	
Number	141	None		Wi-Fi	
Shaded	Y	At Site		Fishing	Y
By Water	Y	Spigots	Y	Hiking	
Paved		**Sewer**		Biking	Y
Pull Thru	Y	None		Swimming	Y
ADA	Y	At Site		Watch Wildlife	Y
Max RV Size	45	Dump Station	Y	Pets	Y
Electric		**Amenities**		**Security**	
None		Restrooms	Y	Host(s)	Y
20 Amp	Y	Showers	Y	Rangers(s)	
30 Amp	Y	Reserve Sites	Y	Gate	Y
50 Amp	Y	Store	Y	Patrolled	Y
		Grill/Table	Y		

[6] Cherry Glen Campground
I-35, Exit 90
North of Des Moines
N41 43.905 W93 40.792
COE Rate: $20-$24
America/Beautiful Rate: $10-$12
(515) 964-8792
www.recreation.gov/

Directions

7 miles. From Exit 90 turn west and follow
Hwy 160 (Oralabor Rd), which becomes Hwy
415, for 6.1 miles. Turn west (left) on 94th
Ave for 0.6 miles to the Park.

Points of Interest

Try the 24 mile paved Neal Smith Trail which runs
from Des Moines to Big Creek State Park, and
connects the campground to all recreation areas
on the east side of the lake. It is used for biking,
hiking, jogging, walking, & in-line skating.

RV Sites		Water		Laundry	
Number	125	None		Wi-Fi	
Shaded	Y	At Site	few	Fishing	Y
By Water	Y	Spigots	Y	Hiking	Y
Paved		**Sewer**		Biking	Y
Pull Thru		None		Swimming	Y
ADA	Y	At Site	Y	Watch Wildlife	Y
Max RV Size	45	Dump Station	Y	Pets	Y
Electric		**Amenities**		**Security**	
None		Restrooms	Y	Host(s)	Y
20 Amp	Y	Showers	Y	Rangers(s)	Y
30 Amp	Y	Reserve Sites	Y	Gate	
50 Amp	Y	Store		Patrolled	Y
		Grill/Table	Y		

[7] Briggs Woods County Park
I-35, Exit 142
South of Webster City
N42 25.917 W93 48.092
County Rate: $18-$24
(515) 832-9570
www.mycountyparks.com/

Directions

15.5 miles. From Exit 142 go 12.2 miles west on Hwy 20 to Hwy 17. Turn south 2.3 miles to Briggs Wood Trail. Turn left for 0.9 miles to the Park.

Points of Interest

The Park, located in the heart of some of the most fertile land in the world, has a 62 acre lake and 18 hole golf course, which is one of Iowa's most challenging golf courses. There are numerous multi-recreational trails, including one going to Webster City, a great bike outing.

RV Sites		Water		Laundry	
Number	81	None		Wi-Fi	Y
Shaded	Y	At Site	Y	Fishing	Y
By Water	Y	Spigots		Hiking	Y
Paved		**Sewer**		Biking	Y
Pull Thru	Y	None		Swimming	Y
ADA	Y	At Site	Y	Watch Wildlife	
Max RV Size	45	Dump Station		Pets	Y
Electric		**Amenities**		**Security**	
None		Restrooms	Y	Host(s)	Y
20 Amp	Y	Showers	Y	Rangers(s)	
30 Amp	Y	Reserve Sites	Y	Gate	Y
50 Amp	Y	Store		Patrolled	Y
		Grill/Table	Y		

[8] Clear Lake State Park
I-35, Exit 193
South side of Clear Lake
N43 06.657 W93 23.316
State Rate: $6-$19
(641) 357-4212
www.iowadnr.gov/Destinations/StateParksRecAreas/IowasStateParks.aspx

Directions

3 miles. From Exit 193 go 1 mile west on Hwy 106 (255 St.). Turn south on Hwy 107 (S. 8th St.) for 1.5 miles, then turn west on 27th Ave. for 0.5 mile. Turn left on S Shore Dr, then an immediate right to the Park entrance.

Points of Interest

One of the states most popular parks, Clear Lake's premier attraction is the Surf Ballroom, the site of Buddy Holly's last concert in 1959. The Ballroom still hosts a variety of musical acts.

RV Sites		Water		Laundry	
Number	200	None		Wi-Fi	
Shaded	Y	At Site	Y	Fishing	Y
By Water	Y	Spigots	Y	Hiking	Y
Paved		**Sewer**		Biking	Y
Pull Thru	Y	None		Swimming	Y
ADA	Y	At Site	Y	Watch Wildlife	Y
Max RV Size	45	Dump Station	Y	Pets	Y
Electric		**Amenities**		**Security**	
None		Restrooms	Y	Host(s)	Y
20 Amp	Y	Showers	Y	Rangers(s)	Y
30 Amp	Y	Reserve Sites	Y	Gate	
50 Amp	Y	Store		Patrolled	Y
		Grill/Table	Y		

[9] Prairie Rose State Park
I-80, Exit 46
North of Avoca
N41 36.004 W95 12.704
State Rate: $6-$19
(712) 773-2701
www.iowadnr.gov/Destinations/StateParksRecAreas/IowasStateParks.aspx

Directions

7.5 miles. From Exit 46 go 7.5 miles north on Cty Hwy M47 (York Rd.) to the Park entrance on your left.

Points of Interest

The terraced hillside provides wonderful views of the lake and the surrounding hills. An interpretive trail winds along the shoreline and provides opportunities to observe a variety of plants and wildlife. The Prairie Rose beach provides good swimming and sunbathing.

RV Sites		Water		Laundry	
Number	95	None		Wi-Fi	
Shaded	7	At Site	Y	Fishing	Y
By Water	Y	Spigots	Y	Hiking	Y
Paved		**Sewer**		Biking	
Pull Thru		None		Swimming	Y
ADA	Y	At Site	Y	Watch Wildlife	Y
Max RV Size	45	Dump Station	Y	Pets	Y
Electric		**Amenities**		**Security**	
None		Restrooms	Y	Host(s)	Y
20 Amp	Y	Showers	Y	Rangers(s)	Y
30 Amp	Y	Reserve Sites	Y	Gate	
50 Amp	Y	Store	Y	Patrolled	Y
		Grill/Table	Y		

[10] Lake Anita State Park
I-80, Exit 70
South of Anita
N41 25.962 W94 45.705
State Rate: $6-$19
(712) 762-3564
www.iowadnr.gov/Destinations/StatePark-sRecAreas/IowasStateParks.aspx

Directions

4.5 miles. From Exit 70 go south on Hwy 148 (through Anita) for 4.5 miles in total to the Park entrance on your right.

Points of Interest

The Park is one of the most popular recreation facilities in the region. Using the self-guided nature trail provides an opportunity to learn about many of the shrubs & trees found in southwest Iowa. Lake Anita also offers a 4-mile walking trail which winds around the entire lake.

RV Sites		Water		Laundry	
Number	144	None		Wi-Fi	
Shaded	Y	At Site	Y	Fishing	Y
By Water	Y	Spigots	Y	Hiking	Y
Paved		Sewer		Biking	Y
Pull Thru		None		Swimming	
ADA	Y	At Site	Y	Watch Wildlife	Y
Max RV Size	45	Dump Station	Y	Pets	Y
Electric		Amenities		Security	
None		Restrooms	Y	Host(s)	Y
20 Amp	Y	Showers	Y	Rangers(s)	Y
30 Amp	Y	Reserve Sites	Y	Gate	
50 Amp	Y	Store		Patrolled	Y
		Grill/Table	Y		

[11] Rock Creek State Park
I-80, Exit 173
Northeast of Kellogg
N41 45.635 W92 50.202
State Rate: $6-$16
(641) 236-3722
www.iowadnr.gov/Destinations/StatePark-sRecAreas/IowasStateParks.aspx

Directions

9 miles. From Exit 173 go north on Hwy 224 (through Kellogg) for 5.3 miles to Cty Rd. F27. Turn east for 3.5 miles, crossing over the lake, to the Park entrance on your right.

Points of Interest

The concentrations of teal, bluebills & mallards offer an excellent bird watching opportunity. Kellogg features the five-building Kellogg Museum, with a one-room schoolhouse, country church, factory/bank museum, and blacksmith shop.

RV Sites		Water		Laundry	
Number	200	None		Wi-Fi	
Shaded	Y	At Site		Fishing	Y
By Water	Y	Spigots	Y	Hiking	Y
Paved		Sewer		Biking	Y
Pull Thru	Y	None		Swimming	Y
ADA	Y	At Site	Y	Watch Wildlife	Y
Max RV Size	42	Dump Station	Y	Pets	Y
Electric		Amenities		Security	
None		Restrooms	Y	Host(s)	Y
20 Amp	Y	Showers	Y	Rangers(s)	Y
30 Amp	Y	Reserve Sites	Y	Gate	
50 Amp	Y	Store	Y	Patrolled	Y
		Grill/Table	Y		

[12] Sugar Bottom
I-80, Exit 239
North of Iowa City
N41 46.538 W91 33.519
COE Rate: $20-$26
America/Beautiful Rate: $10-$13
(319) 338-3543
http://www.recreation.gov/

Directions

9 miles. From Exit 239 turn north on I-380 for 4 miles to Exit 4. Go east 2.1 miles on Penn Street to Front St. Turn left, go 3 miles (Front becomes Mehaffey). Just after crossing Mehaffey Bridge, turn right into the Park.

Points of Interest

In Iowa City, Coralville, & North Liberty see the Antique Car Museum of Iowa, Herbert Hoover Presidential Museum, and Riverside Theater. There are also a number of vineyards & wineries.

RV Sites		Water		Laundry	
Number	233	None		Wi-Fi	
Shaded	Y	At Site	Y	Fishing	Y
By Water	Y	Spigots	Y	Hiking	Y
Paved		Sewer		Biking	Y
Pull Thru	Y	None		Swimming	Y
ADA	Y	At Site	Y	Watch Wildlife	Y
Max RV Size	45	Dump Station	Y	Pets	Y
Electric		Amenities		Security	
None		Restrooms	Y	Host(s)	Y
20 Amp	Y	Showers	Y	Rangers(s)	Y
30 Amp	Y	Reserve Sites	Y	Gate	
50 Amp	Y	Store		Patrolled	Y
		Grill/Table	Y		

115

[13] West Lake County Park
I-80, Exit 290
West of Davenport
N41 31.191 W90 41.286
County Rate: $18-$21
(563) 328-3281
http://www.mycountyparks.com

Directions

6 miles. From Exit 290 go 4 miles south on I-280 to Exit 4. Go west on 160th St. 0.6 miles to 110th Ave (Cty Rd Y48). Turn south 1.3 miles to the Park entrance on the left.

Points of Interest

Davenport offers theatre, symphony, riverboats, gaming, Mississippi Valley Blues Festival, Quad City Air Show, & world famous Bix Beiderbecke Memorial Jazz Festival. The Figge Art Institution holds a magnificent collection of paintings/prints by American Regionalist Grant Wood.

RV Sites		Water		Laundry	
Number	150	None		Wi-Fi	
Shaded	Y	At Site	Y	Fishing	Y
By Water	Y	Spigots	Y	Hiking	Y
Paved	Y	Sewer		Biking	Y
Pull Thru	Y	None		Swimming	Y
ADA	Y	At Site	Y	Watch Wildlife	
Max RV Size	42	Dump Station	Y	Pets	Y
Electric		Amenities		Security	
None		Restrooms		Host(s)	Y
20 Amp	Y	Showers	Y	Rangers(s)	
30 Amp	Y	Reserve Sites		Gate	
50 Amp	Y	Store		Patrolled	Y
		Grill/Table	Y		

[14] Squaw Creek County Park
I-380, Exit 24
East of Cedar Rapids
N42 01.210 W91 33.367
County Rate: $20-$30
(319) 377-5954
http://www.mycountyparks.com

Directions

6 miles. From Exit 24 go 6 miles east on Hwy 100. Just before you reach Hwy 13/151 turn right on Banner Dr. into the Park and Golf Course.

Points of Interest

In Cedar Rapids visit Brucemore. The Queen Anne-style mansion/estate has exhibits, music festivals, outdoor theatre, garden walks and holiday events. See the National Motorcycle Museum, Duffy's Collectible Cars Museum, & the Silos & Smokestacks National Heritage Area.

RV Sites		Water		Laundry	
Number	69	None		Wi-Fi	
Shaded	Y	At Site	Y	Fishing	Y
By Water	Y	Spigots	Y	Hiking	Y
Paved	Y	Sewer		Biking	Y
Pull Thru	Y	None		Swimming	
ADA	Y	At Site	Y	Watch Wildlife	Y
Max RV Size	45	Dump Station	Y	Pets	Y
Electric		Amenities		Security	
None		Restrooms	Y	Host(s)	Y
20 Amp	Y	Showers	Y	Rangers(s)	
30 Amp	Y	Reserve Sites	Y	Gate	
50 Amp	Y	Store		Patrolled	Y
		Grill/Table	Y		

[15] Black Hawk County Park
I-380, Exit 72
Northwest of Cedar Falls
N42 33.752 W92 28.655
County Rate: $20
(319) 433-7275
http://www.mycountyparks.com

Directions

12.5 miles. Follow I-380 as it ends at Exit 72 & becomes Hwy 218. Follow Hwy 218 for 9.7 miles (through Waterloo) to Exit 189. Turn west on Lone Tree Rd for 2.7 miles to the Park.

Points of Interest

Bike to Cedar Falls. Take time to visit Heritage Farm, a Percheron horse farm & enjoy a horse drawn wagon ride. See the Cedar Valley Arboretum & Botanical Gardens; Cedar Falls Raceway (1/4 mile drag strip with 350' concrete launch pads) & the Hearst Sculpture Gardens.

RV Sites		Water		Laundry	
Number	197	None		Wi-Fi	
Shaded	Y	At Site	Y	Fishing	Y
By Water	Y	Spigots	Y	Hiking	Y
Paved		Sewer		Biking	Y
Pull Thru	Y	None		Swimming	
ADA	Y	At Site	Y	Watch Wildlife	Y
Max RV Size	45	Dump Station	Y	Pets	Y
Electric		Amenities		Security	
None		Restrooms	Y	Host(s)	Y
20 Amp	Y	Showers	Y	Rangers(s)	
30 Amp	Y	Reserve Sites	Y	Gate	
50 Amp	Y	Store		Patrolled	Y
		Grill/Table	Y		

[16] Viking Lake State Park
Hwy 34, at Cty Rd M-65
East of Red Oak
N40 58.384 W95 02.732
State Rate: $6-$19
(712) 829-2235
www.iowadnr.gov/Destinations/StatePark-sRecAreas/IowasStateParks.aspx

Directions

11 miles. From Red Oak go 9.7 miles east on Hwy 34 to Cty Rd M-65. Turn south for 0.5 miles to Cty Rd H-43, turn east again for 0.8 mile to the Park.

Points of Interest

Stroll or drive Red Oak's historic Heritage Hill Tour. The tour embodies a wide range of architectural styles including excellent examples of Queen Anne, Georgian, Italianate, English Tudor, Colonial Revival, & Frank Lloyd Wright's Prairie Style.

RV Sites		Water		Laundry	
Number	120	None		Wi-Fi	
Shaded	Y	At Site	Y	Fishing	Y
By Water	Y	Spigots	Y	Hiking	Y
Paved		**Sewer**		Biking	Y
Pull Thru		None		Swimming	
ADA	Y	At Site	Y	Watch Wildlife	Y
Max RV Size	45	Dump Station	Y	Pets	Y
Electric		**Amenities**		**Security**	
None		Restrooms	Y	Host(s)	Y
20 Amp	Y	Showers	Y	Rangers(s)	Y
30 Amp	Y	Reserve Sites	Y	Gate	
50 Amp	Y	Store	Y	Patrolled	Y
		Grill/Table	Y		

[17] Green Valley State Park
Hwy 34, Lincoln St in Creston
North of Creston
N41 06.872 W94 22.740
State Rate: $6-$19
(641) 782-5131
www.iowadnr.gov/Destinations/StatePark-sRecAreas/IowasStateParks.aspx

Directions

3.5 miles. From Northwest Creston go north on Lincoln St for 3.0 miles to 130th St and turn left for 0.4 miles to the park.

Points of Interest

Green Valley is base camp for anglers trying their luck at four area lakes (Three Mile, Twelve Mile, Summit Lake and Green Valley Lake), all within 10 miles of each other. A 3 mile paved trail passes through Mitchell Marsh, and it's worth a stop to watch waterfowl & other wetland species of birds.

RV Sites		Water		Laundry	
Number	100	None		Wi-Fi	
Shaded	Y	At Site	Y	Fishing	Y
By Water	Y	Spigots	Y	Hiking	Y
Paved		**Sewer**		Biking	Y
Pull Thru	Y	None		Swimming	
ADA	Y	At Site	Y	Watch Wildlife	Y
Max RV Size	45	Dump Station	Y	Pets	Y
Electric		**Amenities**		**Security**	
None		Restrooms	Y	Host(s)	Y
20 Amp	Y	Showers	Y	Rangers(s)	Y
30 Amp	Y	Reserve Sites	Y	Gate	
50 Amp	Y	Store		Patrolled	Y
		Grill/Table	Y		

[18] Geode State Park
Hwy 34, From Middletown
Southwest of Danville
N40 48.953 W91 22.843
State Rate: $6-$16
(319) 392-4601
www.iowadnr.gov/Destinations/StatePark-sRecAreas/IowasStateParks.aspx

Directions

At Middletown, 3.8 miles southeast of Danville, take Cty Rd J-20/Hwy 79 west for 6.7 miles to the main entrance of the park.

Points of Interest

Geodes bring "rock hounds" to the Park and local area. Events in the area include Dragon Boat Races (May), Lake Geode Challenge Triathlon (July), Burlington Steamboat Days (June), West Point Sweet Corn Festival (August) & Old Thresher's Reunion in Mt. Pleasant (before Labor Day).

RV Sites		Water		Laundry	
Number	168	None		Wi-Fi	
Shaded	Y	At Site		Fishing	Y
By Water	Y	Spigots	Y	Hiking	Y
Paved		**Sewer**		Biking	Y
Pull Thru	Y	None		Swimming	Y
ADA	Y	At Site		Watch Wildlife	Y
Max RV Size	45	Dump Station	Y	Pets	Y
Electric		**Amenities**		**Security**	
None		Restrooms	Y	Host(s)	Y
20 Amp	Y	Showers	Y	Rangers(s)	Y
30 Amp	Y	Reserve Sites	Y	Gate	
50 Amp		Store		Patrolled	Y
		Grill/Table	Y		

[19] Black Hawk State Park
Hwy 20, Sac City
South of Sac City
N42 18.161 W95 02.921
State Rate: $6-$19
(712) 657-8712
www.iowadnr.gov/Destinations/StateParks-sRecAreas/IowasStateParks.aspx

Directions

11 miles. From Sac City go south on Cty Rd M54 for 8.2 miles to Hwy 71. Turn west for 2.1 miles to Madison St in Lake View. Turn south for 0.4 miles and go east 0.3 mile on 3rd St to Blossom St. Turn south to the Park entrance.

Points of Interest

The lake has no motor size restrictions & is a boating/fishing enthusiast's dream. The Stubb Stevenson Nature Trail offers a chance to learn about shrubs & trees in the park (20 marked sites).

RV Sites		Water		Laundry	
Number	128	None		Wi-Fi	
Shaded	Y	At Site	Ycc	Fishing	Y
By Water	Y	Spigots	Y	Hiking	Y
Paved		**Sewer**		Biking	Y
Pull Thru	Y	None		Swimming	
ADA	Y	At Site		Watch Wildlife	Y
Max RV Size	45	Dump Station	Y	Pets	Y
Electric		**Amenities**		**Security**	
None		Restrooms	Y	Host(s)	Y
20 Amp	Y	Showers	Y	Rangers(s)	Y
30 Amp	Y	Reserve Sites	Y	Gate	
50 Amp	Y	Store		Patrolled	Y
		Grill/Table	Y		

[20] Brushy Creek State Recreation Area
Hwy 20, at Duncombe
South of Ft. Dodge
N42 23.816 W93 59.766
State Rate: $11-$19
(515) 543-8298
www.iowadnr.gov/Destinations/StateParks-sRecAreas/IowasStateParks.aspx

Directions

4 miles. From Hwy 20 go 3.3 miles south on Cty Rd P73 (Union Ave). For the West Entrance go 0.8 miles east on Lake View Dr (270th).

Points of Interest

There is a specific non-equestrian campground. Equestrian users can enjoy a modern camp facility. Fishing & the shooting range are popular. With 45 miles of multi-use trails, there are activities for horseback riding, hiking, snowmobiling, cross country skiing, & mountain biking.

RV Sites		Water		Laundry	
Number	234	None		Wi-Fi	
Shaded	Y	At Site	Y	Fishing	y
By Water	Y	Spigots	Y	Hiking	y
Paved	some	**Sewer**		Biking	y
Pull Thru	Y	None		Swimming	y
ADA	Y	At Site	Y	Watch Wildlife	y
Max RV Size	45	Dump Station	Y	Pets	Y
Electric		**Amenities**		**Security**	
None		Restrooms	Y	Host(s)	Y
20 Amp	Y	Showers	Y	Rangers(s)	Y
30 Amp	Y	Reserve Sites	Y	Gate	
50 Amp	Y	Store		Patrolled	Y
		Grill/Table	Y		

[21] Backbone State Park
Hwy 20, at Hwy 13, Exit 275
North of Manchester
N42 36.044 W91 31.961
State Rate: $6-$19
(563) 924-2000
www.iowadnr.gov/Destinations/StateParks-sRecAreas/IowasStateParks.aspx

Directions

15.5 miles. Take Hwy 13 for 8.6 miles north to 150th St. Turn left, go 4.3 miles into Dundee to Cty Rd W69 (Center St). Turn north 2.5 miles to the Park.

Points of Interest

Climbers and rappellers will find many challenging cliffs. Bicyclists can pedal through scenic splendor; or do the Northeast State Park Bike Route. Lake activities abound. Backbone also has 21 miles of hiking and multi-use trails.

RV Sites		Water		Laundry	
Number	125	None		Wi-Fi	
Shaded	Y	At Site		Fishing	Y
By Water	Y	Spigots	Y	Hiking	Y
Paved		**Sewer**		Biking	
Pull Thru	Y	None		Swimming	Y
ADA	Y	At Site		Watch Wildlife	Y
Max RV Size	45	Dump Station	Y	Pets	Y
Electric		**Amenities**		**Security**	
None		Restrooms	Y	Host(s)	Y
20 Amp	Y	Showers	Y	Rangers(s)	Y
30 Amp	Y	Reserve Sites	Y	Gate	
50 Amp	Y	Store	Y	Patrolled	Y
		Grill/Table	Y		

About Kansas's Public Campgrounds

The Kansas Department of Wildlife and Parks manages 24 state parks. You will find information and a helpful brochure at -

http://kdwpt.state.ks.us/State-Parks

Many parks host annual events such as concerts, festivals, and competitions. The Parks are pet friendly but pets must be restrained by a leash no longer than 10 feet. Reservation can be made online. In most parks about half of the sites can be reserved. The rest will be available on a first-come, first-served basis. To made a reservation go to -

http://www.reserveamerica.com/

Camping Fees. A camping permit is required in addition to the motor vehicle permit for overnight stays. All daily camping permits expire at 2:00 p.m. Prime site fee applies to designated sites from April 1 - September 30. In addition to the fees below, there is a $3.00 per stay transaction fee for all overnight stays.

Daily Camping	$ 7.00 - $8.00
Prime Site Fee	$ 2.00
One Utility (year round, in addition to camping fee)	$ 7.50
Two Utilities (year round, in addition to camping fee)	$ 9.50
Three Utilities (year round, in addition to camping fee)	$10.50

The Corps of Engineers provides a number of good campgrounds as well and a number are listed here.

[1] El Dorado State Park	[8] Clinton State Park
[2] Riverside East - John Redmond Reservoir	[9] Cheney State Park - West
	[10] Hillsboro Cove
[3] Eisenhower State Park	[11] Venango Campground
[4] Hillsdale State Park	[12] Elk City State Park
[5] Cedar Bluff State Park - Bluffton	[13] Cross Timbers State Park
[6] Wilson Lake - Lucas Camp	[14] Glen Elder State Park
[7] West Rolling Hills	[15] Lovewell State Park

NOTES:

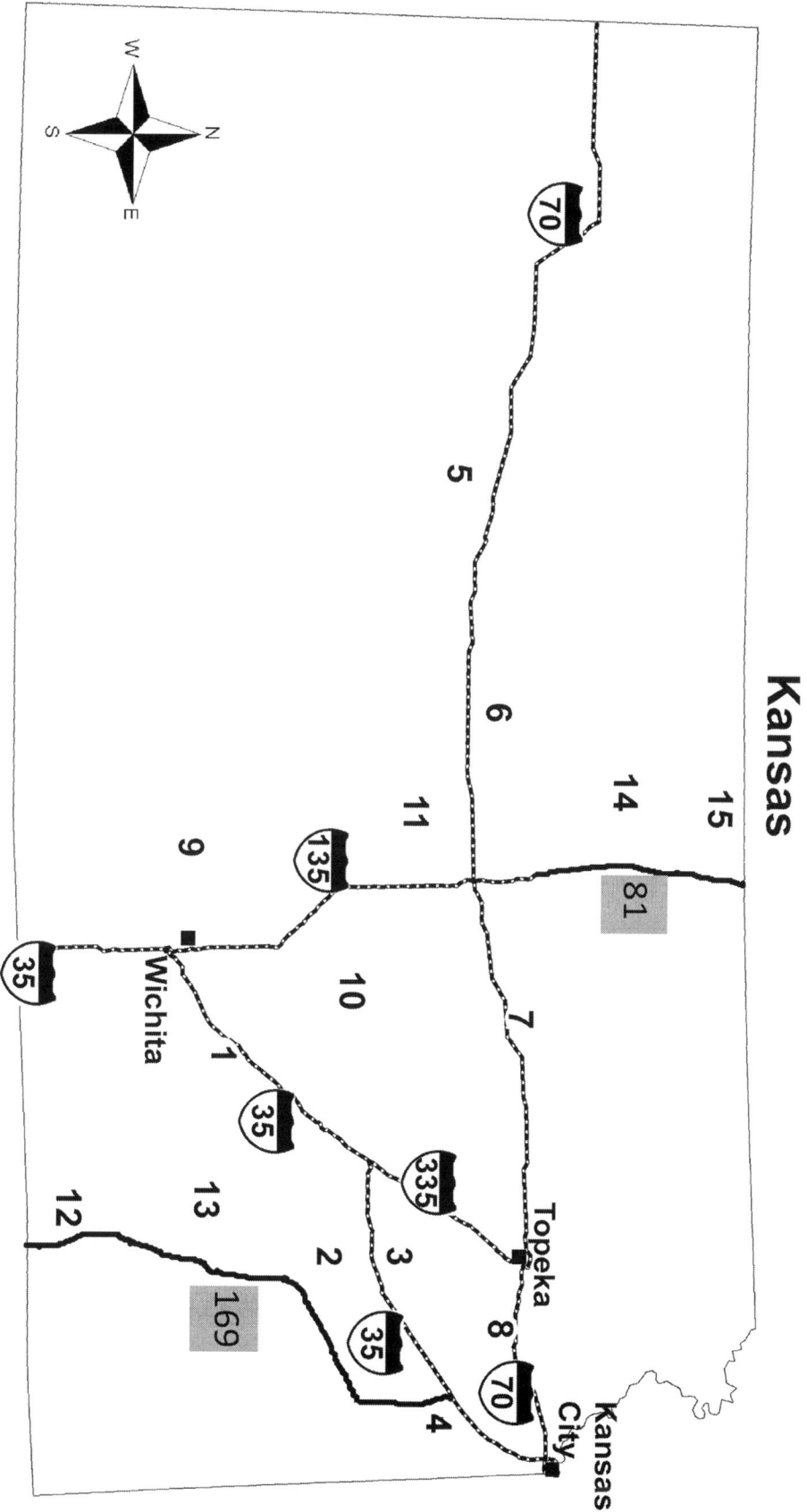

Kansas

[1] El Dorado State Park
I-35, Exit 71
East of El Dorado
N37 49.981 W96 47.136
State Rate: $15-$30
(316) 321-7180
http://kdwpt.state.ks.us/news/State-Parks/
Locations/El-Dorado

Directions

8 miles. From Exit 71 turn east for 6.1 miles on Hwy 54/254 to Bluestem Rd. Turn north for 1.7 miles to Shady Creek Access Rd and the park entrance on your right.

Points of Interest

El Dorado provides an opportunity to relive the Kansas oil boom at the Butler County History Center & Kansas Oil Museum. Local history is captured in works at the Coutts Memorial Museum of Art. There are fine art galleries, upscale shops.

RV Sites		Water		Laundry	Y
Number	471	None		Wi-Fi	
Shaded	Y	At Site	Y	Fishing	Y
By Water	Y	Spigots	Y	Hiking	Y
Paved		Sewer		Biking	Y
Pull Thru	Y	None		Swimming	Y
ADA	5	At Site	Y	Watch Wildlife	Y
Max RV Size	45	Dump Station	Y	Pets	Y
Electric		Amenities		Security	
None		Restrooms	Y	Host(s)	Y
20 Amp	Y	Showers	Y	Rangers(s)	Y
30 Amp	Y	Reserve Sites	Y	Gate	
50 Amp	Y	Store	Y	Patrolled	Y
		Grill/Table	Y		

[2] Riverside East - John Redmond Reservoir
I-35, Exit 155
North of Burlington
N38 14.978 W95 45.227
COE: $15
America/Beautiful Rate: $8
(620) 364-8613
http://www.recreation.gov/

Directions

13 miles. From Exit 155 turn south for 11.8 miles on Hwy 75 to New Strawn. Turn west on 16th (Lake St.) for 0.3 miles to Embankment Rd. Bear left, go 1 mile to the campground.

Points of Interest

The spillway is a popular fishing areas & there is a two-mile hiking trail, providing numerous year around wildlife observation & photography opportunities. Burlington main street is 3 miles south.

RV Sites		Water		Laundry	
Number	43	None		Wi-Fi	
Shaded	Y	At Site	Y	Fishing	Y
By Water	Y	Spigots	Y	Hiking	Y
Paved		Sewer		Biking	Y
Pull Thru	Y	None		Swimming	
ADA	Y	At Site	Y	Watch Wildlife	Y
Max RV Size	45	Dump Station	Y	Pets	Y
Electric		Amenities		Security	
None		Restrooms	Y	Host(s)	Y
20 Amp	Y	Showers	Y	Rangers(s)	Y
30 Amp	Y	Reserve Sites	Y	Gate	
50 Amp		Store		Patrolled	Y
		Grill/Table	Y		

[3] Eisenhower State Park
I-35, Exit 155
Northeast of Emporia
N38 32.140 W95 44.846
State Rate: $15-$30
(785) 528-4102
http://kdwpt.state.ks.us/news/State-Parks/Locations/Eisenhower

Directions

11 miles. From Exit 155 turn north for 8.2 miles on Hwy 75 to Hwy 278. Go west for 3 miles to the Park entrance on your left.

Points of Interest

Go to Ike's General Store in Doud Campground to pay campground fees. Emporia is notable for structures on the National Register of Historic Places such as the Old Emporia Public Library, Finney (Warren Wesley) House, & the Granada Theater (known as the Fox Theater).

RV Sites		Water		Laundry	Y
Number	186	None		Wi-Fi	Y
Shaded	Y	At Site	Y	Fishing	Y
By Water	Y	Spigots	Y	Hiking	Y
Paved		Sewer		Biking	Y
Pull Thru	Y	None		Swimming	Y
ADA	Y	At Site	Y	Watch Wildlife	Y
Max RV Size	45	Dump Station	Y	Pets	Y
Electric		Amenities		Security	
None		Restrooms	Y	Host(s)	Y
20 Amp	Y	Showers	Y	Rangers(s)	Y
30 Amp	Y	Reserve Sites	Y	Gate	
50 Amp	Y	Store	Y	Patrolled	Y
		Grill/Table	Y		

[4] Hillsdale State Park
I-35, Exit 207
Southwest of Olathe
N38 39.889 W94 53.250
State Rate: $15-$30
(913) 783-4507
http://kdwpt.state.ks.us/news/State-Parks/
Locations/Hillsdale

Directions

10 miles. From Exit 207 turn south for 9.7 miles on Gardener Rd, which becomes Tontzville Rd, crosses the lake, then becomes Harmony Rd, to 255th St (Lake Rd). Go right for 0.3 miles to the Park entrance

Points of Interest

See the John Brown Museum in Osawatomie, a stop on the Underground Railroad. In Olathe visit the Mahaffie Stagecoach Stop and Farm, Ernie Miller Park and Nature Center, or Heritage Park.

RV Sites		Water		Laundry	Y
Number	181	None		Wi-Fi	
Shaded	Y	At Site	Y	Fishing	Y
By Water	Y	Spigots	Y	Hiking	Y
Paved		Sewer		Biking	Y
Pull Thru	Y	None		Swimming	Y
ADA	Y	At Site		Watch Wildlife	
Max RV Size	45	Dump Station	Y	Pets	Y
Electric		Amenities		Security	
None		Restrooms	Y	Host(s)	Y
20 Amp	Y	Showers	Y	Rangers(s)	Y
30 Amp	Y	Reserve Sites	Y	Gate	
50 Amp	Y	Store		Patrolled	Y
		Grill/Table	Y		

[5] Cedar Bluff State Park - Bluffton
I-70, Exit 135
South of Wakeney
N38 48.761 W99 43.593
State Rate: $15-$30
(785) 726-3212
http://kdwp.state.ks.us/news/State-Parks/Locations/Cedar-Bluff

Directions

13 miles. From Exit 135 turn south for 13 miles on Hwy 147 to the park entrance on your right.

Points of Interest

Threshing Machine Canyon, site of an 1850s Indian attack on a wagon train bearing a threshing machine, is west of the park. In the historic canyon, you find carvings dating to the mid 1800s. For a stunning view, drive to the top of the 150-foot tall, cedar covered limestone bluffs.

RV Sites		Water		Laundry	
Number	126	None		Wi-Fi	Y
Shaded	Y	At Site	Y	Fishing	Y
By Water	Y	Spigots	Y	Hiking	Y
Paved		Sewer		Biking	Y
Pull Thru	Y	None		Swimming	Y
ADA	Y	At Site	Y	Watch Wildlife	Y
Max RV Size	Y	Dump Station	Y	Pets	Y
Electric		Amenities		Security	
None		Restrooms	Y	Host(s)	Y
20 Amp	Y	Showers	Y	Rangers(s)	Y
30 Amp	Y	Reserve Sites	Y	Gate	
50 Amp	Y	Store		Patrolled	Y
		Grill/Table	Y		

[6] Wilson Lake - Lucas Camp
I-70, Exit 206
North of Wilson
N38 58.159 W98 30.174
COE: $8-$18
America/Beautiful Rate: $4-$9
(785) 658-2551
http://www.recreation.gov/

Directions

9 miles. From Exit 206 turn north for 8 miles on Hwy 232 to Hwy 181. Turn west for 1 mile to the campground on the right.

Points of Interest

The Wilson Lake area has 3 other excellent campgrounds as well. You will pass Wilson State Park and Sylvan (COE) on the way to Lucas. From Wilson State Park you can drive west to Minooka (COE). The three provide over 200 additional sites and can accommodate large RVs.

RV Sites		Water		Laundry	
Number	94	None		Wi-Fi	
Shaded	Y	At Site	Y	Fishing	Y
By Water	Y	Spigots	Y	Hiking	Y
Paved		Sewer		Biking	Y
Pull Thru	Y	None		Swimming	Y
ADA	Y	At Site	Y	Watch Wildlife	Y
Max RV Size	Y	Dump Station	Y	Pets	Y
Electric		Amenities		Security	
None		Restrooms	Y	Host(s)	Y
20 Amp	Y	Showers	Y	Rangers(s)	Y
30 Amp	Y	Reserve Sites	Y	Gate	
50 Amp	Y	Store		Patrolled	Y
		Grill/Table	Y		

[7] West Rolling Hills
I-70, Exit 290
Northwest of Junction City
N39 03.582 W96 56.347
COE: $12-$19
America/Beautiful Rate: $6-$9
(785) 238-5714
http://www.recreation.gov/

Directions

5 miles. From Exit 290 turn north on Milford Lake Rd for 4.3 miles to Hwy 244. Turn east for 0.3 mile to the campground on the left.

Points of Interest

The Milford Lake area has 3 other excellent campgrounds within 5 miles of Rolling Hills - Milford State Park, Curtis Creek & Farnum Creek (both COE). See the U. S. Calvary Museum, Custer House, and 1st Infantry Division Museum in Fort Riley's historic main post district.

RV Sites		Water		Laundry	
Number	44	None		Wi-Fi	
Shaded	Y	At Site	Y	Fishing	Y
By Water	Y	Spigots	Y	Hiking	Y
Paved		**Sewer**		Biking	Y
Pull Thru	Y	None		Swimming	Y
ADA	Y	At Site		Watch Wildlife	Y
Max RV Size	45	Dump Station	Y	Pets	Y
Electric		**Amenities**		**Security**	
None		Restrooms	Y	Host(s)	Y
20 Amp	Y	Showers	Y	Rangers(s)	Y
30 Amp	Y	Reserve Sites	Y	Gate	
50 Amp	Y	Store		Patrolled	Y
		Grill/Table	Y		

[8] Clinton State Park
I-70, Exit 197 of I-70 Kansas Turnpike
Southwest of Lawrence
N38 56.496 W95 21.224
State Rate: $15-$30
(785) 842-8562
http://kdwpt.state.ks.us/State-Parks/Locations/Clinton

Directions

5 miles. From Exit 197 turn south on Hwy 10 for 4 miles to 2nd exit (N 1400 Rd). Turn right, then right again at E 900th Rd. Turn left at N 1415 Rd, go 1 mile to the Park entrance.

Points of Interest

Lawrence claims one of the most beautiful downtowns. Do the 'Gallery Walk.' See the Battle of Black Jack Battlefield. Visit Atchison, birthplace of Amelia Earhart. Her grandparents' Victorian home (where Earhart was born) is a museum.

RV Sites		Water		Laundry	Y
Number	240	None		Wi-Fi	
Shaded	Y	At Site	Y	Fishing	Y
By Water	Y	Spigots	Y	Hiking	Y
Paved		**Sewer**		Biking	Y
Pull Thru	Y	None		Swimming	Y
ADA	Y	At Site	Y	Watch Wildlife	Y
Max RV Size	45	Dump Station	Y	Pets	Y
Electric		**Amenities**		**Security**	
None		Restrooms	Y	Host(s)	Y
20 Amp	Y	Showers	Y	Rangers(s)	Y
30 Amp	Y	Reserve Sites	Y	Gate	
50 Amp	Y	Store	Y	Patrolled	Y
		Grill/Table	Y		

[9] Cheney State Park - West
I-135, Exit 6 or I-235, Exit 7
West of Wichita
N37 43.139 W97 50.070
State Rate: $15-$30
(316) 542-3664
http://kdwpt.state.ks.us/index.php/State-Parks/Locations/Cheney

Directions

26 or 31 miles. From Exit 6 of I-135 turn west for 26 miles or 21 miles from Exit 7 of I-235 on Hwy 400 to Hwy 251. Go north 3.4 miles to 21st, turn west for 2.5 miles to the park.

Points of Interest

The Park contains one of the top U. S. sailing lakes. A marina on the East Shore offers supplies & services for boaters/anglers. The Wildlife Area adjacent to the park provides a variety of wildlife watching & nature photography.

RV Sites		Water		Laundry	
Number	223	None		Wi-Fi	
Shaded	Y	At Site	Y	Fishing	Y
By Water	Y	Spigots	Y	Hiking	Y
Paved	Y	**Sewer**		Biking	Y
Pull Thru	Y	None		Swimming	Y
ADA	Y	At Site	Y	Watch Wildlife	Y
Max RV Size	45	Dump Station	Y	Pets	Y
Electric		**Amenities**		**Security**	
None		Restrooms	Y	Host(s)	Y
20 Amp	Y	Showers	Y	Rangers(s)	Y
30 Amp	Y	Reserve Sites	Y	Gate	
50 Amp	Y	Store	Y	Patrolled	Y
		Grill/Table	Y		

[10] Hillsboro Cove
I-135, Exit 60
East of McPherson
N38 21.757 W97 06.453
COE: $17-$23
America/Beautiful Rate: $9-$12
(620) 382-2101
http://www.recreation.gov/

Directions

28 miles. From Exit 60 turn east on Hwy 56 for 27.7 miles. Turn left on Nighthawk Rd, then right on 200th for 0.3 miles to the campground.

Points of Interest

The nearby communities of Hillsboro & Marion offer many opportunities for visitors, with festivals, art & craft events scheduled throughout the year. The shopping and dining choices in the towns, as well as a welcoming atmosphere will give you a small town's comfort and feel.

RV Sites		Water		Laundry	
Number	52	None		Wi-Fi	
Shaded	Y	At Site	Y	Fishing	Y
By Water	Y	Spigots	Y	Hiking	Y
Paved		Sewer		Biking	Y
Pull Thru	Y	None		Swimming	Y
ADA	Y	At Site		Watch Wildlife	Y
Max RV Size	45	Dump Station	Y	Pets	Y
Electric		Amenities		Security	
None		Restrooms	Y	Host(s)	Y
20 Amp	Y	Showers	Y	Rangers(s)	Y
30 Amp	Y	Reserve Sites	Y	Gate	
50 Amp		Store		Patrolled	Y
		Grill/Table	Y		

[11] Venango Campground
I-135, Exit 78
Southwest of Salina
N38 38.009 W97 59.270
COE: $12-$36
America/Beautiful Rate: $6-$18
(785) 546-2294
http://www.recreation.gov/

Directions

27 miles. From Exit 78 turn southwest on Hwy 81 Bus for 4.5 miles to Lindsborg. Continue west on Hwy 4 for 16.1 miles to Hwy 141. Turn north for 5.2 miles to Venango Rd. Turn left, go 0.6 miles to the campground.

Points of Interest

Visit the Eisenhower Presidential Library and Museum in Abilene. The Coronado-Quivira Museum in Lyons focuses on Spanish explorers, and the Santa Fe Trail.

RV Sites		Water		Laundry	
Number	141	None		Wi-Fi	
Shaded	Y	At Site	Y	Fishing	Y
By Water	Y	Spigots	Y	Hiking	Y
Paved		Sewer		Biking	Y
Pull Thru	Y	None		Swimming	Y
ADA	Y	At Site	Y	Watch Wildlife	Y
Max RV Size	45	Dump Station	Y	Pets	Y
Electric		Amenities		Security	
None		Restrooms	Y	Host(s)	Y
20 Amp	Y	Showers	Y	Rangers(s)	Y
30 Amp	Y	Reserve Sites	Y	Gate	Y
50 Amp	Y	Store		Patrolled	Y
		Grill/Table	Y		

[12] Elk City State Park
Hwy 169, at Hwy 160
West of Independence
N37 15.582 W95 46.080
State Rate: $15-$30
(620) 331-6295
http://kdwpt.state.ks.us/news/State-Parks/Locations/Elk-City

Directions

12 miles. From Hwy 169 at Hwy 160 go west for 8.5 miles through Independence to "Peter Pan Road" (CR 3525). Turn north for 2 miles to CR 4800. Turn west for 1.5 miles to the park.

Points of Interest

A nationally-recognized trails system invites you to take a closer look at the rich flora & fauna in Elk City State Park. Elk City Reservoir offers good to excellent fishing opportunities for channel catfish, flathead catfish, white bass and crappie.

RV Sites		Water		Laundry	Y
Number	150	None		Wi-Fi	Y
Shaded	Y	At Site	Y	Fishing	Y
By Water	Y	Spigots	Y	Hiking	Y
Paved		Sewer		Biking	Y
Pull Thru	Y	None		Swimming	Y
ADA	Y	At Site	Y	Watch Wildlife	Y
Max RV Size	45	Dump Station	Y	Pets	Y
Electric		Amenities		Security	
None		Restrooms	Y	Host(s)	Y
20 Amp	Y	Showers	Y	Rangers(s)	Y
30 Amp	Y	Reserve Sites	Y	Gate	
50 Amp	Y	Store		Patrolled	Y
		Grill/Table	Y		

[13] Cross Timbers State Park
West of Yates Center
Hwy 54, West of Hwy 169
N37 46.651 W95 56.588
State Rate: $15-$30
(620) 637-2213
http://kdwpt.state.ks.us/news/State-Parks/
Locations/Cross-Timbers

Directions

17 miles. From Yates Center go 12.8 miles west to Hwy 105. Turn south & east for 3 miles in all to S. Point Rd. Go south again 1.5 miles to the Park.

Points of Interest

The forested flood plains, surrounded by terraces of prairie & hills of oak savannah, provide you an opportunity to immerse yourself in some of the most diverse flora & fauna in Kansas. This was a favored hunting & camping ground of Native Americans of the Osage Nation.

RV Sites		Water		Laundry	
Number	77	None		Wi-Fi	
Shaded	Y	At Site	Y	Fishing	Y
By Water	Y	Spigots	Y	Hiking	Y
Paved		Sewer		Biking	Y
Pull Thru	Y	None		Swimming	
ADA	Y	At Site	Y	Watch Wildlife	Y
Max RV Size	45	Dump Station	Y	Pets	Y
Electric		Amenities		Security	
None		Restrooms	Y	Host(s)	Y
20 Amp	Y	Showers	Y	Rangers(s)	Y
30 Amp	Y	Reserve Sites	Y	Gate	
50 Amp	Y	Store		Patrolled	Y
		Grill/Table	Y		

[14] Glen Elder State Park
Hwy 81, at Hwy 24
West of Glen Elder
N39 30.953 W98 20.348
State Rate: $15-$30
(785) 545-3345
http://kdwpt.state.ks.us/State-Parks/Locations/Glen-Elder

Directions

39 miles. At the Hwy 81/24 junction go west through Beloit and Glen Elder on Hwy 24 to the Park.

Points of Interest

On the shores of Waconda Lake near the Park, Cawker City offers some of the finest hunting, fishing, camping and boating in the state. Try out the nine hole artificial green golf course with a second nine holes as well. And don't miss the World's Largest Ball of Twine.

RV Sites		Water		Laundry	
Number	120	None		Wi-Fi	
Shaded	Y	At Site	Y	Fishing	Y
By Water	Y	Spigots	Y	Hiking	Y
Paved		Sewer		Biking	Y
Pull Thru	Y	None		Swimming	Y
ADA	Y	At Site	Y	Watch Wildlife	Y
Max RV Size	45	Dump Station	Y	Pets	Y
Electric		Amenities		Security	
None		Restrooms	Y	Host(s)	Y
20 Amp	Y	Showers	Y	Rangers(s)	Y
30 Amp	Y	Reserve Sites	Y	Gate	
50 Amp	Y	Store		Patrolled	Y
		Grill/Table	Y		

[15] Lovewell State Park
Hwy 81, at Hwy 36
Northwest of Scandia
N39 54.844 W98 02.581
State Rate: $15-$30
(785) 753-4971
http://kdwpt.state.ks.us/State-Parks/Locations/
Lovewell

Directions

50 miles. Go 36 miles west of Hwy 81 on Hwy 36, then 9 miles north on Hwy 14. Turn east at Y Road. Travel 4 miles and turn south at 4-way stop. Park entrance is 0.5 mile south.

Points of Interest

A haven for outdoor lovers who look for variety in their vacations, Lovewell offers a blend of camping, fishing, wildlife watching, & events. An historic limestone schoolhouse hosts summer church services. A restaurant & groceries are available.

RV Sites		Water		Laundry	
Number	157	None		Wi-Fi	
Shaded	Y	At Site	Y	Fishing	Y
By Water	Y	Spigots	Y	Hiking	Y
Paved		Sewer		Biking	Y
Pull Thru	Y	None		Swimming	Y
ADA	Y	At Site	Y	Watch Wildlife	Y
Max RV Size	45	Dump Station	Y	Pets	Y
Electric		Amenities		Security	
None		Restrooms	Y	Host(s)	Y
20 Amp	Y	Showers	Y	Rangers(s)	Y
30 Amp	Y	Reserve Sites	Y	Gate	
50 Amp	Y	Store	Y	Patrolled	Y
		Grill/Table	Y		

About Kentucky's Public Campgrounds

Wherever you travel in Kentucky, you are never far from one of the 49 Kentucky State Parks. Thirty-two of the Parks offer nearly 3,000 improved camp sites. Find them at -

http://parks.ky.gov/

Kentucky State Parks offer nearly 300 miles of trails suitable for all levels of enjoyment. The state parks oversee 15 marinas that offer pontoon and fishing boat rentals. All 17 resort parks have themed restaurants that serve both regional and specialty dishes. With 19 State Park golf courses, there is sure to be something for everyone. Several parks are equipped with seasonal riding stables. The parks operate more than two dozen swimming pools and 11 lake beaches. Leashed pets are allowed in park campgrounds and on many trails.

You can reserve a Kentucky State Parks campsite up to a year in advance with a credit card. Reservations are allowed for stays of up to two weeks. There is no Park general admission fee. There is a Senior Discount of 10 percent on lodging and camping fees with proof of age for those 62 and older. Get reservations at -

http://kentuckystateparks.reserveamerica.com/

There is an online reservation fee (around $8) and a Holiday Premium fee ($2-$8). Firewood brought in from out-of-state is prohibited unless it is bundled, stamped USDA certified clean wood.

[1] Kentucky Dam Village State Resort Park	**[8] Mammoth Cave Headquarters Campground**
[2] Hurricane Creek	**[9] General Butler State Resort**
[3] Taylorsville Lake Park	**[10] Big Bone Lick State Park**
[4] Kentucky Horse Resort Campground	**[11] Grove Recreation Area**
[5] Twin Knobs	**[12] Baileys Point**
[6] Grayson Lake State Park	**[13] Kendall Campground**
[7] Tailwater - Barren River Lake	**[14] Levi Jackson State Park**
	[15] Jenny Wiley State Resort Park

NOTES:

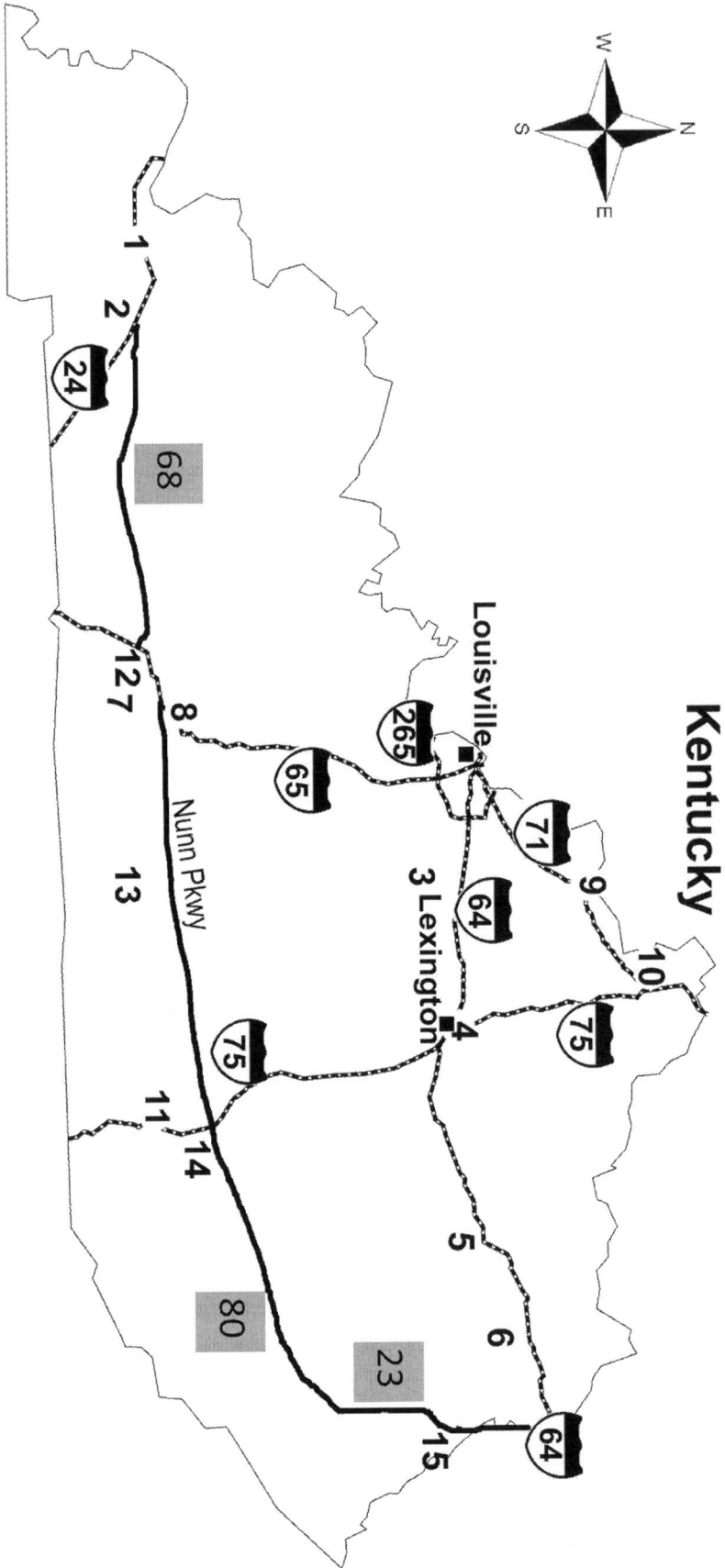

Kentucky

Louisville

Lexington

Nunn Pkwy

[1] Kentucky Dam Village State Resort Park
I-24, Exit 27
East of Paducah
N37 00.733 W88 16.903
State Rate: $22, Senior Discount
(270) 362-4271
parks.ky.gov/parks/resortparks/ky-dam-village/

Directions

3 miles. From Exit 27 turn east for 2 miles on Hwy 62. Exit north (left) on Hwy 282 (Gilbertsville Hwy) for 0.7 miles to the camp registration.

Points of Interest:

This is one of Kentucky's most popular resort campgrounds. The Village Inn Lodge and Harbor Lights Restaurant provide a nice view of the Tennessee River and the marina. In Paducah visit the Lowertown Arts District, National Quilt Museum, and the River Discovery Center.

RV Sites		Water		Laundry	
Number	205	None		Wi-Fi	
Shaded	Y	At Site	Y	Fishing	Y
By Water		Spigots		Hiking	Y
Paved	Y	Sewer		Biking	Y
Pull Thru		None		Swimming	Y
ADA	Y	At Site		Watch Wildlife	
Max RV Size	45	Dump Station	Y	Pets	Y
Electric		Amenities		Security	
None		Restrooms	Y	Host(s)	Y
20 Amp	Y	Showers	Y	Rangers(s)	Y
30 Amp	Y	Reserve Sites	Y	Gate	
50 Amp	Y	Store	Y	Patrolled	Y
		Grill/Table	Y		

[2] Hurricane Creek
I-24, Exit 56
South of Eddyville
N36 55.212 W87 58.502
COE Rate: $16-$22
America/Beautiful Rate: $8-$11
(270) 522-8821
http://www.reserveamerica.com/

Directions

8 miles. From Exit 56 turn south for 1.2 miles on Hwy 139 to Hwy 276 (Hurricane Rd.). Turn west (right) for 6 miles to Hwy 274. Turn right, go 0.5 miles to Hurricane Camp Rd and the campground on the left.

Points of Interest

You are close to 'Land Between the Lakes National Recreation Area,' which offers hunting, fishing, horseback riding, plus motorcycle/ATV trails. 'Patti's 1880's Settlement' is a unique destination.

RV Sites		Water		Laundry	Y
Number	45	None		Wi-Fi	
Shaded	Y	At Site	Y	Fishing	Y
By Water	Y	Spigots		Hiking	Y
Paved		Sewer		Biking	Y
Pull Thru	Y	None		Swimming	Y
ADA	Y	At Site		Watch Wildlife	Y
Max RV Size	40	Dump Station	Y	Pets	Y
Electric		Amenities		Security	
None		Restrooms	Y	Host(s)	Y
20 Amp	Y	Showers	Y	Rangers(s)	Y
30 Amp	Y	Reserve Sites	Y	Gate	
50 Amp	Y	Store		Patrolled	Y
		Grill/Table	Y		

[3] Taylorsville Lake Park
I-64, Exit 35
East of Louisville
N38 02.023 W85 13.823
State Rate: $23, Senior Discount
(502) 477-8713
http://parks.ky.gov/parks/recreationparks/taylorsville-lake/

Directions

14 miles. From Exit 35 go south for 5.8 miles on Hwy 53 to Southville. Turn right on Hwy 44, go 6.2 miles to Hwy 248. Turn left, go 2 miles to Park Rd and the park on the right.

Points of Interest

The trail system in this park is multi-use for hikers, mountain bikers, & horseback riders. In Taylorsville visit the Sanctuary Arts Center, enjoy it's storytellers, music makers, and artists. The art center offers classes, & art works of every kind.

RV Sites		Water		Laundry	Y
Number	55	None		Wi-Fi	
Shaded	Y	At Site	Y	Fishing	Y
By Water	Y	Spigots		Hiking	Y
Paved		Sewer		Biking	Y
Pull Thru	Y	None		Swimming	
ADA	Y	At Site		Watch Wildlife	Y
Max RV Size	45	Dump Station	Y	Pets	Y
Electric		Amenities		Security	
None		Restrooms	Y	Host(s)	Y
20 Amp	Y	Showers	Y	Rangers(s)	Y
30 Amp	Y	Reserve Sites	Y	Gate	
50 Amp	Y	Store		Patrolled	Y
		Grill/Table	Y		

[4] Kentucky Horse Resort Campground
I-64, Exit 75; I-75, Exit 120
North of Lexington
N38 08.474 W84 30.814
State Rate: $25-$35; Senior Discount
(859) 259-4257
http://kyhorsepark.com/

Directions

3 miles from I-64. From Exit 75 go 2 miles north on I-75 to Exit 120. Turn east on Cty Rd. 1973 for 1 mile to Campground Rd & the park on the left. **1 mile from I-75.** From Exit 120 turn east on Cty Rd. 1973 for 1 mile to Campground Rd.

Points of Interest

If you are into horses or want to see what the thoroughbred horse community is all about, this is the place. Visit the Kentucky Horse Park at a discounted rate. Go to the Hall of Champions, American Saddlebred Museum, etc.

RV Sites		Water		Laundry	
Number	260	None		Wi-Fi	Y
Shaded	Y	At Site	Y	Fishing	
By Water		Spigots		Hiking	Y
Paved	Y	**Sewer**		Biking	Y
Pull Thru	Y	None		Swimming	Y
ADA	Y	At Site		Watch Wildlife	
Max RV Size	45	Dump Station	Y	Pets	Y
Electric		**Amenities**		**Security**	
None		Restrooms	Y	Host(s)	Y
20 Amp	Y	Showers	Y	Rangers(s)	Y
30 Amp	Y	Reserve Sites	Y	Gate	
50 Amp	Y	Store	Y	Patrolled	Y
		Grill/Table	Y		

[5] Twin Knobs
I-64, Exit 133
Southwest of Morehead
N38 05.747 W83 29.464
Daniel Boone NF: $24-$35
America/Beautiful Rate: $12-$18
(606) 784-8816
http://www.recreation.gov/

Directions

9 miles. From Exit 133 turn south for 9 miles on Hwy 801 to Twin Knobs Rd and the campground on the right.

Points of Interest

The camp has a lot to offer for all interests and activities. Paved walkways make walking and exploring easier across the 10 camping loops. Photographers will like the views of Cave Run Lake and the wind surfers. Enjoy the large sandy beach, partake in the Interpretive Programs.

RV Sites		Water		Laundry	
Number	64	None		Wi-Fi	
Shaded	Y	At Site		Fishing	Y
By Water	Y	Spigots	Y	Hiking	Y
Paved	Y	**Sewer**		Biking	Y
Pull Thru		None		Swimming	Y
ADA	Y	At Site		Watch Wildlife	Y
Max RV Size	45	Dump Station	Y	Pets	Y
Electric		**Amenities**		**Security**	
None		Restrooms	Y	Host(s)	Y
20 Amp	Y	Showers	Y	Rangers(s)	Y
30 Amp	Y	Reserve Sites	Y	Gate	
50 Amp	Y	Store	Y	Patrolled	Y
		Grill/Table	Y		

[6] Grayson Lake State Park
I-64, Exit 172
South of Grayson
N38 12.740 W83 00.916
State Rate: $21-$28; Senior Discount
(606) 474-9727
http://parks.ky.gov/parks/recreationparks/grayson-lake/

Directions

11 miles. From Exit 172 go 11.2 miles south on Hwy 7 in to the park. Turn right at Grayson Lake State Park Rd.

Points of Interest

The rolling terrain presents challenging play for golfers on a 18 hole course that encircles the lake. Hidden Cove was rated #4 by Golf Digest in 2005. For non-golfers the Beech-Hemlock Forest Trail is an opportunity to discover the distinctive plants, rock formations, and wildlife of the park.

RV Sites		Water		Laundry	Y
Number	71	None		Wi-Fi	
Shaded	Y	At Site	Y	Fishing	Y
By Water	Y	Spigots		Hiking	Y
Paved	Y	**Sewer**		Biking	Y
Pull Thru	Y	None		Swimming	
ADA	Y	At Site		Watch Wildlife	Y
Max RV Size	45	Dump Station	Y	Pets	Y
Electric		**Amenities**		**Security**	
None		Restrooms	Y	Host(s)	Y
20 Amp	Y	Showers	Y	Rangers(s)	Y
30 Amp	Y	Reserve Sites	Y	Gate	
50 Amp	Y	Store	Y	Patrolled	Y
		Grill/Table	Y		

[7] Tailwater-Barren River Lake
I-65, Exit 38
South of Smiths Grove
N36 53.162 W86 07.701
COE Rate: $19
America/Beautiful Rate: $10
(270) 622-7732
http://www.recreation.gov/

Directions

14.5 miles. From Exit 38 turn south for 11.2 miles on Hwy 101 to Hwy 1533 (Meader-Port Oliver Rd). Turn left for 3.1 miles to Hwy 252. Turn left, go 0.2 miles to Riverbend Rd and the campground on the left.

Points of Interest

Local area attractions include the National Corvette Museum, Kentucky Down Under, and Diamond Caverns. In Bowling Green visit Aviation Heritage Park, Historic Railpark & Train Museum.

RV Sites		Water		Laundry	
Number	48	None		Wi-Fi	
Shaded	Y	At Site	Y	Fishing	Y
By Water	Y	Spigots		Hiking	Y
Paved		Sewer		Biking	Y
Pull Thru	Y	None		Swimming	Y
ADA	Y	At Site		Watch Wildlife	Y
Max RV Size	45	Dump Station	Y	Pets	Y
Electric		Amenities		Security	
None		Restrooms	Y	Host(s)	Y
20 Amp	Y	Showers	Y	Rangers(s)	Y
30 Amp	Y	Reserve Sites	Y	Gate	
50 Amp	Y	Store		Patrolled	Y
		Grill/Table	Y		

[8] Mammoth Cave Headquarters Camp
I-65, Exit 48
North of Park City
N37 07.778 W86 04.016
NP Rate: $17
America/Beautiful Rate: $9
(270) 758-2180
http://www.nps.gov/maca/planyourvisit/camping.htm

Directions

3 miles. From Exit 48 turn north for 3 miles on Hwy 255 (Mammoth Cave Parkway) into the park. Follow signs to Headquarters.

Points of Interest

Tour part of the world's longest known cave system. Plan your cave tour in advance and buy reserve tickets. Other park activities include nature walks, evening programs, surface hikes, canoeing, horseback riding, and bicycling.

RV Sites		Water		Laundry	Y
Number	105	None		Wi-Fi	Y
Shaded	Y	At Site		Fishing	Y
By Water		Spigots	Y	Hiking	Y
Paved		Sewer		Biking	Y
Pull Thru	Y	None		Swimming	
ADA	Y	At Site		Watch Wildlife	Y
Max RV Size	40	Dump Station	Y	Pets	Y
Electric		Amenities		Security	
None	Y	Restrooms	Y	Host(s)	Y
20 Amp		Showers	Y	Rangers(s)	Y
30 Amp		Reserve Sites	Y	Gate	
50 Amp		Store	Y	Patrolled	Y
		Grill/Table	Y		

[9] General Butler State Resort Park
I-71, Exit 44
Southeast side of Carrollton
N38 40.009 W85 08.625
State Rate: $23-$29; Senior Discount
(502) 732-4384
http://parks.ky.gov/parks/resortparks/general-butler/default.aspx

Directions

2 miles. From Exit 44 turn north for 1.8 miles on Hwy 227 to General Butler Park Rd and the park on the left.

Points of Interest

Visit the Butler-Turpin State Historic House, built in 1859, recalls one of Kentucky's foremost military families from Colonial times, American Revolution, War of 1812, Mexican War & the Civil War.

RV Sites		Water		Laundry	Y
Number	111	None		Wi-Fi	
Shaded	Y	At Site	Y	Fishing	Y
By Water	Y	Spigots	Y	Hiking	Y
Paved	Y	Sewer		Biking	Y
Pull Thru	Y	None		Swimming	Y
ADA		At Site	Y	Watch Wildlife	Y
Max RV Size	45	Dump Station	Y	Pets	Y
Electric		Amenities		Security	
None		Restrooms	Y	Host(s)	Y
20 Amp	Y	Showers	Y	Rangers(s)	Y
30 Amp	Y	Reserve Sites	Y	Gate	
50 Amp	Y	Store	Y	Patrolled	Y
		Grill/Table	Y		

[10] Big Bone Lick State Park
I-71/75, Exit 175
South of Cincinnati
N38 53.342 W84 44.855
State Rate: $23-$27; Senior Discount
(859) 384-3522
http://parks.ky.gov/parks/historicsites/big-bone-lick/default.aspx

Directions

8 miles. From Exit 175 go 7.6 miles southwest on Hwy 338 (Richwood then Beaver Rd) to the park.

Points of Interest

Designated as a National Natural Landmark, the park is significant for its combination of salt springs and late Pleistocene bone beds, where the mammoth, mastodon, ground sloth and bison roamed. Walk recreated grasslands/wet-lands/savannas leading to a "bog" diorama.

RV Sites		Water		Laundry	Y
Number	62	None		Wi-Fi	
Shaded	Y	At Site	Y	Fishing	Y
By Water		Spigots		Hiking	Y
Paved	Y	Sewer		Biking	Y
Pull Thru		None		Swimming	Y
ADA	Y	At Site		Watch Wildlife	Y
Max RV Size	42	Dump Station	Y	Pets	Y
Electric		Amenities		Security	
None		Restrooms	Y	Host(s)	Y
20 Amp	Y	Showers	Y	Rangers(s)	Y
30 Amp	Y	Reserve Sites	Y	Gate	
50 Amp		Store	Y	Patrolled	Y
		Grill/Table	Y		

[11] Grove Recreation Area
I-75, Exit 25
West of Corbin
N36 56.414 W84 13.032
Daniel Boone NF Rate: $16
America/Beautiful Rate: $8
(606) 528-6156
http://www.recreation.gov/

Directions

11 miles. From Exit 25 turn southwest for 4.7 miles on Hwy 25W to Hwy 1193 (Bee Creek Rd.) Turn right for 2.8 miles to Grove Rd. Turn right, follow Grove Rd. for 3 miles to the campground.

Points of Interest

In Corbin go to Harland Sanders Museum & Café, dine where it all began at Colonel Sander's original restaurant. Tour the Corbin Railroad Museum.

RV Sites		Water		Laundry	
Number	60	None		Wi-Fi	
Shaded	Y	At Site	Y	Fishing	Y
By Water	Y	Spigots		Hiking	Y
Paved		Sewer		Biking	Y
Pull Thru		None		Swimming	Y
ADA	Y	At Site		Watch Wildlife	Y
Max RV Size	45	Dump Station	Y	Pets	Y
Electric		Amenities		Security	
None		Restrooms	Y	Host(s)	Y
20 Amp	Y	Showers	Y	Rangers(s)	Y
30 Amp	Y	Reserve Sites	Y	Gate	
50 Amp		Store		Patrolled	Y
		Grill/Table	Y		

[12] Baileys Point
Nunn Parkway, South on Hwy 31-E
Southwest of Glasgow
N36 52.869 W86 05.385
COE Rate: $17-$23
America/Beautiful Rate: $9-$12
(270) 622-6959
http://www.recreation.gov/

Directions

19 miles. South of Glasgow, from Louie B. Nunn Cumberland Parkway, take 31-E south 15 miles to Hwy 252. Turn right, go 1.5 miles to Hwy 517, turn right & follow signs to Park.

Points of Interest

Take day trips to the National Corvette Museum, Kentucky Down Under, Diamond Caverns, and Mammoth Cave National Park. Hikers can explore the C.E. Rager Nature Trail and the Robert Foster Hiking Trail.

RV Sites		Water		Laundry	Y
Number	203	None		Wi-Fi	
Shaded	Y	At Site	Y	Fishing	Y
By Water	Y	Spigots		Hiking	Y
Paved	some	Sewer		Biking	Y
Pull Thru	Y	None		Swimming	Y
ADA	Y	At Site		Watch Wildlife	Y
Max RV Size	45	Dump Station	Y	Pets	Y
Electric		Amenities		Security	
None		Restrooms	Y	Host(s)	Y
20 Amp	Y	Showers	Y	Rangers(s)	Y
30 Amp	Y	Reserve Sites	Y	Gate	
50 Amp	Y	Store		Patrolled	Y
		Grill/Table	Y		

[13] Kendall Campground
Nunn Parkway, South on Hwy 127
South of Russell Springs
N36 52.348 W85 07.967
COE Rate: $12-$22
America/Beautiful Rate: $6-$11
(270) 343-4660
http://www.recreation.gov/

Directions

16 miles. Take US Highway 127 south from the Nunn Parkway for 16 miles and turn right on Kendall Dam Rd just before crossing the dam.

Points of Interest

The campground overlooks the river, offering sweeping scenic views. Find convenient access to a cold water trout stream, stocked with rainbow, brook and brown trout. Wolf Creek Dam National Fish Hatchery is within walking distance of the campground.

RV Sites		Water		Laundry	Y
Number	116	None		Wi-Fi	
Shaded	Y	At Site	Y	Fishing	Y
By Water	Y	Spigots		Hiking	Y
Paved		**Sewer**		Biking	Y
Pull Thru	Y	None		Swimming	
ADA	Y	At Site		Watch Wildlife	Y
Max RV Size	45	Dump Station	Y	Pets	Y
Electric		**Amenities**		**Security**	
None		Restrooms	Y	Host(s)	Y
20 Amp	Y	Showers	Y	Rangers(s)	Y
30 Amp	Y	Reserve Sites	Y	Gate	
50 Amp	Y	Store		Patrolled	Y
		Grill/Table	Y		

[14] Levi Jackson State Park
I-75, Exit 38
South of London
N37 04.801 W84 02.542
State Rate: $24-$38; Senior Discount
(606) 330-2130
http://parks.ky.gov/parks/recreationparks/
levi-jackson/default.aspx

Directions

9 miles. From the Daniel Boone Parkway (Hwy 80) go 2.7 miles south on I-75 to Hwy 192. Exit and go east 1.9 miles to Hwy 229. Turn right for 4.6 miles to the Park.

Points of Interest

Hike historic Wilderness Road & Boone's Trace. These trails carried more than 200,000 settlers to the western frontier between 1774-1796. See the Mountain Life Museum & McHargue's Mill, tributes to 19th century pioneer ingenuity

RV Sites		Water		Laundry	Y
Number	146	None		Wi-Fi	Y
Shaded	Y	At Site	Y	Fishing	
By Water		Spigots		Hiking	Y
Paved		**Sewer**		Biking	Y
Pull Thru	some	None		Swimming	
ADA	Y	At Site	Y	Watch Wildlife	Y
Max RV Size	45	Dump Station	Y	Pets	Y
Electric		**Amenities**		**Security**	
None		Restrooms	Y	Host(s)	Y
20 Amp	Y	Showers	Y	Rangers(s)	Y
30 Amp	Y	Reserve Sites	Y	Gate	
50 Amp	Y	Store	Y	Patrolled	Y
		Grill/Table	Y		

[15] Jenny Wiley State Resort Park
Hwy 23, East on Hwy 3 (Hwy 1370)
In Prestonsburg
N37 43.631 W82 44.753
State Rate: $21-$31; Senior Discount
(606) 889-1790
http://parks.ky.gov/parks/resortparks/jenny-wiley/default.aspx

Directions

2.2 miles. North of Prestonsburg, off Hwy 23, take Hwy 3 (Hwy 1370) for 2.2 miles to the west entrance. Some suggest using the east entrance.

Points of Interest

Attractions include Butcher Hollow, David Appalachian Crafts, Mountain Home Place, Pioneer Village, the Kentucky Appalachian Artisan Center, the Samuel May House, Van Lear Historical Coal Camp Museum, the grave of Jenny Wiley, Augusta Dils York Mansion, & Elkhorn City Railroad Museum.

RV Sites		Water		Laundry	Y
Number	121	None		Wi-Fi	
Shaded	Y	At Site	Y	Fishing	Y
By Water	Y	Spigots		Hiking	Y
Paved		**Sewer**		Biking	Y
Pull Thru	Y	None		Swimming	Y
ADA	Y	At Site		Watch Wildlife	Y
Max RV Size	45	Dump Station	Y	Pets	Y
Electric		**Amenities**		**Security**	
None		Restrooms	Y	Host(s)	Y
20 Amp	Y	Showers	Y	Rangers(s)	Y
30 Amp	Y	Reserve Sites	Y	Gate	
50 Amp	Y	Store	Y	Patrolled	Y
		Grill/Table	Y		

About Louisiana's Public Campgrounds

Louisiana's 22 State Parks, 17 Historic Sites, and one Preservation Area offer a uniquely rewarding experience of natural beauty and historical riches. Each of the parks is also located in a high recreation potential area. You can hike, fish, bike and enjoy birding and nature trails. Most State Parks feature a waterfront location, campsites and picnic areas. Any pet brought in to a State Park must be on a leash (not to exceed 6 feet in length). See the state website for more details and information -

http://www.crt.state.la.us/louisiana-state-parks/index

Visitors who hold an America the Beautiful Pass (or already have a Golden Age/Golden Access Passport) are entitled to a 50% reduction on camping fees at Louisiana State Parks. Parks may have $2 per person entrance fee (waived for people 62 and older).

Reservations can be made 11 months to the day in advance online at -

http://reservations2.usedirect.com/LAStateParksHome/

or call the reservation center at (877) 226-7652.

State Park Overnight Camping Fees are as follows:

Premium Campsite (Improved Campsite with sewerage or pull-through or prime location)	$20 per night, Oct-Mar $28 per night, Apr-Sept
Improved Campsite (water and electrical hookup)	$18 per night, Oct-Mar $22 per night, Apr-Sept
Unimproved Campsite (without hookup)	$14 per night

[1] Sam Houston Jones State Park	[7] Indian Creek Recreation Area
[2] Bayou Segnette State Park	[8] Kincaid Camp
[3] Fontainebleau State Park	[9] Tickfaw State Park
[4] Beaver Dam	[10] Palmetto Island
[5] Lake Claiborne State Park	[11] South Toledo Bend State Park
[6] Chicot State Park, North Loop	[12] North Toledo Bend State Park

NOTES:

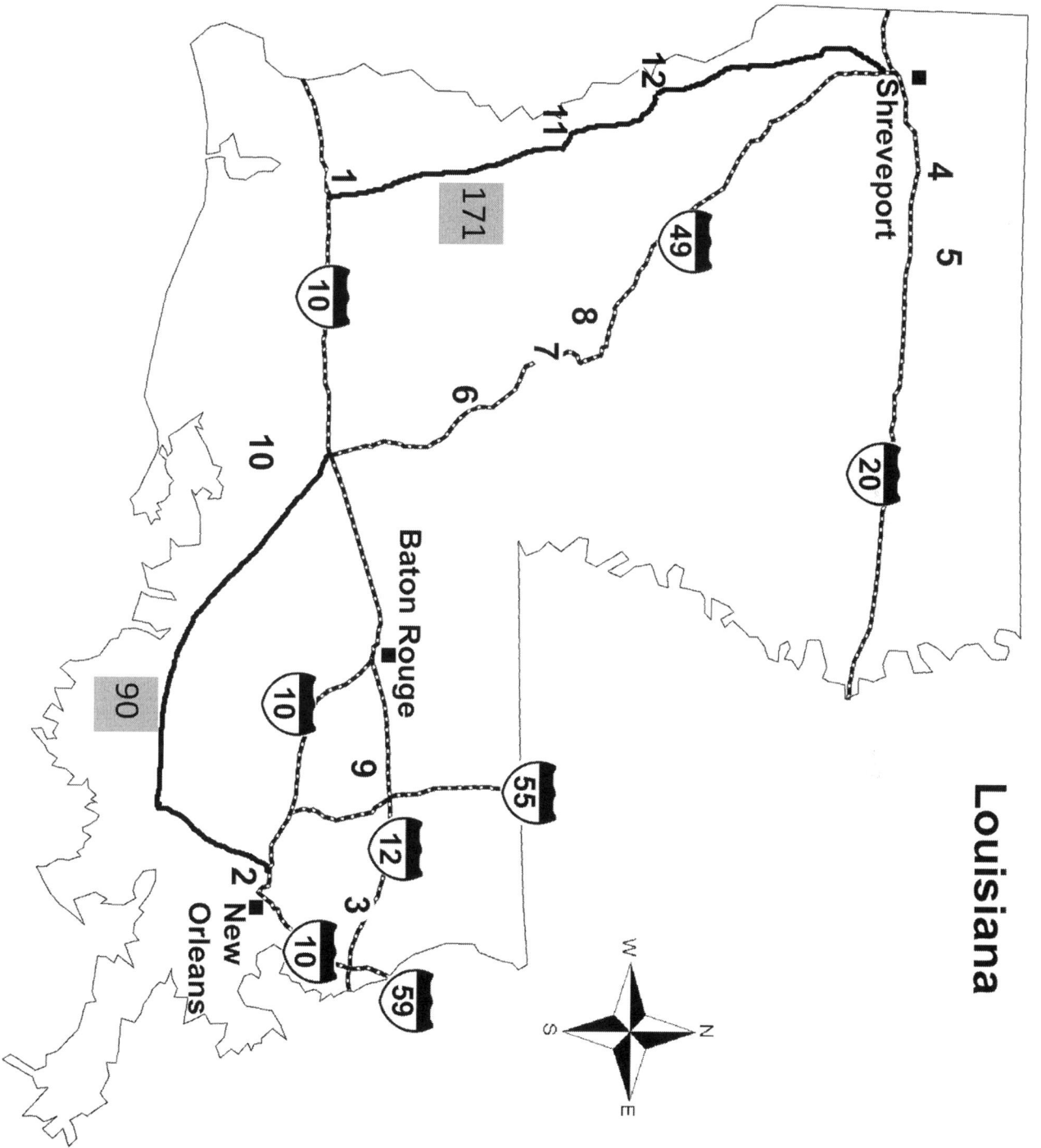

Louisiana

[1] Sam Houston Jones State Park
I-10, Exit 27
North of Lake Charles
N30 18.043 W93 14.669
State Rate: See Introduction
America/Beautiful Rate: See Introduction
(888) 677-7264
http://www.crt.state.la.us/louisiana-state-parks/parks/sam-houston-jones-state-park/index

Directions

5 miles. From Exit 27 go 5 miles north on Hwy 378 to the entrance, on your left.

Points of Interest

The area is known as the "Festival Capital," with over 75 annual festivals. In Lake Charles visit the Charpentier Historical District, the Port of Lake Charles, Millennium and Adventure Cove Parks for dining, shopping, entertainment.

RV Sites		Water		Laundry	
Number	62	None		Wi-Fi	
Shaded	Y	At Site	Y	Fishing	
By Water	Y	Spigots		Hiking	Y
Paved		**Sewer**		Biking	Y
Pull Thru	Y	None		Swimming	
ADA	Y	At Site	Y	Watch Wildlife	
Max RV Size	45	Dump Station	Y	Pets	Y
Electric		**Amenities**		**Security**	
None		Restrooms		Host(s)	Y
20 Amp	Y	Showers		Rangers(s)	Y
30 Amp	Y	Reserve Sites	Y	Gate	
50 Amp	Y	Store		Patrolled	Y
		Grill/Table	Y		

[2] Bayou Segnette State Park
I-10 Exit 234
South of New Orleans
N29 54.013 W90 09.327
State Rate: See Introduction
America/Beautiful Rate: See Introduction
(888) 677-2296
http://www.crt.state.la.us/louisiana-state-parks/parks/bayou-segnette-state-park/index

Directions

12 miles. From Exit 234 go 12 miles south on Expressway 90 (Pontchartrain Expressway, then Westbank Expressway). The Park will be on your left at Drake Dr. (blinking yellow light). Avoid rush hours.

Points of Interest

Camp in the scenic bayou. Just 20-30 minutes from New Orleans and the French Quarter, a multitude of recreational opportunities awaits.

RV Sites		Water		Laundry	Y
Number	98	None		Wi-Fi	Y
Shaded	Y	At Site	Y	Fishing	
By Water		Spigots		Hiking	Y
Paved	Y	**Sewer**		Biking	Y
Pull Thru		None		Swimming	Y
ADA	Y	At Site	Y	Watch Wildlife	
Max RV Size	45	Dump Station	Y	Pets	Y
Electric		**Amenities**		**Security**	
None		Restrooms	Y	Host(s)	Y
20 Amp	Y	Showers	Y	Rangers(s)	Y
30 Amp	Y	Reserve Sites	Y	Gate	
50 Amp	Y	Store	Y	Patrolled	Y
		Grill/Table	Y		

[3] Fontainebleau State Park
I-12, Exit 65
North shore of Lake Pontchartrain
N30 20.729 W90 01.354
State Rate: See Introduction
America/Beautiful Rate: See Introduction
(888) 677-3668
http://www.crt.state.la.us/louisiana-state-parks/parks/fontainebleau-state-park/index

Directions

6.5 miles. From Exit 65 follow Hwy 59 south for 3.6 miles to Hwy 190. Turn left, go 2.6 miles to Group Campground Rd on the right.

Points of Interest

The Park has beautiful views! Enjoy the beach, boardwalk and the pier. Another option would be the Global Wildlife Center, the largest free-roaming wildlife preserve of its kind in the country, with over 4,000 exotic, endangered animals.

RV Sites		Water		Laundry	Y
Number	163	None		Wi-Fi	Y
Shaded	Y	At Site	Y	Fishing	Y
By Water	Y	Spigots		Hiking	
Paved	Y	**Sewer**		Biking	Y
Pull Thru	Y	None		Swimming	Y
ADA	Y	At Site	some	Watch Wildlife	Y
Max RV Size	45	Dump Station	Y	Pets	Y
Electric		**Amenities**		**Security**	
None		Restrooms	Y	Host(s)	Y
20 Amp	Y	Showers	Y	Rangers(s)	Y
30 Amp	Y	Reserve Sites	Y	Gate	
50 Amp	Y	Store	Y	Patrolled	Y
		Grill/Table	Y		

[4] Beaver Dam Campground
I-20, Exit 47
North of Minden
N32 40.575 W93 18.349
Kisatchie N F Rate: $11
America/Beautiful Rate: $6
(318) 377-6727
http://www.recreation.gov/

Directions

9 miles. From Exit 47 go 1.6 miles north on Hwy 7 to Hwy 79. Go right for 0.5 mile to Hwy 159. Go left for 4.6 mile to Cty Rd 111 (Caney Lake Rd), then left 2.4 mile to Caney Lake camp sign, turn left on NF 810 to the camp.

Points of Interest

The Minden red-bricked Main Street generates nostalgic images of a time gone by. The old-time charm extends to restaurants and quaint shops. Minden has an historic residential district.

RV Sites		Water		Laundry	
Number	28	None		Wi-Fi	
Shaded	Y	At Site	Y	Fishing	Y
By Water	Y	Spigots		Hiking	Y
Paved	Y	Sewer		Biking	Y
Pull Thru		None		Swimming	Y
ADA	Y	At Site		Watch Wildlife	Y
Max RV Size	45	Dump Station	Y	Pets	Y
Electric		Amenities		Security	
None		Restrooms	Y	Host(s)	Y
20 Amp	Y	Showers	Y	Rangers(s)	Y
30 Amp	Y	Reserve Sites	Y	Gate	
50 Amp	Y	Store		Patrolled	Y
		Grill/Table	Y		

[5] Lake Claiborne State Park
I-20, Exit 67
North of Arcadia
N32 42.780 W92 55.401
State Rate: See Introduction
America/Beautiful Rate: See Introduction
(888) 677-2524
http://www.crt.state.la.us/louisiana-state-parks/parks/lake-claiborne-state-park/index

Directions

17 miles. From Exit 67 go 7.6 miles northwest to Athens. Turn east, then bear north, on Hwy 518 for 8.2 miles to Hwy 146. Go east (right) 1 mile to the Park entrance.

Points of Interest

Visit the Bonnie and Clyde Historic Site, near Arcadia. Tour Poverty Point Historic Site (East of Monroe), a complex of Native American ceremonial mounds built between 1700 and 700 B.C

RV Sites		Water		Laundry	Y
Number	87	None		Wi-Fi	Y
Shaded	Y	At Site	Y	Fishing	Y
By Water	Y	Spigots		Hiking	Y
Paved	Y	Sewer		Biking	Y
Pull Thru	Y	None		Swimming	Y
ADA	Y	At Site		Watch Wildlife	Y
Max RV Size	45	Dump Station	Y	Pets	Y
Electric		Amenities		Security	
None		Restrooms	Y	Host(s)	Y
20 Amp	Y	Showers	Y	Rangers(s)	Y
30 Amp	Y	Reserve Sites	Y	Gate	
50 Amp	Y	Store	Y	Patrolled	Y
		Grill/Table	Y		

[6] Chicot State Park, North Loop
I-49 Exit 46
North of Opelousas
N30 47.379 W92 17.269
State Rate: See Introduction
America/Beautiful Rate: See Introduction
(888) 677-2442
http://www.crt.state.la.us/louisiana-state-parks/parks/chicot-state-park/index

Directions

11 miles. From Exit 46 go 7.1 miles west on Hwy 106 to Hwy 3042. Turn south on Hwy 3042 for 4 miles to the main entrance on the left.

Points of Interest

Visit the Acadian town of Ville Platte ("flat town"). Cajun traditions/cultural are found in the spoken French, music & food. Opelousas was the boyhood home of Jim Bowie. Don't miss the "Rendez-vous des Cajuns" live radio show in Eunice.

RV Sites		Water		Laundry	Y
Number	100	None		Wi-Fi	Y
Shaded	Y	At Site	Y	Fishing	Y
By Water		Spigots		Hiking	Y
Paved	Y	Sewer		Biking	Y
Pull Thru	Y	None		Swimming	Y
ADA	Y	At Site		Watch Wildlife	Y
Max RV Size	45	Dump Station	Y	Pets	Y
Electric		Amenities		Security	
None		Restrooms	Y	Host(s)	Y
20 Amp	Y	Showers	Y	Rangers(s)	Y
30 Amp	Y	Reserve Sites	Y	Gate	
50 Amp	Y	Store	Y	Patrolled	Y
		Grill/Table	Y		

[7] Indian Creek Recreation Area
I-49, Exit 73
Southeast of Woodworth
N31 06.817 W92 28.228
LA Dept of Ag. Rate: $18-$25
(318) 487-5058
http://townofwoodworth.com/recreation/indiancreek.html

Directions

6 miles. From Exit 73 go 2.5 miles southwest on Hwy 3265 (Robinson Bridge Rd) to just east of Woodworth. Turn south on Indian Creek Rd for 1.2 miles to Camp Ground Rd. Turn left and go 2.1 miles to the Park.

Points of Interest

In Alexandria/Pineville, visit the Frogmore Cotton Plantation & Gins, Louisiana Maneuvers & Military Museum, Tunica-Biloxi Indian Museum, Alexandria Antique Mall, & many restaurants.

RV Sites		Water		Laundry	
Number	101	None		Wi-Fi	Y
Shaded	Y	At Site	Y	Fishing	Y
By Water	Y	Spigots		Hiking	Y
Paved	Y	Sewer		Biking	Y
Pull Thru	Y	None		Swimming	Y
ADA		At Site		Watch Wildlife	
Max RV Size	45	Dump Station	Y	Pets	Y
Electric		Amenities		Security	
None		Restrooms	Y	Host(s)	Y
20 Amp	Y	Showers	Y	Rangers(s)	
30 Amp	Y	Reserve Sites		Gate	Y
50 Amp	Y	Store		Patrolled	Y
		Grill/Table	Y		

[8] Kincaid Camp
I-49, Exit 86
West of Alexandria
N31 15.494 W92 37.915
Kisatchie N F Rate: $15
America/Beautiful Rate: $8
(318) 793-9427
http://www.fs.usda.gov/recarea/kisatchie/null/recarea/?recid=34621&actid=82

Directions

21 miles. From Exit 86 go 2 miles west on Hwy 165 to Hwy 28, then west for 12.7 miles to Hwy 121. Turn south for 0.3 miles to Kincaid/Valentine Lakes sign. Turn left, go 4 miles to Forest Rd 200. Go left for 2.4 miles to the camp.

Points of Interest

See **[7]** above.

RV Sites		Water		Laundry	
Number	40	None		Wi-Fi	
Shaded	Y	At Site		Fishing	Y
By Water	Y	Spigots	Y	Hiking	Y
Paved	Y	Sewer		Biking	Y
Pull Thru		None		Swimming	Y
ADA		At Site		Watch Wildlife	Y
Max RV Size	45	Dump Station	Y	Pets	Y
Electric		Amenities		Security	
None		Restrooms	Y	Host(s)	
20 Amp	Y	Showers	Y	Rangers(s)	
30 Amp	Y	Reserve Sites		Gate	
50 Amp		Store		Patrolled	Y
		Grill/Table	Y		

[9] Tickfaw State Park
I-55, Exit 26
West of Springfield
N30 23.451 W90 37.658
State Rate: See Introduction
America/Beautiful Rate: See Introduction
(888) 981-2020
http://www.crt.state.la.us/louisiana-state-parks/parks/tickfaw-state-park/index

Directions

13 miles. From Exit 26 go west for 5.4 miles on Hwy 22 to Springfield. Continue west on Hwy 1037 (Blood River Rd) for 6.2 miles to Patterson Rd, then bear left for 1.2 miles to the park.

Points of Interest

Ponchatoula is said to be "America's Antique City," with the quality of the antiques and collectibles combined with the experience of the dealers. Try the "Swamp Walk."

RV Sites		Water		Laundry	Y
Number	30	None		Wi-Fi	Y
Shaded	Y	At Site	Y	Fishing	Y
By Water		Spigots		Hiking	Y
Paved	Y	Sewer		Biking	Y
Pull Thru		None		Swimming	Y
ADA	Y	At Site		Watch Wildlife	Y
Max RV Size	45	Dump Station	Y	Pets	Y
Electric		Amenities		Security	
None		Restrooms	Y	Host(s)	Y
20 Amp	Y	Showers	Y	Rangers(s)	Y
30 Amp	Y	Reserve Sites	Y	Gate	Y
50 Amp	Y	Store	Y	Patrolled	Y
		Grill/Table	Y		

[10] Palmetto Island
From Hwy 90, west of New Iberia
South of Abbeville on Hwy 82
N29 52.252 W92 09.023
State Rate: See Introduction
America/Beautiful Rate: See Introduction
(888) 677-0094
http://www.crt.state.la.us/louisiana-state-parks/parks/palmetto-island-state-park/index

Directions

10.5 miles. In Abbeville, from Hwy 14 go south on Hwy 82 (State Street) out of town for 7.5 miles, turn left onto LA 690, go 1 mile, then right onto Pleasant Drive 2 miles to the park.

Points of Interest

In Abbeville visit the Museum & Art Gallery where the Acadian culture is preserved; the Museum of Erath highlights the Cajun & Creole cultures of south Louisiana, & the history of the Acadian settlement.

RV Sites		Water		Laundry	Y
Number	96	None		Wi-Fi	Y
Shaded	Y	At Site	Y	Fishing	
By Water	Y	Spigots		Hiking	
Paved		Sewer		Biking	Y
Pull Thru		None		Swimming	Y
ADA	Y	At Site		Watch Wildlife	Y
Max RV Size	45	Dump Station	Y	Pets	Y
Electric		Amenities		Security	
None		Restrooms	Y	Host(s)	Y
20 Amp	Y	Showers	Y	Rangers(s)	Y
30 Amp	Y	Reserve Sites	Y	Gate	
50 Amp	Y	Store		Patrolled	Y
		Grill/Table	Y		

[11] South Toledo Bend State Park
Off Hwy 171, Hwy 11/392 from Anacoco
West of Anacoco
N31 12.325 W93 34.483
State Rate: See Introduction
America/Beautiful Rate: See Introduction
(888) 398-4770
http://www.crt.state.la.us/louisiana-state-parks/parks/south-toledo-bend-state-park/index

Directions

15.6 miles. From Anacoco, turn west 15 miles on Hwy 11/392, then north on Hwy 191 for 0.1 mile. Turn west on Bass Haven Rd 0.5 mile to the park.

Points of Interest

The Museum of West Louisiana in Leesville, housed in the old Kansas City Southern depot offers exhibits on the culture and life of southwest Louisiana residents.

RV Sites		Water		Laundry	Y
Number	55	None		Wi-Fi	Y
Shaded	Y	At Site	Y	Fishing	Y
By Water	Y	Spigots		Hiking	Y
Paved	Y	Sewer		Biking	Y
Pull Thru	Y	None		Swimming	Y
ADA	Y	At Site		Watch Wildlife	Y
Max RV Size	45	Dump Station	Y	Pets	Y
Electric		Amenities		Security	
None		Restrooms	Y	Host(s)	Y
20 Amp	Y	Showers	Y	Rangers(s)	Y
30 Amp	Y	Reserve Sites	Y	Gate	
50 Amp	Y	Store	Y	Patrolled	Y
		Grill/Table	Y		

[12] North Toledo Bend State Park
Off Hwy 171, Hwy 482 from Zwolle
Southwest of Zwolle
N31 34.153 W93 44.013
State Rate: See Introduction
America/Beautiful Rate: See Introduction
(888) 677-6400
http://www.crt.state.la.us/louisiana-state-parks/parks/north-toledo-bend-state-park/index

Directions

9 miles. In Zwolle go west 0.8 miles on Hwy 482, turn right on Hwy 191, go 1.0 mile to Hwy 3229. Turn left, go 4.7 miles to North Toledo Park Road. Go left 2.3 miles to the park.

Points of Interest

Natchitoches is the oldest settlement in the Louisiana Purchase. It has a 33-block Historic Landmark District featuring Creole architecture, bed & breakfasts, restaurants, shops & historic homes.

RV Sites		Water		Laundry	Y
Number	63	None		Wi-Fi	Y
Shaded	Y	At Site	Y	Fishing	
By Water	Y	Spigots		Hiking	Y
Paved	Y	Sewer		Biking	Y
Pull Thru		None		Swimming	
ADA	Y	At Site		Watch Wildlife	Y
Max RV Size	45	Dump Station	Y	Pets	Y
Electric		Amenities		Security	
None		Restrooms	Y	Host(s)	Y
20 Amp	Y	Showers	Y	Rangers(s)	Y
30 Amp	Y	Reserve Sites	Y	Gate	
50 Amp	Y	Store		Patrolled	Y
		Grill/Table	Y		

About Maine's Public Campgrounds

Maine's State Park system is as varied as the state's landscape. In Maine, there are more than 30 state parks dedicated to the visitor's enjoyment. Twelve state parks and the Allagash Wilderness Waterway provide camping opportunities. After Labor Day most facilities are closed for the season. The Maine State Parks website is -

http://www.maine.gov/dacf/parks/index.shtml

Make camping reservations at-

http://www.maine.gov/dacf/parks/camping/reservations/index.shtml

State parks sites offer a number of accommodations for people with disabilities and special needs - reserved parking spaces; wheelchair ramps; beach wheelchairs; hardened surfaces on trails and walkways; accessible restrooms; roll-in showers; benches in showers and changing rooms; TTY; and easy-to-reach campsites. Each park or historic site is rated by the state for overall ease of access.

Pets must be on a leash not exceeding four feet in length and must not be left unattended. Pets are not allowed on beaches or in the Sebago Lake State Park campground.

Acadia National Park is an exceptional RV campground destination so 2 campgrounds, either near or in the Park, were added even though the locations exceed the 'within 30 minutes of an Interstate' guideline.

[1] Sebago Lake State Park	**[5] Bradbury Mountain State Park**
[2] Lake St. George State Park	**[6] Camden Hills State Park**
[3] Lamoine State Park	**[7] Cobscook Bay State Park**
[4] Blackwoods Campground	

NOTES:

Maine

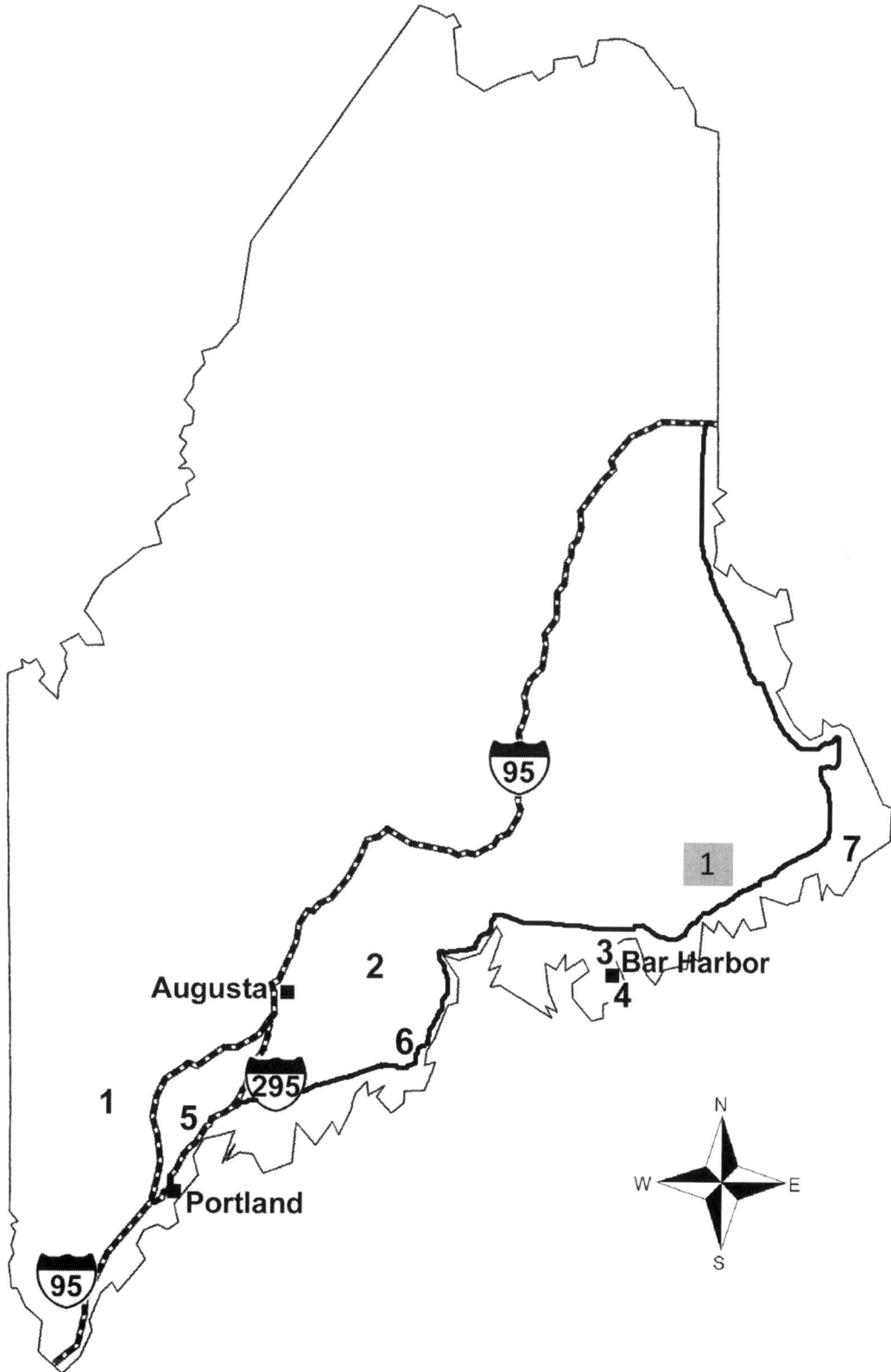

[1] Sebago Lake State Park
I-95, Exit 63
Sebago Lake - North Shore
N43 56.526 W70 32.778
State Rate: $15-$35
(207) 693-6613
http://www.maine.gov/cgi-bin/online/doc/park-search/index.pl

Directions

17 miles. From Exit 63 turn southwest on Hwy 202 (Gray Rd.) for 6.4 miles to Hwy 302. Turn northwest (right) on 302 for 10.2 miles. Turn left on State Park Rd into the Park.

Points of Interest

Ride the Songo River Queen on Sebago-Long Lake. Enjoy auctions, antiquing, craft fairs and bazaars. Bridgton is a haven for old books, antiques, china, porcelain, Shaker items and quilts.

RV Sites		Water		Laundry	
Number	250	None		Wi-Fi	
Shaded	Y	At Site	Y	Fishing	Y
By Water	Y	Spigots		Hiking	Y
Paved		**Sewer**		Biking	Y
Pull Thru		None		Swimming	Y
ADA	Y	At Site		Watch Wildlife	Y
Max RV Size	40	Dump Station	Y	Pets	N
Electric		**Amenities**		**Security**	
None		Restrooms	Y	Host(s)	Y
20 Amp	Y	Showers	Y	Rangers(s)	Y
30 Amp	Y	Reserve Sites	Y	Gate	
50 Amp		Store	Y	Patrolled	Y
		Grill/Table	Y		

[2] Lake St. George State Park
I-95, Exit 109
East of Augusta
N44 23.884 W69 20.861
State Rate: $15-$25
(207) 589-4255
http://www.maine.gov/cgi-bin/online/doc/park-search/index.pl

Directions

28 miles. From Exit 109 turn east on Hwy 202 (Western Ave) for 3 miles, where the road joins with Hwy 3. Now follow Hwy 3 for 25 miles to the Park, just north of Sherman's Corner.

Points of Interest

Visit Belfast, where the decades long presence of artists, artisans, studios and galleries is a big reason it is called "the funkiest little town in Maine."

RV Sites		Water		Laundry	
Number	38	None		Wi-Fi	
Shaded	Y	At Site		Fishing	Y
By Water	Y	Spigots	Y	Hiking	Y
Paved		**Sewer**		Biking	Y
Pull Thru		None		Swimming	Y
ADA	Y	At Site		Watch Wildlife	Y
Max RV Size	40	Dump Station	Y	Pets	Y
Electric		**Amenities**		**Security**	
None	Y	Restrooms	Y	Host(s)	Y
20 Amp		Showers	Y	Rangers(s)	Y
30 Amp		Reserve Sites	Y	Gate	
50 Amp		Store		Patrolled	Y
		Grill/Table	Y		

[3] Lamoine State Park
I-95, Exit 182
Southeast of Ellsworth
N44 27.332 W68 17.855
State Rate: $15-$25
(207) 667-4778
http://www.maine.gov/cgi-bin/online/doc/park-search/index.pl

Directions

37 miles. From Exit 182 go 4.6 miles east on I-395 to exit 6. Go southeast (right) for 23 miles on Hwy 1a to Ellsworth. Continue on Hwy 1 for 2 miles to Hwy 184. Turn right on Hwy 184 for 7.7 miles to the Park on your right.

Points of Interest

Located in one of the most sought-after vacation regions in the state. The Park's location provides easy access to Bar Harbor, Acadia National Park, rockbound islands, and area lighthouses.

RV Sites		Water		Laundry	
Number	62	None		Wi-Fi	
Shaded	Y	At Site		Fishing	Y
By Water	Y	Spigots	Y	Hiking	Y
Paved		**Sewer**		Biking	Y
Pull Thru		None		Swimming	Y
ADA	Y	At Site		Watch Wildlife	
Max RV Size	45	Dump Station	Y	Pets	Y
Electric		**Amenities**		**Security**	
None	Y	Restrooms	Y	Host(s)	Y
20 Amp		Showers	Y	Rangers(s)	Y
30 Amp		Reserve Sites	Y	Gate	
50 Amp		Store		Patrolled	Y
		Grill/Table	Y		

[4] Blackwoods Campground
I-95, Exit 182
Southeast of Ellsworth
N44 18.804 W68 12.849
Arcadia NP Rate: $10-$20
America/Beautiful Rate: $5-$10
(207) 288-3274
www.nps.gov/acad/planyourvisit/blackwood-scampground.htm

Directions

54 miles. From Exit 182 go 4.6 miles east on I-395 to Exit 6. Go southeast for 23 miles on Hwy 1a to Ellsworth. Continue on Hwy 1 for 1 mile. Bear right onto Hwy 3 & go 25 miles to the Park.

Points of Interest

Acadia's carriage roads, designed by John D. Rockefeller so he could travel via horse and carriage, provide you an excellent way to explore Acadia by auto, horseback or bicycle.

RV Sites		Water		Laundry	
Number	61	None		Wi-Fi	
Shaded	Y	At Site		Fishing	
By Water		Spigots	Y	Hiking	Y
Paved		Sewer		Biking	Y
Pull Thru	Y	None		Swimming	
ADA	Y	At Site		Watch Wildlife	Y
Max RV Size	35	Dump Station	Y	Pets	Y
Electric		Amenities		Security	
None	Y	Restrooms	Y	Host(s)	Y
20 Amp		Showers		Rangers(s)	Y
30 Amp		Reserve Sites	Y	Gate	
50 Amp		Store		Patrolled	Y
		Grill/Table	Y		

[5] Bradbury Mountain State Park
I-295, Exit 22
Northwest of Freeport
N43 53.982 W70 10.724
State Rate: $11-$19
(207) 688-4712
http://www.maine.gov/cgi-bin/online/doc/park-search/index.pl

Directions

5 miles. From Exit 22 go northwest on Hwy 125 to Durham Rd. turn left, go 0.2 miles to Pownal Rd. Go right for 4.2 miles (becomes Elmwood). Turn right on Hwy 9 (Hallowell Rd) for 0.6 mile to the Park.

Points of Interest

Sculpted by a glacier, Bradbury Mountain is the park's outstanding natural feature. In Freeport, a beautiful coastal village, find over 200 outlets, designer shops, eclectic boutiques, great restaurants, casual cafes, and L.L.Bean.

RV Sites		Water		Laundry	
Number	35	None		Wi-Fi	
Shaded	Y	At Site		Fishing	
By Water		Spigots	Y	Hiking	Y
Paved		Sewer		Biking	Y
Pull Thru		None	Y	Swimming	
ADA	Y	At Site		Watch Wildlife	Y
Max RV Size	35	Dump Station		Pets	Y
Electric		Amenities		Security	
None	Y	Restrooms	Y	Host(s)	Y
20 Amp		Showers	Y	Rangers(s)	Y
30 Amp		Reserve Sites	Y	Gate	
50 Amp		Store		Patrolled	Y
		Grill/Table	Y		

[6] Camden Hills State Park
Hwy 1
North of Camden
N44 13.922 W69 02.792
State Rate: $15-$35
(207) 236-3109
http://www.maine.gov/cgi-bin/online/doc/park-search/index.pl

Directions

1.5 Miles. Go 1.5 miles north from the center of Camden on Hwy 1 to the Park.

Points of Interest

The Park's signature location is the scenic vista high atop Mt. Battie. The park is a few minutes north of Camden, a quintessential New England town with shops in walking distance to the harbor. Harbor cruises, whale and puffin watches are available daily.

RV Sites		Water		Laundry	
Number	100	None		Wi-Fi	Y
Shaded	Y	At Site	Y	Fishing	Y
By Water	Y	Spigots		Hiking	Y
Paved		Sewer		Biking	Y
Pull Thru		None		Swimming	
ADA	Y	At Site		Watch Wildlife	Y
Max RV Size	45	Dump Station	Y	Pets	Y
Electric		Amenities		Security	
None		Restrooms	Y	Host(s)	Y
20 Amp	Y	Showers	Y	Rangers(s)	Y
30 Amp	Y	Reserve Sites	Y	Gate	
50 Amp		Store		Patrolled	Y
		Grill/Table	Y		

[7] Cobscook Bay State Park
Hwy 1
North of Machias
N44 50.893 W67 10.171
State Rate: $14-$24
(207) 726-4412
http://www.maine.gov/cgi-bin/online/doc/
parksearch/index.pl

Directions

22 miles. Take Hwy 1 north of Machias for 21.5 miles to park signs marking the turnoff onto South Edmunds Rd. The park entrance is on the right 0.5 miles from the turnoff.

Points of Interest

Cobscook, the Maliseet-Passamaquoddy tribal word for "boiling tides," describes this setting, The wildlife-rich waters of Cobscook Bay surround the 888-acre park on three sides, providing opportunities to watch 200+ bird species.

RV Sites		Water		Laundry	
Number	106	None		Wi-Fi	
Shaded	Y	At Site		Fishing	clamming
By Water	Y	Spigots	Y	Hiking	Y
Paved		Sewer		Biking	Y
Pull Thru	Y	None		Swimming	
ADA	Y	At Site		Watch Wildlife	Y
Max RV Size	40	Dump Station	Y	Pets	Y
Electric		Amenities		Security	
None	Y	Restrooms	Y	Host(s)	Y
20 Amp		Showers	Y	Rangers(s)	Y
30 Amp		Reserve Sites	Y	Gate	
50 Amp		Store		Patrolled	Y
		Grill/Table	Y		

About Massachusetts Public Campgrounds

Public campgrounds in Massachusetts are essentially limited to the State Park System. For folks with larger rigs, 35-40 feet is generally the length limit. Massachusetts State Park camping information can be found at -

http://www.mass.gov/eea/agencies/dcr/massparks/recreational-activities/massparks-camping-info-generic.html#5

Camping fees at Department of Conservation & Recreation campgrounds are:

Coastal Campground

Out Of State Resident - $17 a night

MA Resident - $15 a night

Inland Campground

Out Of State Resident - $14 a night

MA Resident - $12 a night

Advanced reservations are available for 29 state forests and park campgrounds. Reservations may be made as early as six months prior to the date of arrival, and as late as one day prior to arrival. The reservation transaction charge is $8.65 per reservation. Call (877) 422-6762 or go online to ReserveAmerica at -

http://www.reserveamerica.com/unifSearch.do

Pets are allowed but must be leashed (10 foot maximum) at all times. There may be areas posted off-limits to pets.

[1] October Mountain State Forest	**[7] Pearl Hill State Park**
[2] Tolland State Forest	**[8] Scusett Beach State Reservation**
[3] Wells State Park	**[9] Lake Dennison Recreation Area**
[4] DAR State Forest	**[10] Mohawk Trail State Forest**
[5] Harold Parker State Forest	**[11] Clarksburg State Park**
[6] Salisbury Beach State Reservation	

NOTES:

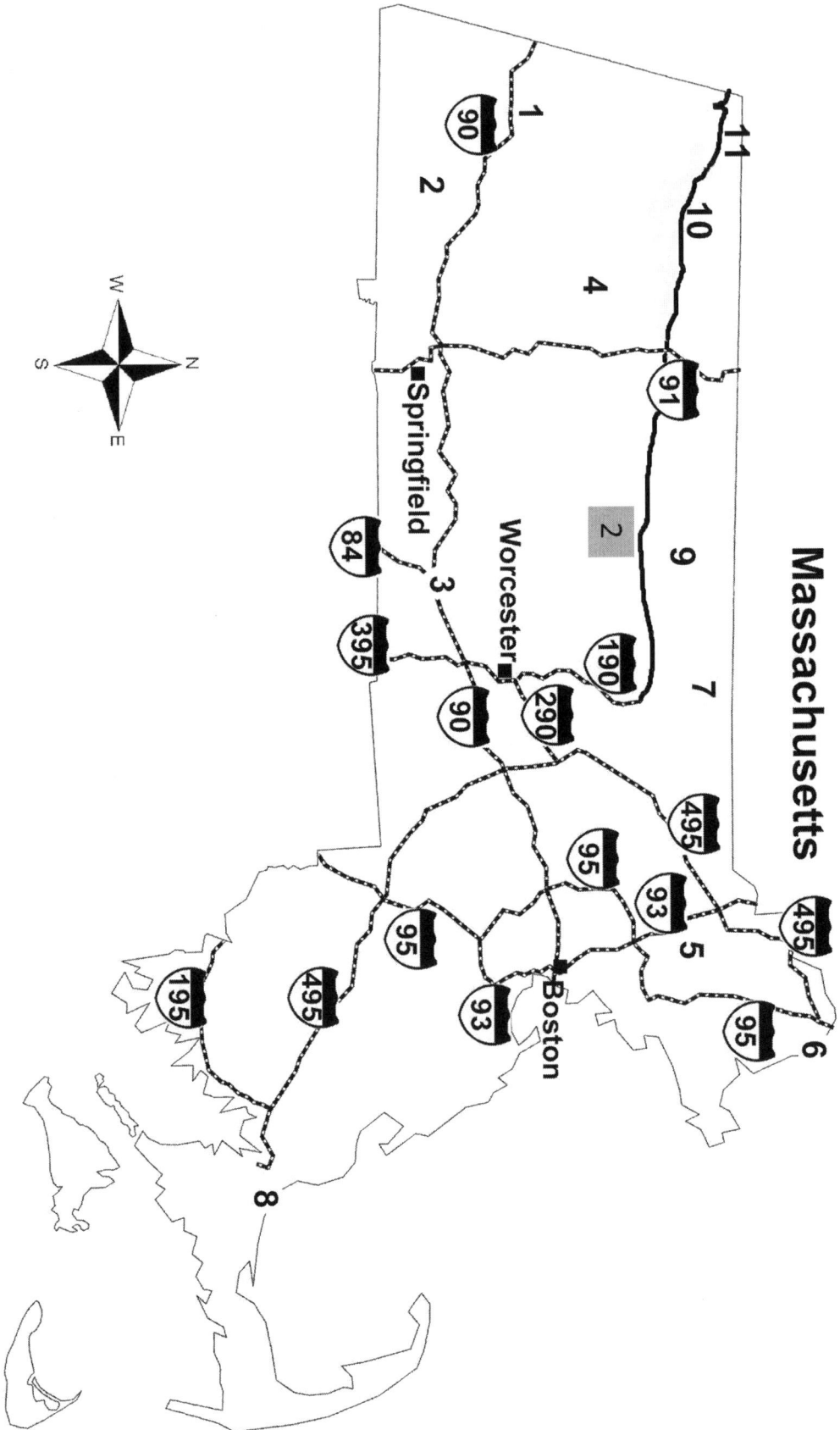

Massachusetts

Springfield

Worcester

Boston

90 1

2

11

10

4

91

2

84

3

395

9

190

7

90

290

495

95

93

495

5

95

93

6

95

195

495

8

[1] October Mountain State Forest
I-90, Exit 2
North of Lee
N42 20.178 W73 14.036
State Rate: $12-$14
(413) 243-1778
http://www.mass.gov/eea/agencies/dcr/
massparks/region-west/october-mountain-
state-forest-generic.html

Points of Interest

3.5 miles. From Exit 2 follow Hwy 20 north-west 1.1 mile through Lee to Center St. Turn right, go 0.3 miles, bear left on Columbia St. for 0.8 miles. Go straight at the merge onto Bradley St. Go 1.1 miles (becomes Woodland Rd), following brown signs to the park.

Points of Interest

You are in the midst of the Berkshire Region, with the Appalachian Trail. Visit Tanglewood.

RV Sites		Water		Laundry	
Number	23	None		Wi-Fi	
Shaded	Y	At Site		Fishing	Y
By Water	Y	Spigots	Y	Hiking	Y
Paved		Sewer		Biking	Y
Pull Thru	Y	None		Swimming	
ADA	Y	At Site		Watch Wildlife	Y
Max RV Size	35	Dump Station	Y	Pets	Y
Electric		Amenities		Security	
None	Y	Restrooms	Y	Host(s)	Y
20 Amp		Showers	Y	Rangers(s)	Y
30 Amp		Reserve Sites	Y	Gate	
50 Amp		Store		Patrolled	Y
		Grill/Table	Y		

[2] Tolland State Forest
I-90, Exit 3
West of Westfield
N42 08.680 W73 02.996
State Rate: $12-$14
(413) 269-6002
http://www.mass.gov/eea/agencies/dcr/massparks/
region-west/tolland-state-forest-generic.html

Directions

22 miles. From Exit 3 go 1.5 mi. south on Hwy 10/202 to Hwy 20. Go west for 5.8 mi. to Hwy 23 (Blandford). Turn left & go 11.8 mi. (through East Otis). A mi. past the East Otis townline, go left on West Shore Rd for 1.7 mi., then left 1.3 mi. on Tolland Rd. to the camp.

Points of Interest

See Hancock Shaker Village, Berkshire & Norman Rockwell Museums. Browse Mews in Stockbridge, unique shops includes many local artists' designs.

RV Sites		Water		Laundry	
Number	44	None		Wi-Fi	
Shaded	Y	At Site		Fishing	Y
By Water	Y	Spigots	Y	Hiking	Y
Paved		Sewer		Biking	Y
Pull Thru		None		Swimming	Y
ADA	Y	At Site		Watch Wildlife	Y
Max RV Size	35	Dump Station	Y	Pets	Y
Electric		Amenities		Security	
None	Y	Restrooms	Y	Host(s)	Y
20 Amp		Showers	Y	Rangers(s)	Y
30 Amp		Reserve Sites	Y	Gate	
50 Amp		Store		Patrolled	Y
		Grill/Table	Y		

[3] Wells State Park
I-90, Exit 9; I-84, Exit 3A
North of Sturbridge
N42 08.482 W72 02.496
State Rate: $12-$14
(508) 347-9257
http://www.mass.gov/eea/agencies/dcr/
massparks/region-central/wells-state-park.html

Directions

2.5 miles. From either Interstate Exit, follow Hwy 131/20 for 1.4 miles east to Hwy 49. Turn north (left) on Hwy 49. Go 0.9 mile to the Park.

Points of Interest

Visit Old Sturbridge Village. Discover rural New England life of the 1700s & 1800s. 'OSV,' on 200+ acres of historical land features over 40 reproduction, reconstructed buildings reminiscent of centuries-old New England. The Village is the largest outdoor living history in the northeast.

RV Sites		Water		Laundry	
Number	48	None		Wi-Fi	
Shaded	Y	At Site		Fishing	Y
By Water	Y	Spigots	Y	Hiking	Y
Paved		Sewer		Biking	Y
Pull Thru	Y	None		Swimming	Y
ADA	Y	At Site		Watch Wildlife	Y
Max RV Size	35	Dump Station	Y	Pets	Y
Electric		Amenities		Security	
None	Y	Restrooms	Y	Host(s)	Y
20 Amp		Showers	Y	Rangers(s)	Y
30 Amp		Reserve Sites	Y	Gate	
50 Amp		Store		Patrolled	Y
		Grill/Table	Y		

[4] DAR State Forest
I-91, Exit 19
Northwest of Northampton
N42 27.376 W72 47.448
State Rate: $12-$14
(413) 268-7098
http://www.mass.gov/eea/agencies/dcr/massparks/region-west/dar-state-forest-generic.html

Directions

15.5 miles. From Exit 19 in Northampton follow Hwy 9 west & northwest for 13.9 miles to just past Goshen. Turn right onto Hwy 112 and continue for 0.7 miles to Moore Hill Rd. Turn right, go 0.8 miles to the Park entrance.

Points of Interest

In 1851, opera singer Jenny Lind, the "Swedish Nightingale", called Northampton the "Paradise of America." The city is an arts destination, once named "Number One Best Small Arts Town."

RV Sites		Water		Laundry	
Number	34	None		Wi-Fi	
Shaded	Y	At Site		Fishing	Y
By Water	Y	Spigots	Y	Hiking	Y
Paved		**Sewer**		Biking	Y
Pull Thru		None		Swimming	Y
ADA	Y	At Site		Watch Wildlife	Y
Max RV Size	28	Dump Station	Y	Pets	Y
Electric		**Amenities**		**Security**	
None	Y	Restrooms	Y	Host(s)	Y
20 Amp		Showers	Y	Rangers(s)	Y
30 Amp		Reserve Sites	Y	Gate	
50 Amp		Store		Patrolled	Y
		Grill/Table	Y		

[5] Harold Parker State Forest
I-93, Exit 41; also I-95, Exit 47
Northwest of Danvers
N42 36.649 W71 05.436
State Rate: $12-$14
(978) 475-7972
http://www.mass.gov/eea/agencies/dcr/massparks/region-north/harold-parker-state-forest.html

Directions

4.5 miles. From Exit 41 go 2.6 miles northeast on Hwy 125. Turn right on Harold Parker Rd, go 1.5 miles to Jenkins Rd. Turn right on Jenkins Rd, go 0.2 miles to the Park entrance.

Points of Interest

You are within an hour of most of the sites and activities that the Boston metropolitan area has to offer. The 3,000 acre Park forest offers 35 miles of hiking and biking trails.

RV Sites		Water		Laundry	
Number	25	None		Wi-Fi	
Shaded	Y	At Site	Y	Fishing	Y
By Water	Y	Spigots	Y	Hiking	Y
Paved		**Sewer**		Biking	Y
Pull Thru		None		Swimming	Y
ADA	Y	At Site		Watch Wildlife	Y
Max RV Size	40	Dump Station	Y	Pets	Y
Electric		**Amenities**		**Security**	
None	Y	Restrooms	Y	Host(s)	Y
20 Amp		Showers	Y	Rangers(s)	Y
30 Amp		Reserve Sites	Y	Gate	
50 Amp		Store		Patrolled	Y
		Grill/Table	Y		

[6] Salisbury Beach State Reservation
I-95, Exit 58
East of Salisbury
N42 50.507 W70 49.361
State Rate: $15-$17
(978) 462-4481
http://www.mass.gov/eea/agencies/dcr/massparks/region-north/salisbury-beach-state-reservation.html

Directions

4 miles. From Exit 58 follow Hwy 110 east for 2 miles to Salisbury & the intersection with Hwy 1. Turn north 0.2 miles, then turn right on Hwy 1a (Beach Rd) & follow it 2 miles to the Park (State Beach Rd) on the right.

Points of Interest

Over-the-dune boardwalks, playground, & pavilion area make this a popular ocean destination. There are also many towns south & north to visit & enjoy.

RV Sites		Water		Laundry	
Number	403	None		Wi-Fi	
Shaded		At Site	Y	Fishing	Y
By Water	Y	Spigots		Hiking	Y
Paved	Y	**Sewer**		Biking	Y
Pull Thru		None		Swimming	Y
ADA	Y	At Site		Watch Wildlife	
Max RV Size	40	Dump Station	Y	Pets	Y
Electric		**Amenities**		**Security**	
None		Restrooms	Y	Host(s)	Y
20 Amp	Y	Showers	Y	Rangers(s)	Y
30 Amp	Y	Reserve Sites	Y	Gate	
50 Amp	Y	Store		Patrolled	Y
		Grill/Table	Y		

[7] Pearl Hill State Park
I-190, Exit 8
North of Fitchburg
N42 39.274 W71 45.457
State Rate: $12-$14
(978) 597-8802
http://www.mass.gov/eea/agencies/dcr/
massparks/region-central/pearl-hill-state-park.html

Directions

16 miles. From Exit 8 go 1.9 mile west on Hwy 2 to exit 32. Go north onto Hwy 13, 10 miles to Hwy 119 in Townsend. Turn left on Hwy 119, go 2.1 miles to New Fitchburg Rd Turn left, go 1.8 miles to the parK.

Points of Interest

Leominster has over 20 antique shops. Visit the Fitchburg Art Museum with paintings, prints, drawings, ceramics & decorative arts as well as Greek, Roman, Asian & pre-Columbian antiquities.

RV Sites		Water		Laundry	
Number	51	None		Wi-Fi	
Shaded	Y	At Site		Fishing	Y
By Water	Y	Spigots	Y	Hiking	Y
Paved		**Sewer**		Biking	Y
Pull Thru	Y	None		Swimming	Y
ADA	Y	At Site		Watch Wildlife	Y
Max RV Size	35	Dump Station	Y	Pets	Y
Electric		**Amenities**		**Security**	
None	Y	Restrooms		Host(s)	Y
20 Amp		Showers	Y	Rangers(s)	Y
30 Amp		Reserve Sites	Y	Gate	
50 Amp		Store		Patrolled	Y
		Grill/Table	Y		

[8] Scusset Beach State Reservation
I-495, Exit 1
On the Cape Cod Canal
N41 46.680 W70 30.345
State Rate: $15-$17
(508) 888-0859
http://www.mass.gov/eea/agencies/dcr/
massparks/region-south/scusset-beach-state-reservation.html

Directions

15.5 miles. From Exit 1 go east 10 miles on Hwy 25 to Hwy 6 exit. Go east on Hwy 6 for 3.5 miles to the Hwy 3/6 rotary. Go east on Meetinghouse Lane (becomes Scusset Beach Rd) for 2 miles to the camp.

Points of Interest

Scusset Beach is a popular swimming, salt water angling & ship watching area. Bicycling along the canal is fun. You are at the gateway to Cape Cod!

RV Sites		Water		Laundry	
Number	92	None		Wi-Fi	
Shaded	some	At Site	Y	Fishing	Y
By Water	Y	Spigots		Hiking	Y
Paved	Y	**Sewer**		Biking	Y
Pull Thru		None		Swimming	Y
ADA	Y	At Site		Watch Wildlife	Y
Max RV Size	40	Dump Station	Y	Pets	Y
Electric		**Amenities**		**Security**	
None		Restrooms	Y	Host(s)	Y
20 Amp	Y	Showers	Y	Rangers(s)	Y
30 Amp	Y	Reserve Sites	Y	Gate	
50 Amp		Store	Y	Patrolled	Y
		Grill/Table			

[9] Lake Dennison Recreation Area
Hwy 2, North on Hwy 202
North of Phillipston North Corners
N42 38.879 W72 04.852
State Rate: $12-$14
(978) 939-8962
http://www.mass.gov/eea/agencies/dcr/
massparks/region-central/lake-dennison-recreation-area.html

Directions

Hwy 2 West bound to Exit 20 then right on Baldwinville Rd 2.4 miles to the end. Then right on Hwy 202 North 3.5 miles to park. **Hwy 2 East bound** to Exit 19, Hwy 202 North 7.5 miles to the park

Points of Interest

The Park offers camping on a 85 acre lake, swimming, fishing, a ramp for non-power boats & 50 miles of mountain biking trails close by.

RV Sites		Water		Laundry	
Number	142	None		Wi-Fi	
Shaded	Y	At Site		Fishing	Y
By Water	Y	Spigots	Y	Hiking	Y
Paved		**Sewer**		Biking	Y
Pull Thru	Y	None		Swimming	Y
ADA	Y	At Site		Watch Wildlife	Y
Max RV Size	38	Dump Station	Y	Pets	Y
Electric		**Amenities**		**Security**	
None	Y	Restrooms	Y	Host(s)	Y
20 Amp		Showers	Y	Rangers(s)	Y
30 Amp		Reserve Sites	Y	Gate	
50 Amp		Store		Patrolled	Y
		Grill/Table	Y		

[10] Mohawk Trail State Forest
Hwy 2, west of Charlemont
West of Charlemont
N42 38.196 W72 56.130
State Rate: $12-$14
(413) 339-5504
http://www.mass.gov/eea/agencies/dcr/
massparks/region-west/mohawk-trail-state-
forest.html

Directions

4 miles. From Charlemont go 4 miles west on
Hwy 2 to the Park entrance at Cold Water Rd.

Points of Interest

This is one of the most scenic woodland areas
in Massachusetts. Many of the original Indian
trails, including the Mahican-Mohawk Trail, are
open for hiking. Over 18 miles of rivers and
streams make for excellent trout fishing and
swimming.

RV Sites		Water		Laundry	
Number	36	None		Wi-Fi	
Shaded	Y	At Site		Fishing	Y
By Water	Y	Spigots	Y	Hiking	Y
Paved		**Sewer**		Biking	Y
Pull Thru		None		Swimming	Y
ADA	Y	At Site		Watch Wildlife	Y
Max RV Size	25	Dump Station	Y	Pets	Y
Electric		**Amenities**		**Security**	
None	Y	Restrooms	Y	Host(s)	Y
20 Amp		Showers	Y	Rangers(s)	Y
30 Amp		Reserve Sites	Y	Gate	
50 Amp		Store		Patrolled	Y
		Grill/Table	Y		

[11] Clarksburg State Park
Hwy 2, North on Hwy 8
North of North Adams
N42 43.990 W73 04.672
State Rate: $12-$14
(413) 664-8345
http://www.mass.gov/eea/agencies/dcr/
massparks/region-west/clarksburg-state-park.html

Directions

3.2 miles. From downtown North Adams, take
Hwy 8 north 3 miles to Middle Rd. Turn left and
continue 0.1 mile to the park.

Points of Interest

The Park offers unspoiled northern hardwood
forest with breathtaking views of the Hoosac
Range, Mount Greylock and the Green Mountains. Mauserts Pond is surrounded by 9.5 miles
of foot trails, where visitors can observe a variety
of wildlife, possibly a moose!

RV Sites		Water		Laundry	
Number	39	None		Wi-Fi	
Shaded	Y	At Site		Fishing	Y
By Water	Y	Spigots	Y	Hiking	Y
Paved		**Sewer**		Biking	Y
Pull Thru		None	Y	Swimming	Y
ADA	Y	At Site		Watch Wildlife	Y
Max RV Size	23	Dump Station		Pets	Y
Electric		**Amenities**		**Security**	
None	Y	Restrooms	Y	Host(s)	Y
20 Amp		Showers	Y	Rangers(s)	Y
30 Amp		Reserve Sites	Y	Gate	
50 Amp		Store		Patrolled	Y
		Grill/Table	Y		

About Michigan's Public Campgrounds

Michigan is predominately populated with State Park and National Forest campgrounds. There are around 125 State Park and Forest as well as over 60 National Forest campgrounds statewide. It can be said that you are never more than half an hour from a Michigan State Park, State Forest or National Forest Campground. The Michigan Department of Natural Resources and Environment is responsible for the State's Parks and Forest, and can be found at -

http://www.michigan.gov/dnr/0,1607,7-153-10365---,00.html

Reservations for campsites may be made up to 6 months in advance of your arrival date. The reservation fee is $8, cancellation fee is $10. The Recreation Passport has replaced the vehicle window sticker for entry into state parks, recreation areas, state forest campgrounds and non-motorized trail head and boat launch parking ($11 - Michigan registered vehicles; $31.10 - Non-Michigan registered vehicles). The Michigan Department of Natural Resources State Park Campground and Harbor Reservation page can be found at - **https://www. midnrreservations.com/**

State Park and Recreation Area Fees

Full Hook-Up Campsite - $33 per night: Full hook-up campsites feature direct sewer, water and electrical hook-ups with 20/30 or 50 amp service.

Premium Modern Campsite - $29-$28 per night: Premium campsites feature 50-amp electric hookups, modern toilet buildings, showers, wheelchair-accessible sites and sanitation stations. In addition, some campgrounds have pull-through sites for larger vehicles.

Modern Campsite - $27-$16 per night: Modern campsites feature electric hookups (amps will vary), modern toilet buildings, showers, wheelchair-accessible sites and sanitation stations. In addition, some campgrounds have pull-through sites for larger vehicles

Semi-Modern Campsite - $18-$16 per night: There are two distinct options in this classification. The first offers electrical service but no modern toilet/shower buildings. Vault toilets are available on location and water is available from a hand pump. The second option provides modern toilet and shower buildings but no electrical hookups.

Rustic Campsite - $10-$14 per night: Vault toilets and hand pump water. No showers or flush toilets

Many parks require as much as 100 feet of electric extension cord. With few exceptions, pets are welcomed in Michigan state parks and recreation areas. Pets are not allowed on designated beaches or areas used for wading or swimming. Always keep your pet on a leash not to exceed six feet in length.

[1] Sleepy Hollow State Park

[2] Metamora-Hadley Recreation Area

[3] Lakeport State Park

[4] Sterling State Park

[5] Pontiac Lake Recreation Area

[6] Seven Lakes State Park

[7] Bay City State Recreation Area

[8] South Higgins Lake State Park

[9] Hartwick Pines State Park

[10] Burt Lake State Park

[11] Wilderness State Park

[12] Foley Creek Campground

[13] Brimley State Park

[14] Warren Dunes State Park

[15] Fort Custer Recreation Area

[16] Waterloo Portage Lake

[17] Hoffmaster State Park

[18] Ionia State Recreation Area

[19] Proud Lake Recreation Area

[20] Van Buren State Park

[21] Holland State Park

[22] Ludington State Park

[23] Sleeping Bear Dunes

[24] Petoskey State Park

[25] Port Crescent State Park

[26] Harrisville State Park

[27] P. H. Hoeft State Park

NOTES:

Michigan

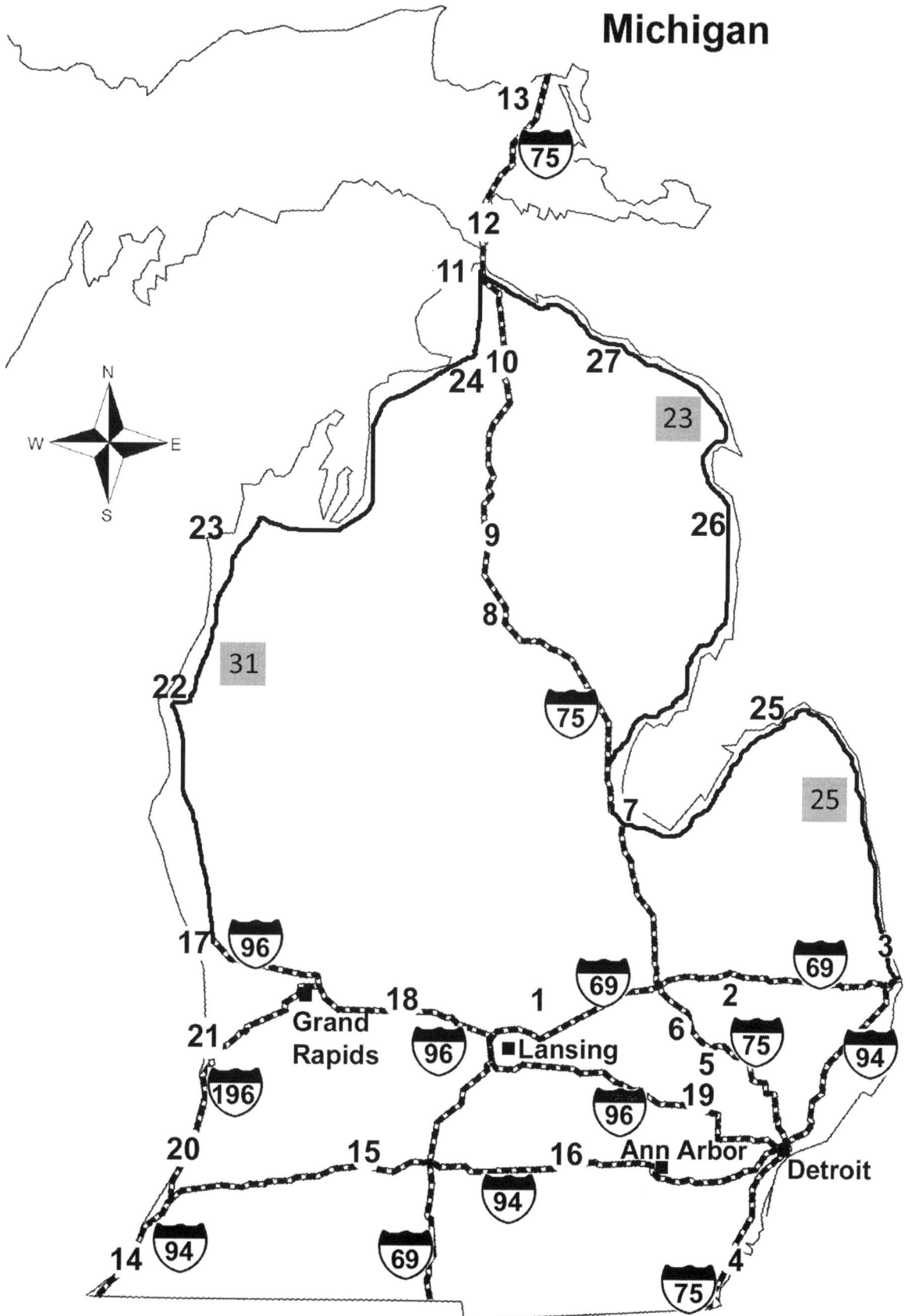

[1] Sleepy Hollow State Park
I-69, Exit 89
North of Lansing
N42 55.747 W84 24.461
State Rate: $19 (Modern)
(517) 651-6217
http://www.michigandnr.com/parksandtrails/Details.aspx?id=495&type=SPRK

Directions

14 miles. From Exit 89 go north on Hwy 127 for 8 miles to Price Rd. Turn east on Price for 6 miles to the Park entrance at State Park Rd.

Points of Interest

Greater Lansing area destinations include Curwood Castle, Abrams Planetarium, Kresge Art Museum, Cooley Gardens, Michigan Women's Historical Center, and the Meridian Historical Village. For food/beverages try Uncle John's Cider Mill or the Michigan Brewing Company.

RV Sites		Water		Laundry	
Number	181	None		Wi-Fi	
Shaded	Y	At Site		Fishing	Y
By Water		Spigots	Y	Hiking	Y
Paved	Y	Sewer		Biking	Y
Pull Thru		None		Swimming	Y
ADA	Y	At Site		Watch Wildlife	Y
Max RV Size	45	Dump Station	Y	Pets	Y
Electric		Amenities		Security	
None		Restrooms	Y	Host(s)	Y
20 Amp	Y	Showers	Y	Rangers(s)	Y
30 Amp	Y	Reserve Sites	Y	Gate	
50 Amp		Store	Y	Patrolled	Y
		Grill/Table	Y		

[2] Metamora-Hadley Recreation Area
I-69, Exit 155
Southeast of Flint
N42 56.702 W83 21.425
State Rate: $23 (Modern)
(810) 797-4439
http://www.michigandnr.com/parksandtrails/details.aspx?id=472&type=SPRK

Directions

8 miles. From Exit 155 go 5 miles south on Hwy 24. Turn west on Cty Hwy 62 (Pratt Rd) for 2.3 miles to Herd Rd. Turn south for 0.7 miles to the Park entrance.

Points of Interest

Visit the Buick Gallery - a large collection of vintage Buicks, automotive memorabilia & research archives. At Crossroads Village wander through 35 historic buildings & shops. Ride the Genesee Belle Riverboat for a scenic cruise on Mott Lake

RV Sites		Water		Laundry	
Number	214	None		Wi-Fi	
Shaded	Y	At Site		Fishing	Y
By Water	Y	Spigots	Y	Hiking	Y
Paved		Sewer		Biking	Y
Pull Thru	Y	None		Swimming	Y
ADA	Y	At Site		Watch Wildlife	Y
Max RV Size	45	Dump Station	Y	Pets	Y
Electric		Amenities		Security	
None		Restrooms	Y	Host(s)	Y
20 Amp	Y	Showers	Y	Rangers(s)	Y
30 Amp	Y	Reserve Sites	Y	Gate	
50 Amp		Store	Y	Patrolled	Y
		Grill/Table	Y		

[3] Lakeport State Park
I-69/I-94, Exit 274
North of Port Huron
N43 07.466 W82 29.837
State Rate: $23 (Modern)
(810) 327-6224
http://www.michigandnr.com/parksandtrails/Details.aspx?id=466&type=SPRK

Directions

9.5 miles. From Exit 274 go 9.5 miles north on Hwy 25. North of Burtchville, bear right at the south side of the Park on M-25, Lakeshore Rd, to the campground.

Points of Interest

Tour the retired Coast Guard Cutter Bramble & the Huron Lightship. Find out why antique collectors treasure Marine City. Stroll the world's longest wooden freshwater boardwalk in St. Clair.

RV Sites		Water		Laundry	
Number	250	None		Wi-Fi	
Shaded	Y	At Site		Fishing	
By Water	Y	Spigots	Y	Hiking	Y
Paved	some	Sewer		Biking	Y
Pull Thru	Y	None		Swimming	Y
ADA	Y	At Site		Watch Wildlife	Y
Max RV Size	45	Dump Station	Y	Pets	Y
Electric		Amenities		Security	
None		Restrooms	Y	Host(s)	Y
20 Amp	Y	Showers	Y	Rangers(s)	Y
30 Amp	Y	Reserve Sites	Y	Gate	
50 Amp		Store	Y	Patrolled	Y
		Grill/Table	Y		

[4] Sterling State Park
I-75, Exit 15
East of Monroe on Lake Erie
N41 55.206 W83 20.292
State Rate: $24-$33 (Modern, Full Hook-up)
(734) 289-2715
http://www.michigandnr.com/parksandtrails/Details.aspx?id=497&type=SPRK

Directions

2 miles. From Exit 15 go northeast for 0.7 mile on Dixie Hwy. Turn right on State Park Rd for 1 mile to the Park entrance.

Points of Interest

The Park is in Monroe County, one of Michigan's oldest communities. Historic treasures abound giving Monroe County both national and global appeal. With Lake Erie and the River Raisin, the area is Michigan's top visitor destination. Learn more at - http://www.monroeinfo.com/

RV Sites		Water			Laundry	
Number	256	None			Wi-Fi	
Shaded		At Site	Y		Fishing	Y
By Water	Y	Spigots	Y		Hiking	Y
Paved	Y	Sewer			Biking	Y
Pull Thru	Y	None			Swimming	Y
ADA	Y	At Site	some		Watch Wildlife	Y
Max RV Size	45	Dump Station	Y		Pets	Y
Electric		Amenities			Security	
None		Restrooms	Y		Host(s)	Y
20 Amp	Y	Showers	Y		Rangers(s)	Y
30 Amp	Y	Reserve Sites	Y		Gate	
50 Amp	some	Store			Patrolled	Y
		Grill/Table	Y			

[5] Pontiac Lake Recreation Area
I-75, Exit 93
Northwest of Pontiac
N42 41.199 W83 29.390
State Rate: $18 (Modern)
(248) 666-1020
http://www.michigandnr.com/parksandtrails/details.aspx?id=196&type=SPCG

Directions

6.5 miles. From Exit 93 go southeast 1.5 miles on Dixie Hwy to White Lake Rd. Turn south for 1.7 miles to Anderson Rd. Turn west for 0.5 miles to White Lake Rd. (not Old White Lake). Turn left for 2.2 miles to Teggerdine Rd. Turn south 0.5 miles to Maceday Rd & the park.

Points of Interest

Visit Pontiac, known for the Arts, Beats & Eats Festival. Pontiac participates in the annual Woodward Dream Cruise celebrating Woodward's hot-rod history.

RV Sites		Water			Laundry	
Number	176	None			Wi-Fi	
Shaded	Y	At Site			Fishing	
By Water		Spigots	Y		Hiking	
Paved		Sewer			Biking	Y
Pull Thru		None			Swimming	
ADA	Y	At Site			Watch Wildlife	
Max RV Size	45	Dump Station	Y		Pets	Y
Electric		Amenities			Security	
None		Restrooms	Y		Host(s)	Y
20 Amp	Y	Showers	Y		Rangers(s)	Y
30 Amp	Y	Reserve Sites	Y		Gate	
50 Amp		Store			Patrolled	Y
		Grill/Table	Y			

[6] Seven Lakes State Park
I-75, Exit 101
South of Flint
N42 49.006 W83 38.886
State Rate: $19 (Modern)
(248) 634-7271
http://www.michigandnr.com/parksandtrails/Details.aspx?id=492&type=SPRK

Directions

5 miles. From Exit 101 go west on Grange Hall Rd for 4.1 miles to Fish Lake Rd. Turn north 0.8 mile to the Park entrance on you left.

Points of Interest

Flint's dramatic history as the birthplace of General Motors comes to life at Sloan Museum. The museum's newest gallery takes visitors on a fascinating journey through Flint in the 20th century - from the birth of General Motors to the present. Visit Durand Union Station.

RV Sites		Water			Laundry	
Number	70	None			Wi-Fi	
Shaded	some	At Site			Fishing	Y
By Water	Y	Spigots	Y		Hiking	
Paved	Y	Sewer			Biking	Y
Pull Thru		None			Swimming	Y
ADA	Y	At Site			Watch Wildlife	
Max RV Size	40	Dump Station	Y		Pets	Y
Electric		Amenities			Security	
None		Restrooms	Y		Host(s)	Y
20 Amp	Y	Showers	Y		Rangers(s)	Y
30 Amp	Y	Reserve Sites	Y		Gate	
50 Amp		Store	Y		Patrolled	Y
		Grill/Table	Y			

[7] Bay City State Recreation Area
I-75, Exit 168
North of Saginaw
N43 40.041 W83 54.451
State Rate: $19-$21 (Modern)
(989) 684-3020
http://www.michigandnr.com/parksandtrails/Details.aspx?type=SPRK&id=437

Directions

5 miles. From Exit 168 go 5 miles east on Beaver Rd to the Park.

Points of Interest

The Park has one of the largest remaining freshwater, coastal wetlands on the Great Lakes (the Tobico Marsh). You will be on Saginaw Bay with paved trails, a boardwalk, 2 observation towers, multiple observation platforms and photo opportunities.

RV Sites		Water		Laundry	
Number	193	None		Wi-Fi	
Shaded	Y	At Site		Fishing	Y
By Water	Y	Spigots	Y	Hiking	Y
Paved		**Sewer**		Biking	Y
Pull Thru		None		Swimming	Y
ADA	Y	At Site		Watch Wildlife	Y
Max RV Size	45	Dump Station	Y	Pets	Y
Electric		**Amenities**		**Security**	
None		Restrooms	Y	Host(s)	Y
20 Amp	Y	Showers	Y	Rangers(s)	Y
30 Amp	Y	Reserve Sites	Y	Gate	
50 Amp		Store		Patrolled	Y
		Grill/Table	Y		

[8] South Higgins Lake State Park
I-75, Exit 239
South of Grayling
N44 25.383 W84 40.684
State Rate: $25-$33 (Modern, Full Hook-up)
(989) 821-6374
http://www.michigandnr.com/parksandtrails/details.aspx?id=496&type=SPRK

Directions

6.5 miles. From Exit 239 turn southwest, just after the off ramp, immediately turn right on Cty Rd 103 (Robinson Lake Rd.). Go 3.2 miles to Higgins Lake Rd. Turn south 3.1 miles to State Park Dr and the Park.

Points of Interest

The morel beckons visitors to this area during the spring. Crawford County has ample state & federal property which may be mushroom hunted at will.

RV Sites		Water		Laundry	
Number	400	None		Wi-Fi	
Shaded	Y	At Site	some	Fishing	Y
By Water	Y	Spigots	Y	Hiking	Y
Paved		**Sewer**		Biking	Y
Pull Thru	Y	None		Swimming	Y
ADA	Y	At Site	some	Watch Wildlife	Y
Max RV Size	45	Dump Station	Y	Pets	Y
Electric		**Amenities**		**Security**	
None		Restrooms	Y	Host(s)	Y
20 Amp	Y	Showers	Y	Rangers(s)	Y
30 Amp	Y	Reserve Sites	Y	Gate	
50 Amp	some	Store	Y	Patrolled	Y
		Grill/Table	Y		

[9] Hartwick Pines State Park
I-75, Exit 259
North of Grayling
N44 44.120 W84 40.179
State Rate: $25-$33 (Modern, Full Hook-up)
(989) 348-7068
http://www.michigandnr.com/parksandtrails/details.aspx?id=126&type=SPCG

Directions

2 miles. From Exit 259 go 2 miles northeast on Hwy 93 (Hartwick Pines Rd) to State Park Dr and the entrance on your left.

Points of Interest

Visit the Park logging museum. Forest hikes are special along the Old Growth Pine Trail of 300 year old trees. Gaylord, Michigan's Alpine Village, offers a quaint setting & much shopping. Enjoy weekend entertainment, a twice weekly farmers market & vast array of events & activities.

RV Sites		Water		Laundry	
Number	100	None		Wi-Fi	
Shaded	Y	At Site	some	Fishing	Y
By Water		Spigots	Y	Hiking	Y
Paved	Y	**Sewer**		Biking	Y
Pull Thru	Y	None		Swimming	
ADA	Y	At Site	some	Watch Wildlife	Y
Max RV Size	45	Dump Station	Y	Pets	Y
Electric		**Amenities**		**Security**	
None		Restrooms	Y	Host(s)	Y
20 Amp	Y	Showers	Y	Rangers(s)	Y
30 Amp	Y	Reserve Sites	Y	Gate	
50 Amp	some	Store		Patrolled	Y
		Grill/Table	Y		

[10] Burt Lake State Park
I-75, Exit 310
Southeast side of Indian River
N45 24.083 W84 37.151
State Rate: $24-$26 (Modern)
(231) 238-9392
http://www.michigandnr.com/parksandtrails/details.aspx?id=107&type=SPCG

Directions

1 mile. From Exit 310 go west, 0.4 mile, then south 0.3 mile on Hwy 68 to State Park Dr and the Park entrance on your right.

Points of Interest

In Indian River visit the 55 foot Cross In The Woods. Go to Ocqueoc Falls, on the Ocqueoc Falls Bicentennial Pathway. There are two falls. See one of only three known surviving examples of deck truss highway bridges in Michigan, built in 1937.

RV Sites		Water			Laundry	
Number	306	None			Wi-Fi	
Shaded	Y	At Site			Fishing	Y
By Water	Y	Spigots		Y	Hiking	Y
Paved	some	**Sewer**			Biking	Y
Pull Thru	Y	None			Swimming	Y
ADA	Y	At Site			Watch Wildlife	Y
Max RV Size	45	Dump Station		Y	Pets	Y
Electric		**Amenities**			**Security**	
None		Restrooms		Y	Host(s)	Y
20 Amp	Y	Showers		Y	Rangers(s)	Y
30 Amp	Y	Reserve Sites		Y	Gate	
50 Amp	some	Store			Patrolled	Y
		Grill/Table		Y		

[11] Wilderness State Park
I-75, Exit 337
West of Mackinaw City
N45 44.739 W84 53.999
State Rate: $16-$27 (Modern)
(231) 436-5381
http://www.michigandnr.com/parksandtrails/details.aspx?id=240&type=SPCG

Directions

10 miles From Exit 337 turn south on Hwy 108 (Nicolet), immediately turn right on Trails End Rd. Go 2.5 miles to the shoreline & Wilderness Park Dr. Turn south, follow Wilderness Park Dr for 7.5 miles to the camp at Swamp Line Rd.

Points of Interest

Discover Mackinaw City, one of Michigan's top tourist destinations and gateway to Mackinac Island. Check out the 'Icebreaker Mackinaw' Maritime Museum & McGulpin Point Lighthouse.

RV Sites		Water			Laundry	
Number	250	None			Wi-Fi	
Shaded	Y	At Site			Fishing	
By Water	Y	Spigots		Y	Hiking	Y
Paved		**Sewer**			Biking	Y
Pull Thru	Y	None			Swimming	
ADA	Y	At Site			Watch Wildlife	Y
Max RV Size	45	Dump Station		Y	Pets	Y
Electric		**Amenities**			**Security**	
None		Restrooms		Y	Host(s)	Y
20 Amp	Y	Showers		Y	Rangers(s)	Y
30 Amp	Y	Reserve Sites		Y	Gate	
50 Amp		Store			Patrolled	Y
		Grill/Table		Y		

[12] Foley Creek Campground
I-75, Exit 352
North of St. Ignace
N45 55.979 W84 44.982
Hiawatha USFS Rate: $16
America/Beautiful Rate: $8
(906) 643-7900
http://www.fs.usda.gov/recarea/hiawatha/recarea/?recid=13294

Directions

2 miles. From Exit 352 go east to Mackinac Trail Rd. Turn south 2.2 miles to the Park entrance.

Points of Interest

St. Ignace, the third oldest continuously inhabited settlement in the United States, has a variety of activities including restaurants, golfing, shady beaches, shopping, and ferry service to Mackinac Island. Explore the Straits of Mackinac Lighthouses, and Father Marquette National Memorial.

RV Sites		Water			Laundry	
Number	48	None			Wi-Fi	
Shaded		At Site			Fishing	Y
By Water		Spigots		Y	Hiking	Y
Paved		**Sewer**			Biking	Y
Pull Thru	Y	None			Swimming	
ADA		At Site			Watch Wildlife	Y
Max RV Size	45	Dump Station			Pets	Y
Electric		**Amenities**			**Security**	
None	Y	Restrooms		Y	Host(s)	
20 Amp		Showers			Rangers(s)	Y
30 Amp		Reserve Sites			Gate	
50 Amp		Store			Patrolled	Y
		Grill/Table		Y		

[13] Brimley State Park
I-75, Exit 386
West of Sault Ste. Marie
N46 24.759 W84 33.364
State Rate: $21-$23 (Modern)
(906) 248-3422
http://www.michigandnr.com/parksandtrails/details.aspx?id=414&type=SPRK

Directions

10.5 miles. From Exit 386 go 7.2 miles west on Hwy 28 to Hwy 221. Turn north for 2.5 miles to W. 6 Mile Road. Turn east 0.8 miles to S. Park St. and the Park entrance.

Points of Interest

Tahquamenon Falls, two national fish hatcheries, the Tower of History, the Museum of Ship Valley Camp, the Soo Locks, Sault Ste. Marie, the Coast Guard Station, the International Bridge and the Mackinaw Bridge are all in the local area.

RV Sites		Water		Laundry	
Number	237	None		Wi-Fi	
Shaded	Y	At Site		Fishing	Y
By Water	Y	Spigots	Y	Hiking	Y
Paved		**Sewer**		Biking	Y
Pull Thru	some	None		Swimming	Y
ADA	Y	At Site		Watch Wildlife	
Max RV Size	45	Dump Station	Y	Pets	Y
Electric		**Amenities**		**Security**	
None		Restrooms	Y	Host(s)	Y
20 Amp	Y	Showers	Y	Rangers(s)	Y
30 Amp	Y	Reserve Sites	Y	Gate	
50 Amp	some	Store		Patrolled	Y
		Grill/Table	Y		

[14] Warren Dunes State Park
I-94, Exits 12 or 16
South of Benton Harbor
N41 54.080 W86 35.690
State Rate: $16-$27 (Semi-Modern, Modern)
(269) 426-4013
http://www.michigandnr.com/parksandtrails/details.aspx?id=504&type=SPRK

Directions

2 miles. **From Exit 12** turn west on Sawyer Rd for 0.3 miles to the Red Arrow Hwy. Turn northeast (right) for 1.4 miles to State Park Rd. **From Exit 16** turn west to the Red Arrow Hwy. Go 2.2 miles south to the entrance.

Points of Interest

Near by destinations includes the Silver Beach Carousel Museum, Box Factory for the Arts, Fort St Joseph Museum, Horn Archaeological Museum, Krasl Art Center, & Michigan Flywheelers Museum.

RV Sites		Water		Laundry	
Number	182	None		Wi-Fi	
Shaded	Y	At Site		Fishing	
By Water	Y	Spigots	Y	Hiking	Y
Paved		**Sewer**		Biking	Y
Pull Thru	some	None		Swimming	Y
ADA	Y	At Site		Watch Wildlife	Y
Max RV Size	45	Dump Station	Y	Pets	Y
Electric		**Amenities**		**Security**	
None		Restrooms	Y	Host(s)	Y
20 Amp	Y	Showers	Y	Rangers(s)	Y
30 Amp	Y	Reserve Sites	Y	Gate	
50 Amp	some	Store	Y	Patrolled	Y
		Grill/Table	Y		

[15] Fort Custer Recreation Area
I-94, Exit 92
West of Battle Creek
N42 20.072 W85 20.302
State Rate: $21 (Modern)
(269) 731-4200
http://www.michigandnr.com/parksandtrails/details.aspx?id=448&type=SPRK

Directions

9 miles. From Exit 92 go 4 miles northeast on Hwy 37 to Hwy 96. Turn northwest, go 5.2 miles on Hwy 96 to Fort Custer Dr Turn left into the Park.

Points of Interest

Area attractions include the American Museum of Magic; the Arcadia Brewing Company; Cherry Creek Wine Cellar; Cornwell's Turkeyville, USA; the Critchlow Alligator Sanctuary; Historic Adventist Village; the Southern Exposure Herb Farm; and the Marshall Postal Museum.

RV Sites		Water		Laundry	
Number	219	None		Wi-Fi	
Shaded	Y	At Site		Fishing	Y
By Water	Y	Spigots	Y	Hiking	Y
Paved	some	**Sewer**		Biking	Y
Pull Thru		None		Swimming	Y
ADA	Y	At Site		Watch Wildlife	Y
Max RV Size	45	Dump Station	Y	Pets	Y
Electric		**Amenities**		**Security**	
None		Restrooms	Y	Host(s)	Y
20 Amp	Y	Showers	Y	Rangers(s)	Y
30 Amp	Y	Reserve Sites	Y	Gate	
50 Amp		Store	Y	Patrolled	Y
		Grill/Table	Y		

[16] Waterloo Portage Lake
I-94, Exit 147
Northeast of Jackson
N42 19.513 W84 14.497
State Rate: $22-$24 (Modern)
(734) 475-8307
http://www.dnr.state.mi.us/parksandtrails/Details.aspx?id=234&type=SPCG

Directions

3 miles. From Exit 147 go north on Race Rd for 2 miles to Seymore Ave. Turn east and go 1 mile to the Park entrance on your left.

Points of Interest

Jackson is ringed with a number of vineyards and wineries. Enjoy Cascade Falls, all manmade - 500 feet in length, a vertical height of 64 feet, total width of 60 feet, 6 fountains, 16 Falls (11 are illuminated), 1,230 Colored Electric Lights, and a 2,000 gallon per minute flow rate.

RV Sites		Water			Laundry	
Number	136	None			Wi-Fi	
Shaded	Y	At Site			Fishing	Y
By Water	Y	Spigots		Y	Hiking	Y
Paved	some	Sewer			Biking	Y
Pull Thru	some	None			Swimming	Y
ADA	Y	At Site			Watch Wildlife	Y
Max RV Size	45	Dump Station		Y	Pets	Y
Electric		Amenities			Security	
None		Restrooms		Y	Host(s)	Y
20 Amp	Y	Showers		Y	Rangers(s)	Y
30 Amp	Y	Reserve Sites		Y	Gate	
50 Amp	some	Store			Patrolled	Y
		Grill/Table		Y		

[17] Hoffmaster State Park
I-96, Exit 1
South of Muskegon
N43 08.411 W86 16.291
State Rate: $18-$29 (Semi-Modern, Modern)
(231) 798-3711
http://www.michigandnr.com/parksandtrails/details.aspx?id=457&type=SPRK

Directions

6 miles From Exit 1 turn south for 2.5 miles on Hwy 31 to Pontaluna Rd. Go west for 2.7 miles. As you approach the shoreline Pontaluna turns northwest and becomes Lake Harbor. Go 0.6 miles to the Park entrance on your left.

Points of Interest

Try the Park's Dune Climb Stairway with an observation deck & view of the dunes & Lake Michigan. In Muskegon visit the Hackley & Hume Historic site, Fire Barn Museum, & Scolnik House.

RV Sites		Water			Laundry	
Number	293	None			Wi-Fi	
Shaded	Y	At Site			Fishing	
By Water	Y	Spigots		Y	Hiking	Y
Paved		Sewer			Biking	Y
Pull Thru	some	None			Swimming	Y
ADA	Y	At Site			Watch Wildlife	Y
Max RV Size	45	Dump Station		Y	Pets	Y
Electric		Amenities			Security	
None		Restrooms		Y	Host(s)	Y
20 Amp	Y	Showers		Y	Rangers(s)	Y
30 Amp	Y	Reserve Sites		Y	Gate	
50 Amp	some	Store		Y	Patrolled	Y
		Grill/Table		Y		

[18] Ionia State Recreation Area
I-96, Exit 64
East of Grand Rapids
N42 55.783 W85 08.045
State Rate: $19 (Modern)
(616) 527-3750
http://www.michigandnr.com/parksandtrails/details.aspx?id=461&type=SPRK

Directions

4 miles. From Exit 64 go 3.5 miles north on Jordan Lake Rd to the Park entrance.

Points of Interest

Grand Rapids touts its walkable downtown for shopping and food, all within a 1/2 mile radius, with riverwalks, bridges, and unique architecture. Visit the Grand Rapids Art Museum and Gerald R. Ford Presidential Museum. Try the Opera or treat yourself to the Symphony Pops.

RV Sites		Water			Laundry	
Number	100	None			Wi-Fi	
Shaded	Y	At Site			Fishing	Y
By Water	Y	Spigots		Y	Hiking	Y
Paved		Sewer			Biking	Y
Pull Thru		None			Swimming	Y
ADA	Y	At Site			Watch Wildlife	Y
Max RV Size	45	Dump Station		Y	Pets	Y
Electric		Amenities			Security	
None		Restrooms		Y	Host(s)	Y
20 Amp	Y	Showers		Y	Rangers(s)	Y
30 Amp	Y	Reserve Sites		Y	Gate	
50 Amp		Store			Patrolled	Y
		Grill/Table		Y		

[19] Proud Lake Recreation Area
I-96, Exit 159
Northwest of Farmington Hills
N42 33.560 W83 31.745
State Rate: $22 (Modern)
(248) 685-2433
http://www.dnr.state.mi.us/parksandtrails/Details.aspx?id=487&type=SPRK

Directions

5 miles. From Exit 159 go 4.3 miles north on Wixom Rd. Turn east on Glengary Rd for 0.5 miles to the Park entrance, Proud Lake Rec Rd.

Points of Interest

The Park, on the scenic Huron River, offers more than 20 miles of trails covering several diverse habitats. In spring, hepatica (liverwort), marsh marigold, violets and many other wildflowers abound. Guided interpretive walks and other nature activities are offered.

RV Sites		Water		Laundry	
Number	130	None		Wi-Fi	
Shaded	Y	At Site		Fishing	Y
By Water	Y	Spigots	Y	Hiking	Y
Paved		Sewer		Biking	Y
Pull Thru		None		Swimming	Y
ADA	Y	At Site		Watch Wildlife	
Max RV Size	45	Dump Station	Y	Pets	Y
Electric		Amenities		Security	
None		Restrooms	Y	Host(s)	Y
20 Amp	Y	Showers	Y	Rangers(s)	Y
30 Amp	Y	Reserve Sites	Y	Gate	
50 Amp	some	Store	Y	Patrolled	Y
		Grill/Table	Y		

[20] Van Buren State Park
I-196, Exit 18
North of Benton Harbor
N42 20.074 W86 18.249
State Rate: $21-$23 (Modern)
(269) 637-2788
http://www.michigandnr.com/parksandtrails/details.aspx?id=227&type=SPCG

Directions

3.5 miles. From Exit 18, turn north on Hwy 140 for 0.2 miles to 14th Ave. Turn west for 0.8 mile to the Blue Star Hwy. Turn south 1.4 miles, bear right at the Five Star Hwy (Ruggles) & continue for 1.1 mile to the park.

Points of Interest

Visit South Haven, don't miss the World-Famous Lighthouse, a great photo opportunity. Antiquing, museums, wineries, beach sights and walks all are good choices in this area.

RV Sites		Water		Laundry	
Number	220	None		Wi-Fi	
Shaded	some	At Site		Fishing	
By Water	Y	Spigots	Y	Hiking	Y
Paved		Sewer		Biking	Y
Pull Thru		None		Swimming	Y
ADA	Y	At Site		Watch Wildlife	
Max RV Size	45	Dump Station	Y	Pets	Y
Electric		Amenities		Security	
None		Restrooms	Y	Host(s)	Y
20 Amp	Y	Showers	Y	Rangers(s)	Y
30 Amp	Y	Reserve Sites	Y	Gate	
50 Amp	some	Store		Patrolled	Y
		Grill/Table	Y		

[21] Holland State Park (Beach)
I-196, Exit 44
West of Holland
N42 46.415 W86 12.475
State Rate: $27-$33 (Modern, Full Hook-up)
(616) 399-9390
http://www.michigandnr.com/parksandtrails/details.aspx?id=458&type=SPRK

Directions

14 miles. From Exit 44 go 7 miles north on Hwy 31. Exit at Lakewood and go west. Along the way Lakewood will become Douglas, then Ottawa Beach. Go 7.2 miles in all to the Park.

Points of Interest

Visit Holland! Spring is for tulips, making it one of the best times to visit the many parks, gardens, and Dutch attractions. In summer, enjoy the beaches, ride the trails, or sail on Lake Michigan. Autumn brings a harvest of orchards, fall color.

RV Sites		Water		Laundry	
Number	211	None		Wi-Fi	
Shaded	Y	At Site	some	Fishing	Y
By Water	Y	Spigots	Y	Hiking	Y
Paved	Y	Sewer		Biking	Y
Pull Thru	Y	None		Swimming	Y
ADA	Y	At Site	some	Watch Wildlife	
Max RV Size	45	Dump Station	Y	Pets	Y
Electric		Amenities		Security	
None		Restrooms	Y	Host(s)	Y
20 Amp	Y	Showers	Y	Rangers(s)	Y
30 Amp	Y	Reserve Sites	Y	Gate	
50 Amp	some	Store	Y	Patrolled	Y
		Grill/Table	Y		

[22] Ludington State Park (3 Campgrounds)
Hwy 31, West on Hwy 10
North of Ludington
N43 59.626 W86 28.110
State Rate: $27-$29 (Premium, Modern)
(231) 843-2423
http://www.michigandnr.com/parksandtrails/details.aspx?id=468&type=SPRK

Directions

7 miles. At Hwy 10 & Hwy 31 go 1.9 miles west on Hwy 10 (Ludington Ave) to Jebavy Rd, then north for 1 mile to Bryant Rd, and 2 miles west to Hwy 116. Follow Hwy 116 north for 2 miles to the Park.

Points of Interest

Walk through White Pine Village, just south of Ludington. The Village is over thirty museum buildings and sites of local history. Take a dune ride or take the children for a morning or afternoon at Sandcastles Children's Museum.

RV Sites		Water		Laundry	
Number	352	None		Wi-Fi	
Shaded	Y	At Site		Fishing	Y
By Water	Y	Spigots	Y	Hiking	Y
Paved		Sewer		Biking	Y
Pull Thru	Y	None		Swimming	
ADA	Y	At Site		Watch Wildlife	Y
Max RV Size	45	Dump Station	Y	Pets	Y
Electric		Amenities		Security	
None		Restrooms	Y	Host(s)	Y
20 Amp	Y	Showers	Y	Rangers(s)	Y
30 Amp	Y	Reserve Sites	Y	Gate	
50 Amp	some	Store	Y	Patrolled	Y
		Grill/Table	Y		

[23] Sleeping Bear Dunes Nat'l Lakeshore: Platte River Campground
Hwy 31, West on Hwy 706 (Platte Rd)
West of Traverse City
N44 42.926 W86 07.284
Sleeping Bears Dunes NP Rate: $19
America/Beautiful Rate: $10
(231) 326-4700
http://www.nps.gov/slbe/index.htm

Directions

6.5 miles. Take Hwy 706 (Platte Rd) west from Hwy 31 for 5.2 miles to Hwy 22 (Northland Hwy). Go right for 0.9 miles to Lake Michigan Rd, turn left, go 0.3 miles to the Campground.

Points of Interest

Sand beaches, 450' bluffs, an island lighthouse, inland lakes, unique flora & fauna make up the Sleeping Bear Dunes. Coastal villages & picturesque farmsteads will add to your experience.

RV Sites		Water		Laundry	
Number	100	None		Wi-Fi	
Shaded	Y	At Site		Fishing	Y
By Water	Y	Spigots	Y	Hiking	Y
Paved	Y	Sewer		Biking	Y
Pull Thru	Y	None		Swimming	
ADA	Y	At Site		Watch Wildlife	Y
Max RV Size	40	Dump Station	Y	Pets	Y
Electric		Amenities		Security	
None		Restrooms	Y	Host(s)	Y
20 Amp	Y	Showers	Y	Rangers(s)	Y
30 Amp	Y	Reserve Sites	Y	Gate	
50 Amp	Y	Store		Patrolled	Y
		Grill/Table	Y		

[24] Petoskey State Park
Hwy 31, North on Hwy 119
Northeast of Petoskey
N45 24.477 W84 54.128
State Rate: $27-$29 (Premium, Modern)
(231) 347-2311
http://www.michigandnr.com/parksandtrails/Details.aspx?type=SPRK&id=483

Directions

3.5 miles. Two miles northeast of Petoskey on Hwy 31 turn left on Hwy 119 for 1.5 miles to the Park.

Points of Interest

The Oden Fish Hatchery is a short drive from the Park & one of the most advanced facilities of its kind. Two near by towns, Harbor Springs & Petoskey, are both known for their shopping districts, local arts and crafts shops, shows and restaurants. Drive the Tunnel of Trees scenic byway.

RV Sites		Water		Laundry	
Number	180	None		Wi-Fi	
Shaded	Y	At Site		Fishing	
By Water	Y	Spigots	Y	Hiking	Y
Paved	some	Sewer		Biking	Y
Pull Thru		None		Swimming	Y
ADA	Y	At Site		Watch Wildlife	Y
Max RV Size	45	Dump Station	Y	Pets	Y
Electric		Amenities		Security	
None		Restrooms	Y	Host(s)	Y
20 Amp	Y	Showers	Y	Rangers(s)	Y
30 Amp	Y	Reserve Sites	Y	Gate	
50 Amp	some	Store		Patrolled	Y
		Grill/Table	Y		

[25] Port Crescent State Park
Hwy 25
West of Port Austin
N44 00.455 W83 03.079
State Rate: $27 (Modern)
(989) 738-8663
http://www.michigandnr.com/parksandtrails/
details.aspx?id=486&type=SPRK

Directions

4.5 miles. From Port Austin go west 4.5 miles to the Park.

Points of Interest

On the shores of beautiful Lake Huron, with 90 miles of shoreline. Port Austin and the surrounding areas are quiet, picturesque, and enhanced by the beauty of the lake. The area offers spectacular sunsets and sunrises. To the east are many historic areas as well as Lighthouse Park featuring historic Pointe Aux Barques lighthouse.

RV Sites		Water		Laundry	
Number	135	None		Wi-Fi	
Shaded	Y	At Site		Fishing	Y
By Water	Y	Spigots	Y	Hiking	Y
Paved	some	**Sewer**		Biking	Y
Pull Thru		None		Swimming	Y
ADA	Y	At Site		Watch Wildlife	Y
Max RV Size	45	Dump Station	Y	Pets	Y
Electric		**Amenities**		**Security**	
None		Restrooms	Y	Host(s)	Y
20 Amp	Y	Showers	Y	Rangers(s)	Y
30 Amp	Y	Reserve Sites	Y	Gate	
50 Amp		Store		Patrolled	
		Grill/Table	Y		

[26] Harrisville State Park
Hwy 23
South side of Harrisville
N44 38.876 W83 18.103
State Rate: $23-$25 (Modern)
(989) 724-5126
http://www.michigandnr.com/parksandtrails/
details.aspx?id=451&type=SPRK

Directions

0.8 miles. Go south on Hwy 23 from Harrisville for less than a mile to the Park.

Points of Interest

The park is within walking distance of the resort town of Harrisville and close to Sturgeon Point Light House. There are numerous summer concerts in Harrisville. The harbor is a center for salmon and trout fishing. The beaches in and around Harrisville have been recognized as being among the "top ten in Michigan."

RV Sites		Water		Laundry	
Number	195	None		Wi-Fi	
Shaded	Y	At Site		Fishing	Y
By Water	Y	Spigots	Y	Hiking	Y
Paved	some	**Sewer**		Biking	Y
Pull Thru	some	None		Swimming	Y
ADA	Y	At Site		Watch Wildlife	
Max RV Size	45	Dump Station	Y	Pets	Y
Electric		**Amenities**		**Security**	
None		Restrooms	Y	Host(s)	Y
20 Amp	Y	Showers	Y	Rangers(s)	Y
30 Amp	Y	Reserve Sites	Y	Gate	
50 Amp	some	Store		Patrolled	Y
		Grill/Table	Y		

[27] P. H. Hoeft State Park
Hwy 23
Northwest of Rogers City
N45 27.822 W83 53.015
State Rate: $22 (Modern)
(989) 734-2543
http://www.michigandnr.com/parksandtrails/
Details.aspx?type=SPRK&id=456

Directions

4.5 miles. Go north on Hwy 23 from Rogers City for 4.5 miles to the Park.

Points of Interest

Sites are a short, easy walk to Lake Huron & swim beach. Bicyclists can use the bike trail to Rogers City just 4.5 miles away. Be sure to visit 40 Mile Point Lighthouse. Its been a welcoming beacon to sailors since May 1897 and is still operating today. The lighthouse museum, pilot house and gift shop are open Tuesday - Sunday.

RV Sites		Water		Laundry	
Number	144	None		Wi-Fi	
Shaded	Y	At Site		Fishing	Y
By Water	Y	Spigots	Y	Hiking	Y
Paved		**Sewer**		Biking	Y
Pull Thru	Y	None		Swimming	Y
ADA	Y	At Site		Watch Wildlife	Y
Max RV Size	45	Dump Station	Y	Pets	Y
Electric		**Amenities**		**Security**	
None		Restrooms	Y	Host(s)	Y
20 Amp	Y	Showers	Y	Rangers(s)	Y
30 Amp	Y	Reserve Sites	Y	Gate	
50 Amp		Store		Patrolled	Y
		Grill/Table	Y		

About Minnesota's Public Campgrounds

The Minnesota Parks and Recreation Division oversees 66 parks, six recreation areas, and eight waysides that contain examples of Minnesota's most scenic lands. You can explore specifics about these resources at -

http://www.dnr.state.mn.us/index.html

All vehicles entering a state park must display a valid Minnesota State Park vehicle permit (annual and day permits can be purchased at a park). The park system is working to make facilities accessible to people of all abilities. You should call the specific state park you are planning to visit for up-to-date information on accessibility. Gathering firewood in a park is not permitted, however, firewood can be purchased at the park office. Pets are welcome in state parks but must be kept on a leash of not more than six feet and must be personally attended at all times.

RV reservations can be made up to one year in advance. You can search by date to find the perfect time for your overnight stay. Typically, 30% of campsites in parks and state recreation areas are only rented on a first-come, first-serve basis. Reservations can be made by phone, 8 a.m. to 8 p.m., seven days a week at (866) 857-2757 [TDD (218) 336-2189]. For online reservations go to -

http://www.dnr.state.mn.us/state_parks/reservations.html

Fees are -

Standard campsites: $12-$23	Reservation fees: Online - $7.00,
Electricity: add $8	Call - $8.50
Water and Sewer: add $6	Daily Vehicle Permit: $5

There are also some excellent County and Town Parks. While the County/Town fees are a bit higher, they are comparable to the State Parks (after miscellaneous State fees are added).

[1] Myre - Big Island State Park	[12] Whitewater State Park
[2] Rice Lake State Park	[13] Great River Bluffs State Park
[3] Nerstrand - Big Woods State Park	[14] Buffalo River State Park
[4] Lebanon Hills Regional Park	[15] Lake Carlos State Park
[5] Interstate Park	[16] Camden State Park
[6] Banning State Park	[17] Upper Sioux Agency State Park
[7] Moose Lake State Park	[18] Sibley State Park
[8] Indian Point Campground	[19] Pokegama Dam Campground
[9] Blue Mounds State Park	[20] Lake Bemidji State Park
[10] Adrian Municipal Park	[21] Red River State Recreation Area
[11] Pihl's Park	

Minnesota

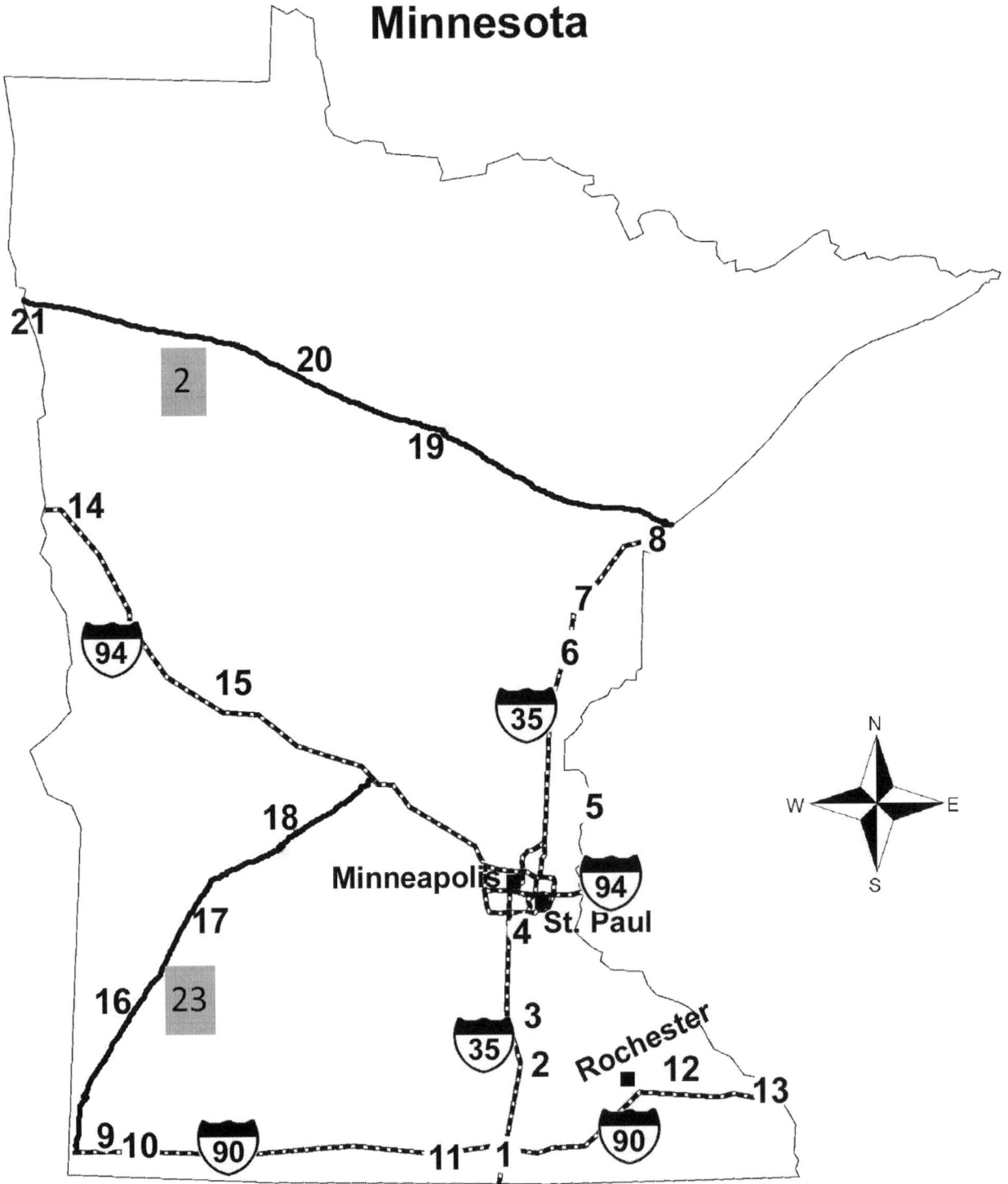

21

2

20

19

14

94

15

8

7

6

35

5

18

94

Minneapolis

St. Paul

17

4

16 23

3

35

2 Rochester 12

13

9 10 90

11 1 90

N

W — E

S

[1] Myre - Big Island State Park
I-35, Exit 11
Southeast of Albert Lea
N43 38.190 W93 18.526
State Rate: See Introduction
(507) 379-3403
http://www.dnr.state.mn.us/state_parks/myre_
big_island/index.html

Directions

2 miles. From Exit 11 go east for 0.5 mile on Cty Rd. 46 to Cty Rd. 38. Turn south 1.5 miles to the campground.

Points of Interest

Albert Lea, "The Land Between the Lakes," is between Fountain & Albert Lea Lake. Take a tour on the Pelican Breeze II Cruise Boat. Tour Historical Museum/Village, Albert Lea Art Center & Story Lady Doll/Toy Museum. Shop historic downtown specialty, craft, gift and antique shops.

RV Sites		Water		Laundry	
Number	93	None		Wi-Fi	
Shaded	Y	At Site		Fishing	
By Water	Y	Spigots	Y	Hiking	Y
Paved		Sewer		Biking	Y
Pull Thru		None		Swimming	Y
ADA	Y	At Site		Watch Wildlife	
Max RV Size	45	Dump Station	Y	Pets	Y
Electric		Amenities		Security	
None		Restrooms	Y	Host(s)	Y
20 Amp	Y	Showers	Y	Rangers(s)	Y
30 Amp	Y	Reserve Sites	Y	Gate	
50 Amp	Y	Store	Y	Patrolled	Y
		Grill/Table	Y		

[2] Rice Lake State Park
I-35, Exit 42
East of Owatonna
N44 05.535 W93 03.862
State Rate: See Introduction
(507) 455-5871
http://www.dnr.state.mn.us/state_parks/rice_
lake/index.html

Directions

10 miles. From Exit 42 go east and south on Hoffman Dr for 1.2 miles. Turn east (left) on Cty Rd 19 (Rose St.). Go 9 miles to Cty Rd 40. Turn south into the Park.

Points of Interest

Stroll Owatonna Downtown Retail District's specialty shops & boutiques. Shop at Cabela's, the second most popular tourist attraction in Minnesota. Experience what life was like in Owatonna at the turn of the 20th Century at the Village of Yesteryear.

RV Sites		Water		Laundry	
Number	40	None		Wi-Fi	
Shaded	Y	At Site		Fishing	
By Water	Y	Spigots	Y	Hiking	Y
Paved		Sewer		Biking	Y
Pull Thru		None		Swimming	
ADA	Y	At Site		Watch Wildlife	Y
Max RV Size	45	Dump Station	Y	Pets	Y
Electric		Amenities		Security	
None		Restrooms	Y	Host(s)	Y
20 Amp	Y	Showers	Y	Rangers(s)	Y
30 Amp	Y	Reserve Sites	Y	Gate	
50 Amp		Store		Patrolled	Y
		Grill/Table	Y		

[3] Nerstrand - Big Woods State Park
I-35, Exit 56
Northeast of Faribault
N44 20.498 W93 06.484
State Rate: See Introduction
(507) 333-4840
http://www.dnr.state.mn.us/state_parks/ner-
strand_big_woods/index.html

Directions

12.5 miles. From Exit 56 go 2.6 miles east on Hwy 60. Turn left on Shumway Ave for one block then bear right on Cty Rd. 20 (St Paul Ave). Go 3.7 miles to Cty Rd. 27. Turn right, go 3.4 miles to Hall Ave. Turn north for 1 mile to Cty Rd 88. Go east 1.7 miles to the Park.

Points of Interest

In Northfield discover outlets for your arts, history or nature curiosities. When you are ready to wine, dine and relax, enjoy one-of-a-kind restaurants.

RV Sites		Water		Laundry	
Number	51	None		Wi-Fi	
Shaded	Y	At Site		Fishing	
By Water		Spigots	Y	Hiking	Y
Paved		Sewer		Biking	Y
Pull Thru		None		Swimming	
ADA	Y	At Site		Watch Wildlife	Y
Max RV Size	45	Dump Station	Y	Pets	Y
Electric		Amenities		Security	
None		Restrooms	Y	Host(s)	Y
20 Amp	Y	Showers	Y	Rangers(s)	Y
30 Amp	Y	Reserve Sites	Y	Gate	
50 Amp		Store		Patrolled	Y
		Grill/Table	Y		

[4] Lebanon Hills Regional Park
I-35, Exit north of Exit 87 @ I-35E/I-35W split
South of Eagan (next to the MN Zoo)
N44 46.375 W93 11.241
County Rate: $25-$35
(651) 688-1376
http://www.co.dakota.mn.us/parks/ReservationsPasses/Campgrounds/Pages/default.aspx

Directions

7 miles. At I-35E/I-35W split take I-35E northeast 5.1 miles to Exit 93. Go east for 0.6 mile on Cliff Rd to Johnny Cake Ridge Rd Turn south 1.2 mile to the campground on the left.

Points of Interest

The Park is on the south edge of Minneapolis and St. Paul and provides a gateway to all the Twin Cities have to offer. You are near the Minnesota Zoo, Fort Snelling State Park, and the Mall of America.

RV Sites		Water		Laundry	
Number	93	None		Wi-Fi	Y
Shaded	Y	At Site	Y	Fishing	
By Water	Y	Spigots		Hiking	Y
Paved		**Sewer**		Biking	Y
Pull Thru	Y	None		Swimming	
ADA	Y	At Site	Y	Watch Wildlife	
Max RV Size	42	Dump Station	Y	Pets	Y
Electric		**Amenities**		**Security**	
None		Restrooms	Y	Host(s)	Y
20 Amp	Y	Showers	Y	Rangers(s)	Y
30 Amp	Y	Reserve Sites	Y	Gate	
50 Amp	Y	Store	Y	Patrolled	Y
		Grill/Table	Y		

[5] Interstate Park
I-35, Exit 135
Northeast of Forest Lake
N45 23.692 W92 40.073
State Rate: See Introduction
(651) 465-5711
http://www.dnr.state.mn.us/state_parks/interstate/index.html

Directions

19 miles. From Exit 135 go east 0.2 miles on Viking to Hwy 61 (Forest). Turn south 0.3 miles to Hwy 98 (Wyoming). Go east 5 miles to Hwy 8. Proceed 13.7 miles northeast on Hwy. 8 to the campground entrance on the right.

Points of Interest

Interstate is a lovely state park in the Dalles of the St. Croix. Two hundred foot basalt sheer cliffs with huge rock resembling human profiles are the hallmark.

RV Sites		Water		Laundry	
Number	37	None		Wi-Fi	
Shaded	Y	At Site		Fishing	
By Water	Y	Spigots	Y	Hiking	Y
Paved		**Sewer**		Biking	Y
Pull Thru		None		Swimming	
ADA	Y	At Site	Y	Watch Wildlife	Y
Max RV Size	45	Dump Station	Y	Pets	Y
Electric		**Amenities**		**Security**	
None		Restrooms	Y	Host(s)	Y
20 Amp	Y	Showers	Y	Rangers(s)	Y
30 Amp	Y	Reserve Sites	Y	Gate	
50 Amp		Store		Patrolled	Y
		Grill/Table	Y		

[6] Banning State Park
I-35, Exit 195
North of Sandstone
N46 10.275 W92 50.887
State Rate: See Introduction
(320) 245-2668
http://www.dnr.state.mn.us/state_parks/banning/index.html

Directions

Adjoins I-35. From Exit 195 go east 0.3 miles on Hwy 23 to Banning Park Rd on your right

Points of Interest

Sandstone is well known as home of the "Midwest Country Music Theater," aired on RFD TV. Enjoy live performances throughout the year. The History & Art Center (on the National Registry), contains quarry artifacts and exhibits of the Great Hinckley Fire and the Railroad of by-gone days.

RV Sites		Water		Laundry	
Number	33	None		Wi-Fi	
Shaded	Y	At Site		Fishing	Y
By Water		Spigots	Y	Hiking	Y
Paved		**Sewer**		Biking	Y
Pull Thru		None		Swimming	
ADA	Y	At Site		Watch Wildlife	Y
Max RV Size	42	Dump Station	Y	Pets	Y
Electric		**Amenities**		**Security**	
None		Restrooms	Y	Host(s)	Y
20 Amp	Y	Showers	Y	Rangers(s)	Y
30 Amp	Y	Reserve Sites	Y	Gate	
50 Amp		Store		Patrolled	Y
		Grill/Table	Y		

[7] Moose Lake State Park
I-35, Exit 214
Southeast of Moose Lake
N46 26.180 W92 44.149
State Rate: See Introduction
(218) 485-5420
http://www.dnr.state.mn.us/state_parks/moose_lake/index.html

Directions

0.5 miles. From Exit 214 go east for 0.5 mile on Cty Rd. 137 to the campground on the right.

Points of Interest

Duluth is within an hour of the Park, where there is much to see and do. Visit the Great Lakes Aquarium, Lake Superior & Mississippi Railroad excursion and museum, Renegade Theater Company, S.S. William A. Irvin Ore Boat Museum, Tweed Museum of Art. Take a lake cruise.

RV Sites		Water		Laundry	
Number	33	None		Wi-Fi	
Shaded	Y	At Site		Fishing	Y
By Water	Y	Spigots	Y	Hiking	Y
Paved		**Sewer**		Biking	Y
Pull Thru		None	Y	Swimming	Y
ADA	Y	At Site		Watch Wildlife	Y
Max RV Size	40	Dump Station		Pets	Y
Electric		**Amenities**		**Security**	
None		Restrooms	Y	Host(s)	Y
20 Amp	Y	Showers	Y	Rangers(s)	Y
30 Amp	Y	Reserve Sites	Y	Gate	
50 Amp		Store		Patrolled	Y
		Grill/Table	Y		

[8] Indian Point Campground
I-35, Exit 251
South of Duluth
N46 43.326 W92 11.112
County Rate: $33-$53
(855) 777-0652
http://www.duluthindianpointcampground.com/campsites

Directions

2 miles. **Northbound**, from Exit 251a (Cody St) go 0.3 miles to 63rd Ave. Turn right, go 0.6 miles to Hwy 23 (Grand Ave). Turn right, go 1.0 miles to 75th Ave. (Pulaski St.). Turn left to the campground. **Southbound**, from Exit 251b (Grand Ave) go 1.2 miles to 75th Ave. (Pulaski St). Turn left to campground.

Points of Interest

There is much to see and do in Duluth. See **[7]** for more information.

RV Sites		Water		Laundry	Y
Number	74	None		Wi-Fi	Y
Shaded	Y	At Site	Y	Fishing	
By Water	Y	Spigots		Hiking	Y
Paved		**Sewer**		Biking	Y
Pull Thru	Y	None		Swimming	
ADA	Y	At Site	Y	Watch Wildlife	
Max RV Size	45	Dump Station	Y	Pets	Y
Electric		**Amenities**		**Security**	
None		Restrooms	Y	Host(s)	Y
20 Amp	Y	Showers	Y	Rangers(s)	
30 Amp	Y	Reserve Sites	Y	Gate	
50 Amp	Y	Store	Y	Patrolled	Y
		Grill/Table	Y		

[9] Blue Mounds State Park
I-90, Exit 12
North of Luverne
N43 43.046 W96 11.515
State Rate: See Introduction
(507) 283-1307
http://www.dnr.state.mn.us/state_parks/blue_mounds/index.html

Directions

6.5 miles. From Exit 12 go 5.4 miles north on Hwy 75 to Cty Rd 20. Turn east for 1.1 mile into the park.

Points of Interest

Enjoy the Park's natural features. The Sioux quartzite cliff rises 100 feet above the plains. Get close up with bison (fenced) grazing on the prairie. Walk the rolling hills among a sea of prairie grasses & flowers swaying in the wind. Don't miss the annual Luverne dachshund races!

RV Sites		Water		Laundry	
Number	73	None		Wi-Fi	
Shaded	Y	At Site		Fishing	
By Water	Y	Spigots	Y	Hiking	Y
Paved		**Sewer**		Biking	Y
Pull Thru		None		Swimming	Y
ADA	Y	At Site	Y	Watch Wildlife	Y
Max RV Size	45	Dump Station	Y	Pets	Y
Electric		**Amenities**		**Security**	
None		Restrooms	Y	Host(s)	Y
20 Amp	Y	Showers	Y	Rangers(s)	Y
30 Amp	Y	Reserve Sites	Y	Gate	
50 Amp		Store		Patrolled	Y
		Grill/Table	Y		

[10] Adrian Municipal Park
I-90, Exit 26
North of Adrian
N43 38.424 W95 56.416
Town Rate: $16-$25
(507) 483-2820
http://www.adrian.govoffice2.com/index.
asp?Type=B_LOC&SEC={37BF5E1E-0906-
41FC-9285-598A01179A51}

Directions

0.5 miles. From Exit 26 go 0.2 miles south to
Franklin St. Turn right, go 0.3 miles to the Park.

Points of Interest

Visit Luverne. Go to Blue Mounds State Park.
The Sioux quartzite cliff rises 100 feet above the
plains. Get close up with bison (fenced) grazing
on the prairie. Walk the rolling hills among a sea
of prairie grasses & flowers swaying in the wind.
See [9]

RV Sites		Water		Laundry	Y
Number	110	None		Wi-Fi	Y
Shaded	Y	At Site	Y	Fishing	
By Water		Spigots		Hiking	
Paved		**Sewer**		Biking	Y
Pull Thru	Y	None		Swimming	Y
ADA	Y	At Site	Y	Watch Wildlife	
Max RV Size	45	Dump Station	Y	Pets	Y
Electric		**Amenities**		**Security**	
None		Restrooms	Y	Host(s)	Y
20 Amp	Y	Showers	Y	Rangers(s)	
30 Amp	Y	Reserve Sites	Y	Gate	
50 Amp	Y	Store		Patrolled	Y
		Grill/Table	Y		

[11] Pihl's Park
I-90, Exit 138
South of Wells
N43 38.460 W93 43.851
County Rate: $18-$20
(507) 553-5864
http://www.co.faribault.mn.us/index.
php?option=com_content&view=article&id=13
&Itemid=22#Pihls_About

Directions

1.5 miles. From Exit 138 go 1.2 miles south on
Hwy 22 to the Park entrance on the right.

Points of Interest

Albert Lea, "The Land Between the Lakes," is
between Fountain & Albert Lea Lake. Take a tour
on the Pelican Breeze II Cruise Boat. Tour the
Historical Museum/Village, Albert Lea Art Center
& Story Lady Doll/Toy Museum. Shop historic
downtown specialty, craft, gift & antique shops.

RV Sites		Water		Laundry	
Number	30	None		Wi-Fi	
Shaded	Y	At Site	Y	Fishing	Y
By Water	Y	Spigots		Hiking	
Paved		**Sewer**		Biking	Y
Pull Thru	Y	None		Swimming	Y
ADA	Y	At Site	Y	Watch Wildlife	
Max RV Size	40	Dump Station	Y	Pets	Y
Electric		**Amenities**		**Security**	
None		Restrooms	Y	Host(s)	Y
20 Amp	Y	Showers	Y	Rangers(s)	
30 Amp	Y	Reserve Sites		Gate	Y
50 Amp		Store		Patrolled	Y
		Grill/Table	Y		

[12] Whitewater State Park
I-90, Exit 233
North of St. Charles
N44 03.779 W92 02.595
State Rate: See Introduction
(507) 932-3007
http://www.dnr.state.mn.us/state_parks/white-
water/index.html

Directions

8 miles. From Exit 233 go 8 miles north on
Hwy 74 through St. Charles to the Park.

Points of Interest

Rochester, the "Best Small City in America,"
is home to the renowned Mayo Clinic & the
largest IBM complex under one roof. There are
many upscale shops & nice restaurants. Drive
to historic Mantorville to enjoy the Melodramas
at the Opera House and have a steak at the
Hubbell House.

RV Sites		Water		Laundry	
Number	104	None		Wi-Fi	
Shaded	Y	At Site		Fishing	Y
By Water	Y	Spigots	Y	Hiking	Y
Paved		**Sewer**		Biking	Y
Pull Thru	Y	None		Swimming	Y
ADA	Y	At Site	Y	Watch Wildlife	Y
Max RV Size	40	Dump Station	Y	Pets	Y
Electric		**Amenities**		**Security**	
None		Restrooms	Y	Host(s)	Y
20 Amp	Y	Showers	Y	Rangers(s)	Y
30 Amp	Y	Reserve Sites	Y	Gate	
50 Amp	Y	Store		Patrolled	Y
		Grill/Table	Y		

[13] Great River Bluffs State Park (aka O. L. Kipp State Park)
I-90, Exit 266
South of Winona
N43 56.355 W91 24.546
State Rate: See Introduction
(507) 643-6849
http://www.dnr.state.mn.us/state_parks/great_river_bluffs/index.html

Directions

2 miles. From Exit 266 turn north to Cty Rd. 3. Go right for 1 mile to Lynch Rd (Kipp Dr). Turn right into the Park. Drive 1 miles to the camp.

Points of Interest

The Park's King's Bluff trail offers a breathtaking view of the Mississippi River Valley. Drive north to Winona, on the Mississippi, and enjoy this riverfront town, or visit the National Eagle Center in Wabasha (of Grumpy Old Men fame).

RV Sites		Water		Laundry	
Number	31	None		Wi-Fi	
Shaded	Y	At Site		Fishing	
By Water		Spigots	Y	Hiking	Y
Paved		**Sewer**		Biking	Y
Pull Thru		None	Y	Swimming	
ADA	Y	At Site		Watch Wildlife	Y
Max RV Size	45	Dump Station		Pets	Y
Electric		**Amenities**		**Security**	
None	Y	Restrooms	Y	Host(s)	Y
20 Amp		Showers	Y	Rangers(s)	Y
30 Amp		Reserve Sites	Y	Gate	
50 Amp		Store		Patrolled	Y
		Grill/Table	Y		

[14] Buffalo River State Park
I-94, Exit 6
East of Fargo - Moorhead
N46 52.175 W96 28.421
State Rate: See Introduction
(218) 498-2124
http://www.dnr.state.mn.us/state_parks/buffalo_river/index.html

Directions

10 miles. From Exit 6 go 2 miles north on Hwy 336 to Hwy 10. Turn east for 8.3 miles to the Cty Hwy 44 and the park entrance.

Points of Interest

In Fargo-Moorhead walk the Walk with more than 100 celebrity signatures, handprints and footprints in cement at the Celebrity Walk Of Fame. The Fargo Air Museum is home to the only flying F2G-1D Super Corsair in the world, & one of four flying Japanese Zero's in the world.

RV Sites		Water		Laundry	
Number	44	None		Wi-Fi	
Shaded	Y	At Site		Fishing	Y
By Water		Spigots	Y	Hiking	Y
Paved		**Sewer**		Biking	Y
Pull Thru		None		Swimming	Y
ADA	Y	At Site		Watch Wildlife	Y
Max RV Size	45	Dump Station	Y	Pets	Y
Electric		**Amenities**		**Security**	
None		Restrooms	Y	Host(s)	Y
20 Amp	Y	Showers	Y	Rangers(s)	Y
30 Amp	Y	Reserve Sites	Y	Gate	
50 Amp	Y	Store		Patrolled	Y
		Grill/Table	Y		

[15] Lake Carlos State Park
I-94, Exit 103
North of Alexandria
N46 00.021 W95 20.153
State Rate: See Introduction
(320) 852-7200
http://www.dnr.state.mn.us/state_parks/lake_carlos/index.html

Directions

13.5 miles. From Exit 103 take Hwy 29 through Alexandria, 11.8 miles in all to Cty Rd 38. Turn left, go 1.5 miles into the Park to the campground.

Points of Interest

In Alexandria, the Runestone Museum allows visitors to decide if the artifact is authentic - were the first visitors to America the Vikings in 1362? Enjoy summer stock theatre productions, or nationally known musicians. Eat on the lake marina.

RV Sites		Water		Laundry	
Number	121	None		Wi-Fi	
Shaded	Y	At Site		Fishing	Y
By Water	Y	Spigots	Y	Hiking	Y
Paved		**Sewer**		Biking	Y
Pull Thru		None		Swimming	Y
ADA	Y	At Site		Watch Wildlife	Y
Max RV Size	42	Dump Station	Y	Pets	Y
Electric		**Amenities**		**Security**	
None		Restrooms	Y	Host(s)	Y
20 Amp	Y	Showers	Y	Rangers(s)	Y
30 Amp	Y	Reserve Sites	Y	Gate	
50 Amp		Store		Patrolled	Y
		Grill/Table	Y		

[16] Camden State Park
Hwy 23
Southwest of Marshall
N44 21.340 W95 55.069
(507) 865-4530
http://www.dnr.state.mn.us/state_parks/camden/index.html

Directions

10 miles. From Marshall, go 10 miles southwest on Hwy 23 to the Park entrance.

Points of Interest

You can spend a whole day birding in the Park, especially during spring and fall songbird migration. Check out the many unique stores and shops in and around Marshall, there are 3 antiquestore tours. Check out the Fagen Fighters WWII Museum, End-O-Line Railroad Park and Museum, and Minnesota Machinery Museum.

RV Sites		Water		Laundry	
Number	80	None		Wi-Fi	
Shaded	Y	At Site		Fishing	Y
By Water	Y	Spigots	Y	Hiking	Y
Paved		Sewer		Biking	Y
Pull Thru	Y	None		Swimming	Y
ADA	Y	At Site		Watch Wildlife	Y
Max RV Size	45	Dump Station	Y	Pets	Y
Electric		Amenities		Security	
None		Restrooms	Y	Host(s)	Y
20 Amp	Y	Showers	Y	Rangers(s)	Y
30 Amp	Y	Reserve Sites	Y	Gate	
50 Amp		Store		Patrolled	Y
		Grill/Table	Y		

[17] Upper Sioux Agency State Park
Hwy 67
Southeast of Granite Falls
N44 44.072 W95 27.388
State Rate: See Introduction
(320) 564-4777
http://www.dnr.state.mn.us/state_parks/upper_sioux_agency/index.html

Directions

7.6 miles. From the intersection of Hwy 23 & Hwy 67 go south on Hwy 67 7.6 miles to the park. *(Dump Station at Granite Falls water treatment plant).

Points of Interest

The Park, site of the Upper Sioux or Yellow Medicine Agency, was established in 1963 to preserve & interpret the remains of the old Agency site. The Treaty of Traverse Des Sioux of 1851 moved the Dakota Indians to a reservation along the Minnesota River Valley.

RV Sites		Water		Laundry	
Number	34	None		Wi-Fi	
Shaded	Y	At Site		Fishing	Y
By Water	Y	Spigots	Y	Hiking	Y
Paved		Sewer		Biking	Y
Pull Thru		None		Swimming	
ADA	Y	At Site		Watch Wildlife	Y
Max RV Size	45	Dump Station	*	Pets	Y
Electric		Amenities		Security	
None		Restrooms	Y	Host(s)	Y
20 Amp	Y	Showers	Y	Rangers(s)	Y
30 Amp	Y	Reserve Sites	Y	Gate	
50 Amp	Y	Store		Patrolled	Y
		Grill/Table	Y		

[18] Sibley State Park
Hwy 9
West of New London
N45 18.675 W95 00.637
State Rate: See Introduction
(320) 354-2055
http://www.dnr.state.mn.us/state_parks/sibley/index.html

Distance

4.5 miles. From New London, take Hwy 9 west 0.4 mile to County Rd 40 (4th Ave, then 180th Ave). Go left on County Rd 40 for 3 miles. Then go 1 mile north on 71 to the park.

Points of Interest

Hike to Mount Tom. A canoe route invites adventurers to portage and canoe on Henschien Lake and Swan Lake. The Interpretive Center has been remodeled and a new, engaging oak savanna exhibit has been installed.

RV Sites		Water		Laundry	
Number	132	None		Wi-Fi	
Shaded	Y	At Site		Fishing	Y
By Water	Y	Spigots	Y	Hiking	Y
Paved		Sewer		Biking	Y
Pull Thru	Y	None		Swimming	Y
ADA	Y	At Site		Watch Wildlife	
Max RV Size	45	Dump Station	Y	Pets	Y
Electric		Amenities		Security	
None		Restrooms	Y	Host(s)	Y
20 Amp	Y	Showers	Y	Rangers(s)	Y
30 Amp	Y	Reserve Sites	Y	Gate	
50 Amp	Y	Store	Y	Patrolled	Y
		Grill/Table	Y		

[19] Pokegama Dam Campground
Hwy 2
West of Grand Rapids
N47 15.051 W93 35.166
COE Rate: $26
America/Beautiful Rate: $13
(218) 326-6128
http://www.recreation.gov/

Directions

3 miles. Go west from Hwys 2/38 in Grand Rapids for 3 miles on Hwy 2 to the park on the left.

Points of Interest

The picturesque Grand Rapids area has been a favorite of those planning Minnesota family vacations, fishing trips, and couple's getaways for over 100 years. Children will be delighted by the Children's Museum, while "Wizard of Oz" fans will love the Judy Garland Museum - Judy Garland was born in Grand Rapids.

RV Sites		Water		Laundry	
Number	19	None		Wi-Fi	
Shaded	Y	At Site		Fishing	Y
By Water	Y	Spigots	Y	Hiking	Y
Paved		Sewer		Biking	
Pull Thru		None		Swimming	
ADA	Y	At Site		Watch Wildlife	Y
Max RV Size	45	Dump Station	Y	Pets	Y
Electric		Amenities		Security	
None		Restrooms	Y	Host(s)	Y
20 Amp	Y	Showers	Y	Rangers(s)	Y
30 Amp	Y	Reserve Sites	Y	Gate	
50 Amp	Y	Store		Patrolled	Y
		Grill/Table	Y		

[20] Lake Bemidji State Park
Hwy 71, from Hwy 2
North of Bemidji
N47 32.436 W94 50.174
State Rate: See Introduction
(218) 308-2300
http://www.dnr.state.mn.us/state_parks/lake_bemidji/index.html

Directions

7.3 miles. From Hwys 2/71 go north on Hwy 71 for 4.8 miles to Glidden Rd NE. Turn right, go 0.8 miles to Cty Rd 21, then left for 0.3 miles to Cty Rd 20 (Birchmont Beach Rd). Turn right, go 1.4 miles to the Park.

Points of Interest

This park is the perfect playground, offering visitors swimming, boating, fishing, bird watching, hiking, camping, biking, picnicking, and year-round naturalist-led activities.

RV Sites		Water		Laundry	
Number	95	None		Wi-Fi	Y
Shaded	Y	At Site		Fishing	Y
By Water	Y	Spigots	Y	Hiking	Y
Paved		Sewer		Biking	Y
Pull Thru	Y	None		Swimming	Y
ADA	Y	At Site		Watch Wildlife	Y
Max RV Size	40	Dump Station	Y	Pets	Y
Electric		Amenities		Security	
None		Restrooms	Y	Host(s)	Y
20 Amp	Y	Showers	Y	Rangers(s)	Y
30 Amp	Y	Reserve Sites	Y	Gate	
50 Amp		Store		Patrolled	Y
		Grill/Table	Y		

[21] Red River State Recreation Area
Hwy 2
In East Grand Forks
N47 55.746 W97 01.687
State Rate: See Introduction
(218) 773-4950
http://www.dnr.state.mn.us/state_parks/red_river/index.html

Directions

Adjacent to Hwy 2 and just east of the Red River. Off 4th St NW and adjoining Cabela's and the Riverwalk Center Mall. Follow the Avenue of Flags to the park. Look for the Blue Moose Restaurant.

Points of Interest

A grass roots effort, as a result of the flood of 1997, the 1,200 acre greenway, setting in an urban area offers visitors access to recreational opportunities, as well as shopping & dining facilities within walking distance of one another.

RV Sites		Water		Laundry	
Number	109	None		Wi-Fi	Y
Shaded	Y	At Site	Y	Fishing	Y
By Water	Y	Spigots		Hiking	Y
Paved		Sewer		Biking	Y
Pull Thru	Y	None		Swimming	Y
ADA	Y	At Site	Y	Watch Wildlife	
Max RV Size	45	Dump Station		Pets	Y
Electric		Amenities		Security	
None		Restrooms	Y	Host(s)	Y
20 Amp	Y	Showers	Y	Rangers(s)	Y
30 Amp	Y	Reserve Sites	Y	Gate	
50 Amp	Y	Store	Y	Patrolled	Y
		Grill/Table	Y		

About Mississippi's Public Campgrounds

Mississippi has one of the most diverse collections of parklands. Lands and park management is provided by the State as well as the Corp of Engineers, some Counties, the National Forest Service, and the National Park Service. The Mississippi Department of Wildlife, Fisheries and Parks (MDWFP) is found at -

http://www.mdwfp.com/parks-destinations/ms-state-parks.aspx

MDWFP oversees the 25 State Parks but has given Reserve America primary responsibility for providing park information and oversight of reservations. Reservations can be made up to two years in advance. Reservations can be made at -

http://mississippistateparks.reserveamerica.com/welcome.do

Sites are classified as follows -

Full Hook-up: $20

Standard (electric and water): $18

Premium (waterfront): $24

Pets are allowed but must be on a leash up to 6 feet long.

[1] Davis Bayou Campground	[10] Hugh White State Park
[2] Shepard State Park	[11] Wallace Creek Campground
[3] Roosevelt State Park	[12] John W. Kyle State Park
[4] Marathon Lake	[13] Hernando Point
[5] Twiltley Branch Campground	[14] Paul B. Johnson State Park
[6] Percy Quin State Park	[15] Clarkco State Park
[7] Lake Lincoln State Park	[16] Lake Lowndes State Park
[8] Timberlake Campground	[17] Tombigbee State Park
[9] Holmes County State Park	[18] Wall Doxey State Park

NOTES:

Mississippi

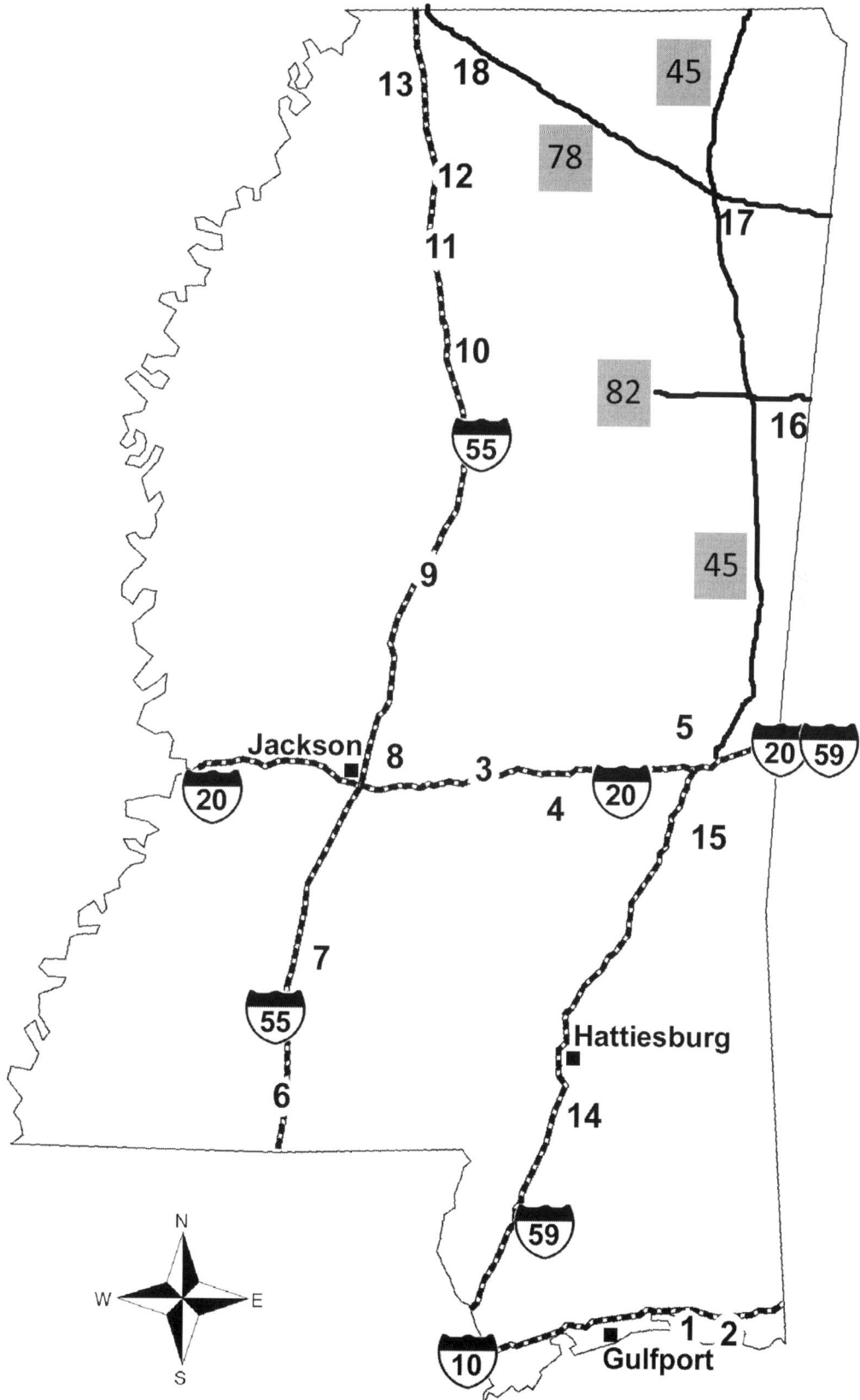

[1] Davis Bayou Campground
I-10, Exit 50
In Ocean Springs
N30 23.831 W88 47.746
Gulf Islands NPS Rate: $22
America/Beautiful Rate: $11
(228) 875-2358
http://www.nps.gov/guis/planyourvisit/davis-bayou-camping.htm

Directions

8 miles. From Exit 50 go 2.7 miles south on Hwy 609 to Hwy 90 (Bienville Blvd.). Turn east, go 3 miles to Gulf Island National Seashore Parkway. Turn south, follow the road 2.4 miles to the Park.

Points of Interest

Explore Ocean Springs, the 'City of Discovery.' This community is one of the most sought out destinations on the Mississippi Gulf Coast for culture, history, beaches and entertainment.

RV Sites		Water		Laundry	
Number	51	None		Wi-Fi	
Shaded	Y	At Site	Y	Fishing	Y
By Water	Y	Spigots		Hiking	Y
Paved	Y	**Sewer**		Biking	Y
Pull Thru		None		Swimming	
ADA	Y	At Site		Watch Wildlife	Y
Max RV Size	45	Dump Station		Pets	Y
Electric		**Amenities**		**Security**	
None		Restrooms	Y	Host(s)	Y
20 Amp	Y	Showers	Y	Rangers(s)	Y
30 Amp	Y	Reserve Sites		Gate	
50 Amp	Y	Store		Patrolled	Y
		Grill/Table	Y		

[2] Shepard State Park
I-10, Exit 61
East of Pascagoula
N30 22.356 W88 37.566
State Rate: See Introduction
(228) 497-2244
http://www.mdwfp.com/parks-destinations/ms-state-parks/shepard.aspx

Directions

8 miles. From Exit 61 go south for 3 miles on Gautier Vancleave Rd to Hwy 90. You are advised to call for the best 'final miles' directions.

Points of Interest

Some species found in the Pascagoula River can be found nowhere else in the U.S. For bird-watchers, the Audubon Center in Moss Point can point you to the best sites. You are a few miles away from casino action in Biloxi.

RV Sites		Water		Laundry	
Number	28	None		Wi-Fi	
Shaded	Y	At Site	Y	Fishing	Y
By Water	Y	Spigots		Hiking	
Paved		**Sewer**		Biking	Y
Pull Thru	Y	None		Swimming	
ADA	Y	At Site		Watch Wildlife	
Max RV Size	40	Dump Station	Y	Pets	Y
Electric		**Amenities**		**Security**	
None		Restrooms	Y	Host(s)	Y
20 Amp	Y	Showers	Y	Rangers(s)	Y
30 Amp	Y	Reserve Sites	Y	Gate	
50 Amp		Store		Patrolled	Y
		Grill/Table	Y		

[3] Roosevelt State Park
I-20, Exit 77
South of Morton
N32 19.144 W89 39.967
State Rate: See Introduction
(601) 732-6316
http://www.mdwfp.com/parks-destinations/ms-state-parks/roosevelt.aspx

Directions

0.6 miles. From Exit 77 go north for 0.6 miles on Hwy 13 to Park Rd. and the entrance.

Points of Interest

Visit Jackson, the 'City with Soul.' There are many museums, attractions, Civil War and Civil Rights venues. Stir your soul with great blues, gospel, & jazz. Bring your appetite & savor "down home" southern cooking & gourmet Southern Fusion. Ride the Fondern Trolley.

RV Sites		Water		Laundry	Y
Number	109	None		Wi-Fi	
Shaded	Y	At Site	Y	Fishing	Y
By Water	Y	Spigots		Hiking	Y
Paved	Y	**Sewer**		Biking	Y
Pull Thru	Y	None		Swimming	Y
ADA	Y	At Site	Y	Watch Wildlife	Y
Max RV Size	40	Dump Station	Y	Pets	Y
Electric		**Amenities**		**Security**	
None		Restrooms	Y	Host(s)	Y
20 Amp	Y	Showers	Y	Rangers(s)	Y
30 Amp	Y	Reserve Sites	Y	Gate	
50 Amp	Y	Store	Y	Patrolled	Y
		Grill/Table	Y		

[4] Marathon Lake
I-20, Exit 88
South of Forest
N32 12.295 W89 21.842
Bienville NF Rate: $20
America/Beautiful Rate: $10
(601) 469-3811
http://www.fs.usda.gov/recarea/mississippi/recreation/camping-cabins/recarea/?recid=28791&actid=29

Directions

14 miles. From Exit 88 turn north & immediately go right on Erle Johston Dr for 1 mile to Hwy 501. Go southeast for 9.5 miles to Morton Marathon Rd. Turn left, go 1.5 miles to Smith Cty Rd 506 & continue 1.6 miles to Shopping Center Rd 520. Turn 0.4 miles to camp on left.

Points of Interest Also see [5].

Ride the Dentzel Carousel. Tour the Jimmy Rodgers Museum.

RV Sites		Water		Laundry	
Number	34	None		Wi-Fi	
Shaded	Y	At Site	Y	Fishing	Y
By Water	Y	Spigots		Hiking	Y
Paved	Y	**Sewer**		Biking	Y
Pull Thru		None		Swimming	Y
ADA	Y	At Site		Watch Wildlife	Y
Max RV Size	45	Dump Station	Y	Pets	Y
Electric		**Amenities**		**Security**	
None		Restrooms	Y	Host(s)	Y
20 Amp	Y	Showers	Y	Rangers(s)	Y
30 Amp	Y	Reserve Sites		Gate	
50 Amp		Store		Patrolled	Y
		Grill/Table	Y		

[5] Twiltley Branch Campground
I-20, Exit 150
North of Meridian
N32 29.722 W88 48.791
COE Rate: $12-$20
America/Beautiful Rate: $6-$10
(601) 626-8068
http://www.recreation.gov/

Directions

15.5 miles. From Exit 150 go 13 miles north on Hwy 19 to Collinsville. Turn east on West Lauderdale Rd for 1 mile. Turn right on Hamrick Rd, go 1.1 miles to Barrett Rd. Turn right, go 0.4 mile to the Park.

Points of Interest Also see [4].

For Meridian, download the Tour Guide for all kinds of ideas for things to do and see, great pictures too! (*http://www.visitmeridian.com/index.cfm/visitors-guide-map-app/*)

RV Sites		Water		Laundry	
Number	64	None		Wi-Fi	
Shaded	Y	At Site	Y	Fishing	Y
By Water	Y	Spigots		Hiking	Y
Paved		**Sewer**		Biking	Y
Pull Thru	Y	None		Swimming	Y
ADA	Y	At Site		Watch Wildlife	Y
Max RV Size	45	Dump Station	Y	Pets	Y
Electric		**Amenities**		**Security**	
None		Restrooms	Y	Host(s)	Y
20 Amp	Y	Showers	Y	Rangers(s)	Y
30 Amp	Y	Reserve Sites	Y	Gate	
50 Amp	Y	Store		Patrolled	Y
		Grill/Table	Y		

[6] Percy Quin State Park
I-55, Exit 15
South of McComb
N31 11.496 W90 29.810
State Rate: See Introduction
(601) 684-3938
http://www.mdwfp.com/parks-destinations/ms-state-parks/percy-quin.aspx

Directions

3.5 miles. From Exit 15 go west for 1.5 miles on Hwy 24 to Hwy 48. Turn south for 2 miles to Percy Quin Dr. Turn west into the Park.

Points of Interest

McComb was selected as "The Hospitality City" of "The Hospitality State" three years running. Antiquing is popular here, with 8 shops to explore. Magnolia has 2 historic districts, one with three of Mississippi's premier Queen Anne residences and an antebellum Greek Revival cottage.

RV Sites		Water		Laundry	Y
Number	100	None		Wi-Fi	
Shaded	Y	At Site	Y	Fishing	Y
By Water	Y	Spigots		Hiking	Y
Paved	Y	**Sewer**		Biking	Y
Pull Thru		None		Swimming	Y
ADA	Y	At Site	Y	Watch Wildlife	Y
Max RV Size	40	Dump Station	Y	Pets	Y
Electric		**Amenities**		**Security**	
None		Restrooms	Y	Host(s)	Y
20 Amp	Y	Showers	Y	Rangers(s)	Y
30 Amp	Y	Reserve Sites	Y	Gate	
50 Amp	Y	Store	Y	Patrolled	Y
		Grill/Table	Y		

[7] Lake Lincoln State Park
I-55, Exit 51
East of Wesson
N31 40.401 W90 20.470
State Rate: See Introduction
(601) 643-9044
http://www.mdwfp.com/parks-destinations/ms-state-parks/lake-lincoln.aspx

Directions

10 miles. From Exit 51 go east 1.6 miles on Sylvarena, then left on Lowery Rd for 1.7 miles to Hwy 51. Turn south for 1 mile to Bahala Rd. Turn east, go 0.4 miles to Hardy St. & turn south. Go 0.7 mile to Timberlane Rd. Turn east, go 2.2 miles to Sunset Rd. Turn south again for 2 miles to the Park.

Points of Interest

Stop in Crystal Springs, Visit the Tomato Museum & Art Gallery, Robert Johnson Blues Museum, numerous antique shops, or join in one of festivals.

RV Sites		Water		Laundry	Y
Number	71	None		Wi-Fi	
Shaded	Y	At Site	Y	Fishing	Y
By Water	Y	Spigots		Hiking	Y
Paved	Y	Sewer		Biking	Y
Pull Thru	some	None		Swimming	Y
ADA	Y	At Site	Y	Watch Wildlife	Y
Max RV Size	45	Dump Station	Y	Pets	Y
Electric		Amenities		Security	
None		Restrooms	Y	Host(s)	Y
20 Amp	Y	Showers	Y	Rangers(s)	Y
30 Amp	Y	Reserve Sites	Y	Gate	
50 Amp	Y	Store		Patrolled	Y
		Grill/Table	Y		

[8] Timberlake Campground
I-55, Exit 105
Northeast of Jackson
N32 23.146 W90 02.374
Water District Rate: $20-$24; Senior Discount
(601) 992-9100
http://www.therez.ms/Camping/timberlake.html

Directions

7.5 miles. From Exit 105 go 1.7 miles east on Natchez Trace Pkwy to the Old Canton Rd exit. Turn south for 1.1 miles to Lake Harbour Dr. Turn east, go 4.5 miles (the road changes to Spillway Rd) to Northshore Pkwy. Turn left, go 0.2 miles to the Park.

Points of Interest

In Jackson, the 'City with Soul' there are many museums, attractions, Civil War, & Civil Rights venues. Stir your soul with blues, gospel & jazz. Bring your appetite and savor "down home" southern cooking.

RV Sites		Water		Laundry	Y
Number	61	None		Wi-Fi	Y
Shaded	Y	At Site	Y	Fishing	Y
By Water	Y	Spigots		Hiking	Y
Paved	Y	Sewer		Biking	Y
Pull Thru		None		Swimming	Y
ADA	Y	At Site	Y	Watch Wildlife	
Max RV Size	42	Dump Station		Pets	Y
Electric		Amenities		Security	
None		Restrooms	Y	Host(s)	Y
20 Amp	Y	Showers	Y	Rangers(s)	
30 Amp	Y	Reserve Sites		Gate	
50 Amp	Y	Store		Patrolled	Y
		Grill/Table	Y		

[9] Holmes County State Park
I-55, Exit 150
South of Durant
N33 01.643 W89 55.211
State Rate: See Introduction
(662) 653-3351
http://www.mdwfp.com/parks-destinations/ms-state-parks/holmes-county.aspx

Directions

1.2 miles. From Exit 150 go east for 1.2 miles on Hwy 424 (State Park Rd) into the Park.

Points of Interest

Kosciusko, one of "America's 100 Best Small Towns," & one of the "Top Sixty Prettiest Painted places in America" is Oprah Winfrey's birthplace. A downtown driving/walking tour through historic downtown features 28 historic homes, many on the National Register of Historic Places.

RV Sites		Water		Laundry	Y
Number	28	None		Wi-Fi	
Shaded	Y	At Site	Y	Fishing	Y
By Water	Y	Spigots		Hiking	Y
Paved	Y	Sewer		Biking	Y
Pull Thru	some	None		Swimming	Y
ADA	Y	At Site		Watch Wildlife	Y
Max RV Size	40	Dump Station	Y	Pets	Y
Electric		Amenities		Security	
None		Restrooms	Y	Host(s)	Y
20 Amp	Y	Showers	Y	Rangers(s)	Y
30 Amp	Y	Reserve Sites	Y	Gate	
50 Amp		Store		Patrolled	Y
		Grill/Table	Y		

[10] Hugh White State Park
I-55, Exit 206
East of Grenada
N33 48.198 W89 43.732
State Rate: See Introduction
(662) 226-4934
http://www.mdwfp.com/parks-destinations/ms-state-parks/hugh-white.aspx

Directions

7.5 miles. From Exit 206 go east on Hwy 8/333 (Sunset Dr) to Grenada. Continue on Hwy 8 (now Lakeview Dr) for 4.4 miles total. Turn left on Hwy 333 & Old Hwy 8 (while Hwy 8 goes straight). Follow Old Hwy 8 for 3 miles to the Park.

Points of Interest

Outdoor enthusiasts will enjoy Grenada and all it has to offer from Grenada Lake to the Lofton Archery Classic and the National Fox Hunt. Antiquing and downtown shopping will keep you busy.

RV Sites		Water		Laundry	
Number	125	None		Wi-Fi	
Shaded	Y	At Site	Y	Fishing	Y
By Water	Y	Spigots		Hiking	Y
Paved		Sewer		Biking	Y
Pull Thru		None		Swimming	
ADA	Y	At Site		Watch Wildlife	Y
Max RV Size	40	Dump Station	Y	Pets	Y
Electric		Amenities		Security	
None		Restrooms	Y	Host(s)	Y
20 Amp	Y	Showers	Y	Rangers(s)	Y
30 Amp	Y	Reserve Sites	Y	Gate	
50 Amp		Store		Patrolled	Y
		Grill/Table	Y		

[11] Wallace Creek Campground
I-55, Exit 233
South of Batesville
N34 09.992 W89 53.771
COE Rate: $12-$18
America/Beautiful Rate: $6-$9
(662) 563-4571
http://www.recreation.gov/

Directions

1.6 miles from I-55. From Exit 233 go east for 0.8 miles on Cty Rd 36. Go left on Cty Rd 38 (Enid Dam Rd) for 0.8 miles to the Park on your right.

Points of Interest Also see [12]

"A popular poster in Oxford Mississippi proclaims, 'The Square is the Center of the Universe.' After a visit to this downtown's mecca of shops & restaurants, that statement is hard to deny." William Faulkner's home is nearby.

RV Sites		Water		Laundry	
Number	99	None		Wi-Fi	
Shaded	Y	At Site	Y	Fishing	Y
By Water	Y	Spigots	Y	Hiking	Y
Paved	Y	Sewer		Biking	Y
Pull Thru	Y	None		Swimming	Y
ADA	Y	At Site	Y	Watch Wildlife	Y
Max RV Size	45	Dump Station	Y	Pets	Y
Electric		Amenities		Security	
None		Restrooms	Y	Host(s)	Y
20 Amp	Y	Showers	Y	Rangers(s)	Y
30 Amp	Y	Reserve Sites	Y	Gate	
50 Amp	Y	Store		Patrolled	Y
		Grill/Table	Y		

[12] John W. Kyle State Park
I-55, Exit 252
East of Sardis
N34 24.749 W89 48.663
State Rate: See Introduction
(662) 487-1345
http://www.mdwfp.com/parks-destinations/ms-state-parks/john-w-kyle.aspx

Directions

7 miles. From Exit 252 go east & south for 7 miles on Hwy 315 to the Park on your right. Note the campground is on the Lower Lake.

Points of Interest Also see [11]

Oxford, one of the South's crown jewels, is home to The University of Mississippi & hosts an array of athletic events, performing arts programs, scholarly presentations, museums & exhibits. Springtime brings the colors of blooming azaleas, wisteria & dogwood.

RV Sites		Water		Laundry	Y
Number	199	None		Wi-Fi	
Shaded	Y	At Site	Y	Fishing	Y
By Water	Y	Spigots	Y	Hiking	Y
Paved	Y	Sewer		Biking	Y
Pull Thru		None		Swimming	Y
ADA	Y	At Site	Y	Watch Wildlife	Y
Max RV Size	40	Dump Station	Y	Pets	Y
Electric		Amenities		Security	
None		Restrooms	Y	Host(s)	Y
20 Amp	Y	Showers	Y	Rangers(s)	Y
30 Amp	Y	Reserve Sites	Y	Gate	
50 Amp	Y	Store		Patrolled	Y
		Grill/Table	Y		

[13] Hernando Point
I-55, Exit 271
Southwest of Hernando
N34 44.277 W90 04.486
COE Rate: $16-$20
America/Beautiful Rate: $8-$10
(662) 562-6261
http://www.recreation.gov/

Directions

9 miles. From Exit 271 go west on Hwy 306 for 0.8 miles to Hwy 51. Turn north for 3.1 miles to Wheeler Rd. Turn west for 5.1 miles to the end of Wheeler, which is the campground.

Points of Interest

If you like Bar-B-Q, visit Southaven, whose Springfest is the largest barbecue contest in Mississippi. Southaven is home to the nationally famous 'Interstate Bar-B-Q.' Take in an event at the Desoto Civic Center.

RV Sites		Water		Laundry	
Number	83	None		Wi-Fi	
Shaded	Y	At Site	Y	Fishing	Y
By Water	Y	Spigots	Y	Hiking	Y
Paved		**Sewer**		Biking	Y
Pull Thru	Y	None		Swimming	
ADA	Y	At Site		Watch Wildlife	Y
Max RV Size	45	Dump Station	Y	Pets	Y
Electric		**Amenities**		**Security**	
None		Restrooms	Y	Host(s)	Y
20 Amp	Y	Showers	Y	Rangers(s)	Y
30 Amp	Y	Reserve Sites	Y	Gate	
50 Amp	Y	Store		Patrolled	Y
		Grill/Table	Y		

[14] Paul B. Johnson State Park
I-59, Exit 59
South of Hattiesburg
N31 08.093 W89 13.807
State Rate: See Introduction
(601) 582-7721
http://www.mdwfp.com/parks-destinations/ms-state-parks/paul-b-johnson.aspx

Directions

11 miles. From Exit 59 go east for 3 miles on Hwy 98. Turn south on Hwy 49 for 7.5 miles to the campground on your right.

Points of Interest

In Hattiesburg, visit the All-American Rose Garden at the University of Southern Mississippi (750 award-winning bushes). At the Historic Saenger Theater swing to the sounds of the theater's original 1929 pipe organ. Both are free. Shop for antiques, 'eclectibles' & bargains.

RV Sites		Water		Laundry	Y
Number	125	None		Wi-Fi	
Shaded	Y	At Site	Y	Fishing	Y
By Water		Spigots	Y	Hiking	Y
Paved	Y	**Sewer**		Biking	Y
Pull Thru	Y	None		Swimming	Y
ADA	Y	At Site	Y	Watch Wildlife	Y
Max RV Size	45	Dump Station	Y	Pets	Y
Electric		**Amenities**		**Security**	
None		Restrooms	Y	Host(s)	Y
20 Amp	Y	Showers	Y	Rangers(s)	Y
30 Amp	Y	Reserve Sites	Y	Gate	
50 Amp	Y	Store		Patrolled	Y
		Grill/Table	Y		

[15] Clarkco State Park
I-59/I-20, Exit 157
South of Meridian
N32 06.241 W88 42.219
State Rate: See Introduction
(601) 776-6651
http://www.mdwfp.com/parks-destinations/ms-state-parks/clarkco.aspx

Directions

22 miles. From Exit 157 go south for 22 miles on Hwy 45 to Hwy 145. Turn left, go 0.5 miles to the Park entrance on the right.

Points of Interest Also see [4].

For Meridian, download the Tour Guide for all kinds of ideas for things to do and see, great pictures too (see [4])! Visit the Causeyville General Store, opened in 1895 as a general store and gristmill.

RV Sites		Water		Laundry	Y
Number	43	None		Wi-Fi	
Shaded	Y	At Site	Y	Fishing	Y
By Water	Y	Spigots	Y	Hiking	Y
Paved	Y	**Sewer**		Biking	Y
Pull Thru	Y	None		Swimming	Y
ADA	Y	At Site	Y	Watch Wildlife	Y
Max RV Size	40	Dump Station	Y	Pets	Y
Electric		**Amenities**		**Security**	
None		Restrooms	Y	Host(s)	Y
20 Amp	Y	Showers	Y	Rangers(s)	Y
30 Amp	Y	Reserve Sites	Y	Gate	
50 Amp	Y	Store	Y	Patrolled	Y
		Grill/Table	Y		

[16] Lake Lowndes State Park
Hwy 45/182 Main St. Exit in Columbus
Southeast of Columbus
State Rate: See Introduction
N33 26.378 W88 18.324
(662) 328-2110
http://www.mdwfp.com/parks-destinations/
ms-state-parks/lake-lowndes.aspx

Directions

10.7 miles. On Hwy 45, take the Downtown (Main St.) exit south & follow Hwy 182 for 2.8 miles. Turn right on Hwy 69, go 4.8 miles to Lake Lowndes Rd. Turn left, go 3.1 miles to the Park.

Points of Interest

The Park Visitor's Center features indoor tennis, basketball, card room & a game room with pool & ping pong. Columbus, a town that thrives on its rich heritage and Southern charm, has 676 historic properties & 23 National Register properties.

RV Sites		Water		Laundry	Y
Number	50	None		Wi-Fi	
Shaded	Y	At Site	Y	Fishing	Y
By Water	Y	Spigots	Y	Hiking	Y
Paved	Y	Sewer		Biking	Y
Pull Thru		None		Swimming	
ADA	Y	At Site	Y	Watch Wildlife	Y
Max RV Size	40	Dump Station	Y	Pets	Y
Electric		Amenities		Security	
None		Restrooms	Y	Host(s)	Y
20 Amp	Y	Showers	Y	Rangers(s)	Y
30 Amp	Y	Reserve Sites	Y	Gate	
50 Amp	Y	Store	Y	Patrolled	Y
		Grill/Table	Y		

[17] Tombigbee State Park
Hwy 45
Southeast of Tupelo
State Rate: See Introduction
N34 13.991 W88 37.829
(662) 842-7669
http://www.mdwfp.com/parks-destinations/ms-state-parks/tombigbee.aspx

Directions

5.4 miles. South side of Tupelo on Hwy 45. Take the Hwys 6/178/278 exit east. Follow Hwy 6 for 2.8 miles to State Park Rd. Turn left, go 2.6 miles to the Park.

Points of Interest

Tupelo is the Birthplace of Elvis Presley, is the headquarters to the scenic Natchez Trace Parkway, and home to the incredible Tupelo Automobile Museum. The Battle of Tupeolo was fought here on the Tupelo National Battlefield

RV Sites		Water		Laundry	Y
Number	20	None		Wi-Fi	
Shaded	Y	At Site	Y	Fishing	Y
By Water	Y	Spigots	Y	Hiking	Y
Paved	Y	Sewer		Biking	Y
Pull Thru		None		Swimming	
ADA	Y	At Site	Y	Watch Wildlife	Y
Max RV Size	45	Dump Station	Y	Pets	Y
Electric		Amenities		Security	
None		Restrooms	Y	Host(s)	Y
20 Amp	Y	Showers	Y	Rangers(s)	Y
30 Amp	Y	Reserve Sites	Y	Gate	Y
50 Amp	Y	Store		Patrolled	
		Grill/Table	Y		

[18] Wall Doxey State Park
Hwy 78, South on Hwys 4/7
South of Holly Springs
State Rate: See Introduction
N34 39.881 W89 27.669
(662) 252-423
http://www.mdwfp.com/parks-destinations/ms-state-parks/wall-doxey.aspx

Directions

5.9 miles. From Hwy 78, south of Holly Springs, go 0.3 mile south on Hwy 4, then left on Hwy 7 for 5.6 miles to the Park Entrance.

Points of Interest

The Park is just seven miles from the splendid antebellum homes of Holly Springs. The to-do list could also include the Town Square, Marshall County Museum, and Rowan Oak, Home of William Faulkner. The University of Mississippi ("Ole Miss") is just a twenty five minute drive.

RV Sites		Water		Laundry	Y
Number	64	None		Wi-Fi	
Shaded	Y	At Site	Y	Fishing	Y
By Water	Y	Spigots	Y	Hiking	Y
Paved	Y	Sewer		Biking	Y
Pull Thru		None		Swimming	
ADA	Y	At Site		Watch Wildlife	Y
Max RV Size	40	Dump Station	Y	Pets	Y
Electric		Amenities		Security	
None		Restrooms	Y	Host(s)	Y
20 Amp	Y	Showers	Y	Rangers(s)	Y
30 Amp	Y	Reserve Sites	Y	Gate	
50 Amp	Y	Store		Patrolled	Y
		Grill/Table	Y		

About Missouri's Public Campgrounds

Missouri State Parks and Historic Sites are administered by the Division of State Parks. Missouri's state park system, which on four occasions has been ranked as one of the top four state park systems in the nation, contains 85 state parks and historic sites, 40 of which offer camping opportunities. You can find details about the State Parks system at - **http://www.mostateparks.com/**

To ensure that the state park system can be used and enjoyed by everyone, a major effort was undertaken to make facilities, activities and programs accessible to all persons, regardless of abilities. Facilities such as campgrounds, showers, picnic areas, fishing docks and other areas have been renovated to comply with the Americans with Disabilities Act.

Keep your pet on a leash, not longer than 10 feet, at all times. Pets are not allowed inside any park or historic site building, or in public swimming areas and beaches.

The Missouri state park system does not charge entrance fees. However, there are fees associated with camping, lodging, tours, museums and certain special events. Reservations are accepted in 36 of Missouri's 40 state park and historic site campgrounds and can be made online or by phone up to six months in advance or as close as two days. The reservation fee is $8.50. To make reservations visit -

http://www.mostateparks.com/page/54942/camping-reservation-system

A **$2 per night camping discount is available year-round for senior citizens (65 years and older) and persons with disabilities.** An official document such as a driver's license certifying proof of age or disability must be presented when registering. Campsite fees (first number is off-season, second is on-season) typically are -

Basic:	$12 - $13
Electric:	$19 - $23
Electric/Water:	$21 - $25
Sewer/Electric/Water:	$22 - $28
Senior/Disabilities Discount:	$2

[1] Weston Bend State Park	[10] Hawn State Park
[2] Lewis and Clark State Park	[11] Blue Springs Campground
[3] Big Lake State Park	[12] Knob Noster State Park
[4] Wallace State Park	[13] Arrow Rock State Historic Site
[5] Bennett Springs State Park	[14] Finger Lakes State Park
[6] Lane Spring Recreation Area	[15] Graham Cave State Park
[7] Meramec State Park	[16] Indian Point COE Park
[8] Babler Memorial State Park	[17] Harry S. Truman State Park
[9] Trail of Tears State Park	[18] Crowder State Park

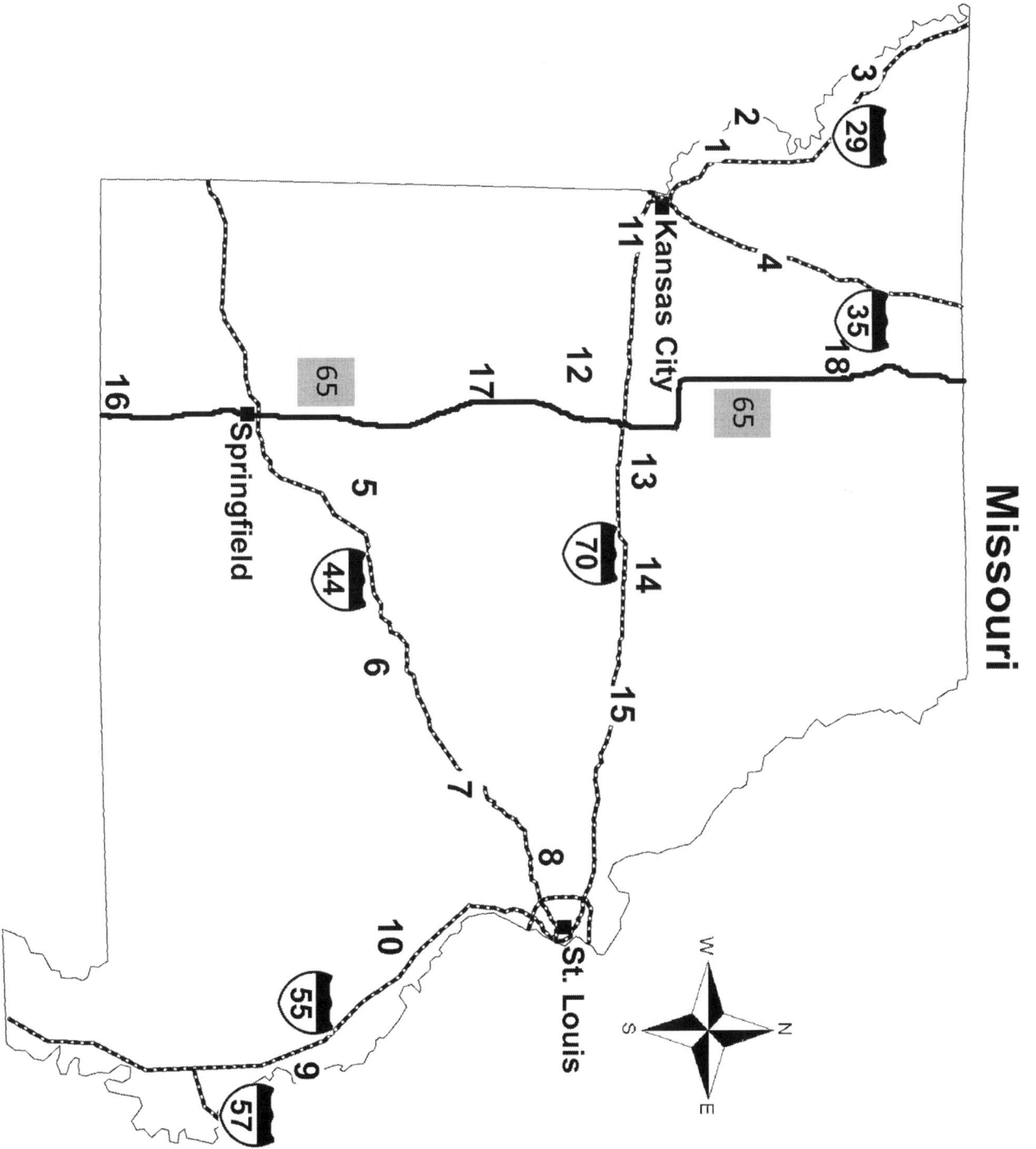

Missouri

Kansas City

Springfield

St. Louis

N W S E

65

65

3
2
1
29

11
4
35
18

16
17
12

13
5
70
14

44
6
15

7

8

10
55

9
57

[1] Weston Bend State Park
I-29, Exit 20
West of Platte City
N39 23.638 W94 52.264
State Rate: See Introduction
(816) 640-5443
www.mostateparks.com/park/weston-bend-state-park

Directions

5 miles. From Exit 20 turn west on Hwy 273 for 4.6 miles to Hwy 45. Turn south 0.4 miles to the Park Entrance.

Points of Interest

Visit Weston, nestled among the high bluffs of the Missouri River and voted Kansas City's #1 Day Trip. Experience unique shopping in lovely pre-Civil War buildings. Enjoy the variety of shops, restaurants, pubs, brewery, wineries, entertainment and places to see in this historic town.

RV Sites		Water			Laundry	Y
Number	34	None			Wi-Fi	Y
Shaded	Y	At Site			Fishing	
By Water	Y	Spigots	Y		Hiking	Y
Paved	Y	Sewer			Biking	Y
Pull Thru	Y	None			Swimming	
ADA	Y	At Site			Watch Wildlife	Y
Max RV Size	40	Dump Station	Y		Pets	Y
Electric		Amenities			Security	
None		Restrooms	Y		Host(s)	Y
20 Amp	Y	Showers	Y		Rangers(s)	Y
30 Amp	Y	Reserve Sites	Y		Gate	Y
50 Amp	Y	Store			Patrolled	Y
		Grill/Table	Y			

[2] Lewis and Clark State Park
I-29, Exit 30
Southwest of St. Joseph
N39 32.328 W95 03.207
State Rate: See Introduction
(816) 579-5564
www.mostateparks.com/park/lewis-and-clark-state-park

Directions

23 miles. From Exit 30 go west 0.7 mi. on Cty Rd H to Hwy 371. Go north 3 mi. to Hwy 116. Go west, 15.2 mi. to Hwy 59. Go south, 2.2 mi. When Hwy 59 turns west, go straight on Hwy 45 for 1.1 mi. to Hwy 138. Turn west 0.6 mi. to the Park.

Points of Interest Also see [4]

St. Joseph was recently named the Top Western Town by True West Magazine. Visit some if its 13 museums and 50+ listings on the National Register of Historic Places.

RV Sites		Water			Laundry	Y
Number	69	None			Wi-Fi	
Shaded	Y	At Site			Fishing	Y
By Water	Y	Spigots	Y		Hiking	Y
Paved	some	Sewer			Biking	Y
Pull Thru	Y	None			Swimming	Y
ADA	Y	At Site			Watch Wildlife	Y
Max RV Size	45	Dump Station	Y		Pets	Y
Electric		Amenities			Security	
None		Restrooms	Y		Host(s)	Y
20 Amp	Y	Showers	Y		Rangers(s)	Y
30 Amp	Y	Reserve Sites	Y		Gate	
50 Amp	Y	Store			Patrolled	Y
		Grill/Table	Y			

[3] Big Lake State Park
I-29, Exit 79
Southwest of Mound City
N40 05.174 W95 20.549
State Rate: See Introduction
(660) 442-3770
www.mostateparks.com/park/big-lake-state-park
(Check to see if park has reopened since flood)

Directions

12.5 miles. From Exit 79 go 10 miles west on Hwy 159 to Hwy 111. Turn north for 2.4 miles to State Park Rd on your left.

Points of Interest

Visit the Squaw Creek Wildlife Refuge & ten-mile, self-guided auto tour. This loop road provides an excellent opportunity to enjoy wildlife in a natural setting from the comfort of a vehicle and/or stop for wildlife observation and photography. There are three hiking trails.

RV Sites		Water			Laundry	Y
Number	75	None			Wi-Fi	
Shaded	Y	At Site			Fishing	Y
By Water	Y	Spigots	Y		Hiking	Y
Paved		Sewer			Biking	Y
Pull Thru	Y	None			Swimming	Y
ADA	Y	At Site			Watch Wildlife	y
Max RV Size	40	Dump Station	Y		Pets	Y
Electric		Amenities			Security	
None		Restrooms	Y		Host(s)	Y
20 Amp	Y	Showers	Y		Rangers(s)	Y
30 Amp	Y	Reserve Sites	Y		Gate	
50 Amp		Store	Y		Patrolled	Y
		Grill/Table	Y			

[4] Wallace State Park
I-35, Exit 48
South of Cameron
N39 39.646 W94 12.798
State Rate: See Introduction
(816) 632-3745
www.mostateparks.com/park/wallace-state-park

Directions

2 miles. From Exit 48 turn southeast and go 0.4 miles on Hwy 69 to Hwy 121. Turn east and go 1.2 miles to the Park entrance.

Points of Interest Also see [2]

With 11 antique shopping destinations and numerous specialty shops, St. Joseph should keep any serious collector/browser busy. St. Joseph's cultural arts, from a world-class art museum to a renowned symphony orchestra, will also give you much to enjoy.

RV Sites		Water		Laundry	Y
Number	77	None		Wi-Fi	
Shaded	Y	At Site		Fishing	Y
By Water		Spigots	Y	Hiking	Y
Paved	some	Sewer		Biking	Y
Pull Thru	Y	None		Swimming	Y
ADA	Y	At Site		Watch Wildlife	Y
Max RV Size	45	Dump Station	Y	Pets	Y
Electric		Amenities		Security	
None		Restrooms	Y	Host(s)	Y
20 Amp	Y	Showers	Y	Rangers(s)	Y
30 Amp	Y	Reserve Sites	Y	Gate	Y
50 Amp		Store		Patrolled	Y
		Grill/Table	Y		

[5] Bennett Springs State Park
I-44, Exit 129
West of Lebanon
N37 44.275 W92 51.552
State Rate: See Introduction
(417) 532-4338
www.mostateparks.com/park/bennett-spring-state-park

Directions

13.5 miles. From Exit 129 turn northwest and go 1.5 miles through Lebanon on Hwy 5. Continue straight on Hwy 64 for 12 miles. Turn into the Park on Hwy 64A on your left.

Points of Interest

Car racing enthusiasts, check out the Lebanon I-44 Speedway & Midway Speedway. Other stops include the Gunter Farms Pumpkin Patch & Maze, Heartland Arena, & the Laclede County Historical Society Museum & Old Jail.

RV Sites		Water		Laundry	Y
Number	191	None		Wi-Fi	Y
Shaded	Y	At Site	Y	Fishing	Y
By Water	Y	Spigots	Y	Hiking	Y
Paved	some	Sewer		Biking	Y
Pull Thru	Y	None		Swimming	Y
ADA	Y	At Site	Y	Watch Wildlife	Y
Max RV Size	45	Dump Station	Y	Pets	Y
Electric		Amenities		Security	
None		Restrooms	Y	Host(s)	Y
20 Amp	Y	Showers	Y	Rangers(s)	Y
30 Amp	Y	Reserve Sites	Y	Gate	
50 Amp	Y	Store	Y	Patrolled	Y
		Grill/Table	Y		

[6] Lane Spring Recreation Area
I-44, Exit 184
South of Rolla
N37 47.941 W91 48.932
Mark Twain NF Rate: $8-$15
America/Beautiful Rate: $4-$8
(573) 364-4621
http://www.fs.usda.gov/recarea/mtnf/recarea/?recid=21780

Directions

13 miles. From Exit 184 go southeast to Kings Hwy & go east 0.8 miles to Hwy 63. Turn south & go 11.5 miles to Cty Rd. 726 (Lake Springs Rd). Go right & follow signs to campground.

Points of Interest

The surroundings have made it a popular spot for weddings. In Rolla see the Blue Bonnet Special Steam Train & visit the Edward L. Clark Museum. There also a number of local wineries.

RV Sites		Water		Laundry	
Number	18	None		Wi-Fi	
Shaded	Y	At Site		Fishing	Y
By Water	Y	Spigots	Y	Hiking	Y
Paved	Y	Sewer		Biking	Y
Pull Thru	Y	None	Y	Swimming	
ADA	Y	At Site		Watch Wildlife	Y
Max RV Size	34	Dump Station		Pets	Y
Electric		Amenities		Security	
None		Restrooms	Y	Host(s)	Y
20 Amp	Y	Showers		Rangers(s)	Y
30 Amp	Y	Reserve Sites		Gate	
50 Amp		Store		Patrolled	Y
		Grill/Table	Y		

[7] Meramec State Park
I-44, Exit 226
East of Oak Grove and Sullivan
N38 12.444 W91 06.132
State Rate: See Introduction
(573) 468-6072
www.mostateparks.com/park/meramec-state-park

Directions

3 miles. From Exit 226 turn southeast on Hwy 185 for 3 miles to the Park Entrance.

Points of Interest

The Park combines the beauty of the Meramec River and its surrounding bluffs, caves and forests. Guided tours of Fisher Cave, one of more than 40 caves in the park, are provided on a seasonal basis for a nominal fee. The Visitor Center offers a mix of educational exhibits.

RV Sites		Water		Laundry	Y
Number	209	None		Wi-Fi	Y
Shaded	Y	At Site	Y	Fishing	Y
By Water	Y	Spigots	Y	Hiking	Y
Paved	Y	Sewer		Biking	Y
Pull Thru	Y	None		Swimming	Y
ADA	Y	At Site	Y	Watch Wildlife	
Max RV Size	45	Dump Station	Y	Pets	Y
Electric		Amenities		Security	
None		Restrooms	Y	Host(s)	Y
20 Amp	Y	Showers	Y	Rangers(s)	Y
30 Amp	Y	Reserve Sites	Y	Gate	Y
50 Amp	Y	Store		Patrolled	Y
		Grill/Table	Y		

[8] Babler Memorial State Park
I-44, Exit 264
West of St. Louis
N38 37.050 W90 41.356
State Rate: See Introduction
(636) 458-3813
www.mostateparks.com/park/dr-edmund-babler-memorial-state-park

Directions

9.5 miles. From Exit 264 turn north 7.7 miles on Hwy 109 to Cty BA (Babler Park Dr). Turn left for 1.9 miles to Guy Park Dr. Turn left into the Park.

Points of Interest

At the Park you can spend a peaceful night camping and still be less than a hour from downtown St. Louis and all the city has to offer. You can discover the visitor options at *www.explorestlouis.com/visitors/index.asp*.

RV Sites		Water		Laundry	
Number	73	None		Wi-Fi	Y
Shaded	Y	At Site		Fishing	
By Water		Spigots	Y	Hiking	Y
Paved	Y	Sewer		Biking	Y
Pull Thru		None		Swimming	
ADA	Y	At Site		Watch Wildlife	Y
Max RV Size	45	Dump Station	Y	Pets	Y
Electric		Amenities		Security	
None		Restrooms	Y	Host(s)	Y
20 Amp	Y	Showers	Y	Rangers(s)	Y
30 Amp	Y	Reserve Sites	Y	Gate	Y
50 Amp	Y	Store		Patrolled	Y
		Grill/Table	Y		

[9] Trail of Tears State Park
I-55, Exit 105
Southwest of Mound City
N37 26.111 W89 29.083
State Rate: See Introduction
(573) 290-5268
www.mostateparks.com/park/trail-tears-state-park

Directions

13 miles. From Exit 105 go 1 mile north on Hwy 61 to Hwy 177. Turn right, south later, for 11.5 miles to the Park entrance, Moccasin Springs Rd, on your left.

Points of Interest

The Park is a memorial to the Cherokee Indians that lost their lives in a forced relocation. Visit Jackson, which Money magazine ranks 59th best small town in the United States. The National Park Service has also recognized Jackson's attractive uptown historic district.

RV Sites		Water		Laundry	Y
Number	52	None		Wi-Fi	
Shaded	Y	At Site	Y	Fishing	Y
By Water	Y	Spigots	Y	Hiking	Y
Paved	Y	Sewer		Biking	
Pull Thru	Y	None		Swimming	Y
ADA	Y	At Site	Y	Watch Wildlife	
Max RV Size	45	Dump Station	Y	Pets	Y
Electric		Amenities		Security	
None		Restrooms	Y	Host(s)	Y
20 Amp	Y	Showers	Y	Rangers(s)	Y
30 Amp	Y	Reserve Sites	Y	Gate	Y
50 Amp		Store		Patrolled	Y
		Grill/Table	Y		

[10] Hawn State Park
I-55, Exit 150
East of Farmington
N37 50.037 W90 14.432
State Rate: See Introduction
(573) 883-3603
www.mostateparks.com/park/hawn-state-park

Directions

14.5 miles. From Exit 150 turn west on Hwy 32. Go 11.2 miles to Hwy 144. Turn south and go 3.1 miles to the Park entrance.

Points of Interest

Hawn is considered "the loveliest of all Missouri State Parks." Enjoy Farmington's historical sites - the Missouri Mines Historical Site and the Fort Davidson State Historic Site. Take a tour of vineyards or just relax with some delicious food and live music at one of the area's wineries.

RV Sites		Water			Laundry	Y
Number	45	None			Wi-Fi	Y
Shaded	Y	At Site			Fishing	Y
By Water	Y	Spigots	Y		Hiking	Y
Paved	Y	**Sewer**			Biking	Y
Pull Thru		None			Swimming	
ADA	Y	At Site			Watch Wildlife	Y
Max RV Size	45	Dump Station	Y		Pets	Y
Electric		**Amenities**			**Security**	
None		Restrooms	Y		Host(s)	Y
20 Amp	Y	Showers	Y		Rangers(s)	Y
30 Amp	Y	Reserve Sites	Y		Gate	Y
50 Amp		Store			Patrolled	Y
		Grill/Table	Y			

[11] Blue Springs Campground
I-70, Exit 15
Southeast of Kansas City
N39 00.305 W94 21.062
County Park Rate: $21-$28
(816) 503-4805
http://www.jacksongov.org/content/7894/8081/default.aspx#Jacomo

Directions

3 miles. From Exit 15 turn south on I-470 and go 2.3 miles to Exit 14. Go 0.4 miles east on NE Bowlin Rd. Turn north into the Park.

Points of Interest

At the Park you can spend a peaceful night camping and still be less than a hour from downtown Kansas City and all the city has to offer. You can discover the visitor options at *www.visitkc.com/things-to-do/index.aspx*.

RV Sites		Water			Laundry	Y
Number	82	None			Wi-Fi	
Shaded	Y	At Site	Y		Fishing	
By Water		Spigots			Hiking	Y
Paved		**Sewer**			Biking	Y
Pull Thru	Y	None			Swimming	Y
ADA	Y	At Site	Y		Watch Wildlife	
Max RV Size	40	Dump Station	Y		Pets	Y
Electric		**Amenities**			**Security**	
None		Restrooms	Y		Host(s)	Y
20 Amp	Y	Showers	Y		Rangers(s)	
30 Amp	Y	Reserve Sites	Y		Gate	
50 Amp	Y	Store			Patrolled	Y
		Grill/Table	Y			

[12] Knob Noster State Park
I-70, Exit 58
South of Concordia
N38 45.182 W93 34.645
State Rate: See Introduction
(660) 563-2463
http://www.mostateparks.com/park/knob-noster-state-park

Directions

18.5 miles. From Exit 58 turn south and follow Hwy 23. Go 18.5 miles to SE 10 Rd and the Park entrance on your right.

Points of Interest

Sedalia is called the home of rails, trails, and ragtime. Depending on your timing, go to the Missouri State Fair, the foot-tapping Scott Joplin Festival, or just explore beautiful historic buildings (such as the Bothwell Lodge State Historic Site), museums and discover antique finds galore.

RV Sites		Water			Laundry	Y
Number	68	None			Wi-Fi	
Shaded	Y	At Site			Fishing	Y
By Water	Y	Spigots	Y		Hiking	Y
Paved		**Sewer**			Biking	Y
Pull Thru		None			Swimming	
ADA	Y	At Site			Watch Wildlife	
Max RV Size	40	Dump Station	Y		Pets	Y
Electric		**Amenities**			**Security**	
None		Restrooms	Y		Host(s)	Y
20 Amp	Y	Showers	Y		Rangers(s)	Y
30 Amp	Y	Reserve Sites	Y		Gate	Y
50 Amp		Store			Patrolled	Y
		Grill/Table	Y			

[13] Arrow Rock State Historic Site
I-70, Exit 98
East of Marshall
N39 03.793 W92 56.789
State Rate: See Introduction
(660) 837-3330
http://www.mostateparks.com/park/arrow-rock-state-historic-site

Directions

12.5 miles. From Exit 98 turn north to Hwy 41. Go west on Hwy 41 for 12.3 miles to the Park entrance.

Points of Interest

Walk to Arrow Rock Village, a National Historic Landmark. Limestone gutters line main street. Wooden sidewalks & overhead canopies line store fronts, recalling the grace of times past. Go to the Lyceum Theater, eat at the Huston Tavern. Visit the George Caleb Bingham Home.

RV Sites		Water		Laundry	
Number	46	None		Wi-Fi	Y
Shaded	Y	At Site		Fishing	Y
By Water		Spigots	Y	Hiking	Y
Paved	Y	Sewer		Biking	Y
Pull Thru	Y	None		Swimming	
ADA	Y	At Site		Watch Wildlife	
Max RV Size	45	Dump Station	Y	Pets	Y
Electric		Amenities		Security	
None		Restrooms	Y	Host(s)	Y
20 Amp	Y	Showers	Y	Rangers(s)	Y
30 Amp	Y	Reserve Sites	Y	Gate	Y
50 Amp	Y	Store	Y	Patrolled	Y
		Grill/Table	Y		

[14] Finger Lakes State Park
I-70, Exit 128
North of Columbia
N39 04.615 W92 19.792
State Rate: See Introduction
(573) 443-5315
http://www.mostateparks.com/park/finger-lakes-state-park

Directions

9 miles. From Exit 128 turn north on Hwy 63 for 9 miles to E Peabody Rd, the Park entrance on your right.

Points of Interest

Columbia's eclectic mix of restaurants, shops, art galleries, music venues, sporting events, & coffee houses means there's never a shortage of things to do. Twenty-five art galleries or museums and nine antique shops guarantee plenty of shopping or places to see.

RV Sites		Water		Laundry	
Number	35	None		Wi-Fi	
Shaded	Y	At Site		Fishing	Y
By Water		Spigots	Y	Hiking	Y
Paved	Y	Sewer		Biking	Y
Pull Thru		None		Swimming	Y
ADA	Y	At Site		Watch Wildlife	
Max RV Size	45	Dump Station	Y	Pets	Y
Electric		Amenities		Security	
None		Restrooms	Y	Host(s)	Y
20 Amp	Y	Showers	Y	Rangers(s)	Y
30 Amp	Y	Reserve Sites	Y	Gate	Y
50 Amp	Y	Store		Patrolled	Y
		Grill/Table	Y		

[15] Graham Cave State Park
I-70, Exit 170
West of St. Louis
N38 54.531 W91 34.567
State Rate: See Introduction
(573) 564-3476
http://www.mostateparks.com/park/graham-cave-state-park

Directions

2 miles. From Exit 170 turn north and immediately turn left on Hwy TT. Go 2 miles to the Park entrance.

Points of Interest Also see [8]

Graham Cave became historically significant when archaeologists discovered how long ago human occupancy had occurred. Archaeologists uncovered artifacts revealing human use of the cave dating back to as early as 10,000 years ago. The Park is an hour from St. Louis.

RV Sites		Water		Laundry	
Number	52	None		Wi-Fi	Y
Shaded	Y	At Site		Fishing	Y
By Water		Spigots	Y	Hiking	Y
Paved	Y	Sewer		Biking	Y
Pull Thru	Y	None		Swimming	
ADA	Y	At Site		Watch Wildlife	Y
Max RV Size	42	Dump Station	Y	Pets	Y
Electric		Amenities		Security	
None		Restrooms	Y	Host(s)	Y
20 Amp	Y	Showers	Y	Rangers(s)	Y
30 Amp	Y	Reserve Sites	Y	Gate	
50 Amp	Y	Store		Patrolled	Y
		Grill/Table	Y		

[16] Indian Point COE
Hwy 65, Hwy 465 Exit
West of Branson
N36 37.772 W93 20.671
COE Rate: $16-$21
America/Beautiful Rate: $8-$11
(417)338-2121
http://www.recreation.gov/

Directions

12 miles. Exit Hwy 65 at Hwy 465 (Ozark Mountain High Rd). Go 7.7 miles to the end at Hwy 76. Go left (same as for Silver Dollar City), go 1.1 miles to Indian Point Rd (2nd light). Turn left, go 3.2 miles (past SDC) to the Park.

Points of Interest

Branson is a top 25 U.S. family destination, and the live music capital of the US. Set aside lots of time to see live shows, you can do 3 a day! Silver Dollar City is worth a full day visit.

RV Sites		Water		Laundry	
Number	76	None		Wi-Fi	Y
Shaded	Y	At Site	Y	Fishing	Y
By Water	Y	Spigots		Hiking	Y
Paved	Y	Sewer		Biking	Y
Pull Thru	Y	None		Swimming	
ADA	Y	At Site		Watch Wildlife	Y
Max RV Size	45	Dump Station	Y	Pets	Y
Electric		Amenities		Security	
None		Restrooms	Y	Host(s)	Y
20 Amp	Y	Showers	Y	Rangers(s)	Y
30 Amp	Y	Reserve Sites	Y	Gate	
50 Amp	Y	Store		Patrolled	Y
		Grill/Table	Y		

[17] Harry S. Truman State Park
Hwy 65, Hwy 7 west
West of Warsaw
N38 16.248 W93 26.807
State Rate: See Introduction
(660) 438-7711
http://www.mostateparks.com/park/harry-s-truman-state-park

Directions

8.5 Miles. From Hwy 65 in Warsaw take Hwy 7 west for 6 miles to Hwy Uu. Turn right, go 2.4 miles to the Park.

Points of Interest

Sedalia is a great day trip for historic architecture, railroad history, world class art, or events like the Missouri State Fair, the Scott Joplin Ragtime Festival, or the Pow-Wow. Tour Bothwell Lodge State Historic Site.

RV Sites		Water		Laundry	Y
Number	198	None		Wi-Fi	Y
Shaded	Y	At Site		Fishing	Y
By Water	Y	Spigots	Y	Hiking	Y
Paved	Y	Sewer		Biking	Y
Pull Thru		None		Swimming	Y
ADA	Y	At Site		Watch Wildlife	Y
Max RV Size	45	Dump Station	Y	Pets	Y
Electric		Amenities		Security	
None		Restrooms	Y	Host(s)	Y
20 Amp	Y	Showers	Y	Rangers(s)	Y
30 Amp	Y	Reserve Sites	Y	Gate	
50 Amp	Y	Store		Patrolled	Y
		Grill/Table	Y		

[18] Crowder State Park
Hwy 65, Hwy 6 west
West of Trenton
N40 05.039 W93 40.191
State Rate: See Introduction
(660) 359-6473
http://www.mostateparks.com/park/crowder-state-park

Directions

5.4 miles. From Hwy 65 in Trenton go west on Hwy 6 for 4.6 miles to Hwy 146. Turn right for 1.2 mile to Hwy 128. Turn right & proceed into the Park.

Points of Interest

Visit Jamesport. Enjoy an informative "Step Back in Time" tour, daily, through the Amish Farmlands, Amish Homes & Farm, Country Shops & Stores. Learn all about the Amish, their customs, life style, beliefs, & ask all those questions you always wanted to know.

RV Sites		Water		Laundry	Y
Number	41	None		Wi-Fi	
Shaded	Y	At Site		Fishing	Y
By Water		Spigots	Y	Hiking	Y
Paved	Y	Sewer		Biking	Y
Pull Thru	Y	None		Swimming	Y
ADA	Y	At Site		Watch Wildlife	
Max RV Size	45	Dump Station	Y	Pets	Y
Electric		Amenities		Security	
None		Restrooms	Y	Host(s)	Y
20 Amp	Y	Showers	Y	Rangers(s)	Y
30 Amp	Y	Reserve Sites	Y	Gate	Y
50 Amp		Store		Patrolled	Y
		Grill/Table	Y		

About Montana's Public Campgrounds

The State Park System is the responsibility of Montana Fish, Wildlife & Parks. At their main website you can plan your stay by searching for a park by name, nearest city, regional area, closest water body, activity, or facility. Go to -

http://stateparks.mt.gov/

You can select a cultural park (Montana's storied past & diverse culture), natural park (natural beauty & scenic wonders), or recreational park (boating, fishing, swimming, water skiing, camping). There is no entrance fee for Montana residents.

Twenty of Montana's 54 state parks have more than 500 campsites to reserve. Reservations can be made nine months in advance of your stay, but no later than two days prior to your arrival. Twenty-five percent of the campsites are designated "walk-up" sites, available on a first-come, first-served basis for campers arriving without reservations. For those parks that charge an entrance fee, nonresidents must purchase a Day Pass ($5/vehicle) or Annual Pass ($25/vehicle). Additional fees are charged at state parks for camping, showers, some guided tours, and special events. There is a $10 reservation fee for reserving campsites. You can reserve a campsite by calling **(855) 922- 6768** or through Reserve America at -   **http://montanastateparks.reserveamerica.com/**

Most camp sites include picnic table and fire ring. Parks with electricity are: Beavertail Hill, Black Sandy, Brush Lake, Cooney, Finley Point, Hell Creek, Lewis and Clark Caverns, Placid Lake, Salmon Lake, Tongue River Reservoir, West Shore. All campgrounds have vault toilets unless noted otherwise.

Camping Fees (1st amount is peak season, 2nd amount is off-season)

	RESIDENT		NONRESIDENT	
	General	Senior/Disabled	General	with Park Pass
Campsite	$15 - $12	$7.5 - $6	$23 - $20	$18 - $15
Site with Electricity	$20 - $17	$12.50 - $11	$28 - $25	$23 - $20

All pets must be on a leash not over 10 feet long. Pets are not permitted on swimming beaches, in sanitary facilities, or in any other area posted to exclude them.

Given the presence of ten forests across the state, there are also a number of National Forest Campgrounds.

[1] Clark Canyon Recreation Area	**[9] Cooney State Park**
[2] Bannack State Park	**[10] Tongue River Reservoir State Park**
[3] Black Sandy State Park	**[11] Makoshika State Park**
[4] Cabin City Campground	**[12] Logan State Park**
[5] Slowey Campground	**[13] Whitefish Lake State Park**
[6] Quartz Flat Campground	**[14] Summit Campground**
[7] Lewis & Clark Caverns State Park	**[15] Great Northern Fair & Campground**
[8] Pine Creek Campground	

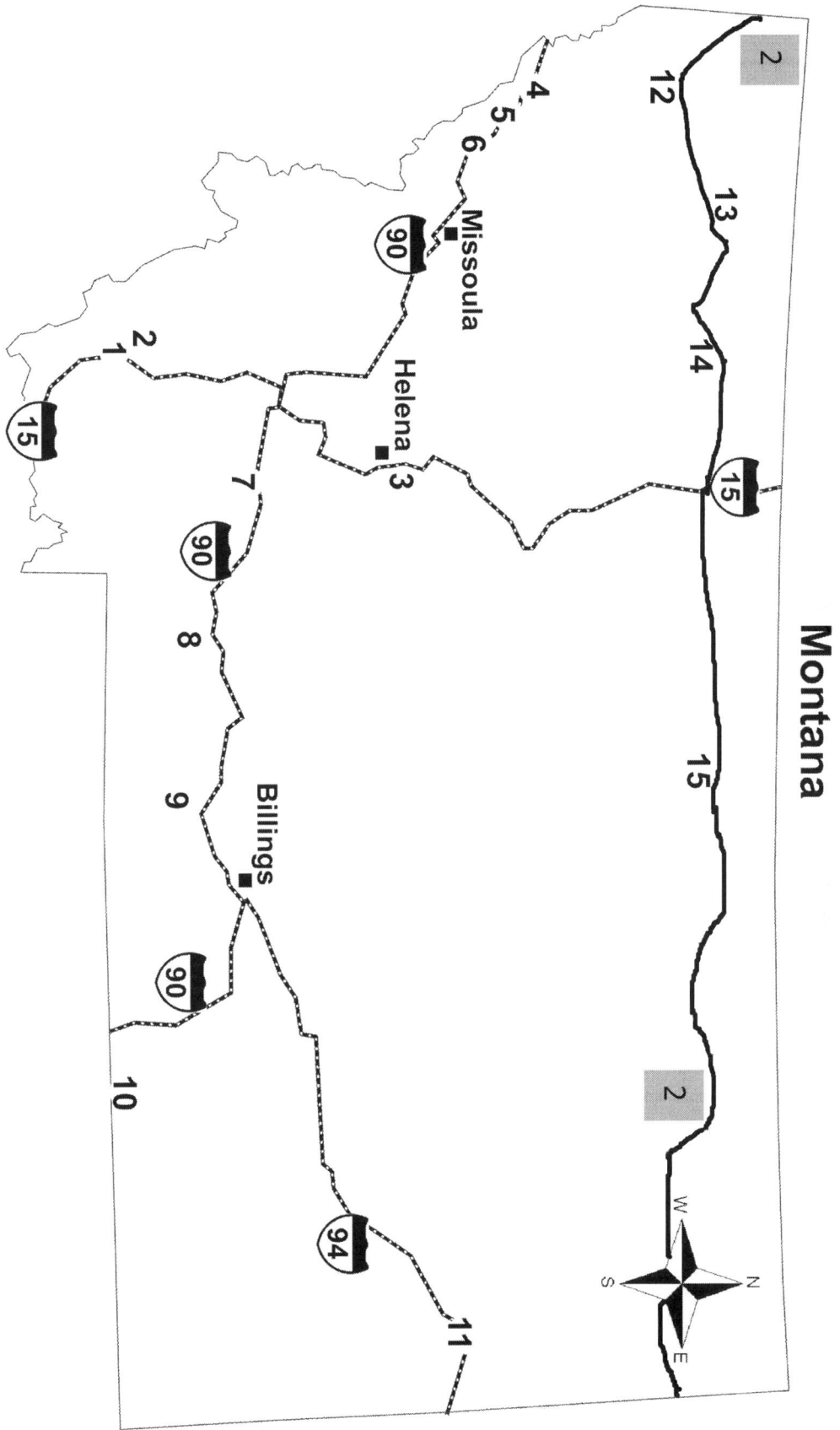

Montana

[1] Clark Canyon Recreation Area
I-15, Exit 44
Southwest of Grayling
N44 59.748 W112 52.250
Bureau of Reclamation Rate: $30
America/Beautiful Rate: $15
(406) 683-6472
http://www.usbr.gov/gp/recreation/ccrrec.htm

Directions

1.2 miles. From Exit 44 go west 1.2 miles on Hwy 324 to the campground on your left.

Points of Interest

This is the site of Camp Fortunate, a significant spot along the Lewis and Clark Trail. It was here that Lewis and Clark met the Lemhi Shoshoni Tribe, and cached their canoes and supplies for the return trip. Sacagawea was reunited with her people here.

RV Sites		Water		Laundry	
Number	55	None		Wi-Fi	
Shaded		At Site	Y	Fishing	Y
By Water	Y	Spigots		Hiking	Y
Paved		**Sewer**		Biking	Y
Pull Thru		None		Swimming	Y
ADA		At Site	Y	Watch Wildlife	Y
Max RV Size	45	Dump Station		Pets	Y
Electric		**Amenities**		**Security**	
None		Restrooms	Y	Host(s)	Y
20 Amp	Y	Showers		Rangers(s)	Y
30 Amp	Y	Reserve Sites		Gate	
50 Amp	Y	Store		Patrolled	Y
		Grill/Table	Y		

[2] Bannack State Park
I-15, Exit 59
West of Dillon
N45 09.653 W112 59.614
State Rate: See Introduction
(406) 834-3413
http://stateparks.mt.gov/bannack/

Directions

21 miles. From Exit 59 go west on Hwy 278 for 17.2 miles. Turn south at Bannack Bench Rd. and go 4 miles. The Park entrance is on the left.

Points of Interest

The Park is a National Historic Landmark and the site of Montana's first major gold discovery in 1862. The Park is actually a preserved abandoned mining town managed by the state. Over 50 buildings line Main Street; the historic log & frame structures recall Montana's formative years.

RV Sites		Water		Laundry	
Number	24	None		Wi-Fi	
Shaded	Y	At Site		Fishing	Y
By Water	Y	Spigots	Y	Hiking	Y
Paved		**Sewer**		Biking	Y
Pull Thru	some	None	Y	Swimming	
ADA	Y	At Site		Watch Wildlife	Y
Max RV Size	45	Dump Station		Pets	Y
Electric		**Amenities**		**Security**	
None	Y	Restrooms	Y	Host(s)	Y
20 Amp		Showers		Rangers(s)	Y
30 Amp		Reserve Sites	Y	Gate	
50 Amp		Store	Y	Patrolled	Y
		Grill/Table	Y		

[3] Black Sandy State Park
I-15, Exit 200
Northeast of Helena
N46 44.718 W111 53.219
State Rate: See Introduction
(406) 495-3270
http://stateparks.mt.gov/black-sandy/

Directions

8 miles. From Exit 200 go east for 5.1 miles on Hwy 453 (Lincoln Rd.) to Hauser Dam Rd. Turn north, then go 3.1 miles to the Park.

Points of Interest

Yellow metal transformed remote 'Last Chance Gulch' into Montana's golden capital. The "Queen City of the Rockies" lives up to its nickname. Helena's nineteenth century architecture dazzles, its gold rush history compels, and its arts and culture reflect a richly talented community

RV Sites		Water		Laundry	
Number	29	None		Wi-Fi	
Shaded	some	At Site		Fishing	Y
By Water	Y	Spigots	Y	Hiking	Y
Paved		**Sewer**		Biking	Y
Pull Thru		None		Swimming	Y
ADA	Y	At Site		Watch Wildlife	Y
Max RV Size	35	Dump Station	Y	Pets	Y
Electric		**Amenities**		**Security**	
None		Restrooms	Y	Host(s)	Y
20 Amp	Y	Showers		Rangers(s)	Y
30 Amp	Y	Reserve Sites	Y	Gate	
50 Amp	Y	Store		Patrolled	Y
		Grill/Table	Y		

[4] Cabin City Campground
I-90, Exit 22
East of De Borgia
N47 22.540 W115 15.817
Lolo National Forest Rate: $7
America/Beautiful Rate: $4
(406) 822-4233
http://www.publiclands.org/explore/site.php?id=2909

Directions

2.5 miles. From Exit 22 go east 1.6 miles, just past Cabin City, on 12 Mile Rd. (aka Mullan Gulch Rd or 2148). Bear left on 12 Mile Rd 353 for 0.3 miles to the campground entrance on your left.

Points of Interest

Try a day trip to the Savenac Historic Tree Nursery in Haugan (I-90, exit 16). It is one of the oldest U.S. Forest Service nurseries in the West. A self-guided tour provides insight to the nursery's history and recovery from the 1910 "Big Burn."

RV Sites		Water		Laundry	
Number	24	None		Wi-Fi	
Shaded	Y	At Site		Fishing	Y
By Water		Spigots	Y	Hiking	Y
Paved		**Sewer**		Biking	Y
Pull Thru		None	Y	Swimming	
ADA		At Site		Watch Wildlife	
Max RV Size	22	Dump Station		Pets	Y
Electric		**Amenities**		**Security**	
None	Y	Restrooms	Y	Host(s)	Y
20 Amp		Showers		Rangers(s)	Y
30 Amp		Reserve Sites		Gate	
50 Amp		Store		Patrolled	Y
		Grill/Table	Y		

[5] Slowey Campground
I-90, Exit 37
South of St. Regis
N47 14.077 W115 01.581
Lolo National Forest Rate: $10
America/Beautiful Rate: $5
(406) 822-4233
http://www.fs.usda.gov/recarea/lolo/recreation/camping-cabins/recarea/?recid=10332&actid=29

Directions

2.5 miles. From Exit 37 turn west and immediately go left on the frontage road, Old US 10, for 2.5 miles to the campground.

Points of Interest Also see [4]

The campground is popular for fly fishing enthusiasts and rafters, kayakers, and canoeists. Try a day trip to the Savenac Historic Tree Nursery in Haugan, MT (I-90, exit 16). It is one of the oldest U.S. Forest Service nurseries in the West.

RV Sites		Water		Laundry	
Number	27	None		Wi-Fi	
Shaded	Y	At Site		Fishing	Y
By Water	Y	Spigots	Y	Hiking	Y
Paved		**Sewer**		Biking	Y
Pull Thru	Y	None	Y	Swimming	
ADA	Y	At Site		Watch Wildlife	Y
Max RV Size	40	Dump Station		Pets	Y
Electric		**Amenities**		**Security**	
None	Y	Restrooms	Y	Host(s)	Y
20 Amp		Showers		Rangers(s)	Y
30 Amp		Reserve Sites		Gate	
50 Amp		Store		Patrolled	Y
		Grill/Table	Y		

[6] Quartz Flat Campground
I-90, Exit Mile Marker 58 Rest Area
North of Quartz
N47 04.484 W114 45.902
Lolo National Forest Rate: $10
America/Beautiful Rate: $5
(406) 822-4233
http://www.fs.usda.gov/recarea/lolo/recreation/ohv/recarea/?recid=10331&actid=31

Directions

Adjoins I-90. From Rest Area to west side of I-90. **The tunnel from the westbound side has a 14 foot clearance.** Some traffic noise.

Points of Interest Also see [4]

Try a day trip to the Savenac Historic Tree Nursery in Haugan, MT (I-90, exit 16). It is one of the oldest U.S. Forest Service nurseries in the West.

RV Sites		Water		Laundry	
Number	7	None		Wi-Fi	
Shaded	Y	At Site		Fishing	Y
By Water		Spigots	Y	Hiking	Y
Paved	Y	**Sewer**		Biking	Y
Pull Thru	Y	None		Swimming	
ADA	Y	At Site		Watch Wildlife	
Max RV Size	45	Dump Station	Y	Pets	Y
Electric		**Amenities**		**Security**	
None	Y	Restrooms	Y	Host(s)	Y
20 Amp		Showers		Rangers(s)	Y
30 Amp		Reserve Sites		Gate	
50 Amp		Store		Patrolled	Y
		Grill/Table	Y		

[7] Lewis & Clark Caverns State Park
I-90, Exit 256
South of Cardwell
N45 49.351 W111 51.080
State Rate: See Introduction
(406) 287-3541
http://stateparks.mt.gov/lewis-and-clark-caverns/

Directions

7.5 miles. From Exit 256 turn south and immediately go left on Hwy 2 for 7.5 miles to the Park entrance on your left.

Points of Interest

This is Montana's first and best-known state park and showcases one of the most highly decorated limestone caverns in the Northwest The caverns tour is said to be worth your time to experience (there is a fee). Butte's vintage architecture and colorful past will draw you to make a visit

RV Sites		Water			Laundry	
Number	39	None			Wi-Fi	
Shaded	some	At Site			Fishing	Y
By Water		Spigots		Y	Hiking	Y
Paved		Sewer			Biking	Y
Pull Thru	Y	None			Swimming	
ADA	Y	At Site			Watch Wildlife	Y
Max RV Size	45	Dump Station		Y	Pets	Y
Electric		Amenities			Security	
None		Restrooms		Y	Host(s)	Y
20 Amp	Y	Showers		Y	Rangers(s)	Y
30 Amp	Y	Reserve Sites		Y	Gate	
50 Amp	Y	Store		Y	Patrolled	Y
		Grill/Table		Y		

[8] Pine Creek Campground
I-90, Exit 333
South of Livingston
N45 29.886 W110 31.473
Gallatin National Forest Rate: $13
America/Beautiful Rate: $7
(877) 646-1012
http://www.recreation.gov/

Directions

14 miles. From Exit 333 go 3.1 miles south on Hwy 89 to E. River Rd. (Hwy 540). Turn left, go through Pine Creek, 7.7 mile in all to Luccock Park Rd. (FS Rd. 202). Turn left, go 2.7 miles to the campground on left.

Points of Interest

Surrounded by majestic mountain ranges, Livingston is steeped in the history of Lewis & Clark, Calamity Jane & Yellowstone National Park. Enjoy a blend of shops, museums, galleries & restaurants.

RV Sites		Water			Laundry	
Number	23	None			Wi-Fi	
Shaded	Y	At Site			Fishing	Y
By Water	Y	Spigots		Y	Hiking	Y
Paved		Sewer			Biking	Y
Pull Thru	Y	None		Y	Swimming	
ADA	Y	At Site			Watch Wildlife	Y
Max RV Size	45	Dump Station			Pets	Y
Electric		Amenities			Security	
None	Y	Restrooms		Y	Host(s)	
20 Amp		Showers			Rangers(s)	Y
30 Amp		Reserve Sites			Gate	
50 Amp		Store			Patrolled	Y
		Grill/Table		Y		

[9] Cooney State Park
I-90, Exit 434
Southwest of Laurel
N45 26.540 W109 12.231
State Rate: See Introduction
(406) 445-2326
http://stateparks.mt.gov/cooney/

Directions

31 miles. From Exit 434 go south for 23 miles on Hwy 212 to Cooney Dam Rd in Boyd. Turn right, go west 8.2 miles to the Park.

Points of Interest

Visit Billings and the land where General Custer fought the Sioux and Cheyenne, where Sitting Bull and Crazy Horse led their people through struggles and to victories, where the Lewis & Clark Expedition passed through, and where Calamity Jane raised a ruckus.

RV Sites		Water			Laundry	
Number	83	None			Wi-Fi	
Shaded	Y	At Site			Fishing	Y
By Water	Y	Spigots		Y	Hiking	Y
Paved		Sewer			Biking	Y
Pull Thru	Y	None			Swimming	Y
ADA	Y	At Site			Watch Wildlife	Y
Max RV Size	45	Dump Station		Y	Pets	Y
Electric		Amenities			Security	
None		Restrooms		Y	Host(s)	Y
20 Amp	Y	Showers		Y	Rangers(s)	Y
30 Amp	Y	Reserve Sites		Y	Gate	
50 Amp	Y	Store			Patrolled	Y
		Grill/Table		Y		

[10] Tongue River Reservoir State Park
I-90, Exit 16 in Wyoming
East of Aberdeen
N45 06.097 W106 47.922
State Rate: See Introduction
(406) 757-2298
http://stateparks.mt.gov/tongue-river-reservoir/

Directions

24 miles. From Exit 16 in Wyoming turn east on Hwy 339 for 1 mile to Hwy 338. Turn north for 21.5 miles. Along the way you will cross into Montana and the road will become Hwy 314. Turn right at Cty Hwy 180, go 1.5 miles into the Park.

Points of Interest

Visit Little Bighorn Battlefield where the U.S. Army's 7th Cavalry fought the Sioux & Cheyenne in one of the Indians last armed efforts to preserve their way of life. South is Sheridan, with a fabled Western history and dramatic mountain vistas.

RV Sites		Water		Laundry	
Number	156	None		Wi-Fi	
Shaded		At Site		Fishing	Y
By Water	Y	Spigots	Y	Hiking	Y
Paved	some	Sewer		Biking	Y
Pull Thru	Y	None		Swimming	Y
ADA	Y	At Site		Watch Wildlife	Y
Max RV Size	45	Dump Station	Y	Pets	Y
Electric		Amenities		Security	
None		Restrooms	Y	Host(s)	Y
20 Amp	Y	Showers	Y	Rangers(s)	Y
30 Amp	Y	Reserve Sites	Y	Gate	
50 Amp	Y	Store	Y	Patrolled	Y
		Grill/Table	Y		

[11] Makoshika State Park
I-94, Exit 213
South side of Glendive
N47 05.414 W104 42.598
State Rate: See Introduction
(406) 377-6256
http://stateparks.mt.gov/makoshika/

Directions

3 miles. From Exit 213 go south 0.5 mi. to W. Towne St. Turn left, go 1.1 mi. to Merrill. Turn right, go 0.3 mi., bearing left on Douglas to E. Berry, go 0.3 mi. to S. Taylor. Turn right, go 0.4 mi. to Snyder, go left, 0.3 mi. to the Park entrance.

Points of Interest

To the Sioux Indians, Ma-ko-shi-ka meant bad earth or 'bad land.' the pine & juniper studded badland formations, one of the most geologically spectacular in the region, houses the fossil remains of tyrannosaurus rex and triceratops.

RV Sites		Water		Laundry	
Number	21	None		Wi-Fi	
Shaded		At Site		Fishing	
By Water		Spigots	Y	Hiking	Y
Paved	Y	Sewer		Biking	Y
Pull Thru	Y	None	Y	Swimming	
ADA	Y	At Site		Watch Wildlife	Y
Max RV Size	45	Dump Station		Pets	Y
Electric		Amenities		Security	
None	Y	Restrooms	Y	Host(s)	Y
20 Amp		Showers		Rangers(s)	Y
30 Amp		Reserve Sites	Y	Gate	
50 Amp		Store	Y	Patrolled	Y
		Grill/Table	Y		

[12] Logan State Park
Hwy 2
West of Kalispell
N48 01.988 W115 03.901
State Rate: See Introduction
(406) 293-7190
http://stateparks.mt.gov/logan/

Directions

44 miles. Forty-four miles west of Kalispell on Hwy 2.

Points of Interest

The Park has frontage on the north shore of Middle Thompson Lake, Logan is heavily forested with western larch, Douglas-fir, and ponderosa pine. This is a great stop to relax, enjoy the scenery, take a swim, fish or other water sports. The Park is about 80 miles from West Glacier and the entrance to Glacier National Park.

RV Sites		Water		Laundry	
Number	37	None		Wi-Fi	
Shaded	Y	At Site		Fishing	Y
By Water	Y	Spigots	Y	Hiking	Y
Paved		Sewer		Biking	
Pull Thru	Y	None		Swimming	Y
ADA	Y	At Site		Watch Wildlife	Y
Max RV Size	42	Dump Station	Y	Pets	Y
Electric		Amenities		Security	
None	Y	Restrooms	Y	Host(s)	Y
20 Amp		Showers	Y	Rangers(s)	Y
30 Amp		Reserve Sites	Y	Gate	
50 Amp		Store		Patrolled	Y
		Grill/Table	Y		

[13] Whitefish Lake State Park
Hwy 2, West on Hwy 40
North west side of Whitefish
N48 25.396 W114 22.168
State Rate: See Introduction
(406) 862-3991
http://stateparks.mt.gov/whitefish-lake/

Directions

9.2 miles. At Halfmoon, southeast of Whitefish, turn left on Hwy 40, go 4.4 miles to Spokane Ave. Turn right, go 2.2 miles to Hwy 93 (2nd St.) Turn left go 1.5 miles to State Park Rd. turn right, follow State Park Rd. to the Park.

Points of Interest

The park is your base for the Whitefish hiking & biking trail system, and/or a short drive to Whitefish Mountain ski resort. Check out the Whitefish Downtown Farmers Market, every Tuesday evening from Memorial Day through September.

RV Sites		Water		Laundry	
Number	25	None		Wi-Fi	
Shaded	Y	At Site		Fishing	Y
By Water	Y	Spigots	Y	Hiking	Y
Paved		Sewer		Biking	Y
Pull Thru	Y	None	Y	Swimming	Y
ADA	Y	At Site		Watch Wildlife	Y
Max RV Size	42	Dump Station		Pets	Y
Electric		Amenities		Security	
None		Restrooms	Y	Host(s)	Y
20 Amp	Y	Showers	Y	Rangers(s)	Y
30 Amp	Y	Reserve Sites	Y	Gate	
50 Amp	Y	Store		Patrolled	Y
		Grill/Table	Y		

[14] Summit Campground
Hwy 2
Summit of Marias Pass
N48 19.207 W113 21.082
Lewis & Clark National Forest Rate: $10
America/Beautifal Rate: $5
(406) 466-5341
http://www.fs.usda.gov/recarea/lcnf/recreation/ohv/recarea/?recid=61568&actid=31

Directions

12 miles west of East Glacier. Forty-four miles east of West Glacier. On Hwy 2.

Points of Interest

A 3 mile trail connects the campground to the Continental Divide Scenic Trail. Nearby, a memorial commemorates Theodore Roosevelt and the Blackfeet tribe with a miniature Washington Monument.

RV Sites		Water		Laundry	
Number	17	None		Wi-Fi	
Shaded	Y	At Site		Fishing	
By Water		Spigots	Y	Hiking	Y
Paved		Sewer		Biking	Y
Pull Thru		None		Swimming	
ADA	Y	At Site		Watch Wildlife	Y
Max RV Size	30	Dump Station	Y	Pets	Y
Electric		Amenities		Security	
None	Y	Restrooms	Y	Host(s)	Y
20 Amp		Showers		Rangers(s)	Y
30 Amp		Reserve Sites		Gate	
50 Amp		Store		Patrolled	Y
		Grill/Table	Y		

[15] Great Northern Fair & Campground
Hwy 2
In Havre
N48 33.183 W109 42.563
County Rate: $20
(406) 265-7121
http://centralmontana.com/listings/3191.htm

Directions

0.5 mile. Located 0.5 mile west of Havre on the Great Northern Fairgrounds, south side of the Rd.

Points of Interest

The campground is a convenient stop on the way to/from Glacier National Park. Restaurants, supplies, and shopping are within walking distance. You can also arrange to have tours of a 1870s army fort and a bison kill site used by native bison hunters for over 2,000 years.

RV Sites		Water		Laundry	
Number	24	None		Wi-Fi	
Shaded		At Site	Y	Fishing	
By Water		Spigots		Hiking	
Paved		Sewer		Biking	Y
Pull Thru	Y	None		Swimming	
ADA		At Site		Watch Wildlife	
Max RV Size	45	Dump Station	Y	Pets	Y
Electric		Amenities		Security	
None		Restrooms	Y	Host(s)	Y
20 Amp	Y	Showers	Y	Rangers(s)	
30 Amp	Y	Reserve Sites		Gate	
50 Amp	Y	Store	Y	Patrolled	Y
		Grill/Table	Y		

About Nebraska's Public Campgrounds

Nebraska's state system encompasses 87 areas across the state (State Parks, Recreation Areas, Historical Parks), 24 of which will accommodate RVs. You will find lands to suit virtually every outdoor taste, whether you're seeking the ultimate in modern conveniences in a picturesque outdoor setting or want to get back to nature amid the unspoiled beauty of the wilderness. The Park system is the responsibility of the Nebraska Game and Parks Commission (NGPC), whose website is -

http://outdoornebraska.ne.gov/parks/

Relevant NGPC regulations state the following: (1) Dogs, cats and other pets are prohibited unless under physical restrictive control at all times. Leashes may not exceed six feet in length. Pets which become a nuisance shall be removed from the area. Pets are prohibited in public eating places and food stores, public buildings, and on designated swimming beaches; (2) The reservation of campsites designated as "reservable" in designated campgrounds is permitted through the NGPC reservation system.

NGPC has joined with ReserveAmerica to make reservations. The system includes easy-to-use maps, photographs and a shopping cart so users can reserve multiple arrival dates or multiple type of units. Users may go online to book reservations ($7 fee) up to 12 months in advance at:

http://nebraskastateparks.reserveamerica.com/

Reservations can also be made through the call center at (402) 471-1414.

A Nebraska State Park Permit is required when entering all state parks, state historical parks and state recreation areas. The daily fee is $5. All motor vehicles, operated within the boundaries of a designated fee area, must properly display a valid permit.

[1] Lake McConaughy State Rec. Area	[7] Eugene T. Mahoney State Park
[2] Johnson Lake State Rec. Area	[8] Two Rivers State Recreation Area
[3] Fort Kearny State Rec. Area	[9] Fort Robinson State Park
[4] Windmill State Rec. Area	[10] Merritt Reservoir State Recreation Area
[5] Mormon Island State Rec. Area	[11] Willow Creek State Recreation Area
[6] Pawnee Lake State Rec. Area	[12] Ponca State Park

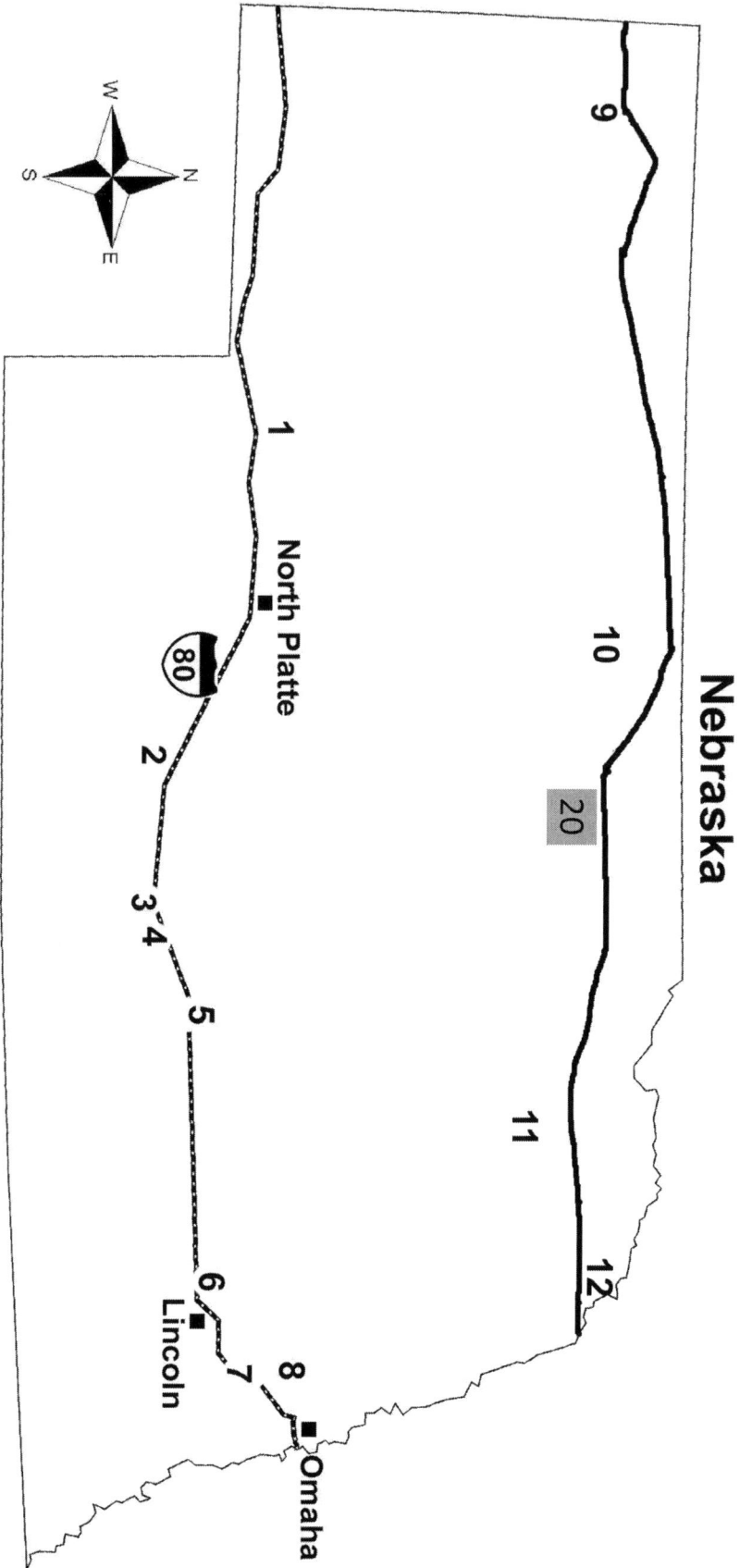

Nebraska

1
North Platte
80
2
3 4
5
6
Lincoln
7 8
Omaha
9
10
20
11
12

[1] Lake McConaughy State Recreation Area
I-80, Exit 126
North of Ogallala
N41 13.176 W101 40.289
State Rate: $8-$26
(308) 284-8800
http://outdoornebraska.ne.gov/parks/guides/
parksearch/showpark.asp?Area_No=99

Directions

10-13 miles. From Exit 126 go north, follow Hwy 61 for 10-13 miles to the campground of your choice - Lake Ogallala (electric/water, paved); Lone Eagle (full service, water front); Little Thunder (full service, paved).

Points of Interest

There is much to see & do in this large recreation area. In all there are over 200 sites, which accommodate 45 foot RVs, with every combination of utilities/services available. Some have sewers and there is a dump station.

RV Sites		Water		Laundry	
Number	243	None		Wi-Fi	
Shaded	Y	At Site	Y	Fishing	Y
By Water	Y	Spigots	Y	Hiking	
Paved	Y	**Sewer**		Biking	Y
Pull Thru		None		Swimming	
ADA	Y	At Site	Y	Watch Wildlife	Y
Max RV Size	45	Dump Station	Y	Pets	Y
Electric		**Amenities**		**Security**	
None		Restrooms	Y	Host(s)	Y
20 Amp	Y	Showers	Y	Rangers(s)	Y
30 Amp	Y	Reserve Sites	Y	Gate	
50 Amp	Y	Store	Y	Patrolled	Y
		Grill/Table	Y		

[2] Johnson Lake State Recreation Area
I-80, Exit 237
South of Lexington
N40 40.757 W99 49.798
State Rate: $13-$20
(308) 785-2685
http://outdoornebraska.ne.gov/parks/guides/
parksearch/showpark.asp?Area_No=94

Directions

8 miles. From Exit 237 go south for 8 miles on Hwy 283. Turn right on E Park Dr 25A into the Park.

Points of Interest

Lexington offers numerous antique shops. Several century old homes have been restored to their original beauty. See the McCabe Aeroplane or "Baby Biplane" with its unique elliptical wing design at the Dawson County Historical Society Museum.

RV Sites		Water		Laundry	
Number	63	None		Wi-Fi	
Shaded	Y	At Site		Fishing	Y
By Water	Y	Spigots	Y	Hiking	Y
Paved	some	**Sewer**		Biking	Y
Pull Thru		None		Swimming	Y
ADA	Y	At Site		Watch Wildlife	Y
Max RV Size	42	Dump Station	Y	Pets	Y
Electric		**Amenities**		**Security**	
None		Restrooms	Y	Host(s)	Y
20 Amp	Y	Showers	Y	Rangers(s)	Y
30 Amp	Y	Reserve Sites	Y	Gate	
50 Amp	Y	Store		Patrolled	Y
		Grill/Table	Y		

[3] Fort Kearny State Recreation Area
I-80, Exit 279
South of Kearny
N40 39.130 W98 59.366
State Rate: $13-$20
(308) 865-5305
http://outdoornebraska.ne.gov/parks/guides/
parksearch/showpark.asp?Area_No=98

Directions

6 miles. From Exit 279, go south on Hwy 10 for 3 miles. Turn west on Hwy 50A for 2 miles to Rd 30. Turn north for 0.8 miles to the Park.

Points of Interest

For Sandhill Crane viewing and photography go to Rowe Sanctuary. In Kearny visit the Trails and Rails Museum, Nebraska Firefighters Museum, Museum of Nebraska Art, or Fort Kearny Museum. Tour the Cedar Hills Vineyard or Geo Spencer Vineyards.

RV Sites		Water		Laundry	
Number	38	None		Wi-Fi	
Shaded	Y	At Site		Fishing	Y
By Water	Y	Spigots	Y	Hiking	Y
Paved		**Sewer**		Biking	Y
Pull Thru		None		Swimming	Y
ADA	Y	At Site		Watch Wildlife	Y
Max RV Size	45	Dump Station	Y	Pets	Y
Electric		**Amenities**		**Security**	
None		Restrooms	Y	Host(s)	Y
20 Amp	Y	Showers	Y	Rangers(s)	Y
30 Amp	Y	Reserve Sites	Y	Gate	
50 Amp	Y	Store		Patrolled	Y
		Grill/Table	Y		

[4] Windmill State Recreation Area
I-80, Exit 285
East of Kearny
N40 42.441 W98 50.730
State Rate: $13-$20
(308) 468-5700
http://outdoornebraska.ne.gov/parks/guides/
parksearch/showpark.asp?Area_No=196

Directions

Adjoins I-80. From Exit 285 go north on Hwy 10C (Lowell Rd) for 0.3 miles and turn right in to the Park

Points of Interest

Windmill Crossing is where the Pawnee Indians forded the Platte River during annual buffalo hunts. The old-time windmills on site add much to the character of the Park. They have all been restored to working order. For Sandhill Crane viewing and photography go to Rowe Sanctuary.

RV Sites		Water		Laundry	Y
Number	32	None		Wi-Fi	
Shaded	Y	At Site		Fishing	Y
By Water		Spigots	Y	Hiking	Y
Paved	Y	Sewer		Biking	Y
Pull Thru	Y	None		Swimming	
ADA	Y	At Site		Watch Wildlife	Y
Max RV Size	45	Dump Station	Y	Pets	Y
Electric		Amenities		Security	
None		Restrooms	Y	Host(s)	Y
20 Amp	Y	Showers	Y	Rangers(s)	Y
30 Amp	Y	Reserve Sites	Y	Gate	
50 Amp	Y	Store		Patrolled	Y
		Grill/Table	Y		

[5] Mormon Island State Recreation Area
I-80, Exit 312
South of Grand Island
N40 49.416 W98 22.666
State Rate: $13-$20
(308) 385-6211
http://outdoornebraska.ne.gov/parks/guides/
parksearch/showpark.asp?Area_No=123

Directions

Adjoins I-80. From Exit 312 go north on Hwy 34/281 for 0.2 miles and turn right in to the Park.

Points of Interest

The early spring Sandhill Crane viewing and photography are excellent. In Grand Island experience live thoroughbred racing at Fonner Park. Explore the area's pioneer heritage at Stuhr Museum. Try your hand at clay or skeet shooting. Visit art galleries and a myriad of shopping venues.

RV Sites		Water		Laundry	Y
Number	34	None		Wi-Fi	
Shaded	Y	At Site		Fishing	Y
By Water		Spigots	Y	Hiking	Y
Paved	Y	Sewer		Biking	Y
Pull Thru	Y	None		Swimming	Y
ADA	Y	At Site		Watch Wildlife	Y
Max RV Size	45	Dump Station	Y	Pets	Y
Electric		Amenities		Security	
None		Restrooms	Y	Host(s)	Y
20 Amp	Y	Showers	Y	Rangers(s)	Y
30 Amp	Y	Reserve Sites	Y	Gate	
50 Amp	Y	Store		Patrolled	Y
		Grill/Table	Y		

[6] Pawnee Lake State Rec. Area
I-80, Exit 388
West of Lincoln
N40 51.034 W96 51.796
State Rate: $8-$20
(402) 796-2362
http://outdoornebraska.ne.gov/parks/guides/
parksearch/showpark.asp?Area_No=135

Directions

7.5 miles. From Exit 388 go 0.5 miles south on Hwy 103. Go east on Hwy 6 for 4 miles. Turn north on NW. 98th St. for 2 miles to W. Adams St. Turn west for 0.9 miles to the Park.

Points of Interest

Lincoln is home to many of the nation's prized historical monuments. Examples include the Germans from Russia Museum, the Home of William Jennings Bryan, or Historic Haymarket. The International Quilt Study Center & Museum is an excellent stop.

RV Sites		Water		Laundry	
Number	68	None		Wi-Fi	
Shaded	Y	At Site		Fishing	Y
By Water	Y	Spigots	Y	Hiking	Y
Paved	Y	Sewer		Biking	Y
Pull Thru		None		Swimming	Y
ADA	Y	At Site		Watch Wildlife	Y
Max RV Size	45	Dump Station	Y	Pets	Y
Electric		Amenities		Security	
None		Restrooms	Y	Host(s)	Y
20 Amp	Y	Showers	Y	Rangers(s)	Y
30 Amp	Y	Reserve Sites	Y	Gate	
50 Amp	Y	Store	Y	Patrolled	Y
		Grill/Table	Y		

[7] Eugene T. Mahoney State Park
I-80, Exit 426
Southwest of Omaha
N41 00.967 W96 19.013
State Rate: $22-$28
(402) 944-2523
http://outdoornebraska.gov/parks/park_pages/Mahoney_SP/

Directions

Adjoins I-80. From Exit 426 go northwest 0.5 miles and turn right, just before the Strategic Air & Space Museum, into the Park.

Points of Interest

Dine in the Lodge restaurant (with the scenic Platte River as a backdrop). Mahoney has many recreational activities - aquatic center, miniature golf, driving range, tennis, horseback rides, crafts, observation tower, and nature conservatory. Visit the Strategic Air & Space Museum.

RV Sites		Water		Laundry	Y
Number	74	None		Wi-Fi	Y
Shaded	Y	At Site	Y	Fishing	Y
By Water		Spigots	Y	Hiking	Y
Paved	Y	**Sewer**		Biking	Y
Pull Thru		None		Swimming	
ADA	Y	At Site	Y	Watch Wildlife	Y
Max RV Size	45	Dump Station	Y	Pets	Y
Electric		**Amenities**		**Security**	
None		Restrooms	Y	Host(s)	Y
20 Amp	Y	Showers	Y	Rangers(s)	Y
30 Amp	Y	Reserve Sites	Y	Gate	
50 Amp	Y	Store	Y	Patrolled	Y
		Grill/Table	Y		

[8] Two Rivers State Recreation Area
I-80, Exit 445
West of Omaha
N41 13.148 W96 20.969
State Rate: $13-$23
(402) 359-5165
http://outdoornebraska.ne.gov/parks/guides/parksearch/showpark.asp?Area_No=175

Directions

15 miles. From Exit 445 go west 12.7 miles on Hwy 92/275 (becomes Center Rd). Follow 92 when 275 turns north. Turn south for 1 mile on S 264th St to F St. Turn right for 1 mile to the Park entrance.

Points of Interest

Omaha has the world's largest indoor rainforest. Visit the Durham Western Heritage Museum or Joslyn Art Museum. Shop in the Old Market district - restaurants, pubs & galleries line authentic cobblestone streets. Savor a legendary Omaha steak.

RV Sites		Water		Laundry	
Number	207	None		Wi-Fi	
Shaded	Y	At Site		Fishing	Y
By Water	Y	Spigots	Y	Hiking	Y
Paved	Y	**Sewer**		Biking	Y
Pull Thru		None		Swimming	Y
ADA	Y	At Site	Y	Watch Wildlife	Y
Max RV Size	45	Dump Station	Y	Pets	Y
Electric		**Amenities**		**Security**	
None		Restrooms	Y	Host(s)	Y
20 Amp	Y	Showers	Y	Rangers(s)	Y
30 Amp	Y	Reserve Sites	Y	Gate	
50 Amp	Y	Store	Y	Patrolled	Y
		Grill/Table	Y		

[9] Fort Robinson State Park
Hwy 20
Southwest of Crawford
N42 40.035 W103 27.928
State Rate: $7-$24
(308) 665-2900
http://outdoornebraska.ne.gov/parks/guides/parksearch/showpark.asp?Area_No=77

Directions

3.5 miles. Go west on Hwy 20 from Crawford for 3.5 miles to the park on Hwy 20.

Points of Interest

This was the site of the 1879 Cheyenne Outbreak and death of Sioux Chief Crazy Horse. The State Historical Society operates a museum and many exhibit buildings to interpret the Fort's history. Tour the new exhibit The Clash of the Mammoths at the Trailside Museum of Natural History.

RV Sites		Water		Laundry	Y
Number	125	None		Wi-Fi	
Shaded	Y	At Site	Y	Fishing	Y
By Water		Spigots	Y	Hiking	Y
Paved	Y	**Sewer**		Biking	Y
Pull Thru	some	None		Swimming	Y
ADA	Y	At Site	Y	Watch Wildlife	
Max RV Size	45	Dump Station	Y	Pets	Y
Electric		**Amenities**		**Security**	
None		Restrooms	Y	Host(s)	Y
20 Amp	Y	Showers	Y	Rangers(s)	Y
30 Amp	Y	Reserve Sites	Y	Gate	
50 Amp	Y	Store	Y	Patrolled	Y
		Grill/Table	Y		

[10] Merritt Reservoir State Recreation Area
Hwy 97
Southwest of Valentine
N42 37.924 W100 52.011
State Rate: $7-$15
(402) 376-3320
http://outdoornebraska.ne.gov/parks/guides/
parksearch/showpark.asp?Area_No=115

Directions

26 miles. Go south on Hwy 97 from Valentine for 26 miles to the park on Hwy 97.

Points of Interest

Merritt Reservoir offers some of Nebraska's best fishing. Area attractions include the Valentine National Wildlife Refuge, Snake River Falls, the Valentine State Fish Hatchery, and Fort Niobrara Wildlife Refuge. In Valentine see historic cantilevered Bryan Bridge over the Niobrara River. It is one of the highest railroad bridges in the US.

RV Sites		Water		Laundry	
Number	48	None		Wi-Fi	
Shaded	Y	At Site		Fishing	Y
By Water		Spigots	Y	Hiking	
Paved	some	**Sewer**		Biking	Y
Pull Thru	Y	None		Swimming	
ADA	Y	At Site		Watch Wildlife	
Max RV Size	45	Dump Station	Y	Pets	Y
Electric		**Amenities**		**Security**	
None		Restrooms	Y	Host(s)	Y
20 Amp	Y	Showers	Y	Rangers(s)	Y
30 Amp	Y	Reserve Sites	Y	Gate	
50 Amp	Y	Store	Y	Patrolled	Y
		Grill/Table	Y		

[11] Willow Creek State Recreation Area
Hwy 20, South on Hwy 13
South of Plainview
N42 10.423 W97 33.765
State Rate: $12-$18
(402) 329-4053
http://outdoornebraska.ne.gov/parks/guides/
parksearch/showpark.asp?Area_No=256

Directions

24 miles. From Hwy 20 take Hwy 13 (just west of Plainview) south for 20 miles to 852 Rd. Turn west for 2 miles (on gravel), turn South (left) on 549 Avenue 0.5 miles to 851 Rd. Go 1 mile right, then north (right) 0.5 mile to enter park

Points of Interest

Just northwest is Ashfall Fossil Beds State Historical Park. Here you can watch ongoing excavations of prehistoric animals preserved under layers of volcanic ash deposited eons ago

RV Sites		Water		Laundry	Y
Number	55	None		Wi-Fi	
Shaded	Y	At Site		Fishing	Y
By Water	Y	Spigots	Y	Hiking	Y
Paved	Y	**Sewer**		Biking	Y
Pull Thru		None		Swimming	Y
ADA	Y	At Site		Watch Wildlife	Y
Max RV Size	45	Dump Station	Y	Pets	Y
Electric		**Amenities**		**Security**	
None		Restrooms	Y	Host(s)	Y
20 Amp	Y	Showers	Y	Rangers(s)	Y
30 Amp	Y	Reserve Sites	Y	Gate	
50 Amp	Y	Store		Patrolled	Y
		Grill/Table	Y		

[12] Ponca State Park
Hwy 20, North on Hwy 12
Northwest of Sioux City
N42 36.021 W96 42.895
State Rate: $12-$18
(402) 755-2284
http://www.outdoornebraska.ne.gov/parks/
guides/parksearch/showpark.asp?Area_No=143

Directions

10.8 miles. South of Ponca take Hwy 12, from Hwy 20, north for 7.8 miles to Ponca. Turn right on Spur 26E, follow it 3 miles north to the park.

Points of Interest

Ponca State Park features one of the state's most comprehensive outdoor/environmental education programs. With 20 miles of trails, the park provides hikers and mountain bikers many opportunities to explore the park's backcountry.

RV Sites		Water		Laundry	
Number	57	None		Wi-Fi	
Shaded	Y	At Site	Y	Fishing	Y
By Water	Y	Spigots	Y	Hiking	Y
Paved	Y	**Sewer**		Biking	Y
Pull Thru	Y	None		Swimming	Y
ADA	Y	At Site		Watch Wildlife	Y
Max RV Size	45	Dump Station	Y	Pets	Y
Electric		**Amenities**		**Security**	
None		Restrooms	Y	Host(s)	Y
20 Amp	Y	Showers	Y	Rangers(s)	Y
30 Amp	Y	Reserve Sites	Y	Gate	
50 Amp	Y	Store		Patrolled	Y
		Grill/Table	Y		

About Nevada's Public Campgrounds

The Nevada Division of State Parks is responsible for the 23 park system, 17 of which have RV camping facilities. The website is -

http://parks.nv.gov/

There is no online registration system. Fees for an RV site are variable and determined by adding the sum of - Entrance fee ($7-$12/vehicle) plus Camping fee (the numbers that are given in this book, varies from $14 - $20) plus Utilities fee ($10). Your Entrance Fee may count toward the camping site fee, so ask. Pets are welcome, but they must be kept on a leash of not more than six feet in length. They are not allowed in Visitor Centers.

[1] Valley of Fire State Park	**[6] Angel Creek Campground**
[2] Washoe Lake State Park	**[7] Pahranagat National Wildlife Refuge**
[3] Lahontan State Recreation Area	**[8] Cathedral Gorge State Park**
[4] Rye Patch State Recreation Area	**[9] Cave Lake State Park**
[5] South Fork State Recreation Area	

NOTES:

Nevada

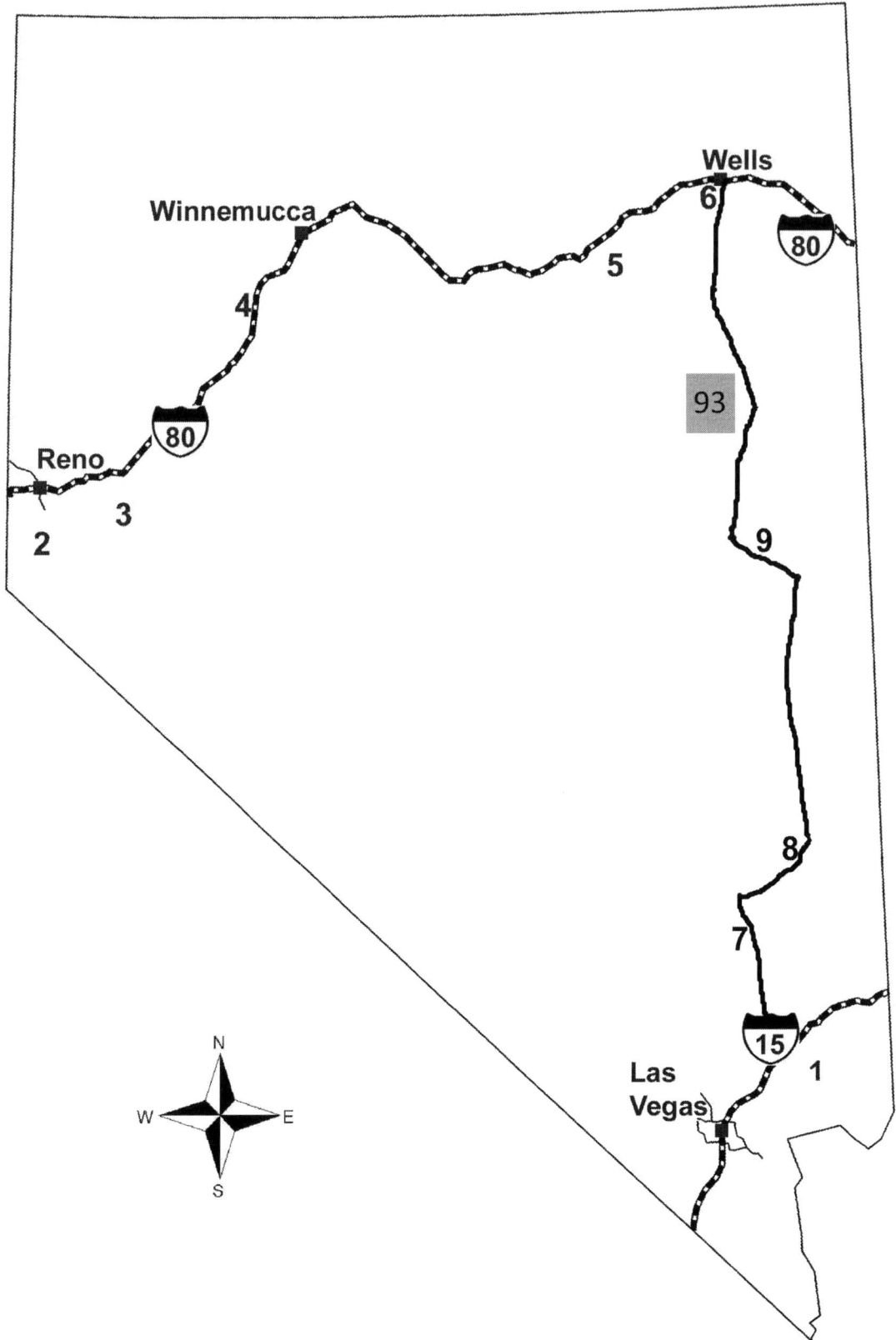

[1] Valley of Fire State Park
I-15, Exit 75
Northeast of Las Vegas
N36 25.814 W114 31.093
State Rate: $20-$30
(702) 397-2088
http://parks.nv.gov/parks/valley-of-fire-state-park/

Directions

19 miles. From Exit 75 turn southeast on Hwy 169 (Valley of Fire Highway) for 19 miles into the Park. Entry fee may count toward site fee.

Points of Interest

There are many beautiful sites within the Park. Lake Mead National Recreation Area borders the park. Lost City Museum in Overton offers fine displays of Indian artifacts and reconstruction of the original pit dwellings and pueblo found in the Moapa Valley.

RV Sites		Water		Laundry	
Number	72	None		Wi-Fi	
Shaded		At Site	Y	Fishing	
By Water		Spigots	Y	Hiking	Y
Paved		**Sewer**		Biking	Y
Pull Thru	Y	None		Swimming	
ADA	Y	At Site		Watch Wildlife	Y
Max RV Size	45	Dump Station	Y	Pets	Y
Electric		**Amenities**		**Security**	
None		Restrooms	Y	Host(s)	Y
20 Amp	Y	Showers	Y	Rangers(s)	Y
30 Amp	Y	Reserve Sites		Gate	
50 Amp	Y	Store	Y	Patrolled	Y
		Grill/Table	Y		

[2] Washoe Lake State Park
I-80, Exit 15
South of Reno
N39 14.489 W119 45.795
State Rate: $17
(775) 687-4319
http://parks.nv.gov/parks/washoe-lake-state-park/

Directions

24 miles. From Exit 15 turn south on Hwy 395 for 17 miles to the East Lake Blvd. Turn left, go south 7 miles to the Park entrance.

Points of Interest Also see [3]

A day trip to Virginia City is a step back in time. The 19th century mining boom turned Virginia City and its grubby prospectors into instant millionaires. They built mansions, imported furniture & fashions from Europe & the Orient. Find it as it was then. See *www.virginiacity-nv.org/*

RV Sites		Water		Laundry	
Number	49	None		Wi-Fi	
Shaded	ramada	At Site		Fishing	Y
By Water		Spigots	Y	Hiking	Y
Paved		**Sewer**		Biking	Y
Pull Thru	Y	None		Swimming	Y
ADA	Y	At Site		Watch Wildlife	Y
Max RV Size	45	Dump Station	Y	Pets	Y
Electric		**Amenities**		**Security**	
None	Y	Restrooms	Y	Host(s)	Y
20 Amp		Showers	Y	Rangers(s)	Y
30 Amp		Reserve Sites		Gate	
50 Amp		Store		Patrolled	Y
		Grill/Table	Y		

[3] Lahontan State Recreation Area
I-80, Exit 46
N39 22.668 W119 12.078
South of Fernley
State Rate: $15
(775) 577-2235
http://parks.nv.gov/lah.htm

Directions

20 miles. From Exit 46 turn south, go 18 miles on Hwy 95 (which turns south again in Fernley). Go east on Fir Ave for 2 miles into the Park. Drive to Silver Springs Beach #7.

Points of Interest Also see [2]

Virginia City was a boisterous town with gold in every hill. The spirits of past Comstock characters still inhabit the places they built, and 150 years later romance thrives in this wondrous place. Learn about Mark Twain and his stint as reporter for the Territorial Enterprise.

RV Sites		Water		Laundry	
Number	25+	None		Wi-Fi	
Shaded		At Site		Fishing	Y
By Water	Y	Spigots	Y	Hiking	Y
Paved	Y	**Sewer**		Biking	Y
Pull Thru		None		Swimming	Y
ADA	Y	At Site		Watch Wildlife	Y
Max RV Size	45	Dump Station	Y	Pets	Y
Electric		**Amenities**		**Security**	
None	Y	Restrooms	Y	Host(s)	Y
20 Amp		Showers	Y	Rangers(s)	Y
30 Amp		Reserve Sites		Gate	
50 Amp		Store		Patrolled	Y
		Grill/Table	Y		

[4] Rye Patch State Recreation Area
I-80, Exit 129
Southwest of Winnemucca
N40 28.130 W118 18.657
State Rate: $14
(775) 538-7321
http://parks.nv.gov/parks/rye-patch-state-recreation-area/

Directions

1 mile. From Exit 129 turn west on Hwy 401 for 1 mile into the Park.

Points of Interest

Winnemucca has much to offer, from 24-hour gaming opportunities, to a rich western history, to renowned Basque festivals and Basque dining. The annual festival in June hosts a variety of traditional Basque games including weight carrying, wood chopping, and Jota dancing.

RV Sites		Water		Laundry	
Number	46	None		Wi-Fi	
Shaded	Y	At Site		Fishing	Y
By Water	Y	Spigots	Y	Hiking	Y
Paved		Sewer		Biking	Y
Pull Thru		None		Swimming	Y
ADA	Y	At Site		Watch Wildlife	Y
Max RV Size	45	Dump Station	Y	Pets	Y
Electric		Amenities		Security	
None	Y	Restrooms	Y	Host(s)	Y
20 Amp		Showers	Y	Rangers(s)	Y
30 Amp		Reserve Sites		Gate	
50 Amp		Store	Y	Patrolled	Y
		Grill/Table	Y		

[5] South Fork State Recreation Area
I-80, Exit 301
South of Elko
N40 39.836 W115 44.464
State Rate: $14
(775) 744-4346
http://parks.nv.gov/parks/south-fork-state-recreation-area//

Directions

18 miles. From Exit 301 turn southeast 0.8 miles on Mountain City Hwy to Idaho St. Turn left for 1 mile to Hwy 227. Turn right for 7 miles to Hwy 228. Go south for 5.5 miles to Cty Rd 715 (South Fork). Go right 3.5 miles to the Park.

Points of Interest

Check out Elko . . . "Nevada with Altitude." You can take a gold mine tour. Visit the Northeastern Nevada Museum. Also see the Western Folklife Center.

RV Sites		Water		Laundry	
Number	25+	None		Wi-Fi	
Shaded		At Site		Fishing	Y
By Water	Y	Spigots	Y	Hiking	Y
Paved		Sewer		Biking	Y
Pull Thru		None		Swimming	Y
ADA	Y	At Site		Watch Wildlife	Y
Max RV Size	30	Dump Station	Y	Pets	Y
Electric		Amenities		Security	
None		Restrooms	Y	Host(s)	Y
20 Amp	few	Showers	Y	Rangers(s)	Y
30 Amp	few	Reserve Sites	some	Gate	
50 Amp		Store	Y	Patrolled	Y
		Grill/Table	Y		

[6] Angel Creek Campground
I-80, Exit 351
South of Wells
N41 01.725 W115 03.053
Humboldt NF Rate: $15-$30
America/Beautiful Rate: $8-$15
(775) 752-3357
http://www.recreation.gov/

Directions

9 miles. From Exit 351 go south and immediately turn right on Hwy 231 (Angel Lake Rd). Go 8 miles to Angel Creek. Turn left and go 1 mile to the campground.

Points of Interest

Visit Wells - cows, cowboys and casinos! Explore Metropolis, a ghost town, with a fascinating history. The grandest hotel between Reno & Salt Lake, a business district with concrete sidewalks, and street lights all sprang up in 1911.

RV Sites		Water		Laundry	
Number	18	None		Wi-Fi	
Shaded	Y	At Site		Fishing	Y
By Water	Y	Spigots	Y	Hiking	Y
Paved	Y	Sewer		Biking	Y
Pull Thru	few	None	Y	Swimming	
ADA	Y	At Site		Watch Wildlife	Y
Max RV Size	45	Dump Station		Pets	Y
Electric		Amenities		Security	
None	Y	Restrooms	Y	Host(s)	Y
20 Amp		Showers		Rangers(s)	Y
30 Amp		Reserve Sites		Gate	
50 Amp		Store		Patrolled	Y
		Grill/Table	Y		

[7] Pahranagat National Wildlife Refuge
Hwy 93
South of Alamo
N37 18.190 W115 07.524
Pahranagat NWR Rate: $1
(775) 725-3417
http://www.fws.gov/refuge/Pahranagat/visit/
visitor_activities.html

Directions

7.3 miles. Go 6.0 miles south of Alamo to the
south tip of Upper Pahranagat Lake. Turn right on
Badger Valley Rd then right again on Upper Lake
Access Rd. Go 1.3 mile north to the campground.

Points of Interest

The 3 mile Upper Lake Trail circles the lake &
provides an excellent opportunity to see waterfowl year around. Refuge naturalists & volunteers
offer a wide variety of free guided programs designed to showcase the amazing refuge wildlife.

RV Sites		Water		Laundry	
Number	14	None	Y	Wi-Fi	
Shaded	Y	At Site		Fishing	Y
By Water	Y	Spigots		Hiking	Y
Paved		**Sewer**		Biking	
Pull Thru	Y	None	Y	Swimming	
ADA		At Site		Watch Wildlife	Y
Max RV Size	45	Dump Station		Pets	Y
Electric		**Amenities**		**Security**	
None	Y	Restrooms	Y	Host(s)	
20 Amp		Showers		Rangers(s)	Y
30 Amp		Reserve Sites		Gate	
50 Amp		Store		Patrolled	Y
		Grill/Table	Y		

[8] Cathedral Gorge State Park
Hwy 93
Northwest of Panaca
N37 48.208 W114 24.415
State Rate: $17-$27
(775) 728-4460
http://parks.nv.gov/parks/cathedral-gorge/

Directions

1 mile. At Hwy 93/319 just west of Panaca go
1 mile north on Hwy 93 to the Park.

Points of Interest

Cathedral Gorge will delight photographers.
Erosion has carved unique and dramatic pat-
terns in the bentonite clay. There are numer-
ous trails to explore the formations and cathe-
dral-like spires - thus the name of the Park.
The walking trails provide great views of the
Park. You are within 25 miles of 4 other State
Parks, check out their special features.

RV Sites		Water		Laundry	
Number	22	None		Wi-Fi	
Shaded	ramada	At Site		Fishing	
By Water		Spigots	Y	Hiking	Y
Paved		**Sewer**		Biking	Y
Pull Thru	Y	None		Swimming	
ADA	Y	At Site		Watch Wildlife	Y
Max RV Size	40	Dump Station	Y	Pets	Y
Electric		**Amenities**		**Security**	
None		Restrooms	Y	Host(s)	Y
20 Amp	Y	Showers	Y	Rangers(s)	Y
30 Amp	Y	Reserve Sites		Gate	
50 Amp		Store		Patrolled	Y
		Grill/Table	Y		

[9] Cave Lake State Park
Hwy 93, east on Hwy 486
Southeast of Ely
N39 11.075 W114 42.946
State Rate: $17
(775) 296-1505
http://parks.nv.gov/parks/cave-lake-state-park/

Directions

13 miles. From Ely go 8 miles south on Hwy
93 to Hwy 486 (Success Summit Rd). Turn
east for 5 miles to the Park.

Points of Interest

The Park is a great camp for trout fishing.
Lehman Caves, in Great Basin National Park,
is a wonderful day trip. This beautiful marble
cave is ornately decorated with stalactites,
stalagmites, helictites, flowstone, popcorn,
and over 300 rare shield formations. Or go to
the Nevada Northern Railway Museum in Ely.

RV Sites		Water		Laundry	
Number	35	None		Wi-Fi	
Shaded	Y	At Site		Fishing	Y
By Water	Y	Spigots	Y	Hiking	Y
Paved		**Sewer**		Biking	Y
Pull Thru	Y	None		Swimming	Y
ADA	Y	At Site		Watch Wildlife	Y
Max RV Size	35	Dump Station	Y	Pets	Y
Electric		**Amenities**		**Security**	
None	Y	Restrooms	Y	Host(s)	Y
20 Amp		Showers	Y	Rangers(s)	Y
30 Amp		Reserve Sites		Gate	
50 Amp		Store		Patrolled	Y
		Grill/Table	Y		

About New Hampshire's Public Campgrounds

The New Hampshire Division of Parks and Recreation oversees the State Park system. Visit their website for detailed information at -

http://www.nhstateparks.org/

There are nineteen State campgrounds. Fees vary from $25 - $50, depending on location, amenities and utilities available. Reservations are taken for all state park campgrounds through -

http://newhampshirestateparks.reserveamerica.com/

or by calling 1-877-nhparks (1-877-647-2757). The maximum reservation window is 11 months in advance. There is a non-refundable reservation fee of $8.75. New Hampshire residents age 65 and older are offered a $5 discount per nightly fee.

Pets are permitted at Bear Brook, Coleman, Deer Mountain, Dry River, Green-field (designated area only), Lake Francis, Milan, Mollidgewock, Moose Brook, Pillsbury, Sunapee, and Umbagog campgrounds. Pets must be leashed and supervised at all times. No pets are permitted on the bathing beaches. Pets are not to be left unattended in any vehicle, camper, carrier or enclosure at any time.

The White Mountain National Forest also provides a number of campground op-portunities.

[1] Storrs Pond Recreation Area	**[6] Ellacoya State Park**
[2] Pawtuckaway State Park	**[7] White Lake State Park**
[3] Campton Campground	**[8] Umbagog Lake State Park**
[4] Cannon Mountain RV Park	**[9] Coleman State Park**
[5] Hampton Beach State Park	

NOTES:

New Hampshire

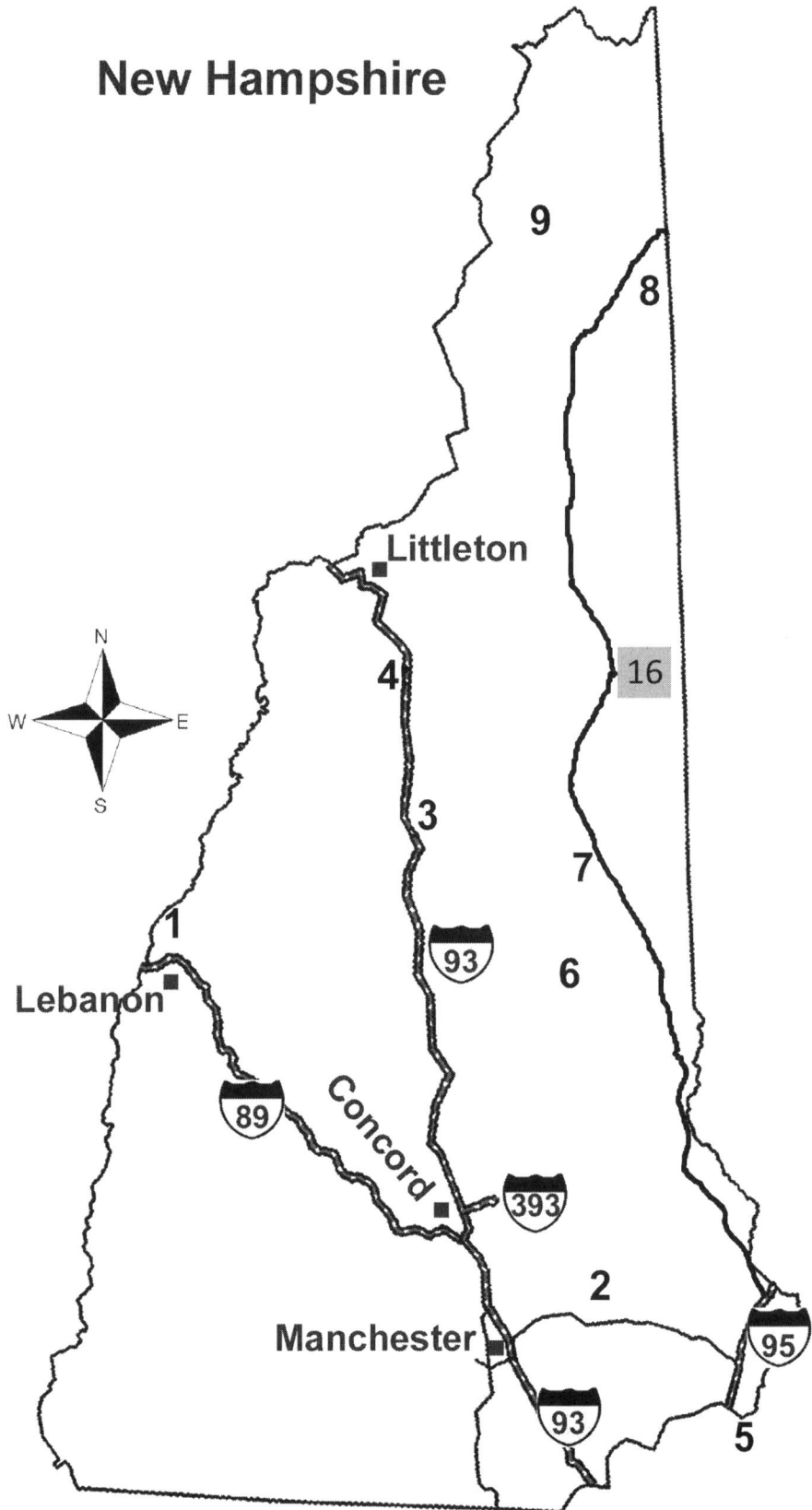

[1] Storrs Pond Recreation Area
I-89, Exit 18
North of Hanover
N43 43.206 W72 15.641
County Park Rate: $38
(603) 643-2134
http://www.storrspond.org/

Directions

7 miles. From Exit 18 go 5 miles north on Hwy 120 to Hwy 10 (Lyme Rd). Turn north (right), go 1 mile to Reservoir Rd. Turn right for 0.7 miles to the Campground.

Points of Interest

The region is a part of what is known as "The Upper Valley." At the region's center are Hanover & Lebanon on the New Hampshire side of the river. Hanover is home to Dartmouth College (one of the Ivies and ninth oldest college in the nation) and enjoys a lively, traditional downtown.

RV Sites		Water		Laundry	
Number	11	None		Wi-Fi	Y
Shaded	Y	At Site	Y	Fishing	
By Water	Y	Spigots	Y	Hiking	Y
Paved		Sewer		Biking	Y
Pull Thru		None		Swimming	Y
ADA	Y	At Site		Watch Wildlife	
Max RV Size	35	Dump Station	Y	Pets	Y
Electric		Amenities		Security	
None		Restrooms	Y	Host(s)	Y
20 Amp	Y	Showers	Y	Rangers(s)	
30 Amp	Y	Reserve Sites	Y	Gate	
50 Amp		Store		Patrolled	Y
		Grill/Table	Y		

[2] Pawtuckaway State Park
I-93, Exit 7
East of Manchester
N43 04.792 W71 10.373
State Rate: $25-$30
(603) 895-3031
http://www.nhstateparks.org/explore/state-parks/pawtuckaway-state-park.aspx

Directions

18 miles. From Exit 7 go 14 mi. east on Hwy 101 to exit 5. Go north 0.6 mi. on Hwy 107/156. Turn left then an immediate right on Hwy 156. Go 1.1 mi. to Harriman Rd. Turn left for 0.2 mi., then right on Mountain Rd. Go 2 mi. to State Park Rd.

Points of Interest

Manchester, nationally ranked among top cities by different Magazines, is home to the Currier Museum, Palace Theatre, New Hampshire Symphony, the Tupelo Music Hall.

RV Sites		Water		Laundry	
Number	55	None		Wi-Fi	
Shaded	Y	At Site		Fishing	Y
By Water	Y	Spigots	Y	Hiking	Y
Paved		Sewer		Biking	Y
Pull Thru		None	Y	Swimming	Y
ADA	Y	At Site		Watch Wildlife	Y
Max RV Size	35	Dump Station		Pets	N
Electric		Amenities		Security	
None	Y	Restrooms	Y	Host(s)	Y
20 Amp		Showers	Y	Rangers(s)	Y
30 Amp		Reserve Sites	Y	Gate	
50 Amp		Store	Y	Patrolled	Y
		Grill/Table	Y		

[3] Campton Campground
I-93, Exit 28
North of Plymouth
N43 52.260 W71 37.819
White Mountain NF Rate: $20
America/Beautiful Rate: $10
(603) 536-6100
http://www.recreation.gov/

Directions

2 miles. From Exit 28 go 2 miles northeast on Hwy 49 to the campground on your left.

Points of Interest

Plymouth, has a rich historical and cultural heritage. Nathaniel Hawthorne, Daniel Webster, Robert Frost, and the Pemigewasset Indians have all played their part in the history of Plymouth. Do the Heritage Trail to get a sense of the past and an appreciation of the town's history.

RV Sites		Water		Laundry	
Number	53	None		Wi-Fi	
Shaded	Y	At Site		Fishing	Y
By Water	Y	Spigots	Y	Hiking	Y
Paved		Sewer		Biking	Y
Pull Thru		None	Y	Swimming	
ADA	Y	At Site		Watch Wildlife	Y
Max RV Size	45	Dump Station		Pets	Y
Electric		Amenities		Security	
None	Y	Restrooms	Y	Host(s)	Y
20 Amp		Showers	Y	Rangers(s)	Y
30 Amp		Reserve Sites	Y	Gate	
50 Amp		Store		Patrolled	Y
		Grill/Table	Y		

[4] Cannon Mountain RV Park
I-93, Exit 34C
South East of Franconia
N44 10.739 W71 41.657
State Rate: $40
(603) 745-8391
http://www.nhstateparks.org/explore/state-parks/franconia-notch-state-park.aspx

Directions

Adjoins I-93. Accessible directly from Exit 34C

Points of Interest

There are a number of towns nearby, each with a unique flavor and traditional New England attractions. Try the Franconia Heritage Museum or Clark's Trading Post, home of Clark's Trained Bears and the White Mountain Central Railroad. Bretton Woods Lodge is also a special destination.

RV Sites		Water		Laundry	
Number	7	None		Wi-Fi	
Shaded		At Site	Y	Fishing	Y
By Water	Y	Spigots		Hiking	Y
Paved		Sewer		Biking	Y
Pull Thru		None		Swimming	
ADA	Y	At Site	Y	Watch Wildlife	Y
Max RV Size	40	Dump Station		Pets	N
Electric		Amenities		Security	
None		Restrooms	Y	Host(s)	Y
20 Amp	Y	Showers	Y	Rangers(s)	Y
30 Amp	Y	Reserve Sites	Y	Gate	
50 Amp	Y	Store	Y	Patrolled	
		Grill/Table	Y		

[5] Hampton Beach State Park
I-95, Exit 2, to 1A
South of Hampton Beach
N42 53.847 W70 48.840
State Rate: $50
(603) 926-3784
http://www.nhstateparks.org/explore/state-parks/hampton-beach-state-park.aspx

Directions

5 miles. At Exit 2 of I-95 go east toward the ocean on Hwy 101 for 4.3 miles to 1A. Turn south for 1.2 toward Hampton Harbor Inlet. Enter the Park area 0.1 mile north of the Hampton Harbor Inlet.

Points of Interest

Restaurants, entertainment, and other services are offered along 1A, a short walk. The park is close to whale watching, saltwater fishing charter boats, and sandy beaches.

RV Sites		Water		Laundry	
Number	28	None		Wi-Fi	
Shaded		At Site	Y	Fishing	Y
By Water	Y	Spigots	Y	Hiking	
Paved		Sewer		Biking	Y
Pull Thru	Y	None		Swimming	Y
ADA	Y	At Site	Y	Watch Wildlife	
Max RV Size	40	Dump Station	Y	Pets	N
Electric		Amenities		Security	
None		Restrooms	Y	Host(s)	Y
20 Amp	Y	Showers		Rangers(s)	Y
30 Amp	Y	Reserve Sites	Y	Gate	
50 Amp	Y	Store	Y	Patrolled	Y
		Grill/Table	Y		

[6] Ellacoya State Park
Hwy 16, at Hwy 11; I-93, Exit 20
In Gilford
N43 34.348 W71 21.285
State Rate: $47
(603) 293-7821
http://www.nhstateparks.org/explore/state-parks/ellacoya-state-park.aspx

Directions

27 miles. North of Rochester, from Hwy 16, take Hwy 11, northwest for 27 miles to the Park. Or from I-93, Exit 20, go northeast on Hwy 3 for 12.3 miles to Hwy 11. Turn east, go 4.5 miles to the Park.

Points of Interest

The scenery of the Lakes Region is the main attraction here. Other top attractions include cruising Lake Winnipesaukee aboard the Mt. Washington or touring historic Castle in the Clouds estate.

RV Sites		Water		Laundry	Y
Number	38	None		Wi-Fi	
Shaded	Y	At Site	Y	Fishing	Y
By Water	Y	Spigots	Y	Hiking	Y
Paved		Sewer		Biking	Y
Pull Thru	Y	None		Swimming	Y
ADA	Y	At Site	Y	Watch Wildlife	
Max RV Size	45	Dump Station		Pets	N
Electric		Amenities		Security	
None		Restrooms	Y	Host(s)	Y
20 Amp	Y	Showers	Y	Rangers(s)	Y
30 Amp	Y	Reserve Sites	Y	Gate	
50 Amp		Store		Patrolled	Y
		Grill/Table	Y		

[7] White Lake State Park
Hwy 16
North of West Ossipee
N43 50.191 W71 12.542
State Rate: $25-$30
(603) 323-7350
http://www.nhstateparks.org/explore/state-parks/white-lake-state-park.aspx

Directions

7 miles. From Center Ossipee go 7 miles north on Hwy 16 to the Park.

Points of Interest

Spend a day at the Castle in the Clouds, a 16 room mansion and 5,500 acre mountaintop estate in Moultonborough. Take in the museum, Art Gallery and relax at the Carriage House Cafe'. Drive up to Conway for a day of shopping at the outlet malls and local stores for antiques. Enjoy lunch at one of the many cafes.

RV Sites		Water		Laundry	
Number	200	None		Wi-Fi	
Shaded	Y	At Site		Fishing	Y
By Water	Y	Spigots	Y	Hiking	Y
Paved		Sewer		Biking	Y
Pull Thru		None		Swimming	Y
ADA	Y	At Site		Watch Wildlife	Y
Max RV Size	35	Dump Station	Y	Pets	N
Electric		Amenities		Security	
None	N	Restrooms	Y	Host(s)	Y
20 Amp		Showers	Y	Rangers(s)	Y
30 Amp		Reserve Sites	Y	Gate	
50 Amp		Store	Y	Patrolled	Y
		Grill/Table	Y		

[8] Umbagog Lake State Park
Hwy 16, East on Hwy 26
Southeast of Errol
N44 42.779 W71 04.362
State Rate: $35
(603) 482-7795
http://www.nhstateparks.org/explore/state-parks/umbagog-lake-state-park.aspx#legend

Directions

6 miles. East of Errol at Hwy 16 & 26, take Hwy 26 southeast for 6 miles to the Park.

Points of Interest

The primary delights of this park are the scenic beauty of the lake, the excellent beach and swimming, biking and hiking. Lake Umbagog has been ranked the #5 top kayak spot in New England! Those bringing a boat will have the best time.

RV Sites		Water		Laundry	
Number	27	None		Wi-Fi	
Shaded	Y	At Site	Y	Fishing	Y
By Water	Y	Spigots	Y	Hiking	Y
Paved		Sewer		Biking	Y
Pull Thru	Y	None		Swimming	Y
ADA	Y	At Site	Y	Watch Wildlife	Y
Max RV Size	40	Dump Station	Y	Pets	Y
Electric		Amenities		Security	
None		Restrooms	Y	Host(s)	Y
20 Amp	Y	Showers	Y	Rangers(s)	Y
30 Amp	Y	Reserve Sites	Y	Gate	
50 Amp	few	Store	Y	Patrolled	Y
		Grill/Table	Y		

[9] Coleman State Park
Hwy 16, West on Hwy 26
North of Kidderville
N44 55.957 W71 20.025
State Rate: $25
(603) 237-5382
http://www.nhstateparks.org/explore/state-parks/coleman-state-park.aspx

Directions

20 miles. From Hwy 16/26 in Errol go 15 miles northwest on Hwy 26 to Diamond Pond Rd at Kidderville. Turn north for 5 miles to the Park.

Points of Interest

The excellent trout fishing in Little Diamond Pond and nearby streams makes Coleman an excellent location for fishing enthusiasts. Kayakers will also enjoy use of the Pond. You can also rent a boat.

RV Sites		Water		Laundry	
Number	25	None		Wi-Fi	
Shaded	Y	At Site		Fishing	Y
By Water	Y	Spigots	Y	Hiking	Y
Paved		Sewer		Biking	Y
Pull Thru	Y	None		Swimming	
ADA	Y	At Site		Watch Wildlife	Y
Max RV Size	40	Dump Station	Y	Pets	Y
Electric		Amenities		Security	
None	N	Restrooms	Y	Host(s)	Y
20 Amp		Showers	Y	Rangers(s)	Y
30 Amp		Reserve Sites	Y	Gate	
50 Amp		Store		Patrolled	Y
		Grill/Table	Y		

About New Jersey's Public Campgrounds

With more than 430,000 acres, New Jersey's state parks and forests have much to offer and explore. Chances are there's one less than 30 miles away from your in-state location. The Parks are managed by the Division of Parks and Forestry. Their website is -

http://www.state.nj.us/dep/parksandforests/parks/index.html

Sixteen state campgrounds will accommodate RVs, however, there are no hook ups. Pets are welcome, as long as they are kept on a leash six (6) feet or less in length. Pets are prohibited from all buildings, swimming beaches and swimming waters, non-designated pet friendly campsites and overnight facilities.

ReserveAmerica is New Jersey's reservation system for all overnight facilities. Reservations are now available online or through the ReserveAmerica call center. Online reservations can be made 7 days per week/24 hours a day. To make a reservation through the call center, please contact ReserveAmerica at 1-855-607-3075. The online site is -

http://www.reserveamerica.com/campgroundDirectoryList. do?contractCode=nj

Reservations can be made up to 11 months in advance of the reservation date. Campsites are typically around $20 - $25. Park entrance fees are $5 per vehicle.

[1] Spruce Run Recreation Area	[4] Allaire State Park
[2] Stephens State Park	[5] Belleplain State Forest
[3] Turkey Swamp County Park	[6] Bass River State Forest

NOTES:

New Jersey

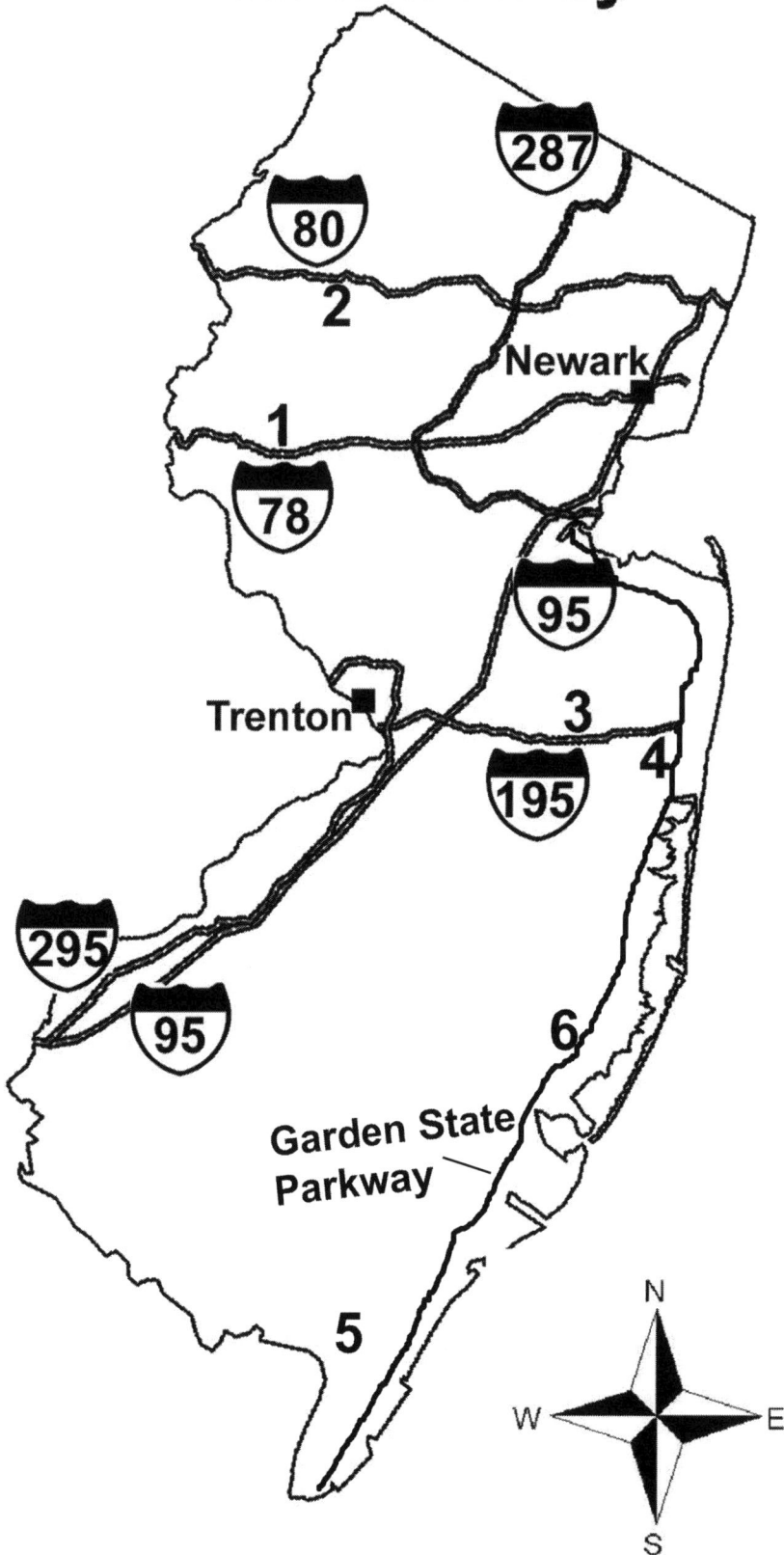

[1] Spruce Run Recreation Area
I-78, Exit 17
North of Annandale
N40 39.771 W74 56.324
State Rate: $20-$25
(908) 638-8572
http://www.state.nj.us/dep/parksandforests/parks/spruce.html#camp

Directions

5 miles. From Exit 17 go north for 3.2 miles on Hwy 31 to Van Syckels Corner Rd. Turn left, go 1.5 miles to the Park entrance on the left.

Points of Interest

Just north visit Oxford Furnace & Shippen Manor. The Furnace, built in 1741, was the third furnace in Colonial New Jersey and the first where iron ore was mined. On a hill overlooking the Furnace sits Shippen Manor, once the home of the ironmaster and now a Museum.

RV Sites		Water		Laundry	
Number	53	None		Wi-Fi	
Shaded	Y	At Site		Fishing	Y
By Water	Y	Spigots	Y	Hiking	Y
Paved	few	**Sewer**		Biking	Y
Pull Thru	Y	None		Swimming	Y
ADA	Y	At Site		Watch Wildlife	
Max RV Size	40+	Dump Station	Y	Pets	N
Electric		**Amenities**		**Security**	
None	Y	Restrooms	Y	Host(s)	Y
20 Amp		Showers	Y	Rangers(s)	Y
30 Amp		Reserve Sites	Y	Gate	
50 Amp		Store		Patrolled	Y
		Grill/Table	Y		

[2] Stephens State Park
I-80, Exit 25
North of Hackettstown
N40 52.300 W74 48.617
State Rate: $20-$25
(908) 852-3790
http://www.state.nj.us/dep/parksandforests/parks/stephens.html

Directions

8 miles. From Exit 25 bear right onto the off ramp to Continental and Kays Rd for 1.8 miles to Cty Rd 604 (Waterloo Rd.). Turn left and go 5.7 miles to the camp on your left.

Points of Interest

Explore Morris Canal & Waterloo Village. The Village is a 400-year old Lenape (Delaware) Indian village along the once prosperous Canal. The restored Village contains a working mill complex with grist & sawmills, a general store, blacksmith & more.

RV Sites		Water		Laundry	
Number	11	None		Wi-Fi	
Shaded	Y	At Site		Fishing	Y
By Water	Y	Spigots	Y	Hiking	Y
Paved		**Sewer**		Biking	Y
Pull Thru	Y	None	Y	Swimming	
ADA	Y	At Site		Watch Wildlife	Y
Max RV Size	40	Dump Station		Pets	N
Electric		**Amenities**		**Security**	
None	Y	Restrooms	Y	Host(s)	Y
20 Amp		Showers	Y	Rangers(s)	Y
30 Amp		Reserve Sites	Y	Gate	
50 Amp		Store		Patrolled	Y
		Grill/Table	Y		

[3] Turkey Swamp County Park
I-195, Exit 22
North of Vista Center
N40 11.825 W74 17.896
CP Rate: $30-$39
(732) 462-7286
http://www.monmouthcountyparks.com/Page.aspx?ID=2522

Directions

3.5 miles. From Exit 22 turn northeast for 2.4 miles on Jackson Mills Rd to Georgia Rd. Go left for 1 mile to the park entrance on your left.

Points of Interest

At historic Longstreet Farm, in Holmdel Park, costumed interpreters share with visitors life as it was in rural Monmouth County during the 1890's. Go to the Creative Arts Center in Thompson Park, with pottery & ceramics studios, and classrooms for painting, drawing, & other crafts.

RV Sites		Water		Laundry	Y
Number	64	None		Wi-Fi	
Shaded	Y	At Site	Y	Fishing	Y
By Water	Y	Spigots		Hiking	Y
Paved		**Sewer**		Biking	Y
Pull Thru	Y	None		Swimming	
ADA	Y	At Site		Watch Wildlife	Y
Max RV Size	40	Dump Station	Y	Pets	Y
Electric		**Amenities**		**Security**	
None		Restrooms	Y	Host(s)	Y
20 Amp	Y	Showers	Y	Rangers(s)	Y
30 Amp	Y	Reserve Sites	Y	Gate	
50 Amp		Store		Patrolled	Y
		Grill/Table	Y		

[4] Allaire State Park
I-195, Exit 31
North of Lakewood
N40 09.732 W74 07.877
State Rate: $20-$25
(732) 938-2371
http://www.state.nj.us/dep/parksandforests/
parks/allaire.html

Directions

1.5 miles. From Exit 31 turn north on Squankum Rd and immediately go right on Cty Rd 524 (Allaire Rd) for 1.3 miles to the Park on your right.

Points of Interest

The Park is best known for its historic 19th-century iron making town, Allaire Village, and its antique steam trains on the Pine Creek Railroad. The Village was known as the Howell Works in the early 19th century, when it was a thriving industrial community producing pig & cast iron.

RV Sites		Water		Laundry	
Number	45	None		Wi-Fi	
Shaded	Y	At Site		Fishing	Y
By Water	Y	Spigots	Y	Hiking	Y
Paved		**Sewer**		Biking	Y
Pull Thru	Y	None		Swimming	
ADA	Y	At Site		Watch Wildlife	Y
Max RV Size	40	Dump Station	Y	Pets	N
Electric		**Amenities**		**Security**	
None	Y	Restrooms	Y	Host(s)	Y
20 Amp		Showers	Y	Rangers(s)	Y
30 Amp		Reserve Sites	Y	Gate	
50 Amp		Store	Y	Patrolled	Y
		Grill/Table	Y		

[5] Belleplain State Forest
Garden State Parkway, Exit 13
South of Belleplain
N39 14.613 W74 50.963
State Rate: $20-$25
(609) 861-2404
http://www.state.nj.us/dep/parksandforests/
parks/belle.html

Directions

12.2 miles. At Exit 13 turn away from the ocean & make an immediate right on Hwy 9. Go 1.8 miles & turn left on Hwy 83. Bear right in 4 miles, merge with Delsea Dr. In 1.2 miles turn right on Tyler Rd (Woodbine) then left in 2.8 miles on Sumner (Kubiak). Go 1.8 miles to the Park.

Points of Interest

The CCC converted Meisle Cranberry Bog into Lake Nummy, a popular swimming & fishing area. You are an hour from Sea Island, Cape May & Atlantic City.

RV Sites		Water		Laundry	Y
Number	168	None		Wi-Fi	
Shaded	Y	At Site		Fishing	Y
By Water	Y	Spigots	Y	Hiking	Y
Paved		**Sewer**		Biking	Y
Pull Thru		None		Swimming	Y
ADA	Y	At Site		Watch Wildlife	Y
Max RV Size	40	Dump Station	Y	Pets	Y
Electric		**Amenities**		**Security**	
None	Y	Restrooms	Y	Host(s)	Y
20 Amp		Showers	Y	Rangers(s)	Y
30 Amp		Reserve Sites	Y	Gate	
50 Amp		Store	Y	Patrolled	Y
		Grill/Table	Y		

[6] Bass River State Forest
Garden State Parkway, Exits 50 & 52
Northwest of Tuckerton
N39 37.221 W74 25.383
State Rate: $20-$25
(609) 296-1114
http://www.state.nj.us/dep/parksandforests/
parks/bass.html

Directions

Southbound, Exit 52, 2.2 miles. Go 1.3 miles on Cty 654 to Stage Rd, turn right, go 0.9 miles to the Park. **Northbound, Exit 50,** 5.5 miles. Proceed 1.8 miles to Maple Ave, turn left. Go 2.4 miles to Stage Rd, turn right, go 1.3 miles to the Park.

Points of Interest

Visit Tuckerton Seaport, a working maritime village. This one-of-a-kind attraction, in the heart of historic Tuckerton NJ, brings the Jersey Shore's maritime traditions of the past and present to life

RV Sites		Water		Laundry	Y
Number	176	None		Wi-Fi	
Shaded	Y	At Site		Fishing	Y
By Water	Y	Spigots	Y	Hiking	Y
Paved		**Sewer**		Biking	Y
Pull Thru		None		Swimming	Y
ADA	Y	At Site		Watch Wildlife	Y
Max RV Size	40	Dump Station	Y	Pets	Y
Electric		**Amenities**		**Security**	
None	Y	Restrooms	Y	Host(s)	Y
20 Amp		Showers	Y	Rangers(s)	Y
30 Amp		Reserve Sites	Y	Gate	
50 Amp		Store	Y	Patrolled	Y
		Grill/Table	Y		

About New Mexico's Public Campgrounds

New Mexico has 35 diverse State Parks to explore, including cool lakes, mountain forests, canyons, desert beauty, and fascinating historical sites, including dinosaur tracks! Information from the New Mexico State Parks Division can be found at -

http://www.emnrd.state.nm.us/

Facilities are available on a first come, first served basis with the exception of parks where the division has established a reservation program and a visitor has reserved the facility. Pet owners must restrain pets on leashes that are not more than 10 feet in length.

Primitive campsites offer no special facilities except a cleared area for camping. Sites may include trash cans, chemical toilets or parking. Developed sites offer additional facilities such as electric and sewage hookups.

Camp sites fees are as follows -

Primitive site -	**$ 8**
Developed site -	**$10**
Developed site with electricity -	**$14**
Developed site with sewage -	**$14**
Developed site with electric/sewage -	**$18**
Electric hookup with annual permit -	**$ 4**
Sewage hookup with annual permit -	**$ 4**
Electric/sewage with annual permit -	**$ 8**
Water hookup (where available) -	**No charge**
Per vehicle entrance fee -	**$ 5**

New Mexico campsites can be reserved from 1 day to 6 months in advance at -

http://newmexicostateparks.reserveamerica.com/

You can also call (877) 664-7787 to make a reservation.

[1] Rockhound State Park	[9] McGaffey Campground
[2] Leasburg Dam State Park	[10] Bluewater Lake State Park
[3] Caballo Lake State Park	[11] Santa Rosa Lake State Park
[4] Elephant Butte Lake State Park	[12] Ute Lake State Park
[5] Cochiti Lake Campground	[13] Brantley Lake State Park
[6] Field Tract Campground	[14] Bottomless Lakes State Park
[7] Storrie Lake State Park	[15] Navajo Lake State Park
[8] Sugarite Canyon State Park	

New Mexico

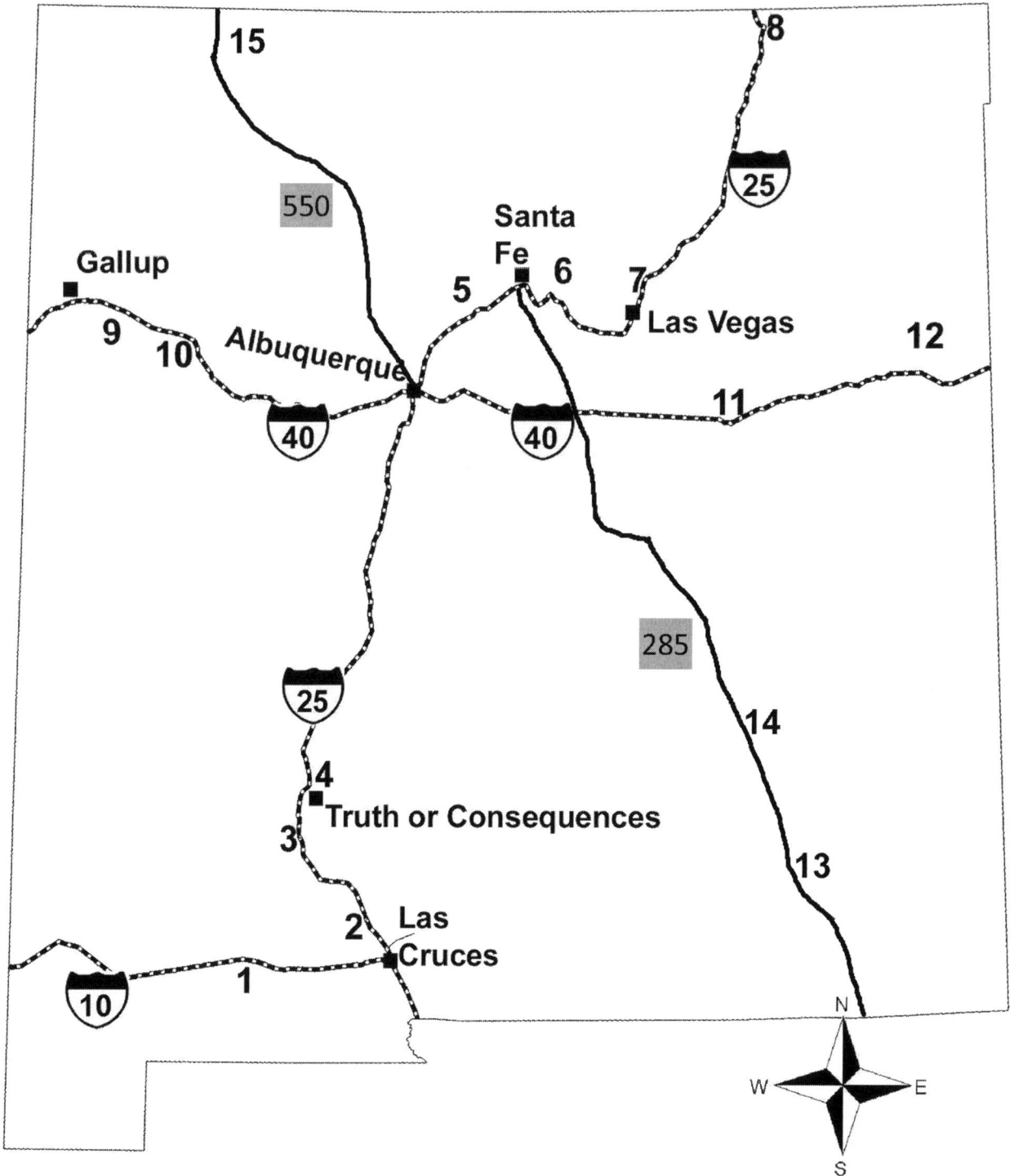

15

8

550

25

Santa
Fe

5   6   7

Gallup

Las Vegas

12

9   10

Albuquerque

11

40   **40**

285

14

25

4

Truth or Consequences

3

13

2   Las
Cruces

10   1

N

W   E

S

[1] Rockhound State Park
I-10, Exit 82
Southeast of Deming
N32 11.134 W107 36.786
State Rate: See Introduction
(575) 546-6182
http://www.emnrd.state.nm.us/SPD/rock-houndstatepark.html

Directions

14 miles. From Exit 82 turn south on Hwy 180, which becomes Hwy 11, for 5.3 miles to Hwy 141. Turn east for 8.5 miles to the park.

Points of Interest

The Park trails are of varying degrees of difficulty, with breathtaking views. Sunsets can be spellbinding from the SW facing camp, especially from the high elevation sites. You are allowed to take up to 15 lbs of rock for your collection (find jasper, quartz, agate, opal, thunder eggs).

RV Sites		Water		Laundry	
Number	29	None		Wi-Fi	
Shaded	ramada	At Site	Y	Fishing	
By Water		Spigots		Hiking	Y
Paved		Sewer		Biking	Y
Pull Thru	Y	None		Swimming	
ADA	Y	At Site		Watch Wildlife	Y
Max RV Size	45	Dump Station	Y	Pets	Y
Electric		Amenities		Security	
None		Restrooms	Y	Host(s)	Y
20 Amp	Y	Showers	Y	Rangers(s)	Y
30 Amp	Y	Reserve Sites	Y	Gate	
50 Amp		Store	Y	Patrolled	Y
		Grill/Table	Y		

[2] Leasburg Dam State Park
I-10, Exit 144; or I-25, Exit 19
North of Las Cruces
N32 29.330 W106 54.888
State Rate: See Introduction
(575) 524-4068
http://www.emnrd.state.nm.us/SPD/leasburg-damstatepark.html

Directions

20 miles. From Exit 144 turn north on I-25 for 19 miles to Exit 19. Turn southwest for 0.5 miles on Hwy 157 to the Park entrance on your right.

Points of Interest

Las Cruces, located between the Organ Mountains and the meandering Rio Grande River, blends a unique variety of attractions, culture, and historical sites such as Old Mesilla. Enjoy excellent weather, with 350 days of sunshine per year, and world-class Mexican food!

RV Sites		Water		Laundry	
Number	31	None		Wi-Fi	Y
Shaded	ramada	At Site	Y	Fishing	Y
By Water	Y	Spigots		Hiking	Y
Paved	Y	Sewer		Biking	Y
Pull Thru	Y	None		Swimming	Y
ADA	Y	At Site		Watch Wildlife	Y
Max RV Size	40	Dump Station	Y	Pets	Y
Electric		Amenities		Security	
None		Restrooms	Y	Host(s)	Y
20 Amp	Y	Showers	Y	Rangers(s)	Y
30 Amp	Y	Reserve Sites	Y	Gate	Y
50 Amp		Store	Y	Patrolled	Y
		Grill/Table	Y		

[3] Caballo Lake State Park
I-25, Exit 59
South of Caballo
N32 54.429 W107 18.702
State Rate: See Introduction
(575) 743-3942
http://www.emnrd.state.nm.us/SPD/caballo-lakestatepark.html

Directions

1 mile. From Exit 59 turn north on Hwy 187 for 1 mile to the Park entrance on your right.

Points of Interest

Try a visit to Silver City. With two dozen art galleries, studios, antique stores and a tile workshop, Silver City will meet your artistic needs. Hike or bike up to Boston Hills, a reclaimed historic mining area overlooking town; or see the Gila Cliff Dwellings.

RV Sites		Water		Laundry	
Number	135	None		Wi-Fi	
Shaded	ramada	At Site	Y	Fishing	Y
By Water	Y	Spigots		Hiking	Y
Paved		Sewer		Biking	Y
Pull Thru	Y	None		Swimming	Y
ADA	Y	At Site	Y	Watch Wildlife	Y
Max RV Size	45	Dump Station	Y	Pets	Y
Electric		Amenities		Security	
None		Restrooms	Y	Host(s)	Y
20 Amp	Y	Showers	Y	Rangers(s)	Y
30 Amp	Y	Reserve Sites	Y	Gate	
50 Amp		Store	Y	Patrolled	Y
		Grill/Table	Y		

[4] Elephant Butte Lake State Park
I-25, Exit 83
North of Truth or Consequences
N33 10.846 W107 12.525
State Rate: See Introduction
(575) 744-5923
http://www.emnrd.state.nm.us/SPD/elephantbuttelakestatepark.html

Directions

4 miles. From Exit 83 turn south to Hwy 195 on the east side of the Interstate. Follow Hwy 195 for 4 miles to the park on your left.

Points of Interest

On the banks of the Rio Grande, Truth or Consequences has long been a preferred vacation site. You can bath in soothing hot springs. Then take in the cultural life, ranging from flying fingers at the New Mexico Old Time Fiddlers Contest to the solemnity of The Geronimo Springs Museum.

RV Sites		Water		Laundry	
Number	173	None		Wi-Fi	Y
Shaded	ramada	At Site	Y	Fishing	Y
By Water	Y	Spigots	Y	Hiking	Y
Paved		Sewer		Biking	Y
Pull Thru	Y	None		Swimming	
ADA	Y	At Site		Watch Wildlife	Y
Max RV Size	45	Dump Station	Y	Pets	Y
Electric		Amenities		Security	
None		Restrooms	Y	Host(s)	Y
20 Amp	Y	Showers	Y	Rangers(s)	Y
30 Amp	Y	Reserve Sites	Y	Gate	
50 Amp	Y	Store	Y	Patrolled	Y
		Grill/Table	Y		

[5] Cochiti Lake Campground
I-25, Exit 259
West of Santa Fe
N35 38.542 W106 19.980
COE Rate: $8-$14
America/Beautiful Rate: $4-$7
(505) 465-0307
 www.recreation.gov/

Directions

13 miles. From Exit 259 go north for 13 miles, through Pena Blanca, on Hwy 22 (Cochiti Hwy) to the campground.

Points of Interest

The Park has many opportunities for both wildlife viewing and recreation. Santa Fe, one of the top travel destinations in the US, is within a hours drive. You can see details about this fascinating city at - *http://www.santafe.org/*

RV Sites		Water		Laundry	
Number	75	None		Wi-Fi	
Shaded	ramada	At Site	Y	Fishing	
By Water		Spigots	Y	Hiking	Y
Paved	Y	Sewer		Biking	Y
Pull Thru	Y	None		Swimming	Y
ADA	Y	At Site	Y	Watch Wildlife	Y
Max RV Size	45	Dump Station	Y	Pets	Y
Electric		Amenities		Security	
None		Restrooms	Y	Host(s)	Y
20 Amp	Y	Showers	Y	Rangers(s)	Y
30 Amp	Y	Reserve Sites	Y	Gate	
50 Amp		Store		Patrolled	
		Grill/Table	Y		

[6] Field Tract Campground
I-25, Exit 307
North of Pecos
N35 41.258 W105 41.672
Santa Fe NF Rate: $8
America/Beautiful Rate: $4
(505) 438-7840
http://www.fs.fed.us/r3/sfe/recreation/districts/pecos/index.html#camping

Directions

15 miles. From Exit 307 go north for 15 miles, through Pecos, on Hwy 63 to the campground.

Points of Interest

Visit Pecos, located between Santa Fe and Las Vegas, New Mexico, at the site of a mountain pass used by travelers for centuries. Pecos is a place to hike, fish, and horseback ride. Relax, wander main street, shop, and enjoy a meal at one of the family owned restaurants.

RV Sites		Water		Laundry	
Number	15	None		Wi-Fi	
Shaded	Y	At Site		Fishing	
By Water		Spigots	Y	Hiking	Y
Paved	Y	Sewer		Biking	Y
Pull Thru	Y	None		Swimming	
ADA	Y	At Site		Watch Wildlife	Y
Max RV Size	45	Dump Station	Y	Pets	Y
Electric		Amenities		Security	
None	Y	Restrooms	Y	Host(s)	Y
20 Amp		Showers	Y	Rangers(s)	Y
30 Amp		Reserve Sites	Y	Gate	
50 Amp		Store		Patrolled	Y
		Grill/Table	Y		

[7] Storrie Lake State Park
I-25, Exit 343
North of Las Vegas, NM
N35 39.463 W105 13.904
State Rate: See Introduction
(505) 425-7278
http://www.emnrd.state.nm.us/SPD/storri-elakestatepark.html

Directions

5 miles. From Exit 343 turn north on Hwy 518 and go 5 miles to the park on your left.

Points of Interest

With the arrival of the Santa Fe Railway in 1879, the Las Vegas area became a hangout for some historic Old West characters, including Doc Holliday, Billy the Kid & Wyatt Earp. Enjoy the many culturally rich opportunities Las Vegas has to offer, from summer Fiestas to art galleries.

RV Sites		Water			Laundry	
Number	45	None			Wi-Fi	
Shaded	ramada	At Site	Y		Fishing	Y
By Water	Y	Spigots			Hiking	Y
Paved		**Sewer**			Biking	Y
Pull Thru	Y	None			Swimming	
ADA	Y	At Site			Watch Wildlife	Y
Max RV Size	40	Dump Station	Y		Pets	Y
Electric		**Amenities**			**Security**	
None		Restrooms	Y		Host(s)	Y
20 Amp	Y	Showers	Y		Rangers(s)	Y
30 Amp	Y	Reserve Sites	Y		Gate	
50 Amp		Store			Patrolled	Y
		Grill/Table	Y			

[8] Sugarite Canyon State Park
I-25, Exit 452
Northeast of Raton
N36 56.306 W104 22.732
State Rate: See Introduction
(575) 445-5607
http://www.emnrd.state.nm.us/SPD/sugarite-canyonstatepark.html

Directions

6 miles. From Exit 452 follow Hwy 72 east for 3.7 miles. Turn north on Hwy 526 for 2 miles to the Visitor Center.

Points of Interest

The Park's Coal Camp Interpretive Trail winds through the ruins of the Sugarite coal camp. Coal mining in the area provided an important economic boost to the region and state. Other area geologic features include the iridium layer, Raton Basin and Capulin National Volcano.

RV Sites		Water			Laundry	
Number	40	None			Wi-Fi	
Shaded	ramada	At Site	Y		Fishing	Y
By Water	Y	Spigots			Hiking	Y
Paved		**Sewer**			Biking	Y
Pull Thru	Y	None			Swimming	Y
ADA	Y	At Site	Y		Watch Wildlife	Y
Max RV Size	40	Dump Station	Y		Pets	Y
Electric		**Amenities**			**Security**	
None		Restrooms	Y		Host(s)	Y
20 Amp	Y	Showers	Y		Rangers(s)	Y
30 Amp	Y	Reserve Sites	Y		Gate	
50 Amp		Store	Y		Patrolled	Y
		Grill/Table	Y			

[9] McGaffey Campground
I-40, Exit 33
Southeast of Gallup
N35 22.232 W108 31.395
Cibola NF Rate: $10-$15
America/Beautiful Rate: $5-$8
(505) 346-3900
http://www.forestcamping.com/dow/southwst/cibcmp.htm#quaking%20aspen

Directions

10.5 miles. From Exit 33 go south on Hwy 400 for 10 miles to the campground sign. Turn right on to a gravel road, go 0.4 miles to campground entrance.

Points of Interest

Go to El Morro National Monument, located on an ancient east-west trail. Close by you'll find the Ice Cave & Bandera Volcano, situated on the Continental Divide, where volcanic craters & lava tubes compare with the lunar landscape.

RV Sites		Water			Laundry	
Number	21	None			Wi-Fi	
Shaded	Y	At Site			Fishing	
By Water		Spigots	Y		Hiking	Y
Paved		**Sewer**			Biking	Y
Pull Thru	Y	None	Y		Swimming	
ADA	Y	At Site			Watch Wildlife	Y
Max RV Size	40+	Dump Station			Pets	Y
Electric		**Amenities**			**Security**	
None		Restrooms	Y		Host(s)	Y
20 Amp	Y	Showers	Y		Rangers(s)	Y
30 Amp	Y	Reserve Sites	Y		Gate	
50 Amp		Store			Patrolled	Y
		Grill/Table	Y			

[10] Bluewater Lake State Park
I-40, Exit 63
Southeast of Thoreau
N35 18.094 W108 06.447
State Rate: See Introduction
(505) 876-2391
http://www.emnrd.state.nm.us/SPD/bluewaterlakestatepark.html

Directions

6 miles. From Exit 63 turn south for 6 miles on Hwy 412. This road will dead end at the Park

Points of Interest

The area is very interesting with many photography opportunities. Things to see include Mt. Taylor, the Zuni Mountains and Zuni Pueblo, El Malpais National Monument, and Indian ruins. Be sure to visit the Northwest New Mexico Visitor Center in Grants.

RV Sites		Water		Laundry	
Number	149	None		Wi-Fi	
Shaded	ramada	At Site		Fishing	Y
By Water	Y	Spigots	Y	Hiking	Y
Paved		**Sewer**		Biking	Y
Pull Thru	Y	None		Swimming	
ADA	Y	At Site		Watch Wildlife	Y
Max RV Size	45	Dump Station	Y	Pets	Y
Electric		**Amenities**		**Security**	
None		Restrooms	Y	Host(s)	Y
20 Amp	Y	Showers	Y	Rangers(s)	Y
30 Amp	Y	Reserve Sites	Y	Gate	Y
50 Amp		Store		Patrolled	Y
		Grill/Table	Y		

---

[11] Santa Rosa Lake State Park
I-40, Exit 275
North of Santa Rosa
N35 01.810 W104 40.067
State Rate: See Introduction
(575) 472-3110
http://www.emnrd.state.nm.us/PRD/santa-rosa.htm

Directions

10 miles. From Exit 275 turn west on Hwy 54/84 for 1 mile to 2nd. St (Hwy 91). Turn right and follow Hwy 91 for 9 miles to the Park.

Points of Interest

Near Santa Rosa visit Puerto de Luna (PDL), an ancient adobe village in a beautiful landscape. PDL was once the most thriving village in the area. Tour Nuestro Señora del Refugio Church. Try PDL's famous "PDL Chile" a unique strain of chile . . . look for local restaurant specials.

RV Sites		Water		Laundry	
Number	76	None		Wi-Fi	
Shaded	ramada	At Site	Y	Fishing	Y
By Water	Y	Spigots	Y	Hiking	Y
Paved		**Sewer**		Biking	Y
Pull Thru	Y	None		Swimming	Y
ADA	Y	At Site	Y	Watch Wildlife	Y
Max RV Size	40	Dump Station	Y	Pets	Y
Electric		**Amenities**		**Security**	
None		Restrooms	Y	Host(s)	Y
20 Amp	Y	Showers	Y	Rangers(s)	Y
30 Amp	Y	Reserve Sites	Y	Gate	
50 Amp		Store	Y	Patrolled	
		Grill/Table	Y		

[12] Ute Lake State Park
I-40, Exit 356
West of Logan
N35 21.356 W103 27.178
State Rate: See Introduction
(575) 487-2284
http://www.emnrd.state.nm.us/SPD/utelakestaetpark.html

Directions

24 miles. From Exit 356 go north for 19.5 miles on Hwy 469 to Hwy 54. Turn north for 2 miles into Logan. Turn west at Martinez St (Hwy 540). Follow Hwy 540 for 2.5 miles to the Park.

Points of Interest

Tucumcari, Heart of the Mother Road & City of Murals on historic Route 66. Visit their world-class Dinosaur & Historical Museums. National, State and Historic Scenic Byways make for great photo opportunities, as do the beautiful vistas.

RV Sites		Water		Laundry	
Number	142	None		Wi-Fi	
Shaded	ramada	At Site	Y	Fishing	Y
By Water	Y	Spigots	Y	Hiking	Y
Paved		**Sewer**		Biking	Y
Pull Thru	Y	None		Swimming	Y
ADA	Y	At Site		Watch Wildlife	Y
Max RV Size	45	Dump Station	Y	Pets	Y
Electric		**Amenities**		**Security**	
None		Restrooms	Y	Host(s)	Y
20 Amp	Y	Showers	Y	Rangers(s)	Y
30 Amp	Y	Reserve Sites	Y	Gate	
50 Amp	Y	Store	Y	Patrolled	Y
		Grill/Table	Y		

[13] Brantley Lake State Park
Hwy 285, East on Cty Rd 30
North of Carlsbad
N32 34.020 W104 21.012
State Rate: See Introduction
(575) 457-2384
http://www.emnrd.state.nm.us/SPD/brantley-lakestatepark.html

Directions

4.2 miles. From Hwy 285 go east on Cty Rd 30 (Capitan Reef Rd) for 4.2 miles then turn left into the park. Campground is 2 miles past the Visitor Center.

Points of Interest

Carlsbad Caverns is about an hour away. Reservations are recommended for all guided cave tours. Self-Guided Tour Tickets are sold at the Visitor Center daily. There are no RV Campgrounds in Carlsbad Caverns National Park.

RV Sites		Water		Laundry	
Number	51	None		Wi-Fi	
Shaded	ramada	At Site	Y	Fishing	Y
By Water	Y	Spigots	Y	Hiking	Y
Paved	Y	**Sewer**		Biking	Y
Pull Thru	Y	None		Swimming	
ADA	Y	At Site	few	Watch Wildlife	
Max RV Size	45	Dump Station	Y	Pets	Y
Electric		**Amenities**		**Security**	
None		Restrooms	Y	Host(s)	Y
20 Amp	Y	Showers	Y	Rangers(s)	Y
30 Amp	Y	Reserve Sites	Y	Gate	
50 Amp	Y	Store		Patrolled	Y
		Grill/Table	Y		

[14] Bottomless Lakes State Park
Hwy 285, East on Hwy 380
Southeast of Roswell
N33 21.313 W104 20.302
State Rate: See Introduction
(575) 624-6058
http://www.emnrd.state.nm.us/SPD/bottomlesslakesstatepark.html

Directions

13.5 miles. Go east from Hwy 285/380 in Roswell for 10.3 miles to Hwy 409. Turn right for 3.2 miles to the Park.

Points of Interest

The unique park lakes are sinkholes, 17 to 90 feet deep. Roswell is known not only for aliens, but for its hospitality in welcoming visitors! Conrad Hilton, Roger Staubach, & Sam Donaldson went to school here. Will Rogers said that Roswell was the prettiest little town west of the Pecos.

RV Sites		Water		Laundry	
Number	37	None		Wi-Fi	Y
Shaded	ramada	At Site	Y	Fishing	Y
By Water	Y	Spigots	Y	Hiking	Y
Paved		**Sewer**		Biking	Y
Pull Thru	Y	None		Swimming	Y
ADA	Y	At Site	Y	Watch Wildlife	
Max RV Size	40	Dump Station	Y	Pets	Y
Electric		**Amenities**		**Security**	
None		Restrooms	Y	Host(s)	Y
20 Amp	Y	Showers	Y	Rangers(s)	Y
30 Amp	Y	Reserve Sites	Y	Gate	
50 Amp	Y	Store		Patrolled	Y
		Grill/Table	Y		

[15] Navajo Lake State Park
Hwy 550, East on Hwy 64
Northeast of Bloomfield
N36 49.116 W107 39.191
State Rate: See Introduction
(505) 632-2278
http://www.emnrd.state.nm.us/SPD/navajo-lakestatepark.html

Directions

23 miles. There are 7 campgrounds. Entering via Hwy 511 will give you the widest choice of locations. From Bloomfield Hwy 550/64 go east on Hwy 64 for 11.6 miles to Hwy 511. Turn north for 10.5 miles to the Park.

Points of Interest

Navajo Lake is the 2nd largest lake in the state, with multiple campgrounds, 2 marinas, and 2 boat docks. The San Juan River is a world-class fly fishing destination.

RV Sites		Water		Laundry	
Number	244	None		Wi-Fi	Y
Shaded	Y	At Site	Y	Fishing	Y
By Water	Y	Spigots	Y	Hiking	Y
Paved	Y	**Sewer**		Biking	Y
Pull Thru	Y	None		Swimming	Y
ADA	Y	At Site	Y	Watch Wildlife	Y
Max RV Size	45	Dump Station	Y	Pets	Y
Electric		**Amenities**		**Security**	
None		Restrooms	Y	Host(s)	Y
20 Amp	Y	Showers	Y	Rangers(s)	Y
30 Amp	Y	Reserve Sites	Y	Gate	
50 Amp	Y	Store	Y	Patrolled	Y
		Grill/Table	Y		

About New York's Public Campgrounds

The New York State Office of Parks, Recreation and Historic Preservation oversees the 178 State Parks, 68 of which have campgrounds. You will find their website at -

http://nysparks.state.ny.us/parks/

The Department of Environmental Conservation (DEC) operates 52 campgrounds located in the Adirondack and Catskill Parks. State campgrounds in this area do not offer utility hookups. The use of electric generators is allowed. You will find their website at -

http://www.dec.ny.gov/outdoor/camping.html

Pets must be kept on a leash at all times and the leash can be no longer than 6 ft. Don't leave pets unattended and always pick up after them. A Rabies certificate is required. A new regulation is now in effect that prohibits the import of firewood into New York unless it has been kiln-dried.

Reservations for both departments can be made from 1 day to 9 months in advance by calling

(800) 456-CAMP or online at -

newyorkstateparks.reserveamerica.com

The fee structure is -

Basic Site Fee -	**$15**
AMENITY ADD-ONS	
Weekend/Holiday (Fri/Sat/Sun) -	**$ 4**
Electric (15/20/30 amps) -	**$ 6**
Electric (50 amps) -	**$ 8**
Prime -	**$ 4**
Prime (Waterfront) -	**$ 6**
Prime (Oceanfront) -	**$12**
Full Hookup (water/electric/prime) -	**$12**
Reservation Fee -	**$ 9**
Out-of-State Visitor	**$ 5**

NOTES:

[1] Greenwood Park

[2] Fillmore Glen State Park

[3] Green Lakes State Park

[4] Southwick Beach State Park

[5] Grass Point State Park

[6] Wellesley Island State Park

[7] Allegany State Park - Quaker Area

[8] Robert H. Treman State Park

[9] Newtown Battlefield State Park

[10] Hickories County Park

[11] Harriman State Park (Beaver Pond)

[12] Mills Norrie State Park
(Margaret Lewis Norrie)

[13] Thacher State Park

[14] Moreau Lake State Park

[15] Cumberland Bay State Park

[16] Chenango Valley State Park

[17] Gilbert Lake State Park

[18] Lake Erie State Park

[19] Darien Lakes State Park

[20] Cayuga Lake State Park

[21] Stony Brook State Park\

[22] Limekiln Lake

[23] Lake Eaton

[24] Meadowbrook

NOTES:

New York

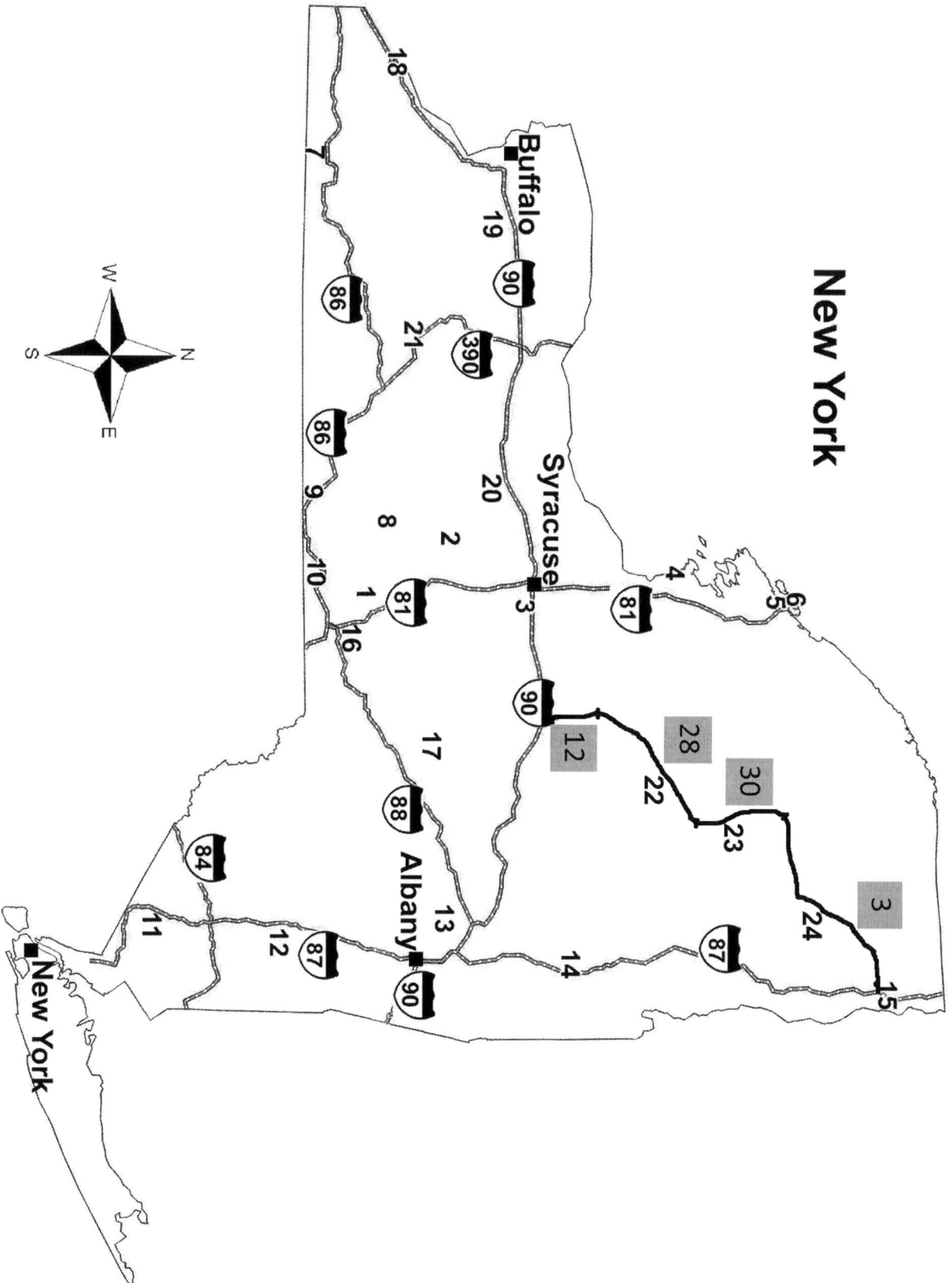

[1] Greenwood Park
I-81, Exit 8
West of Whitney Point
N42 17.280 W76 05.177
County Rate: $18-$22
(607) 778-2193
http://www.gobroomecounty.com/parks/greenwood

Directions

10 miles. From Exit 8; if northbound, turn northeast on Hwy 26 for 0.6 miles too Hwy 11/79, then turn left; if southbound, exit directly onto Hwy 11/79. Follow Hwy 79 northwest for 5 miles to Cty Rd 21 (Caldwell Hill Rd). Turn south for 4 miles, then turn right onto Greenwood Rd for 1 mile to the Park.

Points of Interest

In Binghamton visit farmers' markets, stroll through art galleries or antique shops. Take a spin on a restored, antique carousel.

RV Sites		Water		Laundry	
Number	50	None		Wi-Fi	
Shaded		At Site		Fishing	Y
By Water		Spigots	Y	Hiking	Y
Paved		**Sewer**		Biking	Y
Pull Thru		None		Swimming	Y
ADA	Y	At Site		Watch Wildlife	
Max RV Size	40	Dump Station	Y	Pets	Y
Electric		**Amenities**		**Security**	
None		Restrooms	Y	Host(s)	Y
20 Amp	Y	Showers	Y	Rangers(s)	
30 Amp	Y	Reserve Sites	Y	Gate	
50 Amp		Store	Y	Patrolled	Y
		Grill/Table	Y		

[2] Fillmore Glen State Park
I-81, Exit 12
Northwest of Cortland
N42 42.010 W76 25.223
State Rate: See Introduction
(315) 497-0130
http://nysparks.com/parks/park-results.aspx?n=Fillmore%20Glen&src=1

Directions

16 miles. From Exit 12 go west to Hwy 281. Turn right for 0.4 miles to Hwy 90 (Cayuga St). Turn west on Hwy 90 for 13 miles to Hwy 38. Go 3 miles north to the Park on your right.

Points of Interest

The Park is an oasis of cool, dense woods crowded into a long, narrow gorge. Its hiking trails offer spectacular views, unique geological formations, waterfalls, & a botanically rich glen.

RV Sites		Water		Laundry	
Number	60	None		Wi-Fi	
Shaded	Y	At Site		Fishing	
By Water	Y	Spigots	Y	Hiking	Y
Paved	Y	**Sewer**		Biking	Y
Pull Thru		None		Swimming	Y
ADA	Y	At Site		Watch Wildlife	Y
Max RV Size	45	Dump Station	Y	Pets	Y
Electric		**Amenities**		**Security**	
None		Restrooms	Y	Host(s)	Y
20 Amp	Y	Showers	Y	Rangers(s)	Y
30 Amp	Y	Reserve Sites	Y	Gate	
50 Amp	few	Store		Patrolled	Y
		Grill/Table	Y		

[3] Green Lakes State Park
I-481, Either Exit from I-81, to I-481
East of Syracuse
N43 03.351 W76 00.289
State Rate: See Introduction
(315) 637-6111
http://nysparks.com/parks/park-results.aspx?n=Green%20Lakes&src=1

Directions

4 miles. From the northbound or southbound exits of I-81 onto I-481, proceed on I-481 to Exit 5. Follow Kirkville Rd east for 1.3 miles to Fremont Rd. Turn south for 1.2 miles to Hwy 290. Turn east, follow signs for 1.4 miles to park.

Points of Interest

There are numerous sites to see along the Erie Canal, as well as Revolutionary War destinations. Many orchards, specialty shops, galleries & restaurants are to be found.

RV Sites		Water		Laundry	
Number	132	None		Wi-Fi	
Shaded	Y	At Site	Y	Fishing	
By Water		Spigots	Y	Hiking	Y
Paved		**Sewer**		Biking	Y
Pull Thru	Y	None		Swimming	Y
ADA	Y	At Site		Watch Wildlife	Y
Max RV Size	40	Dump Station	Y	Pets	Y
Electric		**Amenities**		**Security**	
None		Restrooms	Y	Host(s)	Y
20 Amp	Y	Showers	Y	Rangers(s)	Y
30 Amp	Y	Reserve Sites	Y	Gate	
50 Amp	Y	Store		Patrolled	Y
		Grill/Table	Y		

[4] Southwick Beach State Park
I-81, Exit 40
West of Adams
N43 45.878 W76 11.764
State Rate: See Introduction
(315) 846-5338
http://nysparks.com/parks/park-results.
aspx?n=Southwick%20Beach&src=1

Directions
7.5 miles. From Exit 40 go west for 7.5 miles on Hwy 193 to the Park.

Points of Interest
The Park is adjacent to the Lakeview Wildlife Management Area, home to the environmentally-sensitive coastal sand dunes. Park nature and hiking trails adjoin the wildlife management area and its trail system, which visitors are encouraged to use.

RV Sites		Water		Laundry	
Number	100	None		Wi-Fi	
Shaded	Y	At Site		Fishing	Y
By Water	Y	Spigots	Y	Hiking	Y
Paved		**Sewer**		Biking	Y
Pull Thru	Y	None		Swimming	Y
ADA	Y	At Site		Watch Wildlife	
Max RV Size	50	Dump Station	Y	Pets	Y
Electric		**Amenities**		**Security**	
None		Restrooms	Y	Host(s)	Y
20 Amp	Y	Showers	Y	Rangers(s)	Y
30 Amp	Y	Reserve Sites	Y	Gate	
50 Amp	Y	Store		Patrolled	Y
		Grill/Table	Y		

[5] Grass Point State Park
I-81, Exit 50
South of Alexandria Bay
44 16.737 W75 59.723
State Rate: See Introduction
(315) 686-4472
http://nysparks.com/parks/park-results.
aspx?n=Grass%20Point&src=1

Directions
1.5 miles. From Exit 50 go southwest for 1.5 miles on Hwy 12 to the Park.

Points of Interest
This Park puts you in the midst of the beautiful 1000 Islands. Visit the Antique Boat Museum and stroll among a priceless collection of 100 antique boats; or tour the Handweaving Museum and Arts Center. Stop at the Thousand Islands Winery for world class wines and local hospitality.

RV Sites		Water		Laundry	
Number	73	None		Wi-Fi	
Shaded	Y	At Site		Fishing	Y
By Water	Y	Spigots	Y	Hiking	Y
Paved		**Sewer**		Biking	Y
Pull Thru		None		Swimming	Y
ADA	Y	At Site		Watch Wildlife	
Max RV Size	40	Dump Station	Y	Pets	Y
Electric		**Amenities**		**Security**	
None		Restrooms	Y	Host(s)	Y
20 Amp	Y	Showers	Y	Rangers(s)	Y
30 Amp	Y	Reserve Sites	Y	Gate	
50 Amp	Y	Store		Patrolled	Y
		Grill/Table	Y		

[6] Wellesley Island State Park
I-81, Exit 51
On Wellesley Island
N44 18.958 W76 01.168
State Rate: See Introduction
(315) 482-2722
http://nysparks.state.ny.us/parks/52/details.aspx

Directions
2.5 miles. From Exit 51 go southeast for 0.5 miles on Cty Rd 191 to Thousand Island Park Rd. Turn right for 0.5 miles to Cross Island Rd. Turn right for 1.6 miles to the Park.

Points of Interest
The Park's sandy beach offers swimming, sunbathing & a golf course. A main attraction is the Minna Anthony Common Nature Center, which includes a museum & varied habitats - wooded wetlands, miles of shoreline, granite outcrops, miles of trails for hiking, & nature education.

RV Sites		Water		Laundry	Y
Number	400	None		Wi-Fi	
Shaded	Y	At Site	Y	Fishing	Y
By Water	Y	Spigots	Y	Hiking	Y
Paved		**Sewer**		Biking	Y
Pull Thru		None		Swimming	Y
ADA	Y	At Site	Y	Watch Wildlife	Y
Max RV Size	45	Dump Station	Y	Pets	Y
Electric		**Amenities**		**Security**	
None		Restrooms	Y	Host(s)	Y
20 Amp	Y	Showers	Y	Rangers(s)	Y
30 Amp	Y	Reserve Sites	Y	Gate	
50 Amp		Store	Y	Patrolled	Y
		Grill/Table	Y		

[7] Allegany State Park - Quaker Area
I-86, Exit 18
South of Salamanca
N42 02.237 W78 50.759
State Rate: See Introduction
(716) 354-2182
http://nysparks.state.ny.us/parks/1/details.aspx

Directions

7 miles. From Exit 18 go south for 4.5 miles on Hwy 280 (Quaker Run Rd) to ASP Route. Bear left for 2 miles to Quaker Run, turn left then right on Cain Hollow Rd to the campground.

Points of Interest

Salamanca, nestled in the scenic foothills of the Allegheny River, is filled with country charm. It is the only city in the U. S. that lies almost completely on an Indian Reservation. Stop at the Seneca Iroquois National Museum & the Salamanca Rail Museum, or enjoy the gaming facilities.

RV Sites		Water			Laundry	Y
Number	304	None			Wi-Fi	
Shaded	Y	At Site			Fishing	Y
By Water		Spigots	Y		Hiking	Y
Paved		Sewer			Biking	Y
Pull Thru	Y	None			Swimming	
ADA	Y	At Site			Watch Wildlife	Y
Max RV Size	45	Dump Station	Y		Pets	Y
Electric		Amenities			Security	
None		Restrooms	Y		Host(s)	Y
20 Amp	Y	Showers	Y		Rangers(s)	Y
30 Amp	Y	Reserve Sites	Y		Gate	
50 Amp	Y	Store	Y		Patrolled	Y
		Grill/Table	Y			

[8] Robert H. Treman State Park
I-86, Exit 54
South of Ithaca
N42 23.893 W76 32.765
State Rate: See Introduction
(607) 273-3440
http://nysparks.state.ny.us/parks/135/details.aspx

Directions

24 miles. From Exit 54 go north for 24 miles on Hwy 13 to the Park on your left.

Points of Interest

This is an area of exceptional beauty, with the rugged Enfield Glen Gorge as its scenic highlight. Winding trails follow the gorge past 12 waterfalls, including the 115-foot Lucifer Falls, where you can see a mile-and-a-half down the wooded gorge. Don't forget Ithaca, a great town to visit!

RV Sites		Water			Laundry	
Number	71	None			Wi-Fi	
Shaded	Y	At Site			Fishing	Y
By Water	Y	Spigots	Y		Hiking	Y
Paved		Sewer			Biking	Y
Pull Thru		None			Swimming	Y
ADA	Y	At Site			Watch Wildlife	Y
Max RV Size	45	Dump Station	Y		Pets	Y
Electric		Amenities			Security	
None		Restrooms	Y		Host(s)	Y
20 Amp	Y	Showers	Y		Rangers(s)	Y
30 Amp	Y	Reserve Sites	Y		Gate	
50 Amp		Store			Patrolled	Y
		Grill/Table	Y			

[9] Newtown Battlefield State Park
I-86, Near Exit 58
South of Elmira
N42 02.629 W76 44.056
State Rate: See Introduction
(607) 732-6067
http://nysparks.state.ny.us/parks/107/details.aspx

Directions

2 miles. 1.5 miles north of Exit 58 turn northeast on Oneida Rd for 1 mile to Newtown Reservation Rd. Turn right, go 1 mile to the campground.

Points of Interest

Enjoy the park's vistas. The Park and its monument mark the site of the battle of Newtown, which occurred in August of 1779 and was the decisive clash in one of the largest offensive campaigns of the American Revolution. Just north of the Park you can stroll through Elmira.

RV Sites		Water			Laundry	
Number	18	None			Wi-Fi	
Shaded	Y	At Site			Fishing	
By Water		Spigots	Y		Hiking	Y
Paved	Y	Sewer			Biking	Y
Pull Thru		None			Swimming	
ADA	Y	At Site			Watch Wildlife	
Max RV Size	40	Dump Station	Y		Pets	Y
Electric		Amenities			Security	
None	some	Restrooms	Y		Host(s)	Y
20 Amp	few	Showers	Y		Rangers(s)	Y
30 Amp	few	Reserve Sites	Y		Gate	
50 Amp		Store			Patrolled	Y
		Grill/Table	Y			

[10] Hickories County Park
I-86, Exit 65
East of Owego
N42 05.482 W76 13.556
County Rate: $25-$30
(607) 687-1199
http://www.townofowego.com/parksdepartment.html

Directions

1 mile. From Exit 65 go northeast for 0.5 mile on the Hwy 17 Access Rd to the Hickory Park Rd. Turn right into the campground.

Points of Interest

Historic Owego is a charming village along the Susquehanna River in the southeast corner of the Finger Lakes Region. Enjoy over 80 gift & antique shops, local artisans & restaurants. It was named "Coolest Small Town in America" in 2009 by Budget Travel Magazine readers.

RV Sites		Water		Laundry	
Number	57	None		Wi-Fi	
Shaded	Y	At Site	Y	Fishing	Y
By Water	Y	Spigots	Y	Hiking	
Paved	Y	**Sewer**		Biking	Y
Pull Thru		None		Swimming	
ADA	Y	At Site	Y	Watch Wildlife	
Max RV Size	40	Dump Station	Y	Pets	Y
Electric		**Amenities**		**Security**	
None		Restrooms	Y	Host(s)	Y
20 Amp	Y	Showers	Y	Rangers(s)	Y
30 Amp	Y	Reserve Sites		Gate	
50 Amp	Y	Store		Patrolled	Y
		Grill/Table	Y		

[11] Harriman State Park (Beaver Pond)
I-87, Exit 16
East of Harriman
N41 13.750 W74 04.218
State Rate: See Introduction
(845) 947-2792
http://nysparks.state.ny.us/parks/116/details.aspx

Directions

15 miles. From Exit 16 you immediately take the Averill Ave (Hwy 17) exit, & turn left on to Averill. Then turn left again on to Hwy 6 going east. Follow Hwy 6 for 5.5 miles to the Rotary. Take Palisades Interstate Pky. south for 6 miles to Gate Hill Rd. Turn right for 2 miles to the Park.

Points of Interest

The campground adjoins Lake Welch Recreation Area. A beach & plenty of outdoor activities make this a great destination not far from New York City. Stony Point Battlefield State Historic Site is near by.

RV Sites		Water		Laundry	Y
Number	137	None		Wi-Fi	
Shaded	Y	At Site		Fishing	Y
By Water	Y	Spigots	Y	Hiking	Y
Paved		**Sewer**		Biking	Y
Pull Thru		None		Swimming	Y
ADA	Y	At Site		Watch Wildlife	
Max RV Size	38	Dump Station	Y	Pets	N
Electric		**Amenities**		**Security**	
None	Y	Restrooms	Y	Host(s)	Y
20 Amp		Showers	Y	Rangers(s)	Y
30 Amp		Reserve Sites	Y	Gate	
50 Amp		Store		Patrolled	
		Grill/Table	Y		

[12] Mills Norrie State Park
(Margaret Lewis Norrie)
I-87, Exit 19
East of Kingston
N41 50.421 W73 55.901
State Rate: See Introduction
(845) 889-4646
http://nysparks.state.ny.us/parks/171/details.aspx

Directions

19 miles. From Exit 19 turn west on Hwy 28, north on Hwy 209 (becomes Hwy 199), for 8.5 miles in all to Hwy 9G. Turn south for 1.5 miles to Hwy 9. Go right on Hwy 9 for 9 miles to the Park.

Points of Interest

The Park has bluffs overlooking the Hudson River. Visit the Vanderbilt Mansion National Historic Site of 600 acres, known for its grand scale, classical ornament, and look of permanence. The majestic home is also famous for its landscaping.

RV Sites		Water		Laundry	
Number	45	None		Wi-Fi	
Shaded	Y	At Site		Fishing	Y
By Water		Spigots	Y	Hiking	Y
Paved		**Sewer**		Biking	Y
Pull Thru		None		Swimming	
ADA	Y	At Site		Watch Wildlife	Y
Max RV Size	40	Dump Station	Y	Pets	Y
Electric		**Amenities**		**Security**	
None	Y	Restrooms	Y	Host(s)	Y
20 Amp		Showers	Y	Rangers(s)	Y
30 Amp		Reserve Sites	Y	Gate	
50 Amp		Store		Patrolled	Y
		Grill/Table	Y		

[13] Thacher State Park
I-87, Exit 23
Southwest of Albany
N42 39.198 W74 02.735
State Rate: See Introduction
(518) 872-1674
http://nysparks.state.ny.us/parks/99/details.aspx

Directions

20 miles. From Exit 23 turn south on Hwy 9W (Southern Blvd.) for 1.3 miles to Hwy 32. Go right for 3 miles to Elm Ave (Cty Rd. 52). Turn right, go north for 1.7 miles to Hwy 85. Turn left, go 7 miles to Hwy 157. Turn right & follow Hwy 157 for 7 miles to the Park.

Points of Interest

A good first stop to exploring Albany is at the Albany Heritage Area Visitors Center. Tour four centuries of architecture, from the renovated State Capital Million Dollar Staircase to the inspiring 'Egg' at Empire State Plaza.

RV Sites		Water		Laundry	
Number	131	None		Wi-Fi	
Shaded	Y	At Site		Fishing	Y
By Water	Y	Spigots	Y	Hiking	Y
Paved		Sewer		Biking	Y
Pull Thru		None		Swimming	Y
ADA	Y	At Site		Watch Wildlife	
Max RV Size	30	Dump Station	Y	Pets	Y
Electric		Amenities		Security	
None	Y	Restrooms	Y	Host(s)	Y
20 Amp		Showers	Y	Rangers(s)	Y
30 Amp		Reserve Sites	Y	Gate	
50 Amp		Store		Patrolled	Y
		Grill/Table	Y		

[14] Moreau Lake State Park
I-87, Exit 17
North of Saratoga Springs
N43 13.624 W73 42.405
State Rate: See Introduction
(518) 793-0511
http://nysparks.state.ny.us/parks/150/details.aspx

Directions

0.8 miles. From Exit 17 turn southwest on Hwy 9 and immediately turn right on to Old Saratoga Rd for 0.8 miles in all to the Park.

Points of Interest

The Park is home to some of Saratoga's most popular attractions. The mineral springs have been a popular destination for wealthy vacationers since the mid 1800s. The many galleries, boutiques, restaurants, and sights downtown Saratoga Springs will keep you busy.

RV Sites		Water		Laundry	
Number	147	None		Wi-Fi	
Shaded	Y	At Site		Fishing	Y
By Water	Y	Spigots	Y	Hiking	Y
Paved		Sewer		Biking	Y
Pull Thru		None		Swimming	Y
ADA	Y	At Site		Watch Wildlife	Y
Max RV Size	40	Dump Station	Y	Pets	Y
Electric		Amenities		Security	
None	Y	Restrooms	Y	Host(s)	Y
20 Amp		Showers	Y	Rangers(s)	Y
30 Amp		Reserve Sites	Y	Gate	
50 Amp		Store	Y	Patrolled	Y
		Grill/Table	Y		

[15] Cumberland Bay State Park
I-87, Near Exit 39
North of Plattsburgh
N44 43.474 W73 25.586
State Rate: See Introduction
(518) 563-5240
http://nysparks.state.ny.us/parks/34/details.aspx

Directions

1 mile. From Exit 39 turn southeast for 1 mile on Hwy 314 (Cumberland Head Rd) to the Park.

Points of Interest

The Park, on Lake Champlain, is popular because of its sand beach. Visit Ausable Chasm, the oldest natural attraction in the USA (est. 1870)! Walk along towering cliff walks in the midst of a primeval forest that peers into the chasm from many scenic overlooks and vistas.

RV Sites		Water		Laundry	
Number	133	None		Wi-Fi	
Shaded		At Site		Fishing	Y
By Water		Spigots	Y	Hiking	Y
Paved		Sewer		Biking	Y
Pull Thru	Y	None		Swimming	Y
ADA	Y	At Site		Watch Wildlife	
Max RV Size	45	Dump Station	Y	Pets	Y
Electric		Amenities		Security	
None		Restrooms	Y	Host(s)	Y
20 Amp	Y	Showers	Y	Rangers(s)	Y
30 Amp	Y	Reserve Sites	Y	Gate	
50 Amp	Y	Store	Y	Patrolled	Y
		Grill/Table	Y		

[16] Chenango Valley State Park
I-88, Exit 3
North of Binghamton
N42 12.929 W75 49.066
State Rate: See Introduction
(607) 648-5251
http://nysparks.state.ny.us/parks/41/details.aspx

Directions

4 miles. From Exit 3 turn north on Hwy 369 for 4 miles to Cove State Park Rd & the Park.

Points of Interest

The Park is an ice age wonder. Its two kettle lakes were created when the last glacier retreated and left behind huge chunks of buried ice which melted to form the lakes and bog. Birdwatchers and fishermen will especially enjoy this park. Binghamton is close by for town outings.

RV Sites		Water		Laundry	
Number	182	None		Wi-Fi	
Shaded	Y	At Site		Fishing	Y
By Water	Y	Spigots	Y	Hiking	Y
Paved		**Sewer**		Biking	Y
Pull Thru		None		Swimming	Y
ADA	Y	At Site		Watch Wildlife	Y
Max RV Size	45	Dump Station	Y	Pets	Y
Electric		**Amenities**		**Security**	
None		Restrooms	Y	Host(s)	Y
20 Amp	Y	Showers	Y	Rangers(s)	Y
30 Amp	Y	Reserve Sites	Y	Gate	
50 Amp	Y	Store	Y	Patrolled	Y
		Grill/Table	Y		

[17] Gilbert Lake State Park
I-88, Exit 13
North of Oneonta
N42 34.362 W75 07.700
State Rate: See Introduction
(607) 432-2114
http://nysparks.state.ny.us/parks/19/details.aspx

Directions

11 miles. From Exit 13 turn northwest on Hwy 205 for 6.7 miles to Laurens. Turn left at Cty Rd 11A (Waters then south on Main through town) for 0.7 miles to Cty Rd. 12 (Gilbert Lake Rd). Turn north for 3.7 miles to the Park.

Points of Interest

The Park's lake & ponds lie in wooded, hilly terrain of the Catskills. Visit Cooperstown & the Corvette Americana Hall of Fame, Fenimore House & Art Museum, Farmers Museum and of course the National Baseball Hall of Fame & Museum.

RV Sites		Water		Laundry	
Number	135	None		Wi-Fi	
Shaded	Y	At Site		Fishing	Y
By Water	Y	Spigots	Y	Hiking	Y
Paved		**Sewer**		Biking	Y
Pull Thru		None		Swimming	Y
ADA	Y	At Site		Watch Wildlife	
Max RV Size	45	Dump Station	Y	Pets	Y
Electric		**Amenities**		**Security**	
None		Restrooms	Y	Host(s)	Y
20 Amp	Y	Showers	Y	Rangers(s)	Y
30 Amp	Y	Reserve Sites	Y	Gate	
50 Amp		Store		Patrolled	Y
		Grill/Table	Y		

[18] Lake Erie State Park
I-90, Exit 59
West of Dunkirk
N42 25.258 W79 25.715
State Rate: See Introduction
(716) 792-9214
http://nysparks.state.ny.us/parks/129/details.aspx

Directions

10 miles. From Exit 59 turn north toward Dunkirk for 2 miles on Hwy 60. Turn east (left) on Hwy 5 for 7.8 miles to the Park.

Points of Interest

The high bluffs overlooking Lake Erie provide breathtaking views. Enjoy a shoreline, which covers over three quarters of a mile. Visit Dunkirk, check out the 'Wreck & Roll Festival Series' & the 'Music on the Pier Concert Series,' or take in the Chautauqua Lake Erie Art Trail art sale & display.

RV Sites		Water		Laundry	
Number	99	None		Wi-Fi	
Shaded	Y	At Site		Fishing	Y
By Water	Y	Spigots	Y	Hiking	Y
Paved		**Sewer**		Biking	Y
Pull Thru		None		Swimming	
ADA	Y	At Site		Watch Wildlife	
Max RV Size	50	Dump Station	Y	Pets	Y
Electric		**Amenities**		**Security**	
None		Restrooms	Y	Host(s)	Y
20 Amp	Y	Showers	Y	Rangers(s)	Y
30 Amp	Y	Reserve Sites	Y	Gate	
50 Amp	Y	Store		Patrolled	Y
		Grill/Table	Y		

[19] Darien Lakes State Park
I-90, Exit 48A
East of Buffalo
N42 54.130 W78 25.986
State Rate: See Introduction
(585) 547-9242
http://nysparks.state.ny.us/parks/144/details.
aspx

Directions

10 miles. From Exit 48A turn south on Hwy 77 (Allegany Rd) for 7.7 miles to Hwy 20. Turn west on Hwy 20 for 2.3 miles to Harlow & the Park.

Points of Interest

In Buffalo, see one of the world's great collections of modern art. Tour Frank Lloyd Wright's grandest Prairie Style house. Stroll one of America's great neighborhoods. Explore a South American rainforest or discover the birthplace of the American Arts and Crafts Movement.

RV Sites		Water		Laundry	
Number	158	None		Wi-Fi	
Shaded	Y	At Site		Fishing	Y
By Water	Y	Spigots	Y	Hiking	Y
Paved		**Sewer**		Biking	Y
Pull Thru		None		Swimming	Y
ADA	Y	At Site		Watch Wildlife	
Max RV Size	40	Dump Station	Y	Pets	Y
Electric		**Amenities**		**Security**	
None		Restrooms	Y	Host(s)	Y
20 Amp	Y	Showers	Y	Rangers(s)	Y
30 Amp	Y	Reserve Sites	Y	Gate	
50 Amp	Y	Store		Patrolled	Y
		Grill/Table	Y		

[20] Cayuga Lake State Park
I-90, Exit 41
On the Shores of Cayuga Lake
N42 53.762 W76 45.199
State Rate: See Introduction
(315) 568-5163
http://nysparks.state.ny.us/parks/123/details.
aspx

Directions

8 miles. From Exit 41 turn south on Hwy 414, immediately turn left on Hwy 318 & go 4.4 miles in all to the intersection of Hwys 20 and 89. Take Hwy 89 southeast for 3.9 miles to the Park.

Points of Interest

Explore Seneca Falls, the gateway to the Finger Lakes and widely believed to be the inspiration for Frank Capra's holiday classic, "It's A Wonderful Life." Visit the National Women's Hall of Fame. Try one of the many 'Wine Trails.'

RV Sites		Water		Laundry	
Number	267	None		Wi-Fi	
Shaded	Y	At Site		Fishing	Y
By Water	Y	Spigots	Y	Hiking	Y
Paved		**Sewer**		Biking	Y
Pull Thru		None		Swimming	Y
ADA	Y	At Site		Watch Wildlife	
Max RV Size	40	Dump Station	Y	Pets	Y
Electric		**Amenities**		**Security**	
None		Restrooms	Y	Host(s)	Y
20 Amp	Y	Showers	Y	Rangers(s)	Y
30 Amp	Y	Reserve Sites	Y	Gate	
50 Amp		Store		Patrolled	Y
		Grill/Table	Y		

[21] Stony Brook State Park
I-390, Exit 4
South of Dansville
N42 31.584 W77 41.791
State Rate: See Introduction
(585) 335-8111
http://nysparks.state.ny.us/parks/118/details.
aspx

Directions

2 miles. From Exit 4 turn south on Hwy 36 for 2 miles to the Park.

Points of Interest

The Park's terrain comprises hilly woodlands; a deep gorge with rugged cliffs overlooking three waterfalls; and fascinating rock formations. Campsites are scattered in the woodlands above the gorge. Visit Letchworth - 'The Grand Canyon of the East.'

RV Sites		Water		Laundry	
Number	119	None		Wi-Fi	
Shaded	Y	At Site		Fishing	
By Water	Y	Spigots	Y	Hiking	Y
Paved		**Sewer**		Biking	Y
Pull Thru		None		Swimming	Y
ADA	Y	At Site		Watch Wildlife	
Max RV Size	30	Dump Station	Y	Pets	Y
Electric		**Amenities**		**Security**	
None	Y	Restrooms	Y	Host(s)	Y
20 Amp		Showers	Y	Rangers(s)	Y
30 Amp		Reserve Sites	Y	Gate	
50 Amp		Store	Y	Patrolled	Y
		Grill/Table	Y		

[22] Limekiln Lake
Hwy 28, at Limekiln Lake Rd
South of Inlet
N43 43.321 W74 47.536
State Rate: $20
(315) 357-4401
http://www.dec.ny.gov/outdoor/24476.html

Directions

4 miles. Just south of Inlet go 1.7 miles, turn right on Limekiln Lake Road, go 1 7 miles. Turn right at campground sign, go 0.5 mile to booth.

Points of Interest

Browse the various shops in Old Forge. Take in *View*, a multi-arts center with exhibitions, performances, workshops, & special events for all ages. Visit one of the nearby museums including the Adirondack Museum at Blue Mountain Lake.

RV Sites		Water		Laundry	
Number	271	None		Wi-Fi	
Shaded	Y	At Site		Fishing	Y
By Water	Y	Spigots	Y	Hiking	Y
Paved		Sewer		Biking	Y
Pull Thru		None		Swimming	Y
ADA	Y	At Site		Watch Wildlife	Y
Max RV Size	40	Dump Station	Y	Pets	Y
Electric		Amenities		Security	
None	Y	Restrooms	Y	Host(s)	Y
20 Amp		Showers	Y	Rangers(s)	Y
30 Amp		Reserve Sites	Y	Gate	
50 Amp		Store		Patrolled	Y
		Grill/Table	Y		

[23] Lake Eaton
Hwy 30, at Lake Eaton Rd
North of Long Lake town
N43 59.206 W74 27.377
State Rate: $20
(518) 624-2641
http://www.dec.ny.gov/outdoor/24464.html

Directions

2. 5 miles. Go 2.5 miles north of Hwy 28/30 on Hwy 30 from Long Lake Village to the Park, on the left.

Points of Interest

Browse the various shops in Old Forge. Take in *View*, a multi-arts center with exhibitions, performances, workshops, & special events for all ages. Visit one of the nearby museums including the Adirondack Museum at Blue Mountain Lake.

RV Sites		Water		Laundry	
Number	127	None		Wi-Fi	
Shaded	Y	At Site		Fishing	Y
By Water	Y	Spigots	Y	Hiking	Y
Paved		Sewer		Biking	Y
Pull Thru		None		Swimming	Y
ADA	Y	At Site		Watch Wildlife	Y
Max RV Size	30	Dump Station	Y	Pets	Y
Electric		Amenities		Security	
None	Y	Restrooms	Y	Host(s)	Y
20 Amp		Showers	Y	Rangers(s)	Y
30 Amp		Reserve Sites	Y	Gate	
50 Amp		Store		Patrolled	Y
		Grill/Table	Y		

[24] Meadowbrook
Hwy 3, Southeast on Hwy 86
Southeast of Saranac Lake
N44 17.998 W74 04.900
State Rate: $18
(518) 891-4351
http://www.dec.ny.gov/outdoor/24482.html

Directions

3.6 miles. Go southeast from Saranac Lake, on Hwy 86 for 3.6 miles to the campground on the right side, in Ray Brook.

Points of Interest

Meadowbrook is very convenient for those visiting the Lake Placid Olympic Training venues and the Village of Lake Placid. The villages nearby offer a variety of restaurants, gift stores, shopping, golf courses, boating, fishing, and various other activities.

RV Sites		Water		Laundry	
Number	58	None		Wi-Fi	
Shaded	Y	At Site		Fishing	
By Water		Spigots	Y	Hiking	Y
Paved		Sewer		Biking	Y
Pull Thru		None		Swimming	
ADA	Y	At Site		Watch Wildlife	
Max RV Size	30	Dump Station	Y	Pets	Y
Electric		Amenities		Security	
None	Y	Restrooms	Y	Host(s)	Y
20 Amp		Showers	Y	Rangers(s)	Y
30 Amp		Reserve Sites	Y	Gate	
50 Amp		Store		Patrolled	Y
		Grill/Table	Y		

About North Carolina's Public Campgrounds

North Carolina is blessed with beautiful beaches, majestic mountains and countless rivers and streams. The North Carolina Division of Parks and Recreation oversees the State Park System. Their website is located at -

http://www.ncparks.gov/Visit/main.php

Reservations can be made up to 11 months in advance at -

http://www.ncparks.gov/News/special/reservations.php

Another easy way to make reservations is by calling toll-free 877-7-CAMPNC (877-722-6762). There is a $3 surcharge per reservation/per night's stay to support the reservations system.

Only three parks (Falls Lake, Jordan Lake and Kerr Lake) have entrance gate fees. Anyone who is 62 years of age or older is eligible for a senior discount on entrance fees and camping. The discounts are $6 for campsites with electrical hookups and $5 for campsites without electrical hookups. Pets are permitted so long as they are on a leash no longer than 6 feet and under the constant control of the owner.

[1] Lake Powhatan Recreation Area

[2] Curtis Creek

[3] Hagan - Stone County Park

[4] Falls Lake State Recreation Area (Rolling View)

[5] Cliffs of the Neuse State Park

[6] Carolina Beach State Park

[7] Morrow Mountain State Park

[8] Pilot Mountain State Park

[9] McDowell Nature Center & Preserve

[10] Stone Mountain State Park

[11] Dan Nicholas Park

[12] Kerr Lake State Recreation Area (Bullocksville Campground)

[13] Jones Lake State Park

NOTES:

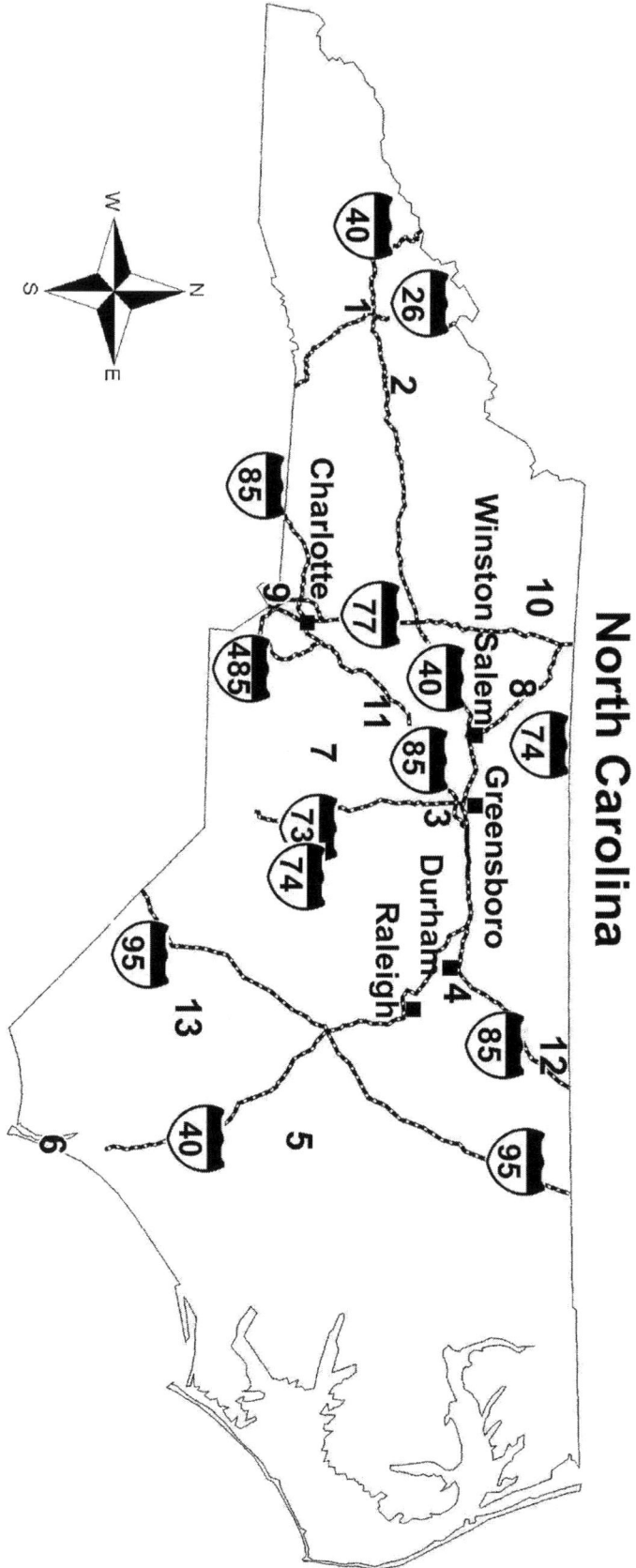

North Carolina

[1] Lake Powhatan Recreation Area
I-26, Exit 33
South of Asheville
N35 29.126 W82 37.781
Pisgah NF Rate: $22-$44
America/Beautiful Rate: $11-$22
(828) 670-5627
http://www.recreation.gov

Directions

5 miles. From Exit 33 go southwest for 2 miles on Hwy 191 (Bevard Rd) to Bent Creek Ranch Rd. Turn right for 0.3 miles, then left on Wesley Branch Rd for 2.4 miles to the camp.

Points of Interest

Asheville has many events. Lovers of art, crafts & live music will enjoy the city. The Park is near the North Carolina Arboretum, Biltmore Estate & the Blue Ridge Parkway Folk Art Center & Destination Center, hot springs, and mountain lookouts.

RV Sites		Water		Laundry	
Number	54	None		Wi-Fi	
Shaded	Y	At Site	Y	Fishing	Y
By Water	Y	Spigots	Y	Hiking	Y
Paved	Y	**Sewer**		Biking	Y
Pull Thru	Y	None		Swimming	Y
ADA	Y	At Site	Y	Watch Wildlife	
Max RV Size	45	Dump Station	Y	Pets	Y
Electric		**Amenities**		**Security**	
None		Restrooms	Y	Host(s)	Y
20 Amp	Y	Showers	Y	Rangers(s)	Y
30 Amp	Y	Reserve Sites	Y	Gate	
50 Amp	Y	Store		Patrolled	Y
		Grill/Table	Y		

[2] Curtis Creek
I-40, Exit 73
North of Old Fort
N35 41.420 W82 11.792
Pisgah NF Rate: $5
America/Beautiful Rate: $3
(828) 652-2144
http://www.forestcamping.com/dow/southern/pisgcmp.htm#curtis%20creek

Directions

7 miles. From Exit 73 go north on Catawba for 0.4 miles to Hwy 70. Turn right for 2 miles to State Rt 1227 (Curtis Creek Rd). Turn left and go 4.7 miles to campground.

Points of Interest

Visit Little Switzerland, named because of its deep valleys & distant ranges resembling the foothills of the Swiss Alps. Explore Emerald Village or the apple orchards, museums, & historic mines.

RV Sites		Water		Laundry	
Number	14	None		Wi-Fi	
Shaded		At Site		Fishing	Y
By Water		Spigots	Y	Hiking	Y
Paved	Y	**Sewer**		Biking	Y
Pull Thru		None		Swimming	
ADA	Y	At Site	Y	Watch Wildlife	
Max RV Size	40	Dump Station		Pets	Y
Electric		**Amenities**		**Security**	
None	Y	Restrooms	Y	Host(s)	Y
20 Amp		Showers		Rangers(s)	Y
30 Amp		Reserve Sites		Gate	
50 Amp		Store		Patrolled	Y
		Grill/Table	Y		

[3] Hagan-Stone Park
I-40/I-85, Exit 38
South of Greensboro
N35 56.931 W79 44.179
County Rate: $20, Senior Discount
(336) 641-7275
http://haganstone.guilfordparks.com/

Directions

9 miles. From Exit 38 go south on Hwy 421 for 6.7 miles to Hagan-Stone Park Rd. Turn south for 2.3 miles to the Park.

Points of Interest

With much to offer in Greensboro it is hard to choose. Examples include Castle McCulloch (Crystal Gardens and Gem Panning), Blandwood Mansion, and Carolina Model Railroaders. Or visit some of the many art galleries, museums, performing arts, venues & theater.

RV Sites		Water		Laundry	
Number	70	None		Wi-Fi	
Shaded	Y	At Site		Fishing	Y
By Water		Spigots	Y	Hiking	Y
Paved		**Sewer**		Biking	Y
Pull Thru		None		Swimming	Y
ADA	Y	At Site	Y	Watch Wildlife	
Max RV Size	45	Dump Station	Y	Pets	Y
Electric		**Amenities**		**Security**	
None		Restrooms	Y	Host(s)	Y
20 Amp	Y	Showers	Y	Rangers(s)	
30 Amp	Y	Reserve Sites	Y	Gate	
50 Amp	Y	Store		Patrolled	Y
		Grill/Table	Y		

[4] Falls Lake SRA (Rolling View)
I-40, Exit 283
North of Raleigh
N36 00.271 W78 43.633
State Rate: $17-$34, Senior Discount
(919) 676-1027
http://www.ncparks.gov/Visit/parks/fala/main.php

Directions

24 miles. From Exit 283 go east on I-540 for 9 miles to exit 9 (Hwy 50, Creedmoor Rd). Turn north for 5 miles to Hwy 98 (Durham Rd). Turn west for 5.6 miles to Baptist Rd. Turn northeast for 4 miles to the Park.

Points of Interest

With so much to offer in the Raleigh-Durham area, a good way to start planning a local tour to the region would be the following two websites:
- *http://www.visitraleigh.com/*
- *http://www.durham-nc.com/*

RV Sites		Water		Laundry	
Number	117	None		Wi-Fi	
Shaded	Y	At Site	Y	Fishing	Y
By Water	Y	Spigots	Y	Hiking	Y
Paved		Sewer		Biking	Y
Pull Thru	Y	None		Swimming	Y
ADA	Y	At Site		Watch Wildlife	
Max RV Size	45	Dump Station	Y	Pets	Y
Electric		Amenities		Security	
None		Restrooms	Y	Host(s)	Y
20 Amp	Y	Showers	Y	Rangers(s)	Y
30 Amp	Y	Reserve Sites	Y	Gate	
50 Amp		Store		Patrolled	Y
		Grill/Table	Y		

[5] Cliffs of the Neuse State Park
I-40, Exit 355
South of Goldsboro
N35 14.038 W77 53.942
State Rate: $17, Senior Discount
(919) 778-6234
http://www.ncparks.gov/Visit/parks/clne/main.php

Directions

23 miles. From Exit 355 go northeast on Hwy 1783 (joined by Hwy 117) for 10 miles to Hwy 55. Turn right, go 10.7 miles to Hwy 111. Turn left, go 2.4 miles, turn right on Cliff Park Rd to the Park.

Points of Interest

Turn of the century visitors to the area drank mineral water from local springs to cure their ills and take riverboat excursions to the cliffs. Visit the CCS Neuse, one of 22 ironclads commissioned by the Confederate navy.

RV Sites		Water		Laundry	
Number	35	None		Wi-Fi	
Shaded	Y	At Site		Fishing	Y
By Water	Y	Spigots	Y	Hiking	Y
Paved		Sewer		Biking	Y
Pull Thru		None		Swimming	Y
ADA	Y	At Site		Watch Wildlife	
Max RV Size	45	Dump Station	Y	Pets	Y
Electric		Amenities		Security	
None	Y	Restrooms	Y	Host(s)	Y
20 Amp		Showers	Y	Rangers(s)	Y
30 Amp		Reserve Sites	Y	Gate	
50 Amp		Store	Y	Patrolled	Y
		Grill/Table	Y		

[6] Carolina Beach State Park
I-40, Exit 420
South side of Wilmington
N34 02.718 W77 54.246
State Rate: $17, Senior Discount
(910) 458-8206
http://www.ncparks.gov/Visit/parks/cabe/main.php

Directions

16 miles. Beyond Exit 420 proceed on Hwy 117 for 5 miles. Go straight for 10.4 miles on Hwy 132 (which is joined by Hwy 421). After Snow's Cut Bridge turn right on to Spencer Farlow Dr then left on Old Dow Rd, 0.7 miles to the Park.

Points of Interest

Tour the Wilmington historic district, with historic houses, plantations and the Airlie Gardens. There are also many museums including the WWII battleship North Carolina.

RV Sites		Water		Laundry	
Number	83	None		Wi-Fi	
Shaded	Y	At Site		Fishing	Y
By Water	Y	Spigots	Y	Hiking	Y
Paved		Sewer		Biking	Y
Pull Thru	Y	None		Swimming	
ADA	Y	At Site		Watch Wildlife	Y
Max RV Size	35	Dump Station	Y	Pets	Y
Electric		Amenities		Security	
None	Y	Restrooms	Y	Host(s)	Y
20 Amp		Showers	Y	Rangers(s)	Y
30 Amp		Reserve Sites	Y	Gate	Y
50 Amp		Store		Patrolled	Y
		Grill/Table	Y		

[7] Morrow Mountain State Park
I-73/74, Exit Hwy 24/27 Briscoe
East of Albemarie
N35 22.255 W80 06.276
State Rate: $17_$22, Senior Discount
(704) 982-4402

http://www.ncparks.gov/Visit/parks/momo/main.php

Directions

27 miles. From Hwy 24/27 Briscoe Exit go west on Hwy 24 for 23 miles. Turn north (right) on Valley Drive for 3.3 miles to Morrow Mountain Rd. Turn right to the Park

Points of Interest

Your are in the Albemarie Region, which is rich in Civil War and military history, unique shops, wineries and vineyards. Go to this website to discover your options -

http://www.albemarle-nc.com/attractions/

RV Sites		Water		Laundry		tub
Number	124	None		Wi-Fi		
Shaded	Y	At Site		Fishing	Y	
By Water		Spigots	Y	Hiking	Y	
Paved		Sewer		Biking	Y	
Pull Thru	Y	None		Swimming	Y	
ADA	Y	At Site		Watch Wildlife	Y	
Max RV Size	45	Dump Station	Y	Pets	Y	
Electric		Amenities		Security		
None		Restrooms	Y	Host(s)	Y	
20 Amp	Y	Showers	Y	Rangers(s)	Y	
30 Amp	Y	Reserve Sites	Y	Gate		
50 Amp	Y	Store		Patrolled	Y	
		Grill/Table	Y			

[8] Pilot Mountain State Park
I-74, Exit South of Pilot Mountain
South of Pilot Mountain
N36 20.623 W80 27.958
State Rate: $15, Senior Discount
(336) 325-2355

http://www.ncparks.gov/Visit/parks/pimo/main.php

Directions

Exit south of Pilot Mountain on to Pilot Mountain Park Rd. Turn west into the Park.

Points of Interest

From any direction you see Pilot Mountain rising over 1,400 feet above the countryside of the upper Piedmont plateau. Visit Horne Creek Farm, a historical farm near Pinnacle. The farm is a North Carolina State Historic Site depicting farm life in the northwest Piedmont area, circa 1900.

RV Sites		Water		Laundry	
Number	49	None		Wi-Fi	
Shaded	Y	At Site		Fishing	Y
By Water		Spigots	Y	Hiking	Y
Paved		Sewer		Biking	Y
Pull Thru	Y	None		Swimming	
ADA	Y	At Site		Watch Wildlife	
Max RV Size	35	Dump Station	Y	Pets	Y
Electric		Amenities		Security	
None	Y	Restrooms	Y	Host(s)	Y
20 Amp		Showers	Y	Rangers(s)	Y
30 Amp		Reserve Sites	Y	Gate	
50 Amp		Store		Patrolled	Y
		Grill/Table	Y		

[9] McDowell Nature Center & Preserve
I-77, Exit 1
Southwest of Charlotte
N35 06.038 W81 01.350
County Rate: $26-$33
(704) 583-1284

http://charmeck.org/mecklenburg/county/ParkandRec/StewardshipServices/NaturePreserves/Pages/McDowell.aspx

Directions

8 miles. From Exit 1 of I-77 go northwest on I-485 for 1 mile to exit 1 of I-485. Go southwest on Hwy 49 (S Tryon St, then York Rd) for 7 miles to McDowell Park Dr. Turn north to the Park.

Points of Interest

In Charlotte step aboard the Historic Charlotte Trolley in South End, or stroll along the tree-lined streets of Dilworth to experience the warmth & Queen City Southern hospitality.

RV Sites		Water		Laundry	
Number	56	None		Wi-Fi	
Shaded	Y	At Site	Y	Fishing	Y
By Water	Y	Spigots	Y	Hiking	Y
Paved	Y	Sewer		Biking	Y
Pull Thru	Y	None		Swimming	
ADA	Y	At Site		Watch Wildlife	Y
Max RV Size	40	Dump Station	Y	Pets	Y
Electric		Amenities		Security	
None		Restrooms	Y	Host(s)	Y
20 Amp	Y	Showers	Y	Rangers(s)	
30 Amp	Y	Reserve Sites	Y	Gate	Y
50 Amp	Y	Store		Patrolled	Y
		Grill/Table	Y		

[10] Stone Mountain State Park
I-77, Exits 83 or 85
Southwest of Mt. Airy
N36 22.626 W81 01.128
State Rate: $17-$22, Senior Discount
(336) 957-8185
http://www.ncparks.gov/Visit/parks/stmo/main.php

Directions

18 miles. **Northbound**, Exit 83 on to Hwy 21. **Southbound**, Exit 85, turn west on CC Camp Rd for 1 mi. to Hwy 21 & turn right. All follow Hwy 21 for 10 miles to Traphill Rd. Turn west 4.3 mi. to John P. Frank Pkwy. Turn right 2.5 mi. to the Park.

Points of Interest

Visit Mount Airy. A stroll down Main Street in the "Friendly City" reminds you of Mayberry on the popular '60s TV series. Show fans can visit Floyd's City Barber Shop, the Old Mayberry Jail, Snappy Lunch, even Andy's childhood home.

RV Sites		Water		Laundry	Y
Number	90	None		Wi-Fi	
Shaded	Y	At Site	Y	Fishing	Y
By Water	Y	Spigots	Y	Hiking	Y
Paved	Y	Sewer		Biking	Y
Pull Thru		None		Swimming	Y
ADA	Y	At Site		Watch Wildlife	Y
Max RV Size	45	Dump Station	Y	Pets	Y
Electric		Amenities		Security	
None		Restrooms	Y	Host(s)	Y
20 Amp	Y	Showers	Y	Rangers(s)	Y
30 Amp	Y	Reserve Sites	Y	Gate	
50 Amp	Y	Store		Patrolled	Y
		Grill/Table	Y		

[11] Dan Nicholas Park
I-85, Exit 76
South of Salisbury
N35 37.926 W80 21.256
County Rate: $17-$24
(704) 216-7808
http://www.dannicholas.net/

Directions

8 miles. From Exit 76 go south 0.4 miles on Hwy 52 to Newsome Rd. Turn left, go 1.0 mile to Bringle Ferry Rd. Turn right for 6 miles to the Park on your left.

Points of Interest

The Park is an adventure in itself. "Haden's Carousel" was given to Dan Nicholas Park in memory of Haden Holmes Hurley. Ride the narrow gauge train at Hurley Train Station. The New Aquarium, in a simulated habitat, includes a Nature Center.

RV Sites		Water		Laundry	
Number	70	None		Wi-Fi	
Shaded	Y	At Site	Y	Fishing	Y
By Water	Y	Spigots	Y	Hiking	Y
Paved		Sewer		Biking	Y
Pull Thru	Y	None		Swimming	
ADA	Y	At Site		Watch Wildlife	
Max RV Size	40	Dump Station	Y	Pets	Y
Electric		Amenities		Security	
None		Restrooms	Y	Host(s)	Y
20 Amp	Y	Showers	Y	Rangers(s)	Y
30 Amp	Y	Reserve Sites	Y	Gate	
50 Amp	Y	Store	Y	Patrolled	
		Grill/Table	Y		

[12] Kerr Lake SRA (Bullocksville Camp)
I-85, Exit 223
North of Henderson
N36 27.526 W78 21.885
State Rate: $17-$45, Senior Discount
(252) 438-7791
http://www.ncparks.gov/Visit/parks/kela/main.php

Directions

6 miles. From Exit 223 go 2 miles northwest on Manson Rd to Drewry Crossroads. Go straight through the crossroads onto Bullocksville Park Rd. Proceed 3.6 miles west to the camp.

Points of Interest

Kerr Lake, with over 850 miles of shoreline, is one of the largest lakes in the Southeast. It's also one of the most beautiful, from wooded shores to secluded coves to tranquil picnic areas. Classic cars are a reoccurring theme for the region, with many events to choose from.

RV Sites		Water		Laundry	
Number	60	None		Wi-Fi	
Shaded	Y	At Site	Y	Fishing	Y
By Water	Y	Spigots	Y	Hiking	Y
Paved		Sewer		Biking	Y
Pull Thru		None		Swimming	Y
ADA	Y	At Site		Watch Wildlife	Y
Max RV Size	45	Dump Station	Y	Pets	Y
Electric		Amenities		Security	
None		Restrooms	Y	Host(s)	Y
20 Amp	Y	Showers	Y	Rangers(s)	Y
30 Amp	Y	Reserve Sites	Y	Gate	
50 Amp	Y	Store	Y	Patrolled	Y
		Grill/Table	Y		

[13] Jones Lake State Park
I-95, Exit 20
Southeast of Fayetteville
N34 41.911 W78 36.248
State Rate: $17-$22, Senior Discount
(910) 588-4550
http://www.ncparks.gov/Visit/parks/jone/main.php

Directions

30 miles. From Exit 20 go southeast on Hwy 211 for 1.3 miles to Hwy 41. Turn left, go 23 miles on Hwy 41. Just north of Elizabethtown, turn north on Hwy 242. Proceed 5.4 miles to the park.

Points of Interest

Fayetteville knows what it means to be ready at a moment's notice and golf is no exception. With 20 courses by the likes of Davis Love III, Willard Byrd and Stuart Gooden, 360 holes and 19 miles of beautiful fairways, enjoy the fastest tee times, and best deals

RV Sites		Water		Laundry	
Number	20	None		Wi-Fi	
Shaded	Y	At Site		Fishing	Y
By Water		Spigots	Y	Hiking	Y
Paved		Sewer		Biking	Y
Pull Thru	few	None		Swimming	Y
ADA	Y	At Site		Watch Wildlife	Y
Max RV Size	40	Dump Station	Y	Pets	Y
Electric		Amenities		Security	
None	Y	Restrooms	Y	Host(s)	Y
20 Amp		Showers	Y	Ranger(s)	Y
30 Amp		Reserve Sites	Y	Gate	
50 Amp		Store		Patrolled	Y
		Grill/Table	Y		

NOTES:

About North Dakota's Public Campgrounds

The North Dakota Parks and Recreation Department manages state parks and recreation areas, most of which take camping reservations. The website for information is -

http://www.parkrec.nd.gov/index.html

Pets are welcome, provided they are restrained either by a 6 ft. leash or portable enclosure. Animals are not allowed on any designated swimming areas, playgrounds, in buildings, or other posted areas in a state park, except for animals used to assist the disabled. You are advised to leave out-of-state firewood at home. Firewood may be purchased through the park.

All motor vehicles entering a state park are required by statute to display a valid daily vehicle entrance permit or annual vehicle permit year-round. The daily fee is $5 per vehicle. There is a $4 online reservation fee, $8 Call Center fee. The remaining sites are first come, first serve. You are advised to make a reservation on holiday weekends and at selected parks on special event weekends. Campsite reservations may be made online. Campsite reservations have a 95-day advance window. The reservation website is -

https://apps.nd.gov/pnr/sp/services/public/reserve/mapview.htm

Campsite reservations may also be made by phoning (800) 807-4723.

The camping fees structure is:

Daily entrance fee (all parks):	**$ 5**
Electrical site -	**$18 - $20**
Electrical site with sewer hookup -	**$28 - $30**
Site without electricity -	**$10 - $12**
Little Missouri electricity -	**$12**
Cross Ranch electrical site -	**$15**

Little Missouri/Sully Creek site without electricity - $10

100% of North Dakota State Parks' visitor fees are used to maintain and operate the park system.

[1] Lindenwood Campground	**[6] Eggerts Landing Campground**
[2] Turtle River State Park	**[7] Fort Stevenson State Park**
[3] Icelandic State Park	**[8] Lewis and Clark State Park**
[4] Cottonwood Campground	**[9] Grahams Island State Park**
[5] Fort Abraham Lincoln State Park	

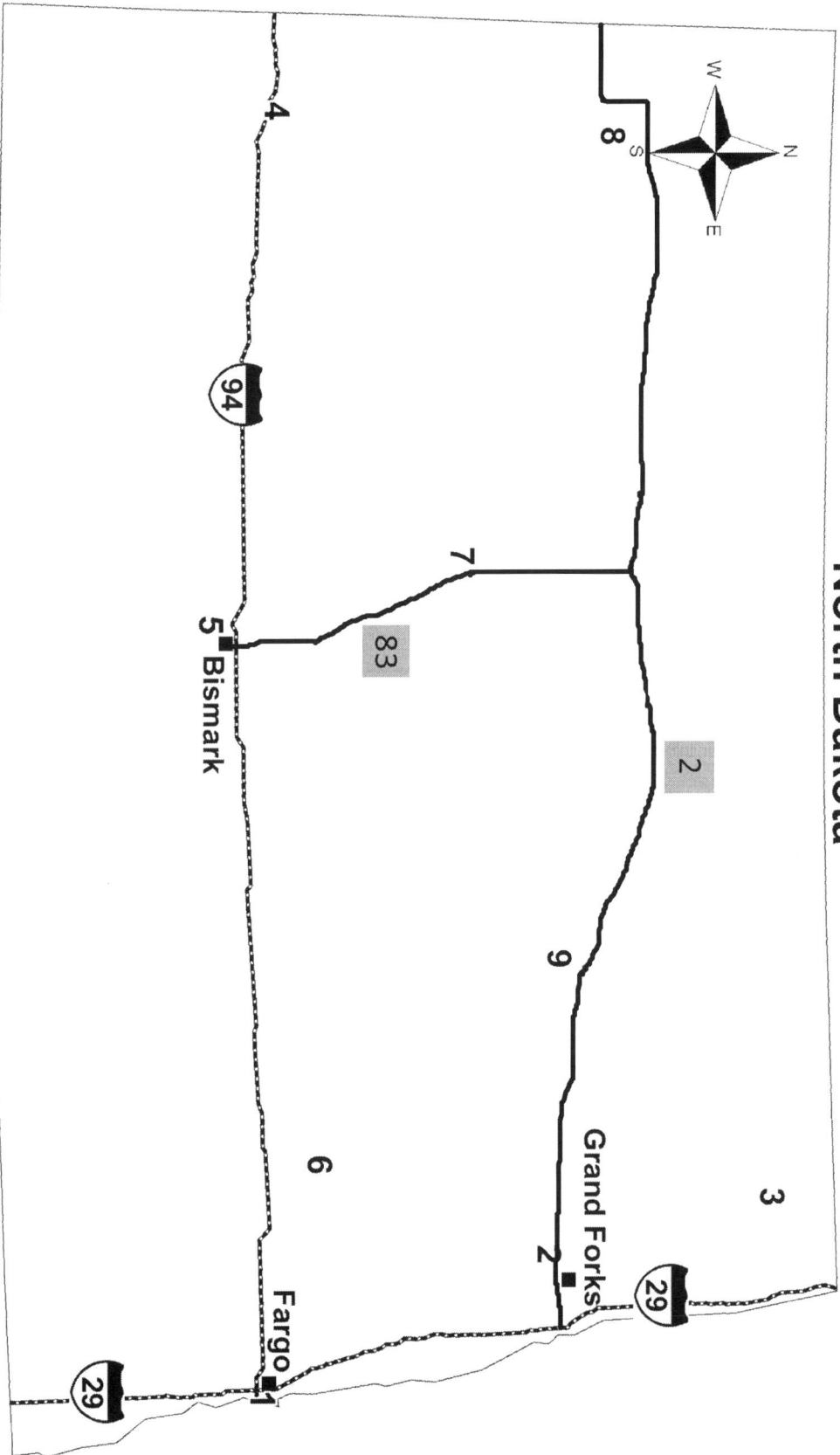

North Dakota

[1] Lindenwood Campground
I-29, Exit 63; I-94, Exit 351
South side of Fargo
N46 51.260 W96 47.257
County Rate: $28
(701) 232-3987
http://www.fargoparks.com/facility_camp.html

Directions

3 miles. From Exit 63 of I-29 go east for 2 miles on I-94 to Exit 351. Go north on University Dr. for 0.4 miles to 17th Ave. S. Turn east for 0.5 miles to the Park.

Points of Interest

There are a number of 'should see' destinations in Fargo - The Fargo Air Museum, the Celebrity Walk Of Fame with over 100 signatures, the 1926 restored Fargo Theatre vintage movie palace, Bonanzaville with 15 acres of historic buildings, & the Plains Art Museum.

RV Sites		Water		Laundry	
Number	46	None		Wi-Fi	
Shaded	Y	At Site	Y	Fishing	
By Water	Y	Spigots	Y	Hiking	
Paved	Y	Sewer		Biking	Y
Pull Thru		None		Swimming	
ADA	Y	At Site		Watch Wildlife	
Max RV Size	40	Dump Station	Y	Pets	Y
Electric		Amenities		Security	
None		Restrooms	Y	Host(s)	Y
20 Amp	Y	Showers	Y	Rangers(s)	Y
30 Amp	Y	Reserve Sites	Y	Gate	
50 Amp	Y	Store	Y	Patrolled	Y
		Grill/Table	Y		

[2] Turtle River State Park
I-29, Exit 141
West of Grand Forks
N47 55.968 W97 29.006
State Rate: See Introduction
(701) 594-4445
http://www.parkrec.nd.gov/parks/trsp/trsp.html

Directions

18 miles. From Exit 141 go west for 18 miles on Hwy 2. The Park entrance is just after Cty. Rd. 2 (30th St. NE).

Points of Interest

In Grand Forks visit Heritage Village, with it's steam engine threshing machines, museum displays, and demonstrations. Go downtown East Grand Forks to the Cabela's store. Enjoy the North Dakota Museum of Art, "a cultural jewel on the prairie."

RV Sites		Water		Laundry	
Number	125	None		Wi-Fi	
Shaded	Y	At Site	Y	Fishing	Y
By Water	Y	Spigots	Y	Hiking	Y
Paved		Sewer		Biking	Y
Pull Thru	Y	None		Swimming	
ADA	Y	At Site		Watch Wildlife	
Max RV Size	45	Dump Station	Y	Pets	Y
Electric		Amenities		Security	
None		Restrooms	Y	Host(s)	Y
20 Amp	Y	Showers	Y	Rangers(s)	Y
30 Amp	Y	Reserve Sites	Y	Gate	
50 Amp	Y	Store		Patrolled	Y
		Grill/Table	Y		

[3] Icelandic State Park
I-29, Exit 203
West of Joliette
N48 46.364 W97 44.373
State Rate: See Introduction
(701) 265-4561
http://www.parkrec.nd.gov/parks/isp/isp.html

Directions

24 miles. From Exit 203 go west for 24 miles on Hwy 5. The Park entrance is a mile after Cty Rd 12.

Points of Interest

Nearby attractions include Pembina County Museum, the Pioneer Machinery Site, Pembina State Museum, Gingras State Historic Site, Kittson Trading Post State Historic Site, Jay Wessel Wildlife Management Area, Frost Fire Mountain, and Pembina Gorge.

RV Sites		Water		Laundry	
Number	159	None		Wi-Fi	
Shaded	Y	At Site	Y	Fishing	Y
By Water	Y	Spigots	Y	Hiking	Y
Paved		Sewer		Biking	Y
Pull Thru	Y	None		Swimming	Y
ADA	Y	At Site		Watch Wildlife	Y
Max RV Size	45	Dump Station	Y	Pets	Y
Electric		Amenities		Security	
None		Restrooms	Y	Host(s)	Y
20 Amp	Y	Showers	Y	Rangers(s)	Y
30 Amp	Y	Reserve Sites	Y	Gate	
50 Amp	few	Store		Patrolled	Y
		Grill/Table	Y		

[4] Cottonwood Campground
I-94, Exit 24
Theodore Roosevelt National Park
N46 56.904 W103 31.682
NP Rate: $10
America/Beautiful Rate: $5
(701) 623-4466
http://www.nps.gov/thro/planyourvisit/camping.htm

Directions

7 miles. From Exit 24 go 1.5 miles south on Pacific Ave. to East River Rd. Turn north, follow East River Rd. for 5.6 miles to the Campground.

Points of Interest

Buffalo are know to wander through the campground. A major feature of the South Unit is the paved, 36 mile Scenic Loop Drive with pullouts & interpretive signs. The Painted Canyon Visitors Center provides unparalleled panoramic views of the North Dakota badlands.

RV Sites		Water		Laundry	
Number	76	None		Wi-Fi	
Shaded	Y	At Site		Fishing	Y
By Water	Y	Spigots	Y	Hiking	Y
Paved		Sewer		Biking	Y
Pull Thru	Y	None	Y	Swimming	
ADA	Y	At Site		Watch Wildlife	Y
Max RV Size	45	Dump Station		Pets	Y
Electric		Amenities		Security	
None	Y	Restrooms	Y	Host(s)	Y
20 Amp		Showers		Rangers(s)	Y
30 Amp		Reserve Sites		Gate	
50 Amp		Store		Patrolled	Y
		Grill/Table	Y		

[5] Fort Abraham Lincoln State Park
I-94, Exit 152
South of Mandan
N46 44.870 W100 50.360
State Rate: See Introduction
(701) 667-6340
http://www.parkrec.nd.gov/parks/flsp.htm

Directions

9 miles. From Exit 152 go south for 1.3 miles on Hwy 6 to Main St. Turn east (left), go 0.9 miles to Hwy 1806, turn south and go 3 miles to Pleasant Valley Rd. Bare right for 4 miles to the Park entrance on the left.

Points of Interest

The Fort was an important infantry & cavalry post. George Armstrong Custer & the Seventh Cavalry rode out on their ill-fated expedition against the Sioux at the Little Big Horn. Portions of the military post have been reconstructed.

RV Sites		Water		Laundry	
Number	57	None		Wi-Fi	
Shaded	Y	At Site	Y	Fishing	Y
By Water	Y	Spigots	Y	Hiking	Y
Paved		Sewer		Biking	Y
Pull Thru	Y	None		Swimming	
ADA	Y	At Site	Y	Watch Wildlife	Y
Max RV Size	45	Dump Station	Y	Pets	Y
Electric		Amenities		Security	
None		Restrooms	Y	Host(s)	Y
20 Amp	Y	Showers	Y	Rangers(s)	Y
30 Amp	Y	Reserve Sites	Y	Gate	
50 Amp	Y	Store	Y	Patrolled	Y
		Grill/Table	Y		

[6] Eggerts Landing Campground
I-94, Exit 292
North of Valley City
N47 05.736 W98 00.514
COE Rate: $26
America/Beautiful Rate: $13
(701) 845-2970
http://www.recreation.gov/

Directions

14 miles. From Exit 292 follow Cty Rd 21 signs through Valley City, 0.8 miles north on 8th Ave, then east for 0.5 miles on Main to 5th Ave, then turn north, still on Cty 21 for 12.3 miles to 22nd St. Turn west for 0.5 miles to the camp.

Points of Interest

Stop at the Valley City Visitor Center, which houses "Rosebud," an 1881 Northern Pacific Railcar. Browse Sheyenne Valley shops for antiques, artist wares, quilting supplies & unique dining.

RV Sites		Water		Laundry	
Number	37	None		Wi-Fi	
Shaded	Y	At Site		Fishing	Y
By Water	Y	Spigots	Y	Hiking	Y
Paved		Sewer		Biking	Y
Pull Thru		None		Swimming	Y
ADA	Y	At Site		Watch Wildlife	Y
Max RV Size	45	Dump Station	Y	Pets	Y
Electric		Amenities		Security	
None		Restrooms	Y	Host(s)	Y
20 Amp	Y	Showers	Y	Rangers(s)	Y
30 Amp	Y	Reserve Sites	Y	Gate	
50 Amp		Store		Patrolled	Y
		Grill/Table	Y		

[7] Fort Stevenson State Park
Hwy 83, West on Hwy 1804
South of Garrison
N47 35.770 W101 25.235
State Rate: See Introduction
(701) 337-5576
http://www.parkrec.nd.gov/parks/fssp/fssp.html

Directions

9.5 miles. At Hwy 83/1804 go west on Hwy 1804 for 6 miles to Garrison & Cty Rd 15 (41st Ave NW). Turn south for 3.5 miles to the Park.

Points of Interest

The Park is know as the walleye capital of North Dakota. Notable day trips could be the Audubon National Wildlife Refuge, Fort Mandan National Historic Site, Knife River Indian Villages National Historic Site, and North Dakota Lewis and Clark Interpretive Center.

RV Sites		Water		Laundry	
Number	125	None		Wi-Fi	
Shaded	Y	At Site	Y	Fishing	Y
By Water	Y	Spigots	Y	Hiking	Y
Paved		Sewer		Biking	Y
Pull Thru	Y	None		Swimming	Y
ADA	Y	At Site	Y	Watch Wildlife	Y
Max RV Size	45	Dump Station	Y	Pets	Y
Electric		Amenities		Security	
None		Restrooms	Y	Host(s)	Y
20 Amp	Y	Showers	Y	Rangers(s)	Y
30 Amp	Y	Reserve Sites	Y	Gate	
50 Amp	Y	Store	Y	Patrolled	Y
		Grill/Table	Y		

[8] Lewis and Clark State Park
Hwy 2, East on Broadway
East of Williston
N48 07.479 W103 14.164
State Rate: See Introduction
(701) 859-3071
http://www.parkrec.nd.gov/parks/lcsp/lcsp.html

Directions

20 miles. From Williston, take Broadway (becomes Hwy 1804) east for 17 miles to Cty Rd 15. Turn south for 3 miles to the Park.

Points of Interest

The rugged buttes of the North Dakota Badlands provide a towering backdrop to the camp. Meriwether Lewis and William Clark camped nearby on April 17, 1805. Lake Sakakawea offers excellent fishing (Walleye, Sauger, Northern Pike); two rare species, the pallid sturgeon & prehistoric-looking paddlefish, can occasionally be found.

RV Sites		Water		Laundry	
Number	63	None		Wi-Fi	Y
Shaded	Y	At Site	Y	Fishing	Y
By Water	Y	Spigots	Y	Hiking	Y
Paved		Sewer		Biking	Y
Pull Thru	Y	None		Swimming	Y
ADA	Y	At Site	Y	Watch Wildlife	Y
Max RV Size	45	Dump Station	Y	Pets	Y
Electric		Amenities		Security	
None		Restrooms	Y	Host(s)	Y
20 Amp	Y	Showers	Y	Rangers(s)	Y
30 Amp	Y	Reserve Sites	Y	Gate	
50 Amp	Y	Store	Y	Patrolled	Y
		Grill/Table	Y		

[9] Grahams Island State Park
Hwy 2, West on Hwy 19
West of Devils Lake
N48 03.199 W99 04.25
State Rate: See Introduction
(701) 766-4015
http://www.parkrec.nd.gov/parks/gisp/gisp.html

Directions

12.6 miles. In Devils Lake, take Hwy 19 west, 9.6 miles to 72nd Ave NE. Turn south for 3 miles over the elevated embankment to the park.

Points of Interest

Take a day trip to Fort Totten, one of the best preserved military forts of the frontier era, west of the Mississippi River. The Fort is operated by Fort Totten State Historic Site Foundation & located within the Historic Site. Take a walking tour of 16 original 1870 buildings. Have a meal at the Totten Trail Historic Inn.

RV Sites		Water		Laundry	
Number	144	None		Wi-Fi	
Shaded	some	At Site	Y	Fishing	Y
By Water	Y	Spigots	Y	Hiking	Y
Paved		Sewer		Biking	Y
Pull Thru	Y	None		Swimming	Y
ADA	Y	At Site	Y	Watch Wildlife	Y
Max RV Size	45	Dump Station	Y	Pets	Y
Electric		Amenities		Security	
None		Restrooms	Y	Host(s)	Y
20 Amp	Y	Showers	Y	Rangers(s)	Y
30 Amp	Y	Reserve Sites	Y	Gate	
50 Amp	Y	Store	Y	Patrolled	Y
		Grill/Table	Y		

About Ohio's Public Campgrounds

The Division of Parks, a unit of the Ohio Department of Natural Resources, is responsible for the System of 74 State Parks. Spread across the Parks are nine resort lodges, three dining lodges, six golf courses, more than 9,000 campsites in 57 family campgrounds, 36 visitor/nature centers, 80 swimming beaches and 19 swimming pools, 188 boat ramps and 7,583 boat docks, and 1,167 miles of trails. Most Ohio State Park campgrounds are open year-round. You can find information at - **http://parks.ohiodnr.gov/**

The state park resort lodges, along with newer state park facilities and older facilities that have been renovated, offer a variety of accessible features such as fishing piers, launch ramps, trails, picnic sites and campsites. Campsites with accessible features may include extra wide paved pads on level grades, berms, modified picnic tables, fire rings and/or grills, or water fountains, and may be close to restroom buildings with entrance ramps, accessible fixtures, grab bars and wide stalls. All state park campgrounds allow pets, and many have designated areas for pets. Pets must be on a leash not exceeding 6 feet in length and must be under control at all times. Proof of rabies shots and a physical description of the animals is required upon request. You should not bring your own firewood.

Ohio remains one of the few states in the country that does not charge a general admission or parking fee at its 74 state parks. Camping reservations are encouraged, but not required. You can make your reservation up to 6 months in advance of arrival. Most campgrounds offer dump stations free of charge to registered campers. Ice and firewood are available at most campgrounds. You can make reservations (there is a $8.25 fee) at -

http://www.ohio.reserveworld.com/

You can also contact the Call Center at (866) 644-6727.

Ohio has six national parks. Cuyahoga Valley National offers camping and a variety of outdoor recreational activities. Perry's Victory and International Peace Memorial is located at Put-in-Bay on South Bass Island. The James A. Garfield National Historic Site is in Mentor. The Hopewell Culture National Historic Park is located near Chillicothe. The Dayton Aviation Heritage National Historic Park includes three landmarks around town. The William Howard Taft National Historic Site is located in Cincinnati.

NOTES:

[1] Hueston Woods State Park	[13] Maumee Bay State Park
[2] Buck Creek State Park	[14] Mill Creek (Berlin Reservoir)
[3] Dillon State Park	[15] Wolf Run State Park
[4] Barkcamp State Park	[16] Salt Fork State Park
[5] Caesar Creek State Park	[17] Harrison Lake State Park
[6] Deer Creek State Park	]18] East Harbor State Park
[7] Alum Creek State Park	[19] Geneva State Park
[8] Mt. Gilead State Park	[20] Miami Whitewater Forest Camp
[9] Mohican State Park	[21] Stonelick State Park
[10] Findley State Park	[22] Gallia County Junior Fairgrounds
[11] Lake Loramie State Park	[23] Jackson Lake State Park
[12] Indian Lake State Park	[24] Scioto Trail State Park

NOTES:

Ohio

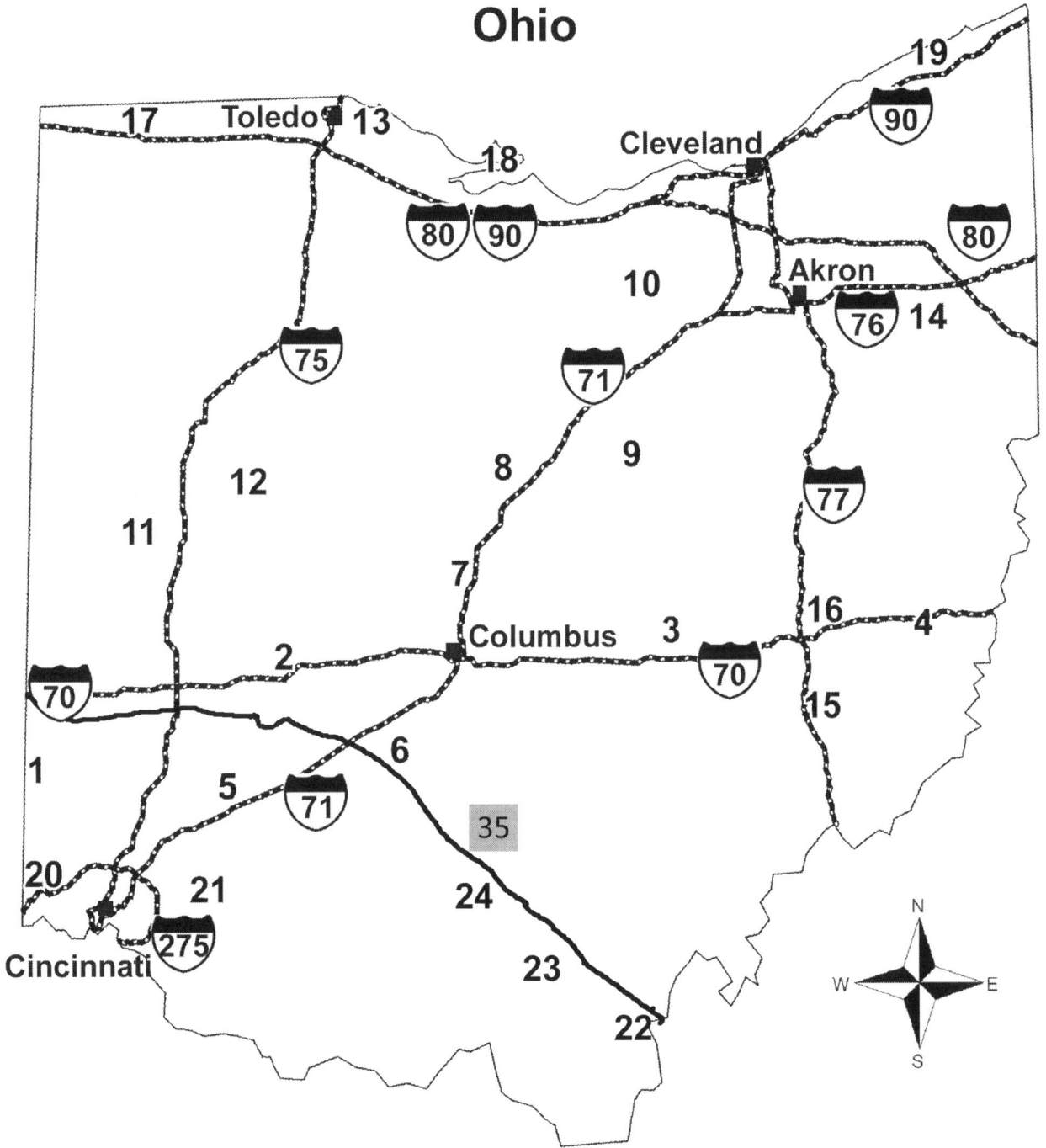

[1] Hueston Woods State Park
I-70, Exit 10
South of Eaton
N39 35.678 W84 45.896
State Rate: $20-$25
(513) 523-6347
http://parks.ohiodnr.gov/huestonwoods

Directions

24 miles. From Exit 10 go south for 14.7 miles (through Eaton) to Camden. In Camden turn west on W Central (Hwy 725), go 6 mi. to Hwy 177. Turn south for 1.8 miles, then west on Camden-College Corner Rd for 1.5 miles to the Park.

Points of Interest

Enjoy a meal at the Lodge, situated on a bluff overlooking Acton Lake. At the Nature Center, attend bird and flower walks, slide talks, and fossil hunts. Lake access for dogs offers a place for your pets to frolic and swim.

RV Sites		Water		Laundry	Y
Number	488	None		Wi-Fi	Y
Shaded	Y	At Site		Fishing	Y
By Water	Y	Spigots	Y	Hiking	Y
Paved	Y	Sewer		Biking	Y
Pull Thru	Y	None		Swimming	Y
ADA	Y	At Site		Watch Wildlife	Y
Max RV Size	45	Dump Station	Y	Pets	Y
Electric		Amenities		Security	
None		Restrooms	Y	Host(s)	Y
20 Amp	Y	Showers	Y	Rangers(s)	Y
30 Amp	Y	Reserve Sites	Y	Gate	
50 Amp		Store	Y	Patrolled	Y
		Grill/Table	Y		

[2] Buck Creek State Park
I-70, Exit 62
Northeast side of Springfield
N39 56.759 W83 43.768
State Rate: $23-$27
(937) 322-5284
http://parks.ohiodnr.gov/buckcreek

Directions

4 miles. From Exit 62 go west for 2.4 miles on Hwy 40 (National Rd) to N. Bird Rd. Turn right, go 1.7 miles to the Park entrance.

Points of Interest

Springfield offers amenities such as awesome antiquing, the Clark State Performing Arts Center, the Springfield Museum of Art and Frank Lloyd Wright's Westcott House. The city's architectural heritage is on full display around every corner.

RV Sites		Water		Laundry	
Number	111	None		Wi-Fi	
Shaded	Y	At Site		Fishing	Y
By Water	Y	Spigots	Y	Hiking	Y
Paved	Y	Sewer		Biking	
Pull Thru		None		Swimming	Y
ADA	Y	At Site		Watch Wildlife	
Max RV Size	35	Dump Station	Y	Pets	Y
Electric		Amenities		Security	
None		Restrooms	Y	Host(s)	Y
20 Amp	Y	Showers	Y	Rangers(s)	Y
30 Amp	Y	Reserve Sites	Y	Gate	
50 Amp		Store		Patrolled	Y
		Grill/Table	Y		

[3] Dillon State Park
I-70, Exit 153 (State St.)
Northeast of Zanesville
N40 01.744 W82 06.181
State Rate: $19-$25
(740) 452-1083
http://parks.ohiodnr.gov/dillon

Directions

8 miles. From Exit 153: **westbound**, at State St. turn right 0.3 mi. to Hwy 146, then turn left; **eastbound**, from the off ramp immediately turn right on Jackson St, go 2 blocks and turn right on Old Newark Rd, go 0.5 mi. to Hwy 146, turn left. All travelers, go 7.3 mi. on Hwy 146 to Clay Littick Dr, turn left into the Park.

Points of Interest

Downtown Zanesville is becoming one of the premiere artist communities in Ohio. Visit Dresden, birthplace of the Longaberger Basket.

RV Sites		Water		Laundry	Y
Number	195	None		Wi-Fi	Y
Shaded	Y	At Site		Fishing	Y
By Water	Y	Spigots	Y	Hiking	Y
Paved	Y	Sewer		Biking	Y
Pull Thru		None		Swimming	Y
ADA	Y	At Site		Watch Wildlife	
Max RV Size	45	Dump Station	Y	Pets	Y
Electric		Amenities		Security	
None		Restrooms	Y	Host(s)	Y
20 Amp	Y	Showers	Y	Rangers(s)	Y
30 Amp	Y	Reserve Sites	Y	Gate	
50 Amp	Y	Store	Y	Patrolled	Y
		Grill/Table	Y		

[4] Barkcamp State Park
I-70, Exit 208
Southeast of Morristown
N40 02.810 W81 01.867
State Rate: $22
(740) 484-4064
http://parks.ohiodnr.gov/barkcamp

Directions

1.6 miles. From Exit 208 go south for 0.7 miles on Hwy 149. Turn east on Hwy 92 (Barkcamp Park Rd) for 0.9 miles to the Park.

Points of Interest

The Belmont County Museum, an impressive Romanesque-style mansion, built in 1888 with 26 rooms, houses a quilt collection, antique farm implements and interesting relics of the "Gay 90's" period. The nearby Quaker Friends Meeting House, a large restored building was built in 1914.

RV Sites		Water		Laundry	
Number	123	None		Wi-Fi	
Shaded	Y	At Site		Fishing	Y
By Water	Y	Spigots	Y	Hiking	Y
Paved	Y	Sewer		Biking	Y
Pull Thru		None		Swimming	Y
ADA	Y	At Site		Watch Wildlife	Y
Max RV Size	35	Dump Station	Y	Pets	Y
Electric		Amenities		Security	
None		Restrooms	Y	Host(s)	Y
20 Amp	Y	Showers	Y	Rangers(s)	Y
30 Amp	Y	Reserve Sites	Y	Gate	
50 Amp	Y	Store	Y	Patrolled	Y
		Grill/Table	Y		

[5] Caesar Creek State Park
I-71, Exit 45
Northeast of Lebanon
N39 32.318 W83 58.440
State Rate: $28
(513) 897-3055
http://parks.ohiodnr.gov/caesarcreek

Directions

4.7 miles. From Exit 45 go a short distance east and just past Denny Rd turn left on Hwy 380. Go 3 miles to Center Rd. Turn left, go 1.6 miles to the Park.

Points of Interest

Explore the Caesar Creek Gorge nature preserve, featuring a 180 foot deep gorge displaying unique geologic formations. The Little Miami Scenic River offers canoeing and spectacular scenery. USA Today called Lebanon one of the "Ten Great Places to Browse for Antiques."

RV Sites		Water		Laundry	
Number	283	None		Wi-Fi	
Shaded		At Site		Fishing	Y
By Water	Y	Spigots	Y	Hiking	Y
Paved	Y	Sewer		Biking	Y
Pull Thru		None		Swimming	Y
ADA	Y	At Site		Watch Wildlife	
Max RV Size	40	Dump Station	Y	Pets	Y
Electric		Amenities		Security	
None		Restrooms	Y	Host(s)	Y
20 Amp	Y	Showers	Y	Rangers(s)	Y
30 Amp	Y	Reserve Sites	Y	Gate	
50 Amp	Y	Store		Patrolled	Y
		Grill/Table	Y		

[6] Deer Creek State Park
I-71, Exit 84
Southwest of Columbus
N39 39.137 W83 14.733
State Rate: $28
(740) 869-3124
http://parks.ohiodnr.gov/deercreek

Directions

9 miles. From Exit 84 go 3.3 miles south on Hwy 56 into Mt. Sterling. Turn right on Hwy 207 (Columbus St) and go 0.3 miles, then bare left on Hwy 207 for 3.9 miles to Crooks-Yankeetown Rd. Turn left, go 1.4 miles to the Park entrance.

Points of Interest

The Park is central Ohio's vacation showplace. A collage of meadows & woodlands surround a scenic reservoir. This resort park features a modern lodge, cottages, campground, golf course, swimming beach and boating for outdoor enthusiasts.

RV Sites		Water		Laundry	
Number	227	None		Wi-Fi	
Shaded	Y	At Site		Fishing	Y
By Water	Y	Spigots	Y	Hiking	Y
Paved	Y	Sewer		Biking	Y
Pull Thru		None		Swimming	Y
ADA	Y	At Site		Watch Wildlife	Y
Max RV Size	45	Dump Station	Y	Pets	Y
Electric		Amenities		Security	
None		Restrooms	Y	Host(s)	Y
20 Amp	Y	Showers	Y	Rangers(s)	Y
30 Amp	Y	Reserve Sites	Y	Gate	
50 Amp	Y	Store	Y	Patrolled	Y
		Grill/Table	Y		

[7] Alum Creek State Park
I-71, Exit 131
North of Columbus
N40 14.217 W82 59.235
State Rate: $29-$38
(740) 548-4631
http://parks.ohiodnr.gov/alumcreek

Directions

6 miles. From Exit 131 go 3 miles west on Hwy 36/37 to Lacky Old State Rd 10. Turn south for 3 miles to the Park Welcome Center on the left.

Points of Interest

Tour the Olentangy Indian Caverns, learn the techniques of historic gem mining. Visit the Delaware County Fairgrounds, renowned for the Little Brown Jug harness race. Shop Easton Town Center, wander the Short North Arts District, buy your fresh food items at North Market.

RV Sites		Water		Laundry	
Number	286	None		Wi-Fi	
Shaded	Y	At Site	Y	Fishing	Y
By Water	Y	Spigots	Y	Hiking	Y
Paved	Y	Sewer		Biking	Y
Pull Thru		None		Swimming	Y
ADA	Y	At Site	Y	Watch Wildlife	
Max RV Size	45	Dump Station	Y	Pets	Y
Electric		Amenities		Security	
None		Restrooms	Y	Host(s)	Y
20 Amp	Y	Showers	Y	Rangers(s)	Y
30 Amp	Y	Reserve Sites	Y	Gate	
50 Amp	Y	Store		Patrolled	Y
		Grill/Table	Y		

[8] Mt. Gilead State Park
I-71, Exit 151
East side of Mt. Gilead
N40 32.746 W82 48.533
State Rate: $22
(419) 946-1961
http://parks.ohiodnr.gov/mountgilead

Directions

6 miles. From Exit 151 go west for 6 miles on Hwy 95 to the Park entrance on the right, which you will find just before entering Mt. Gilead.

Points of Interest

Places to visit include the Fostoria Glass Museum, Seneca Caverns, Sorrowful Mother Shrine, the home of William G. Harding, and the Tiffin Glass Museum. You will also find many antiquing opportunities, fairs, festivals, farm days, and lots of home cooking!

RV Sites		Water		Laundry	
Number	59	None		Wi-Fi	
Shaded	Y	At Site		Fishing	Y
By Water	Y	Spigots	Y	Hiking	Y
Paved		Sewer		Biking	Y
Pull Thru		None		Swimming	
ADA	Y	At Site	Y	Watch Wildlife	
Max RV Size	45	Dump Station	Y	Pets	Y
Electric		Amenities		Security	
None		Restrooms	Y	Host(s)	Y
20 Amp	Y	Showers		Rangers(s)	Y
30 Amp	Y	Reserve Sites	Y	Gate	
50 Amp	Y	Store		Patrolled	Y
		Grill/Table	Y		

[9] Mohican State Park
I-71, Exit 165
Southeast of Mansfield
N40 36.578 W82 15.446
State Rate: $21-$39
(419) 994-5125
http://parks.ohiodnr.gov/mohican

Directions

19 miles. From Exit 165 go east for 18.6 miles on Hwy 97, passing through Bellville and Butler. Turn left at Hwy 3, go 0.3 miles to the Park entrance on your left.

Points of Interest

Enjoy a meal at the Park lodge. The Pine Run Grist Mill, in the Park, features an overshot waterwheel that powers two millstones where grain was ground into flour. Visit Malabar Farm State Park, home of noted conservationist Louis Bromfield.

RV Sites		Water		Laundry	
Number	186	None		Wi-Fi	Y
Shaded	Y	At Site	Y	Fishing	Y
By Water	Y	Spigots	Y	Hiking	Y
Paved	Y	Sewer		Biking	Y
Pull Thru		None		Swimming	Y
ADA	Y	At Site	Y	Watch Wildlife	Y
Max RV Size	45	Dump Station	Y	Pets	Y
Electric		Amenities		Security	
None		Restrooms	Y	Host(s)	Y
20 Amp	Y	Showers	Y	Rangers(s)	Y
30 Amp	Y	Reserve Sites	Y	Gate	
50 Amp	Y	Store	Y	Patrolled	Y
		Grill/Table	Y		

[10] Findley State Park
I-71, Exit 186
Southwest of Cleveland
N41 08.028 W82 13.144
State Rate: $23-$27
(440) 647-5749
http://parks.ohiodnr.gov/findley

Directions

23 miles. From Exit 186 go west on Hwy 250 for 1.4 miles to Hwy 42. Go north on Hwy 42 for 1 mile to the Hwy 250 Bypass. Take the Bypass west for 1.5 miles & exit on to Hwy 58 north. Follow Hwy 58 for 18.7 miles north to the Park.

Points of Interest

Findley State Park, once a state forest, is heavily wooded with stately pines and various hardwoods. The scenic hiking trails allow nature lovers to view spectacular wildflowers and observe wildlife.

RV Sites		Water			Laundry	Y
Number	271	None			Wi-Fi	
Shaded	Y	At Site			Fishing	Y
By Water	Y	Spigots	Y		Hiking	Y
Paved		Sewer			Biking	Y
Pull Thru	Y	None			Swimming	
ADA	Y	At Site			Watch Wildlife	Y
Max RV Size	45	Dump Station	Y		Pets	Y
Electric		Amenities			Security	
None		Restrooms	Y		Host(s)	Y
20 Amp	Y	Showers	Y		Rangers(s)	Y
30 Amp	Y	Reserve Sites	Y		Gate	
50 Amp	Y	Store			Patrolled	Y
		Grill/Table	Y			

[11] Lake Loramie State Park
I-75, Exit 99
Northwest of Sidney
N40 21.455 W84 21.437
State Rate: $21-$27
(937) 295-2011
http://parks.ohiodnr.gov/lakeloramie

Directions

14 miles. From Exit 99 go west on Hwy 119 for 10.8 miles to Paris St on the east edge of Minster. Turn south for 0.5 miles to Hwy 362. Turn left, go 2.5 miles to the Park entrance on your left.

Points of Interest Also see [11]

Named in honor of Neil Armstrong, first man to set foot on the moon, the museum in Wapakoneta chronicles Ohio's contributions to space flight. Among the items on display are the F5D Sky Lancer, the Gemini VIII spacecraft, Apollo 11 artifacts and a moon rock.

RV Sites		Water			Laundry	
Number	175	None			Wi-Fi	Y
Shaded		At Site			Fishing	Y
By Water	Y	Spigots	Y		Hiking	Y
Paved	Y	Sewer			Biking	Y
Pull Thru	Y	None			Swimming	Y
ADA	Y	At Site			Watch Wildlife	Y
Max RV Size	45	Dump Station	Y		Pets	Y
Electric		Amenities			Security	
None		Restrooms	Y		Host(s)	Y
20 Amp	Y	Showers	Y		Rangers(s)	Y
30 Amp	Y	Reserve Sites	Y		Gate	
50 Amp	Y	Store	Y		Patrolled	Y
		Grill/Table	Y			

[12] Indian Lake State Park
I-75, Exit 110
East of Wapakoneta
N40 31.119 W83 54.027
State Rate: $26-$36
(937) 843-2717
http://parks.ohiodnr.gov/indianlake

Directions

16 miles. From Exit 110 go east and south for 14 miles on Hwy 33. Continue to follow Hwy 33 when it turns south in New Hampshire. Turn east on Hwy 366, continue straight on Hwy 235, when 366 turns south, for 1.8 miles in all to the Park.

Points of Interest Also see [11]

Tour the Piatt Castles. These 19th century homes opened in the 1910s. The castles contain collections of Native American tools, books, military artifacts & family furnishings from 2 centuries.

RV Sites		Water			Laundry	Y
Number	452	None			Wi-Fi	
Shaded	Y	At Site	Y		Fishing	Y
By Water	Y	Spigots	Y		Hiking	Y
Paved	Y	Sewer			Biking	Y
Pull Thru		None			Swimming	Y
ADA	Y	At Site	Y		Watch Wildlife	Y
Max RV Size	45	Dump Station	Y		Pets	Y
Electric		Amenities			Security	
None		Restrooms	Y		Host(s)	Y
20 Amp	Y	Showers	Y		Rangers(s)	Y
30 Amp	Y	Reserve Sites	Y		Gate	
50 Amp	Y	Store	Y		Patrolled	Y
		Grill/Table	Y			

[13] Maumee Bay State Park
I-75, Exit 208
East of Toledo
N41 40.482 W83 22.260
State Rate: $28
(419) 836-7758
http://parks.ohiodnr.gov/maumeebay

Directions

12.5 miles. From Exit 208 go 3.5 miles south on I-280 to Exit 7. Turn east on Hwy 2 (Navarre Ave) and go 6.3 miles to N Curtice Rd. Turn north for 2.5 miles to the Park entrance.

Points of Interest

Enjoy a meal at Quilter Lodge, which overlooks the Maumee Bay of Lake Erie. Trautman Nature Center is equipped with inter-active displays, a programming auditorium, research laboratory and viewing windows. Toledo is close by and has many sites and destinations.

RV Sites		Water		Laundry	Y
Number	252	None		Wi-Fi	Y
Shaded	Y	At Site		Fishing	Y
By Water	Y	Spigots	Y	Hiking	Y
Paved	Y	Sewer		Biking	Y
Pull Thru		None		Swimming	Y
ADA	Y	At Site		Watch Wildlife	Y
Max RV Size	45	Dump Station	Y	Pets	Y
Electric		Amenities		Security	
None		Restrooms	Y	Host(s)	Y
20 Amp	Y	Showers	Y	Rangers(s)	Y
30 Amp	Y	Reserve Sites	Y	Gate	
50 Amp	Y	Store	Y	Patrolled	Y
		Grill/Table	Y		

[14] Mill Creek (Berlin Reservoir)
I-76, Exit 54
East of Akron
N41 00.623 W80 59.174
COE Rate: $14-$24
America/Beautiful Rate: $7-$12
(330) 547-8180
http://www.recreation.gov/

Directions

8.5 miles. From Exit 54 go 5.4 miles south on Hwy 534 (Pricetown Rd) to Hwy 224. Turn west, go 2.1 miles to Bedell Rd. Turn south for 1 mile. Turn west to Mill Creek Campground.

Points of Interest

Berlin Lake is renowned for its excellent walleye fishing. Berlin Lake also has nesting ospreys, beaver, and occasional sightings of bald eagles. Also visit Noah's Lost Ark Animal Sanctuary.

RV Sites		Water		Laundry	
Number	348	None		Wi-Fi	
Shaded	Y	At Site		Fishing	Y
By Water	Y	Spigots	Y	Hiking	Y
Paved		Sewer		Biking	Y
Pull Thru		None		Swimming	Y
ADA	Y	At Site		Watch Wildlife	Y
Max RV Size	45	Dump Station	Y	Pets	Y
Electric		Amenities		Security	
None		Restrooms	Y	Host(s)	Y
20 Amp	Y	Showers	Y	Rangers(s)	Y
30 Amp	Y	Reserve Sites	Y	Gate	
50 Amp	Y	Store	Y	Patrolled	
		Grill/Table	Y		

[15] Wolf Run State Park
I-77, Exit 28
South of Cambridge
N39 47.387 W81 32.411
State Rate: $20-$24
(740) 732-5035
http://parks.ohiodnr.gov/wolfrun

Directions

1 mile. From Exit 28 go south but immediately turn left on Main St. Proceed straight on to and follow Cty Rd 126 (Wolf Run Rd), 1 mile in all to the Park entrance on your left.

Points of Interest Also see [15]

Cambridge is the birthplace of John Glenn, U.S. Senator & American Astronaut & William "Hopalong Cassidy" Boyd - both have historic sites. Glass is a major attraction, including the National Museum of Cambridge Glass & Degenhart Paperweight & Glass Museum.

RV Sites		Water		Laundry	Y
Number	138	None		Wi-Fi	
Shaded	Y	At Site		Fishing	Y
By Water	Y	Spigots	Y	Hiking	Y
Paved	Y	Sewer		Biking	Y
Pull Thru		None		Swimming	Y
ADA	Y	At Site		Watch Wildlife	Y
Max RV Size	45	Dump Station	Y	Pets	Y
Electric		Amenities		Security	
None		Restrooms	Y	Host(s)	Y
20 Amp	Y	Showers	Y	Rangers(s)	Y
30 Amp	Y	Reserve Sites	Y	Gate	
50 Amp	Y	Store	Y	Patrolled	Y
		Grill/Table	Y		

[16] Salt Fork State Park
I-77, Exit 47
N40 04.930 W81 27.583
Northeast of Cambridge
State Rate: $27-$36
(740) 439-3521
http://parks.ohiodnr.gov/saltfork

Directions

6 mile. From Exit 47 go east for 6 miles on Hwy 22 (Cadiz Rd) to Hwy 1. Turn north into the Park.

Points of Interest Also see [15]

Salt Fork Lodge features a dining room, coffee shop, & gift shop. A miniature golf course is at the beach, near the park's nature center. History buffs will enjoy Roscoe Village in Coshocton, a restored early 1800s canal town featuring historic buildings and special activities.

RV Sites		Water			Laundry	
Number	212	None			Wi-Fi	Y
Shaded	some	At Site	Y		Fishing	Y
By Water	Y	Spigots	Y		Hiking	Y
Paved	Y	Sewer			Biking	Y
Pull Thru		None			Swimming	Y
ADA	Y	At Site	Y		Watch Wildlife	Y
Max RV Size	45	Dump Station	Y		Pets	Y
Electric		Amenities			Security	
None		Restrooms	Y		Host(s)	Y
20 Amp	Y	Showers	Y		Rangers(s)	Y
30 Amp	Y	Reserve Sites	Y		Gate	
50 Amp	Y	Store	Y		Patrolled	Y
		Grill/Table	Y			

[17] Harrison Lake State Park
I-80/90, Exit 25
N41 38.232 W84 21.737
Northeast of West Unity
State Rate: $19-$25
(419) 237-2593
http://parks.ohiodnr.gov/harrisonlake

Directions

5.5 miles. From Exit 25 go north on Hwy 66 for 3.5 miles to Cty Rd M. Turn west, go 2 miles to the Park Check-in Station on your right.

Points of Interest

Visit the Sauder Museum, Farm and Craft Village. The large complex includes an 1860s home, barnyard, the Craft Village, a museum displaying antique tools and farm implements, and a restored barn housing a restaurant with country-style cooking.

RV Sites		Water			Laundry	Y
Number	173	None			Wi-Fi	
Shaded	Y	At Site			Fishing	Y
By Water	Y	Spigots	Y		Hiking	Y
Paved	Y	Sewer			Biking	Y
Pull Thru		None			Swimming	Y
ADA	Y	At Site			Watch Wildlife	
Max RV Size	45	Dump Station	Y		Pets	Y
Electric		Amenities			Security	
None		Restrooms	Y		Host(s)	Y
20 Amp	Y	Showers	Y		Rangers(s)	Y
30 Amp	Y	Reserve Sites	Y		Gate	
50 Amp	Y	Store	Y		Patrolled	Y
		Grill/Table	Y			

[18] East Harbor State Park
I-80/90, Exit 91
East of Port Clinton
N41 32.495 W82 49.218
State Rate: $21-$36
(419) 734-4424
http://parks.ohiodnr.gov/eastharbor

Directions

21 miles. From Exit 91 go northeast for 10 miles on Hwy 53 (W Freemont Rd). Turn east on Hwy 2 for 7.1 miles to Hwy 269. Follow Hwy 269 for 3.8 miles to the Park entrance.

Points of Interest

Tour Marblehead Lighthouse, in the village of Marblehead, the oldest lighthouse in operation on the Great Lakes. Other activities include Stonehenge Estate, riding the ferry, or relaxing at Crystal Cave and Heineman's Winery, or Mon Ami Winery.

RV Sites		Water			Laundry	Y
Number	571	None			Wi-Fi	Y
Shaded	Y	At Site	Y		Fishing	Y
By Water	Y	Spigots	Y		Hiking	Y
Paved	Y	Sewer			Biking	Y
Pull Thru	Y	None			Swimming	Y
ADA	Y	At Site	Y		Watch Wildlife	Y
Max RV Size	40	Dump Station	Y		Pets	Y
Electric		Amenities			Security	
None		Restrooms	Y		Host(s)	Y
20 Amp	Y	Showers	Y		Rangers(s)	Y
30 Amp	Y	Reserve Sites	Y		Gate	
50 Amp	Y	Store	Y		Patrolled	Y
		Grill/Table	Y			

[19] Geneva State Park
I-90, Exit 218
North of Geneva
N41 50.748 W80 57.565
State Rate: $21-$34
(440) 466-8400
http://parks.ohiodnr.gov/geneva

Directions

5.5 miles. From Exit 218 go 5.5 miles north on Hwy 534, through Geneva, to the Park entrance.

Points of Interest

The Lodge and Conference Center at Geneva-on-the-Lake provides beautiful views of Lake Erie. Enjoy a meal at the full-service restaurant. You are in Ashtabula County, home to 16 covered bridges, 15 award-winning wineries, nineteen museums, and two wild & scenic rivers

RV Sites		Water		Laundry	Y
Number	100	None		Wi-Fi	Y
Shaded	Y	At Site	Y	Fishing	Y
By Water	Y	Spigots	Y	Hiking	Y
Paved	Y	**Sewer**		Biking	Y
Pull Thru		None		Swimming	Y
ADA	Y	At Site	Y	Watch Wildlife	
Max RV Size	45	Dump Station	Y	Pets	Y
Electric		**Amenities**		**Security**	
None		Restrooms	Y	Host(s)	Y
20 Amp	Y	Showers	Y	Rangers(s)	Y
30 Amp	Y	Reserve Sites	Y	Gate	
50 Amp		Store		Patrolled	Y
		Grill/Table	Y		

[20] Miami Whitewater Forest Camp
I-275, Exit 25; to I-74, Exit 3
Northwest of Cincinnati
N39 15.252 W84 45.734
Hamilton County Rate: $28; Senior Discount
(513) 367-9632
http://greatparks.org/parks/miami-whitewater-forest/miami-whitewater-forest-camp-ground

Directions

4 miles. From Exit 25 of I-275 go northwest on I-74 for 2 miles to Exit 3. Take Dry Fork Rd north for 1 mile. Turn right on West Rd, then turn left into the Park. Follow signs to the harbor, check-in at the boathouse.

Points of Interest Also see [21]

Visit the Cincinnati Art Museum, Cincinnati Museum Center, Contemporary Arts Center, National Underground Railroad Freedom Center, Behringer-Crawford Museum, & Cincinnati Observatory.

RV Sites		Water		Laundry	
Number	46	None		Wi-Fi	
Shaded	Y	At Site	Y	Fishing	
By Water	Y	Spigots	Y	Hiking	
Paved		**Sewer**		Biking	Y
Pull Thru		None		Swimming	
ADA	Y	At Site	Y	Watch Wildlife	
Max RV Size	40	Dump Station	Y	Pets	Y
Electric		**Amenities**		**Security**	
None		Restrooms	Y	Host(s)	Y
20 Amp	Y	Showers	Y	Rangers(s)	
30 Amp	Y	Reserve Sites	Y	Gate	
50 Amp		Store		Patrolled	Y
		Grill/Table	Y		

[21] Stonelick State Park
I-275, Exit 257
East of Cincinnati
N39 12.811 W84 04.926
State Rate: $20-$26
(513) 734-4323
http://parks.ohiodnr.gov/stonelick

Directions

14 miles. From Exit 28 go east for 10.3 miles on Hwy 28. Turn south at Edenton-Pleasant Plain Rd. After 1.1 miles turn right, then left on Newtonsville Rd and go 1.5 miles, joining Hwy 727. Go 1 more mile to the Park.

Points of Interest Also see [20]

In Cincinnati you will find nostalgic rides at Cincinnati Railway's Lebanon Station. Visit the famous Findlay Farmer's Market, Pyramid Hill Sculpture Park and Museum, Taft Museum of Art and the GOLD Cincinnati Museum Center.

RV Sites		Water		Laundry	Y
Number	114	None		Wi-Fi	
Shaded	Y	At Site	few	Fishing	Y
By Water	Y	Spigots	Y	Hiking	Y
Paved	Y	**Sewer**		Biking	Y
Pull Thru		None		Swimming	Y
ADA	Y	At Site	few	Watch Wildlife	Y
Max RV Size	45	Dump Station	Y	Pets	Y
Electric		**Amenities**		**Security**	
None		Restrooms	Y	Host(s)	Y
20 Amp	Y	Showers	Y	Rangers(s)	Y
30 Amp	Y	Reserve Sites	Y	Gate	
50 Amp	Y	Store	Y	Patrolled	Y
		Grill/Table	Y		

[22] Gallia County Junior Fairgrounds
Hwy 35
North of Gallipolis
N38 50.651 W82 14.398
County Rate: $20
(740) 446-4120
http://galliacountyfair.org/

Directions
1 mile. Just west of the Kentucky State Line in Ohio, exit Hwy 35 at Business 35/Hwy 160 (Jackson Pky). Go west on Jackson Pky 0.6 mile to the Fairground Camping area on the left.

Points of Interest
A good one night stopover. Open all year. Be sure to check the Fairground calender to determine of you'll arrive in the middle of a fair event. Convenient to shopping for supplies. The Gallia County Farmers Market is on Thursdays and Saturdays. Check the exhibit at the French Art Colony.

RV Sites		Water		Laundry	
Number	200	None		Wi-Fi	
Shaded		At Site	Y	Fishing	
By Water		Spigots	Y	Hiking	
Paved		Sewer		Biking	Y
Pull Thru		None		Swimming	
ADA	Y	At Site	Y	Watch Wildlife	
Max RV Size	40	Dump Station		Pets	Y
Electric		Amenities		Security	
None		Restrooms	Y	Host(s)	Y
20 Amp	Y	Showers		Rangers(s)	
30 Amp	Y	Reserve Sites		Gate	
50 Amp	Y	Store		Patrolled	Y
		Grill/Table			

[23] Jackson Lake State Park
Hwy 35, south on Hwy 93
South of Jackson
N38 54.136 W82 35.808
State Rate: $20-$24
(740) 682-6197
http://parks.ohiodnr.gov/jacksonlake

Directions
13.5 miles In Jackson, on Main St (becomes Hwy 93) go south for 11.5 miles to Hwy 279 in Oak Hill. Turn right, go 1.3 miles to Tommy Been Rd. Turn right, go 0.7 miles to the Park.

Points of Interest
Visit the Buckeye Iron Furnace State Memorial, which preserves the history of the Ohio iron-producing days. The Leo Petroglyph State Memorial site features well-preserved rock carvings cut into sandstone by prehistoric Indians. Figures represent animals, humans and other life forms.

RV Sites		Water		Laundry	
Number	34	None		Wi-Fi	Y
Shaded	Y	At Site		Fishing	Y
By Water	Y	Spigots	Y	Hiking	Y
Paved		Sewer		Biking	Y
Pull Thru		None		Swimming	Y
ADA	Y	At Site		Watch Wildlife	Y
Max RV Size	40	Dump Station	Y	Pets	Y
Electric		Amenities		Security	
None		Restrooms	Y	Host(s)	Y
20 Amp	Y	Showers	Y	Rangers(s)	Y
30 Amp	Y	Reserve Sites	Y	Gate	
50 Amp	Y	Store		Patrolled	Y
		Grill/Table	Y		

[24] Scioto Trail State Park
Hwy 35, south on Hwy 23
South of Chillicothe
N39 13.418 W82 55.872
State Rate: $16-$24
(740) 887-4818
http://parks.ohiodnr.gov/sciototrail

Directions
In Chillicothe take Hwy 23/35 south, follow Hwy 23 for 8 miles to Hwy 372 (Stoney Creek Rd). Turn left and proceed on Hwy 372 for 3.5 miles to the Park.

Points of Interest
The Mound City/Hopewell Culture Group National Historic Park is a prehistoric Indian complex of 23 burial mounds, Museum and Visitors' Center. The Ross County Historical Society in Chillicothe features exhibits of pioneer crafts, firearms, furniture, toys and clothing.

RV Sites		Water		Laundry	
Number	55	None		Wi-Fi	
Shaded	Y	At Site		Fishing	Y
By Water	Y	Spigots	Y	Hiking	Y
Paved		Sewer		Biking	Y
Pull Thru	Y	None		Swimming	Y
ADA	Y	At Site		Watch Wildlife	Y
Max RV Size	45	Dump Station	Y	Pets	Y
Electric		Amenities		Security	
None		Restrooms	Y	Host(s)	Y
20 Amp	Y	Showers		Rangers(s)	Y
30 Amp	Y	Reserve Sites	Y	Gate	
50 Amp	Y	Store	Y	Patrolled	Y
		Grill/Table	Y		

About Oklahoma's Public Campgrounds

The Oklahoma Tourism & Recreation Department oversees the State Park Website. There are thirty-five State Parks. Most campsites at Oklahoma State Parks are first come, first served; however, eight take reservations. The Parks generally allow pets on a leash.

Campsite fees are:

Primitive RV camp site -	$12.00
Semi-modern site (electric and water) -	$20.00-$25.00
Modern site (electric, sewer and water) -	$23.00-$25.00
Premium sites (at water's edge) -	$ 5.00 additional
Senior Discount (over 62) -	$ 2.00
Park Entrance Fee -	None

You will find park and reservation details at -

http://www.travelok.com/state_parks

There are a number of County and Federal Lands which enrich the mix of RV campgrounds.

[1] Lake Murray State Park	[10] Kiowa 1 Campground COE
[2] Chandler City Park (Tilghman Park)	[11] Heyburn Park Campground COE
[3] Arcadia Park	[12] Hawthorn Bluff Campground COE
[4] Lake Carl Blackwell - Pine Grove	[13] Burns Run West COE
[5] Osage Cove, Kaw Lake COE	[14] McGee Creek State Park
[6] Foss State Park	[15] Rocky Point (Fort Gibson) COE
[7] Red Rock Canyon State Park	[16] Kiamichi Park COE
[8] Lake Thunderbird State Park	[17] Okmulgee State Park
[9] Lake Eufaula State Park	[18] Washington Cove COE

NOTES:

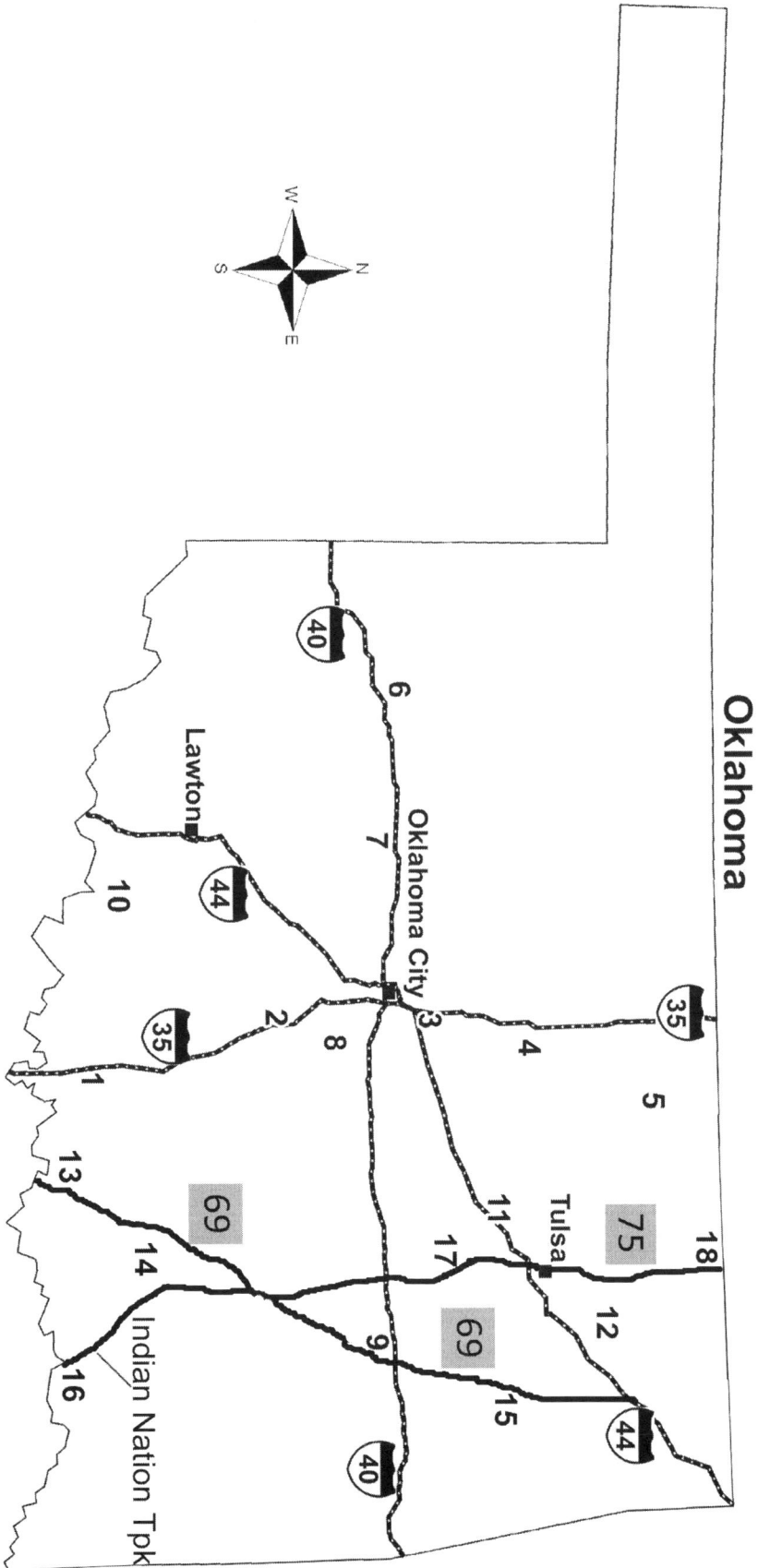

Oklahoma

[1] Lake Murray State Park
I-35, Exit 29
Southeast of Ardmore
N34 08.151 W97 06.533
State Rate: See Introduction
(580) 223-4044
http://www.travelok.com/listings/view.profile/
id.4358/type.lodging

Directions

2.6 miles. From Exit 29 go east for 2.6 miles on Hwy 70 to Hwy 77S. Turn right in to the Park.

Points of Interest

WPA and CCC laborers built this 12,000 acre park and lake. You have access to Murray Lodge, miniature golf, horseback riding, tennis courts and a pool. Tucker Tower, much like a lighthouse, built out of rock and sitting at the top of a cliff out on a point, watches over the lake.

RV Sites		Water		Laundry	Y
Number	329	None		Wi-Fi	
Shaded	Y	At Site	Y	Fishing	Y
By Water	Y	Spigots	Y	Hiking	Y
Paved	Y	**Sewer**		Biking	Y
Pull Thru	Y	None		Swimming	Y
ADA	Y	At Site	Y	Watch Wildlife	Y
Max RV Size	45	Dump Station	Y	Pets	Y
Electric		**Amenities**		**Security**	
None		Restrooms	Y	Host(s)	Y
20 Amp	Y	Showers	Y	Rangers(s)	Y
30 Amp	Y	Reserve Sites		Gate	some
50 Amp	Y	Store	Y	Patrolled	Y
		Grill/Table	Y		

[2] Chandler City Park (Tilghman Park)
I-35, Exit 91
In Chandler
N34 59.165 W97 22.590
City Rate: $22
(405) 527-5114
http://chandlerok.com/recreation/parks

Directions

1 mile. From Exit 91 go northeast on Hwy 74 for 0.3 miles to Chandler Rd. Turn west (left), go 0.5 miles to Park Rd on your right.

Points of Interest Also see [8]

In Norman visit Campus Corner. From unique boutiques to worldwide cuisine, the 627,000 square feet of Campus Corner can cater to all your wants and desires. With 47 boutiques & shops and 23 restaurants and nightclubs Campus Corner is a great destination in Norman.

RV Sites		Water		Laundry	Y
Number	40	None		Wi-Fi	
Shaded	Y	At Site	Y	Fishing	
By Water	Y	Spigots	Y	Hiking	
Paved	Y	**Sewer**		Biking	Y
Pull Thru	Y	None		Swimming	Y
ADA	Y	At Site	Y	Watch Wildlife	
Max RV Size	45	Dump Station	near	Pets	Y
Electric		**Amenities**		**Security**	
None		Restrooms	Y	Host(s)	Y
20 Amp	Y	Showers	Y	Rangers(s)	
30 Amp	Y	Reserve Sites		Gate	
50 Amp	Y	Store		Patrolled	Y
		Grill/Table	Y		

[3] Arcadia Lake Park
I-35, Exit 141
East of Edmond
N35 39.158 W97 22.721
City Rate: $15-$25; Senior Discount
(405) 216-7470
http://www.shopoklahoma.com/arcadia_park.htm

Directions

2.5 miles. From Exit 141 go east on Hwy 66 for 2.2 miles to the Park on your right.

Points of Interest

Between Oklahoma City and Edmond, there is much to see and do. A few examples are the National Cowboy Hall of Fame, Express Ranches Clydesdale Center, The Rodeo Opry, Overholser Mansion, Oklahoma Indian Art Gallery, and the American Banjo Museum.

RV Sites		Water		Laundry	
Number	100	None		Wi-Fi	
Shaded	Y	At Site	Y	Fishing	Y
By Water	Y	Spigots	Y	Hiking	Y
Paved	Y	**Sewer**		Biking	Y
Pull Thru	Y	None		Swimming	Y
ADA	Y	At Site	Y	Watch Wildlife	Y
Max RV Size	40	Dump Station	Y	Pets	Y
Electric		**Amenities**		**Security**	
None		Restrooms	Y	Host(s)	Y
20 Amp	Y	Showers	Y	Rangers(s)	
30 Amp	Y	Reserve Sites		Gate	
50 Amp	Y	Store		Patrolled	Y
		Grill/Table	Y		

[4] Lake Carl Blackwell - Pine Grove
I-35, Exit 174
West of Stillwater
N36 07.476 W97 12.607
Oklahoma State University Rate: $20
(405) 372-5157
http://lcb.okstate.edu/campgrounds

Directions

9 miles. From Exit 174 go east on Hwy 51 for 7.8 miles to Hwy 51C. Turn north, go 1.4 miles to the Park.

Points of Interest

If you like Red Dirt Music, Stillwater is the home to Red Dirt Music and top musical talent such as Garth Brooks. Wrestling fans will want to stop at the National Wrestling Hall of Fame & Museum. The Sheerar Museum houses outstanding exhibits of Stillwater and A&M/OSU history.

RV Sites		Water		Laundry	
Number	140	None		Wi-Fi	
Shaded	Y	At Site	Y	Fishing	Y
By Water	Y	Spigots	Y	Hiking	Y
Paved	Y	Sewer		Biking	Y
Pull Thru	Y	None		Swimming	Y
ADA	Y	At Site		Watch Wildlife	
Max RV Size	40	Dump Station		Pets	Y
Electric		Amenities		Security	
None		Restrooms	Y	Host(s)	Y
20 Amp	Y	Showers	Y	Rangers(s)	
30 Amp	Y	Reserve Sites		Gate	
50 Amp	Y	Store		Patrolled	Y
		Grill/Table	Y		

[5] Osage Cove, Kaw Lake COE
I-35, Exit 214
East of Ponca City
N36 42.809 W96 53.272
COE Rate: $18
America/Beautiful Rate: $9
(580) 762-5611
http://www.recreation.gov/

Directions

27 miles. From Exit 214 go east on Hwy 60 for 25 miles (through Ponca City) to Kaw Dam Rd. Turn north 0.4 miles to Osage Cove Rd. Turn right, go 1.7 miles to Osage Park Rd on your left.

Points of Interest

Ponca City got its name from the Ponca Native American people. Explore the Native American culture through pow-wows, social & ceremonial dances. A day tour might include Marland Mansion & the Pioneer Women Museum.

RV Sites		Water		Laundry	
Number	97	None		Wi-Fi	
Shaded	Y	At Site		Fishing	Y
By Water	Y	Spigots	Y	Hiking	Y
Paved	Y	Sewer		Biking	Y
Pull Thru		None		Swimming	
ADA	Y	At Site		Watch Wildlife	Y
Max RV Size	45	Dump Station	Y	Pets	Y
Electric		Amenities		Security	
None		Restrooms	Y	Host(s)	Y
20 Amp	Y	Showers	Y	Rangers(s)	Y
30 Amp	Y	Reserve Sites	Y	Gate	
50 Amp		Store		Patrolled	Y
		Grill/Table	Y		

[6] Foss State Park
I-40, Exit 53
West of Clinton
N35 31.805 W99 11.460
State Rate: See Introduction
(580) 592-4433
http://www.travelok.com/listings/view.profile/id.2848/type.lodging

Directions

7 miles. From Exit 53 go 6.3 miles north on Hwy 44, which is joined by Hwy 73. Follow Hwy 73 when it turns west, go 0.2 to Marina Rd and the Park entrance.

Points of Interest

In Clinton visit the Oklahoma Route 66 Museum. Visit the Washita Battlefield, where George A. Custer led the 7th U.S. Cavalry on a surprise attack against the Southern Cheyenne village of Peace Chief Black Kettle.

RV Sites		Water		Laundry	
Number	110	None		Wi-Fi	
Shaded	Y	At Site	Y	Fishing	Y
By Water	Y	Spigots	Y	Hiking	Y
Paved	Y	Sewer		Biking	Y
Pull Thru	Y	None		Swimming	Y
ADA	Y	At Site	Y	Watch Wildlife	Y
Max RV Size	45	Dump Station	Y	Pets	Y
Electric		Amenities		Security	
None		Restrooms	Y	Host(s)	Y
20 Amp	Y	Showers	Y	Rangers(s)	Y
30 Amp	Y	Reserve Sites		Gate	
50 Amp	Y	Store	Y	Patrolled	Y
		Grill/Table	Y		

[7] Red Rock Canyon State Park
I-40, Exit 101
West of Oklahoma City
N35 27.381 W98 21.556
State Rate: See Introduction
(405) 542-6344
http://www.travelok.com/listings/view.profile/id.6275/type.lodging

Directions

6 miles. From Exit 101 go south for 6 miles on Hwy 8/281 (through Hinton) to the Park entrance on your left.

Points of Interest

The park and campsites are located down in a canyon (short steep entry road) among red rock canyon walls. The canyon walls are a favorite for rappelling and exploration. Visit the Chisholm Trail Museum and Governor Seay Mansion, and the American Indian Hall of Fame.

RV Sites		Water		Laundry	
Number	56	None		Wi-Fi	
Shaded	Y	At Site	Y	Fishing	Y
By Water	Y	Spigots	Y	Hiking	Y
Paved	Y	**Sewer**		Biking	Y
Pull Thru	Y	None		Swimming	Y
ADA	Y	At Site	Y	Watch Wildlife	Y
Max RV Size	40	Dump Station	Y	Pets	Y
Electric		**Amenities**		**Security**	
None		Restrooms	Y	Host(s)	Y
20 Amp	Y	Showers	Y	Rangers(s)	Y
30 Amp	Y	Reserve Sites	Y	Gate	
50 Amp	Y	Store	Y	Patrolled	Y
		Grill/Table	Y		

[8] Lake Thunderbird State Park
I-40, Exit 166
East of Norman
N35 13.940 W97 14.853
State Rate: See Introduction
(405) 360-3572
http://www.travelok.com/listings/view.profile/id.4386/type.lodging

Directions

12 miles. From Exit 166 go south for 11 miles on 120th Ave (Choctaw Rd). Turn east for 1 mile to the Park.

Points of Interest Also see [2]

See ancient artifacts of the Five Civilized Tribes at the Jacobson House in Norman. Visit the ecological woodlands at the Oliver Nature Preserve. Tour the Crucible Foundry, Gallery & Sculpture Garden, with bronze sculptures from around the country in their sculpture garden.

RV Sites		Water		Laundry	
Number	200	None		Wi-Fi	Y
Shaded	Y	At Site	Y	Fishing	Y
By Water	Y	Spigots	Y	Hiking	Y
Paved	Y	**Sewer**		Biking	Y
Pull Thru	Y	None		Swimming	Y
ADA	Y	At Site	Y	Watch Wildlife	Y
Max RV Size	40	Dump Station	Y	Pets	Y
Electric		**Amenities**		**Security**	
None		Restrooms	Y	Host(s)	Y
20 Amp	Y	Showers	Y	Rangers(s)	Y
30 Amp	Y	Reserve Sites	Y	Gate	
50 Amp	Y	Store	Y	Patrolled	Y
		Grill/Table	Y		

[9] Lake Eufaula State Park
I-40, Exit 259
South of Checotah
N35 23.972 W95 36.313
State Rate: See Introduction
(918) 689-5311
http://www.travelok.com/listings/view.profile/id.4336/type.lodging

Directions

5.5 miles. From Exit 259 go south for 5.5 miles on Hwy 150 to the Visitors Center on your left.

Points of Interest

Checotah is home to a number of antique malls, the Honey Springs Civil War battle site & an historic district. It claims to be Steerwrestling Capital of the World. It is the hometown of 2005 American Idol winner & Country Star Carrie Underwood, & country music singer Mel McDaniel.

RV Sites		Water		Laundry	
Number	94	None		Wi-Fi	Y
Shaded	Y	At Site	Y	Fishing	Y
By Water	Y	Spigots	Y	Hiking	Y
Paved	Y	**Sewer**		Biking	Y
Pull Thru	Y	None	Y	Swimming	Y
ADA	Y	At Site	Y	Watch Wildlife	Y
Max RV Size	45	Dump Station		Pets	Y
Electric		**Amenities**		**Security**	
None		Restrooms	Y	Host(s)	Y
20 Amp	Y	Showers	Y	Rangers(s)	Y
30 Amp	Y	Reserve Sites	Y	Gate	
50 Amp	Y	Store	Y	Patrolled	Y
		Grill/Table	Y		

[10] Kiowa 1 Campground COE
I-44, Exit 5
Southeast of Lawton
N34 15.654 W98 05.208
COE Rate: $14-$18
America/Beautiful Rate: $7-$9
(580) 963-9031
http://www.reserveamerica.com/

Directions

31 miles. From Exit 5 go east on Hwy 70/277 for 24 miles. Turn north at N2750 Rd for 7 miles to E1900 Rd. Turn right in to the Park.

Points of Interest

Lawton is the third largest city in Oklahoma. Local attractions include Fort Sill National Historic Landmark; Comanche National Museum & Cultural Center; Historic Mattie Beal Home; the Holy City of the Wichitas; Museum of the Great Plains & Wichita Mountains Wildlife Refuge.

RV Sites		Water			Laundry	
Number	180	None			Wi-Fi	
Shaded	Y	At Site	Y		Fishing	Y
By Water	Y	Spigots	Y		Hiking	Y
Paved	Y	Sewer			Biking	Y
Pull Thru	Y	None			Swimming	Y
ADA	Y	At Site			Watch Wildlife	Y
Max RV Size	45	Dump Station	Y		Pets	Y
Electric		Amenities			Security	
None		Restrooms	Y		Host(s)	Y
20 Amp	Y	Showers	Y		Rangers(s)	Y
30 Amp	Y	Reserve Sites	Y		Gate	
50 Amp	Y	Store			Patrolled	Y
		Grill/Table	Y			

[11] Heyburn Park Campground COE
I-44, Exit 196
Southwest of Tulsa
N35 56.689 W96 18.449
COE Rate: $14-$16
America/Beautiful Rate: $7-$8
(918) 247-6601
http://www.recreation.gov/

Directions

11 miles. From Exit 196 go north on Hwy 48/66 for 2.5 miles and bare right on Hwy 66. Go 5.7 miles on Hwy 66 to Hwy 273 Rd. Turn north for 2.3 miles to Lake Heyburn Rd. Turn west for 0.6 miles to the Park entrance.

Points of Interest

Tulsa's cultural scene shines with ballet and symphony, sharing the spotlight with cultural events, activities, architecture, and art including 18 of Frederic Remington's 22 bronzes.

RV Sites		Water			Laundry	
Number	45	None			Wi-Fi	
Shaded	Y	At Site	Y		Fishing	Y
By Water	Y	Spigots	Y		Hiking	Y
Paved		Sewer			Biking	Y
Pull Thru	Y	None			Swimming	Y
ADA	Y	At Site			Watch Wildlife	Y
Max RV Size	45	Dump Station	Y		Pets	Y
Electric		Amenities			Security	
None		Restrooms	Y		Host(s)	Y
20 Amp	Y	Showers	Y		Rangers(s)	Y
30 Amp	Y	Reserve Sites	Y		Gate	
50 Amp	Y	Store			Patrolled	Y
		Grill/Table	Y			

[12] Hawthorn Bluff Campground COE
I-44, Exit 255
Northeast of Tulsa
N36 25.920 W95 40.863
COE Rate: $16-$20
America/Beautiful Rate: $8-$10
(918) 443-2319
http://www.recreation.gov/

Directions

13 miles. From Exit 255 follow Hwy 20 west in to Claremore. Hwy 88 joins Hwy 20 after 1.5 miles. Now follow Hwy 88 north for 11.5 miles to the Park on your right.

Points of Interest

Claremore is the home of Will Rogers. Visit the Will Rogers Memorial & Birthplace Ranch. Other sights include the J.M. Davis Arms & Historical Museum and The Belvidere Mansion. See the world's largest totem pole in Foyil.

RV Sites		Water			Laundry	
Number	56	None			Wi-Fi	
Shaded	Y	At Site	Y		Fishing	Y
By Water	Y	Spigots	Y		Hiking	Y
Paved		Sewer			Biking	Y
Pull Thru	Y	None			Swimming	Y
ADA	Y	At Site			Watch Wildlife	Y
Max RV Size	45	Dump Station	Y		Pets	Y
Electric		Amenities			Security	
None		Restrooms	Y		Host(s)	Y
20 Amp	Y	Showers	Y		Rangers(s)	Y
30 Amp	Y	Reserve Sites	Y		Gate	
50 Amp	Y	Store			Patrolled	Y
		Grill/Table	Y			

[13] Burns Run West COE
Hwy 69/75, Exit 72
Northwest of Denison
N33 51.852 W96 35.531
COE Rate: $20-$24
America/Beautiful Rate: $10-$12
(580) 965-4922
http://www.recreation.gov/

Directions

6.3 miles, **from the south**. From Hwy 69/75 take Exit 72. On Hwy 91 go 4.3 miles north to the second left onto E Burns Run. Follow signs 1.5 miles. Or 5.2 miles, **from the north** take the Hwy 75a Exit off Hwy 69/75. Follow 75a (becomes E Burns Run) 5.2 miles, to the Park.

Points of Interest

Lake Texoma is considered the "Playground of the Southwest," & "Striper Capital of the World," where fishing, boating, and hiking abound.

RV Sites		Water		Laundry	
Number	117	None		Wi-Fi	
Shaded	Y	At Site	Y	Fishing	Y
By Water	Y	Spigots	Y	Hiking	Y
Paved	Y	**Sewer**		Biking	Y
Pull Thru	Y	None		Swimming	Y
ADA	Y	At Site	Y	Watch Wildlife	Y
Max RV Size	45	Dump Station	Y	Pets	Y
Electric		**Amenities**		**Security**	
None		Restrooms	Y	Host(s)	Y
20 Amp	Y	Showers	Y	Rangers(s)	Y
30 Amp	Y	Reserve Sites	Y	Gate	
50 Amp	Y	Store		Patrolled	Y
		Grill/Table	Y		

[14] McGee Creek State Park
Hwy 69, east on Hwy 3
East of Atoka
N34 18.917 W95 52.767
State Rate: See Introduction
(580) 889-5822
http://www.travelok.com/listings/view.profile/id.4972

Directions

21.4 miles. Go east from Atoka on Hwy 3, 17.2 miles to McGee Creek Dam Rd. Turn north for 4.2 miles to the Park. You can also reach the Park on Hwy 3 from Hwy 75 (Indian Nation Turnpike).

Points of Interest

Visitors enjoy water recreation along 64 miles of shoreline. The Atoka museum covers the history of the Civil War in Oklahoma as well as a shootout between local lawmen & Clyde Barrow, to homegrown talents such as Reba McEntire.

RV Sites		Water		Laundry	
Number	150	None		Wi-Fi	Y
Shaded	Y	At Site	Y	Fishing	Y
By Water		Spigots	Y	Hiking	Y
Paved	Y	**Sewer**		Biking	Y
Pull Thru	Y	None		Swimming	Y
ADA	Y	At Site	Y	Watch Wildlife	Y
Max RV Size	45	Dump Station	Y	Pets	Y
Electric		**Amenities**		**Security**	
None		Restrooms	Y	Host(s)	Y
20 Amp	Y	Showers	Y	Rangers(s)	Y
30 Amp	Y	Reserve Sites	Y	Gate	
50 Amp	Y	Store	Y	Patrolled	Y
		Grill/Table	Y		

[15] Rocky Point (Fort Gibson) COE
Hwy 69
North of Wagoner
N36 01.697 W95 18.901
COE Rate: $14-$20
America/Beautiful Rate: $7-$10
(918) 462-2042
http://www.recreation.gov/

Directions

8 miles. From Wagoner, travel 4.3 miles north on Hwy 69, then 3 miles east on E 0690 Rd (Whitehorn Cove Rd). Follow signs north 0.8 miles on Rocky Point Rd to campground.

Points of Interest

The lake is named for Fort Gibson, a National Historical Landmark with volunteers reenacting the lifestyle and military history of the state. The Wagoner Historical Museum has one of the finest regional collections of histoThereric fashions.

RV Sites		Water		Laundry	
Number	62	None		Wi-Fi	
Shaded	Y	At Site	Y	Fishing	Y
By Water	Y	Spigots	Y	Hiking	Y
Paved	Y	**Sewer**		Biking	Y
Pull Thru	Y	None		Swimming	Y
ADA	Y	At Site	Y	Watch Wildlife	Y
Max RV Size	45	Dump Station	Y	Pets	Y
Electric		**Amenities**		**Security**	
None		Restrooms	Y	Host(s)	Y
20 Amp	Y	Showers	Y	Rangers(s)	Y
30 Amp	Y	Reserve Sites	Y	Gate	Y
50 Amp	Y	Store		Patrolled	Y
		Grill/Table	Y		

[16] Kiamichi Park COE
Indian National Turnpike, East on Hwy 70
East of Hugo
N34 00.712 W95 24.507
COE Rate: $12-$22
America/Beautiful Rate: $6-$11
(580) 326-3345
http://www.recreation.gov/

Directions

7.4 miles. From Hugo take Hwy 70 east for 6.4 miles. Turn north on the Road just after Fallon and follow the posted signs 1 mile to the campground.

Points of Interest

Hugo is notable in the history of American railroad culture, visit the historic Frisco Depot Museum. Circus culture also distinguishes Hugo, three of America's largest active circuses spend their winters here because of the climate.

RV Sites		Water		Laundry	
Number	86	None		Wi-Fi	
Shaded	Y	At Site	Y	Fishing	Y
By Water	Y	Spigots	Y	Hiking	Y
Paved		**Sewer**		Biking	Y
Pull Thru		None		Swimming	
ADA	Y	At Site		Watch Wildlife	Y
Max RV Size	45	Dump Station	Y	Pets	Y
Electric		**Amenities**		**Security**	
None		Restrooms	Y	Host(s)	Y
20 Amp	Y	Showers	Y	Rangers(s)	Y
30 Amp	Y	Reserve Sites	Y	Gate	
50 Amp	Y	Store		Patrolled	Y
		Grill/Table	Y		

[17] Okmulgee State Park
Hwy 75, West on Hwy 56
West of Okmulgee
N35 37.313 W96 04.063
State Rate: See Introduction
(918) 756-5971
http://www.travelok.com/listings/view.profile/id.5520/type.lodging

Directions

On the west side of Okmulgee take Hwy 56 for 4.7 mile to Hwy 561. Bear left for 0.7 mile to the Park. The Park is located adjacent to Dripping Springs State Park.

Points of Interest

The 'one of a kind' Creek Indian Council House Museum, in Okmulgee, was created to preserve Muscogee (Creek) culture. Meticulous restoration, in 1993, garnered a National Historic Preservation Award. Will Rogers helped save the structure

RV Sites		Water		Laundry	
Number	47	None		Wi-Fi	
Shaded	Y	At Site	Y	Fishing	Y
By Water	Y	Spigots	Y	Hiking	Y
Paved		**Sewer**		Biking	Y
Pull Thru	Y	None		Swimming	Y
ADA	Y	At Site		Watch Wildlife	Y
Max RV Size	45	Dump Station	Y	Pets	Y
Electric		**Amenities**		**Security**	
None		Restrooms	Y	Host(s)	Y
20 Amp	Y	Showers	Y	Rangers(s)	Y
30 Amp	Y	Reserve Sites	Y	Gate	
50 Amp		Store		Patrolled	Y
		Grill/Table	Y		

[18] Washington Cove COE
Hwy 75, West on Hwy 10
South of Copan
N36 54.429 W95 56.106
COE Rate: $16
America/Beautiful Rate: $8
(918) 532-4129
http://www.recreation.gov/

Directions

2.5 miles. South of Copan take Hwy 10 1 mile west to N 3970 Rd. Turn north for 1.5 miles to the campground.

Points of Interest

The lake is home to many species of game fish. Hikers & horseback riders will enjoy exploring the area. Visit the Tom Mix Museum in Dewey. The collection is both Tom Mix memorabilia & other items that actually belonged to Tom & were used by him in his daily activities.

RV Sites		Water		Laundry	
Number	101	None		Wi-Fi	
Shaded	some	At Site	Y	Fishing	Y
By Water	Y	Spigots	Y	Hiking	Y
Paved		**Sewer**		Biking	Y
Pull Thru	Y	None		Swimming	
ADA	Y	At Site	Y	Watch Wildlife	Y
Max RV Size	45	Dump Station	Y	Pets	Y
Electric		**Amenities**		**Security**	
None		Restrooms	Y	Host(s)	Y
20 Amp	Y	Showers	Y	Rangers(s)	Y
30 Amp	Y	Reserve Sites	Y	Gate	
50 Amp		Store		Patrolled	Y
		Grill/Table	Y		

About Oregon's Public Campgrounds

The Oregon Parks & Recreation Department oversees the State Park System. Their website is - **http://www.oregonstateparks.org/**

Oregon State Parks offers over 50 campgrounds. Twenty-eight accept reservations year-round. The others are first-come, first-served. Forty of the 50 are parks with RV camp sites, restrooms, & showers. For information about campgrounds (including seasonal opening and closing dates) visit the park web page.

Most Oregon State Parks can accommodate RVs up to 50 feet in length. You must be able to fit your towed vehicle onto the campsite. The Parks along the Columbia River are generally near railroad tracks, however Parks were selected with moderate (by most standards) sound levels. Pets are allowed in the parks but must be confined by the owner, or on a leash not more than six (6) feet long, and kept under physical control at all times.

Reservations are accepted year-round. You can make reservations as far in advance as 9 months, or as few as 2 days before your stay. When you make a reservation, you must pay the entire amount due for the length of your stay plus a nonrefundable reservation fee. Reservation and transaction fees are nonrefundable. Reservations may be made online with a credit card, or by calling (800) 452-5687. Online reservations are handled by ReserveAmerica at -

http://www.reserveamerica.com/campgroundDirectoryList.do?contractCode=or

No other website is authorized to handle Oregon state park reservations. There are two types of campsites of primary interest to RVers:

Full hookup sites – sewer, electricity & water; paved parking area adjacent to site.

Electrical sites – electricity and water; paved parking adjacent to site.

Oregon also has a notably fine collection of County and Federal Parks.

[1] Emigrant Lake (Point Park)	[12] Bullards Beach State Park
[2] Valley of the Rogue State Park	[13] Honeyman State Park
[3] Pine Meadows Campground COE	[14] Devil's Lake State Recreation Area
[4] Gills Landing RV Park	[15] Fort Stevens State Park
[5] Champoeg State Heritage Area	[16] Crater Lake NP (Mazama Village)
[6] Umatilla Marina and RV Park	[17] Tumalo State Park
[7] Ainsworth State Park	[18] Jefferson County Fair Complex
[8] Deschutes River State Recreation Area	[19] Camp Creek NF
[9] Boardman Marina Park	[20] Grant County RV Park
[10] Emigrant Springs State Heritage Area	[21] Unity Lake State Recreation Area
[11] Farewell Bend State Recreation Area	

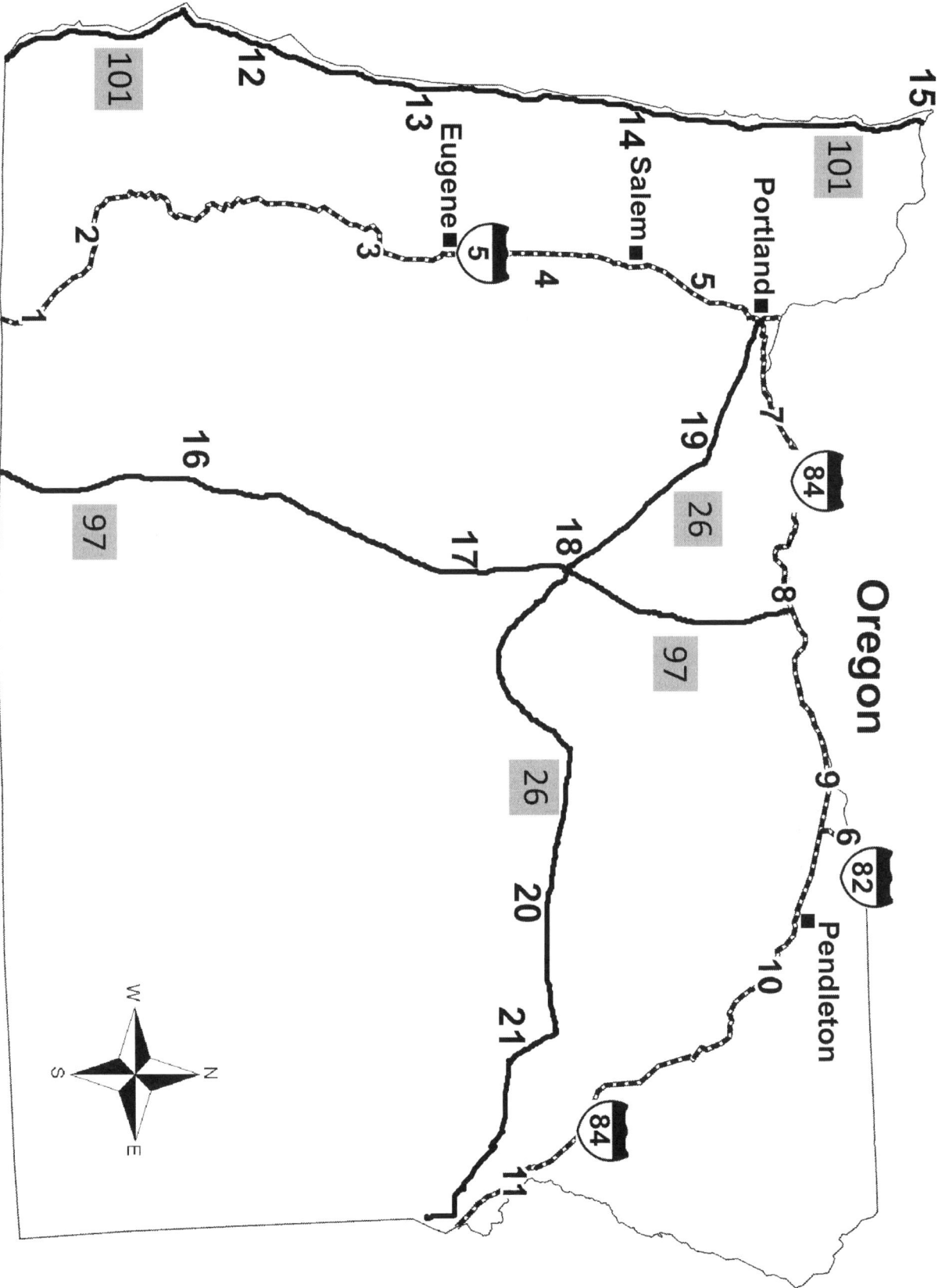

Oregon

101
12
101
15
13
Eugene ■
5
14 Salem ■
Portland ■
4
5
2
3
7
19
84
16
26
17
18
8
97
97
26
9
6
82
20
Pendleton ■
10
21
84
11

W
S   N
E

[1] Emigrant Lake (Point Park)
I-5, Exit 14
Southeast of Ashland
N42 09.208 W122 37.596
County Rate: $30
(541) 774-8183
http://jacksoncountyor.org/parks/Camping/
Emigrant-Lake

Directions

3 miles. From Exit 14 go southeast for 3 miles on Hwy 66 to Emigrant Lake Rd. Turn left and follow Emigrant Lake Rd to the campground.

Points of Interest

Ashland is home of the Oregon Shakespeare Festival & other visual & vocal artistry. Talented chefs prepare locally grown cuisine to pair with award winning local wines. The Crater Rock Museum in Central Point features exhibits of minerals, gemstones, fossils & petrified wood.

RV Sites		Water		Laundry	
Number	32	None		Wi-Fi	
Shaded	some	At Site	Y	Fishing	Y
By Water	Y	Spigots	Y	Hiking	Y
Paved	Y	Sewer		Biking	Y
Pull Thru	Y	None		Swimming	Y
ADA	Y	At Site	Y	Watch Wildlife	
Max RV Size	45	Dump Station	Y	Pets	Y
Electric		Amenities		Security	
None		Restrooms	Y	Host(s)	Y
20 Amp	Y	Showers	Y	Rangers(s)	
30 Amp	Y	Reserve Sites	Y	Gate	
50 Amp	Y	Store		Patrolled	Y
		Grill/Table	Y		

[2] Valley of the Rogue State Park
I-5, Exit 45b
East of Grants Pass
N42 24.616 W123 07.798
State Rate: $20-$28
(541) 582-3128
http://www.jacksoncountyparks.com/emi-grant_lake.htm

Directions

Along I-5. From Exit 45b: **southbound**, turn right at the end of the off ramp to the registration area; **northbound**, proceed to Rogue River Rd, turn right and proceed to the registration area.

Points of Interest

Camp along the river made famous by novelist & avid fisherman Zane Grey. Go to Crater Lake, the Oregon Caves National Monument, Jacksonville, Ashland's Shakespeare Festival, the Britt Music Festival, & historic Wolf Creek Inn

RV Sites		Water		Laundry	Y
Number	139	None		Wi-Fi	
Shaded	Y	At Site	Y	Fishing	Y
By Water	Y	Spigots	Y	Hiking	Y
Paved	Y	Sewer		Biking	Y
Pull Thru	Y	None		Swimming	Y
ADA	Y	At Site	Y	Watch Wildlife	
Max RV Size	45	Dump Station	Y	Pets	Y
Electric		Amenities		Security	
None		Restrooms	Y	Host(s)	Y
20 Amp	Y	Showers	Y	Rangers(s)	Y
30 Amp	Y	Reserve Sites	Y	Gate	
50 Amp	Y	Store		Patrolled	Y
		Grill/Table	Y		

[3] Pine Meadows Campground COE
I-5, Exits 172 and 174
South of Eugene
N43 42.021 W123 03.376
COE Rate: $12-$18
America/Beautiful Rate: $5-$8
(541) 942-8657
http://www.recreation.gov/

Directions

6-8 miles. **Northbound**, use Exit 174, turn southbound 2 miles to Exit 172. All travelers, now southbound, take exit 172, go 3.5 miles south on 6th St (London Rd). Take a left on Cottage Grove Reservoir Rd. Campground is 2.6 miles on the right.

Points of Interest

In Eugene browse and shop at the legendary Saturday Market. Take in the Hult Center for the Performing Arts. Visit the Jordan Schnitzer Museum of Art on the University of Oregon campus.

RV Sites		Water		Laundry	
Number	97	None		Wi-Fi	
Shaded	Y	At Site		Fishing	Y
By Water	Y	Spigots	Y	Hiking	Y
Paved	Y	Sewer		Biking	Y
Pull Thru	Y	None		Swimming	Y
ADA	Y	At Site		Watch Wildlife	Y
Max RV Size	45	Dump Station	Y	Pets	Y
Electric		Amenities		Security	
None	Y	Restrooms	Y	Host(s)	Y
20 Amp		Showers	Y	Rangers(s)	Y
30 Amp		Reserve Sites	Y	Gate	
50 Amp		Store		Patrolled	Y
		Grill/Table	Y		

[4] Gills Landing RV Park
I-5, Exit 228
East of Corvallis, in Lebanon
N44 32.258 W122 53.525
County Rate: $24
(541) 258-4917
http://www.ci.lebanon.or.us/index.aspx?page=125

Directions

9 miles. From Exit 228 go east, 7.7 miles on Hwy 34 (Corvallis-Lebanon Hwy) into Lebanon to Hwy 20. Turn south on Main St for 0.5 miles to Grant St. Follow Grant east 0.7 miles to the Park.

Points of Interest

With 38 arts and culture options or 21 culinary and wineries possibilities, you're sure to find plenty to do in Corvallis. Shoppers will be happy too. There are also walking tours - the Historic Homes Trolley Tour, Historical Walking Tours, or do a Corvallis GPS Waymarking Hunt.

RV Sites		Water		Laundry	
Number	20	None		Wi-Fi	Y
Shaded	Y	At Site	Y	Fishing	Y
By Water	Y	Spigots	Y	Hiking	Y
Paved	Y	**Sewer**		Biking	Y
Pull Thru		None		Swimming	
ADA	Y	At Site	Y	Watch Wildlife	
Max RV Size	45	Dump Station		Pets	Y
Electric		**Amenities**		**Security**	
None		Restrooms	Y	Host(s)	Y
20 Amp	Y	Showers	Y	Rangers(s)	
30 Amp	Y	Reserve Sites	Y	Gate	
50 Amp	Y	Store		Patrolled	Y
		Grill/Table	Y		

[5] Champoeg State Heritage Area
I-5, Exit 278
South of Portland
N45 14.896 W122 53.651
State Rate: $22-$28
(503) 678-1251
http://www.oregonstateparks.org/park_113.php

Directions

6 miles. From Exit 278 go 3.5 miles west on Ehlen (then Yergen Rd) to Case Rd. Turn north for 1.3 miles to Champoeg Rd, then west for 0.9 miles to the Park.

Points of Interest

Champoeg features a unique combination of history, nature, & recreation. This is the site where Oregon's first provisional government was formed in 1843. Tour the park's Visitor Center, Newell House, & Pioneer Mothers Log Cabin museums to discover pioneer life at Champoeg.

RV Sites		Water		Laundry	
Number	79	None		Wi-Fi	
Shaded	Y	At Site	Y	Fishing	Y
By Water	Y	Spigots	Y	Hiking	Y
Paved	Y	**Sewer**		Biking	Y
Pull Thru	Y	None		Swimming	Y
ADA	Y	At Site	Y	Watch Wildlife	Y
Max RV Size	40	Dump Station	Y	Pets	Y
Electric		**Amenities**		**Security**	
None		Restrooms	Y	Host(s)	Y
20 Amp	Y	Showers	Y	Rangers(s)	Y
30 Amp	Y	Reserve Sites	Y	Gate	
50 Amp	Y	Store	Y	Patrolled	Y
		Grill/Table	Y		

[6] Umatilla Marina and RV Park
I-82, Exit 1 of I-82
On the Columbia River at Umatilla
N45 55.392 W119 19.850
County Rate: $30
(541) 922-3939
http://www.umatillarvpark.com/

Directions

1 mile. From Exit 1 turn west on Hwy 730 and immediately turn right on Brownell Blvd. Go 0.4 miles north to 3rd. Turn left, go 0.3 miles to Quincy St. Turn right to the Park.

Points of Interest

Visit Columbia Crest Winery, Fort Henrietta or Pendleton Woolen Mills. Enjoy the Hermiston's Farm City Pro Rodeo or Pendleton Roundup. McNary Dam has a number of sights, including an Interpretive Center. Take your walk at the McNary Wildlife Nature Area.

RV Sites		Water		Laundry	
Number	26	None		Wi-Fi	Y
Shaded	Y	At Site	Y	Fishing	Y
By Water	Y	Spigots	Y	Hiking	Y
Paved		**Sewer**		Biking	Y
Pull Thru	Y	None		Swimming	Y
ADA	Y	At Site	Y	Watch Wildlife	
Max RV Size	40	Dump Station	Y	Pets	Y
Electric		**Amenities**		**Security**	
None		Restrooms	Y	Host(s)	Y
20 Amp	Y	Showers	Y	Rangers(s)	
30 Amp	Y	Reserve Sites	Y	Gate	
50 Amp	Y	Store		Patrolled	Y
		Grill/Table	Y		

[7] Ainsworth State Park
I-84, Exit 35
West of Hood River
N45 35.745 W122 03.180
State Rate: $20-$24

(503) 695-2301
http://www.oregonstateparks.org/park_146.php

Directions

1 mile. From Exit 35 go southwest on the historic Columbia River Hwy for 1 mile to the Park.

Points of Interest

Enjoy breathtaking views of the Columbia River Gorge from the Historic Columbia River Highway State Trail. The Mosier Twin Tunnels stretch is a paved five-mile route between two trailheads. There is gorge scenery from the Bridge of the Gods at Cascade Locks.

RV Sites		Water		Laundry	
Number	43	None		Wi-Fi	
Shaded	Y	At Site	Y	Fishing	
By Water	Y	Spigots	Y	Hiking	Y
Paved	Y	Sewer		Biking	Y
Pull Thru	Y	None		Swimming	
ADA	Y	At Site	Y	Watch Wildlife	Y
Max RV Size	45	Dump Station	Y	Pets	Y
Electric		Amenities		Security	
None		Restrooms	Y	Host(s)	Y
20 Amp	Y	Showers	Y	Rangers(s)	Y
30 Amp	Y	Reserve Sites		Gate	
50 Amp		Store		Patrolled	Y
		Grill/Table	Y		

[8] Deschutes River State Recreation Area
I-84, Exit 97
East of The Dalles
N45 38.075 W120 54.502
State Rate: $18-$22

(541) 739-2322
http://www.oregonstateparks.org/park_37.php

Directions

3 miles. From Exit 97 go east on Hwy 206, just across the Deschutes River to the Park entrance.

Points of Interest

Enjoy a bike ride, following the 'Old Railbed Trail,' up the canyon. The trail is an easy, flat grade but mountain bikes are recommended. Be prepared with a patch kit. Visit The Dalles, where pioneers once loaded their wagons onto rafts or barges & floated down the Columbia.

RV Sites		Water		Laundry	
Number	34	None		Wi-Fi	
Shaded	Y	At Site	Y	Fishing	Y
By Water	Y	Spigots	Y	Hiking	Y
Paved	Y	Sewer		Biking	Y
Pull Thru		None		Swimming	
ADA	Y	At Site		Watch Wildlife	Y
Max RV Size	42	Dump Station	Y	Pets	Y
Electric		Amenities		Security	
None		Restrooms	Y	Host(s)	Y
20 Amp	Y	Showers	Y	Rangers(s)	Y
30 Amp	Y	Reserve Sites	Y	Gate	
50 Amp	Y	Store		Patrolled	Y
		Grill/Table	Y		

[9] Boardman Marina Park
I-84, Exit 164
North side of Boardman
N45 50.592 W119 42.486
County Rate: $27-$32

(541) 481-7217
http://www.boardmanmarinapark.com/

Directions

1 mile. From Exit 164 turn north for 0.4 miles on Main St. Turn west for 0.3 miles on Marine Dr to the Park on your right.

Points of Interest

Visit Columbia Crest Winery, Fort Henrietta or Pendleton Woolen Mills. Enjoy the Hermiston's Farm City Pro Rodeo or Pendleton Roundup. McNary Dam has a number of sights, including an Interpretive Center. Take your walk at the McNary Wildlife Nature Area.

RV Sites		Water		Laundry	Y
Number	63	None		Wi-Fi	Y
Shaded	Y	At Site	Y	Fishing	Y
By Water	Y	Spigots	Y	Hiking	Y
Paved	Y	Sewer		Biking	Y
Pull Thru		None		Swimming	
ADA	Y	At Site	Y	Watch Wildlife	
Max RV Size	40	Dump Station	Y	Pets	Y
Electric		Amenities		Security	
None		Restrooms	Y	Host(s)	Y
20 Amp	Y	Showers	Y	Rangers(s)	
30 Amp	Y	Reserve Sites	Y	Gate	
50 Amp	Y	Store		Patrolled	Y
		Grill/Table	Y		

[10] Emigrant Springs State Heritage Area
I-84, Exit 234
Southeast of Pendleton
N45 32.411 W118 27.631
State Rate: $18-$24
(541) 983-2277

http://www.oregonstateparks.org/park_23.php

Directions

1 mile. **Eastbound**, from Exit 234 go 0.6 miles south on the Frontage Rd to the Park. **Westbound**, from Exit 234 go 0.6 miles northwest on the Frontage Rd to the Park.

Points of Interest

The Park preserves a site near the summit of the Blue Mountains where Oregon Trail travelers once replenished their water supplies. At the Oregon Trail Interpretive Park experience the Oregon Trail as the pioneers did - some of the best-preserved traces of the Old Emigrant Road await.

RV Sites		Water		Laundry	
Number	18	None		Wi-Fi	
Shaded	Y	At Site	Y	Fishing	
By Water		Spigots	Y	Hiking	Y
Paved	Y	Sewer		Biking	Y
Pull Thru		None		Swimming	
ADA	Y	At Site	Y	Watch Wildlife	Y
Max RV Size	40	Dump Station	near	Pets	Y
Electric		Amenities		Security	
None		Restrooms	Y	Host(s)	Y
20 Amp	Y	Showers	Y	Rangers(s)	Y
30 Amp	Y	Reserve Sites	Y	Gate	
50 Amp	Y	Store		Patrolled	Y
		Grill/Table	Y		

[11] Farewell Bend State Recreation Area
I-84, Exit 353
North of Ontario
N44 18.212 W117 13.658
State Rate: $18-$24
(541) 869-2365

http://www.oregonstateparks.org/park_7.php

Directions

1 mile. From Exit 353 turn north for 1 mile on Huntington Hwy 30 to the Park entrance.

Points of Interest

The Park offers a beautiful desert experience on the banks of the Snake River's Brownlee Reservoir. Pioneers took a final rest here before traveling to Oregon City. Oregon Trail wagon ruts are still visible. Historic markers provide information on Farewell Bend's significance.

RV Sites		Water		Laundry	
Number	80	None		Wi-Fi	
Shaded	Y	At Site	Y	Fishing	Y
By Water	Y	Spigots	Y	Hiking	Y
Paved	Y	Sewer		Biking	Y
Pull Thru	Y	None		Swimming	
ADA	Y	At Site	Y	Watch Wildlife	Y
Max RV Size	45	Dump Station	Y	Pets	Y
Electric		Amenities		Security	
None		Restrooms	Y	Host(s)	Y
20 Amp	Y	Showers	Y	Rangers(s)	Y
30 Amp	Y	Reserve Sites	Y	Gate	
50 Amp	Y	Store		Patrolled	Y
		Grill/Table	Y		

[12] Bullards Beach State Park
Hwy 101
North of Bandon
N43 09.104 W124 23.738
State Rate: $22-$28
(541) 347-2209

http://www.oregonstateparks.org/index.cfm?do=parkPage.dsp_parkPage&parkId=50

Directions

2.3 miles. In Bandon go 2.3 miles north of the Hwy 101/42S junction on Hwy 101 to the Park.

Points of Interest

Historic Coquille River Lighthouse is at the end of the beach access road in the park. Visit Bandon by the Sea, with its many shops, galleries, and restaurants. Bandon is called "The Cranberry Capitol of the World." Coos Bay is 21 miles north of the Park.

RV Sites		Water		Laundry	
Number	162	None		Wi-Fi	
Shaded	Y	At Site	Y	Fishing	Y
By Water	Y	Spigots	Y	Hiking	Y
Paved	Y	Sewer		Biking	Y
Pull Thru	few	None		Swimming	
ADA	Y	At Site	Y	Watch Wildlife	Y
Max RV Size	45	Dump Station	Y	Pets	Y
Electric		Amenities		Security	
None		Restrooms	Y	Host(s)	Y
20 Amp	Y	Showers	Y	Rangers(s)	Y
30 Amp	Y	Reserve Sites	Y	Gate	
50 Amp	Y	Store		Patrolled	Y
		Grill/Table	Y		

[13] Honeyman State Park
Hwy 101
South of Florence
N43 55.815 W124 06.452
State Rate: $24-$31
(541) 997-3851
http://www.oregonstateparks.org/index.
cfm?do=parkPage.dsp_parkPage&parkId=95

Directions

3.2 miles. In Florence go 3.2 miles south of the Hwy 101/126 junction on Hwy 101 to the Park.

Points of Interest

Take the challenge, walk the two miles of sand dunes from the park to the ocean. Visit the Heceta Head Lighthouse and Scenic Viewpoint. Time your Park visit - spring brings out the pink rhododendrons; in fall, huckleberries and blackberries are ripe for the picking.

RV Sites		Water		Laundry	
Number	156	None		Wi-Fi	
Shaded	Y	At Site	Y	Fishing	Y
By Water	Y	Spigots	Y	Hiking	Y
Paved	Y	Sewer		Biking	Y
Pull Thru	Y	None		Swimming	Y
ADA	Y	At Site	Y	Watch Wildlife	
Max RV Size	42	Dump Station	Y	Pets	Y
Electric		Amenities		Security	
None		Restrooms	Y	Host(s)	Y
20 Amp	Y	Showers	Y	Rangers(s)	Y
30 Amp	Y	Reserve Sites	Y	Gate	
50 Amp	Y	Store		Patrolled	Y
		Grill/Table	Y		

[14] Devil's Lake State Recreation Area
Hwy 101
North of Lincoln City
N44 58.250 W124 00.870
State Rate: $24-$31
(541) 994-2002
http://www.oregonstateparks.org/index.
cfm?do=parkPage.dsp_parkPage&parkId=155

Directions

In Lincoln City. On the northwest shore of Devil's Lake at NE 6th Dr in Lincoln City.

Points of Interest

The only Oregon coast campground located in a city, you are within walking distance of the ocean and town, yet very secluded with nature trails. One of the largest outlet malls in Oregon is a short drive away. A great location to stock up on supplies, shop the town and enjoy the ocean.

RV Sites		Water		Laundry	
Number	30	None		Wi-Fi	
Shaded	Y	At Site	Y	Fishing	Y
By Water	Y	Spigots	Y	Hiking	
Paved	Y	Sewer		Biking	Y
Pull Thru		None		Swimming	
ADA	Y	At Site	Y	Watch Wildlife	Y
Max RV Size	45	Dump Station	Y	Pets	Y
Electric		Amenities		Security	
None		Restrooms	Y	Host(s)	Y
20 Amp	Y	Showers	Y	Rangers(s)	Y
30 Amp	Y	Reserve Sites	Y	Gate	
50 Amp	Y	Store		Patrolled	Y
		Grill/Table	Y		

[15] Fort Stevens State Park
Hwy 101
North of Warrenton
State Rate: $25-$32
N46 11.058 W123 57.396
(503) 861-3170, ext 21
http://www.oregonstateparks.org/index.
cfm?do=parkPage.dsp_parkPage&parkId=129

Directions

4.6 miles. South of Warrenton turn off Hwy 101, west on to Hwy 104, go 1.4 miles to Delaura Beach Ln (SW 18th St). Turn left, proceed (merges into NW Ridge Rd) 3.2 miles to the Park.

Points of Interest

Tour Fort Stevens, which was in service for 84 years, beginning during the Civil War & closing at the end of World War II. Walk the beach, do some beach-combing. Don't miss the Astoria Bridge, a drive across is an experience in itself.

RV Sites		Water		Laundry	
Number	450	None		Wi-Fi	
Shaded	Y	At Site	Y	Fishing	Y
By Water	Y	Spigots	Y	Hiking	Y
Paved	Y	Sewer		Biking	Y
Pull Thru	Y	None		Swimming	Y
ADA	Y	At Site	Y	Watch Wildlife	Y
Max RV Size	45	Dump Station	Y	Pets	Y
Electric		Amenities		Security	
None		Restrooms	Y	Host(s)	Y
20 Amp	Y	Showers	Y	Rangers(s)	Y
30 Amp	Y	Reserve Sites	Y	Gate	
50 Amp	Y	Store		Patrolled	Y
		Grill/Table	Y		

[16] Crater Lake NP (Mazama Village)
Hwy 97, North on Hwy 62
North of Klamath Falls
N42 51.947 W122 10.148
NPS Rate: $29-$35
America/Beautiful Rate: $15-$18
(888) 774-2728
http://www.craterlakelodges.com/lodging/mazama-village-campground/

Directions

From Hwy 97/62 go northwest on Hwy 62 for 30 miles to the Mazama Village Campground.

Points of Interest

Located seven miles from the rim of Crater Lake, the Mazama Village Campground is open mid-June to late September/early October. Reservations highly recommended, some sites are first-come-first- serve. For details visit - *http://www.nps.gov/crla/index.htm*

RV Sites		Water		Laundry	Y
Number	212	None		Wi-Fi	
Shaded	Y	At Site		Fishing	
By Water		Spigots	Y	Hiking	Y
Paved		Sewer		Biking	Y
Pull Thru	Y	None		Swimming	Y
ADA	Y	At Site		Watch Wildlife	Y
Max RV Size	45	Dump Station	Y	Pets	Y
Electric		Amenities		Security	
None		Restrooms	Y	Host(s)	Y
20 Amp	few	Showers	Y	Rangers(s)	Y
30 Amp	few	Reserve Sites	Y	Gate	
50 Amp	few	Store	Y	Patrolled	Y
		Grill/Table	Y		

[17] Tumalo State Park
Hwy 97, Northwest on Hwy 20
Northwest of Bend
N44 07.560 W121 19.807
State Rate: $26-$30
(541) 388-6055
http://www.oregonstateparks.org/index.cfm?do=parkPage.dsp_parkPage&parkId=34

Directions

2.6 miles. At the junction of Hwy 97 & Hwy 20 go northwest on Hwy 20 for 1.4 miles to Old Bend-Redmond Hwy. Turn left, then right on O. B. Riley Rd in 0.2 miles. Proceed 1 mile to the Park.

Points of Interest

A day of sightseeing in Bend is a good choice. Bend, known for outdoor pursuits and pristine beauty, is the "outdoor playground of the West." Also nearby are Newberry National Volcanic Monument & Cline Falls.

RV Sites		Water		Laundry	
Number	22	None		Wi-Fi	
Shaded	Y	At Site	Y	Fishing	Y
By Water	Y	Spigots	Y	Hiking	Y
Paved	Y	Sewer		Biking	Y
Pull Thru		None		Swimming	Y
ADA	Y	At Site	Y	Watch Wildlife	
Max RV Size	45	Dump Station	Y	Pets	Y
Electric		Amenities		Security	
None		Restrooms	Y	Host(s)	Y
20 Amp	Y	Showers	Y	Rangers(s)	Y
30 Amp	Y	Reserve Sites	Y	Gate	
50 Amp		Store		Patrolled	Y
		Grill/Table	Y		

[18] Jefferson County Fair Complex
Hwy 97/26
In Madras
N44 37.075 W121 08.247
County Rate: $20-$23
(541) 475-6288
http://www.jcfairgrounds.org/rv-park

Directions

Adjoins Hwy 97/26. 1 mile north of the junction of Hwy 97 and Hwy 26.

Points of Interest

A good one night stopover. Open all year. Be sure to check the Fairground calender to determine of you'll arrive in the middle of a fair event. Convenient to shopping for supplies. Named for the fabric, Madras offers rock-hounding, fishing, pleasure boating, rafting, water-skiing, golfing, hiking; or enjoy culture sampling the community.

RV Sites		Water		Laundry	
Number	65	None		Wi-Fi	
Shaded		At Site	Y	Fishing	
By Water		Spigots	Y	Hiking	
Paved		Sewer		Biking	
Pull Thru	Y	None		Swimming	
ADA	Y	At Site	Y	Watch Wildlife	
Max RV Size	45	Dump Station		Pets	Y
Electric		Amenities		Security	
None		Restrooms	Y	Host(s)	Y
20 Amp	Y	Showers	Y	Rangers(s)	
30 Amp	Y	Reserve Sites		Gate	
50 Amp	Y	Store		Patrolled	Y
		Grill/Table	Y		

[19] Camp Creek NF
Hwy 26
East of Rhododendron
Mount Hood NF Rate: $16-$41
America/Beautiful Rate: $8-$21
N45 18.475 W121 50.949
(541) 328-0909
http://www.recreation.gov/

Directions

3 miles. From Rhododendron go 3 miles east on Hwy 26 to the campground on your right.

Points of Interest

The campground sits next to a babbling forest creek in the country's scenic Pacific Northwest region and is not far from the base of snow-covered Mt. Hood. Surrounding the campground are a variety of hiking and mountain biking trails. A variety of trout and whitefish populate the nearby creek and river.

RV Sites		Water		Laundry	
Number	12	None		Wi-Fi	
Shaded	Y	At Site		Fishing	Y
By Water	Y	Spigots	Y	Hiking	Y
Paved		Sewer		Biking	Y
Pull Thru	Y	None	Y	Swimming	
ADA	Y	At Site		Watch Wildlife	Y
Max RV Size	25	Dump Station		Pets	Y
Electric		Amenities		Security	
None	Y	Restrooms	Y	Host(s)	Y
20 Amp		Showers		Rangers(s)	Y
30 Amp		Reserve Sites	Y	Gate	
50 Amp		Store		Patrolled	Y
		Grill/Table	Y		

[20] Grant County RV Park
Hwy 26/395
In John Day
N44 25.215 W118 57.265
County Rate: $15-$27
(541) 575-1900
http://www.grantcountyfairgrounds.com/rvpark.php

Directions

0.3 miles. From the junction of Hwy 26 and Hwy 395 in John Day go one block west on Hwy 26/395 (West Main) to NW Bridge St. Turn north for 4 blocks to the Park & Fairgrounds.

Points of Interest

The Grant County RV Park is next to the John Day River & the Grant County Fairgrounds. Only blocks from the City Park & swimming pool, downtown, restaurants, and shopping but still feels as if you're in the country.

RV Sites		Water		Laundry	
Number	25	None		Wi-Fi	Y
Shaded	Y	At Site	Y	Fishing	
By Water		Spigots	Y	Hiking	
Paved	Y	Sewer		Biking	
Pull Thru	Y	None		Swimming	
ADA		At Site	Y	Watch Wildlife	
Max RV Size	45	Dump Station	Y	Pets	Y
Electric		Amenities		Security	
None		Restrooms	Y	Host(s)	Y
20 Amp	Y	Showers	Y	Rangers(s)	
30 Amp	Y	Reserve Sites	Y	Gate	
50 Amp	Y	Store		Patrolled	Y
		Grill/Table	Y		

[21] Unity Lake State Recreation Area
Hwy 26, North on Hwy 245
West of Unity
N44 29.680 W118 11.252
State Rate: $19-$24
(541) 446-3470
http://www.oregonstateparks.org/index.cfm?do=parkPage.dsp_parkPage&parkId=7

Directions

4.3 miles. From the Post Office in Unity go 1.9 miles west to Hwy 245. Turn north, 2.4 miles to the Park.

Points of Interest

The high desert surroundings of this park and the smell of juniper provider a unique environment. The cool grass of the park, with the lake as background, formed by the Burnt River, make for a relaxing campground experience.

RV Sites		Water		Laundry	
Number	35	None		Wi-Fi	
Shaded	Y	At Site	Y	Fishing	Y
By Water	Y	Spigots	Y	Hiking	Y
Paved	Y	Sewer		Biking	Y
Pull Thru	Y	None		Swimming	
ADA	Y	At Site	Y	Watch Wildlife	Y
Max RV Size	45	Dump Station	Y	Pets	Y
Electric		Amenities		Security	
None		Restrooms	Y	Host(s)	Y
20 Amp	Y	Showers	Y	Rangers(s)	Y
30 Amp	Y	Reserve Sites	Y	Gate	
50 Amp	Y	Store		Patrolled	Y
		Grill/Table	Y		

About Pennsylvania's Public Campgrounds

Pennsylvania's state parks are managed by the Pennsylvania Department of Conservation and Natural Resources (DCNR). The Department competed with the best systems in the country and was awarded the top honor as the 2009 National Gold Medal Award for Excellence in Park and Recreation Management. The DCNR website for State Parks is - **http://www.dcnr.state.pa.us/stateparks/**

Pets are welcome in designated locations: day-use areas, on designated sites in campgrounds, and all areas not otherwise closed to pets. Pets are prohibited in swimming areas, inside buildings, in non-pet overnight areas, or in any area designated as an area closed to pets.

Make online reservations or call toll-free (888) 727-2757, 7 a.m. to 5 p.m. Monday to Saturday, for state park information and reservations, or e-mail them your postal address for an information packet. Campsites can be reserved from 11 months up to noon of the day of arrival. To reserve online go to -

http://www.pa.reserveworld.com/

Campground fees are set park-by-park. Entry is free. General Fee Guidelines are:

Amenities (Per Night)	Resident Price	Non-resident Price
Site Base Price	$15.00	$17.00
Premium (Fri. Sat. Holiday, Events)	$ 4.00	$ 4.00
Electricity	$ 6.50	$ 6.50
Water	$ 8.00	$ 8.00
Water and Sewer	$13.00	$13.00
Designated Pet Campsite	$ 2.00	$ 2.00
Senior Citizen/ADA Discount	- $ 4.50	- $ 4.50
Transient RV Overnight Camping	$ 6.00	$ 6.00

[1] Laurel Hill State Park

[2] Shawnee State Park

[3] Cowans Gap State Park

[4] French Creek State Park

[5] Pymatuning State Park

[6] Shenango Recreation Area Campground

[7] Clear Creek State Park

[8] Bald Eagle State Park

[9] Hickory Run State Park

[10] Caledonia State Park

[11] Locust Lake State Park

[12] Lackawanna State Park

[13] Gifford Pinchot State Park

[14] Promised Land State Park

[15] Blue Knob State Park

[16] Black Moshannon State Park

[17] Tobyhanna State Park

[18] Chapman State Park

[19] Lyman Run State Park

[20] Hills Creek State Park

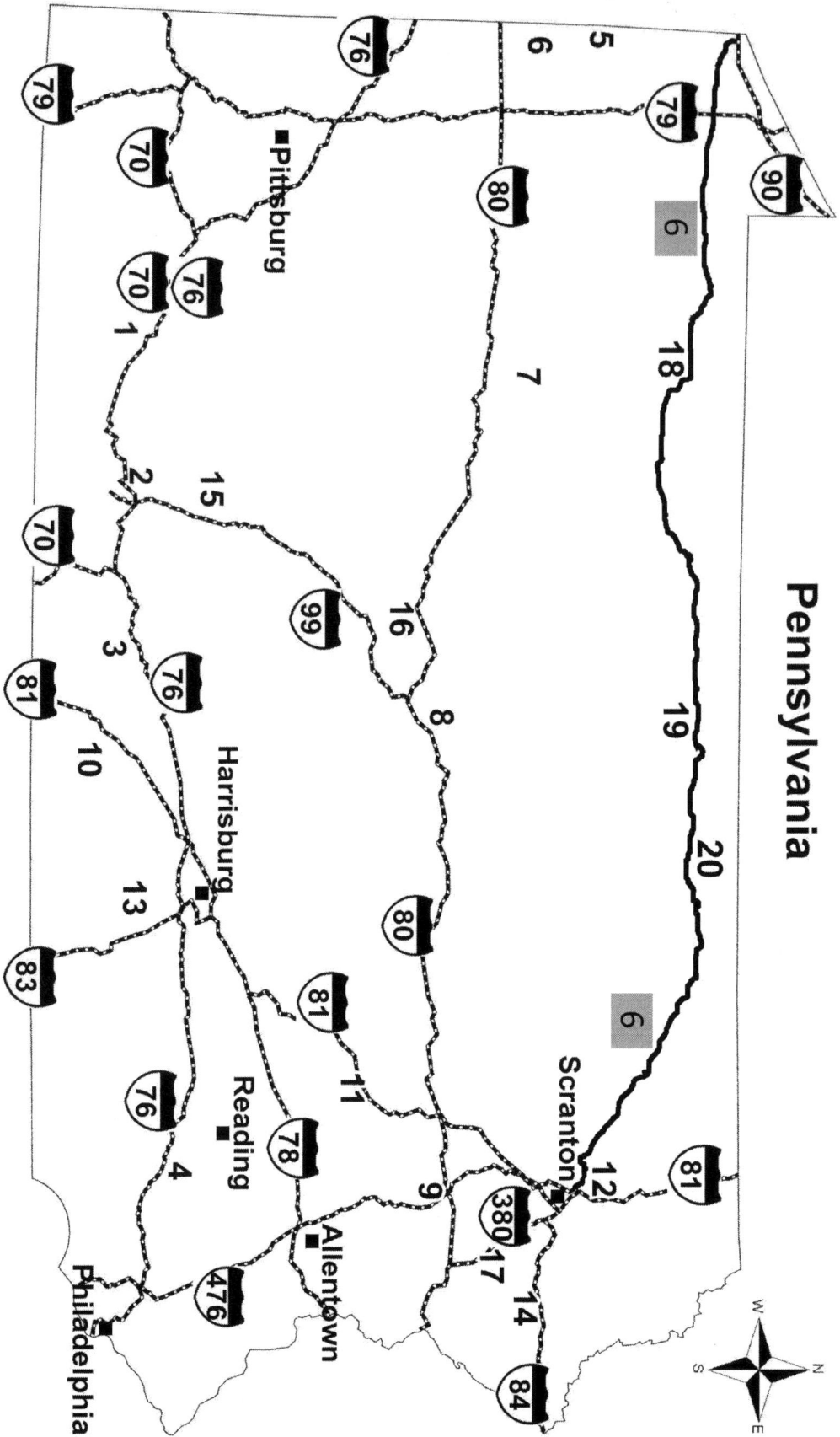

Pennsylvania

[1] Laurel Hill State Park
I-70/76, Exits 91 or 110
West of Somerset
N40 00.547 W79 13.100
State Rates: See Introduction
(814) 445-7725
http://www.dcnr.state.pa.us/stateparks/find-apark/laurelhill/index.htm

Directions

11-14 miles. **From Exit 91**, go 12 miles southeast on Hwy 31 to Trent Rd. Turn right for 2 miles to the Park. **From Exit 110,** go south 0.5 miles on Hwy 601 to Hwy 31. Turn east, go 8 miles to Trent Rd. Turn left for 2 miles to the Park.

Points of Interest

History buffs will want to visit French & Indian War sites including Fort Necessity and Fort Ligonier where a key strategic battle of the French & Indian War occurred. Stop by Frank Lloyd Wright's Fallingwater®.

RV Sites		Water			Laundry	Y
Number	264	None			Wi-Fi	
Shaded	Y	At Site			Fishing	Y
By Water	Y	Spigots	Y		Hiking	Y
Paved	Y	Sewer			Biking	Y
Pull Thru		None			Swimming	Y
ADA	Y	At Site			Watch Wildlife	Y
Max RV Size	45	Dump Station	Y		Pets	some
Electric		Amenities			Security	
None		Restrooms	Y		Host(s)	Y
20 Amp	Y	Showers	Y		Rangers(s)	Y
30 Amp	Y	Reserve Sites	Y		Gate	
50 Amp	Y	Store			Patrolled	Y
		Grill/Table	Y			

[2] Shawnee State Park
I-70/76 & I-99 Junction, Exit 146
West of I-99 Junction
N40 03.040 W78 37.414
State Rates: See Introduction
(814) 733-4218
http://www.dcnr.state.pa.us/stateparks/find-apark/shawnee/index.htm

Directions

9 miles. From I-70/76 & I-99, turn south on I-99 for 2 miles to Hwy 30 exit. Go west for 7 miles to the Park entrance on your left (just after Harrison Rd).

Points of Interest

At Old Bedford Village & Fort Bedford enjoy military & civilian re-enactments, colonial crafts, exhibits & instructions, and festivals. The only fossilized coral reef cavern known to be in existence is found at Coral Caverns.

RV Sites		Water			Laundry	Y
Number	293	None			Wi-Fi	
Shaded	Y	At Site			Fishing	Y
By Water		Spigots	Y		Hiking	Y
Paved		Sewer			Biking	Y
Pull Thru	few	None			Swimming	Y
ADA	Y	At Site			Watch Wildlife	Y
Max RV Size	45	Dump Station	Y		Pets	some
Electric		Amenities			Security	
None		Restrooms	Y		Host(s)	Y
20 Amp	Y	Showers	Y		Rangers(s)	Y
30 Amp	Y	Reserve Sites	Y		Gate	
50 Amp	Y	Store			Patrolled	Y
		Grill/Table	Y			

[3] Cowans Gap State Park
I-76, Exit 180
West of Hustontown
N39 59.929 W77 55.255
State Rates: See Introduction
(717) 485-3948
http://www.dcnr.state.pa.us/stateparks/find-apark/cowansgap/index.htm

Directions

12 miles. From I-76, turn north on Hwy 522 for 5 miles to Burnt Cabins. Bare right on to Hwy 1010 (Grist Mill Rd) for 0.8 miles. Turn south on Hwy 1005 (Allens Valley Rd). Follow Hwy 1005 for 6 miles to the Park entrance.

Points of Interest

Tour the Historic Burnt Cabins Grist Mill. This operating mill produces cornmeal, buckwheat, whole wheat and rye flour. Visit President James Buchanan's birthplace.

RV Sites		Water			Laundry	
Number	201	None			Wi-Fi	
Shaded	Y	At Site			Fishing	Y
By Water	Y	Spigots	Y		Hiking	Y
Paved		Sewer			Biking	Y
Pull Thru	few	None			Swimming	Y
ADA	Y	At Site			Watch Wildlife	Y
Max RV Size	45	Dump Station	Y		Pets	some
Electric		Amenities			Security	
None		Restrooms	Y		Host(s)	Y
20 Amp	Y	Showers	Y		Rangers(s)	Y
30 Amp	Y	Reserve Sites	Y		Gate	
50 Amp		Store	Y		Patrolled	Y
		Grill/Table	Y			

[4] French Creek State Park
I-76, Exits 298
Southeast of Reading
N40 11.774 W75 47.802
State Rates: See Introduction
(610) 582-9523
http://www.dcnr.state.pa.us/stateparks/find-apark/frenchcreek/index.htm

Directions

6 miles. From Exit 298 go east 0.4 miles on Reading, then right for 1 mile on Joanna Rd, then right for 0.6 miles on Elverson Rd to Hopewell. Go left on Hopewell, which becomes Park Rd, for 3.6 miles to the Park entrance.

Points of Interest

French Creek offers two lakes, extensive forests, & 40 miles of hiking trails. Nearby the Hopewell Furnace National Historic Site features a cold-blast furnace restored to its 1830s appearance.

RV Sites		Water		Laundry	
Number	201	None		Wi-Fi	
Shaded	Y	At Site		Fishing	Y
By Water		Spigots	Y	Hiking	Y
Paved		Sewer		Biking	Y
Pull Thru		None		Swimming	Y
ADA	Y	At Site		Watch Wildlife	Y
Max RV Size	40	Dump Station	Y	Pets	some
Electric		Amenities		Security	
None		Restrooms	Y	Host(s)	Y
20 Amp	Y	Showers	Y	Rangers(s)	Y
30 Amp	Y	Reserve Sites	Y	Gate	
50 Amp	Y	Store		Patrolled	Y
		Grill/Table	Y		

[5] Pymatuning State Park
I-79, Exit 147
West of Meadville
N41 29.938 W80 28.169
State Rates: See Introduction
(724) 932-3142
http://www.dcnr.state.pa.us/stateparks/find-apark/pymatuning/index.htm

Directions

20 miles. From Exit 147 follow Hwy 322 for 20 miles to the Park

Points of Interest

This is the largest state park in the Common-wealth, within Pennsylvania's Great Lakes Region. Ride in a train or be entertained at a dinner theatre. There is also a century-old amusement park, the state's largest agricultural fair and museums of all types.

RV Sites		Water		Laundry	Y
Number	388	None		Wi-Fi	
Shaded	Y	At Site	Y	Fishing	Y
By Water	Y	Spigots	Y	Hiking	Y
Paved		Sewer		Biking	Y
Pull Thru	few	None		Swimming	Y
ADA	Y	At Site	Y	Watch Wildlife	Y
Max RV Size	45	Dump Station	Y	Pets	some
Electric		Amenities		Security	
None		Restrooms	Y	Host(s)	Y
20 Amp	Y	Showers	Y	Rangers(s)	Y
30 Amp	Y	Reserve Sites	Y	Gate	
50 Amp	Y	Store	Y	Patrolled	Y
		Grill/Table	Y		

[6] Shenango Recreation Area Camp
I-80, Exit 4
North of Sharon-Hermitage
N41 17.854 W80 25.826
COE Rate: $19-$24
America/Beautiful Rate: $10-$12
(724) 646-1124
http://www.recreation.gov/

Directions

12 miles. From Exit 4 go north on I-376 & Hwy 18 north, crossing the causeway, 9.7 mi. in all. The park is on the left of the divided highway. Continue north, exit to the right at Rutledge Dr, make the turn-around, go south on Hwy 18 for 1.7 mi. Before the causeway go right on West Lake Rd, & 0.4 mi. to the Park.

Points of Interest

In the summer, concerts are held at the Buhl Farm Park. Do part of the Underground Railroad Driving tour. See the following website -

www.discovermercercountypa.org/urr.asp

RV Sites		Water		Laundry	
Number	322	None		Wi-Fi	
Shaded	Y	At Site		Fishing	Y
By Water	Y	Spigots	Y	Hiking	Y
Paved		Sewer		Biking	Y
Pull Thru	Y	None		Swimming	
ADA	Y	At Site		Watch Wildlife	Y
Max RV Size	45	Dump Station	Y	Pets	Y
Electric		Amenities		Security	
None		Restrooms	Y	Host(s)	Y
20 Amp	Y	Showers	Y	Rangers(s)	Y
30 Amp	Y	Reserve Sites	Y	Gate	
50 Amp	Y	Store		Patrolled	Y
		Grill/Table	Y		

[7] Clear Creek State Park
I-80, Exit 78
Northeast of Clarion
N41 19.345 W79 04.598
State Rates: See Introduction
(814) 752-2368
http://www.dcnr.state.pa.us/stateparks/find-apark/clearcreek/index.htm

Directions

11.5 miles. From Exit 78, go 7.5 miles north on Hwy 36 to Hwy 949. Turn right, go 4 miles to the Park.

Points of Interest

During the summer, an environmental educator presents guided walks, hands-on activities & evening campfire programs. The Visitor Center has logging and nature exhibits. Clarion County Festivals and attractions include The Horsethief Festival, and Autumn Leaf Festival.

RV Sites		Water		Laundry	
Number	53	None		Wi-Fi	
Shaded	Y	At Site		Fishing	Y
By Water	Y	Spigots	Y	Hiking	Y
Paved		**Sewer**		Biking	Y
Pull Thru		None		Swimming	
ADA	Y	At Site		Watch Wildlife	Y
Max RV Size	45	Dump Station	Y	Pets	some
Electric		**Amenities**		**Security**	
None		Restrooms	Y	Host(s)	Y
20 Amp	Y	Showers	Y	Rangers(s)	Y
30 Amp	Y	Reserve Sites	Y	Gate	
50 Amp	Y	Store		Patrolled	Y
		Grill/Table	Y		

[8] Bald Eagle State Park
I-80, Exit 158
West of I-99 Junction
N41 02.160 W77 39.113
State Rates: See Introduction
(814) 625-2775
http://www.dcnr.state.pa.us/stateparks/find-apark/baldeagle/index.htm

Directions

8.5 miles. From Exit 158, turn northeast on Hwy 150 for 8.2 miles to the Park entrance on your right.

Points of Interest

Visit the Nature Inn at Bald Eagle. Tour Penn's Cave by boat, one of the only all water caverns in the United States. See the PA Military Museum in Boalsburg, with 20th Century armed services exhibits. Have dinner at the Gamble Mill in Bellefonte, a once working grist mill.

RV Sites		Water		Laundry	
Number	97	None		Wi-Fi	
Shaded	Y	At Site		Fishing	Y
By Water	Y	Spigots	Y	Hiking	Y
Paved	Y	**Sewer**		Biking	Y
Pull Thru		None		Swimming	Y
ADA	Y	At Site		Watch Wildlife	Y
Max RV Size	45	Dump Station	Y	Pets	some
Electric		**Amenities**		**Security**	
None		Restrooms	Y	Host(s)	Y
20 Amp	Y	Showers	Y	Rangers(s)	Y
30 Amp	Y	Reserve Sites	Y	Gate	
50 Amp	Y	Store	Y	Patrolled	Y
		Grill/Table	Y		

[9] Hickory Run State Park
I-80, Exit 274
West of I-476
N41 01.569 W75 41.788
State Rates: See Introduction
(570) 443-0400
http://www.dcnr.state.pa.us/stateparks/find-apark/hickoryrun/index.htm

Directions

6 miles. From Exit 274, turn south on Hwy 534, go 6 miles to the Park entrance.

Points of Interest

Do the Lehigh Gorge State Park and Hickory Run State Park "Auto Tour." Tour Eckley, one of the hundreds of company mining towns or "patches" built in the anthracite region of Pennsylvania during the nineteenth century. Go on down to Pocono Raceway.

RV Sites		Water		Laundry	
Number	381	None		Wi-Fi	
Shaded	Y	At Site		Fishing	Y
By Water	Y	Spigots	Y	Hiking	Y
Paved		**Sewer**		Biking	
Pull Thru		None		Swimming	Y
ADA	Y	At Site		Watch Wildlife	Y
Max RV Size	45	Dump Station	Y	Pets	Y
Electric		**Amenities**		**Security**	
None		Restrooms	Y	Host(s)	Y
20 Amp	Y	Showers	Y	Rangers(s)	Y
30 Amp	Y	Reserve Sites	Y	Gate	
50 Amp	Y	Store	Y	Patrolled	Y
		Grill/Table	Y		

[10] Caledonia State Park
I-81, Exit 16
East of Chambersburg
N39 54.488 W77 28.630
State Rates: See Introduction
(717) 352-2161
http://www.dcnr.state.pa.us/stateparks/find-apark/caledonia/index.htm

Directions

9 miles. From Exit 16 go 8.5 miles east on Hwy 30 to Hwy 233. Turn north for 0.2 miles to the Park entrance.

Points of Interest

A Park naturalist offers campfire programs, guided hikes and environmental education programs in the summer months. The Thaddeus Stevens Blacksmith Shop is a historical center. Be sure to visit nearby Gettysburg National Military Park/Battlefield.

RV Sites		Water		Laundry	
Number	175	None		Wi-Fi	
Shaded	Y	At Site		Fishing	Y
By Water	Y	Spigots	Y	Hiking	Y
Paved		**Sewer**		Biking	Y
Pull Thru	Y	None		Swimming	Y
ADA	Y	At Site		Watch Wildlife	
Max RV Size	45	Dump Station	Y	Pets	some
Electric		**Amenities**		**Security**	
None		Restrooms	Y	Host(s)	Y
20 Amp	Y	Showers	Y	Rangers(s)	Y
30 Amp	Y	Reserve Sites	Y	Gate	
50 Amp	Y	Store		Patrolled	Y
		Grill/Table	Y		

[11] Locust Lake State Park
I-81, Exit 131
South of Mahanoy City
N40 47.097 W76 07.187
State Rates: See Introduction
(570) 467-2404
http://www.dcnr.state.pa.us/stateparks/parks/locustlake.aspx

Directions

6 miles. At Exit 131 ramp to Mahanoy City (Locust SP), on the west side of I-81, turn southwest on to Hwy 1008 (Morea Rd). Go 1.1 miles to Hwy 1006 (Burma Rd). Turn left, go 1 miles to Hwy 1011 (Brockton Mtn Rd). Turn left, go 1.6 miles to Rd 489 (Locust Lake Rd). Turn right for 1.2 miles to the Park.

Points of Interest

This is Schuylkill County, with America's Oldest Brewery. Tour a coal mine or visit a classic car museum. Taste the offerings from five wineries.

RV Sites		Water		Laundry	
Number	282	None		Wi-Fi	
Shaded	Y	At Site		Fishing	Y
By Water	Y	Spigots	Y	Hiking	Y
Paved		**Sewer**		Biking	Y
Pull Thru		None		Swimming	Y
ADA	Y	At Site		Watch Wildlife	
Max RV Size	40	Dump Station	Y	Pets	some
Electric		**Amenities**		**Security**	
None		Restrooms	Y	Host(s)	Y
20 Amp	Y	Showers	Y	Rangers(s)	Y
30 Amp	Y	Reserve Sites	Y	Gate	
50 Amp	Y	Store	Y	Patrolled	Y
		Grill/Table	Y		

[12] Lackawanna State Park
I-81, Exit 199
North of Scranton
N41 33.922 W75 42.475
State Rates: See Introduction
(570) 945-3239
http://www.dcnr.state.pa.us/stateparks/find-apark/lackawanna/index.htmpx

Directions

3.5 miles. From Exit 199 go 3.1 miles on Hwy 524 (Kennedy Creek Rd) to Hwy 407. Turn north for 0.4 miles to Lake View Dr. Turn left in to the Park.

Points of Interest

Lacka-wanna is Indian for "the meeting of two streams." In Scranton take a trip underground - tour a coal mine. Take a trolley ride to Montage Mountain. Check out America's largest collection of steam locomotives.

RV Sites		Water		Laundry	
Number	61	None		Wi-Fi	
Shaded	Y	At Site		Fishing	Y
By Water	Y	Spigots	Y	Hiking	Y
Paved	Y	**Sewer**		Biking	Y
Pull Thru		None		Swimming	Y
ADA	Y	At Site		Watch Wildlife	
Max RV Size	40	Dump Station	Y	Pets	some
Electric		**Amenities**		**Security**	
None		Restrooms	Y	Host(s)	Y
20 Amp	Y	Showers	Y	Rangers(s)	Y
30 Amp	Y	Reserve Sites	Y	Gate	
50 Amp	Y	Store		Patrolled	Y
		Grill/Table	Y		

[13] Gifford Pinchot State Park
I-83, Exit 32
North of York
N40 03.264 W76 54.626
State Rates: See Introduction
(717) 292-4112
http://www.dcnr.state.pa.us/stateparks/find-apark/giffordpinchot/index.htm

Directions

10 miles. From Exit 32, go east on Hwy 382 (Lewisberry Rd) for 3.5 miles. Turn left on Hwy 177, go 6 miles to Hwy 74. Turn left for 0.7 miles to the Park entrance.

Points of Interest

The Park is with 2 hours of Gettysburg, Hershey, Lancaster County (Amish Country) & Baltimore. Some options include the Antique Auto Museum, National Watch & Clock Museum, and The Daylily Farm.

RV Sites		Water		Laundry	
Number	339	None		Wi-Fi	
Shaded	Y	At Site		Fishing	Y
By Water	Y	Spigots	Y	Hiking	Y
Paved	Y	Sewer		Biking	Y
Pull Thru		None		Swimming	Y
ADA	Y	At Site		Watch Wildlife	
Max RV Size	45	Dump Station	Y	Pets	some
Electric		Amenities		Security	
None		Restrooms	Y	Host(s)	Y
20 Amp	Y	Showers	Y	Rangers(s)	Y
30 Amp	Y	Reserve Sites	Y	Gate	
50 Amp	Y	Store		Patrolled	Y
		Grill/Table	Y		

[14] Promised Land State Park
I-84, Exit 26
East of Scranton
N41 19.170 W75 12.584
State Rates: See Introduction
(570) 676-3428
http://www.dcnr.state.pa.us/stateparks/find-apark/promisedland/index.htm

Directions

3 miles. From Exit 26, go south on Hwy 390 for 3 miles to the Park.

Points of Interest

The Delaware Water Gap National Recreation Area is near by and has much to offer in outdoor hikes and sights. Streams tumble off the Pocono plateau and rush through dark hemlock groves to the river. Watch the watershed in action at Dingmans Falls, Raymondskill, or Childs Park.

RV Sites		Water		Laundry	
Number	447	None		Wi-Fi	
Shaded	Y	At Site	Y	Fishing	Y
By Water	Y	Spigots	Y	Hiking	Y
Paved		Sewer		Biking	Y
Pull Thru	Y	None		Swimming	Y
ADA	Y	At Site	Y	Watch Wildlife	
Max RV Size	45	Dump Station	Y	Pets	some
Electric		Amenities		Security	
None		Restrooms	Y	Host(s)	Y
20 Amp	Y	Showers	Y	Rangers(s)	Y
30 Amp	Y	Reserve Sites	Y	Gate	
50 Amp	Y	Store		Patrolled	Y
		Grill/Table	Y		

[15] Blue Knob State Park
I-99, Exit 23 of
South of Altoona
N40 17.717 W78 34.744
State Rates: See Introduction
(814) 276-3576
http://www.dcnr.state.pa.us/stateparks/find-apark/blueknob/index.htm

Directions

12.5 miles. From Exit 23, turn east to the first intersection, then south and east on Hwy 164, for 8 miles to Hwy 3003/4035 (Blue Knob Rd). Turn south for 4.5 miles and in to the Park.

Points of Interest

Overlooking the scenic Ridge and Valley Province to the east, Blue Knob has spectacular views. Unique photographic opportunities are available during low humidity weather and with changes of season.

RV Sites		Water		Laundry	
Number	48	None		Wi-Fi	
Shaded	some	At Site		Fishing	Y
By Water		Spigots	Y	Hiking	Y
Paved		Sewer		Biking	Y
Pull Thru		None		Swimming	Y
ADA	Y	At Site		Watch Wildlife	Y
Max RV Size	40	Dump Station	Y	Pets	some
Electric		Amenities		Security	
None		Restrooms	Y	Host(s)	Y
20 Amp	Y	Showers	Y	Rangers(s)	Y
30 Amp	Y	Reserve Sites	Y	Gate	
50 Amp	Y	Store		Patrolled	Y
		Grill/Table	Y		

[16] Black Moshannon State Park
I-99, Exits 61 or 62
Northwest of State College
N40 54.911 W78 03.513
State Rates: See Introduction
(814) 342-5960
http://www.dcnr.state.pa.us/stateparks/find-apark/blackmoshannon/index.htm

Directions

20 miles. From Exits 61/62 go northwest for 11.5 miles on Hwy 322 to Hwy 504, near north Phillipsburg. Turn east for 8.5 miles to the Park.

Points of Interest

College Station has many cultural, entertainment, shopping, and dining opportunities. The presence of Penn State University opens up possibilities for campus programs open to the public plus an attractive place to walk and sightsee.

RV Sites		Water		Laundry	Y
Number	80	None		Wi-Fi	
Shaded	Y	At Site		Fishing	Y
By Water	Y	Spigots	Y	Hiking	Y
Paved		Sewer		Biking	Y
Pull Thru		None		Swimming	Y
ADA	Y	At Site		Watch Wildlife	Y
Max RV Size	45	Dump Station	Y	Pets	some
Electric		Amenities		Security	
None		Restrooms	Y	Host(s)	Y
20 Amp		Showers	Y	Rangers(s)	Y
30 Amp	Y	Reserve Sites	Y	Gate	
50 Amp	Y	Store	Y	Patrolled	Y
		Grill/Table	Y		

[17] Tobyhanna State Park
I-380, Exit 8
Northeast of Tobyhanna
N41 12.405 W75 23.798
State Rates: See Introduction
(570) 894-8336
http://www.dcnr.state.pa.us/stateparks/parks/tobyhanna.aspx

Directions

3 miles. At Exit 8 proceed to and turn east on Hwy 423, go 2.5 miles to the Park.

Points of Interest

The list if things to do in the Poconos is too long to mention. Theaters, concerts, museums, shopping, dining . . its all there.

Go to - *http://www.800poconos.com/things-to-do/*

RV Sites		Water		Laundry	
Number	140	None		Wi-Fi	
Shaded	Y	At Site		Fishing	Y
By Water	Y	Spigots	Y	Hiking	Y
Paved		Sewer		Biking	Y
Pull Thru		None		Swimming	Y
ADA	Y	At Site		Watch Wildlife	
Max RV Size	35	Dump Station	Y	Pets	some
Electric		Amenities		Security	
None	Y	Restrooms	Y	Host(s)	Y
20 Amp		Showers	Y	Rangers(s)	Y
30 Amp		Reserve Sites	Y	Gate	
50 Amp		Store		Patrolled	Y
		Grill/Table	Y		

[18] Chapman State Park
GAR Hwy 6
West of Clarendon
N41 45.241 W79 10.234
State Rates: See Introduction
(814) 723-0250
http://www.dcnr.state.pa.us/stateparks/find-apark/chapman/index.htm

Directions

5 miles. In Claredon at Railroad Rd turn west & go 5 miles on Chapman Dam Rd to the Park.

Points of Interest

The park adjoins game lands & Allegheny National Forest There is a sand beach along Chapman Lake, & concessions with snacks & supplies. Chapman Lake has fishing for cold-water and warm-water fish; trout fishing exists in the West Branch of Tionesta Creek and Farnsworth Run.

RV Sites		Water		Laundry	
Number	82	None		Wi-Fi	
Shaded	Y	At Site		Fishing	Y
By Water	Y	Spigots	Y	Hiking	Y
Paved		Sewer		Biking	Y
Pull Thru		None		Swimming	Y
ADA	Y	At Site		Watch Wildlife	Y
Max RV Size	45	Dump Station	Y	Pets	Y
Electric		Amenities		Security	
None		Restrooms	Y	Host(s)	Y
20 Amp	Y	Showers	Y	Rangers(s)	Y
30 Amp	Y	Reserve Sites	Y	Gate	
50 Amp	Y	Store	Y	Patrolled	Y
		Grill/Table	Y		

[19] Lyman Run State Park
GAR Hwy 6, at Galeton
West of Galeton
N41 42.725 W77 44.600
State Rates: See Introduction
(814) 435-5010
http://www.dcnr.state.pa.us/stateparks/find-apark/lymanrun/index.htm

Directions

6 miles. From Galeton take West St (becomes W Branch Rd) for 5.4 miles to Lyman Run Rd. Turn right, go 0.7 miles to the Park.

Points of Interest

The sand beach, modern bathhouse with flush toilets, changing rooms, snack bar & boat rental are centerpieces of the Park lake area. Lyman Run Lake is noted for exceptional water quality & provides excellent trout fishing. Upper Lyman Run basin is a wild brook trout enhancement area.

RV Sites		Water		Laundry	
Number	35	None		Wi-Fi	
Shaded	Y	At Site		Fishing	Y
By Water	Y	Spigots	Y	Hiking	Y
Paved		**Sewer**		Biking	Y
Pull Thru		None		Swimming	Y
ADA	Y	At Site		Watch Wildlife	Y
Max RV Size	45	Dump Station	Y	Pets	Y
Electric		**Amenities**		**Security**	
None		Restrooms	Y	Host(s)	Y
20 Amp	Y	Showers	Y	Rangers(s)	Y
30 Amp	Y	Reserve Sites	Y	Gate	
50 Amp	Y	Store	Y	Patrolled	Y
		Grill/Table	Y		

[20] Hills Creek State Park
GAR Hwy 6
West of Mansfield
N41 48.287 W77 11.198
State Rates: See Introduction
(570) 724-4246
http://www.dcnr.state.pa.us/stateparks/find-apark/hillscreek/index.htm

Directions

3.2 miles. On Hwy 6, 4.8 miles west of Mansfield, take Bullock Rd north 2.3 miles to Cobb Rd. Turn right, go 0.5 miles to Lake Rd. Turn left, go 0.4 miles to the Park.

Points of Interest

Osprey, loon & waterfowl visit the lake that also boasts a variety of fish species. Ride the Tioga Central Railroad on a 34 mile excursion from Wellsboro to near Corning, New York. The Grand Canyon of Pennsylvania is not far.

RV Sites		Water		Laundry	Y
Number	85	None		Wi-Fi	
Shaded	some	At Site		Fishing	Y
By Water	Y	Spigots	Y	Hiking	Y
Paved		**Sewer**		Biking	Y
Pull Thru		None		Swimming	Y
ADA	Y	At Site		Watch Wildlife	Y
Max RV Size	35	Dump Station	Y	Pets	Y
Electric		**Amenities**		**Security**	
None		Restrooms	Y	Host(s)	Y
20 Amp	Y	Showers	Y	Rangers(s)	Y
30 Amp	Y	Reserve Sites	Y	Gate	
50 Amp	Y	Store	Y	Patrolled	Y
		Grill/Table	Y		

About South Carolina's Public Campgrounds

Be it Blue Ridge Mountains or the dunes of the Atlantic; South Carolina State and County Parks, and National Forests have much to offer. Discover forested mountains, waterfalls, rivers and scenic inland lakes, white sand beaches, island shores, American historic sites and cultural treasures. Find out specific information, for example, for the 47 State Parks at -

http://www.southcarolinaparks.com/

RVers who are at least 65 years of age, legally blind or disabled, qualify for certain rate reductions at selected Parks. Pets must be on a leash up to 6 feet or other physical restraint at all times.

Depending on services, the basic camping fee (before extra fees, if any) will vary, generally sites are Standard (water & electricity) or Full Hook-up (sewer, water & electricity).

Reservations at state parks may be made up to 11 months in advance. There are three ways to make reservations at South Carolina State Parks:

- Call toll free 1-866-345-7275;
- Online at **http://southcarolinaparks.reserveamerica.com/**;
- At the park of your choice, by calling the park directly.

[1] Aiken State Natural Area	**[10] Coneross Campground**
[2] Sesquicentennial State Park	**[11] Paris Mountain State Park**
[3] Lee State Natural Area	**[12] Colleton State Park**
[4] Croft State Natural Area	**[13] Little Pee Dee State Park**
[5] Givhans Ferry State Park	**[14] Hunting Island State Park**
[6] James Island County Park	**[15] Buck Hall Recreation Area**
[7] Lake Wateree State Recreation Area	**[16] Huntington Beach State Park**
[8] Chester State Park	**[17] Bakers Creek State Park**
[9] Lake Hartwell State Park	**[18] Calhoun Falls State Park**

NOTES:

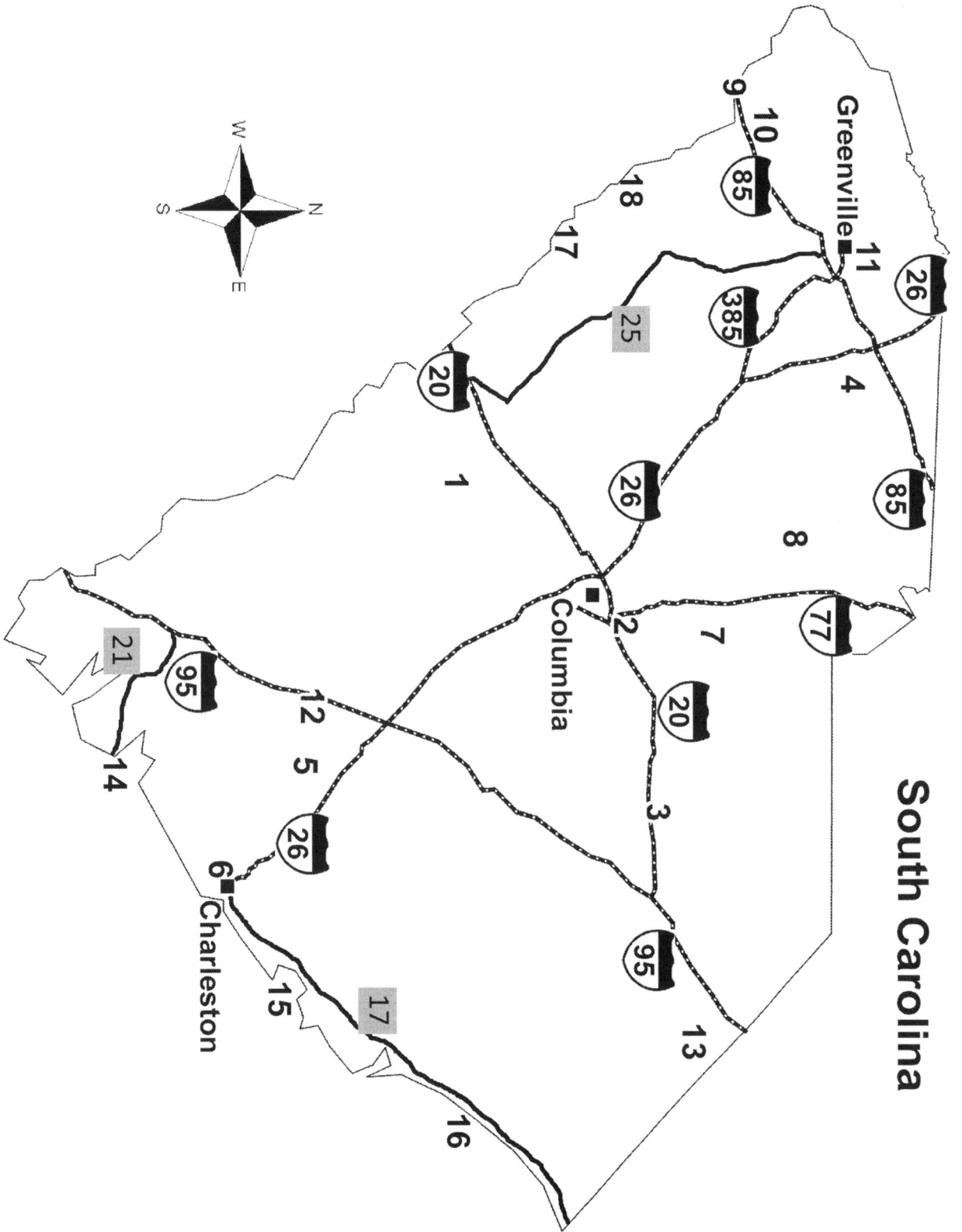

South Carolina

[1] Aiken State Natural Area
I-20, Exit 22
Northeast of Augusta, GA
N33 33.024 W81 29.365
State Rate: $14
(803) 649-2857
http://www.southcarolinaparks.com/aiken/

Directions

26 miles. From Exit 22, go south for 8 miles on Hwy 1 to Aiken. Turn east (left) on Hwy 78 for 13 miles to State Park Rd. Turn north (left), go 5 miles to the Park.

Points of Interest

Spring is a wonderful time to see the beautiful South Fork of the Edisto River. From its broad parkways to rambling "cottages," Aiken is one of the most picturesque communities in the southeast. Augusta, GA is also close, with many sites and events to enjoy.

RV Sites		Water		Laundry	
Number	25	None		Wi-Fi	
Shaded	Y	At Site	Y	Fishing	Y
By Water	Y	Spigots		Hiking	Y
Paved		Sewer		Biking	Y
Pull Thru	few	None		Swimming	
ADA	Y	At Site		Watch Wildlife	Y
Max RV Size	45	Dump Station	Y	Pets	Y
Electric		Amenities		Security	
None		Restrooms	Y	Host(s)	Y
20 Amp	Y	Showers	Y	Rangers(s)	Y
30 Amp	Y	Reserve Sites	Y	Gate	Y
50 Amp		Store		Patrolled	Y
		Grill/Table	Y		

[2] Sesquicentennial State Park
I-20, Exit 74
Northeast of Columbia
N34 06.148 W80 54.641
State Rate: $18
(803) 788-2706
http://www.southcarolinaparks.com/sesqui/

Directions

3 miles. From Exit 74 turn northeast (left) for 3 miles on Hwy 1 (Two Notch Rd) The Park will be on the right.

Points of Interest

There is 2-acre dog park, fenced-in, for dogs to run off-leash. The Columbia area offers a variety of year-round attractions. You'll find historical & cultural attractions, festivals, parks & sporting events. Browse over 80 Columbia attractions at **www.columbiacvb.com/attractions/**

RV Sites		Water		Laundry	
Number	84	None		Wi-Fi	
Shaded	Y	At Site	Y	Fishing	Y
By Water	Y	Spigots		Hiking	Y
Paved		Sewer		Biking	Y
Pull Thru	Y	None		Swimming	
ADA	Y	At Site		Watch Wildlife	Y
Max RV Size	35	Dump Station	Y	Pets	Y
Electric		Amenities		Security	
None		Restrooms	Y	Host(s)	Y
20 Amp	Y	Showers	Y	Rangers(s)	Y
30 Amp	Y	Reserve Sites	Y	Gate	
50 Amp		Store		Patrolled	Y
		Grill/Table	Y		

[3] Lee State Natural Area
I-20, Exit 123
West of Florence
N34 12.263 W80 10.487
State Rate: $18
(803) 428-5307
http://www.southcarolinaparks.com/lee/

Directions

1 mile. From Exit 123 turn north for 1 mile on Cty Rd 22 (Lee State Park Rd) to Loop Rd and the Park on the left.

Points of Interest

If engines and speed are your thing then Florence and the Pee Dee Region is for you, with Darlington Raceway, Florence Motor Speedway and the annual Pee Dee Air Show. Bargain hunters will enjoy the Pee Dee State Farmers' Market and the Florence Flea Market for deals galore.

RV Sites		Water		Laundry	
Number	25	None		Wi-Fi	
Shaded	Y	At Site	Y	Fishing	Y
By Water	Y	Spigots		Hiking	Y
Paved		Sewer		Biking	Y
Pull Thru		None		Swimming	Y
ADA	Y	At Site		Watch Wildlife	Y
Max RV Size	40	Dump Station	Y	Pets	Y
Electric		Amenities		Security	
None		Restrooms	Y	Host(s)	Y
20 Amp	Y	Showers	Y	Rangers(s)	Y
30 Amp	Y	Reserve Sites	Y	Gate	
50 Amp		Store	Y	Patrolled	Y
		Grill/Table	Y		

[4] Croft State Natural Area
I-26, Exit 22
Southeast of Spartanburg
N34 53.495 W81 52.282
State Rate: $14-$18
(864) 585-1283
http://www.southcarolinaparks.com/croft/

Directions

9 miles. From Exit 22, go 1 mile east on Hwy 296 (Reidville Rd) to Hwy 295 (Southport Rd). Turn right & follow Southport for 6 miles to Hwy 56 (Cedar Springs Rd). Turn right, go 2 miles to Dairy Ridge Rd. Turn left in to the Park.

Points of Interest

In the foothills of the Blue Ridge Mountains, Spartanburg has top museums, a thriving art community, unique boutique & antique shopping. Start at the Spartanburg Regional History Museum.

RV Sites		Water		Laundry	
Number	50	None		Wi-Fi	
Shaded	Y	At Site	Y	Fishing	Y
By Water	Y	Spigots		Hiking	Y
Paved		Sewer		Biking	Y
Pull Thru	Y	None		Swimming	
ADA	Y	At Site		Watch Wildlife	Y
Max RV Size	45	Dump Station	Y	Pets	Y
Electric		Amenities		Security	
None		Restrooms	Y	Host(s)	Y
20 Amp	Y	Showers	Y	Rangers(s)	Y
30 Amp	Y	Reserve Sites	Y	Gate	
50 Amp	Y	Store		Patrolled	Y
		Grill/Table	Y		

[5] Givhans Ferry State Park
I-26, Exit 187
West of Summerville
N33 01.638 W80 23.112
State Rate: $14
(843) 873-0692
http://www.southcarolinaparks.com/givhansferry/

Directions

13 miles. From Exit 187, go 1 mile south on Hwy 27 to Hwy 78. Turn left, go 0.4 miles, then turn right on Hwy 27. Follow Hwy 27 for 8 miles to Hwy 61. Turn right, go 3.1 miles to Givhans Ferry Rd. Turn right to the Park entrance.

Points of Interest

From June through December, Charleston hosts a variety of public festivals and events. Experience destinations like Ft. Sumter or The Battery. For ideas go to - **www.charlestoncvb.com/**. **Also see [6].**

RV Sites		Water		Laundry	
Number	25	None		Wi-Fi	
Shaded	Y	At Site	Y	Fishing	Y
By Water	Y	Spigots		Hiking	Y
Paved		Sewer		Biking	Y
Pull Thru		None		Swimming	
ADA	Y	At Site	Y	Watch Wildlife	Y
Max RV Size	45	Dump Station	Y	Pets	Y
Electric		Amenities		Security	
None		Restrooms	Y	Host(s)	Y
20 Amp	Y	Showers	Y	Rangers(s)	Y
30 Amp	Y	Reserve Sites	Y	Gate	
50 Amp	Y	Store		Patrolled	Y
		Grill/Table	Y		

[6] James Island County Park
I-26, Exit 220
Southwest side of Charleston
N32 44.157 W79 58.949
County Rate: $35-$49
(843) 795-4386
http://www.ccprc.com/index.aspx?nid=68

Directions

7 miles From Exit 220, take Hwy 17S, 1.5 miles to the Lockwood Blvd exit. Turn left, then bare right, take the Scarborough Bridge & join Hwy 30W for 2.7 miles to Hwy 171 (Folly Rd). Turn left for 1.1 miles to Camp Rd. Turn right, go 0.8 miles to Riverland Dr. Turn right, go 0.2 miles to the Park entrance.

Points of Interest

Walk the French Quarter & Battery. Go to the Mount Pleasant Farmers Market. Visit Boone Hall. Enjoy sea food & wine. **Also see [5]**.

RV Sites		Water		Laundry	Y
Number	124	None		Wi-Fi	Y
Shaded	Y	At Site	Y	Fishing	Y
By Water	Y	Spigots		Hiking	Y
Paved		Sewer		Biking	Y
Pull Thru	Y	None		Swimming	
ADA	Y	At Site	Y	Watch Wildlife	
Max RV Size	45	Dump Station	Y	Pets	Y
Electric		Amenities		Security	
None		Restrooms	Y	Host(s)	Y
20 Amp	Y	Showers	Y	Rangers(s)	
30 Amp	Y	Reserve Sites	Y	Gate	Y
50 Amp	Y	Store	Y	Patrolled	Y
		Grill/Table	Y		

[7] Lake Wateree State Recreation Area
I-77, Exit 41
North of Columbia
N34 25.849 W80 52.229
State Rate: $16-$22
(803) 482-6401
http://www.southcarolinaparks.com/lakewateree/

Directions

10 miles. From Exit 41 turn east for 2.4 miles on Old River Rd to Hwy 21. Turn north & go 2.1 miles to Hwy 101 (River Rd). Turn east, go 5.1 miles to State Park Rd. Turn left to the Park.

Points of Interest

Camden & Kershaw County are places where tradition mingles with the fast-paced world of steeplechase racing & other recreational offerings. Whether it's historic sightseeing, antique shopping, fine dining or joining the crowds at the Catfish Stomp Festival, this area is first rate.

RV Sites		Water		Laundry	
Number	72	None		Wi-Fi	
Shaded	Y	At Site	Y	Fishing	Y
By Water	Y	Spigots		Hiking	Y
Paved	Y	**Sewer**		Biking	Y
Pull Thru	Y	None		Swimming	
ADA	Y	At Site		Watch Wildlife	Y
Max RV Size	40	Dump Station	Y	Pets	Y
Electric		**Amenities**		**Security**	
None		Restrooms	Y	Host(s)	Y
20 Amp	Y	Showers	Y	Rangers(s)	Y
30 Amp	Y	Reserve Sites	Y	Gate	
50 Amp		Store		Patrolled	Y
		Grill/Table	Y		

[8] Chester State Park
I-77, Exit 65
Southwest of Chester
N34 41.010 W81 14.932
State Rate: $14
(803) 385-2680
http://www.southcarolinaparks.com/chester/

Directions

14 miles. From Exit 65 go west for 9.5 miles on Hwy 9 to the Chester Hwy 9/72/121 Bypass. Go southwest for 3 miles to Hwy 72/121. Turn southwest for 1.4 miles to State Park Rd.

Points of Interest

Discover the charm of the true South in South Carolina's 'Olde English District.' Visit antique stores, artists studios, & numerous historic sites. A few 'must sees' are the Hill Plantation State Historic Site & Gist Mansion, Historic Brattonsville, and the South Carolina Railroad Museum.

RV Sites		Water		Laundry	
Number	25	None		Wi-Fi	
Shaded	Y	At Site	Y	Fishing	Y
By Water	Y	Spigots		Hiking	Y
Paved		**Sewer**		Biking	Y
Pull Thru	Y	None		Swimming	
ADA	Y	At Site		Watch Wildlife	Y
Max RV Size	35	Dump Station	Y	Pets	Y
Electric		**Amenities**		**Security**	
None		Restrooms	Y	Host(s)	Y
20 Amp	Y	Showers	Y	Rangers(s)	Y
30 Amp	Y	Reserve Sites	Y	Gate	
50 Amp		Store		Patrolled	Y
		Grill/Table	Y		

[9] Lake Hartwell State Park
I-85, Exit 1
West of Anderson
N34 29.585 W83 01.673
State Rate: $16-$21
(864) 972-3352
http://www.southcarolinaparks.com/lakehartwell/

Directions

0.4 miles. From Exit 1, go northwest for 0.4 miles to the Park entrance on the left.

Points of Interest

The Parks main attraction is fishing, with a reputation for excellent angling. The lakefront park's information center displays a wide variety of vintage fishing equipment. This location is a gateway to South Carolina's mountain country on the Cherokee Foothills National Scenic Highway.

RV Sites		Water		Laundry	Y
Number	115	None		Wi-Fi	Y
Shaded	Y	At Site	Y	Fishing	Y
By Water	Y	Spigots		Hiking	Y
Paved	Y	**Sewer**		Biking	Y
Pull Thru	Y	None		Swimming	
ADA	Y	At Site		Watch Wildlife	Y
Max RV Size	40	Dump Station	Y	Pets	Y
Electric		**Amenities**		**Security**	
None		Restrooms	Y	Host(s)	Y
20 Amp	Y	Showers	Y	Rangers(s)	Y
30 Amp	Y	Reserve Sites	Y	Gate	
50 Amp		Store	Y	Patrolled	Y
		Grill/Table	Y		

[10] Coneross Campground
I-85, Exit 11
Northwest of Anderson
N34 35.559 W82 53.547
COE Rate: $18-$24
America/Beautiful Rate: $9-$12
(888) 893-0678
http://www.recreation.gov/

Directions

8 miles. From Exit 11, go 6 miles north on Hwy 24, through Townville, to Hwy 37/184. Turn right, go 0.6 miles to Coneross Creek Rd. Turn right, go 1 mile to the camp.

Points of Interest

Pendleton boasts an entire district on the National Register of Historic Places. The charming community offers the opportunity to dine, shop and step back in time with guided tours of the nearby antebellum plantations such as Woodburn & Ashtabula.

RV Sites		Water		Laundry	
Number	106	None		Wi-Fi	
Shaded	Y	At Site	Y	Fishing	Y
By Water	Y	Spigots		Hiking	Y
Paved		**Sewer**		Biking	Y
Pull Thru	Y	None		Swimming	Y
ADA	Y	At Site		Watch Wildlife	Y
Max RV Size	45	Dump Station	Y	Pets	Y
Electric		**Amenities**		**Security**	
None		Restrooms	Y	Host(s)	Y
20 Amp	Y	Showers	Y	Rangers(s)	Y
30 Amp	Y	Reserve Sites	Y	Gate	
50 Amp	Y	Store		Patrolled	Y
		Grill/Table	Y		

[11] Paris Mountain State Park
I-85, Exit 51
North of Greenville
N34 55.512 W82 21.919
State Rate: $18-$19
(864) 244-5565
http://www.southcarolinaparks.com/parismountain/

Directions

10 miles. From Exit 51, go 3.5 miles north on I-385 to exit 40. Exit north on Hwy 291 (N Pleasantburg Rd), go 2.5 miles to Piney Mountain Rd. Turn right, go 1.3 miles to Hwy 253 (Paris Mountain Rd). Turn right, go 1.2 miles to Cty Rd 344. Bare left for 0.8 miles to the Park.

Points of Interest

In the Greenville area, experience breathtaking views and Southern charm, from the Liberty Bridge. Visit museums, shop, enjoy fine eateries.

RV Sites		Water		Laundry	
Number	39	None		Wi-Fi	Y
Shaded	Y	At Site	Y	Fishing	Y
By Water	Y	Spigots		Hiking	Y
Paved	Y	**Sewer**		Biking	Y
Pull Thru	Y	None		Swimming	Y
ADA	Y	At Site		Watch Wildlife	Y
Max RV Size	40	Dump Station	Y	Pets	Y
Electric		**Amenities**		**Security**	
None		Restrooms	Y	Host(s)	Y
20 Amp	Y	Showers	Y	Rangers(s)	Y
30 Amp	Y	Reserve Sites	Y	Gate	Y
50 Amp		Store	Y	Patrolled	Y
		Grill/Table	Y		

[12] Colleton State Park
I-95, Exit 68
North of Walterboro
N33 03.657 W80 36.955
State Rate: $15
(843) 538-8206
http://www.southcarolinaparks.com/colleton/

Directions

3 miles. From Exit 68, go southeast for 2.8 miles on Hwy 61 to Hwy 15 (Jefferies Hwy). Take Hwy 15 north (left) for 0.4 miles to the Park.

Points of Interest

Walterboro is a town of summer tree-lined streets with quaint homes with broad porches surrounded by azaleas, camellias, & beautiful 18th century churches. Wander streets of antiques shops and restaurants. There's a farmers' market.

RV Sites		Water		Laundry	
Number	25	None		Wi-Fi	
Shaded	Y	At Site	Y	Fishing	Y
By Water	Y	Spigots		Hiking	Y
Paved		**Sewer**		Biking	Y
Pull Thru	Y	None		Swimming	
ADA	Y	At Site		Watch Wildlife	Y
Max RV Size	40	Dump Station	Y	Pets	Y
Electric		**Amenities**		**Security**	
None		Restrooms	Y	Host(s)	Y
20 Amp	Y	Showers	Y	Rangers(s)	Y
30 Amp	Y	Reserve Sites	Y	Gate	
50 Amp		Store		Patrolled	Y
		Grill/Table	Y		

[13] Little Pee Dee State Park
I-95, Exit 193
South of Dillon
N34 19.764 W79 17.035
State Rate: $16
(843) 774-8872
http://www.southcarolinaparks.com/lpd/

Directions

13 miles. From Exit 193 go southeast on Hwy 57/9 (through Dillon). Stay with Hwy 57 for 11 miles in all to Cty Rd 22 (State Park Rd). Go left for 2 miles to the Park on your right.

Points of Interest

Dillon County is home to one of the most famous traveler stops on I-95 . . . South of the Border, the unique Mexican-motif mini-resort. Take in the Dillon Motor Speedway, a 4/10 mile asphalt racetrack. Originally a dirt track, it was completely refurbished and reopened.

RV Sites		Water		Laundry	
Number	32	None		Wi-Fi	
Shaded	Y	At Site	Y	Fishing	Y
By Water	Y	Spigots		Hiking	Y
Paved		Sewer		Biking	Y
Pull Thru	Y	None		Swimming	
ADA	Y	At Site		Watch Wildlife	Y
Max RV Size	45	Dump Station	Y	Pets	Y
Electric		Amenities		Security	
None		Restrooms	Y	Host(s)	Y
20 Amp	Y	Showers	Y	Rangers(s)	Y
30 Amp	Y	Reserve Sites	Y	Gate	Y
50 Amp		Store		Patrolled	Y
		Grill/Table	Y		

[14] Hunting Island State Park
Hwy 21, from I-95
East of Beaufort
N32 23.262 W80 26.189
State Rate: $17-$38
(843) 838-2011
http://www.southcarolinaparks.com/huntingisland/

Directions

15.7 miles. From I-95, exit 33, take Hwys 17 & 21 to Beaufort. Continue following Hwy 21 which ends at the park.

Points of Interest

South Carolina's most popular state park, Hunting Island boasts a large variety of land and marine wildlife. The lighthouse here is the only one in the state accessible to the public. Also enjoy 5 miles of beaches. Try your hand at crabbing! Hilton Head Island and Savannah are both close by to the south, Charleston is to the north.

RV Sites		Water		Laundry	
Number	171	None		Wi-Fi	Y
Shaded	Y	At Site	Y	Fishing	Y
By Water	Y	Spigots		Hiking	Y
Paved		Sewer		Biking	Y
Pull Thru	Y	None		Swimming	Y
ADA	Y	At Site		Watch Wildlife	Y
Max RV Size	42	Dump Station	Y	Pets	Y
Electric		Amenities		Security	
None		Restrooms	Y	Host(s)	Y
20 Amp	Y	Showers	Y	Rangers(s)	Y
30 Amp	Y	Reserve Sites	Y	Gate	Y
50 Amp	Y	Store	Y	Patrolled	Y
		Grill/Table	Y		

[15] Buck Hall Recreation Area
Hwy 17
Between Awendaw and McClellanville
N33 02.800 W79 34.014
NF Rate: $20
America/Beautiful Rate: $10
(843) 336-3248
www.recreation.gov

Directions

23.5 miles. Go north from I-526 in Charleston, SC, on Hwy 17 to Buck Hall Landing Road (Forest Road 242). Turn right into the recreation area.

Points of Interest

This location on the Intracoastal Waterway provides the best access to Cape Romain National Wildlife Refuge and Bulls Bay, the best area for shrimp baiting on the coast. Charleston is just a short drive away.

RV Sites		Water		Laundry	
Number	14	None		Wi-Fi	
Shaded	Y	At Site	Y	Fishing	Y
By Water	Y	Spigots		Hiking	Y
Paved	Y	Sewer		Biking	Y
Pull Thru		None		Swimming	
ADA	Y	At Site		Watch Wildlife	Y
Max RV Size	40	Dump Station	Y	Pets	Y
Electric		Amenities		Security	
None		Restrooms	Y	Host(s)	Y
20 Amp	Y	Showers	Y	Rangers(s)	Y
30 Amp	Y	Reserve Sites	Y	Gate	
50 Amp	Y	Store		Patrolled	Y
		Grill/Table	Y		

[16] Huntington Beach State Park
Hwy 17
South of Murrells Inlet
N33 30.822 W79 04.365
State Rate: $21-$47
(843) 237-4440
http://www.southcarolinaparks.com/huntingtonbeach/

Directions

3 miles. From Murrells Inlet drive 3 miles south on Hwy 17 to the Park entrance.

Points of Interest

From amazing beaches, known as Grand Strand, and views, to watchable wildlife, this park has to be at the top of your list. Don't miss the Nature Center. Fishermen will be pleased with the surf fishing. Art lovers will enjoy the Atalaya Arts & Crafts Festival in September. See about tours of the Moorish-style winter home of Archer & Anna Hyatt Huntington.

RV Sites		Water			Laundry	
Number	107	None			Wi-Fi	
Shaded	Y	At Site	Y		Fishing	Y
By Water	Y	Spigots			Hiking	Y
Paved		Sewer			Biking	Y
Pull Thru	Y	None			Swimming	Y
ADA	Y	At Site	some		Watch Wildlife	Y
Max RV Size	45	Dump Station	Y		Pets	Y
Electric		Amenities			Security	
None		Restrooms	Y		Host(s)	Y
20 Amp	Y	Showers	Y		Rangers(s)	Y
30 Amp	Y	Reserve Sites	Y		Gate	
50 Amp	Y	Store	Y		Patrolled	Y
		Grill/Table	Y			

[17] Bakers Creek State Park
Hwy 25, west on Hwy 378
Southwest of McCormick
N33 52.920 W82 20.892
State Rate: $18
(864) 443-2457
http://www.southcarolinaparks.com/bakercreek/

Directions

18.6 miles. From the intersection of Hwy 25 & Hwy 378 go west on Hwy 378, through McCormick to the Park. Open March 1 - Sept. 30.

Points of Interest

The ideal park for campers looking for serene, lake side sites, and boat access to fish on 71,000 acre Lake Thurmond. A large pavilion is great for family and friends to get together. Or, if you enjoy mountain biking, take on the challenge of 10 miles of hilly trails through oak and pine woodlands.

RV Sites		Water			Laundry	
Number	50	None			Wi-Fi	
Shaded	Y	At Site	Y		Fishing	Y
By Water	Y	Spigots			Hiking	Y
Paved		Sewer			Biking	Y
Pull Thru	Y	None			Swimming	
ADA	Y	At Site	Y		Watch Wildlife	Y
Max RV Size	40	Dump Station	Y		Pets	Y
Electric		Amenities			Security	
None		Restrooms	Y		Host(s)	Y
20 Amp	Y	Showers	Y		Rangers(s)	Y
30 Amp	Y	Reserve Sites	Y		Gate	Y
50 Amp		Store			Patrolled	Y
		Grill/Table	Y			

[18] Calhoun Falls State Park
Hwy 25, west on Hwy 72
North of Calhoun Falls
N34 06.459 W82 35.898
State Rate: $19-$21
(864) 447-8267
http://www.southcarolinaparks.com/calhounfalls/

Directions

28 miles. North of Greenwood at Hwy 25 & 72 go west on Hwy 72 for 26.8 miles into Calhoun Falls. Turn north on Hwy 81, go 1.2 miles to the Park.

Points of Interest

The State Park System claims Calhoun Falls is " . . . one of the most coveted in the park system, with spacious RV and tent sites complete with forested, shoreline views of the lake." In addition the park attracts campers to various events during the year - fishing tournaments and the *South Carolina Campground Cookoff*.

RV Sites		Water			Laundry	Y
Number	86	None			Wi-Fi	
Shaded	Y	At Site	Y		Fishing	Y
By Water	Y	Spigots			Hiking	Y
Paved	Y	Sewer			Biking	Y
Pull Thru	Y	None			Swimming	Y
ADA	Y	At Site	Y		Watch Wildlife	Y
Max RV Size	45	Dump Station	Y		Pets	Y
Electric		Amenities			Security	
None		Restrooms	Y		Host(s)	Y
20 Amp	Y	Showers	Y		Rangers(s)	Y
30 Amp	Y	Reserve Sites	Y		Gate	
50 Amp	Y	Store	Y		Patrolled	Y
		Grill/Table	Y			

About South Dakota's Public Campgrounds

Follow the Lewis and Clark Trail. Explore old cabins, military forts, and prehistoric sites. The 60 South Dakota State Parks are the largest outdoor museums in the state. The State Park system is overseen by the South Dakota Game, Fish and Parks (GFP). You can find much information about the Parks statewide at -

http://gfp.sd.gov/state-parks/

In addition there are close to 40 Country Parks to choose from. These can be found at -

www.allstays.com/Campgrounds/South-Dakota-county-campgrounds-map.htm#Mapp

Your pet is allowed in State Parks. Pets should be kept on a leash no longer than 10 feet and you should not leave your pet alone.

There are two options for park entrance - an annual entrance license ($30) or daily licenses (available @ $4 per person or $6 per vehicle; not available at Custer; motorcoach license fee of $3 per person per continuous visit). See more information at: **http://gfp.sd.gov/state-parks/permits/**.

Camping fees vary based on the facilities available at the individual park. Entrance fees are in addition to camping fees. Call the reservation line at (800) 710-2267 or make reservations online at **www.campSD.com**. Reservations for accessible campsites, are available at the same number. There is a $7.70 per site non-refundable reservation fee (not applicable to South Dakota residents).

[1] Union Grove State Park	**[7] Cedar Pass Campground**
[2] Oakwood Lakes State Park	**[8] Lake Mitchell Campground**
[3] Pelican Lake Recreation Area	**[9] Big Sioux Recreation Area**
[4] Roy Lake State Park	**[10] Oahe Downstream Recreation Area**
[5] Spearfish Campground	**[11] West Whitlock Recreation Area**
[6] Pactola Campground	**[12] Indian Creek Recreation Area**

NOTES:

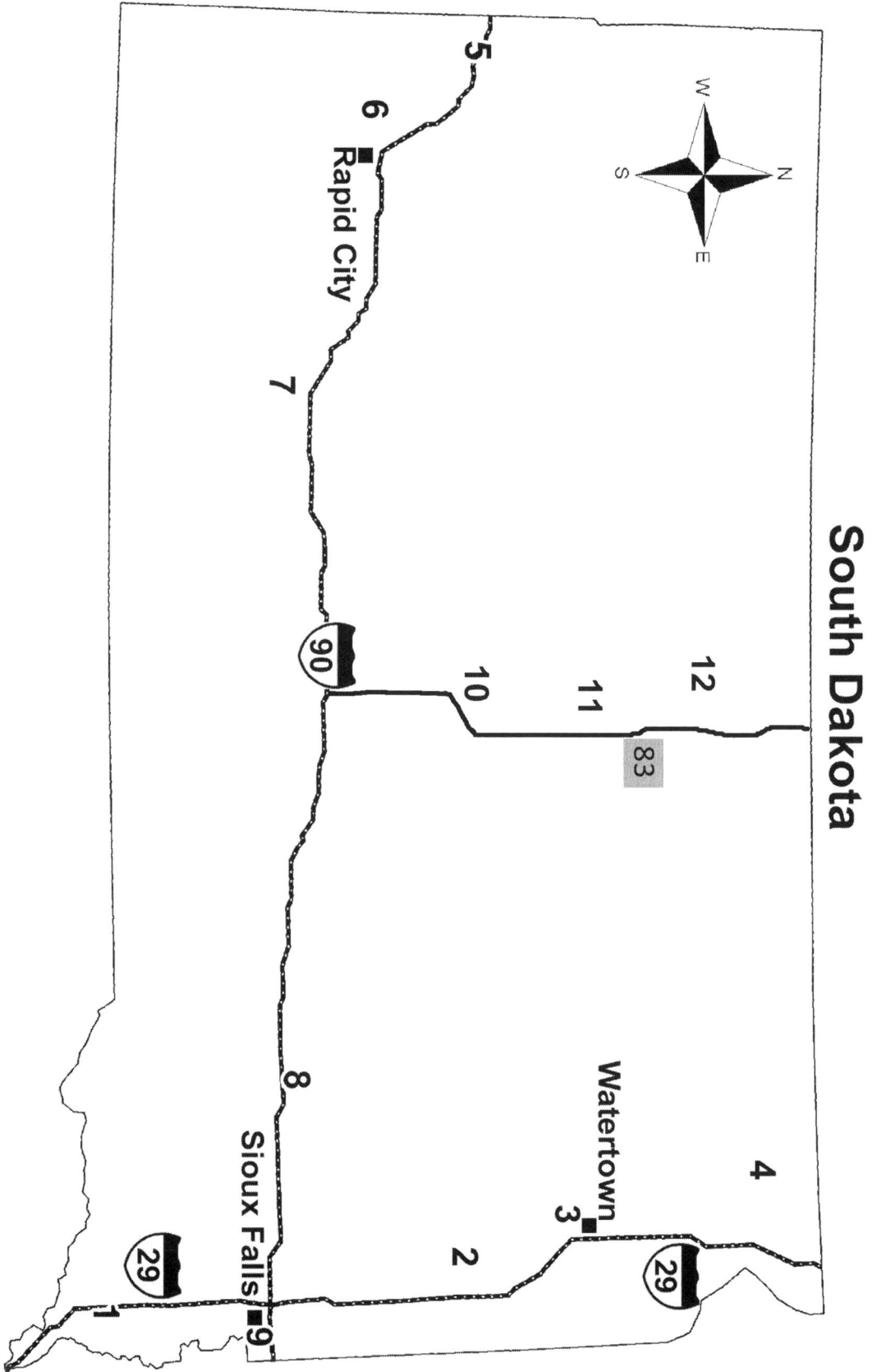

South Dakota

[1] Union Grove State Park
I-29, Exits 31 or 38
South of Beresford
N42 55.245 W96 47.134
State Rate: $10-$24
(605) 987-2263
http://gfp.sd.gov/state-parks/directory/union-grove/

Directions

3 or 5 miles. **Northbound**, from Exit 31, go east 0.4 miles to Cty Rd 1. Turn north 4.4 miles to the Park. **Southbound**, from Exit 38, go east 0.4 miles to Cty Rd 1. Turn south 2.2 miles to the Park.

Points of Interest

Climb Sprit Mound, where Lewis & Clark had heard legends of little spirits. Tour W. H. Over Museum, which features exhibits of life in the upper Midwest. Visit the Austin-Whittemore House, an 1883 Italian villa filled with Victorian furnishings.

RV Sites		Water		Laundry	
Number	25	None		Wi-Fi	
Shaded	Y	At Site		Fishing	
By Water	Y	Spigots	Y	Hiking	Y
Paved		Sewer		Biking	Y
Pull Thru	Y	None		Swimming	
ADA	Y	At Site		Watch Wildlife	Y
Max RV Size	45	Dump Station	Y	Pets	Y
Electric		Amenities		Security	
None		Restrooms	Y	Host(s)	Y
20 Amp	Y	Showers	Y	Rangers(s)	Y
30 Amp	Y	Reserve Sites	Y	Gate	
50 Amp	Y	Store		Patrolled	Y
		Grill/Table	Y		

[2] Oakwood Lakes State Park
I-29, Exit 140
Northwest of Brookings
N44 26.977 W96 59.305
State Rate: $10-$24
(605) 627-5441
http://gfp.sd.gov/state-parks/directory/oakwood-lakes/

Directions

13 miles. From Exit 140, go west for 11 miles on Hwy 30 (204th St, becomes Cty Rd 6) to Oakwood Shoreline Dr. Turn north for 2 miles to the Park.

Points of Interest

Brookings boasts a downtown with beautiful historic buildings, great shops & restaurants. Join costumed guides to discover Laura Ingalls Wilder with a visit to "The Little Town on the Prairie", in De Smet; including The Loftus Store, & the store from the Wilder's Book, The Long Winter.

RV Sites		Water		Laundry	
Number	135	None		Wi-Fi	
Shaded	Y	At Site		Fishing	Y
By Water	Y	Spigots	Y	Hiking	Y
Paved		Sewer		Biking	Y
Pull Thru	Y	None		Swimming	Y
ADA	Y	At Site		Watch Wildlife	
Max RV Size	45	Dump Station	Y	Pets	Y
Electric		Amenities		Security	
None		Restrooms	Y	Host(s)	Y
20 Amp	Y	Showers	Y	Rangers(s)	Y
30 Amp	Y	Reserve Sites	Y	Gate	
50 Amp	Y	Store		Patrolled	Y
		Grill/Table	Y		

[3] Pelican Lake Recreation Area
I-29, Exit 177
West of Watertown
N44 50.846 W97 12.530
State Rate: $10-$24
(605) 882-5200
http://gfp.sd.gov/state-parks/directory/pelican-lake/

Directions

12 miles. From Exit 177, go west for 8.3 miles on Hwy 212 (9th Ave) to 449th Ave (Thompson Point). Turn south for 3 miles to 175th St. Turn east 1 mile to 450th Ave, then turn north in to the Park.

Points of Interest

On hikes see migrating birds, prairie grasses & wildflowers. Visit Redlin Art Center. Redlin is one of the country's most respected painters of wildlife and Americana. Tour the Mellette House, home of the state's first governor.

RV Sites		Water		Laundry	
Number	76	None		Wi-Fi	
Shaded	some	At Site		Fishing	Y
By Water	Y	Spigots	Y	Hiking	Y
Paved		Sewer		Biking	Y
Pull Thru		None		Swimming	Y
ADA	Y	At Site		Watch Wildlife	Y
Max RV Size	45	Dump Station	Y	Pets	Y
Electric		Amenities		Security	
None		Restrooms	Y	Host(s)	Y
20 Amp	Y	Showers	Y	Rangers(s)	Y
30 Amp	Y	Reserve Sites	Y	Gate	
50 Amp	Y	Store		Patrolled	Y
		Grill/Table	Y		

[4] Roy Lake State Park
I-29, Exit 232
South of Lake City
N45 42.200 W97 25.178
State Rate: $10-$24
(605) 448-5701
http://gfp.sd.gov/state-parks/directory/roy-lake/

Directions

24 miles. From Exit 232 go west for 22.4 miles on Hwy 10 (119th/Walnut St) to where Hwy 25 turns south. Go south on Hwy 25 for 1 mile to Northside Dr (Roy Lake Rd). Turn west to Park Number 2 (East Campground).

Points of Interest

Roy Lake has good walleye, bass, panfish, & pike fishing. Early inhabitants of Roy Lake were from the so-called Woodland Culture. Artifacts found to be over 3,000 years old have been found near the park.

RV Sites		Water		Laundry	
Number	102	None		Wi-Fi	
Shaded	Y	At Site		Fishing	Y
By Water	Y	Spigots	Y	Hiking	Y
Paved		**Sewer**		Biking	Y
Pull Thru	few	None		Swimming	Y
ADA	Y	At Site		Watch Wildlife	
Max RV Size	45	Dump Station	Y	Pets	Y
Electric		**Amenities**		**Security**	
None		Restrooms	Y	Host(s)	Y
20 Amp	Y	Showers	Y	Rangers(s)	Y
30 Amp	Y	Reserve Sites	Y	Gate	
50 Amp		Store		Patrolled	Y
		Grill/Table	Y		

[5] Spearfish Campground
I-90, Exit 12
South side of Spearfish
N44 28.849 W103 51.573
City Rate: $20-$39
(605) 642-1340
http://www.spearfishparksandrec.com/campground/index.html

Directions

1.5 miles. From Exit 12 go west 0.7 miles on Jackson Blvd to Canyon St. Turn left and go 0.7 miles south, past the Spearfish City Park & across the bridge to the Campground.

Points of Interest

Downtown Spearfish is within walking distance. You'll find public laundry facilities, grocery & hardware stores, the D.C. Booth Historic Fish Hatchery & the Matthews Opera House. This is a base for touring the Black Hills & Mt. Rushmore.

RV Sites		Water		Laundry	
Number	212	None		Wi-Fi	Y
Shaded	Y	At Site	Y	Fishing	Y
By Water	Y	Spigots	Y	Hiking	Y
Paved		**Sewer**		Biking	Y
Pull Thru	Y	None		Swimming	
ADA		At Site	Y	Watch Wildlife	
Max RV Size	45	Dump Station	Y	Pets	Y
Electric		**Amenities**		**Security**	
None		Restrooms	Y	Host(s)	Y
20 Amp	Y	Showers	Y	Rangers(s)	
30 Amp	Y	Reserve Sites	Y	Gate	
50 Amp	Y	Store		Patrolled	Y
		Grill/Table	Y		

[6] Pactola Reservoir Campground
I-90, Exit 55
West of Rapid City
N44 03.558 W103 29.854
Black Hills NF Rate: $16-$24
America/Beautiful Rate: $8-$12
(605) 574-4402
http://www.recreation.gov/

Directions

24 miles. From Exit 55 go south for 2.3 miles on Highway 445 (Deadwood Ave) to Hwy 44 (Mountain View Rd). Go south & west on Hwy 44 for 17 miles. Turn south for 2.8 miles on Hwy 385 to Custer Gulch Rd and go 1.4 miles to campground sign (Forest Rt. 545). Turn right, go 0.5 miles to the campground.

Points of Interest

Day trips - Jewel Cave, Badlands, Mt. Rushmore, Custer Park, Crazy Horse Monument & Wind Cave.

RV Sites		Water		Laundry	
Number	57	None		Wi-Fi	
Shaded	Y	At Site		Fishing	Y
By Water	Y	Spigots	Y	Hiking	Y
Paved		**Sewer**		Biking	Y
Pull Thru	one	None	Y	Swimming	Y
ADA	Y	At Site		Watch Wildlife	Y
Max RV Size	38	Dump Station		Pets	Y fee
Electric		**Amenities**		**Security**	
None	Y	Restrooms	Y	Host(s)	Y
20 Amp		Showers		Rangers(s)	Y
30 Amp		Reserve Sites	Y	Gate	
50 Amp		Store		Patrolled	Y
		Grill/Table	Y		

[7] Cedar Pass Campground
I-90, Exit 131
South of Cactus Flat
N43 44.787 W101 56.909
Badlands NP Rate: $30
America/Beautiful Rate: $15
(605) 433-5460
http://cedarpasslodge.com/campground/

Directions

8.5 miles. From Exit 131 go south for 8.5 miles on Hwy 240 to the Campground, which is located just past the Ben Reifel Visitor Center at the Hwy 377 turn.

Points of Interest

Drive the Hwy 240 Loop Road. Take a trip down Sage Creek Rim Rd to Robert's Prairie Dog Town. Attend the Night Sky Program. Visit the tipi village located between the Ben Reifel Visitor Center & the Cedar Pass Lodge.

RV Sites		Water		Laundry	
Number	100	None		Wi-Fi	
Shaded	Ramada	At Site		Fishing	
By Water		Spigots	Y	Hiking	Y
Paved	Y	**Sewer**		Biking	Y
Pull Thru	pullover	None		Swimming	
ADA	Y	At Site		Watch Wildlife	
Max RV Size	40+	Dump Station	$1	Pets	Y
Electric		**Amenities**		**Security**	
None		Restrooms	Y	Host(s)	Y
20 Amp	Y	Showers		Rangers(s)	Y
30 Amp	Y	Reserve Sites		Gate	
50 Amp	Y	Store	Y	Patrolled	Y
		Grill/Table	Y		

[8] Lake Mitchell Campground
I-90, Exit 330
North side of Mitchell
N43 44.081 W98 01.560
City Rate: $28-$32
(605) 995-8457
http://www.cityofmitchell.org/index.asp?SEC=447C1EB0-C4CE-4523-9AEC-EF59B6C993F3&Type=B_BASIC

Directions

3.5 miles. From Exit 330 go 3.5 miles north on the Hwy 37 Bypass to Hwy 37, then north to the Park entrance.

Points of Interest

The Mitchell Corn Palace was established in 1892. Locals displayed their harvests on the building exterior to prove the fertility of South Dakota soil. The exterior decorations are completely stripped down & new murals are created each year.

RV Sites		Water		Laundry	Y
Number	70	None		Wi-Fi	
Shaded	Y	At Site	Y	Fishing	Y
By Water	Y	Spigots	Y	Hiking	
Paved		**Sewer**		Biking	Y
Pull Thru	Y	None		Swimming	Y
ADA	Y	At Site	Y	Watch Wildlife	
Max RV Size	40+	Dump Station	Y	Pets	Y
Electric		**Amenities**		**Security**	
None		Restrooms	Y	Host(s)	Y
20 Amp	Y	Showers	Y	Rangers(s)	
30 Amp	Y	Reserve Sites	Y	Gate	
50 Amp	Y	Store		Patrolled	Y
		Grill/Table	Y		

[9] Big Sioux Recreation Area
I-90, Exit 406
East of Sioux Falls
N43 34.358 W96 35.665
State Rate: $10-$24
(605) 582-7243
http://gfp.sd.gov/state-parks/directory/big-sioux/

Directions

3.5 miles. From Exit 406 go 2.9 miles south on Hwy 11 to Sioux Blvd. Turn right, go 0.3 miles to Park St. Turn left, go 0.3 miles to the Park entrance.

Points of Interest

Sioux Falls is the largest city in South Dakota. Two Information Centers, located at Falls Park and at The Empire Mall, have information you need for your visit, including attraction and event information, maps, and brochures. Also visit:
http://www.siouxfallscvb.com/visitorInfo.cfm

RV Sites		Water		Laundry	
Number	49	None		Wi-Fi	
Shaded	Y	At Site		Fishing	Y
By Water	Y	Spigots	Y	Hiking	
Paved		**Sewer**		Biking	Y
Pull Thru		None		Swimming	
ADA	Y	At Site		Watch Wildlife	
Max RV Size	45	Dump Station	Y	Pets	Y
Electric		**Amenities**		**Security**	
None		Restrooms	Y	Host(s)	Y
20 Amp	Y	Showers	Y	Rangers(s)	Y
30 Amp	Y	Reserve Sites	Y	Gate	
50 Amp	Y	Store		Patrolled	Y
		Grill/Table	Y		

[10] Oahe Downstream Recreation Area
Hwy 83, Hwy 14 in Pierre
North of Pierre
N44 26.194 W100 24.032
State Rate: $10-$24
(605) 223-7722
http://gfp.sd.gov/state-parks/directory/oahe-downstream/

Directions

5.6 miles. In Pierre take Hwy 14 west 1 mile to Hwy 1806. Turn right, go 4 miles to Power House Rd, bear right. Go 0.6 miles to the Welcome Center.

Points of Interest

Enjoy a variety of activities, while staying at one of three campgrounds. Visit the South Dakota prairie butterfly garden. Bike the Trail system connecting Farm Island, the city of Pierre, LaFramboise Island, and Oahe Downstream. Tour the State Capitol in Pierre.

RV Sites		Water		Laundry	
Number	206	None		Wi-Fi	
Shaded	Y	At Site		Fishing	Y
By Water	Y	Spigots	Y	Hiking	Y
Paved	Y	Sewer		Biking	Y
Pull Thru	Y	None		Swimming	Y
ADA	Y	At Site		Watch Wildlife	Y
Max RV Size	45	Dump Station	Y	Pets	Y
Electric		Amenities		Security	
None		Restrooms	Y	Host(s)	Y
20 Amp	Y	Showers	Y	Rangers(s)	Y
30 Amp	Y	Reserve Sites	Y	Gate	
50 Amp	Y	Store		Patrolled	Y
		Grill/Table	Y		

[11] West Whitlock Recreation Area
Hwy 83, Hwy 212
West of Gettysburg
N45 02.941 W100 15.991
State Rate: $10-$24
(605) 765-9410
http://gfp.sd.gov/state-parks/directory/west-whitlock/

Directions

14.3 miles. From Hwy 212 at Hwy 83 go 6.2 miles west to Hwy 1804. Turn right, go 4.3 miles to W. Whitlock Rd. Proceed left 3.8 miles to the Recreation Area.

Points of Interest

Inspect the Arikara earth lodge replica, reminiscent of the lodges sighted by the Lewis & Clark expedition. The park is on a peninsula, situated along he Missouri River, with many camp sites benefiting from the view. Fishing is a favorite activity.

RV Sites		Water		Laundry	
Number	105	None		Wi-Fi	
Shaded	Y	At Site		Fishing	Y
By Water	Y	Spigots	Y	Hiking	Y
Paved		Sewer		Biking	Y
Pull Thru		None		Swimming	Y
ADA	Y	At Site		Watch Wildlife	Y
Max RV Size	45	Dump Station	Y	Pets	Y
Electric		Amenities		Security	
None		Restrooms	Y	Host(s)	Y
20 Amp	Y	Showers	Y	Rangers(s)	Y
30 Amp	Y	Reserve Sites	Y	Gate	
50 Amp	Y	Store		Patrolled	Y
		Grill/Table	Y		

[12] Indian Creek Recreation Area
Hwy 83, Hwy 12
Southwest of Mobridge
N45 31.218 W100 23.120
State Rate: $10-$24
(605) 845-7112
http://gfp.sd.gov/state-parks/directory/indian-creek/

Directions

16.7 miles. At Hwy 12 & Hwy 83 go west on Hwy 12 for 15.5 miles to 288th Rd, just east of Mobridge. Turn south for 1.2 miles to the Park.

Points of Interest

The rolling hills, which create great river views make this a lovely camp site. Inquire about the monuments to Sitting Bull, Sacagawea, and the Jedediah Smith Foot Soldier Band. Visit the Mobridge Auditorium to view the 10 murals mounted inside, done by acclaimed Sioux Indian artist Oscar Howe.

RV Sites		Water		Laundry	
Number	124	None		Wi-Fi	
Shaded	some	At Site		Fishing	Y
By Water	Y	Spigots	Y	Hiking	Y
Paved		Sewer		Biking	Y
Pull Thru		None		Swimming	
ADA	Y	At Site		Watch Wildlife	Y
Max RV Size	45	Dump Station	Y	Pets	Y
Electric		Amenities		Security	
None		Restrooms	Y	Host(s)	Y
20 Amp	Y	Showers	Y	Rangers(s)	Y
30 Amp	Y	Reserve Sites	Y	Gate	
50 Amp	Y	Store		Patrolled	Y
		Grill/Table	Y		

About Tennessee's Public Campgrounds

County, Corp of Engineers, and State Parks represent the majority of camping locations in Tennessee.

There are also a number of sites that are classified either as National Cemeteries, Battlefields, Scenic Trails, Rivers, Areas or Parks in Tennessee.

The Tennessee State Parks were selected best in nation for 2007. The system is managed by the Department of Environment & Conservation. Their website is - **http://tnstateparks.com/**

There are 36 RV friendly State Parks and all of them take reservations. Reservations for campsites at selected parks can be made up to 12 months prior to check-in by accessing the registration system through that park's web site.

RV campsites are available for vehicles ranging in length from 20-76 feet and include water and electricity. Most parks have a centrally located dump station. Some parks offer pull-through and waterfront locations.

Camping rates, for up to 4 people, in Tennessee State Parks are standardized according to the facilities available. The rates are from $8 per night for primitive sites up to $25 for premium sites. A typical campsite (water & electricity) is $20. There is no state park access fee.

Tennessee State Parks provides discounts. Active duty U.S. military, Seniors, and disabled campers should check about discounts when registering.

Dogs, cats and other pets are prohibited unless they are crated, caged or on a leash, or otherwise under physical restrictive control at all times.

[1] Poole Knobs, J Percy Priest Dam	[9] Harrison Bay State Park
[2] Old Stone Fort State Park	[10] Cove Lake State Park
[3] T.O. Fuller State Park	[11] Indian Mountain State Park
[4] Natchez Trace State Park	[12] Warriors' Path State Park
[5] Cedars of Lebanon State Park	[13] Chickasaw State Park
[6] Floating Mill Campground	[14] Pickwick Dam Tailwater
[7] Cumberland Mountain State Park	[15] David Crockett State Park
[8] Henry Horton State Park	

NOTES:

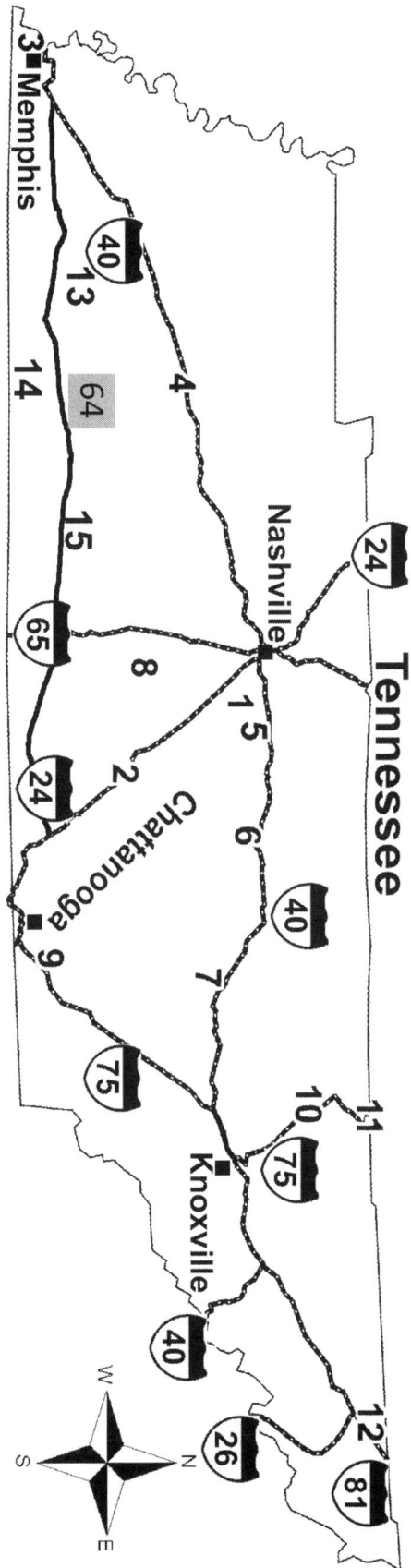

[1] Poole Knobs, J Percy Priest Dam
I-24, Exit 66
Southeast of Nashville
N36 03.155 W86 30.741
COE Rate: $14-$24
America/Beautiful Rate: $7-$12
(615) 459-6948
http://www.recreation.gov/

Directions

9 miles. From Exit 66, go 2.6 miles northeast on Hwy 266 (Sam Ridley Pkwy). Exit north on to Hwy 41N (Murfreesboro Rd), go 1.3 miles to Fergus Rd. Go right 1 mile to Jones Mill Rd. Go right 4 mile to Poole Knobs Camp on the left.

Points of Interest

Nashville, 'Music City,' has much to see and many great venues, attractions, events, tours, shopping, restaurants and live entertainment.

RV Sites		Water		Laundry	
Number	87	None		Wi-Fi	
Shaded	Y	At Site		Fishing	Y
By Water	Y	Spigots	Y	Hiking	Y
Paved		**Sewer**		Biking	Y
Pull Thru	Y	None		Swimming	
ADA	Y	At Site		Watch Wildlife	Y
Max RV Size	40	Dump Station	Y	Pets	Y
Electric		**Amenities**		**Security**	
None		Restrooms	Y	Host(s)	Y
20 Amp	Y	Showers	Y	Rangers(s)	Y
30 Amp	Y	Reserve Sites	Y	Gate	
50 Amp	Y	Store		Patrolled	Y
		Grill/Table	Y		

[2] Old Stone Fort State Park
I-24, Exit 110
Northwest of Manchester
N35 29.668 W86 06.146
State Rate: $20
(931) 723-5073
http://tnstateparks.com/parks/about/old-stone-fort

Directions

1.5 miles. From Exit 110 go 0.8 miles south on Hwy 53 (Woodbury Hwy) to Hwy 2/41. Turn right, go 0.7 miles to the Park entrance on your left. **Note, the bridge into the campground has a 36,000 pound weight limit!**

Points of Interest

Old Stone Fort is a 2,000 year-old American Indian ceremonial site. Local sights include Jack Daniels Distillery; Cumberland Caverns; & Historic Bell Buckle (restored Victorian railroad village).

RV Sites		Water		Laundry	
Number	51	None		Wi-Fi	
Shaded	Y	At Site	Y	Fishing	Y
By Water	Y	Spigots		Hiking	Y
Paved	Y	**Sewer**		Biking	Y
Pull Thru		None		Swimming	
ADA	Y	At Site		Watch Wildlife	Y
Max RV Size	45	Dump Station	Y	Pets	Y
Electric		**Amenities**		**Security**	
None		Restrooms	Y	Host(s)	Y
20 Amp	Y	Showers	Y	Rangers(s)	Y
30 Amp	Y	Reserve Sites	Y	Gate	
50 Amp	Y	Store		Patrolled	Y
		Grill/Table	Y		

[3] T.O. Fuller State Park
I-40, Exit 1e of I-40 to I-240N
Southwest of Memphis
N35 03.826 W90 07.081
State Rate: $20
(901) 543-7581
https://tnstateparks.itinio.com/t-o-fuller

Directions

12 miles. From Exit 1e of I-40 go south on I-240 for 5 miles to I-55N. Take I-55N 1.5 miles to exit 7 (Hwy 61). Go south on Hwy 61 (S 3rd. St) for 1.8 miles to Mitchell Rd. Turn west (right) and follow Mitchell Rd. for 3.6 miles in to the Park.

Points of Interest

Within the Park you can visit the Chucalissa Indian Museum and/or play the 18-hole golf course. Memphis offers Graceland. Don't forget to try the ribs!

RV Sites		Water		Laundry	Y
Number	45	None		Wi-Fi	
Shaded	Y	At Site	Y	Fishing	
By Water		Spigots		Hiking	Y
Paved	some	**Sewer**		Biking	Y
Pull Thru	Y	None		Swimming	Y
ADA	Y	At Site		Watch Wildlife	Y
Max RV Size	45	Dump Station	Y	Pets	Y
Electric		**Amenities**		**Security**	
None		Restrooms	Y	Host(s)	Y
20 Amp	Y	Showers	Y	Rangers(s)	Y
30 Amp	Y	Reserve Sites	Y	Gate	
50 Amp	Y	Store		Patrolled	Y
		Grill/Table	Y		

[4] Natchez Trace State Park
I-40, Exit 116
Northeast of Lexington
N35 47.636 W88 15.947
State Rate: $8 -$25
(731) 968-3742
http://tnstateparks.com/parks/about/natchez-trace

Directions

0.5 miles. From Exit 116 go south on Hwy 114 (Camden Rd) for about 0.5 mile to the Park Office. The campground is a number of miles into the Park.

Points of Interest

Of the three camping areas, the Pin Oak RV Campground is the primary location for RVs. Pin Oak Lodge is situated on the wooded shores of Pin Oak Lake. The Park Inn restaurant, pistol firing range, archery range and assorted outdoor activities will keep everyone busy.

RV Sites		Water		Laundry	Y
Number	208	None		Wi-Fi	
Shaded	some	At Site	Y	Fishing	Y
By Water	Y	Spigots	Y	Hiking	Y
Paved		Sewer		Biking	Y
Pull Thru	Y	None		Swimming	Y
ADA	Y	At Site	Y	Watch Wildlife	Y
Max RV Size	45	Dump Station	Y	Pets	Y
Electric		Amenities		Security	
None		Restrooms	Y	Host(s)	Y
20 Amp	Y	Showers	Y	Rangers(s)	Y
30 Amp	Y	Reserve Sites	Y	Gate	
50 Amp	Y	Store	Y	Patrolled	Y
		Grill/Table	Y		

[5] Cedars of Lebanon State Park
I-40, Exit 238
South of Lebanon
N36 05.637 W86 20.138
State Rate: $20
(615) 443-2769
http://tnstateparks.com/parks/about/cedars-of-lebanon

Directions

6.3 miles. From Exit 238 go south on Hwy 10/231 (Murfreesboro Rd) for 6.3 miles to the Park.

Points of Interest

Lebanon is nicknamed "The Antique City of the South" with over 20 antique stores in the county. Parkland Flea Market & Shopper's Alley are two flea markets that are open on weekends. Nashville Superspeedway is not far. Visit "Fiddler's Grove" and the Fessenden House.

RV Sites		Water		Laundry	Y
Number	117	None		Wi-Fi	
Shaded	Y	At Site	Y	Fishing	
By Water		Spigots		Hiking	Y
Paved	Y	Sewer		Biking	Y
Pull Thru	Y	None		Swimming	Y
ADA	Y	At Site		Watch Wildlife	Y
Max RV Size	40	Dump Station	Y	Pets	Y
Electric		Amenities		Security	
None		Restrooms	Y	Host(s)	Y
20 Amp	Y	Showers	Y	Rangers(s)	Y
30 Amp	Y	Reserve Sites	Y	Gate	
50 Amp	Y	Store	Y	Patrolled	Y
		Grill/Table	Y		

[6] Floating Mill Campground
I-40, Exit 273
Southwest of Cookeville
N36 02.969 W85 45.137
COE Rate: $16-$24
America/Beautiful Rate: $8-$12
(931) 858-4845
http://www.recreation.gov/

Directions

4.5 miles. From Exit 273, go south on Hwy 56 (Smithville, then Cookeville Hwy) for 3.5 miles to Floating Mill Rd. Turn right, go 1 mile to the campground.

Points of Interest

With many antique shops and bookstores, downtown Cookeville should keep you busy. You can buy crafts at the South's premier retailer of fine crafts. Visit the Cookeville History & Depot museums, or view beautiful historic architecture.

RV Sites		Water		Laundry	Y
Number	67	None		Wi-Fi	
Shaded	Y	At Site	Y	Fishing	Y
By Water	Y	Spigots	Y	Hiking	Y
Paved	some	Sewer		Biking	Y
Pull Thru	Y	None		Swimming	Y
ADA	Y	At Site		Watch Wildlife	
Max RV Size	40+	Dump Station	Y	Pets	Y
Electric		Amenities		Security	
None		Restrooms	Y	Host(s)	Y
20 Amp	Y	Showers	Y	Rangers(s)	Y
30 Amp	Y	Reserve Sites	Y	Gate	
50 Amp	Y	Store		Patrolled	Y
		Grill/Table	Y		

[7] Cumberland Mountain State Park
I-40, Exit 317
South of Crossville
N35 53.859 W84 59.576
State Rate: $22.50-$27.50
(931) 484-6138
http://tnstateparks.com/parks/about/cumberland-mountain

Directions

8.5 miles. From Exit 317 go south on Hwy 127, through Crossville, for 8.5 miles. Just past the Homestead Tower Center and Museum, turn right at Pigeon Ridge Rd in to the Park.

Points of Interest

Visit the Homestead Tower Center & Museum. Shop the Cumberland General Store. Take in a play at the Cumberland County Playhouse Theatre. Cumberland Mountain Restaurant is noted for it's Friday catfish dinner.

RV Sites		Water			Laundry	Y
Number	143	None			Wi-Fi	
Shaded	Y	At Site	Y		Fishing	Y
By Water	Y	Spigots			Hiking	Y
Paved	Y	Sewer			Biking	Y
Pull Thru		None			Swimming	Y
ADA	Y	At Site		few	Watch Wildlife	Y
Max RV Size	40	Dump Station	Y		Pets	Y
Electric		Amenities			Security	
None		Restrooms	Y		Host(s)	Y
20 Amp	Y	Showers	Y		Rangers(s)	Y
30 Amp	Y	Reserve Sites	Y		Gate	
50 Amp	few	Store	Y		Patrolled	Y
		Grill/Table	Y			

[8] Henry Horton State Park
I-65, Exit 46
East of Columbia
N35 35.379 W86 41.711
State Rate: $8-$25
(931) 364-2222
http://tnstateparks.com/parks/about/henry-horton

Directions

12.5 miles. From Exit 46, travel 3.8 miles east on Hwy 99/412 to Hwy 431. Turn south and travel 0.7 miles to Hwy 99. Turn east again for 7.5 miles to where 99 dead-ends at Hwy 31A. Turn south, go 0.7 miles to the Park entrance on the left.

Points of Interest

Located on the former estate of Henry H. Horton, 36th governor of Tennessee, is known for its golf course, Inn, campgrounds & trap & skeet range. The Restaurant is said to serve outstanding cuisine.

RV Sites		Water			Laundry	
Number	56	None			Wi-Fi	Y
Shaded	Y	At Site	Y		Fishing	Y
By Water	Y	Spigots			Hiking	Y
Paved		Sewer			Biking	Y
Pull Thru	Y	None			Swimming	Y
ADA	Y	At Site			Watch Wildlife	Y
Max RV Size	40	Dump Station	Y		Pets	Y
Electric		Amenities			Security	
None		Restrooms	Y		Host(s)	Y
20 Amp	Y	Showers	Y		Rangers(s)	Y
30 Amp	Y	Reserve Sites	Y		Gate	
50 Amp	Y	Store	Y		Patrolled	Y
		Grill/Table	Y			

[9] Harrison Bay State Park
I-75, Exit 4
West of Cleveland
N35 10.072 W85 06.694
State Rate: $8-$25
(423) 344-6214
http://tnstateparks.com/parks/about/harrison-bay

Directions

13.5 miles. From Exit 4 go northwest for 4.1 miles on Hwy 153 to Hwy 58 (exit 5). Go right for 8.3 miles to Harrison Bay Rd. Turn left, go 1 mile to the Park entrance.

Points of Interest

Try the Chattanooga River Walk. Visit the Tennessee Aquarium, one of the top aquariums in the USA. Railroaders will want to see the 48 Victorian train cars at the Chattanooga Choo Choo complex. Lookout Mountain is close.

RV Sites		Water			Laundry	
Number	128	None			Wi-Fi	Y
Shaded	Y	At Site	Y		Fishing	Y
By Water	Y	Spigots			Hiking	Y
Paved	Y	Sewer			Biking	Y
Pull Thru	Y	None			Swimming	Y
ADA	Y	At Site			Watch Wildlife	
Max RV Size	45	Dump Station	Y		Pets	Y
Electric		Amenities			Security	
None		Restrooms	Y		Host(s)	Y
20 Amp	Y	Showers	Y		Rangers(s)	Y
30 Amp	Y	Reserve Sites	Y		Gate	
50 Amp	Y	Store	Y		Patrolled	Y
		Grill/Table	Y			

[10] Cove Lake State Park
I-75, Exit 134
Northeast side of Caryville
N36 18.522 W84 12.669
State Rate: $20
(423) 566-9701
http://tnstateparks.com/parks/about/cove-lake

Directions

0.8 miles. From Exit 134 go east and north for 0.8 miles on Hwy 9/63/25W (Veterans Memorial Hwy) to the Park entrance.

Points of Interest

Enjoy badminton, shuffleboard, horseshoes, ping-pong, tennis, and other activities including a paved walking and bicycling trail. Recreation equipment is available on a free check-out system. Hikers should try Devil's Race Track. At dinner time try Rickard Ridge BBQ in the Park

RV Sites		Water			Laundry	
Number	106	None			Wi-Fi	
Shaded	Y	At Site	Y		Fishing	Y
By Water	Y	Spigots			Hiking	Y
Paved		**Sewer**			Biking	Y
Pull Thru	Y	None			Swimming	Y
ADA	Y	At Site			Watch Wildlife	Y
Max RV Size	45	Dump Station	Y		Pets	Y
Electric		**Amenities**			**Security**	
None		Restrooms	Y		Host(s)	Y
20 Amp	Y	Showers	Y		Rangers(s)	Y
30 Amp	Y	Reserve Sites	Y		Gate	
50 Amp		Store			Patrolled	Y
		Grill/Table	Y			

[11] Indian Mountain State Park
I-75, Exit 160
West side of Jellico
N36 35.465 W84 08.541
State Rate: $8-$25
(423) 784-7958
http://tnstateparks.com/parks/about/indian-mountain

Directions

2 miles. From Exit 160 go 0.9 miles northwest on Hwy 9/25W to State Hwy 297 (S Main St). Turn left, go 0.3 miles then make a right on London, go 0.8 miles, turn left on Indian Mountain State Park Circle. Proceed to the Park entrance.

Points of Interest

Take a day trip to the Lenoir Museum Cultural Complex, which includes a Museum, an 18th Century Rice Grist Mill and Crosby Threshing Barn.

RV Sites		Water			Laundry	
Number	47	None			Wi-Fi	
Shaded	Y	At Site	Y		Fishing	Y
By Water	Y	Spigots			Hiking	Y
Paved	Y	**Sewer**			Biking	Y
Pull Thru		None			Swimming	Y
ADA	Y	At Site			Watch Wildlife	Y
Max RV Size	45	Dump Station	Y		Pets	Y
Electric		**Amenities**			**Security**	
None		Restrooms	Y		Host(s)	Y
20 Amp	Y	Showers	Y		Rangers(s)	Y
30 Amp	Y	Reserve Sites	Y		Gate	
50 Amp		Store			Patrolled	Y
		Grill/Table	Y			

[12] Warriors' Path State Park
I-81, Exit 59
Northwest of Colonial Heights
N36 29.937 W82 29.237
State Rate: $8-$25
(423) 239-8531
http://tnstateparks.com/parks/about/warriors-path

Directions

3 miles. From Exit 59 go 1.2 miles northwest on Hwy 36 (Fort Henry Dr) to Hemlock Rd. Turn right & go 1.6 miles to the Park.

Points of Interest

The first country music recordings gave Bristol the title of 'Birthplace of Country Music.' Today you can still enjoy great live performances. The "World's Fastest Half Mile Track," Bristol Motor Speedway/Dragway are favorites for high-powered stock car and drag racing.

RV Sites		Water			Laundry	
Number	134	None			Wi-Fi	
Shaded	Y	At Site	Y		Fishing	Y
By Water		Spigots			Hiking	Y
Paved		**Sewer**			Biking	Y
Pull Thru	Y	None			Swimming	Y
ADA	Y	At Site			Watch Wildlife	Y
Max RV Size	40	Dump Station	Y		Pets	Y
Electric		**Amenities**			**Security**	
None		Restrooms	Y		Host(s)	Y
20 Amp	Y	Showers	Y		Rangers(s)	Y
30 Amp	Y	Reserve Sites	Y		Gate	
50 Amp	Y	Store			Patrolled	Y
		Grill/Table	Y			

[13] Chickasaw State Park
Hwy 64, at Hwy 18
Northeast of Bolivar
N35 23.537 W88 46.913
State Rate: $11-$20
(731) 989-5141.
http://tnstateparks.com/parks/about/chickasaw

Directions

16 miles. In Bolivar go 8.8 miles north on Hwy 18 to Hwy 100. Turn right, go 7.2 miles to the Park.

Points of Interest

There are 3 campgrounds in the Park. You probably want the RV (Trailer) campground. The Park Office is 0.6 miles further east on Hwy 100, beyond the campground Entrance. In Bolivar you'll find historic districts with antebellum homes and other buildings that reflect Bolivar's pre-Civil War prosperity.

RV Sites		Water		Laundry	
Number	52	None		Wi-Fi	
Shaded	Y	At Site	Y	Fishing	Y
By Water	Y	Spigots		Hiking	Y
Paved	Y	**Sewer**		Biking	Y
Pull Thru	Y	None		Swimming	Y
ADA	Y	At Site		Watch Wildlife	
Max RV Size	45	Dump Station	Y	Pets	Y
Electric		**Amenities**		**Security**	
None		Restrooms	Y	Host(s)	Y
20 Amp	Y	Showers	Y	Rangers(s)	Y
30 Amp	Y	Reserve Sites	Y	Gate	
50 Amp		Store		Patrolled	Y
		Grill/Table	Y		

[14] Pickwick Dam Tailwater
Hwy 64, at Hwy 128
South of Savannah, TN
N35 03.948 W88 15.883
TVA Rate: $22
America/Beautiful Rate: $11
(800) 882-5263
http://www.tva.gov/river/recreation/camping.htm#pickwick

Directions

12 miles. From Savannah go 9.3 miles south on Hwy 128 to Wharf Rd. Bear right onto Wharf Rd. Follow Wharf Rd for 2.7 miles to the Park.

Points of Interest

This is a self-service campground. A great location overlooking the Tennessee River. Savannah is rich in Civil War history, and in preserving its heritage and Southern charm.

RV Sites		Water		Laundry	
Number	100	None		Wi-Fi	
Shaded	Y	At Site	Y	Fishing	Y
By Water	Y	Spigots		Hiking	
Paved		**Sewer**		Biking	Y
Pull Thru		None		Swimming	
ADA	Y	At Site		Watch Wildlife	Y
Max RV Size	40+	Dump Station	Y	Pets	Y
Electric		**Amenities**		**Security**	
None		Restrooms	Y	Host(s)	
20 Amp	Y	Showers	Y	Rangers(s)	Y
30 Amp	Y	Reserve Sites		Gate	
50 Amp	Y	Store		Patrolled	Y
		Grill/Table	Y		

[15] David Crockett State Park
Hwy 64
Southwest side of Lawrenceburg
N35 14.540 W87 21.264
State Rate: $8 - $25
(931) 762-9408
http://tnstateparks.com/parks/about/david-crockett

Directions

1.4 miles. In Lawrenceburg on Hwy 64 at Hwy 43 go 1.4 miles west to the Park.

Points of Interest

The Park is named after frontiersman Davy Crockett, who live in Lawrenceburg as a young man. Lawrenceburg is within walking distance. The town square features shopping and antique shops. Tourist attractions include the David Crockett Statue & Mexican War Monument, The city is the birthplace of Southern Gospel Music.

RV Sites		Water		Laundry	
Number	107	None		Wi-Fi	
Shaded	Y	At Site	Y	Fishing	Y
By Water	Y	Spigots		Hiking	Y
Paved	Y	**Sewer**		Biking	Y
Pull Thru		None		Swimming	Y
ADA	Y	At Site		Watch Wildlife	
Max RV Size	42	Dump Station	Y	Pets	Y
Electric		**Amenities**		**Security**	
None		Restrooms	Y	Host(s)	Y
20 Amp	Y	Showers	Y	Rangers(s)	Y
30 Amp	Y	Reserve Sites	Y	Gate	
50 Amp		Store	Y	Patrolled	Y
		Grill/Table	Y		

About Texas's Public Campgrounds

Texas Parks are rich in beauty and history. Texas has multiple regions with a variety of landscapes. Many Parks feature lakes and rivers where you can go boating, fishing, and swimming. Other parks offer trails for hiking, biking, birding and horseback riding.

The Corps of Engineers has almost two dozen project locations in Texas and a number of parks and campgrounds, some included in this chapter.

Texas Parks and Wildlife Department oversee over 90 State Parks. You will find comprehensive statewide information at their website -
http://www.tpwd.state.tx.us/state-parks/

The websites for the individual Parks are extensive and should provide you with information to answer most questions. Reservations can be made at -
http://texas.reserveworld.com/

There are three park fees, which may vary by park:

- Entrance Fee – for day use;
- Facility Fee – stay at a campsite;
- Activity Fee – participate in a special activity;
- Dump Station Fee - $5 (some parks).

Many of the Parks have Wi-Fi. Pets are allowed at the Parks but must be on a leash no more than six feet long.

[1] Hueco Tanks State Park & Historic Site	**[16] McKinney Falls State Park**
[2] Balmorhea State Park	**[17] Jim Hogg Park**
[3] Kerrville-Schreiner Park	**[18] Union Grove - Stillhouse Hollow**
[4] Palmetto State Park	**[19] Midway Camp**
[5] Stephen F. Austin State Park	**[20] Lake Whitney State Park**
[6] Lake Colorado City State Park	**[21] Ray Roberts Lake State Park - Isle du Bois**
[7] Lake Mineral Wells State Park	**[22] Hickory Creek Park**
[8] Holiday Campground	**[23] Padre Island National Seashore**
[9] Cedar Hill State Park	**[24] Lake Corpus Christi State Park**
[10] Tyler State Park	**[25] Galveston Island State Park**
[11] Palo Duro Canyon State Park	**[26] Cagle Recreation Area**
[12] East Fork Campground	**[27] Fairfield Lake State Park**
[13] Cooper Lake (So. Sulphur) State Park	**[28] Waxahachie Creek Park**
[14] Clear Springs/Wright Patman Lake	**[29] Isla Blanca Park**
[15] Potters Creek Campground	**[30] Goose Island State Park**

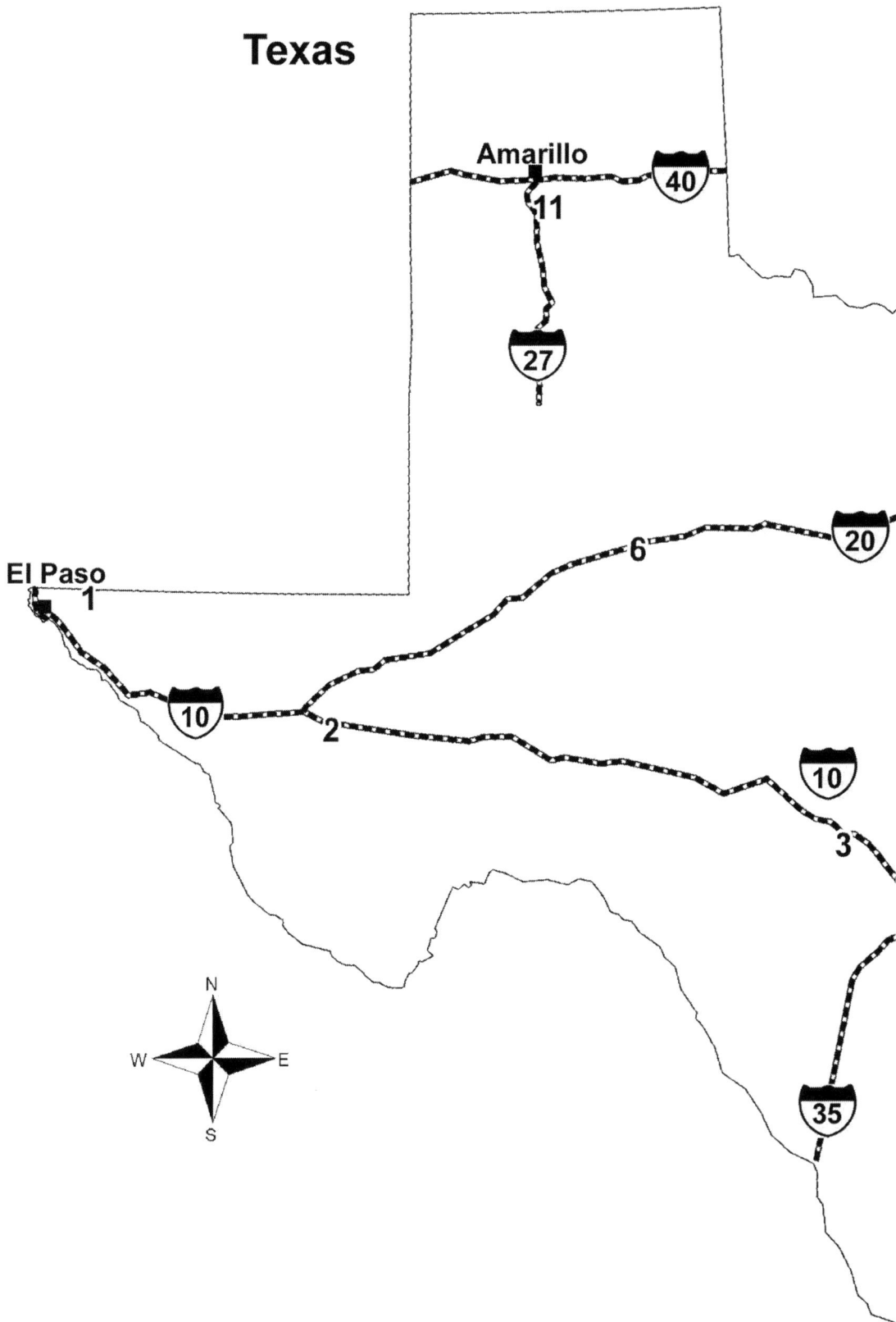

Texas

Amarillo

40

11

27

El Paso

1

6

20

10

2

10

3

35

N

W E

S

Texas

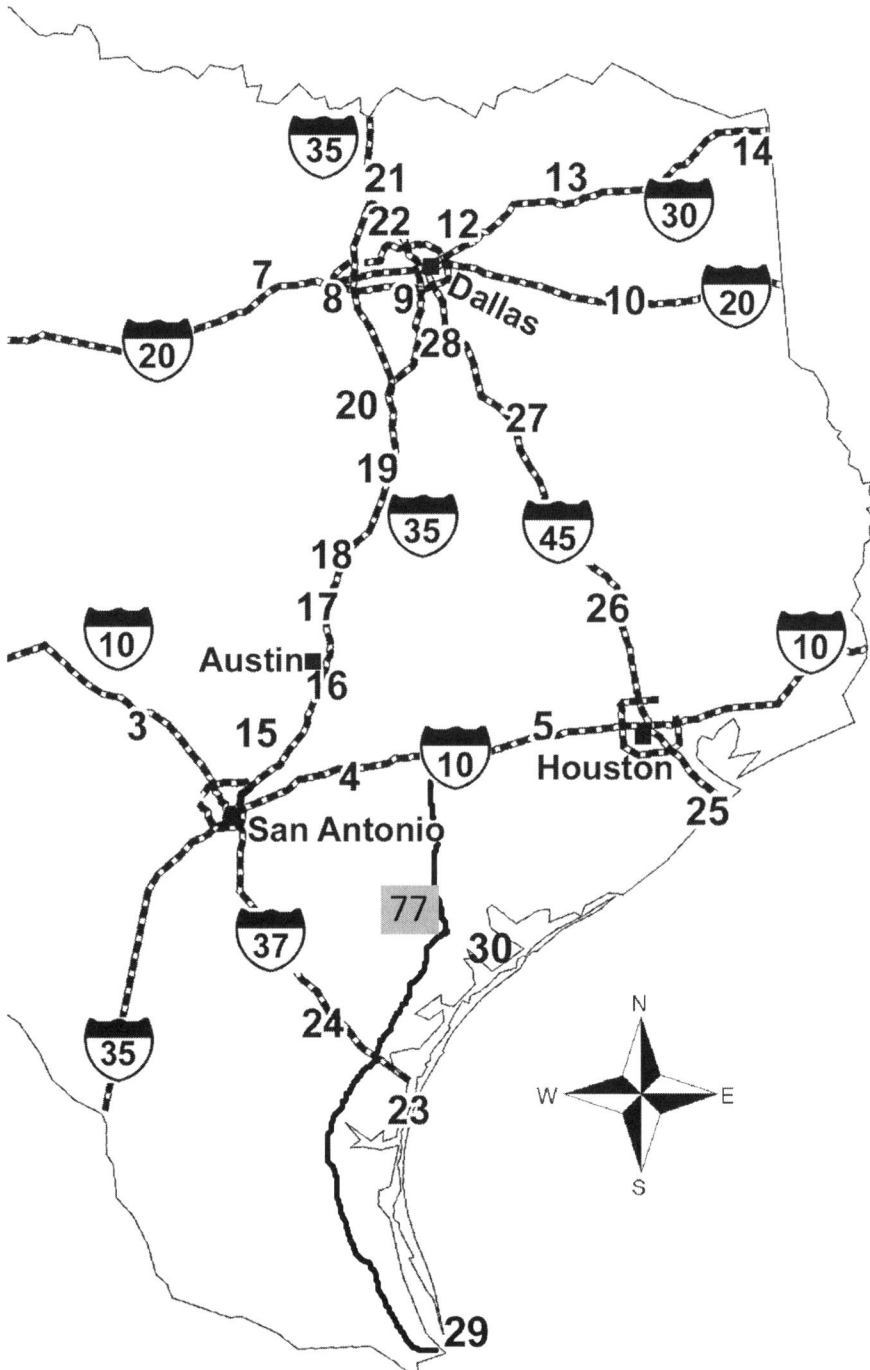

[1] Hueco Tanks State Park and Historic Site
I-10, Exit 23
Northeast of El Paso
N31 55.628 W106 02.572
State Rate: $12-$16
(915) 857-1135
http://www.tpwd.state.tx.us/state-parks/hueco-tanks

Directions

29 miles. From Exit 23 go north and east for 21.5 miles on Hwy 62/180 (Montana Ave) to Ranch Road 2775. Turn north for 7.5 miles to the Park entrance.

Points of Interest

The Park's focus is a unique legacy of fantastic rock paintings. Archaic hunters & recent Native Americans have drawn strange mythological designs & figures on area rocks. For the protection of these resources, visitation is limited. Special reservations are required. Call ahead!

RV Sites		Water		Laundry	
Number	20	None		Wi-Fi	Y
Shaded	Y	At Site	Y	Fishing	
By Water		Spigots	Y	Hiking	Y
Paved	Y	Sewer		Biking	Y
Pull Thru		None		Swimming	
ADA	Y	At Site		Watch Wildlife	Y
Max RV Size	40+	Dump Station	Y	Pets	Y
Electric		Amenities		Security	
None		Restrooms	Y	Host(s)	Y
20 Amp	Y	Showers	Y	Rangers(s)	Y
30 Amp	Y	Reserve Sites	Y	Gate	
50 Amp	Y	Store	Y	Patrolled	
		Grill/Table	Y		

[2] Balmorhea State Park
I-10, Exits 206 or 209
South of Balmorhea
N30 56.732 W103 47.206
State Rate: $11-$17
(432) 375-2370
http://www.tpwd.state.tx.us/state-parks/balmorhea

Directions

6-7 miles. **Eastbound,** from Exit 206 go south 1.7 miles on Ranch Rd 2903 (I-10 Bus) to Hwy 17. Turn right, go 4.2 miles to the Park. **Westbound**, From Exit 209 go south 7 miles to the Park.

Points of Interest

The Park's main attraction is a large artesian spring pool. Two 'must visits' are the renowned McDonald Observatory and Fort Davis, one of the best surviving examples of an Indian Wars' frontier military post in the Southwest.

RV Sites		Water		Laundry	
Number	34	None		Wi-Fi	
Shaded	Y	At Site	Y	Fishing	
By Water		Spigots		Hiking	Y
Paved	Y	Sewer		Biking	
Pull Thru	Y	None		Swimming	Y
ADA	Y	At Site		Watch Wildlife	Y
Max RV Size	45	Dump Station	Y	Pets	Y
Electric		Amenities		Security	
None		Restrooms	Y	Host(s)	Y
20 Amp	Y	Showers	Y	Rangers(s)	Y
30 Amp	Y	Reserve Sites	Y	Gate	
50 Amp		Store		Patrolled	
		Grill/Table	Y		

[3] Kerrville-Schreiner City Park
I-10, Exit 508
South side of Kerrville
N30 00.624 W99 07.253
City Rate: $23-$28
(830) 257-7300
http://www.kerrvilletx.gov/index.aspx?nid=318

Directions

5 miles. From Exit 508 go 0.2 miles to Hwy 534 (Memorial Pkwy). Turn left, go 4.3 miles to Hwy 173. Turn left, go 0.2 miles to the Park Headquarters and Registration, on the left

Points of Interest

Kerrville has the Hill Country Arts Foundation, local craft shops, Museum of Western Art, Kerr Arts and Cultural Center, Kerrville Performing Arts Society and Callioux Theater. Also drive around Hill Country to Bandera, Boerne, Blanco, Fredericksburg, and Ingram.

RV Sites		Water		Laundry	
Number	62	None		Wi-Fi	Y
Shaded	Y	At Site	Y	Fishing	Y
By Water	Y	Spigots	Y	Hiking	Y
Paved		Sewer		Biking	Y
Pull Thru	Y	None		Swimming	
ADA	Y	At Site	Y	Watch Wildlife	Y
Max RV Size	45	Dump Station	Y	Pets	Y
Electric		Amenities		Security	
None		Restrooms	Y	Host(s)	Y
20 Amp	Y	Showers	Y	Rangers(s)	
30 Amp	Y	Reserve Sites	Y	Gate	
50 Amp	Y	Store	Y	Patrolled	Y
		Grill/Table	Y		

[4] Palmetto State Park
I-10, Exit 632
Northwest of Gonzales
N29 35.838 W97 35.079
State Rate: $12-$20
(830) 672-3266
http://www.tpwd.state.tx.us/state-parks/palmetto

Directions

4.3 miles. From Exit 632 go south for 2.5 miles on Hwy 183 (E Pierce St) to Cty Rd 261. Turn right, drive 1.8 miles to the Park.

Points of Interest

The Park is a "hot spot" for birding opportunities. In Gonzales tour the Old Jail Museum, the Pioneer Village Living History Center, and the Gonzales Memorial Museum. Luling offers a year-round Farmers' market, antique and collectible shopping, and dining (including a famous barbecue).

RV Sites		Water		Laundry	
Number	41	None		Wi-Fi	
Shaded	Y	At Site	Y	Fishing	Y
By Water	Y	Spigots	Y	Hiking	Y
Paved	Y	Sewer		Biking	Y
Pull Thru		None		Swimming	Y
ADA	Y	At Site	Y	Watch Wildlife	Y
Max RV Size	45	Dump Station	Y	Pets	Y
Electric		Amenities		Security	
None		Restrooms	Y	Host(s)	Y
20 Amp	Y	Showers	Y	Rangers(s)	Y
30 Amp	Y	Reserve Sites	Y	Gate	
50 Amp	Y	Store	Y	Patrolled	Y
		Grill/Table	Y		

[5] Stephen F. Austin State Park
I-10, Exit 723
West of Houston
N29 48.723 W96 06.488
State Rate: $22
(979) 885-3613
http://www.tpwd.state.tx.us/state-parks/stephen-f-austin

Directions

3 miles. From Exit 723 turn north for 2 miles on FM 1458. Go left on Park Road 38 for 1 mile to the Park Headquarters.

Points of Interest

Walk the old town site of San Felipe, the fabled Cradle of Texas Liberty. Houston is close, with numerous attractions -Hermann Park Zoo, Museum of Natural Science, & NASA. You could also visit the San Jacinto Battleground and Monument as well as the Battleship TEXAS.

RV Sites		Water		Laundry	
Number	40	None		Wi-Fi	Y
Shaded	Y	At Site	Y	Fishing	Y
By Water	Y	Spigots	Y	Hiking	Y
Paved		Sewer		Biking	Y
Pull Thru	Y	None		Swimming	
ADA	Y	At Site	Y	Watch Wildlife	Y
Max RV Size	45	Dump Station	Y	Pets	Y
Electric		Amenities		Security	
None		Restrooms	Y	Host(s)	Y
20 Amp	Y	Showers	Y	Rangers(s)	Y
30 Amp	Y	Reserve Sites	Y	Gate	
50 Amp		Store		Patrolled	Y
		Grill/Table	Y		

[6] Lake Colorado City State Park
I-20, Exit 210
South of Colorado City
N32 18.956 W100 56.123
State Rate: $15-$22
(325) 728-3931
http://www.tpwd.state.tx.us/state-parks/lake-colorado-city

Directions

5.7 miles. From Exit 210 go 5.7 miles south on FM 2836 (Lake Rd) to the Park entrance.

Points of Interest

Colorado City is in the 'Heart of Texas.' Area attractions include Heart of West Texas Museum (where the prehistoric bison roamed), Heritage House, Ruddick Park, and numerous antique stores. Check out the Branding Wall. Walk the historic downtown.

RV Sites		Water		Laundry	
Number	112	None		Wi-Fi	Y
Shaded	Y	At Site	Y	Fishing	Y
By Water	Y	Spigots	Y	Hiking	Y
Paved		Sewer		Biking	Y
Pull Thru	Y	None		Swimming	Y
ADA	Y	At Site	Y	Watch Wildlife	
Max RV Size	45	Dump Station	Y	Pets	Y
Electric		Amenities		Security	
None		Restrooms	Y	Host(s)	Y
20 Amp	Y	Showers	Y	Rangers(s)	Y
30 Amp	Y	Reserve Sites	Y	Gate	
50 Amp		Store		Patrolled	Y
		Grill/Table	Y		

[7] Lake Mineral Wells State Park
I-20, Exit 386
East of Mineral Wells
N32 48.874 W98 02.535
State Rate: $14-$26
(940) 328-1171
http://www.tpwd.state.tx.us/state-parks/lake-mineral-wells/

Directions

19.5 miles. From Exit 386 turn north for 15 miles on Hwy 281 to Hwy 180 in Mineral Wells. Turn east for 4 miles to Park Rd 71. Turn north for 0. 5 miles in to the Park.

Points of Interest

Go fossil collecting at the Mineral Wells Fossil Park. Visit the Clark Botanical Gardens. Walk through the Old Jail Museum, built in 1882 & displaying artifacts of Palo Pinto County. Downtown, explore one of the many antique shops.

RV Sites		Water		Laundry	
Number	88	None		Wi-Fi	Y
Shaded	Y	At Site	Y	Fishing	Y
By Water	Y	Spigots	Y	Hiking	Y
Paved		Sewer		Biking	Y
Pull Thru		None		Swimming	Y
ADA	Y	At Site		Watch Wildlife	
Max RV Size	40+	Dump Station	Y	Pets	Y
Electric		Amenities		Security	
None		Restrooms	Y	Host(s)	Y
20 Amp	Y	Showers	Y	Rangers(s)	Y
30 Amp	Y	Reserve Sites	Y	Gate	
50 Amp	Y	Store	Y	Patrolled	Y
		Grill/Table	Y		

[8] Holiday Campground
I-20, Exit 429
Southwest of Fort Worth
N32 37.092 W97 29.823
COE Rate: $28
America/Beautiful Rate: $14
(817) 292-2400
http://www.recreation.gov/

Directions

7.5 miles. From Exit 429 go 5.7 miles south on Hwy 377 (Benbrook Dr) to S Lakeview Dr. Turn left, go 1.7 miles to the Park.

Points of Interest

Fort Worth, the "City of Cowboys and Culture" offers an array of things to do from museums & galleries to great shopping and historic sites. To discover all you can and want to see, go to -

http://www.fortworth.com/. Also see [9]

RV Sites		Water		Laundry	
Number	74	None		Wi-Fi	
Shaded	Y	At Site	Y	Fishing	Y
By Water	Y	Spigots	Y	Hiking	Y
Paved	Y	Sewer		Biking	Y
Pull Thru	Y	None		Swimming	Y
ADA	Y	At Site		Watch Wildlife	Y
Max RV Size	45	Dump Station	Y	Pets	Y
Electric		Amenities		Security	
None		Restrooms	Y	Host(s)	Y
20 Amp	Y	Showers	Y	Rangers(s)	Y
30 Amp	Y	Reserve Sites	Y	Gate	
50 Amp	Y	Store	Y	Patrolled	Y
		Grill/Table	Y		

[9] Cedar Hill State Park
I-20, Exit 457
South of Arlington & Grand Prairie
N32 37.339 W96 58.780
State Rate: $25-$30
(972) 291-3900
http://www.tpwd.state.tx.us/state-parks/cedar-hill

Directions

4 miles. From Exit 457 go south for 3.7 miles on FM Rd 1382 (Belt Line Rd) to W Spine Rd. Turn right for 0.3 miles in to the Park.

Points of Interest

A few area attractions include Dallas Museum of Art, Dallas Symphony, Dallas Opera, Billy Bob's Texas, horse racing at Lone Star Park, NASCAR racing at Texas Motor Speedway, Traders Village flea market, Farmers Market, and the JFK Memorial. **Also see [8]**

RV Sites		Water		Laundry	
Number	350	None		Wi-Fi	
Shaded	Y	At Site	Y	Fishing	Y
By Water	Y	Spigots	Y	Hiking	Y
Paved		Sewer		Biking	Y
Pull Thru		None		Swimming	Y
ADA	Y	At Site	Y	Watch Wildlife	Y
Max RV Size	40+	Dump Station	Y	Pets	Y
Electric		Amenities		Security	
None		Restrooms	Y	Host(s)	Y
20 Amp	Y	Showers	Y	Rangers(s)	Y
30 Amp	Y	Reserve Sites	Y	Gate	
50 Amp	Y	Store	Y	Patrolled	Y
		Grill/Table	Y		

[10] Tyler State Park
I-20, Exit 562
North of Tyler
N32 28.914 W95 16.832
State Rate: $14-$26
(903) 597-5338
http://www.tpwd.state.tx.us/state-parks/tyler

Directions

2 miles. From Exit 562 go north for 2 miles on State Park Hwy to Park Rd 16. Turn left to the Park entrance.

Points of Interest

Tyler's brick streets lead visitors to an array of attractions, quaint antique shops and unique specialty stores. Noted for its roses and festivals, Tyler also has Broadway and ballet performances, symphony concerts, world-class art museums and cuisine sure to please all.

RV Sites		Water		Laundry	
Number	77	None		Wi-Fi	Y
Shaded	Y	At Site	Y	Fishing	Y
By Water	Y	Spigots	Y	Hiking	Y
Paved	Y	**Sewer**		Biking	Y
Pull Thru	Y	None		Swimming	
ADA	Y	At Site	Y	Watch Wildlife	Y
Max RV Size	40	Dump Station	Y	Pets	Y
Electric		**Amenities**		**Security**	
None		Restrooms	Y	Host(s)	Y
20 Amp	Y	Showers	Y	Rangers(s)	Y
30 Amp	Y	Reserve Sites	Y	Gate	
50 Amp	Y	Store	Y	Patrolled	Y
		Grill/Table	Y		

[11] Palo Duro Canyon State Park
I-27, Exit 106
South of Amarillo
N34 59.078 W101 42.096
State Rate: $24
(806) 488-2227
http://www.tpwd.state.tx.us/state-parks/palo-duro-canyon

Directions

10 miles. From Exit 106 turn east for 10 miles on Hwy 217 to the Park.

Points of Interest

In Amarillo visit the American Quarter Horse Hall of Fame, the Alibates Flint Quarries National Monument, or the Amarillo Botanical Gardens with acres of seasonal themed plantings surrounding the Mary E. Bivins Tropical Conservatory. For a fun dinner go to River Breaks Ranch.

RV Sites		Water		Laundry	
Number	79	None		Wi-Fi	
Shaded	some	At Site	Y	Fishing	
By Water		Spigots	Y	Hiking	Y
Paved	Y	**Sewer**		Biking	Y
Pull Thru	Y	None		Swimming	
ADA	Y	At Site	Y	Watch Wildlife	Y
Max RV Size	45	Dump Station	Y	Pets	Y
Electric		**Amenities**		**Security**	
None		Restrooms	Y	Host(s)	Y
20 Amp	Y	Showers	Y	Rangers(s)	Y
30 Amp	Y	Reserve Sites	Y	Gate	
50 Amp	Y	Store	Y	Patrolled	Y
		Grill/Table	Y		

[12] East Fork Campground
I-30, Exit 68
East of Plano
N33 02.122 W96 30.940
COE Rate: $30
America/Beautiful Rate: $15
(972) 442-3141
http://www.recreation.gov/

Directions

13 miles. From Exit 68 go north on Hwy 205 (S Goliad St) for 8.1 miles to Hwy 78. Turn west, go 3.7 miles to Eubanks Lane. Turn north 0.4 miles, then bare right on Forrest Ross. Continue 0.5 miles north in to the campground.

Points of Interest

Historic downtown Plano offers unique and one-of-a-kind stores and boutiques along its brick street. Stroll through Fairview Farms and Farmer's Market. Go to the Interurban Railway Museum.

RV Sites		Water		Laundry	
Number	50	None		Wi-Fi	
Shaded	some	At Site	Y	Fishing	Y
By Water	Y	Spigots	Y	Hiking	Y
Paved	Y	**Sewer**		Biking	Y
Pull Thru		None		Swimming	Y
ADA	Y	At Site	Y	Watch Wildlife	
Max RV Size	45	Dump Station	Y	Pets	Y
Electric		**Amenities**		**Security**	
None		Restrooms	Y	Host(s)	Y
20 Amp	Y	Showers	Y	Rangers(s)	Y
30 Amp	Y	Reserve Sites	Y	Gate	
50 Amp	Y	Store		Patrolled	Y
		Grill/Table	Y		

[13] Cooper Lake (South Sulphur) State Park
I-30, Exit 122
North of Sulphur Springs
N33 17.199 W95 39.441
State Rate: $16-$20
(903) 945-5256
http://www.tpwd.state.tx.us/state-parks/
cooper-lake

Directions

17 miles. From Exit 122 travel north 11.5 miles on Hwy 19. Turn west for 4.2 miles on FM 71 to FM 3505. Go north for 1.5 miles to the park.

Points of Interest

In Sulphur Springs, shop for antiques on the Town Square, or find the item you desire in one of many factory direct stores. Festivals are a frequent occurrence. You'll want to look for local treasures at the Farmer's Market and Flea Market on the Square.

RV Sites		Water		Laundry	
Number	87	None		Wi-Fi	
Shaded	Y	At Site	Y	Fishing	Y
By Water	Y	Spigots	Y	Hiking	Y
Paved	Y	Sewer		Biking	
Pull Thru	Y	None		Swimming	Y
ADA	Y	At Site	few	Watch Wildlife	Y
Max RV Size	45	Dump Station	Y	Pets	Y
Electric		Amenities		Security	
None		Restrooms	Y	Host(s)	Y
20 Amp	Y	Showers	Y	Rangers(s)	Y
30 Amp	Y	Reserve Sites	Y	Gate	
50 Amp	Y	Store		Patrolled	Y
		Grill/Table	Y		

[14] Clear Springs/Wright Patman Lake
I-30, Exit 220
Southwest of Texarkana
N33 21.506 W94 11.181
COE Rate: $12-$32
America/Beautiful Rate: $6-$16
(903) 838-8781
http://www.recreation.gov/

Directions

11 miles. From Exit 220 go south on Hwy 59, staying with Hwy 59 as it bares right at S Lake St, for 8.1 miles in all to FM 2148. Turn right, go 1.4 miles to Clear Springs Rd. Turn left, go 1.5 miles to Clear Springs Park.

Points of Interest

In Texarkana visit the Ace of Clubs house. Tour Historic Washington State Park. Check out the Perot Theater (an Italian Renaissance Theater built in 1924), & find Photographer's Island.

RV Sites		Water		Laundry	
Number	114	None		Wi-Fi	
Shaded	Y	At Site	Y	Fishing	Y
By Water	Y	Spigots	Y	Hiking	Y
Paved	Y	Sewer		Biking	Y
Pull Thru		None		Swimming	Y
ADA	Y	At Site	Y	Watch Wildlife	Y
Max RV Size	45	Dump Station	Y	Pets	Y
Electric		Amenities		Security	
None		Restrooms	Y	Host(s)	Y
20 Amp	Y	Showers	Y	Rangers(s)	Y
30 Amp	Y	Reserve Sites	Y	Gate	Y
50 Amp	Y	Store		Patrolled	Y
		Grill/Table	Y		

[15] Potters Creek Campground
I-35, Exit 191
North of New Braunfels
N29 54.483 W98 15.791
COE Rate: $26
America/Beautiful Rate: $13
(830) 964-3341
http://www.recreation.gov/

Directions

23 miles. From Exit 191 go north on FM 306 for 20.5 miles to Potters Creek Rd. Turn south for 2.5 miles to the Campground.

Points of Interest

You will enjoy this location, with numerous attractions like the San Antonio River Walk, the Alamo, Natural Bridge Caverns, Wonder World Cavern and Aquamarina Springs in San Marcus, or the Historic town of Gruene - 'gently resisting change since 1872.'

RV Sites		Water		Laundry	
Number	114	None		Wi-Fi	
Shaded	Y	At Site	Y	Fishing	Y
By Water	Y	Spigots	Y	Hiking	Y
Paved	Y	Sewer		Biking	Y
Pull Thru		None		Swimming	Y
ADA	Y	At Site	Y	Watch Wildlife	Y
Max RV Size	45	Dump Station	Y	Pets	Y
Electric		Amenities		Security	
None		Restrooms	Y	Host(s)	Y
20 Amp	Y	Showers	Y	Rangers(s)	Y
30 Amp	Y	Reserve Sites	Y	Gate	Y
50 Amp	Y	Store		Patrolled	Y
		Grill/Table	Y		

[16] McKinney Falls State Park
I-35, Exit 230
South of Austin
N30 10.759 W97 43.275
State Rate: $20-$24
(512) 243-1643
http://www.tpwd.state.tx.us/state-parks/
mckinney-falls

Directions

6 miles. From Exit 230 go east on Hwy 71/290 (Ben White Blvd) for 2.2 miles to Montopolis. Turn right, go 0.5 miles to Burleson Rd. Turn left for 1.5 miles to McKinney Fall Pkwy. Turn right, go 1.8 miles to the Park.

Points of Interest

Enjoy Austin, a creative community filled with designers, painters, sculptors, dancers, filmmakers, musicians and artists of all kinds. Don't forget the best barbeque - ribs & a side of potato salad!

RV Sites		Water		Laundry	
Number	81	None		Wi-Fi	Y
Shaded	Y	At Site	Y	Fishing	Y
By Water	Y	Spigots	Y	Hiking	Y
Paved		**Sewer**		Biking	Y
Pull Thru	Y	None		Swimming	Y
ADA	Y	At Site		Watch Wildlife	Y
Max RV Size	40+	Dump Station	Y	Pets	Y
Electric		**Amenities**		**Security**	
None		Restrooms	Y	Host(s)	Y
20 Amp	Y	Showers	Y	Rangers(s)	
30 Amp	Y	Reserve Sites	Y	Gate	
50 Amp	Y	Store		Patrolled	Y
		Grill/Table	Y		

[17] Jim Hogg Park
I-35, Exit 261
North of Austin
N30 41.192 W97 44.791
COE Rate: $18-$36
America/Beautiful Rate: $9-$18
(512) 930-5253
http://www.recreation.gov/

Directions

8 miles. From Exit 261 go northwest on FM 2338 (Williams Dr) for 5.6 miles to Jim Hogg Rd. Turn south for 1.7 miles to the park entrance. Cedar Breaks Park is another close by COE camp option.

Points of Interest

Enjoy Austin, a creative community filled with designers, painters, sculptors, dancers, filmmakers, musicians & artists of all kinds. Don't forget the best barbeque - ribs & a side of potato salad!

RV Sites		Water		Laundry	
Number	133	None		Wi-Fi	
Shaded	Y	At Site	Y	Fishing	Y
By Water	Y	Spigots	Y	Hiking	Y
Paved	Y	**Sewer**		Biking	Y
Pull Thru		None		Swimming	
ADA	Y	At Site		Watch Wildlife	Y
Max RV Size	45	Dump Station	Y	Pets	Y
Electric		**Amenities**		**Security**	
None		Restrooms	Y	Host(s)	Y
20 Amp	Y	Showers	Y	Rangers(s)	Y
30 Amp	Y	Reserve Sites	Y	Gate	Y
50 Amp	Y	Store		Patrolled	Y
		Grill/Table	Y		

[18] Union Grove - Stillhouse Hollow
I-35, Exit 286
Southwest of Belton
N31 00.646 W97 37.244
COE Rate: $22-$36
America/Beautiful Rate: $11-$18
(254) 947-0072
http://www.recreation.gov/

Directions

8 miles. From Exit 286 go west for 6.5 miles on FM 2484 to Union Grove Park Rd. Turn right, go 1 mile to the Park.

Points of Interest

Visit Salado, the 'Best Art Town in Texas.' Main Street is a marketplace with over 60 shops and artists galleries. Find art, antiques, pottery, crafts, collectibles, Americana, southwest or south-of-the-border decor, handcrafted furniture, gourmet foods and wines.

RV Sites		Water		Laundry	
Number	30	None		Wi-Fi	
Shaded		At Site	Y	Fishing	Y
By Water	Y	Spigots	Y	Hiking	Y
Paved	Y	**Sewer**		Biking	Y
Pull Thru	Y	None		Swimming	Y
ADA	Y	At Site		Watch Wildlife	Y
Max RV Size	45	Dump Station	Y	Pets	Y
Electric		**Amenities**		**Security**	
None		Restrooms	Y	Host(s)	Y
20 Amp	Y	Showers	Y	Rangers(s)	Y
30 Amp	Y	Reserve Sites	Y	Gate	Y
50 Amp	Y	Store		Patrolled	Y
		Grill/Table	Y		

[19] Midway Camp
I-35, Exit 330
Southwest side of Waco
N31 31.537 W97 13.602
COE Rate: $20-$36
America/Beautiful Rate: $10-$16
(254) 756-5359
http://www.recreation.gov/

Directions

6 miles. From Exit 330 go 5 miles west on Hwy 6 (TX Loop 340). Exit right at Midway Park on to Old Fish Pond Rd. Circle under the bridge and go 0.5 miles south, following the service road to the Park.

Points of Interest

Waco's 18 museums and attractions make for a great day trip. Enjoy the restored downtown and warehouse district with restaurants, specialty shops, & scenic River Walk River.

RV Sites		Water		Laundry	
Number	38	None		Wi-Fi	
Shaded	Y	At Site	Y	Fishing	Y
By Water	Y	Spigots	Y	Hiking	Y
Paved	Y	**Sewer**		Biking	Y
Pull Thru	Y	None		Swimming	Y
ADA	Y	At Site	Y	Watch Wildlife	
Max RV Size	45	Dump Station	Y	Pets	Y
Electric		**Amenities**		**Security**	
None		Restrooms	Y	Host(s)	Y
20 Amp	Y	Showers	Y	Rangers(s)	Y
30 Amp	Y	Reserve Sites	Y	Gate	Y
50 Amp	Y	Store		Patrolled	Y
		Grill/Table	Y		

[20] Lake Whitney State Park
I-35, Exit 368
Southwest of Hillsboro
N31 55.815 W97 21.498
State Rate: $14-$24
(254) 694-3793
http://www.tpwd.state.tx.us/state-parks/lake-whitney

Directions

18 miles. From Exit 368 take Hwy 22/171 (Corsicana Hwy) west for 14 miles to the east side of Whitney. Go straight at TX 180 Spur (W Jefferson Ave) for 0.6 miles to S Colorado. Turn south for 0.4 miles to W Lee Ave. Turn west, W Lee becomes FM 1224, go 2.4 miles to the Park.

Points of Interest

From music to theater, Hill College offers free performances to arts enthusiasts.

RV Sites		Water		Laundry	
Number	71	None		Wi-Fi	
Shaded	Y	At Site	Y	Fishing	Y
By Water	Y	Spigots	Y	Hiking	Y
Paved		**Sewer**		Biking	Y
Pull Thru	Y	None		Swimming	Y
ADA	Y	At Site	Y	Watch Wildlife	Y
Max RV Size	40+	Dump Station	Y	Pets	Y
Electric		**Amenities**		**Security**	
None		Restrooms	Y	Host(s)	Y
20 Amp	Y	Showers	Y	Rangers(s)	Y
30 Amp	Y	Reserve Sites	Y	Gate	
50 Amp	Y	Store		Patrolled	Y
		Grill/Table	Y		

[21] Ray Roberts Lake State Park (Isle du Bois Unit)
I-35, Exit 479
North of Denton
N33 21.931 W97 00.809
State Rate: $25-$26
(940) 686-2148
http://www.tpwd.state.tx.us/state-parks/ray-roberts-lake

Directions

11 miles. From Exit 479 go east on FM 455 (Chapman Dr) for 10.5 miles. Turn north on Parkway 4137 for 0.4 mile to the Park.

Points of Interest

Walk Denton's Courthouse Square. Enjoy its music, arts & history. Partake in the many festivals. Denton's restaurants, concerts, shopping and tours will also keep you busy.

RV Sites		Water		Laundry	
Number	115	None		Wi-Fi	Y
Shaded	Y	At Site	Y	Fishing	Y
By Water	Y	Spigots	Y	Hiking	Y
Paved	Y	**Sewer**		Biking	Y
Pull Thru	Y	None		Swimming	Y
ADA	Y	At Site	Y	Watch Wildlife	Y
Max RV Size	40+	Dump Station	Y	Pets	Y
Electric		**Amenities**		**Security**	
None		Restrooms	Y	Host(s)	Y
20 Amp	Y	Showers	Y	Rangers(s)	Y
30 Amp	Y	Reserve Sites	Y	Gate	
50 Amp	Y	Store		Patrolled	Y
		Grill/Table	Y		

[22] Hickory Creek Park
I-35E, Exit 457
North of Lewisville
N33 06.883 W97 02.346
COE Rate: $18-$30
America/Beautiful Rate: $9-$15
(469) 645-9100
http://www.recreation.gov/

Directions

1 mile. **Northbound**, from Exit 457 go on frontage road, to N Denton Dr, take the overpass and turn south on Stemmons to the first right, Tuberville Rd. **Southbound**, from Exit 457, go on to Stemmons to the second right, Tuberville Rd. All travelers go 0.2 mile to Point Vista Rd, turn left, go 0.5 mile to the Park.

Points of Interest

Lewisville's old-town charm is still there when you see and visit the antique shops, specialty stores, and restaurants.

RV Sites		Water			Laundry	Y
Number	121	None			Wi-Fi	
Shaded	Y	At Site	Y		Fishing	Y
By Water	Y	Spigots	Y		Hiking	Y
Paved	Y	Sewer			Biking	Y
Pull Thru	Y	None			Swimming	Y
ADA	Y	At Site			Watch Wildlife	Y
Max RV Size	45	Dump Station	Y		Pets	Y
Electric		Amenities			Security	
None		Restrooms	Y		Host(s)	Y
20 Amp	Y	Showers	Y		Rangers(s)	Y
30 Amp	Y	Reserve Sites	Y		Gate	
50 Amp	Y	Store			Patrolled	Y
		Grill/Table	Y			

[23] Padre Island National Seashore
I-37, Exit 1c
Southeast of Corpus Christi
N27 28.615 W97 16.918
NPS Rate: $8 ($10 vehicle entry fee)
America/Beautiful Rate: $4 ($5 vehicle entry fee?)
(361) 949-8069
http://www.nps.gov/pais/planyourvisit/index.htm

Directions

31 miles. From Exit 1c go 4.7 miles south on Hwy 286 (Crosstown Expy) to Hwy 358. Turn southeast, go 26 miles, follow Hwy 358 (after crossing the JFK Causeway onto Padre Island, Hwy 358 changes to Park Rd 22) to the Visitors Center.

Points of Interest

Bring your beachcombing bucket. Bicycling is a popular activity. With more bird species that any other city in the U.S., Corpus Christi is the Birdiest City in America.

RV Sites		Water			Laundry	
Number	42	None			Wi-Fi	
Shaded	ramada	At Site			Fishing	Y
By Water	Y	Spigots	Y		Hiking	Y
Paved	Y	Sewer			Biking	Y
Pull Thru		None			Swimming	
ADA		At Site			Watch Wildlife	Y
Max RV Size	40+	Dump Station	Y		Pets	Y
Electric		Amenities			Security	
None	Y	Restrooms	Y		Host(s)	Y
20 Amp		Showers	Y		Rangers(s)	Y
30 Amp		Reserve Sites			Gate	
50 Amp		Store			Patrolled	Y
		Grill/Table	Y			

[24] Lake Corpus Christi State Park
I-37, Exit 34
Northwest of Corpus Christi
N28 03.323 W97 52.081
State Rate: $10-$20
(361) 547-2635
http://www.tpwd.state.tx.us/state-parks/lake-corpus-christi

Directions

6 miles. From Exit 34 go southwest on Hwy 359 for 4.6 miles to Park Rd 25. Turn north for 1.2 miles to the campground.

Points of Interest

In Corpus Christi, tour the USS Lexington, ask about the "The Blue Ghost", then consider a purchase at the Ship's store. Walk Heritage Park and Cultural Center with it's historic Victorian homes. Try the Harbor Playhouse community theatre.

RV Sites		Water			Laundry	
Number	91	None			Wi-Fi	
Shaded	Y	At Site	Y		Fishing	Y
By Water	Y	Spigots	Y		Hiking	Y
Paved	Y	Sewer			Biking	Y
Pull Thru	Y	None			Swimming	Y
ADA	Y	At Site	Y		Watch Wildlife	Y
Max RV Size	40+	Dump Station	Y		Pets	Y
Electric		Amenities			Security	
None		Restrooms	Y		Host(s)	Y
20 Amp	Y	Showers	Y		Rangers(s)	Y
30 Amp	Y	Reserve Sites	Y		Gate	
50 Amp	Y	Store			Patrolled	Y
		Grill/Table	Y			

[25] Galveston Island State Park
I-45, Exit 1
Southwest of Galveston
N29 11.863 W94 57.440
State Rate: $20-$25
(409) 737-1222
http://www.tpwd.state.tx.us/state-parks/
galveston-island

Directions

11 miles. From Exit 1 turn south for 1.5 miles on
61st St to Seawall Blvd (FM 3005). Turn right,
go 9.5 miles (the Rd name changes to Termini-
San Luis Pass) to the park at Park Rd 66.

Points of Interest

Attractions in Galveston include; Railroad
Museum; Strand Historic District, the Tall Ship
Elissa (1877 sailing vessel); Seaport Museum;
the Galveston County Museum and Space
Center Houston.

RV Sites		Water		Laundry	
Number	66	None		Wi-Fi	Y
Shaded	Y	At Site	Y	Fishing	Y
By Water	Y	Spigots	Y	Hiking	Y
Paved		Sewer		Biking	Y
Pull Thru		None		Swimming	Y
ADA	Y	At Site		Watch Wildlife	Y
Max RV Size	40+	Dump Station	Y	Pets	Y
Electric		Amenities		Security	
None		Restrooms	Y	Host(s)	Y
20 Amp	Y	Showers	Y	Rangers(s)	Y
30 Amp	Y	Reserve Sites	Y	Gate	Y
50 Amp	Y	Store		Patrolled	Y
		Grill/Table	Y		

[26] Cagle Recreation Area
I-45, Exit 102
South of Huntsville
N30 31.611 W95 35.238
Sam Houston NF Rate: $16-$27
America/Beautiful Rate: $8-$19
(936) 344-6205
http://www.recreation.gov/

Directions

6 miles. From Exit 102 go west for 5.5 miles
on FM 1375 to Rd 238 Kagle Rd. Turn south
(left) 0.2 mile to the Recreation Area.

Points of Interest

Visit Huntsville, Sam Houston's home town.
Huntsville offers places to explore - historic
sites, state institutions, antiques, and hometown hospitality. The town feel and historic
flair of Huntsville helps you appreciate the
'Texas Charm' expression.

RV Sites		Water		Laundry	
Number	47	None		Wi-Fi	
Shaded	Y	At Site	Y	Fishing	Y
By Water	Y	Spigots	Y	Hiking	Y
Paved	Y	Sewer		Biking	Y
Pull Thru		None		Swimming	
ADA	Y	At Site	Y	Watch Wildlife	Y
Max RV Size	45	Dump Station	Y	Pets	Y
Electric		Amenities		Security	
None		Restrooms	Y	Host(s)	Y
20 Amp	Y	Showers	Y	Rangers(s)	Y
30 Amp	Y	Reserve Sites	Y	Gate	
50 Amp	Y	Store		Patrolled	
		Grill/Table	Y		

[27] Fairfield Lake State Park
I-45, Exits 197 or 198
Northeast of Fairfield
N31 45.920 W96 04.328
State Rate: $12-$18
(903) 389-4514
http://www.tpwd.state.tx.us/state-parks/fairfield-lake

Directions

8 miles. From either Exit 197 or 198 go 1.5
miles in to Fairfield, onto Commerce St, then
proceed to Main St. (Ranch Rd 488) Turn left,
go 1.8 miles to Ranch Rd 2570/FM1124. Bare
right, go 1.3 miles to Ranch Rd 3285, Bare
right again, go 3.3 miles to Park Rd 64. Turn
left in to the Park.

Points of Interest

Visit the 'Texas State Railroad' which offers
train excursions. Tour Old Fort Parker. See Confederate Reunion Grounds State Historic Site.

RV Sites		Water		Laundry	
Number	135	None		Wi-Fi	
Shaded	Y	At Site	Y	Fishing	Y
By Water	Y	Spigots	Y	Hiking	Y
Paved		Sewer		Biking	Y
Pull Thru	Y	None		Swimming	Y
ADA	Y	At Site		Watch Wildlife	Y
Max RV Size	40+	Dump Station	Y	Pets	Y
Electric		Amenities		Security	
None		Restrooms	Y	Host(s)	Y
20 Amp	Y	Showers	Y	Rangers(s)	Y
30 Amp	Y	Reserve Sites	some	Gate	
50 Amp		Store		Patrolled	Y
		Grill/Table	Y		

[28] Waxahachie Creek Park
I-45, Exit 247
South of Ennis
N32 17.592 W96 41.476
COE Rate: $16-$18
America/Beautiful Rate: $8-$9
(972) 875-5711
http://www.recreation.gov/

Directions

9 miles. From Exit 247 go 4.3 miles on Hwy 287 to the Bardwell Lake exit (Hwy 34). Turn left onto Hwy 34 and travel 2.8 miles southwest to Bozek Rd. Turn right and travel 1.6 miles to the Waxahachie Creek Park entrance.

Points of Interest

In Ennis you will find Railroad Memorabilia, Crystal Exhibits, Rail Line China Exhibit, the Czech Heritage Exhibit, the National Polka Festival, and Bluebonnet flowers.

RV Sites		Water		Laundry	
Number	71	None		Wi-Fi	
Shaded	Y	At Site	Y	Fishing	Y
By Water	Y	Spigots	Y	Hiking	Y
Paved	Y	**Sewer**		Biking	Y
Pull Thru	Y	None		Swimming	
ADA	Y	At Site		Watch Wildlife	Y
Max RV Size	45	Dump Station	Y	Pets	Y
Electric		**Amenities**		**Security**	
None		Restrooms	Y	Host(s)	Y
20 Amp	Y	Showers	Y	Rangers(s)	Y
30 Amp	Y	Reserve Sites	Y	Gate	Y
50 Amp		Store		Patrolled	Y
		Grill/Table	Y		

[29] Isla Blanca Park
Hwy 77, at Hwy 100
Northeast of Brownsville
N26 04.509 W97 09.780
CP Rate: $18
(956) 761-5494
http://www.co.cameron.tx.us/parks/isla_blanca.htm

Directions

28 miles. From Hwy 100 off Hwy 77 go 27 miles east to South Padre Island. Turn south on Padre Blvd (State Park Rd 100) for 1 mile to the Park.

Points of Interest

Enjoy lots of white sand beach, and your dog is allowed. Local wildlife destinations and sites feature sea turtles, dolphins and birds; as well as nature trails, diving and various water sport activities. Tour the Point Isabel Lighthouse, built in 1852.

RV Sites		Water		Laundry	
Number	535	None		Wi-Fi	Y
Shaded		At Site	Y	Fishing	Y
By Water	Y	Spigots	Y	Hiking	Y
Paved		**Sewer**		Biking	Y
Pull Thru	Y	None		Swimming	Y
ADA		At Site	Y	Watch Wildlife	Y
Max RV Size	45	Dump Station		Pets	Y
Electric		**Amenities**		**Security**	
None		Restrooms	Y	Host(s)	Y
20 Amp	Y	Showers	Y	Rangers(s)	
30 Amp	Y	Reserve Sites	Y	Gate	
50 Amp	Y	Store		Patrolled	Y
		Grill/Table	Y		

[30] Goose Island State Park
Hwy 77, at Sinton
South of Victoria
N28 08.043 W96 59.061
State Rate: $18-$22
(361) 729-2858
http://www.tpwd.state.tx.us/state-parks/goose-island

Directions

47 miles. At Sinton take Hwy 181 southeast for 18 miles to Hwy 35N. Turn north, go 27 miles to Lamar and Hwy P13. Go east for 1.4 miles to Palmetto St. Turn right, go 0.3 mile to the Park.

Points of Interest

Be sure to stop at "The Big Tree." Take a day trip to Aransas National Wildlife Refuge to see and learn about the endangered whooping crane. The Park also does morning shore bird walks.

RV Sites		Water		Laundry	
Number	101	None		Wi-Fi	Y
Shaded	Y	At Site	Y	Fishing	Y
By Water	Y	Spigots	Y	Hiking	Y
Paved		**Sewer**		Biking	Y
Pull Thru	Y	None		Swimming	
ADA	Y	At Site	Y	Watch Wildlife	Y
Max RV Size	40+	Dump Station	Y	Pets	Y
Electric		**Amenities**		**Security**	
None		Restrooms	Y	Host(s)	Y
20 Amp	Y	Showers	Y	Rangers(s)	Y
30 Amp	Y	Reserve Sites	Y	Gate	
50 Amp	some	Store	Y	Patrolled	Y
		Grill/Table	Y		

About Utah's Public Campgrounds

Utah has more than nine million acres in five National Forests and a number of Bureau of Land Management properties; where you'll find many high-mountain lakes, meadows, and woodlands. Some of the many campgrounds across those locations are found in this chapter. For camping reservations in any National Forest, call (877) 444-6777, or visit -

www.recreation.gov/

For BLM facilities go to -

www.blm.gov/wo/st/en.html

Utah State Parks and Recreation manages 43 state parks, with 2,000 camp-sites. Their website with all detailed information, is -

http://stateparks.utah.gov/

Statewide, park restrooms and parking areas are accessible to those with physical challenges and limitations. Many of the parks have accessible ramps, camping, and showers.

Pets are allowed at most Utah State Parks, however, there are a few specific park situations requiring an exception. Check with the park. Pets are not allowed in buildings, on beaches, or in the lakes or reservoirs. Pets must always be on a maximum six-foot leash and never left unattended.

RV camping fees range from $10-$28 per night per site, which includes one RV, one vehicle and up to 8 people. Individual campsite reservations are accepted up to 4 months in advance. Reservations can be made in as little as two days in advance. An $8 reservation fee is charged for a reservation. Reservations can be made through the Reservations webpage or by calling (800) 322-3770, 8 a.m. to 5 p.m. Monday-Friday. To make online reservations go to -

http://stateparks.utah.gov/reservations

[1] Snow Canyon State Park	[7] Castle Rock
[2] Cedar Canyon	[8] Green River State Park
[3] Little Cottonwood	[9] Rockport State Park
[4] Yuba State Park (Oasis Camp)	[10] Sand Island Campground
[5] Utah Lake State Park	[11] Devils Canyon Campground
[6] Anderson Cove	[12] Ken's Lake Campground

Utah

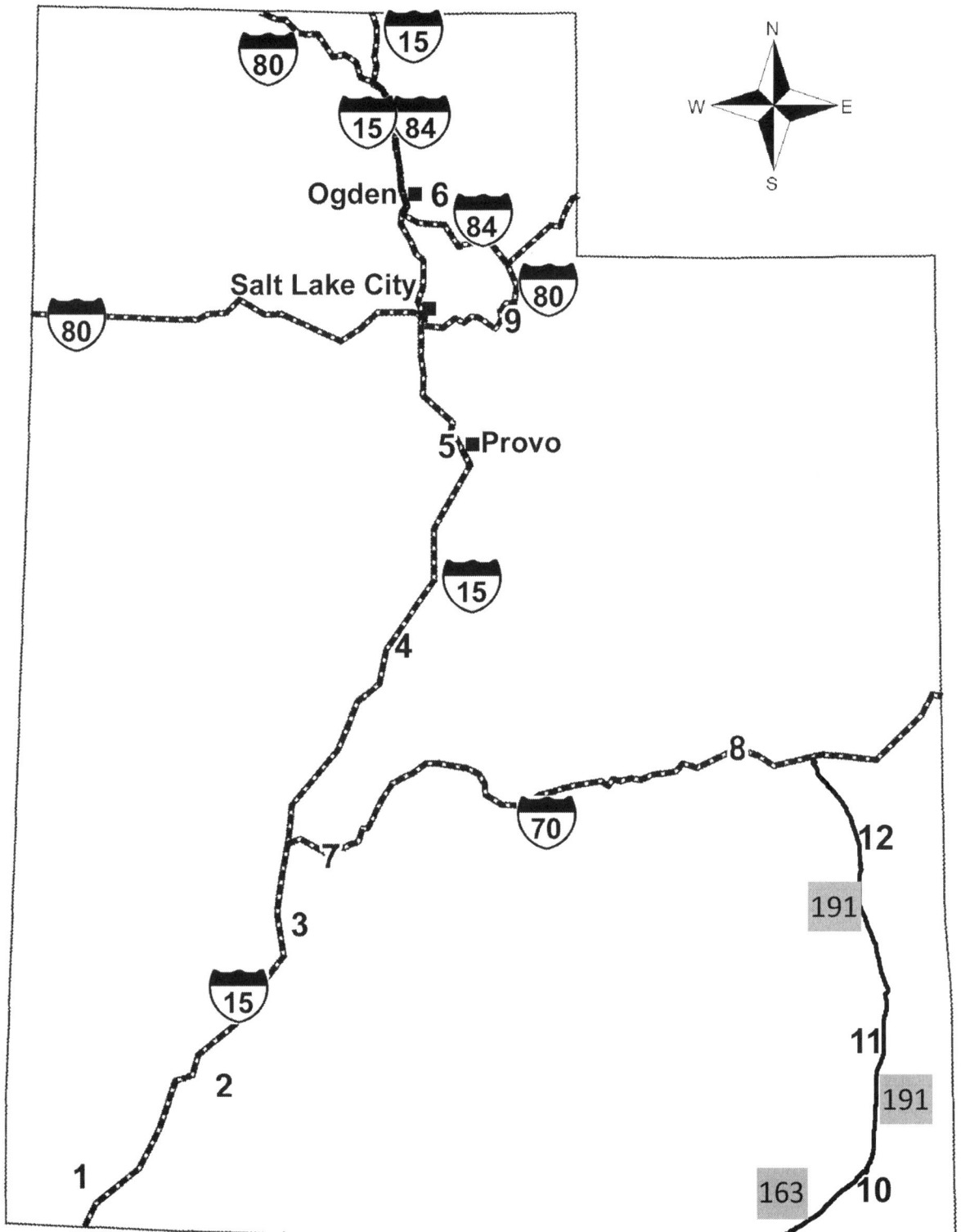

[1] Snow Canyon State Park
I-15, Exit 6
North of St. George
N37 12.169 W113 38.493
State Rate: $16-$20
(435) 628-2255
http://stateparks.utah.gov/park/snow-canyon-state-park

Directions

10 miles. From Exit 6 go north for 3.6 miles on Hwy 18 (Bluff St). Turn west on Snow Canyon Parkway for 4 miles to Hwy 8 (Snow Canyon Dr). Take a right, go 2.6 miles to the south entrance of the park.

Points of Interest

St. George known locally as "Utah's Dixie" has golf all year. Try a Historic Downtown Tour, concert, play, or check out the dinosaur tracks.

RV Sites		Water			Laundry	
Number	24	None			Wi-Fi	
Shaded	ramada	At Site	Y		Fishing	
By Water		Spigots	Y		Hiking	Y
Paved	Y	Sewer			Biking	Y
Pull Thru	Y	None			Swimming	
ADA	Y	At Site			Watch Wildlife	Y
Max RV Size	40+	Dump Station	Y		Pets	Y
Electric		Amenities			Security	
None		Restrooms	Y		Host(s)	Y
20 Amp	Y	Showers	Y		Rangers(s)	Y
30 Amp	Y	Reserve Sites	Y		Gate	
50 Amp		Store			Patrolled	Y
		Grill/Table	Y			

[2] Cedar Canyon
I-15, Exit 59
N37 35.476 W112 54.305
East of Cedar City
Dixie NF Rate: $15
America/Beautiful Rate: $8
(435) 865-3200
http://www.recreation.gov

Directions

14 miles. From Exit 59 go east for 0.9 miles on Hwy 56 (W 200 N St) to Hwy 130 (N Main St). Turn south, go 0.3 miles to Hwy 14 (E Center St). Go east 12.2 miles. Turn in to the left, just below the S curve.

Points of Interest

The Camp is close to Cedar City, Cedar Breaks National Monument, Ashdown Gorge Wilderness and the Virgin River Rim Trail. Other attractions include Bryce Canyon NP and Zion NP.

RV Sites		Water			Laundry	
Number	19	None			Wi-Fi	
Shaded	Y	At Site			Fishing	
By Water	Y	Spigots	Y		Hiking	Y
Paved	Y	Sewer			Biking	Y
Pull Thru		None			Swimming	
ADA	Y	At Site			Watch Wildlife	Y
Max RV Size	40	Dump Station			Pets	Y
Electric		Amenities			Security	
None	Y	Restrooms	Y		Host(s)	Y
20 Amp		Showers			Rangers(s)	Y
30 Amp		Reserve Sites	Y		Gate	
50 Amp		Store			Patrolled	Y
		Grill/Table	Y			

[3] Little Cottonwood
I-15, Exits 109 or 112
East of Beaver
N38 15.304 W112 32.426
Dixie NF Rate: $14
America/Beautiful Rate: $7
(435) 438-2436
http://www.recreation.gov

Directions

7.5 miles. From either Exit 109 or 112 turn east, go 1.7 miles on Hwy 160 in to Beaver. Turn east on Hwy 153 for 6.7 miles to the campground.

Points of Interest

Beaver County claims to have the most beautiful and varied scenery in the West. Notable sites to visit are the ghost towns of Frisco and Newhouse or the historic railroading and mining town of Milford. Walk around Beaver, the birthplace of Butch Cassidy.

RV Sites		Water			Laundry	
Number	14	None			Wi-Fi	
Shaded	Y	At Site			Fishing	Y
By Water	Y	Spigots	Y		Hiking	Y
Paved	Y	Sewer			Biking	
Pull Thru	few	None			Swimming	
ADA	Y	At Site			Watch Wildlife	Y
Max RV Size	40+	Dump Station			Pets	Y
Electric		Amenities			Security	
None	Y	Restrooms	Y		Host(s)	Y
20 Amp		Showers			Rangers(s)	Y
30 Amp		Reserve Sites	Y		Gate	
50 Amp		Store			Patrolled	Y
		Grill/Table	Y			

[4] Yuba State Park (Oasis Camp)
I-15, Exit 202
South of Nephi
N39 22.618 W112 01.694
State Rate: $20-$25
(435) 758-2611
http://stateparks.utah.gov/park/yuba-state-park

Directions

4 miles. From Exit 202 go south for 4 miles on Hwy 78 to the campground on your left.

Points of Interest

The warm waters and sandy beaches make this campground a great place to relax. When you walk along the reservoir you may find evidence of the ancient Native Americans that once lived in the area. Rock art, pieces of pottery, and stone tools are among items that have been found.

RV Sites		Water		Laundry	
Number	28	None		Wi-Fi	
Shaded	Y	At Site	Y	Fishing	Y
By Water	Y	Spigots	Y	Hiking	Y
Paved	Y	**Sewer**		Biking	Y
Pull Thru	Y	None		Swimming	Y
ADA	Y	At Site		Watch Wildlife	Y
Max RV Size	45	Dump Station	Y	Pets	Y
Electric		**Amenities**		**Security**	
None		Restrooms	Y	Host(s)	Y
20 Amp	Y	Showers	Y	Rangers(s)	Y
30 Amp	Y	Reserve Sites	Y	Gate	Y
50 Amp	Y	Store	Y	Patrolled	Y
		Grill/Table	Y		

[5] Utah Lake State Park
I-15, Exit 265
West of Provo
N40 14.230 W111 44.020
State Rate: $25
(801) 375-0731
http://stateparks.utah.gov/park/utah-lake-state-park

Directions

2.5 miles. From Exit 265 go west on Hwy 114 (W Center St) for 2.5 miles to the Park.

Points of Interest

Take a drive to Robert Redford's rustic Sundance Resort. Explore Timpanogos Cave National Monument, with its colorful deposits, beautiful formations, and clear underground pools. Take a time out for some shopping at Cabela's.

RV Sites		Water		Laundry	
Number	47	None		Wi-Fi	
Shaded	Y	At Site	Y	Fishing	Y
By Water	Y	Spigots	Y	Hiking	Y
Paved	Y	**Sewer**		Biking	Y
Pull Thru	Y	None		Swimming	Y
ADA	Y	At Site		Watch Wildlife	Y
Max RV Size	45	Dump Station	Y	Pets	Y
Electric		**Amenities**		**Security**	
None		Restrooms	Y	Host(s)	Y
20 Amp	Y	Showers	Y	Rangers(s)	Y
30 Amp	Y	Reserve Sites	Y	Gate	
50 Amp		Store		Patrolled	Y
		Grill/Table	Y		

[6] Anderson Cove
I-15/84 , Exit 344
East of Ogden
N41 14.978 W111 47.192
Cache NF Rate: $22-$44
America/Beautiful Rate: $11-$22
(801) 745-3215
http://www.recreation.gov

Directions

13 miles. From Exit 344 go 13 miles east on Hwy 39 (Ogden Canyon) to the campground on the left side of highway.

Points of Interest

Visit Fort Buenaventura, the first permanent settlement by people of European descent in the Great Basin on Utah. Tour Hill Aerospace Museum on Hill Air Force Base. The Museum exhibits more than 90 military aircraft, missiles, and aerospace vehicles.

RV Sites		Water		Laundry	
Number	41	None		Wi-Fi	
Shaded	Y	At Site		Fishing	Y
By Water	Y	Spigots	Y	Hiking	Y
Paved	Y	**Sewer**		Biking	Y
Pull Thru		None		Swimming	Y
ADA	Y	At Site		Watch Wildlife	Y
Max RV Size	40+	Dump Station	Y	Pets	Y
Electric		**Amenities**		**Security**	
None	Y	Restrooms	Y	Host(s)	Y
20 Amp		Showers		Rangers(s)	Y
30 Amp		Reserve Sites	Y	Gate	Y
50 Amp		Store	Y	Patrolled	Y
		Grill/Table	Y		

[7] Castle Rock
I-70, Exit 17
Southwest of Richfield
N38 33.489 W112 21.304
Fishlake NF Rate: $13
America/Beautiful Rate: $7
(435) 527-4631
http://www.fs.usda.gov/recarea/fish-lake/recreation/camping-cabins/recarea/?recid=12134&actid=29

Directions

1.3 miles. From Exit 17 go east & on Forest Rt. 478 (gravel) for 1.3 miles to the campground.

Points of Interest

Fremont Indian State Park has a museum, collection of rock art, and access to archaeological sites. Bullion Canyon (Canyon of Gold Driving Tour) will give RVers a chance to glimpse the life and times of the canyon's mines & miners.

RV Sites		Water		Laundry	
Number	30	None		Wi-Fi	
Shaded	Y	At Site		Fishing	
By Water	Y	Spigots	Y	Hiking	Y
Paved		**Sewer**		Biking	Y
Pull Thru	Y	None	Y	Swimming	
ADA	Y	At Site		Watch Wildlife	Y
Max RV Size	45	Dump Station		Pets	Y
Electric		**Amenities**		**Security**	
None	Y	Restrooms	Y	Host(s)	
20 Amp		Showers		Rangers(s)	Y
30 Amp		Reserve Sites	Y	Gate	
50 Amp		Store		Patrolled	Y
		Grill/Table	Y		

[8] Green River State Park
I-70, Exits 160 or 164
At Green River
N38 59.410 W110 09.289
State Rate: $18-$25
(435) 564-3633
http://stateparks.utah.gov/park/green-river-state-park

Directions

2-3 miles. **Eastbound**, from Exit 160 take I-70 Bus 1.7 miles into Green River to Green River Blvd. **Westbound**, from Exit 164 take I-70 Bus 2.6 miles in to Green River to Green River Blvd. All travelers turn south for 0.4 miles to the Park.

Points of Interest

Green River is situated near great scenery, world-class rafting, dinosaur fossils, and Native American rock art panels.

RV Sites		Water		Laundry	
Number	34	None		Wi-Fi	
Shaded	Y	At Site	Y	Fishing	Y
By Water	Y	Spigots	Y	Hiking	Y
Paved	Y	**Sewer**		Biking	Y
Pull Thru	Y	None		Swimming	Y
ADA	Y	At Site		Watch Wildlife	Y
Max RV Size	40+	Dump Station	Y	Pets	Y
Electric		**Amenities**		**Security**	
None		Restrooms	Y	Host(s)	Y
20 Amp	Y	Showers	Y	Rangers(s)	Y
30 Amp	Y	Reserve Sites	Y	Gate	
50 Amp		Store		Patrolled	Y
		Grill/Table	Y		

[9] Rockport State Park (5 camps)
I-80, Exit 155
South of Wanship
N40 45.170 W111 22.558
State Rate: $12-$24
(435) 336-2241
http://stateparks.utah.gov/park/rockport-state-park

Directions

5 miles. From Exit 155 go south for 5 miles on Hwy 32 to the Park.

Points of Interest

In the Park enjoy year-round fishing or warm weather water sports. The Park was named for the rock fort built to protect settlers from Indian uprisings. Take the 'Echo Canyon' driving tour, near Coalville, with over 2 dozen notable sites to stop and see.

RV Sites		Water		Laundry	
Number	75	None		Wi-Fi	
Shaded	Y	At Site		Fishing	Y
By Water	Y	Spigots	Y	Hiking	Y
Paved	Y	**Sewer**		Biking	Y
Pull Thru	Y	None		Swimming	Y
ADA	Y	At Site		Watch Wildlife	Y
Max RV Size	45	Dump Station	Y	Pets	Y
Electric		**Amenities**		**Security**	
None		Restrooms	Y	Host(s)	Y
20 Amp	Y	Showers	Y	Rangers(s)	Y
30 Amp	Y	Reserve Sites	Y	Gate	Y
50 Amp		Store		Patrolled	Y
		Grill/Table	Y		

[10] Sand Island Campground
Hwy 163, at Hwy 191
West of Bluff
N37 15.783 W109 36.790
BLM Rate: $10
America/Beautiful Rate: $5
(435) 587-1504
http://www.blm.gov/ut/st/en/fo/monticello/
recreation/activities/camping/sand_island_
camp_ground.html

RV Sites		Water		Laundry	
Number	24	None		Wi-Fi	
Shaded		At Site		Fishing	
By Water	Y	Spigots	Y	Hiking	Y
Paved		**Sewer**		Biking	Y
Pull Thru	Y	None	Y	Swimming	
ADA		At Site		Watch Wildlife	Y
Max RV Size	45	Dump Station		Pets	Y
Electric		**Amenities**		**Security**	
None	Y	Restrooms	Y	Host(s)	
20 Amp		Showers		Rangers(s)	Y
30 Amp		Reserve Sites		Gate	
50 Amp		Store		Patrolled	Y
		Grill/Table	Y		

Directions

1 mile. At the intersection of Hwys 163/191 go 0.5 mile south on Hwy 191 to Sand Island Rd. Turn left, go 0.5 mile to the campground.

Points of Interest

Explore the area, where Puebloan Native Americans left many cliff dwellings, ruins, pictographs and petroglyphs. Visit the BLM Monticello Field Office for information.

[11] Devils Canyon Campground
Hwy 191
Between Blanding and Monticello
N37 43.752 W109 24.727
Manti-La Sal NF: $10
America/Beautiful Rate: $5
(435) 587-2041
http://www.recreation.gov/

RV Sites		Water		Laundry	
Number	21	None		Wi-Fi	
Shaded	some	At Site		Fishing	
By Water		Spigots	Y	Hiking	Y
Paved		**Sewer**		Biking	Y
Pull Thru	Y	None	Y	Swimming	
ADA		At Site		Watch Wildlife	Y
Max RV Size	45	Dump Station		Pets	Y
Electric		**Amenities**		**Security**	
None	Y	Restrooms	Y	Host(s)	Y
20 Amp		Showers		Rangers(s)	Y
30 Amp		Reserve Sites	Y	Gate	
50 Amp		Store		Patrolled	
		Grill/Table	Y		

Directions

On Hwy 191, 13 miles south of Monticello and 7.7 miles north of Blanding. Look for the campground signs. The camp road is on the west side of the Rd, near Alkali Point Rd.

Points of Interest

A small "moki" ruin (a cliff-face alcove granary) is close by on the "The Forest and Man" interpretive trail out of the campground. Take day trips to one of the many National Parks or Monuments in the area.

[12] Ken's Lake Campground
Hwy 191
South of Moab
N38 27.469 W109 26.528
BLM Rate: $15
America/Beautiful Rate: $8
(435) 259-2100
http://www.blm.gov/ut/st/en/fo/moab/recreation/campgrounds/ken_s_lake.html

RV Sites		Water		Laundry	
Number	31	None	Y	Wi-Fi	
Shaded		At Site		Fishing	Y
By Water	Y	Spigots		Hiking	Y
Paved		**Sewer**		Biking	Y
Pull Thru	Y	None	Y	Swimming	
ADA		At Site		Watch Wildlife	
Max RV Size	45	Dump Station		Pets	Y
Electric		**Amenities**		**Security**	
None	Y	Restrooms	Y	Host(s)	
20 Amp		Showers		Rangers(s)	Y
30 Amp		Reserve Sites		Gate	
50 Amp		Store		Patrolled	Y
		Grill/Table	Y		

Directions

11.6 miles. Go south from Moab for 10 miles to Cty Rd 175 (Steelbender Safari Rd). Turn east for 1.6 miles to the campground.

Point of Interest

Enjoy great views of the Moab Valley. This is a dry camping facility but the location is worth any inconveniences. Day trips are easily done to Arches NP, Dead Horse Canyon SP, or Canyonlands NP. Moab has much to offer for shoppers, or a meal.

About Vermont's Public Campgrounds

The 52 Vermont State Parks are managed by the Department of Forests, Parks, and Recreation. You can start you exploration of the state parks at -

http://www.vtstateparks.com/

Vermont State Parks are said to be more natural and distinctive in character. The State says sites tend to be more private, though not specifically designed for pull-throughs, are charming and accessible. Sites will accommodate RV's from smaller trailers to rigs as large as 40 feet.

Vermont is a dry camping state. At the time this book was printed there were no water, sewer or electric hookups in Vermont State Parks, though water spigots and dump stations can be found. Campgrounds within the parks are usually laid out in loops with water spigots located every few campsites, with centrally located restrooms, most with hot and cold running water and coin operated showers; site surfaces are usually gravel or grass. Parks allow some limited generator use. In Vermont, 'tent' and 'RV' are used to describe the same kind of site. Each site has a fire ring or fireplace with grill for cooking and a picnic table. Most parks sell wood and ice and many have nature programs, performances and other events. Sites are said to be roomy and level. Some are wooded and some open. Most campgrounds permit pets (10 foot leash) but some have specific pet loops.

Campsite fees typically run $18-$22 and you can stay up to 21 consecutive days. There is a pet fee of $1 per night per pet. Reservations can be made up to 11 months in advance, and the inventory for the entire month opens the first business day of the month. Reservations for dates 15 days or more in advance may be made online or through the Reservation Call Center at (888) 409-7579. The online reservation website site is -

https://securevtstateparks.com/cgi-bin/parkCGI.py

During the parks operating season, reservations for dates 14 days or less in advance are made by calling the park directly. There is a $6 reservation fee. Most parks have first come, first serve sites.

[1] Quechee State Park	**[6] Ricker Pond State Park**
[2] Little River State Park	**[7] Woodford State Park**
[3] Grand Isle State Park	**[8] Emerald Lake State Park**
[4] Fort Dummer State Park	**[9] Branbury State Park**
[5] Mt. Ascutney State Park	

Vermont

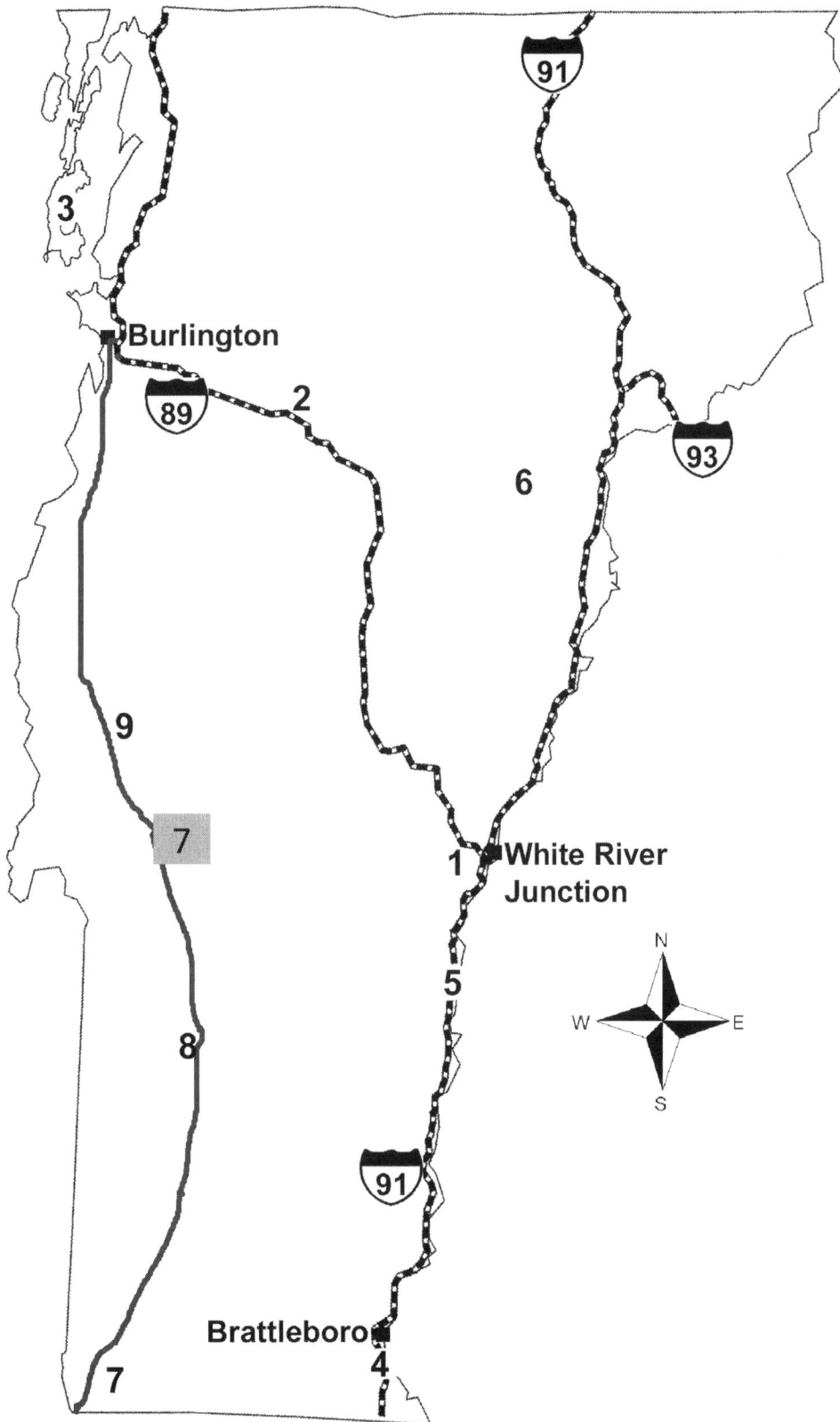

[1] Quechee State Park
I-89, Exit 1
West of White River Junction
N43 38.229 W72 24.070
State Rate: $18-$22
(802) 295-2990
http://www.vtstateparks.com/htm/quechee.htm

Directions

2.5 miles. From Exit 1 go 2.2 miles southwest on Hwy 4 (Woodstock Rd) to the Park.

Points of Interest

The Parks focal point is Vermont's deepest gorge. Visit Woodstock, a quaint village, called "the prettiest small town in America." Walk the village green, with a covered bridge in the middle of town, and stately homes. Browse unique shops, galleries, artisan studios, and country stores. Visit the Calvin Coolidge State Historic Site and Justin Morrill State Historic Site.

RV Sites		Water		Laundry	
Number	45	None		Wi-Fi	Y
Shaded	Y	At Site		Fishing	
By Water	Y	Spigots	Y	Hiking	Y
Paved		**Sewer**		Biking	Y
Pull Thru		None		Swimming	near
ADA	Y	At Site		Watch Wildlife	
Max RV Size	40	Dump Station	Y	Pets	Y
Electric		**Amenities**		**Security**	
None	Y	Restrooms	Y	Host(s)	Y
20 Amp		Showers	Y	Rangers(s)	Y
30 Amp		Reserve Sites	Y	Gate	
50 Amp		Store		Patrolled	Y
		Grill/Table	Y		

[2] Little River State Park
I-89, Exit 10
North of Waterbury
N44 23.382 W72 46.051
State Rate: $18-$22
(802) 244-7103
http://www.vtstateparks.com/htm/littleriver.htm

Directions

5 miles. From Exit 10 go southwest on Hwy 100 for 0.2 miles to Hwy 2 (Main St). Turn right, go 1.3 miles to Little River Rd. Turn north for 3.4 miles to the Park.

Points of Interest

Wander the Waterbury Flea Market. Don't miss Ben and Jerry's Ice Cream Factory and the Cold Hollow Cider Mill. In Barre visit granite quarries & museums. Tour the Vermont State House in Montpelier. Drive up to Moss Glen Falls and to the Trapp Family Lodge in Stowe.

RV Sites		Water		Laundry	
Number	79	None		Wi-Fi	
Shaded	Y	At Site		Fishing	Y
By Water	Y	Spigots	Y	Hiking	Y
Paved		**Sewer**		Biking	Y
Pull Thru		None		Swimming	Y
ADA	Y	At Site		Watch Wildlife	
Max RV Size	40	Dump Station	Y	Pets	Y
Electric		**Amenities**		**Security**	
None	Y	Restrooms	Y	Host(s)	Y
20 Amp		Showers	Y	Rangers(s)	Y
30 Amp		Reserve Sites	Y	Gate	
50 Amp		Store		Patrolled	
		Grill/Table	Y		

[3] Grand Isle State Park
I-89, Exit 17
On South Hero Island
N44 41.257 W73 17.689
State Rate: $18-$22
(802) 372-4300
http://www.vtstateparks.com/htm/grandisle.htm

Directions

13 miles. From Exit 17 go west for 12 miles, follow Hwy 2 over Lake Champlain on to South Hero Island. The park entrance road is just past Pearl St. Turn right on State Park Rd, go 1 mile to the Park.

Points of Interest

The Park is the most visited camp in the state system. With 4,150 feet of shoreline, it is popular with many destination RVers, who spend their entire vacation here. Some local sights include Chazy Reef, Hyde Log Cabin, St. Anne's Shrine, & Hacketts' Orchard.

RV Sites		Water		Laundry	
Number	115	None		Wi-Fi	Y
Shaded	Y	At Site		Fishing	Y
By Water	Y	Spigots	Y	Hiking	Y
Paved		**Sewer**		Biking	Y
Pull Thru	Y	None		Swimming	Y
ADA	Y	At Site		Watch Wildlife	
Max RV Size	40	Dump Station	Y	Pets	Y
Electric		**Amenities**		**Security**	
None	Y	Restrooms	Y	Host(s)	Y
20 Amp		Showers	Y	Rangers(s)	Y
30 Amp		Reserve Sites	Y	Gate	Y
50 Amp		Store	Y	Patrolled	Y
		Grill/Table	Y		

[4] Fort Dummer State Park
I-91, Exit 1
South of Brattleboro
N42 49.459 W72 34.000
State Rate: $18-$20
(802) 254-2610
http://www.vtstateparks.com/htm/fortdummer.htm

Directions

2 miles. From Exit 1 go 0.2 miles north on Hwy 5 (Canal St). Turn right on Fairground Rd, go 0.6 miles to S Main Street. Turn right on S Main, which becomes Old Guilford Rd, go 1.1 miles to the Park.

Points of Interest

In Brattleboro, walk the historic downtown, go shopping and enjoy a meal. Visit the Brattleboro Museum and Art Center, and Estey Organ Museum. Take a scenic drive to Wilmington, stock-up at roadside farmstands, explore downtown Wilmington.

RV Sites		Water		Laundry	
Number	50	None		Wi-Fi	
Shaded	Y	At Site		Fishing	
By Water	Y	Spigots	Y	Hiking	Y
Paved		Sewer		Biking	Y
Pull Thru		None		Swimming	
ADA	Y	At Site		Watch Wildlife	Y
Max RV Size	40	Dump Station	Y	Pets	Y
Electric		Amenities		Security	
None	Y	Restrooms	Y	Host(s)	Y
20 Amp		Showers	Y	Rangers(s)	Y
30 Amp		Reserve Sites	Y	Gate	
50 Amp		Store		Patrolled	Y
		Grill/Table	Y		

[5] Mt. Ascutney State Park
I-91, Exit 8
South of Windsor
N43 26.270 W72 24.344
State Rate: $18-$20
(802) 674-2060
http://www.vtstateparks.com/htm/ascutney.htm

Directions

3 miles. From Exit 8 go east on Hwy 131 for 0.4 miles to Hwy 5. Turn north (left) for 1.1 miles, then bear left on Hwy 44A for 1.1 miles to the Park.

Points of Interest

Drive the Park summit road to the top for excellent views. Hikers can try the 12 plus miles of trails to sites of former quarries and homesteads, relics of past logging operations and other remains of a bygone era. Each trail boasts spectacular viewpoints. **Also see [1]**.

RV Sites		Water		Laundry	
Number	39	None		Wi-Fi	
Shaded	Y	At Site		Fishing	
By Water		Spigots	Y	Hiking	Y
Paved		Sewer		Biking	Y
Pull Thru		None		Swimming	
ADA	Y	At Site		Watch Wildlife	Y
Max RV Size	30	Dump Station	Y	Pets	Y
Electric		Amenities		Security	
None	Y	Restrooms	Y	Host(s)	Y
20 Amp		Showers	Y	Rangers(s)	Y
30 Amp		Reserve Sites	Y	Gate	
50 Amp		Store		Patrolled	Y
		Grill/Table	Y		

[6] Ricker Pond State Park
I-91, Exit 17
South of Windsor
N44 14.733 W72 15.227
State Rate: $18-$22
(802) 584-3821
http://www.vtstateparks.com/htm/ricker.htm

Directions

11 miles. From Exit 17 go northwest on Hwy 302 for 8.5 miles to Hwy 232. Turn north for 2.5 miles to the Park on the right.

Points of Interest

In St. Johnsbury visit the Maple Grove Museum, the Fairbanks Museum and Planetarium or the St. Johnsbury Athenaeum and Art Gallery. In Barre visit granite quarries and museums and the Vermont Historical Society Library. Tour the Vermont State House in Montpelier.

RV Sites		Water		Laundry	
Number	27	None		Wi-Fi	
Shaded	Y	At Site		Fishing	Y
By Water	Y	Spigots	Y	Hiking	Y
Paved		Sewer		Biking	Y
Pull Thru		None		Swimming	Y
ADA	Y	At Site		Watch Wildlife	
Max RV Size	40	Dump Station	Y	Pets	Y
Electric		Amenities		Security	
None	Y	Restrooms	Y	Host(s)	Y
20 Amp		Showers	Y	Rangers(s)	Y
30 Amp		Reserve Sites	Y	Gate	
50 Amp		Store		Patrolled	Y
		Grill/Table	Y		

[7] Woodford State Park
Hwy 7, East on Hwy 9
East of Bennington
N42 53.525 W73 02.111
State Rate: $18-$22
(802) 447-7169
http://www.vtstateparks.com/htm/woodford.htm

Directions

10.7 miles. In Bennington, take Hwy 9 east from Hwy 7 for 10.7 miles to the Park road entrance on the right.

Points of Interest

The Park is on a plateau adjacent to Adams Reservoir. Visit the Bennington Museum, with its extensive collection of paintings and sculpture by Vermont artists. Just north take a day trip to the Norman Rockwell Museum in Arlington. The exhibit focuses on Rockwell's years in Arlington, during which he created many of his famous works.

RV Sites		Water			Laundry	
Number	81	None			Wi-Fi	
Shaded	Y	At Site			Fishing	Y
By Water	Y	Spigots		Y	Hiking	Y
Paved		Sewer			Biking	Y
Pull Thru		None			Swimming	Y
ADA	Y	At Site			Watch Wildlife	Y
Max RV Size	34	Dump Station		Y	Pets	Y
Electric		Amenities			Security	
None	Y	Restrooms		Y	Host(s)	Y
20 Amp		Showers		Y	Rangers(s)	Y
30 Amp		Reserve Sites		Y	Gate	
50 Amp		Store			Patrolled	Y
		Grill/Table		Y		

[8] Emerald Lake State Park
Hwy 7
Between East Dorset and North Dorset
N43 17.026 W73 00.136
State Rate: $18-$22
(802) 362-1655
http://www.vtstateparks.com/htm/emerald.htm

Directions

3.6 miles. From East Dorset take Hwy 7 north. Turn left on Sweeney Lane, then an immediate left onto Emerald Lake Lane.

Points of Interest

Take a day trip to Wilson Castle, a 19th century estate in Proctor. The house (1867) is a mix of architectural styles (Dutch neo-renaissance, Scottish baronial, Queen Anne, & Romanesque Revival). It is operated as a house museum. Visit Hildene, the Abraham Lincoln Family Home, with historic rail cars and a 1,000 pipe organ.

RV Sites		Water			Laundry	
Number	67	None			Wi-Fi	
Shaded	Y	At Site			Fishing	Y
By Water	Y	Spigots		Y	Hiking	Y
Paved		Sewer			Biking	Y
Pull Thru	Y	None			Swimming	Y
ADA	Y	At Site			Watch Wildlife	Y
Max RV Size	40	Dump Station		Y	Pets	Y
Electric		Amenities			Security	
None	Y	Restrooms		Y	Host(s)	Y
20 Amp		Showers		Y	Rangers(s)	Y
30 Amp		Reserve Sites		Y	Gate	
50 Amp		Store		Y	Patrolled	Y
		Grill/Table		Y		

[9] Branbury State Park
Hwy 7, South on Hwy 53
Southeast of Middlebury
N43 54.337 W73 03.962
State Rate: $18-$22
(802) 247-5925
http://www.vtstateparks.com/htm/branbury.htm

Directions

10.6 miles. From Hwy 7 & Hwy 30 in Middlebury go south for 7 miles to Hwy 53. Turn left on Hwy 53 and proceed 3.7 miles southeast to the Park.

Points of Interest

Take a day trip to The University of Vermont Morgan Horse Farm. The farm is home to significant Morgan history and a variety of educational programs. Who can pass up the New England Maple Museum, rated a top ten food museum! Stop by and learn more about Vermont's most famous commodity.

RV Sites		Water			Laundry	
Number	37	None			Wi-Fi	
Shaded	Y	At Site			Fishing	Y
By Water	Y	Spigots		Y	Hiking	Y
Paved		Sewer			Biking	Y
Pull Thru		None			Swimming	Y
ADA	Y	At Site			Watch Wildlife	
Max RV Size	40	Dump Station		Y	Pets	Y
Electric		Amenities			Security	
None	Y	Restrooms		Y	Host(s)	Y
20 Amp		Showers		Y	Rangers(s)	Y
30 Amp		Reserve Sites		Y	Gate	
50 Amp		Store			Patrolled	Y
		Grill/Table		Y		

About Virginia's Public Campgrounds

The 36 Virginia State Parks offer close to 2,000 campsites, hundreds of miles of trails and convenient access to Virginia's major waterways, plus a variety of events and activities at each park. You can start with the Park Systems main website at - **http://www.dcr.virginia.gov/state-parks/**

Twenty-four of the state parks have campgrounds. Site sizes and configurations vary. Some parks provide sites with electric and water hook-ups, which tend to be larger to accommodate RVs. Developed campsites have picnic tables, grills and access to bathhouses.

Virginia State Parks strive to make each park as barrier-free as possible for the convenience of those with limited mobility. Facilities continue to be upgraded for everyone's enjoyment. Each park page has information on the availability of facilities for people with disabilities, under 'Other Info.'

Pets are allowed at all overnight camping facilities. Bring proof of a current rabies vaccination. Your pet must be on a leash no longer than six feet and kept under supervision.

Park fees for standards sites range from $20-$26, electric/water are $30-$35, and full hook ups are $33-$40.

Reservations should be made as early as possible. Unreserved campsites are available on a first-come, first-served basis, but reservations are strongly recommended. Reservations can be made up to 11 months in advance. The system does not generally accept same-day reservations.

Reservations for camping can be made by calling the Reservation Center at (800) 933-7275. Reservations can also be made online, through ReserveAmerica. Each park's web page has a 'Reserve Cabins and Campsites' banner on the left side of the page. Clicking it takes you to the Web reservation page for that park.

Virginia also has a number of excellent County and City Parks that provide good camping options, particularly near the metropolitan areas.

[1] Lake A. Willis Robertson Park	[9] North Bend Campground
[2] First Landing State Park	[10] Pocahontas State Park
[3] Bull Run Regional Park	[11] Pohick Bay Regional Park
[4] Stony Fork Campground	[12] Staunton River State Park
[5] Sugar Hollow Park	[13] Twin Lakes State Park
[6] Hungry Mother State Park	[14] Belle Isle State Park
[7] Claytor Lake State Park	[15] Westmoreland State Park
[8] Natural Chimneys Park	

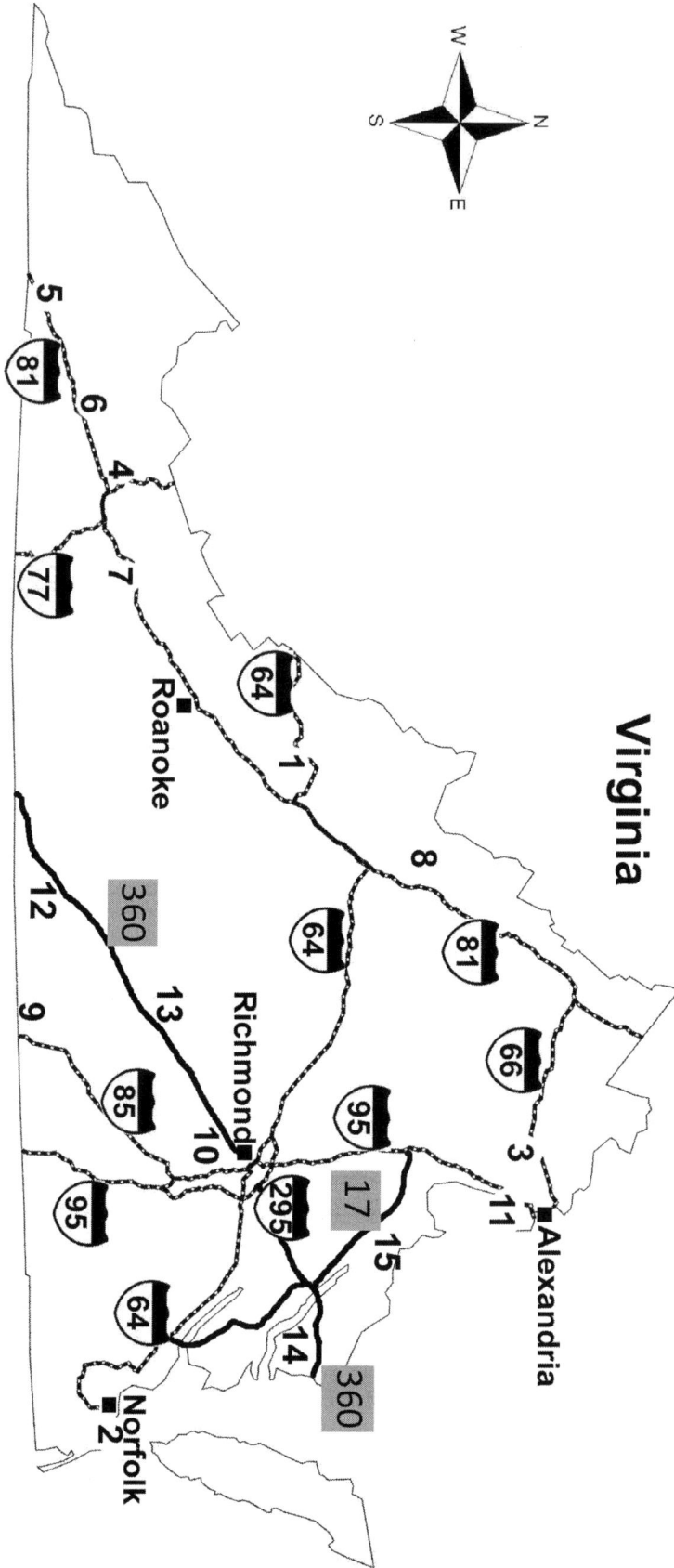

[1] Lake A. Willis Robertson Park
I-64, Exit 55
West of Lexington
N37 47.861 W79 36.599
County Rate: $30
America/Beautiful Discount: $22
(540) 463-4164
http://www.co.rockbridge.va.us/265/Parks-Recreation

Directions

15 miles. From Exit 55 take Hwy 11 southwest for 2.8 mi. to Hwy 251. Continue straight onto Hwy 251. Follow Hwy 251 for 10.3 miles to Collierstown, where 251 merges into Cty 770 (Turnpike Rd). Follow Turnpike Rd for 1.6 miles to the Park.

Points of Interest

Nearby are Natural Bridge, & birthplaces of Sam Houston & Woodrow Wilson. The area also has the tombs of Robert E. Lee & Stonewall Jackson.

RV Sites		Water		Laundry	Y
Number	53	None		Wi-Fi	
Shaded	Y	At Site	Y	Fishing	Y
By Water		Spigots		Hiking	Y
Paved		**Sewer**		Biking	Y
Pull Thru	Y	None		Swimming	Y
ADA		At Site		Watch Wildlife	
Max RV Size	40	Dump Station	Y	Pets	Y
Electric		**Amenities**		**Security**	
None		Restrooms	Y	Host(s)	Y
20 Amp	Y	Showers	Y	Rangers(s)	
30 Amp	Y	Reserve Sites	Y	Gate	
50 Amp		Store		Patrolled	Y
		Grill/Table	Y		

[2] First Landing State Park
I-64, Exit 282
East of Norfolk
N36 55.088 W76 03.097
State Rate: $24-$35
(757) 412-2300
http://www.dcr.virginia.gov/state-parks/first-landing.shtml

Directions

9 miles. From Exit 282 take Hwy 13 (Northampton Blvd) for 4.1 miles to the Shore Drive/Hwy 60 exit (the last exit before the Chesapeake Bay Bridge Tunnel). Go right on to Shore Drive for 4.5 miles to Hwy 343. Turn left at the park entrance.

Points of Interest

The Park, Virginia's most visited, is located by Chesapeake Bay, with shoreline and dunes to walk. In Virginia Beach try a seaside restaurant after a stroll along the 3-mile boardwalk.

RV Sites		Water		Laundry	Y
Number	230	None		Wi-Fi	
Shaded	Y	At Site	Y	Fishing	Y
By Water	Y	Spigots	Y	Hiking	Y
Paved	some	**Sewer**		Biking	Y
Pull Thru	Y	None		Swimming	Y
ADA	Y	At Site		Watch Wildlife	
Max RV Size	45	Dump Station	Y	Pets	Y
Electric		**Amenities**		**Security**	
None		Restrooms	Y	Host(s)	Y
20 Amp	Y	Showers	Y	Rangers(s)	Y
30 Amp	Y	Reserve Sites	Y	Gate	
50 Amp	Y	Store	Y	Patrolled	Y
		Grill/Table	Y		

[3] Bull Run Regional Park
I-66, Exit 52
Southwest of Centerville
N38 48.240 W77 28.613
County Rate: $26-$45
(703) 631-0550
http://www.nvrpa.org/park/bull_run

Directions

4.5 miles. From Exit 52 go west for 2 miles on Hwy 29. Turn south on Bull Run Post Office Rd for 2.5 miles to the park.

Points of Interest

The Park is not far from Washington & Northern Virginia attractions. You are 15 miles from the Vienna Metro Station. Convenient destinations include the Dulles area's Steven F. Udvar-Hazy Center at the National Air & Space Museum & Manassas National Battlefield Park.

RV Sites		Water		Laundry	
Number	144	None		Wi-Fi	
Shaded	Y	At Site	Y	Fishing	
By Water	Y	Spigots	Y	Hiking	Y
Paved		**Sewer**		Biking	Y
Pull Thru	Y	None		Swimming	Y
ADA		At Site	Y	Watch Wildlife	
Max RV Size	40	Dump Station	Y	Pets	Y
Electric		**Amenities**		**Security**	
None		Restrooms	Y	Host(s)	Y
20 Amp	Y	Showers	Y	Rangers(s)	
30 Amp	Y	Reserve Sites	Y	Gate	
50 Amp	Y	Store	Y	Patrolled	Y
		Grill/Table	Y		

[4] Stony Fork Campground
I-77, Exit 47
North of Wytheville
N37 00.619 W81 10.874
Jefferson NF Rate: $12
America/Beautiful Rate: $6
(276) 783-5196
http://www.recreation.gov/

Directions

4 miles. From Exit 47 go west on Hwy 717 (Krenning Rd) for 4 miles to the campground on your left.

Points of Interest

Shoppers should visit the Wytheville Snoopers Antique Mall & the downtown shops. Take a drive up Big Walker Mountain & stop at the Country Store there. For Arts & History try the Wytheville Heritage Museum, or Haller-Gibboney Rock House & Thomas J. Boyd Museum.

RV Sites		Water		Laundry	
Number	50	None		Wi-Fi	
Shaded	Y	At Site	Y	Fishing	Y
By Water	Y	Spigots	Y	Hiking	Y
Paved	Y	Sewer		Biking	Y
Pull Thru	Y	None		Swimming	
ADA	Y	At Site		Watch Wildlife	Y
Max RV Size	45	Dump Station	Y	Pets	Y
Electric		Amenities		Security	
None		Restrooms	Y	Host(s)	Y
20 Amp	Y	Showers	Y	Rangers(s)	Y
30 Amp	Y	Reserve Sites	Y	Gate	
50 Amp		Store		Patrolled	
		Grill/Table	Y		

[5] Sugar Hollow Park
I-81, Exit 7
East of Bristol
N36 38.758 W82 06.631
City Rate: $12-$15
(276) 645-7275
http://www.bristolva.org/index.aspx?NID=149

Directions

1.5 miles. From Exit 7 turn north to Hwy 11 (Lee Hwy). Turn east, drive 0.6 miles to Sugar Hollow Rd. Turn north, follow the road for 0.8 miles to the campground.

Points of Interest

Visit Natural Tunnel, called the Eighth Wonder of the World by William Jennings Bryan. Try a concert or ballet at the Paramount Center for the Arts. Pedal the Virginia Creeper Trail, Virginia's premiere mountain biking trail. Take in the music at the Carter Family Memorial Music Center.

RV Sites		Water		Laundry	
Number	75	None		Wi-Fi	Y
Shaded	Y	At Site	Y	Fishing	Y
By Water		Spigots	Y	Hiking	Y
Paved	Y	Sewer		Biking	Y
Pull Thru	Y	None		Swimming	
ADA	Y	At Site		Watch Wildlife	
Max RV Size	45	Dump Station	Y	Pets	Y
Electric		Amenities		Security	
None		Restrooms	Y	Host(s)	Y
20 Amp	Y	Showers	Y	Rangers(s)	
30 Amp	Y	Reserve Sites	Y	Gate	
50 Amp	few	Store		Patrolled	Y
		Grill/Table	Y		

[6] Hungry Mother State Park
I-81, Exit 47
North of Marion
N36 52.238 W81 31.479
State Rate: $20-$33
(276) 781-7400
http://www.dcr.virginia.gov/state-parks/hungry-mother.shtml

Directions

4 miles. From Exit 47 travel southwest for 1.1 miles on Rt 11. Turn right on Rt 16 north and go 3 miles to the park.

Points of Interest

Marion, in the Blue Ridge Highlands region of Virginia is home of the Lincoln Theater, one of three existing Art Deco Maya Revival-style theaters in America. Built in 1929, this historic landmark hosted legends like Roy Rogers, Ralph Stanley and Roy Acuff.

RV Sites		Water		Laundry	
Number	72	None		Wi-Fi	Y
Shaded	Y	At Site	Y	Fishing	Y
By Water	Y	Spigots	Y	Hiking	Y
Paved	some	Sewer		Biking	Y
Pull Thru	Y	None		Swimming	Y
ADA	Y	At Site	Y	Watch Wildlife	
Max RV Size	35	Dump Station	Y	Pets	Y
Electric		Amenities		Security	
None		Restrooms	Y	Host(s)	Y
20 Amp	Y	Showers	Y	Rangers(s)	Y
30 Amp	Y	Reserve Sites	Y	Gate	
50 Amp	Y	Store	Y	Patrolled	Y
		Grill/Table	Y		

[7] Claytor Lake State Park
I-81, Exit 101
East of Pulaski
N37 03.701 W80 37.428
State Rate: $20-$30
(540) 643-2500
http://www.dcr.virginia.gov/state-parks/clay-tor-lake.shtml

Directions

2.5 miles. From Exit 101 go south 2.2 miles on State Park Rd (State Rt 660) into the park.

Points of Interest

Visit Glencoe Museum and explore the rich heritage of Radford and the New River Valley. Hike the Cascades National Recreation Trail, which ascends a gorge for two miles to the picturesque 66-foot Cascades Waterfall - it is a four-mile round trip. Take the Dixie Caverns Tour.

RV Sites		Water			Laundry	
Number	110	None			Wi-Fi	
Shaded	Y	At Site	Y		Fishing	Y
By Water	Y	Spigots	Y		Hiking	Y
Paved		**Sewer**			Biking	Y
Pull Thru	Y	None			Swimming	Y
ADA	Y	At Site			Watch Wildlife	
Max RV Size	35	Dump Station	Y		Pets	Y
Electric		**Amenities**			**Security**	
None		Restrooms	Y		Host(s)	Y
20 Amp	Y	Showers	Y		Rangers(s)	Y
30 Amp	Y	Reserve Sites	Y		Gate	
50 Amp	Y	Store	Y		Patrolled	Y
		Grill/Table	Y			

[8] Natural Chimneys Park
I-81, Exit 240
Southwest of Harrisonburg
N38 21.122 W79 05.272
County Rate: $24-$41
(540) 350-2510
http://www.co.augusta.va.us/Index.aspx?page=616

Directions

11 miles. From Exit 240 follow Hwy 257 northwest for 3.3 mi. to Hwy 42. Turn left, go 3.6 mi. When Hwy 42 turns south at Hwy 747 (Iron Works Rd, which becomes Mossy Creek) continue straight, following Hwy 747 for 3.4 mi. to Mt. Solon. Turn right on Natural Chimney Rd for 0.6 mi. to Natural Chimney Lane & the Park.

Points of Interest

The Park's rock chimneys are special. From music, arts to bakeries, Harrisonburg is a great destination.

RV Sites		Water			Laundry	
Number	145	None			Wi-Fi	
Shaded	Y	At Site	Y		Fishing	Y
By Water	Y	Spigots	Y		Hiking	Y
Paved		**Sewer**			Biking	Y
Pull Thru	Y	None			Swimming	Y
ADA	Y	At Site	Y		Watch Wildlife	
Max RV Size	40	Dump Station	Y		Pets	Y
Electric		**Amenities**			**Security**	
None		Restrooms	Y		Host(s)	Y
20 Amp	Y	Showers	Y		Rangers(s)	
30 Amp	Y	Reserve Sites	Y		Gate	
50 Amp	Y	Store			Patrolled	Y
		Grill/Table	Y			

[9] North Bend Campground
I-85, Exit 12
Southwest of South Hill
N36 35.689 W78 18.664
COE Rate: $18-$26
America/Beautiful Rate: $9-$13
(434) 738-0059
http://www.recreation.gov/

Directions

17 miles. From Exit 12 go west and follow Hwy 58 for 10.8 miles to Hwy 4 (Buggs Island Rd). Turn south, go 5.9 miles to Hwy 678 (Mays Chapel Rd). Go right for 0.5 miles in to the Campground area. There are multiple camping areas.

Points of Interest

The Tobacco Farm Life Museum presents the region's rich farming heritage & its ties to the "golden leaf." The Model Railroad Museum has a unique & panoramic display of model trains.

RV Sites		Water			Laundry	
Number	238	None			Wi-Fi	
Shaded	Y	At Site	Y		Fishing	Y
By Water	Y	Spigots	Y		Hiking	Y
Paved		**Sewer**			Biking	Y
Pull Thru	Y	None			Swimming	Y
ADA	Y	At Site	Y		Watch Wildlife	Y
Max RV Size	45	Dump Station	Y		Pets	Y
Electric		**Amenities**			**Security**	
None		Restrooms	Y		Host(s)	Y
20 Amp	Y	Showers	Y		Rangers(s)	Y
30 Amp	Y	Reserve Sites	Y		Gate	
50 Amp	Y	Store	Y		Patrolled	Y
		Grill/Table	Y			

[10] Pocahontas State Park
I-95, Exit 62
South of Richmond
N37 21.947 W77 34.344
State Rate: $30
(804) 796-4255
http://www.dcr.virginia.gov/state_parks/poc.shtml

Directions

12 miles. From Exit 62 go west on Hwy 288 for 6 miles to Hwy 10. Exit south on Hwy 10 for 1.8 miles to Hwy 655 (Beach Rd). Turn right and drive 4.1 miles to State Park Rd and the Park.

Points of Interest

The Richmond Region, provides four centuries of history and modern day culture, a unique heritage. Enjoy magnificent architecture, monument lined cobblestone streets, world-class museums, and steeplechase racing.

RV Sites		Water		Laundry	Y
Number	114	None		Wi-Fi	
Shaded	Y	At Site	Y	Fishing	Y
By Water	Y	Spigots	Y	Hiking	Y
Paved		Sewer		Biking	Y
Pull Thru	Y	None		Swimming	Y
ADA	Y	At Site		Watch Wildlife	Y
Max RV Size	45	Dump Station	Y	Pets	Y
Electric		Amenities		Security	
None		Restrooms	Y	Host(s)	Y
20 Amp	Y	Showers	Y	Rangers(s)	Y
30 Amp	Y	Reserve Sites	Y	Gate	
50 Amp	Y	Store	Y	Patrolled	Y
		Grill/Table	Y		

[11] Pohick Bay Regional Park
I-95, Exit 163
Southwest of Alexandria
N38 40.246 W77 10.493
County Rate: $26-$45
(703) 339-6104
http://www.nvrpa.org/park/pohick_bay

Directions

5 miles. From Exit 163 go 0.2 mi. east on Lorton Rd. Turn right on Lorton Market St. Go 1.1 miles (changes to Gunston Rd) to Hwy 1. Go straight through light on Gunston Rd (Hwy 242) for 3.3 miles to Pohick Bay Dr & Park.

Points of Interest

The Park is not far from Washington & Northern Virginia. You are 11 miles from the Springfield Metro Station. Convenient destinations include Mount Vernon, & Gunston Hall Plantation. Trails leads walkers to the waterfront, mini golf and outdoor pool.

RV Sites		Water		Laundry	Y
Number	100	None		Wi-Fi	Y
Shaded	Y	At Site	Y	Fishing	
By Water	Y	Spigots	Y	Hiking	Y
Paved		Sewer		Biking	
Pull Thru	Y	None		Swimming	Y
ADA	Y	At Site	Y	Watch Wildlife	Y
Max RV Size	40	Dump Station	Y	Pets	Y
Electric		Amenities		Security	
None		Restrooms	Y	Host(s)	Y
20 Amp	Y	Showers	Y	Rangers(s)	
30 Amp	Y	Reserve Sites	Y	Gate	
50 Amp	Y	Store	Y	Patrolled	Y
		Grill/Table	Y		

[12] Staunton River State Park
Hwy 360, Southeast on Hwy 344
East of South Boston
N36 42.112 W78 40.778
State Rate: $20-$30
(434) 572-4623
http://www.dcr.virginia.gov/state-parks/staunton-river.shtml

Distance

18.4 miles. From the Hwy 360/58 junction near South Boston take Hwy 360 8.4 miles northeast to Rt 344. Follow Rt 344 southeast for 10 miles to the park

Points of Interest

Check out the South Boston Speedway, which has been hosting NASCAR short track races for 50 years. Take In a play at the Halifax County Little Theatre. Enjoy access to Virginia's largest lake with fishing & aquatic activities.

RV Sites		Water		Laundry	Y
Number	45	None		Wi-Fi	
Shaded	Y	At Site	Y	Fishing	Y
By Water	Y	Spigots	Y	Hiking	Y
Paved		Sewer		Biking	Y
Pull Thru	Y	None		Swimming	Y
ADA	Y	At Site		Watch Wildlife	
Max RV Size	45	Dump Station	Y	Pets	Y
Electric		Amenities		Security	
None		Restrooms	Y	Host(s)	Y
20 Amp	Y	Showers	Y	Rangers(s)	Y
30 Amp	Y	Reserve Sites	Y	Gate	
50 Amp		Store		Patrolled	Y
		Grill/Table	Y		

[13] Twin Lakes State Park
Hwy 360, North on Hwy 613
West of Burkville
N37 10.546 W78 16.722
State Rate: $30
(434) 392-3435
http://www.dcr.virginia.gov/state-parks/twin-lakes.shtml

Directions

6.5 miles. From the Hwy 360/460 junction near Burkville go west on Hwy 360 for 4.7 miles to Hwy 613. Turn north for 1.8 miles to Hwy 629, then east to the Park

Points of Interest

Sailor's Creek Battlefield State Park and other sites on the Lee's Retreat Driving Tour provide an opportunity to visit the final days of the Civil War. In Crewe, visit the Historic Railroad Park.

RV Sites		Water		Laundry	
Number	34	None		Wi-Fi	
Shaded	Y	At Site	Y	Fishing	Y
By Water	Y	Spigots	Y	Hiking	Y
Paved		Sewer		Biking	Y
Pull Thru	Y	None		Swimming	Y
ADA	Y	At Site		Watch Wildlife	
Max RV Size	36	Dump Station	Y	Pets	Y
Electric		Amenities		Security	
None		Restrooms	Y	Host(s)	Y
20 Amp	Y	Showers	Y	Rangers(s)	Y
30 Amp	Y	Reserve Sites	Y	Gate	
50 Amp		Store		Patrolled	Y
		Grill/Table	Y		

[14] Belle Isle State Park
Hwy 360, at Hwy 17
South of Warsaw
N37 46.871 W76 35.256
State Rate: $30
(804) 462-5030
http://www.dcr.virginia.gov/state-parks/belle-isle.shtml

Directions

26.4 miles. On Hwy 360, at Hwy 17, go east over the Rappahannock River for 6.7 miles to Warsaw. Take Hwy 3 southeast for 15.3 miles to Hwy 354. Turn right, go 3 miles to Somers. Turn right onto Belle Isle Rd (Hwy 683) for 1.4 miles to the park.

Points of Interest

Check out the Reedville Fisherman's Museum, Reedville; Morratico Waterfront Museum, Morratico; and the Steamboat Era Museum, Irvington.

RV Sites		Water		Laundry	Y
Number	28	None		Wi-Fi	Y
Shaded	Y	At Site	Y	Fishing	Y
By Water	Y	Spigots	Y	Hiking	Y
Paved		Sewer		Biking	Y
Pull Thru	Y	None		Swimming	Y
ADA	Y	At Site	Y	Watch Wildlife	Y
Max RV Size	45	Dump Station	Y	Pets	Y
Electric		Amenities		Security	
None		Restrooms	Y	Host(s)	Y
20 Amp	Y	Showers	Y	Rangers(s)	Y
30 Amp	Y	Reserve Sites	Y	Gate	
50 Amp	Y	Store		Patrolled	Y
		Grill/Table	Y		

[15] Westmoreland State Park
Hwy 360, at Hwy 17
North of Warsaw
N38 08.801 W76 52.630
State Rate: $20-$30
(804) 493-8821
http://www.dcr.virginia.gov/state-parks/west-moreland.shtml

Directions

24.6 miles. On Hwy 360, at Hwy 17, go east over the Rappahannock River for 6.7 miles to Warsaw. Take Hwy 3 north for 17.9 miles to Hwy 347 and the park.

Points of Interest

Westmoreland is one of the first six state parks opened in June 1936 and built by the Civilian Conservation Corps (CCC). The park is close to George Washington's birthplace and Stratford Hall, the birthplace Robert E. Lee.

RV Sites		Water		Laundry	Y
Number	129	None		Wi-Fi	
Shaded	Y	At Site	Y	Fishing	Y
By Water	Y	Spigots	Y	Hiking	Y
Paved		Sewer		Biking	Y
Pull Thru	Y	None		Swimming	Y
ADA	Y	At Site	Y	Watch Wildlife	Y
Max RV Size	40	Dump Station	Y	Pets	Y
Electric		Amenities		Security	
None		Restrooms	Y	Host(s)	Y
20 Amp	Y	Showers	Y	Rangers(s)	Y
30 Amp	Y	Reserve Sites	Y	Gate	
50 Amp		Store	Y	Patrolled	Y
		Grill/Table	Y		

About Washington's Public Campgrounds

As you might expect, Washington State is rich in campgrounds sponsored by the Corp. of Engineers, National Forest Service, National Park Service, the State and Counties. The Washington State Parks and Recreation Commission oversees close to 100 parks. Their website is - **http://www.parks.wa.gov/**

State Park camping fees (2014) are:

Standard campsites: $17 - $31*. Campsite with water, sink waste, garbage disposal, and flush comfort station.

Partial-utility campsites: $26 - $39*. A standard campsite plus electricity. May have water and/or sewer.

Full-utility campsites: $27 - $42*. A standard campsite with full hook-ups.

Primitive campsites: $12. No nearby flush comfort station. May not have amenities of a standard campsite. Sites accessible by motorized / non-motorized vehicles and water trail camping.

(*There may be additional fees for popular destination parks or select premium campsites.)

You can make a reservation online at - **https://washington.goingtocamp.com/**

You also can call the Reservation Center to make a reservation at (888) 226-7688.

Passes are available for some senior citizens, disabled veterans, and people with disabilities. To obtain a pass call (360) 902-8500 or (360) 902-8844. From April 1 through September 30, the maximum length of stay in any one park is 10 days. Pets are allowed in most state parks, but must be under physical control at all times on a leash no more than eight feet long.

[1] **Battle Ground Lake State Park**	[9] **Big Pines**
[2] **Seaquest State Park**	[10] **Plymouth Campground**
[3] **Millersylvania State Park**	**(John Day Lock and Dam)**
[4] **Flowing Lake Park (Leckies Beach)**	[11] **Grayland Beach State Park**
[5] **Bay View State Park**	[12] **Kalaloch Camp (Olympic National Park)**
[6] **Kachess Campground**	[13] **Bogachiel State Park**
[7] **Ginkgo Petrified Forest State Park**	[14] **Sequim Bay State Park**
[8] **Riverside State Park**	[15] **Dosewallips State Park**

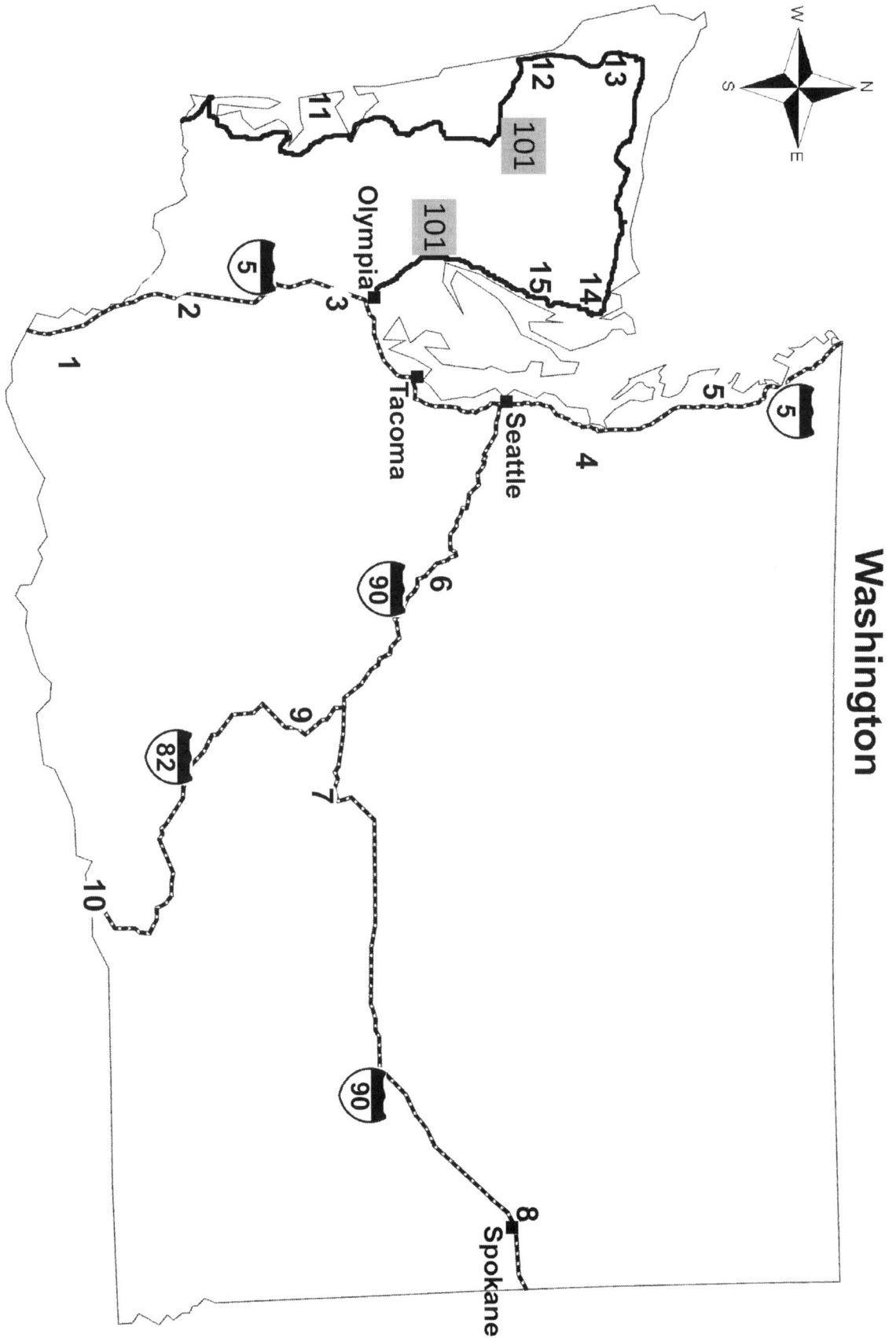

Washington

[1] Battle Ground Lake State Park
I-5, Exit 11
Northeast of Vancouver
N45 48.177 W122 29.199
State Rate: See Introduction
(360) 687-4621
http://www.parks.wa.gov/472/Battle-Ground-Lake

Directions

11 miles. From Exit 11, go east 6 miles on Hwy 502 to Hwy 503. Turn left, go 1.3 mile to 244th. Turn right, go 0.5 mile to 132nd. Turn left, go 0.2 mile to 249th. Turn right, go 1 mile to 152nd. Turn right, go 0.2 mile to 244th, then left, 1.5 mile to the Park.

Points of Interest

Visit Vancouver, it's downtown area has quaint eateries, art galleries, boutiques and antiques. Learn more at the Visitor Center at Fort Vancouver National Site.

RV Sites		Water		Laundry	
Number	31	None		Wi-Fi	
Shaded	Y	At Site	Y	Fishing	Y
By Water	Y	Spigots	Y	Hiking	Y
Paved		**Sewer**		Biking	Y
Pull Thru	Y	None		Swimming	Y
ADA	Y	At Site		Watch Wildlife	Y
Max RV Size	35	Dump Station	Y	Pets	Y
Electric		**Amenities**		**Security**	
None		Restrooms	Y	Host(s)	Y
20 Amp	Y	Showers	Y	Rangers(s)	Y
30 Amp	Y	Reserve Sites	Y	Gate	
50 Amp	Y	Store	Y	Patrolled	Y
		Grill/Table	Y		

[2] Seaquest State Park
I-5, Exit 49
North of Longview
N46 17.742 W122 49.055
State Rate: See Introduction
(360) 274-8633
http://www.parks.wa.gov/581/Seaquest

Directions

5.5 miles. From Exit 49 go east on Hwy 504 (Spirit Lake Hwy) for 5.4 miles to the Park entrance.

Points of Interest

The Park is near Mount St. Helens (Visitor Center at the park), an excellent day trip. The forested park has over a mile of Silver Lake shoreline. Try the one mile wetland trail and six miles of woodland trails for hiking and bicycling. You may also see some spectacular views of wildlife.

RV Sites		Water		Laundry	
Number	33	None		Wi-Fi	
Shaded	Y	At Site	Y	Fishing	Y
By Water	Y	Spigots	Y	Hiking	Y
Paved		**Sewer**		Biking	Y
Pull Thru	Y	None		Swimming	Y
ADA	Y	At Site	Y	Watch Wildlife	Y
Max RV Size	40	Dump Station	Y	Pets	Y
Electric		**Amenities**		**Security**	
None		Restrooms	Y	Host(s)	Y
20 Amp	Y	Showers	Y	Rangers(s)	Y
30 Amp	Y	Reserve Sites	Y	Gate	
50 Amp	Y	Store		Patrolled	
		Grill/Table	Y		

[3] Millersylvania State Park
I-5, Exit 95
South of Olympia
N46 54.576 W122 54.356
State Rate: See Introduction
(360) 753-1519
http://www.parks.wa.gov/546/Millersylvania

Directions

3 miles. From Exit 95 go east on Hwy 121 for 3 miles to the Park entrance on the left.

Points of Interest

Tour Olympia by trolley car or carriage. Sites to see could include the State Capital; Schmidt House, built in 1904 for the owner of the Olympia Brewing Company; Percival Landing (1860) including the "Sandman" Tug Boat; and the End of the Oregon Trail.

RV Sites		Water		Laundry	
Number	48	None		Wi-Fi	
Shaded	Y	At Site	Y	Fishing	Y
By Water	Y	Spigots	Y	Hiking	Y
Paved	Y	**Sewer**		Biking	Y
Pull Thru	Y	None		Swimming	Y
ADA	Y	At Site		Watch Wildlife	Y
Max RV Size	35	Dump Station	Y	Pets	Y
Electric		**Amenities**		**Security**	
None		Restrooms	Y	Host(s)	Y
20 Amp	Y	Showers	Y	Rangers(s)	Y
30 Amp	Y	Reserve Sites	Y	Gate	
50 Amp		Store	Y	Patrolled	Y
		Grill/Table	Y		

[4] Flowing Lake Park (Leckies Beach)
I-5, Exit 194
East of Everett
N47 57.139 W121 59.439
County Rate: $18-$29
(360) 568-2274
http://snohomishcountywa.gov/Facilities/Facility/Details/Flowing-Lake-124

Directions

15 miles. From Exit 194 go east on Hwy 2 for 9.7 miles to Westwick Rd. Turn east & follow Westwick, it will turn north and become 171st Ave SE (Iverson Knutsen Rd), going 5 miles in all to 48 St SE. Turn east 0.5 miles to the Park.

Points of Interest

Everett, home to Boeing, has aerospace & aviation tours. The waterfront is home to a large marina with an authentic 1890's marina marketplace.

RV Sites		Water		Laundry	
Number	30	None		Wi-Fi	
Shaded	Y	At Site	Y	Fishing	Y
By Water	Y	Spigots	Y	Hiking	Y
Paved		**Sewer**		Biking	Y
Pull Thru	Y	None		Swimming	Y
ADA		At Site		Watch Wildlife	
Max RV Size	40	Dump Station	Y	Pets	Y
Electric		**Amenities**		**Security**	
None		Restrooms	Y	Host(s)	Y
20 Amp	Y	Showers	Y	Rangers(s)	
30 Amp	Y	Reserve Sites	Y	Gate	
50 Amp	Y	Store		Patrolled	Y
		Grill/Table	Y		

[5] Bay View State Park
I-5, Exit 230
West of Burlington
N48 29.254 W122 28.81cc3
State Rate: See Introduction
(360) 757-0227
http://www.parks.wa.gov/473/Bay-View

Directions

10 miles. From Exit 230 take Hwy 20 for 6.3 miles west to Whitney-Bayview Rd. Turn north (becomes Bay View-Edison Rd) for 3.6 miles to the park.

Points of Interest

The park is on the coast and offers views of the San Juan Islands, a national marine estuary. When the weather is clear you can see the Olympic Mountains & Mt. Rainier. Plan a day trip down Whidbey Island (book the Clinton Ferry). Stop south of Deception Pass.

RV Sites		Water		Laundry	
Number	30	None		Wi-Fi	
Shaded	Y	At Site	Y	Fishing	Y
By Water	Y	Spigots	Y	Hiking	Y
Paved		**Sewer**		Biking	Y
Pull Thru		None		Swimming	Y
ADA	Y	At Site	Y	Watch Wildlife	
Max RV Size	45	Dump Station	Y	Pets	Y
Electric		**Amenities**		**Security**	
None		Restrooms	Y	Host(s)	Y
20 Amp	Y	Showers	Y	Rangers(s)	Y
30 Amp	Y	Reserve Sites	Y	Gate	
50 Amp	Y	Store		Patrolled	Y
		Grill/Table	Y		

[6] Kachess Campground
I-90, Exit 62
East of Snoqualmie Pass
N47 21.366 W121 14.797
Okanogan-Wenatchee NF Rate: $21-$42
America/Beautiful Rate: $11-$21
(509) 649-3744
http://www.recreation.gov

Directions

5 miles. From Exit 62 go east for 5 miles on Road 49 to the campground.

Points of Interest

The camp is located at the north end of Kachess Lake. Surrounded by high mountains, lakes and forest, the camp is considered one of the most beautiful in the Cle Elum Ranger District. Fish for Kokanee salmon and trout. Enjoy the sandy swimming beach. Hike a section of the Pacific Crest Trail, a premier National Scenic Trail.

RV Sites		Water		Laundry	
Number	129	None		Wi-Fi	
Shaded	Y	At Site	Y	Fishing	Y
By Water	Y	Spigots	Y	Hiking	Y
Paved	Y	**Sewer**		Biking	Y
Pull Thru	Y	None	Y	Swimming	Y
ADA	Y	At Site		Watch Wildlife	Y
Max RV Size	45	Dump Station		Pets	Y
Electric		**Amenities**		**Security**	
None	Y	Restrooms	Y	Host(s)	Y
20 Amp		Showers	Y	Rangers(s)	Y
30 Amp		Reserve Sites	Y	Gate	
50 Amp		Store		Patrolled	Y
		Grill/Table	Y		

[7] Ginkgo Petrified Forest State Park
I-90, Exit 136
East of Ellensburg
N46 54.025 W119 59.571
State Rate: See Introduction
(509) 856-2700
http://www.parks.wa.gov/288/Ginkgo-Petrified-Forest

Directions

3 miles. From Exit 136 turn south on Huntzinger Rd for 2.8 miles to the camping area.

Points of Interest

Ginkgo Petrified Forest is a registered national natural landmark, & is regarded as one of the most unusual fossil forests in the world. Events to look for in Ellensburg are 'The First Friday Artwalk,' Ellensburg Film Festival, Ellensburg Rodeo, Jazz in The Valley, or the Kittitas County Fair. Campground can be windy.

RV Sites		Water		Laundry	Y
Number	50	None		Wi-Fi	
Shaded	Y	At Site	Y	Fishing	Y
By Water	Y	Spigots	Y	Hiking	Y
Paved	Y	Sewer		Biking	Y
Pull Thru	Y	None		Swimming	Y
ADA	Y	At Site	Y	Watch Wildlife	Y
Max RV Size	45	Dump Station		Pets	Y
Electric		Amenities		Security	
None		Restrooms	Y	Host(s)	Y
20 Amp	Y	Showers	Y	Rangers(s)	Y
30 Amp	Y	Reserve Sites	Y	Gate	
50 Amp		Store		Patrolled	
		Grill/Table	Y		

[8] Riverside State Park
I-90, Exit 280
West side of Spokane
N47 41.791 W117 29.769
State Rate: See Introduction
(509) 465-5064
http://www.parks.wa.gov/573/Riverside

Directions

6 miles. From Exit 280 go to Walnut St. Turn north on Walnut, which become Maple, go 1.3 miles to Maxwell Ave. Turn left, go 4.7 miles in all. Maxwell becomes (curve right) Pettit Dr, then W Downriver Park Dr (stay along the river), then (bear left) N. Aubrey L. White Pkwy (Riverside State Park Dr) to the park.

Points of Interest

Take a self-guided tour of Spokane. The Region is "wine country" with some of the country's finest winemakers.

RV Sites		Water		Laundry	
Number	32	None		Wi-Fi	Y
Shaded	Y	At Site	Y	Fishing	Y
By Water	Y	Spigots	Y	Hiking	Y
Paved		Sewer		Biking	Y
Pull Thru	Y	None		Swimming	Y
ADA	Y	At Site	Y	Watch Wildlife	Y
Max RV Size	45	Dump Station	Y	Pets	Y
Electric		Amenities		Security	
None		Restrooms	Y	Host(s)	Y
20 Amp	Y	Showers	Y	Rangers(s)	Y
30 Amp	Y	Reserve Sites	Y	Gate	
50 Amp	Y	Store	Y	Patrolled	Y
		Grill/Table	Y		

[9] Big Pines
I-82, Exit 3 or 26
North of Yakima
N46 47.701 W120 27.491
BLM Rate: $15
America/Beautiful Rate: $8
(509) 665-1200
http://www.blm.gov/or/resources/recreation/site_info.php?siteid=247

Directions

10 or 15 miles. **Eastbound**, from Exit 3 go west for 0.5 miles on Thrall Rd. Turn south on Hwy 821 (Canyon Rd) for 15 miles to the campground. **Westbound**, from Exit 26 go west and north for 9.6 miles to the campground.

Points of Interest

Big Pines is in the very scenic Yakima River Canyon, which cuts through massive basalt cliffs and rolling desert hills.

RV Sites		Water		Laundry	
Number	41	None	Y	Wi-Fi	
Shaded	Y	At Site		Fishing	Y
By Water		Spigots		Hiking	Y
Paved	Y	Sewer		Biking	Y
Pull Thru	Y	None	Y	Swimming	Y
ADA	Y	At Site		Watch Wildlife	Y
Max RV Size	45	Dump Station		Pets	Y
Electric		Amenities		Security	
None	Y	Restrooms	Y	Host(s)	Y
20 Amp		Showers		Rangers(s)	Y
30 Amp		Reserve Sites	Y	Gate	
50 Amp		Store		Patrolled	Y
		Grill/Table	Y		

[10] Plymouth Campground
(John Day Lock & Dam)
I-82, Exit 131
Plymouth, on the Stateline
N45 56.023 W119 21.449
COE Rate: $24-$27
America/Beautiful Rate: $12-$14
(541) 506-4807
http://www.recreation.gov

Directions

2 miles. From Exit 131 go west on Hwy 14 for 0.7 miles to Plymouth Rd. Turn south for 0.7 miles to Christy Rd. Turn west for 0.3 miles to the Park.

Points of Interest

Visit Columbia Crest Winery, Fort Henrietta or Pendleton Woolen Mills. Enjoy the Hermiston's Farm City Pro Rodeo or Pendleton Roundup. McNary Dam has a number of sights, including an Interpretive Center.

RV Sites		Water		Laundry	Y
Number	32	None		Wi-Fi	
Shaded	Y	At Site	Y	Fishing	Y
By Water	Y	Spigots	Y	Hiking	Y
Paved	Y	Sewer		Biking	Y
Pull Thru	Y	None		Swimming	
ADA	Y	At Site	Y	Watch Wildlife	Y
Max RV Size	45	Dump Station	Y	Pets	Y
Electric		Amenities		Security	
None		Restrooms	Y	Host(s)	Y
20 Amp	Y	Showers	Y	Rangers(s)	Y
30 Amp	Y	Reserve Sites	Y	Gate	
50 Amp	Y	Store		Patrolled	Y
		Grill/Table	Y		

[11] Grayland Beach State Park
Hwy 101, Hwy 105 at South Aberdeen
South of Grayland
N46 47.642 W124 05.368
State Rate: See Introduction
(360) 267-4301
http://www.parks.wa.gov/515/Grayland-Beach

Directions

23 miles. In South Aberdeen take Hwy 105 (S. Boone St) south for 23 miles, past Twin Harbors State Park to Cranberry Beach Rd. Turn west into the Park. You can also take Hwy 105 from Howard.

Points of Interest

A beautiful location with a wonderful 1.5 mile ocean beach front. Kite flyers and observers can frequently be seen taking advantage of kite-flying conditions. Five trails lead from the campground to the beach. You can also try clamming, crabbing or saltwater fishing.

RV Sites		Water		Laundry	
Number	100	None		Wi-Fi	
Shaded	Y	At Site	Y	Fishing	Y
By Water	Y	Spigots	Y	Hiking	Y
Paved	Y	Sewer		Biking	Y
Pull Thru	Y	None		Swimming	
ADA	Y	At Site	Y	Watch Wildlife	Y
Max RV Size	45	Dump Station	Y	Pets	Y
Electric		Amenities		Security	
None		Restrooms	Y	Host(s)	Y
20 Amp	Y	Showers	Y	Rangers(s)	Y
30 Amp	Y	Reserve Sites	Y	Gate	
50 Amp	Y	Store		Patrolled	Y
		Grill/Table	Y		

[12] Kalaloch Camp (Olympic National Park)
Hwy 101
North of Queets
N47 36.770 W124 22.481
NPS Rate: $14-$28
America/Beautiful Rate: $7-$14
(360) 565-3130
http://www.recreation.gov

Directions

3.7 miles. Drive 3.7 miles north of Queets to the campground on the left.

Points of Interest

Kalaloch is a "a good place to land" in the Quinault language. The campground is on a bluff overlooking the ocean, there are paths to the beach. Look for crabs and sea urchins at low tide; sea otters float on the surface. Binoculars will come in handy to sight shorebird nests on the beaches, whales and dolphins. Swim with caution.

RV Sites		Water		Laundry	
Number	168	None		Wi-Fi	
Shaded	Y	At Site		Fishing	Y
By Water	Y	Spigots	Y	Hiking	Y
Paved		Sewer		Biking	Y
Pull Thru	Y	None		Swimming	caution
ADA	Y	At Site		Watch Wildlife	Y
Max RV Size	40	Dump Station	Y	Pets	Y
Electric		Amenities		Security	
None	Y	Restrooms	Y	Host(s)	Y
20 Amp		Showers		Rangers(s)	Y
30 Amp		Reserve Sites	Y	Gate	
50 Amp		Store		Patrolled	Y
		Grill/Table	Y		

[13] Bogachiel State Park
Hwy 101
South of Forks
N47 53.689 W124 21.770
State Rate: See Introduction
(360) 374-6356
http://www.parks.wa.gov/478/Bogachiel

Directions

5.6 miles. From the center of Forks go 5.6 miles south to the Park.

Points of Interest

This is a great location to visit the western section of Olympic National Park; the seashore at Mora (the area around La Push, home of the the Quileute Tribe can yield some interesting sights and rewarding cultural discovery), Neah Bay and the rainforest of Hoh. This area has many scenic roadways with exceptional vistas and pull-offs to access miles of trails.

RV Sites		Water			Laundry	
Number	26	None			Wi-Fi	
Shaded	Y	At Site	Y		Fishing	
By Water	Y	Spigots	Y		Hiking	Y
Paved		**Sewer**			Biking	Y
Pull Thru	Y	None			Swimming	
ADA	Y	At Site			Watch Wildlife	Y
Max RV Size	40	Dump Station	Y		Pets	Y
Electric		**Amenities**			**Security**	
None		Restrooms	Y		Host(s)	Y
20 Amp	Y	Showers	Y		Rangers(s)	Y
30 Amp	Y	Reserve Sites			Gate	
50 Amp	Y	Store			Patrolled	Y
		Grill/Table	Y			

[14] Sequim Bay State Park
Hwy 101
Southeast of Sequim
N48 02.446 W123 01.855
State Rate: See Introduction
(360) 683-4235
http://www.parks.wa.gov/582/Sequim-Bay

Directions

4.2 miles. From the center of Sequim drive 4.2 miles southeast on Hwy 101 to the Park.

Points of Interest

If you are into flowers, Sequim is for you. Plan on the Sequim Lavender Weekend, the nations premier lavender celebration. But actually, enjoy Lavender Fields all growing and bloom season. From May through October the Sequim Farmer's Market provides the best of local produce, floral and handcrafts. Or visit the waterfront locations where John Wayne spent many summer weeks.

RV Sites		Water			Laundry	
Number	64	None			Wi-Fi	
Shaded	Y	At Site	Y		Fishing	Y
By Water	Y	Spigots	Y		Hiking	Y
Paved		**Sewer**			Biking	Y
Pull Thru		None			Swimming	Y
ADA	Y	At Site	Y		Watch Wildlife	Y
Max RV Size	45	Dump Station			Pets	Y
Electric		**Amenities**			**Security**	
None		Restrooms	Y		Host(s)	Y
20 Amp	Y	Showers	Y		Rangers(s)	Y
30 Amp	Y	Reserve Sites	Y		Gate	
50 Amp		Store			Patrolled	Y
		Grill/Table	Y			

[15] Dosewallips State Park
Hwy 101, Southside of Brinnon
South of Brinnon
N47 41.254 W122 53.991
State Rate: See Introduction
(360) 796-4415
http://www.parks.wa.gov/499/Dosewallips

Directions

The Park is on Hwy 101 just south of Brinnon.

Points of Interest

This Olympic Peninsula area is geographically unique, consisting of five major landscape settings: temperate rain forest, rugged mountain terrain, large lowland lakes, cascading waterfalls, rivers, and saltwater beaches. The Park reflects this diversity. It offers both freshwater and saltwater activities. A list of activities would include clamming, crabbing, diving, freshwater boating & fishing, saltwater boating & fishing, & swimming.

RV Sites		Water			Laundry	
Number	125	None			Wi-Fi	
Shaded	Y	At Site	Y		Fishing	Y
By Water	Y	Spigots	Y		Hiking	Y
Paved		**Sewer**			Biking	Y
Pull Thru	Y	None			Swimming	Y
ADA	Y	At Site	Y		Watch Wildlife	Y
Max RV Size	45	Dump Station	Y		Pets	Y
Electric		**Amenities**			**Security**	
None		Restrooms	Y		Host(s)	Y
20 Amp	Y	Showers	Y		Rangers(s)	Y
30 Amp	Y	Reserve Sites	Y		Gate	
50 Amp		Store			Patrolled	Y
		Grill/Table	Y			

About West Virginia's Public Campgrounds

The West Virginia Division of Natural Resources (DNR) mission is . . . "to promote conservation by preserving and protecting natural areas of unique or exceptional scenic, scientific, cultural, archaeological, or historical significance and to provide outdoor recreational opportunities for the citizens of this state and its visitors." The Division website is -

http://www.wvstateparks.com/lodging/camping.htm

West Virginia's DNR provides park visitors a choice of primitive tent sites up to full-hook ups at 29 campgrounds. The DNR defines RV sites as follows -

Deluxe: Grill, tent pad, pull-off for trailers, picnic table, electric hookups, some with water and sewer hookups, dumping station, bathhouses with hot showers, flush toilets and laundry facilities.

Standard: Same as deluxe, but generally no hookups are available. Some sites at some areas may have electric hookups.

Rustic: Improved sites with limited facilities, well water and pit toilets.

Dogs and cats are the only pets permitted in state parks and state forests, and they must be restrained on a leash up to ten feet.

Campsite reservations may be made in writing or by calling toll free 1-800-CALL-WVA. Not all parks take reservations. Reservations may be made up to two days in advance. A minimum of two nights, (up to a maximum of 14 nights) is required when making a reservation. The majority of campsites are rented on a first come first serve basis. West Virginia State Parks only offer online reservations for parks with lodges. There are number of fee discount categories, check with the Park you plan to visit.

[1] Beech Fork State Park	[6] Tygart Lake State Park
[2] Coopers Rock State Park	[7] Babcock State Park
[3] Camp Creek State Park	[8] Battle Run COE
[4] Gerald Freeman COE	[9] Mountwood County Park
[5] Stonewall Resort State Park	

NOTES:

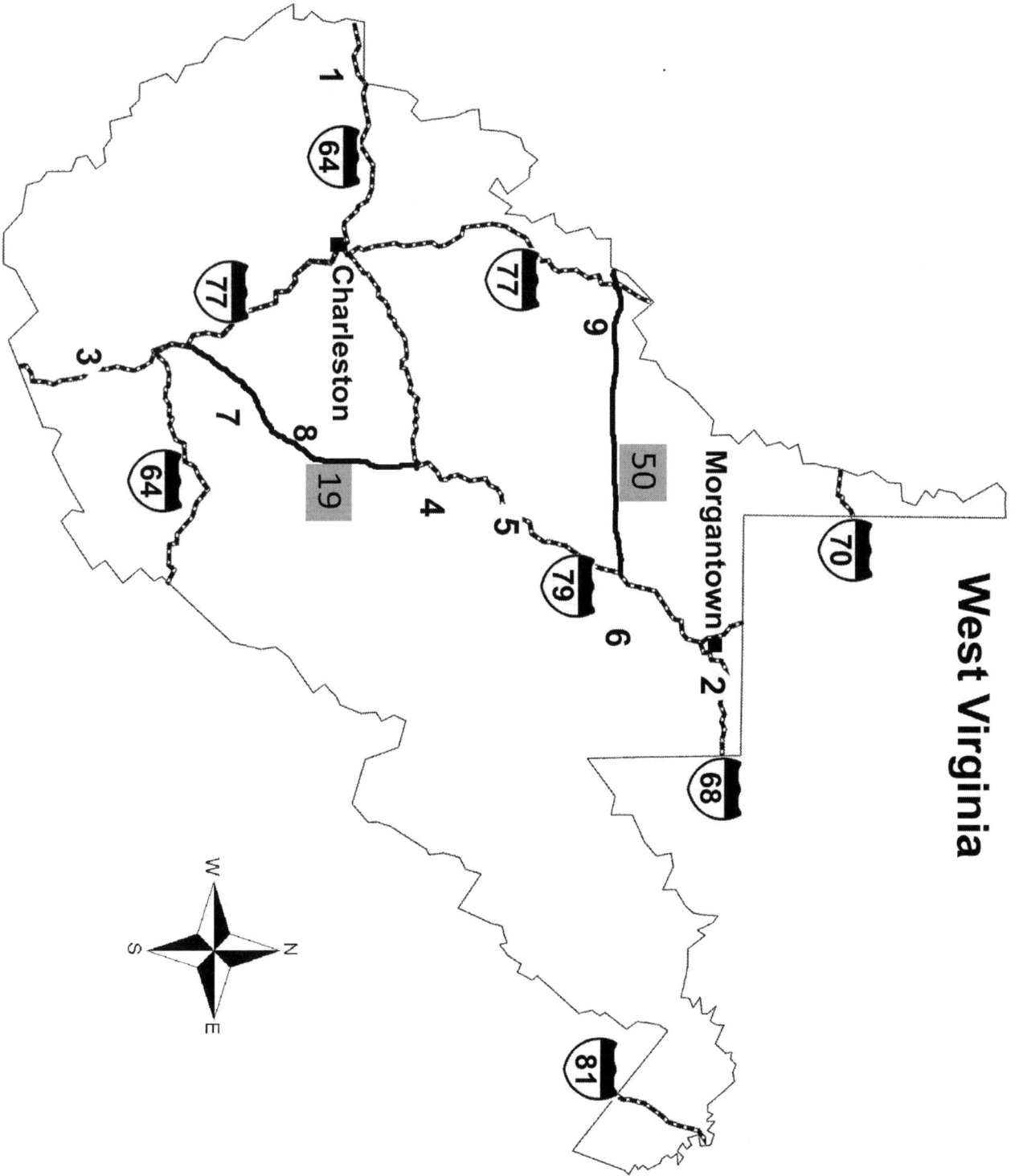

West Virginia

[1] Beech Fork State Park
I-64, Exit 11
South of Huntington
N38 18.482 W82 20.683
State Rate: $23-$29
(304) 528-5794
http://www.beechforksp.com/

Directions

from I-64. There are a few tight curves the last few miles. From Exit 11 take Hwy 10 (Hal Greer Blvd) for 6 miles to Cty Rd 43 (Hughes Branch Rd). Turn right for 3.7 miles to the Park.

Points of Interest

Visit the Blenko Glass Company and observe artisans creating unique handmade glassware famous throughout the world. At the Heritage Farm Museum & Village, experience life as it was in an Appalachian pioneer community.

RV Sites		Water		Laundry	Y
Number	275	None		Wi-Fi	
Shaded	Y	At Site	Y	Fishing	Y
By Water	Y	Spigots	Y	Hiking	Y
Paved		Sewer		Biking	Y
Pull Thru	Y	None		Swimming	Y
ADA	Y	At Site	Y	Watch Wildlife	Y
Max RV Size	40	Dump Station	Y	Pets	Y
Electric		Amenities		Security	
None		Restrooms	Y	Host(s)	Y
20 Amp	Y	Showers	Y	Rangers(s)	Y
30 Amp	Y	Reserve Sites	Y	Gate	
50 Amp	Y	Store		Patrolled	Y
		Grill/Table	Y		

[2] Coopers Rock State Park
I-68, Exit 15
East of Morgantown
N39 38.503 W79 47.644
State Rate: $23
(304) 594-1561
http://www.coopersrockstateforest.com/

Directions

2 miles. From Exit 15 go south for 0.5 miles on Cty Rd 73/12. Continue straight as 73/12 becomes 73/16 for 1.2 miles to the campground.

Points of Interest

Hike to Coopers Rock Overlook. Walk to rock-cliffs, lining the Cheat River Gorge, which provide numerous overlooks. Find Henry Clay Iron Furnace Trail, located in a grassy glade in an otherwise undisturbed forest, a huge stone structure used for producing iron in the 1800's.

RV Sites		Water		Laundry	Y
Number	25	None		Wi-Fi	
Shaded	Y	At Site		Fishing	
By Water		Spigots	Y	Hiking	Y
Paved		Sewer		Biking	Y
Pull Thru	Y	None		Swimming	
ADA	Y	At Site	Y	Watch Wildlife	Y
Max RV Size	40	Dump Station	Y	Pets	Y
Electric		Amenities		Security	
None		Restrooms	Y	Host(s)	Y
20 Amp	Y	Showers	Y	Rangers(s)	Y
30 Amp	Y	Reserve Sites	Y	Gate	
50 Amp		Store	Y	Patrolled	Y
		Grill/Table	Y		

[3] Camp Creek State Park
I-77, Exit 20 of I-77
North of Princeton
N37 30.289 W81 08.068
State Rate: $23-$29
(304) 425-9481
http://www.campcreekstatepark.com/

Directions

2.5 miles. From Exit 20 turn south 0.1 mile on Hwy 19. Go right 2.3 miles on Camp Creek Rd to the Mash Fork Campgrounds.

Points of Interest

Tour Beckley Exhibition Coal Mine, the largest and most popular coal heritage destination in the region. The Bramwell Town Historic District reflects large fortunes amassed by local coal barons and is renowned for having over 14 well preserved Victorian & Tudor style mansions.

RV Sites		Water		Laundry	Y
Number	26	None		Wi-Fi	Y
Shaded	Y	At Site	Y	Fishing	Y
By Water	Y	Spigots	Y	Hiking	Y
Paved	Y	Sewer		Biking	Y
Pull Thru	Y	None		Swimming	
ADA	Y	At Site	Y	Watch Wildlife	Y
Max RV Size	40	Dump Station	Y	Pets	Y
Electric		Amenities		Security	
None		Restrooms	Y	Host(s)	Y
20 Amp	Y	Showers	Y	Rangers(s)	Y
30 Amp	Y	Reserve Sites	Y	Gate	Y
50 Amp	Y	Store	Y	Patrolled	Y
		Grill/Table	Y		

[4] Gerald Freeman Camp
I-79, Exit 67
Southeast of Flatwoods
N38 40.676 W80 32.807
COE Rate: $16-$30
America/Beautiful Rate: $8-$15
(304) 765-7756
http://www.recreation.gov

Directions

13 miles. From Exit 67 turn south then right, go 1.1 mile on Hwy 4 to Hwy 15. Turn left, go 11.5 miles to Government Access Rd, on your right. This will lead you to the campground.

Points of Interest

Just north is Lewis County, with antique shops, glass artists, wineries, and old-fashioned home cooking. There are many fairs and festivals. Board an old steam engine train and ride through the wonderful mountains.

RV Sites		Water		Laundry	Y
Number	159	None		Wi-Fi	
Shaded	Y	At Site	Y	Fishing	Y
By Water	Y	Spigots	Y	Hiking	Y
Paved	Y	Sewer		Biking	Y
Pull Thru	Y	None		Swimming	Y
ADA	Y	At Site	Y	Watch Wildlife	Y
Max RV Size	45	Dump Station	Y	Pets	Y
Electric		Amenities		Security	
None		Restrooms	Y	Host(s)	Y
20 Amp	Y	Showers	Y	Rangers(s)	Y
30 Amp	Y	Reserve Sites	Y	Gate	
50 Amp	Y	Store		Patrolled	Y
		Grill/Table	Y		

[5] Stonewall Resort State Park
I-79, Exit 91
South of Weston
N38 56.529 W80 29.866
State Rate: $43-$45
(304) 269-8889
http://www.stonewallresort.com/

Directions

3.2 miles. From Exit 91 go 2.7 miles south on Hwy 19 to State Park Rd. Turn north for 0.4 miles to the camping area.

Points of Interest

An optional resort fee can be purchased for a Resort Activities Pass for use of resort facilities. In Weston, try the Mountaineer Military Museum or Jackson's Mill Farmstead. See [4] above for other local activities. Did we mention the resort's Arnold Palmer Signature golf course?

RV Sites		Water		Laundry	
Number	40	None		Wi-Fi	Y
Shaded	Y	At Site	Y	Fishing	Y
By Water	Y	Spigots	Y	Hiking	Y
Paved	Y	Sewer		Biking	Y
Pull Thru		None		Swimming	Y
ADA	Y	At Site	Y	Watch Wildlife	Y
Max RV Size	40	Dump Station	Y	Pets	Y
Electric		Amenities		Security	
None		Restrooms	Y	Host(s)	Y
20 Amp	Y	Showers	Y	Rangers(s)	Y
30 Amp	Y	Reserve Sites	Y	Gate	
50 Amp	Y	Store	Y	Patrolled	Y
		Grill/Table	Y		

[6] Tygart Lake State Park
I-79, Exit 124
East of Clarksburg
N39 18.452 W79 59.668
State Rate: $20-$23
(304) 265-6144
http://www.tygartlake.com/

Directions

19.5 miles. From Exit 124 go southeast on Hwy 279 for 2.5 miles to Hwy 50. Turn east for 13 miles to Hwy 119 at Grafton/Blueville. Turn right on Hwy 119, go 1 miles to Bridge St. Turn left, cross the river, 0.1 miles to Barrett St. Turn left, follow Barrett (becomes Knottsville) for 2.9 miles to Bath House Rd (Scab Hollow). Turn right to the Park.

Points of Interest

Visit historic Grafton, tour the Historic B&O Depot museum. Take a drive to Fairmont, explore historic sites there.

RV Sites		Water		Laundry	
Number	40	None		Wi-Fi	Y
Shaded	Y	At Site		Fishing	Y
By Water	Y	Spigots	Y	Hiking	Y
Paved		Sewer		Biking	Y
Pull Thru		None		Swimming	Y
ADA	Y	At Site	Y	Watch Wildlife	Y
Max RV Size	40	Dump Station	Y	Pets	Y
Electric		Amenities		Security	
None		Restrooms	Y	Host(s)	Y
20 Amp	Y	Showers	Y	Rangers(s)	Y
30 Amp	Y	Reserve Sites	Y	Gate	
50 Amp		Store	Y	Patrolled	Y
		Grill/Table	Y		

[7] Babcock State Park
Hwy 19, at Hwy 60
East of Oak Hill
N38 00.424 W80 56.918
State Rate: $20-$24
(304) 438-3004
http://www.babcocksp.com/

Directions

12 miles. From Hwy 19 at Hwy 60 travel east on Hwy 60 for 9.5 miles to Hwy 41. Turn right (south) 1.6 miles to Hwy 11/4, near Clifftop. Turn right for 1 mile to the Park.

Points of Interest

The Park is at the New River Gorge National River, heart of the state's whitewater rafting industry. Visit Carnifex Ferry Battlefield State Park on the Gauley River Canyon. The Battle is re-enacted in odd numbered years with demonstrations of camp life, and military drill.

RV Sites		Water		Laundry	Y
Number	52	None		Wi-Fi	
Shaded	Y	At Site		Fishing	Y
By Water	Y	Spigots	Y	Hiking	Y
Paved		Sewer		Biking	Y
Pull Thru		None		Swimming	Y
ADA	Y	At Site		Watch Wildlife	
Max RV Size	40	Dump Station	Y	Pets	Y
Electric		Amenities		Security	
None		Restrooms	Y	Host(s)	Y
20 Amp	Y	Showers	Y	Rangers(s)	Y
30 Amp	Y	Reserve Sites	Y	Gate	
50 Amp		Store		Patrolled	Y
		Grill/Table	Y		

[8] Battle Run
Hwy 19, at Hwy 129
South of Summersville
N38 13.296 W80 54.585
COE Rate: $24
America/Beautiful Rate: $12
(304) 872-3459
http://www.recreation.gov/

Directions

4 miles. From Hwy 129 (Summersville Lake Rd) go west from Hwy 19 for 3.6 miles to the access road to the Park. Turn right, go 0.3 miles to the campground area.

Points of Interest

The Park's sandstone cliffs and quiet coves along the lake will appeal to outdoor enthusiasts. The lake provides wonderful opportunities for boating, water skiing, swimming and scuba diving. The Carnifex Ferry Battlefield is close by. No pets.

RV Sites		Water		Laundry	Y
Number	107	None		Wi-Fi	
Shaded	Y	At Site		Fishing	Y
By Water	Y	Spigots	Y	Hiking	Y
Paved		Sewer		Biking	Y
Pull Thru	Y	None		Swimming	Y
ADA	Y	At Site		Watch Wildlife	Y
Max RV Size	45	Dump Station	Y	Pets	
Electric		Amenities		Security	
None		Restrooms	Y	Host(s)	Y
20 Amp	Y	Showers	Y	Rangers(s)	Y
30 Amp	Y	Reserve Sites	Y	Gate	
50 Amp		Store		Patrolled	Y
		Grill/Table	Y		

[9] Mountwood County Park
Hwy 50, at Borland Springs Rd
East of Parkersburg
N39 15.002 W81 18.321
Country Rate: $20-$35
(304) 588-1407
http://www.mountwoodpark.org/

Directions

On Hwy 50, just east of I-77, go 11.8 miles east to Borland Springs Rd (Cty 5). Turn right (south) and follow the signs to Mountwood Park.

Points of Interest

The Park hosts festivals and events from Spring through Fall so check their calender when planning your visit. Visit Volcano, where the third oil field in the United States was discovered. The Park celebrates the history of Volcano with a festival the last week in September.

RV Sites		Water		Laundry	
Number	87	None		Wi-Fi	
Shaded	Y	At Site	Y	Fishing	Y
By Water	Y	Spigots	Y	Hiking	Y
Paved		Sewer		Biking	Y
Pull Thru	Y	None		Swimming	
ADA	Y	At Site	Y	Watch Wildlife	Y
Max RV Size	40	Dump Station	Y	Pets	Y
Electric		Amenities		Security	
None		Restrooms	Y	Host(s)	Y
20 Amp	Y	Showers	Y	Rangers(s)	
30 Amp	Y	Reserve Sites	Y	Gate	
50 Amp	some	Store		Patrolled	Y
		Grill/Table	Y		

About Wisconsin's Public Campgrounds

The Wisconsin State Park System provides outdoor recreation, and numerous educational programs about nature & conservation. The State Department of Natural Resources (DNR) reports over 14 million family unit visits a year. Their website is - **http://dnr.wi.gov/topic/parks/.**

In addition to the State Parks, there are a number of County Parks. Go here to discover your options - **http://dnr.wi.gov/topic/parks/coparks.html.** The National Park Service **(http://www.nps.gov/index.htm)** and U. S. Forest Service **(http://www.fs.usda.gov/main/cnnf/home)** are also present in Wisconsin.

A typical RV campsite is in a natural setting with a fire ring, and picnic table. Some sites are accessible for people with disabilities. Pet owners and their pets are welcome in Wisconsin State Parks, but not allowed in buildings, picnic areas and picnic shelters, beaches, except designated "dogs allowed" beaches, or playgrounds.

Camping fees are:

Site only -	$12-$17	Water View -	add $3
Site with Electricity -	$17-$22	Reservations -	$10

Ask about discounts for seniors, disabled veterans and former prisoners of war.

A vehicle doing the towing or carrying must have an annual or daily admission sticker. Any vehicle that is towed or carried into a vehicle admission area is provided free admission.

Camping reservations may be made 11 months in advance or two days before arrival. The online registration system is managed by *ReserveAmerica*. Begin your reservation process at - **http://wisconsinstateparks.reserveamerica.com/.** The reservations website has campground maps and details about each site. You can also call 888-947-2757 (TTY number is 800-274-7275) to make a reservation.

[1] Roche-A-Cri State Park	**[10] Highland Ridge Campground**
[2] DuBay Park	**[11] Black River State Forest**
[3] Council Grounds State Park	**[12] Cliffside Park**
[4] Kohler-Andrae State Park	**[13] Perrot State Park**
[5] Point Beach State Forest	**[14] Interstate Park**
[6] Veterans' Memorial Park	**[15] Pattison State Park**
[7] Rocky Arbor State Park	**[16] Copper Falls State Park**
[8] Mirror Lake State Park	**[17] Potawatomi State Park**
[9] Lake Kegonsa State Park	**[18] Peninsula State Park**

Wisconsin

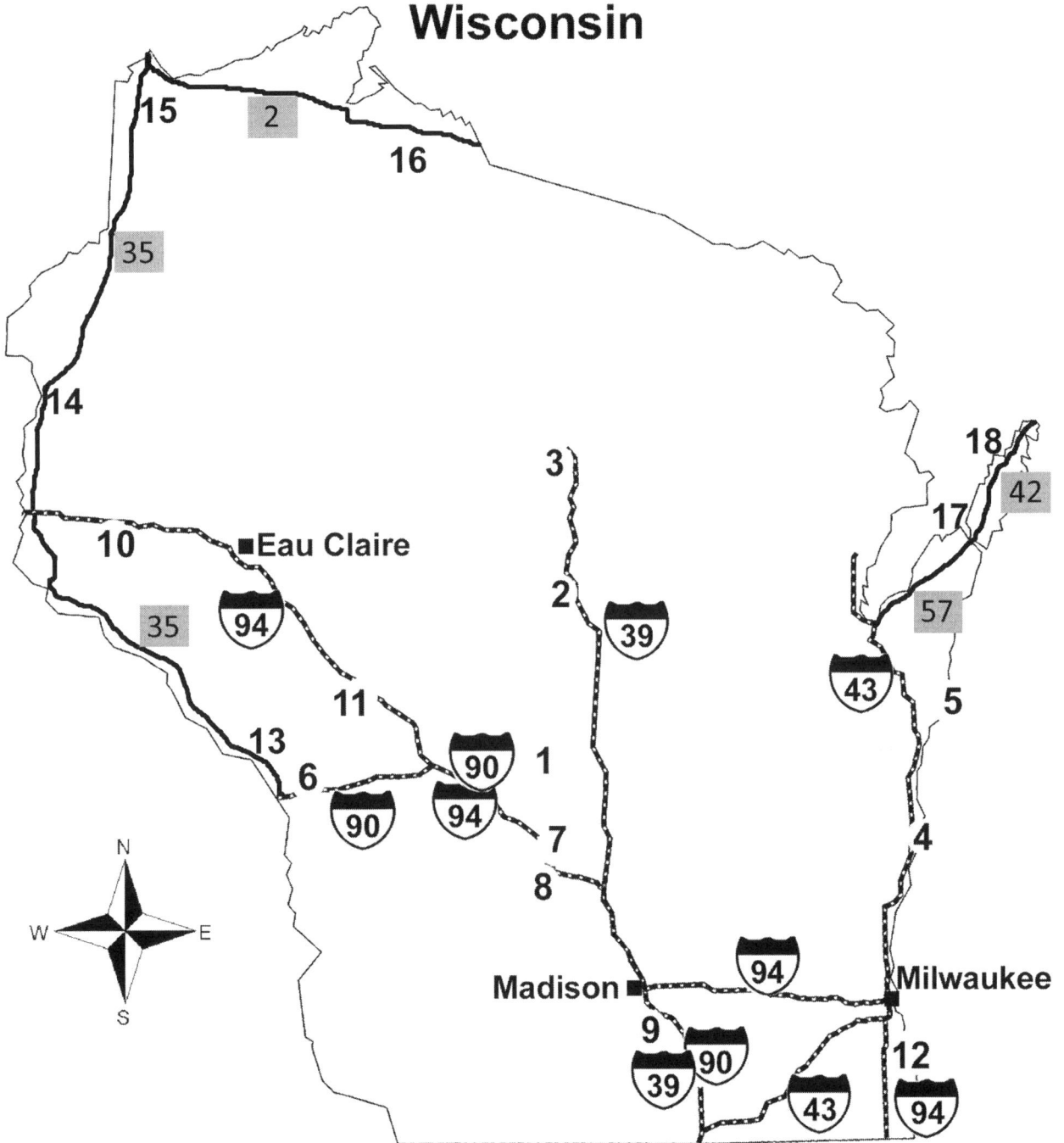

15

2

16

35

14

10 ■Eau Claire

35

94

11

13

6

90 94

7

8

3

2

39

18

42

17

57

43

5

4

1

N

W E

S

Madison■

94

9

39 90

43

Milwaukee■

12

94

[1] Roche-A-Cri State Park
I-39, Exit 124
West of Coloma
N44 00.061 W89 48.737
State Rate: $12-$19
(608) 339-6881
http://dnr.wi.gov/topic/parks/name/rocheacri/

Directions

16 miles. From Exit 124 go west for 14.4 miles on Hwy 21 to Hwy 13. Turn south for 1.7 miles to the Park entrance on your right.

Points of Interest

Hike to the top of the Park's 300 foot high rock. The accessible ramp and observation deck allow all visitors to view the petroglyphs and pictographs. Tour the Petenwell Hydro-electric Plant. Bike the Elroy-Sparta or "400" bike trails. Go to Volk Field and watch military aircraft training.

RV Sites		Water		Laundry	
Number	42	None		Wi-Fi	
Shaded	Y	At Site		Fishing	Y
By Water		Spigots	Y	Hiking	Y
Paved		**Sewer**		Biking	Y
Pull Thru		None		Swimming	
ADA	Y	At Site		Watch Wildlife	Y
Max RV Size	40	Dump Station	Y	Pets	Y
Electric		**Amenities**		**Security**	
None		Restrooms	Y	Host(s)	Y
20 Amp	few	Showers		Rangers(s)	Y
30 Amp	few	Reserve Sites	Y	Gate	
50 Amp	few	Store		Patrolled	Y
		Grill/Table	Y		

[2] DuBay Park
I-39, Exit 175
South of Mosinee
N44 40.655 W89 41.823
County Rate: $16-$22
(715) 346-1433
http://www.co.portage.wi.us/parks/

Directions

6.5 miles. From Exit 175 go southwest on Hwy 34 for 5 miles to Cty Rd E. Turn left, go 1.5 miles to the Park.

Points of Interest

Walk the historic Main St. of Stevens Point, a member of the National Register of Historic Places. See more than 60 buildings of different architectural styles. You will also see murals depicting the area's history. Stop at the Q Gallery Artist's Cooperative and Sculpture Park.

RV Sites		Water		Laundry	
Number	31	None		Wi-Fi	
Shaded	Y	At Site		Fishing	Y
By Water	Y	Spigots	Y	Hiking	Y
Paved		**Sewer**		Biking	Y
Pull Thru		None		Swimming	Y
ADA	Y	At Site		Watch Wildlife	
Max RV Size	35	Dump Station	Y	Pets	Y
Electric		**Amenities**		**Security**	
None		Restrooms	Y	Host(s)	Y
20 Amp	Y	Showers		Rangers(s)	
30 Amp	Y	Reserve Sites	Y	Gate	
50 Amp		Store		Patrolled	Y
		Grill/Table	Y		

[3] Council Grounds State Park
I-39, Exit 208
West side of Merrill
N45 11.075 W89 44.074
State Rate: $15-$22
(715) 536-8773
http://dnr.wi.gov/topic/parks/name/councilgrounds/

Directions

5.5 miles. From Exit 208 go west for 3 miles on Hwy 64. Turn right at Hwy 107 (Grand Ave), go 1.8 miles to Council Grounds Rd. Turn left, go 0.5 miles in to the Park.

Points of Interest

Stroll around Merrill, the 'City of Parks.' Visit the T.B Scott Mansion. Began in 1884, the original owner, said his house was fit for a lumber king and he doubted it had an equal anywhere in Wisconsin. Scott died before the house was finished and the "curse" began . . .

RV Sites		Water		Laundry	
Number	55	None		Wi-Fi	
Shaded	Y	At Site		Fishing	Y
By Water	Y	Spigots	Y	Hiking	Y
Paved		**Sewer**		Biking	Y
Pull Thru		None		Swimming	Y
ADA	Y	At Site		Watch Wildlife	Y
Max RV Size	45	Dump Station	Y	Pets	Y
Electric		**Amenities**		**Security**	
None		Restrooms	Y	Host(s)	Y
20 Amp	Y	Showers	Y	Rangers(s)	Y
30 Amp	Y	Reserve Sites	Y	Gate	
50 Amp		Store		Patrolled	Y
		Grill/Table	Y		

[4] Kohler-Andrae State Park
I-43, Exit 120
South of Sheboygan
N43 40.360 W87 43.079
State Rate: $15-$22
(920) 451-4080
http://dnr.wi.gov/topic/parks/name/kohleran-drae/

Directions

2.5 miles. From Exit 120 go 2.2 miles east on Cty Rd V. Where Cty Rd V turns north, continue straight on Beach Park Lane in to the Park.

Points of Interest

The Park is home to majestic sand dunes & golden beaches. In Sheboygan, South Pier & Riverfront Boardwalk offer fish shanties full of unique gifts, art & food treats. Harbor Centre Downtown offers eclectic shopping, dining, & entertainment in beautifully restored historic buildings.

RV Sites		Water			Laundry	Y
Number	106	None			Wi-Fi	
Shaded	Y	At Site			Fishing	
By Water	Y	Spigots	Y		Hiking	Y
Paved	Y	Sewer			Biking	Y
Pull Thru	Y	None			Swimming	
ADA	Y	At Site			Watch Wildlife	Y
Max RV Size	45	Dump Station	Y		Pets	Y
Electric		Amenities			Security	
None		Restrooms	Y		Host(s)	Y
20 Amp	Y	Showers	Y		Rangers(s)	Y
30 Amp	Y	Reserve Sites	Y		Gate	
50 Amp		Store			Patrolled	Y
		Grill/Table	Y			

[5] Point Beach State Forest
I-43, Exit 154
North of Two Rivers
N44 12.701 W87 30.904
State Rate: $15-$22
(920) 794-7480
http://dnr.wi.gov/topic/parks/name/pointbeach/

Directions

14 miles. From Exit 154 go 8.7 miles east on Hwy 310 into Two Rivers to Hwy 42. Turn left on Hwy 42. After 0.8 miles, when Hwy 42 turns north, go straight on 22nd St, which becomes Sandy Bay Rd and Cty Rd O. Go 4.8 miles to Park Rd.

Points of Interest

Reaching 7 miles into the lake, the point provides a 6-mile beach, dunes & the occasional piece of 19th century sunken ship. The shore is a great place to walk, explore the lighthouse area, and have a good time beachcombing.

RV Sites		Water			Laundry	
Number	131	None			Wi-Fi	
Shaded	Y	At Site	Y		Fishing	
By Water	Y	Spigots	Y		Hiking	Y
Paved		Sewer			Biking	Y
Pull Thru	Y	None			Swimming	Y
ADA	Y	At Site			Watch Wildlife	
Max RV Size	45	Dump Station	Y		Pets	Y
Electric		Amenities			Security	
None		Restrooms	Y		Host(s)	Y
20 Amp	Y	Showers	Y		Rangers(s)	Y
30 Amp	Y	Reserve Sites	Y		Gate	
50 Amp		Store	Y		Patrolled	Y
		Grill/Table	Y			

[6] Veterans' Memorial Park
I-90, Exit 12
Northeast of La Crosse
N43 53.943 W91 06.878
County Rate: $25
(608) 786-4011
http://www.lacrosseriverstatetrail.org/vets.htm

Directions

3 miles. From Exit 12 turn south and then go right for 1.4 miles on Cty Rd C (Buol Rd) to Cty Rd M. Turn north for 0.8 miles to Hwy 16. Turn west 0.7 miles to the Park on your left.

Points of Interest

Step aboard the La Crosse Queen, a replica of the grand riverboats, & one of the few "true" paddlewheelers still in operation, which plied the Mississippi in the early 1900s. Go to the La Crosse Fairgrounds Speedway for NASCAR Racing on Saturdays, April-September.

RV Sites		Water			Laundry	
Number	100	None			Wi-Fi	
Shaded	Y	At Site			Fishing	Y
By Water	Y	Spigots	Y		Hiking	Y
Paved		Sewer			Biking	Y
Pull Thru	Y	None			Swimming	
ADA	Y	At Site			Watch Wildlife	
Max RV Size	40	Dump Station	Y		Pets	Y
Electric		Amenities			Security	
None		Restrooms	Y		Host(s)	Y
20 Amp	Y	Showers	Y		Rangers(s)	
30 Amp	Y	Reserve Sites			Gate	
50 Amp		Store	Y		Patrolled	Y
		Grill/Table	Y			

[7] Rocky Arbor State Park
I-90/94, Exit 85
At the Wisconsin Dells
N43 38.463 W89 48.101
State Rate: $12-$19
(608) 254-8001
http://dnr.wi.gov/topic/parks/name/rockyarbor/

Directions

1 mile. From Exit 85 go east for 0.8 miles on Hwy 12/16 to the park entrance, on your right.

Points of Interest

The Dells' has enhanced its appeal with boutique shopping and additional dining options. The Ducks still provide a great river tour and water lovers will have much to choose from, including the classic Tommy Bartlett Show. Nearby, go to Ringling Bros. Circus World. **Also see [8].**

RV Sites		Water		Laundry	
Number	90	None		Wi-Fi	
Shaded	Y	At Site		Fishing	Y
By Water		Spigots	Y	Hiking	Y
Paved		**Sewer**		Biking	Y
Pull Thru		None		Swimming	
ADA	Y	At Site		Watch Wildlife	Y
Max RV Size	45	Dump Station	Y	Pets	Y
Electric		**Amenities**		**Security**	
None		Restrooms	Y	Host(s)	Y
20 Amp	Y	Showers	Y	Rangers(s)	Y
30 Amp	Y	Reserve Sites	Y	Gate	
50 Amp		Store		Patrolled	Y
		Grill/Table	Y		

[8] Mirror Lake State Park
I-90/94, Exit 92 ,
At Delton
N43 33.681 W89 48.488
State Rate: $15-$22
(608) 254-2333
http://dnr.wi.gov/topic/parks/name/mirror-lake/

Directions

2 miles. From Exit 92 go south for 0.4 miles on Hwy 12 to Fern Dell Rd. Turn west for 1.5 miles to the Park entrance on your right.

Points of Interest

Visit the Seth Peterson Cottage at the Park. It is the only Frank Lloyd Wright-designed house in the world available for rental occupancy. Designed in 1958, it was one of Wright's last commissions. Go here for Dells activities - **http://wisdells.com/**   **Also see [7].**

RV Sites		Water		Laundry	
Number	151	None		Wi-Fi	
Shaded	Y	At Site		Fishing	Y
By Water	Y	Spigots	Y	Hiking	Y
Paved		**Sewer**		Biking	Y
Pull Thru		None		Swimming	Y
ADA	Y	At Site		Watch Wildlife	Y
Max RV Size	45	Dump Station	Y	Pets	Y
Electric		**Amenities**		**Security**	
None		Restrooms	Y	Host(s)	Y
20 Amp	Y	Showers	Y	Rangers(s)	Y
30 Amp	Y	Reserve Sites	Y	Gate	
50 Amp	Y	Store		Patrolled	Y
		Grill/Table	Y		

[9] Lake Kegonsa State Park
I-90/39, Exit 147
Southeast of Madison
N42 58.564 W89 13.816
State Rate: $12-$19
(608) 873-9695
http://dnr.wi.gov/topic/parks/name/lakekegonsa/

Directions

3.5 miles. From Exit 147 take Hwy N south for 0.6 miles to Koshkonong Rd. Turn west, go 1.7 miles to Door Creek Rd. Turn south for 1.1 miles to the end of Door Creek Rd.

Points of Interest

From the historic University of Wisconsin - Madison campus to the beauty of Olbrich Botanical Gardens there is something for everyone, Don't miss the Farmers' Market on the Capital Square, one of the best/biggest in the country. Take a day trip to the 'House on the Rock' or Taliesin.

RV Sites		Water		Laundry	
Number	80	None		Wi-Fi	
Shaded	Y	At Site		Fishing	Y
By Water	Y	Spigots	Y	Hiking	Y
Paved		**Sewer**		Biking	Y
Pull Thru	Y	None		Swimming	Y
ADA	Y	At Site		Watch Wildlife	Y
Max RV Size	45	Dump Station	Y	Pets	Y
Electric		**Amenities**		**Security**	
None		Restrooms	Y	Host(s)	Y
20 Amp	Y	Showers	Y	Rangers(s)	Y
30 Amp	Y	Reserve Sites	Y	Gate	
50 Amp	Y	Store		Patrolled	Y
		Grill/Table	Y		

[10] Highland Ridge Campground
I-94, Exit 24
West of Menomonie
N44 52.746 W92 14.231
COE Rate: $16-$20
America/Beautiful Rate: $8-$10
(715) 778-5562
http://www.recreation.gov

Directions

6 miles. From Exit 24 go south for 2.0 miles on Cty Rd B to Cty Rd N. Turn east for 2 miles to Cty Rd NN. Go south 1.8 miles to the entrance sign.

Points of Interest

Take a day trip drive south to the St. Croix River and Lake Pepin. Drive along Hwy 35 through Maiden Rock, Stockholm, and Pepin. Any of these towns are great lunch stops. In Pepin visit Laura Ingalls Wilder Park and other Wilder landmarks. Go to a Friday fish fry dinner.

RV Sites		Water			Laundry	
Number	38	None			Wi-Fi	
Shaded	Y	At Site			Fishing	Y
By Water	Y	Spigots	Y		Hiking	Y
Paved		Sewer			Biking	Y
Pull Thru		None			Swimming	Y
ADA	Y	At Site			Watch Wildlife	Y
Max RV Size	45	Dump Station	Y		Pets	Y
Electric		Amenities			Security	
None		Restrooms	Y		Host(s)	Y
20 Amp	Y	Showers	Y		Rangers(s)	Y
30 Amp	Y	Reserve Sites	Y		Gate	
50 Amp	Y	Store			Patrolled	Y
		Grill/Table	Y			

[11] Black River State Forest
I-94, Exit 116
Southeast of Black River Falls
N44 17.099 W90 49.804
State Rate: $12-$22
(715) 284-4103
http://dnr.wi.gov/topic/StateForests/blackRiver/

Directions

2.5 miles. From Exit 116 go west for 1 mile on Hwy 54 to Hwy 12/27. Turn south, go 0.5 miles to where Hwy 12 goes east. Turn and drive 0.6 miles to the campground.

Points of Interest

Go scuba diving at Wazee Lake, Wisconsin's deepest lake and a year-round diving destination. Take a country drive, explore the area's many unique shops and antique dealers, or sample brews from one of the fine microbreweries.

RV Sites		Water			Laundry	
Number	98	None			Wi-Fi	
Shaded	Y	At Site			Fishing	Y
By Water	Y	Spigots	Y		Hiking	Y
Paved		Sewer			Biking	Y
Pull Thru	Y	None			Swimming	Y
ADA	Y	At Site			Watch Wildlife	Y
Max RV Size	45	Dump Station	Y		Pets	Y
Electric		Amenities			Security	
None		Restrooms	Y		Host(s)	Y
20 Amp	Y	Showers	Y		Rangers(s)	Y
30 Amp	Y	Reserve Sites	Y		Gate	
50 Amp	Y	Store			Patrolled	Y
		Grill/Table	Y			

[12] Cliffside Park
I-94, Exit 322
North of Racine
N42 49.088 W87 49.531
County Rate: $23
(262) 884-6400
http://publicworks.racineco.com/Parks/Index.aspx

Directions

9 miles. From Exit 322 go east for 3.8 miles on Hwy 100 to Hwy 32. Turn south for 4.2 miles to 6 Mile Rd. Turn east 0.4 miles to Michna Rd. Turn north for 0.3 miles to the park.

Points of Interest

For art, architecture, and scenic gardens, go to the Milwaukee Art Museum. Visit the 1892 Flemish Renaissance Revival Mansion of Captain Frederick Pabst, world famous beer baron and accomplished sea captain. Tour Miller Brewing Company.

RV Sites		Water			Laundry	
Number	92	None			Wi-Fi	
Shaded	Y	At Site	Y		Fishing	
By Water	Y	Spigots	Y		Hiking	Y
Paved		Sewer			Biking	Y
Pull Thru		None			Swimming	
ADA	Y	At Site			Watch Wildlife	
Max RV Size	45	Dump Station	Y		Pets	Y
Electric		Amenities			Security	
None		Restrooms	Y		Host(s)	Y
20 Amp	Y	Showers	Y		Rangers(s)	
30 Amp	Y	Reserve Sites	Y		Gate	
50 Amp	Y	Store			Patrolled	Y
		Grill/Table	Y			

[13] Perrot State Park
Hwy 35, at Trempealeau
West of Trempealeau
N44 00.970 W91 28.511
State Rate: $15-$22
(608) 534-6409
http://dnr.wi.gov/topic/parks/name/perrot/

Directions

2 miles. In Trempealeau, at Hwy 35 and Main St go south on Main St for 4 blocks to First St and turn right. Follow First St (becomes South Park Rd) for 1.9 miles to the Park Headquarters.

Points of Interest

The bluffs around Winona provide a perfect day trip and scenic drive, especially during fall color season. Walk around town & discover the town's historic architecture, abundant stained glass and facades. Numerous arts events, music, film and theater festivals make the trip worthwhile.

RV Sites		Water		Laundry	
Number	102	None		Wi-Fi	
Shaded	Y	At Site		Fishing	
By Water	Y	Spigots	Y	Hiking	Y
Paved		Sewer		Biking	Y
Pull Thru		None		Swimming	
ADA	Y	At Site		Watch Wildlife	Y
Max RV Size	45	Dump Station	Y	Pets	Y
Electric		Amenities		Security	
None		Restrooms	Y	Host(s)	Y
20 Amp	Y	Showers	Y	Rangers(s)	Y
30 Amp	Y	Reserve Sites	Y	Gate	
50 Amp	Y	Store		Patrolled	Y
		Grill/Table	Y		

[14] Interstate Park
Hwy 35, on Hwy 8
West of St. Croix Falls
N45 24.127 W92 38.919
State Rate: $12-$19
(715) 483-3747
http://dnr.wi.gov/topic/parks/name/interstate/

Directions

0.4 miles. The Park is off Hwy 8 on the west side of St. Croix Falls. Just before crossing the St. Croix River into Minnesota turn north into the Park and North Campground.

Points of Interest

This is the state's first park and one of the most beautiful, featuring a deep gorge called the "Dalles of the St. Croix." The town is the headquarters of the St. Croix National Scenic Riverway and the western terminus of the Ice Age HikingTrail.

RV Sites		Water		Laundry	
Number	84	None		Wi-Fi	
Shaded	Y	At Site		Fishing	
By Water	Y	Spigots	Y	Hiking	Y
Paved		Sewer		Biking	Y
Pull Thru		None		Swimming	
ADA	Y	At Site		Watch Wildlife	Y
Max RV Size	45	Dump Station	Y	Pets	Y
Electric		Amenities		Security	
None		Restrooms	Y	Host(s)	Y
20 Amp	Y	Showers	Y	Rangers(s)	Y
30 Amp	Y	Reserve Sites	Y	Gate	
50 Amp	Y	Store	Y	Patrolled	Y
		Grill/Table	Y		

[15] Pattison State Park
Hwy 35
South of Superior
N46 32.216 W92 07.194
State Rate: $15-$22
(715) 399-3111
http://dnr.wi.gov/topic/parks/name/pattison/

Directions

13 miles. From Superior go approximately 13 miles south on Hwy 35. Just past Cty Rd B is the Park entrance.

Points of Interest

Take a day in Superior. Visit the Fairlawn Mansion, an authentically restored 1890 Victorian House Museum. Tour the S.S. Meteor Whaleback Ship Museum, the worlds last remaining, above water, Whaleback ship. Of interest may be the Old Firehouse and Police Museum, the last of Superior's 19th Century Fire Halls.

RV Sites		Water		Laundry	
Number	62	None		Wi-Fi	
Shaded	Y	At Site		Fishing	Y
By Water	Y	Spigots	Y	Hiking	Y
Paved		Sewer		Biking	Y
Pull Thru	Y	None		Swimming	Y
ADA	Y	At Site		Watch Wildlife	
Max RV Size	45	Dump Station	Y	Pets	Y
Electric		Amenities		Security	
None		Restrooms	Y	Host(s)	Y
20 Amp	Y	Showers	Y	Rangers(s)	Y
30 Amp	Y	Reserve Sites	Y	Gate	
50 Amp		Store		Patrolled	Y
		Grill/Table	Y		

[16] Copper Falls State Park
Hwy 2, at Ashland South on Hwy 13
North of Mellen
N46 21.064 W90 38.567
State Rate: $15-$22
(715) 274-5123
http://dnr.wi.gov/topic/parks/name/copper-falls/

Directions

1.7 miles. Take State Highway 13 to the north side of Mellen and turn northeast on State Highway 169. Go about 1.8 miles. The park entrance will be on your left.

Points of Interest

Lava flows, gorges, and wonderful waterfalls make this one of Wisconsin's favorite parks. The Park's structures, including log buildings, were built by the Civilian Conservation Corps. The North Country National Scenic Trail is nearby.

RV Sites		Water		Laundry	
Number	45	None		Wi-Fi	
Shaded	Y	At Site		Fishing	Y
By Water	Y	Spigots	Y	Hiking	Y
Paved		Sewer		Biking	Y
Pull Thru		None		Swimming	
ADA	Y	At Site		Watch Wildlife	Y
Max RV Size	40	Dump Station	Y	Pets	Y
Electric		Amenities		Security	
None		Restrooms	Y	Host(s)	Y
20 Amp	Y	Showers	Y	Rangers(s)	Y
30 Amp	Y	Reserve Sites	Y	Gate	
50 Amp	few	Store	Y	Patrolled	Y
		Grill/Table	Y		

[17] Potawatomi State Park
Hwy 42/57
Southwest side of Sturgeon Bay
N44 51.093 W87 24.158
State Rate: $15-$22
(920) 746-2890
http://dnr.wi.gov/topic/parks/name/potawatomi/

Directions

2.3 miles. From the southwest side of Sturgeon Bay, on Hwy 42/57 turn north on S Duluth Ave and drive 2.3 miles to the Park.

Points of Interest

The Door County Maritime Museum, located on Sturgeon Bay's waterfront, showcases the area's rich maritime roots. Any NFL fan will want to drive to Green Bay for the day to Lambeau Field. The tour is a do-not-miss experience. Be sure to visit the Packers Hall of Fame.

RV Sites		Water		Laundry	
Number	123	None		Wi-Fi	
Shaded	Y	At Site	Y	Fishing	Y
By Water	Y	Spigots	Y	Hiking	Y
Paved		Sewer		Biking	Y
Pull Thru	few	None		Swimming	
ADA	Y	At Site		Watch Wildlife	
Max RV Size	40	Dump Station	Y	Pets	Y
Electric		Amenities		Security	
None		Restrooms	Y	Host(s)	Y
20 Amp	Y	Showers	Y	Rangers(s)	Y
30 Amp	Y	Reserve Sites	Y	Gate	
50 Amp	Y	Store	Y	Patrolled	Y
		Grill/Table	Y		

[18] Peninsula State Park
Hwy 42
Northeast side of Fish Creek
N45 07.581 W87 14.196
State Rate: $15-$22
(920) 868-3258
http://dnr.wi.gov/topic/parks/name/peninsula/

Directions

On Hwy 42 as you reach the northwest side of Fish Creek the Park entrance is on the north side of the Rd.

Points of Interest

Door County has a very New England feel and is well worth a day drive. Fish Creek's main street is also a full and fun day of walking, shopping and eating. One evening attend a local Fish Boil for dinner. The Peninsula Players, America's oldest resident summer theater, is a must to-do evening, The theater property is a marvelous location.

RV Sites		Water		Laundry	
Number	468	None		Wi-Fi	
Shaded	Y	At Site		Fishing	Y
By Water	Y	Spigots	Y	Hiking	Y
Paved		Sewer		Biking	Y
Pull Thru	Y	None		Swimming	Y
ADA	Y	At Site		Watch Wildlife	
Max RV Size	45	Dump Station	Y	Pets	Y
Electric		Amenities		Security	
None		Restrooms	Y	Host(s)	Y
20 Amp	Y	Showers	Y	Rangers(s)	Y
30 Amp	Y	Reserve Sites	Y	Gate	
50 Amp	Y	Store	Y	Patrolled	Y
		Grill/Table	Y		

About Wyoming's Public Campgrounds

The Wyoming State Parks are managed by the Division of State Parks, Historic Sites & Trails. The Division manages 12 State Parks and 21 Historic Sites. Camping is available at 8 Parks and 3 Historic/Recreation Sites. Visit their site for details at - **http://wyoparks.state.wy.us/**

The **overnight camping fee** for a single night (which includes the daily use fee) is:

Resident - $10

Non-resident - $17

Water & Electric - add $ 5

All pets must be in a vehicle or on a leash no longer than ten (10) feet in length and physically controlled at all times. Pets are prohibited in public eating places and food stores, public buildings, and on designated beach areas. Camping is permitted for a maximum of 14 days.

Reservations can be made no more than 90 days in advance at 8 parks. You can make reservations online or by calling the Reservation Center at (877) 996-7275. For online reservations go to - **http://wyoparks.state.wy.us/Reservations/Index.aspx**

The National Parks and National Forests also have a number of good campground locations.

[1] Guernsey State Park	**[7] Alpine Campground (North Loop)**
[2] Glendo State Park	**[8] Warren Bridge Campground**
[3] South Fork Campground	**[9] Colter Bay Village Campground**
[4] Buckboard Crossing	**[10] Bridge Bay Campground**
[5] Curt Gowdy State Park	**[11] Buffalo Bill State Park**
[6] Keyhole State Park	**[12] Sitting Bull Campground**

NOTES:

Wyoming

[1] Guernsey State Park
I-25, Exit 92
Northeast of Wheatland
N42 16.902 W104 46.128
State Rate: $10-$22
(307) 836-2334
http://wyoparks.state.wy.us/Site/SiteInfo.aspx?siteID=7

Directions

15 miles. From Exit 92 go 14 miles west on Hwy 26 to Hwy 317. Turn north for 1 mile to the Park. There are 7 campgrounds.

Points of Interest

This Park is notable for the exceptional building construction done by the Civilian Conservation Corps (CCC) and for artifacts and landmarks from the days of the Oregon Trail. Sites to visit could include Brimmer Point, the Castle, and the Guernsey Museum. Also visit Register Cliff.

RV Sites		Water		Laundry	
Number	216	None		Wi-Fi	
Shaded	Y	At Site	Y	Fishing	Y
By Water	Y	Spigots	Y	Hiking	Y
Paved		Sewer		Biking	Y
Pull Thru	Y	None		Swimming	Y
ADA	Y	At Site		Watch Wildlife	Y
Max RV Size	45	Dump Station	Y	Pets	Y
Electric		Amenities		Security	
None		Restrooms	Y	Host(s)	Y
20 Amp	Y	Showers	Y	Rangers(s)	Y
30 Amp	Y	Reserve Sites	Y	Gate	
50 Amp	Y	Store		Patrolled	Y
		Grill/Table	Y		

[2] Glendo State Park
I-25, Exit 111
Northeast of Glendo
N42 29.097 W105 00.653
State Rate: $10-$17
(307) 735-4433
http://wyoparks.state.wy.us/Site/SiteInfo.aspx?siteID=6

Directions

2 miles. From Exit 111 go east into Glendo, 0.2 miles to Hwy 319 (Yellowstone Hwy). Turn south for 2 blocks to C St. Turn left 1 block to Lincoln Ave. Turn south (Lincoln becomes Glendo Park Rd) for 1.5 miles to the Park. Eleven campgrounds.

Points of Interest

Diggings in the area provides evidence of historic presence of multiple Indian tribes. Near Sandy Beach you'll find sand dunes.

RV Sites		Water		Laundry	
Number	419	None		Wi-Fi	
Shaded	Y	At Site		Fishing	Y
By Water	Y	Spigots	Y	Hiking	Y
Paved		Sewer		Biking	Y
Pull Thru	Y	None		Swimming	Y
ADA	Y	At Site		Watch Wildlife	Y
Max RV Size	45	Dump Station	Y	Pets	Y
Electric		Amenities		Security	
None	Y	Restrooms	Y	Host(s)	Y
20 Amp		Showers	Y	Rangers(s)	Y
30 Amp		Reserve Sites	Y	Gate	
50 Amp		Store	Y	Patrolled	Y
		Grill/Table	Y		

[3] South Fork Campground
I-25, Exit 229
West of Buffalo
N44 16.698 W106 57.029
Bighorn NF Rate: $16
America/Beautiful Rate: $8
(406) 587-9054
http://www.recreation.gov

Directions

17 miles. From Exit 229 go 16.6 miles west on Scenic Hwy 16 to FS Rd 337 (Clear Creek Campground Rd). Turn left to the campground.

Points of Interest

Hwy 16 is a scenic byway. The campground is along the South Fork of Clear Creek, where trout fishing is popular. Sightseeing & photo opportunities are excellent. You can walk to the South Fork Mountain Lodge for a meal &/or check out the Bighorn Mountain adventure options.

RV Sites		Water		Laundry	
Number	14	None		Wi-Fi	
Shaded	Y	At Site		Fishing	Y
By Water	Y	Spigots	Y	Hiking	Y
Paved		Sewer		Biking	Y
Pull Thru		None	Y	Swimming	
ADA	Y	At Site		Watch Wildlife	Y
Max RV Size	45	Dump Station		Pets	Y
Electric		Amenities		Security	
None	Y	Restrooms	Y	Host(s)	
20 Amp		Showers		Rangers(s)	Y
30 Amp		Reserve Sites	Y	Gate	
50 Amp		Store		Patrolled	Y
		Grill/Table	Y		

[4] Buckboard Crossing
I-80, Exit 91
South of Green River
N41 14.944 W109 35.817
Ashley NF Rate: $20
America/Beautiful Rate: $10
(435) 784-3445
http://www.recreation.gov

Directions

25.5 miles. From Exit 91 go southwest to Hwy 530 (Uinta Dr). Follow Hwy 530 for 24 miles, south from Green River, to Buckboard Rd. Turn left, go 1.5 miles to the Campground

Points of Interest

The camp area is famous for trophy lake trout. A number of 30+ pound fish are caught each year. Petroglyphs & artifacts suggest Fremont Indians hunted game here for many centuries. The high elevation keeps temperatures moderate.

RV Sites		Water			Laundry	
Number	66	None			Wi-Fi	
Shaded	ramada	At Site			Fishing	Y
By Water	Y	Spigots		Y	Hiking	Y
Paved		Sewer			Biking	Y
Pull Thru	few	None			Swimming	Y
ADA	Y	At Site			Watch Wildlife	Y
Max RV Size	45	Dump Station		Y	Pets	Y
Electric		Amenities			Security	
None		Restrooms		Y	Host(s)	Y
20 Amp	some	Showers		Y	Rangers(s)	Y
30 Amp	some	Reserve Sites		Y	Gate	
50 Amp	some	Store		Y	Patrolled	Y
		Grill/Table		Y		

[5] Curt Gowdy State Park
I-80, Exit 323
Between Laramie and Cheyenne
N41 11.458 W105 15.274
State Rate: $10-$22
(307) 632-7946
http://wyoparks.state.wy.us/Site/SiteInfo.aspx?siteID=4

Directions

13.5 miles. From Exit 323 turn east on Hwy 210, go 13.3 miles to the Park.

Points of Interest

Both Cheyenne & Laramie are less than an hours drive, each is the best of the Old West - the reality won't disappoint. In Laramie you'll also find unique galleries, shops, boutiques & antiques in its Historic Downtown. In Cheyenne check out the Big Boy Steam Engine, find the 8 'Big Boots.'

RV Sites		Water			Laundry	
Number	139	None			Wi-Fi	
Shaded		At Site		Y	Fishing	Y
By Water	Y	Spigots		Y	Hiking	Y
Paved		Sewer			Biking	Y
Pull Thru	Y	None			Swimming	
ADA	Y	At Site			Watch Wildlife	Y
Max RV Size	45	Dump Station		Y	Pets	Y
Electric		Amenities			Security	
None		Restrooms		Y	Host(s)	Y
20 Amp	Y	Showers		Y	Rangers(s)	Y
30 Amp	Y	Reserve Sites		Y	Gate	
50 Amp	Y	Store		Y	Patrolled	Y
		Grill/Table		Y		

[6] Keyhole State Park
I-90, Exit 165
North of Moorcroft
N44 21.374 W104 45.005
State Rate: $10-$22
(307) 756-3596
http://wyoparks.state.wy.us/Site/SiteInfo.aspx?siteID=10

Directions

6 miles. From Exit 165 go north on the Keyhole Access Rd (Cty Rd 160, then 205) for 5.6 miles to the Park. Nine Campgrounds.

Points of Interest

The Park is on the western edge of the Black Hills and is a mecca for resident and migrating birds of all species. Devils Tower is a short distance north and is an excellent day trip. Visit Sundance and walk the main street, where the 'Kid' got this name.

RV Sites		Water			Laundry	
Number	256	None			Wi-Fi	
Shaded	Y	At Site		Y	Fishing	Y
By Water	Y	Spigots		Y	Hiking	Y
Paved		Sewer			Biking	Y
Pull Thru	Y	None			Swimming	Y
ADA	Y	At Site			Watch Wildlife	Y
Max RV Size	45	Dump Station		Y	Pets	Y
Electric		Amenities			Security	
None		Restrooms		Y	Host(s)	Y
20 Amp	Y	Showers			Rangers(s)	Y
30 Amp	Y	Reserve Sites		Y	Gate	
50 Amp	Y	Store		Y	Patrolled	Y
		Grill/Table		Y		

[7] Alpine Campground (North Loop)
Hwy 26
West of Alpine
N43 11.828 W111 02.460
Caribou-Targhee NF Rate: $12-$14
America/Beautiful Rate: $6-$7
(208) 483-2434
http://www.recreation.gov/

Directions

2.1 miles. From the junction of Hwy 26 and Hwy 89 go 2.1 miles north to the Campground on your left.

Points of Interest

The Palisades Creek Trail leads to Upper Palisades Lake & excellent views of Swan Valley. Alpine should provide for most needs and is 2 miles west. Try to attend Mountain Days in June. You can make day trips to Jackson and Grand Teton National Park from this location.

RV Sites		Water		Laundry	
Number	16	None		Wi-Fi	
Shaded	Y	At Site		Fishing	Y
By Water	Y	Spigots	Y	Hiking	Y
Paved		**Sewer**		Biking	Y
Pull Thru	few	None	Y	Swimming	Y
ADA	Y	At Site		Watch Wildlife	Y
Max RV Size	45	Dump Station		Pets	Y
Electric		**Amenities**		**Security**	
None	Y	Restrooms	Y	Host(s)	Y
20 Amp		Showers		Rangers(s)	
30 Amp		Reserve Sites	Y	Gate	
50 Amp		Store		Patrolled	Y
		Grill/Table			

[8] Warren Bridge Campground
Hwy 26, at Hwy 189/191
Northwest of Pinedale
N43 01.090 W110 07.087
BLM Rate: $10
America/Beautiful Rate: $5
(307) 367-5300
http://www.blm.gov/wy/st/en/field_offices/Pinedale/recreation/developed_sites.html

Directions

21.7 miles. Go 21.7 miles south from Bondurant on Hwy 189/191 to the campground, just south of the Green River.

Points of Interest

The campground is part of the Scab Creek Recreation Area in the foothills of the Wind River Mountains. Discover Pinedale, a significant hunting/outfitting town and a gateway to the Wind River Mountains.

RV Sites		Water		Laundry	
Number	16	None		Wi-Fi	
Shaded		At Site	Y	Fishing	Y
By Water	Y	Spigots	Y	Hiking	Y
Paved		**Sewer**		Biking	Y
Pull Thru	Y	None		Swimming	
ADA	Y	At Site		Watch Wildlife	Y
Max RV Size	45	Dump Station	Y	Pets	Y
Electric		**Amenities**		**Security**	
None	Y	Restrooms	Y	Host(s)	Y
20 Amp		Showers		Rangers(s)	Y
30 Amp		Reserve Sites		Gate	
50 Amp		Store		Patrolled	Y
		Grill/Table	Y		

[9] Colter Bay Village Campground
Hwy 26, at Hwy 89/191
North of Moran in Grand Teton NP
N43 54.691 W110 37.831
Grand Teton NP Rate: $23
America/Beautiful Rate: $12
(307) 739.3300
http://www.gtlc.com/lodging/gtlc-campgrounds-colter-bay-village.aspx

Directions

9.5 miles. From Moran Junction and the Moran Entrance Station go 9.5 miles north on Hwy 89/191 to the campground. The *Village Campground* is next to the *Village RV Park*.

Points of Interest

You're in Colter Bay Village, which has a variety of services. Grand Teton National Park provides a wealth of outdoor opportunities. Go to **http://www.nps.gov/grte/index.htm** for options.

RV Sites		Water		Laundry	
Number	175	None		Wi-Fi	
Shaded	Y	At Site		Fishing	Y
By Water	Y	Spigots	Y	Hiking	Y
Paved		**Sewer**		Biking	Y
Pull Thru		None	Y	Swimming	
ADA	Y	At Site		Watch Wildlife	Y
Max RV Size	45	Dump Station		Pets	Y
Electric		**Amenities**		**Security**	
None		Restrooms	Y	Host(s)	Y
20 Amp	Y	Showers	Y	Rangers(s)	Y
30 Amp	Y	Reserve Sites		Gate	
50 Amp		Store	Y	Patrolled	Y
		Grill/Table	Y		

[10] Bridge Bay Campground
Yellowstone NP Grand Loop
South of Lake Village in Yellowstone NP
N44 32.091 W110 26.077
Yellowtone NP Rate: $22
America/Beautiful Rate: $11
(307) 739-3300
http://www.yellowstonenationalparklodges.
com/lodging/camping/bridge-bay-campground/

Directions

2.5 miles. From Lake Village take the Grand Loop 2.5 miles south to the campground.

Points of Interest

Fishing Bridge RV Park is 4 miles away & is another campground option if Bridge Bay is full or you prefer more amenities (full hook-ups, etc.). The rate is $48. Fishing Bridge only allows hard sided recreational vehicles. See **http://www.nps.gov/yell/index.htm** for all that Yellowstone has to offer.

RV Sites		Water		Laundry	Y
Number	400	None		Wi-Fi	
Shaded	some	At Site		Fishing	Y
By Water	Y	Spigots	Y	Hiking	Y
Paved		Sewer		Biking	Y
Pull Thru	Y	None		Swimming	
ADA	Y	At Site		Watch Wildlife	Y
Max RV Size	40	Dump Station	near	Pets	Y
Electric		Amenities		Security	
None	Y	Restrooms	Y	Host(s)	Y
20 Amp		Showers	near	Rangers(s)	Y
30 Amp		Reserve Sites	Y	Gate	
50 Amp		Store	near	Patrolled	Y
		Grill/Table	Y		

[11] Buffalo Bill State Park
Hwy 14/16
West of Cody
N44 30.219 W109 14.674
State Rate: $10-$22
(307) 587-9227
http://wyoparks.state.wy.us/Site/SiteInfo.
aspx?siteID=3

Directions

10.5 miles. From the center of Cody go 10.5 miles west on Hwy 14/16 to the campground.

Points of Interest

A few days in Cody are a real treat. The Buffalo Bill Center of the West, focusing on the American West, is a two day experience. Take a tour of Old Trail Town, visit Jeremiah Johnson's grave. Take a trolly tour around town, learn much about Buffalo Bill and his influence on the founding & layout of Cody. Then have a meal at the Irma Hotel.

RV Sites		Water		Laundry	
Number	88	None		Wi-Fi	
Shaded	Y	At Site	Y	Fishing	Y
By Water	Y	Spigots	Y	Hiking	Y
Paved		Sewer		Biking	
Pull Thru	Y	None		Swimming	
ADA	Y	At Site	Y	Watch Wildlife	Y
Max RV Size	40	Dump Station	Y	Pets	Y
Electric		Amenities		Security	
None		Restrooms	Y	Host(s)	Y
20 Amp	Y	Showers	Y	Rangers(s)	Y
30 Amp	Y	Reserve Sites	Y	Gate	
50 Amp	Y	Store		Patrolled	
		Grill/Table	Y		

[12] Sitting Bull Campground
Hwy 16
Southwest of Buffalo
N44 11.419 W107 12.662
Bighorn NF Rate: $16
America/Beautiful Rate: $8
(406) 587-9054
http://www.recreation.gov/

Directions

20.7 miles. From Ten Sleep take Hwy 16 east for 20 miles to Forest Service Rd 432. Turn left, go 0.7 mile to campground.

Points of Interest

Park sites give good views of the Bighorn Mountains. Meadowlark Lake is a great place for canoeing and fishing. Trout are plentiful. Off-road vehicle trails are also abundant. Nearby lodges have dining, horseback riding and camping supplies.

RV Sites		Water		Laundry	
Number	41	None		Wi-Fi	
Shaded	Y	At Site		Fishing	Y
By Water	Y	Spigots	Y	Hiking	Y
Paved		Sewer		Biking	Y
Pull Thru		None		Swimming	
ADA	Y	At Site		Watch Wildlife	Y
Max RV Size	45	Dump Station	Y	Pets	Y
Electric		Amenities		Security	
None	Y	Restrooms	Y	Host(s)	Y
20 Amp		Showers		Rangers(s)	Y
30 Amp		Reserve Sites	Y	Gate	
50 Amp		Store		Patrolled	Y
		Grill/Table	Y		

16667188R00202

Made in the USA
San Bernardino, CA
13 November 2014